The
CARTER YEARS
Toward a New Global Order

The Washington Institute for Values in Public Policy

The Washington Institute sponsors research that helps provide the information and fresh insights necessary for formulating policy in a democratic society. Founded in 1982, the Institute is an independent, non-profit educational and research organization which examines current and upcoming issues with particular attention to ethical implications.

ADDITIONAL TITLES

Korean Challenges and American Policy
Edited by Ilpyong J. Kim (1991)

Building Sino-Soviet Relations: An Analysis for the 1990s
Edited by William T. Tow (1991)

Reform and Transformation in Communist Systems: Comparative Perspectives
Edited by Ilpyong J. Kim and Jane Shapiro Zacek (1991)

Asian-Pacific Regional Security
Edited by June Teufel Dreyer (1990)

The Nixon-Kissinger Years: The Reshaping of American Foreign Policy
By Richard C. Thornton (1989)

Confucianism and Economic Development: An Oriental Alternative
Edited by Hung-chao Tai (1989)

Vietnam: Strategy for a Stalemate
By F. Charles Parker (1989)

The East Wind Subsides: Chinese Foreign Policy and the Origins of the Cultural Revolution
By Andrew Hall Wedeman (1987)

The CARTER YEARS
Toward a New Global Order

RICHARD C. THORNTON

PARAGON HOUSE
St. Paul, Minnesota

Published in the United States by
Paragon House Publishers
1925 Oakcrest Avenue
St. Paul, Minnesota 55113

First paperback edition

ISBN 978-1-55778-871-9: $19.95

Original hardcover edition, November 1991

A Washington Institute Press Book

The Library of Congress has catalogued the hardcover edition as follows:

Thornton, Richard C.
The Carter years: toward a new global order / Richard C. Thornton
"A Washington Institute Press book."
Includes index.
ISBN 0-88702-062-3: $26.95
1. United States — Foreign relations — 1977-1981.
2. Carter, Jimmy, 1924– . I. Tide
E872.T46 1991
327.73 — dc 20 91-29701 CIP

Manufactured in the United States of America

The paper used in this publication meets the minimum requirements of American National Standard for Information Sciences—Permanence of Paper for Printed Library Materials, ANSIZ39.48-1984.

10 9 8 7 6 5 4 3 2 1

For current information about all releases from Paragon House, visit the web site at http://www.paragonhouse.com

To my wife Joanne and to our sons Douglas and James, who make the work in this vineyard eminently rewarding

No government can at the same time protect the nation's security and tell its people the truth. All governments seek to bridge the gap to one degree or another, but never succeed completely. The width of the resulting gap between truth and security denotes a government's credibility, or lack of it.

Contents

List of Maps

Preface

This volume is the second of three analyzing American strategy and foreign policy during the period 1968–1988. The first was *The Nixon-Kissinger Years: Reshaping America's Foreign Policy, 1968–1976.* Although the current volume stands by itself and can be read independently of the first, the reader will gain a greater sense of the continuity and change in American foreign policy by reading this volume in conjunction with the preceeding one.

The thesis of this volume is that while the administration of Jimmy Carter came into office fully agreed and prepared to carry forward the general strategy of a new global order initiated by Henry Kissinger in 1973, a major Soviet strategic weapons breakthrough almost immediately forced its reconsideration. Indeed, the basic dynamic within the Carter leadership for virtually his entire term in office was heated debate over the viability of Kissinger's strategy as opposed to a return to some modified form of containment. The result was strategic indecision and policy vacillation.

Containment is best understood in its structural sense as the forward American position on the Eurasian landmass around the periphery of the Soviet bloc. American power provided the essential security shield, and included the political-military-economic relationships to sustain it. The new international order involved the shift of American military power from its forward "containing" positions around the Soviet periphery to a more secure posture created by the establishment and strengthening of collective security structures to ensure stability in the absence of a direct United States presence, and appropriate changes in the political-military-economic relationships.

The new order was a fundamental turn away from containment, whose rationale had been eviscerated during the sixties. Containment as traditionally understood had been sharply undermined as a result of the growth of the Soviet Union's strategic weapons power to parity with the United States' and the rise of West Germany and Japan to economic superpower status. The former development increased the costs as well as the dangers of containment, and the latter raised questions about its very purpose as America's main allies attempted to move into de facto independent positions between Washington and Moscow—even while remaining within the Western alliance.

Essential to the success of the new strategy was detente with the Soviet Union, which would provide the time and opportunity to make the desired changes. The problem was that Moscow declined the proffered bargain of detente and arms control in return for trade and high technology, preferring instead to move toward a design of its own choosing through attempts to alter the correlation of forces by military means. Moreover, Washington's main allies, Bonn and Tokyo, also refused to moderate the neomercantilistic accumulation strategies which were enriching them so rapidly. By the end of 1976 only opening steps had been taken in construction of the new international order, and in some important ways the strategy had left the nation worse off than before.

Nevertheless, the Carter administration, under the leadership of Secretary of State Cyrus Vance, was fully committed to carry the new strategic conception forward. Both President Carter and Secretary of State Vance, for example, sought as the first priority completion of an arms control treaty with the Soviet Union, which they hoped would become a springboard to an improved relationship involving Soviet restraint in return for increased trade and technology. Perhaps as signs of good faith, defense expenditures were to be reduced and arms sales, except for NATO and Japan, were to be cut.

Regarding the United States position in Asia, President Carter had declared his intention to withdraw American forces from South Korea. Moreover, contrary to what eventually developed, early plans included no move toward normalization of relations with China. Indeed, at the first NSC foreign policy meeting, "the subject of China did not come up." In the Southwest Asia–Middle East region, Secretary Vance had in mind the evolution of a "far less intimate" relationship with Iran—the forwardmost American ally in the containment structure around the Soviet periphery. On the other hand, he planned an active role in the Middle East, completing the process initiated by Henry Kissinger after the Yom Kippur War, by shifting the American position westward in the context of Egyptian-Israeli rapprochement and a greatly strengthened Middle East collective security structure.

How far the Carter administration would have gone in revamping the American global position cannot be known in full. Virtually from the outset, within ten days of taking office, the administration received military intelligence that the Soviet Union would soon begin testing a greatly improved guidance system for its MIRVed ICBMs. This information threw all of the administration's plans out the window. The tests indicated that Moscow sought to develop a first-strike, hard-target kill capability against American missiles before the United States had a similar capability against Soviet missiles.

Moreover, if successful, the Soviet Union would have acquired this threatening capability several years earlier than had been anticipated, thoroughly compromising long-term foreign policy planning. Foreign policy planning had proceeded on the assumption that Moscow would not achieve a hard-target kill capability for its MIRVed ICBMs until the mid-eighties, when new American weapons counterbalancing the Soviet advance were scheduled to come on line. This would have meant that American strategic power would retain sufficient advantage to enable the United States to complete its foreign policy shift.

The Soviet breakthrough raised serious questions regarding continued American strategic preeminence, reopening the issue of grand strategy—the new order versus containment—and splitting the top Carter leadership. From the early spring of 1977, virtually every major policy issue would be debated from the perspective of whether the Soviet breakthrough compromised the policy in question or permitted it to go forward. In every case, National Security Adviser Zbigniew Brzczinski recommended policy which would reinforce containment and Secretary of State Cyrus Vance recommended policy which would be consistent with the new order. The president himself would vacillate, sometimes supporting the views of one adviser, sometimes the other. Even though Secretary Vance generally prevailed, the result was that indecision and vacillation marked the foreign policy of the Carter years.

My thanks go to Neil Salonen, director of the Washington Institute, for his continuing support for this project; to Rebecca Salonen, for yet another superb editing of the manuscript; and to the faculty and students of George Washington University's Elliott School of International Affairs and Institute for Sino-Soviet Studies, where I have taught for the past twenty-five years.

PART I

Toward a New Order

CHAPTER 1

The Carter Administration Probes Soviet Intentions

Despite the change of administration from Republican to Democrat, continuity rather than discontinuity marked the transition from President Ford to President Carter. The Carter administration, under Secretary of State Cyrus Vance's direction, sought to carry forward the essential strategic conception of an adjusted global order devised by Henry Kissinger and set in motion in early 1973, despite the fact that the momentum of the new strategy had flagged by 1976. Detente with the Soviet Union was the essential precondition for the successful execution of American strategy, and Secretary Vance assiduously sought to revive it. Only under circumstances of friendly relations with Moscow, particularly as expressed through a satisfactory SALT II agreement, could the United States move confidently to restructure regional balances around the Soviet periphery, in Asia, the Middle East, and Europe, establish stable security structures, redefine security commitments, and reposition American military power.

Almost immediately upon the president's assumption of office, however, a major difficulty arose precipitated by a dramatic and unanticipated adverse shift in the strategic weapons equation in the form of a surprise Soviet breakthrough in ICBM guidance technology. The Soviet breakthrough threatened to deprive the Carter leadership of the time it had assumed would be available, and forced reconsideration of American strategy, which underwent several subsequent revisions. As a result, the four years of the Carter administration were marked by tense and intensive American and Soviet contention in major areas around the globe, as President Carter vacillated over the correct strategy, alternating between attempts to restructure America's global position and attempts to contain Soviet geopolitical activism.

On the other hand, the technological breakthrough promised to give the Soviet Union a first-strike capability against Minuteman several years before American leaders had believed it would arise. This was, afer all, the long-awaited objective for which Moscow had striven since Brezhnev assumed power in 1964. Emerging military strength thus encouraged Soviet leaders to embark upon a major geopolitical offensive to alter the overall correlation of forces while their advantage lasted. In general, then, the Carter years should be understood as a period in which Moscow sought to disrupt United States strategy while pursuing its own geopolitical design. The process was accompanied by extensive Soviet military activity, both directly and through proxies, in the Middle East and Africa, in Southeast and Southwest Asia, and in Central America.

This chapter will focus on the arms control negotiations which took place during the first nine months of the Carter administration, encompassing discovery of Moscow's strategic weapons breakthrough and the Carter administration's response to it. The chapter thus sets the stage for later events leading up to the protracted crisis of 1978–79 centering on the Middle East and Asia, when there occurred in seeming rapid succession the creation and evisceration of the Camp David peace process, the establishment of diplomatic relations between the United States and China, the Vietnamese–Cambodian conflict, the Sino–Vietnamese war, South Yemen's attack on North Yemen, the fall of the shah in Iran, petroleum and monetary crises, the Iran hostage crisis, and the Soviet invasion of Afghanistan. Three other major developments of the Carter administration, the Soviet use of Cuba in a proxy role in the Caribbean, the Nicaraguan revolution, and the Iran–Iraq war, would leave a problem-filled legacy to the Reagan administration.

The Initial Approach to Moscow

Jimmy Carter's initial approach to Moscow was short-lived, lasting only through his first month in office. It is nevertheless useful to sketch the initial set of ideas which underlay the new president's foreign policy in order to better understand the major shift that took place at the very beginning of his administration. At the heart of Carter's foreign policy was his intent to reestablish a cooperative relationship with the Soviet Union based on rapid completion of the SALT II treaty.

During the election campaign Carter had criticized President Ford for allowing the Soviet Union to exploit the detente relationship to the disadvantage of the United States. President Carter entered office vowing to revive detente, which had expired during the crisis over Angola, but on what he hoped would be a more comprehensive and more reciprocal basis. The twin themes that were already apparent during the election campaign were a concentration on human rights and a determination to stabilize and broaden the American–Soviet relationship through arms control and economic cooperation. In other words, President Carter was fully prepared to offer the same quid pro quo that Henry Kissinger had offered earlier, which Moscow had rejected.

The immediate problem was how to correct what the president believed was the Soviet leadership's misperception of American military weakness deriving from the denouement in Vietnam and political stagnation as a result of Watergate. It was, in short, essential to restore United States credibility, without which it would be impossible to dissuade the Soviets from continuing on what appeared to be an assertive foreign policy course based on growing military power. Political and military weakness, real or perceived, would only encourage Moscow on its militant course.

Early on, the president and his advisers chose to attempt to put Moscow on the political defensive with a human rights campaign, while hoping through arms control accommodation and economic incentives to revive detente. The president's national security adviser, Zbigniew Brzezinski, characterized the new emphasis as combining elements of both "cooperation and competition," although he tended to place emphasis on the competitive aspects of the relationship.[1]

While Brzezinski inclined to emphasize "competition," Secretary of State Cyrus Vance was inclined to emphasize "cooperation." Vance, whose policy views were decisive, approached the United States–Soviet relationship with a greater degree of equanimity than did the national security adviser. While he believed that maintaining American military strength and alliances was essential to "managing the global competition" with the Soviets, the secretary also believed that military strength alone was insufficient. As he put it, "central to our strategy as we faced a period of international turbulence" was negotiation of a "fair and verifiable" SALT treaty.[2] An equitable arms control agreement combined with the lifting of trade restrictions imposed by the Jackson–Vanik amendment would establish the basis, Vance believed, for cooperation with Moscow in resolving some of the "turbulence" in places like the Middle East and Southern Africa.

Even before assuming office, Carter had initiated the political offensive against the Soviet Union. His chosen instrument was the concept of human rights, with which he hoped to be able to put Moscow on the defensive.[3] The genesis of the human rights concept was in the heyday of United States–Soviet detente. As part of the effort to restructure its international position, Washington had acquiesced in the frequently proposed Soviet Conference on Security and Cooperation in Europe (CSCE). Preparatory talks for CSCE began in November 1972, and formal deliberations occurred from July 1973 through July 1975.[4]

Moscow had hoped to confine the agenda of the conference to legitimizing the post–World War II boundaries of Europe, reducing American influence, and improving economic ties with Western Europe. The United States, on the other hand, supported by virtually all of the thirty-five participating states (including the Vatican), pressed for a broader agenda, which emphasized human rights. Three sets, or "baskets," of issues—security, economic, and humanitarian—were eventually agreed upon for discussion, and each basket gave birth to an appropriate "declaration" officially sanctioned at the final meeting of the conference in Helsinki.

The Helsinki Agreements, as the conference's work came to be known, produced legislation in the U.S. Congress for the establishment of a Commission on Security and Cooperation in Europe, which President Ford signed into law June 3, 1976. The commission's mandate was to monitor European states' "compliance with or violation of" the Helsinki Agreements. The Helsinki Agreements and the United States commission to monitor them became the basis for the Carter administration's human rights offensive, which initially was directed primarily at the Soviet Union and Eastern Europe.

The concept of human rights replaced the concept of anticommunism as the United States' ideological approach to the world. The concept of anticommunism had been appropriate as long as the United States and the communist powers had remained opposed in two discrete blocs. Rapprochement with the People's Republic of China and detente with the Soviet Union under President Nixon forced a change. Anticommunism was no longer relevant as a means of mobilizing domestic and global public opinion and support. The concept of human rights allowed the United States to differentiate among communists and enabled a more positive ideological mobilization of public opinion. Thus, particularly in the first year of the Carter administration, the instrument of human rights was employed primarily but not exclusively against the Soviet Union and Eastern Europe.[5] Later, the focus would shift to other countries, including various American allies and friends in Latin America and Asia but, perhaps not so curiously, not to China.

The inclusion of provisions on human rights in the CSCE final documents had almost immediate repercussions in the Soviet Union and Eastern Europe. By the fall of 1976 Soviet dissidents were voicing their concerns; there were riots in Poland and unrest in Czechoslovakia and East Germany. And Carter sought to encourage popular assertiveness in the Soviet camp. While president-elect in November, he had sent a telegram expressing his support for Soviet dissident Vladimir Slepak, and Secretary of State–designate Vance in late December had "received" Soviet exile Andrei Amalrik. American and West European news media had given extensive coverage to these events.

Upon Carter's assuming office, this "offensive" continued briefly as the president and other high administration officials praised Soviet dissident Andrei Sakharov, criticized Czechoslovakia for harassing dissidents, and expressed official "concern" over the arrests of Soviet dissidents Alexander Ginsburg and Yuri Orlov. On March 1, President Carter and Vice-President Mondale received Soviet exile Vladimir Bukovsky in the White House.[6] But Carter's human rights campaign lost much of its steam after that as an instrument in the political offensive against Moscow and as a device to drive a wedge between the Soviet Union and Eastern Europe.

Indeed, the United States was abruptly thrown onto the defensive by a development that would overshadow all else, slowing whatever momentum had been generated by the human rights campaign. Almost immediately upon taking office President Carter was faced with what was undoubtedly the single most significant development affecting—no, dominating—his presidency. This was the sudden, unexpected, and disadvantageous turn in the strategic weapons balance produced by the discovery "in early 1977" that Moscow had "perfected the guidance technology that would enable them to liquidate the U.S. Minuteman force."[7]

The Unanticipated Problem of Minuteman Vulnerability

The discovery—within a week of Carter's assuming office—that Moscow had perfected guidance technology for the SS-18, and would soon begin to test it, forced a fundamental, across-the-board reconsideration of United States foreign policy. The resulting reappraisal produced a permanent split in the administration's ranks, which would characterize Carter's term in office. The different emphases which the president's principal advisers placed on relations with the Soviets was natural and desirable, as long as policy differences occurred in the context of agreement over strategy. And in fact, as Vance notes, he and Brzezinski were in general accord at the outset.[8] But it would not last.

The discovery of Moscow's breakthrough precipitated an immediate debate which would thereafter dominate the administration's policymaking focus. The debate was precisely over strategy and, more often than not, produced diametrically opposed policy recommendations from Brzezinski and Vance. In brief terms, which will be explored on a case-by-case basis in more detail below, the differences between the president's two most influential advisers centered around their assessments of the political implications of Moscow's missile breakthrough.

Brzezinski saw a significant accrual of political leverage to Moscow as a result of the missile breakthrough. In an interview given later in the year, but which obviously reflected an earlier judgment, he noted:

> I don't consider nuclear superiority to be politically meaningless. I can fully acknowledge the fact that at a certain point strategic weaponry ceases to exercise military significance in terms of marginal differences and consequences, if used. However, the perception by others or by oneself of someone else having quote unquote

> strategic superiority can influence political behavior. It can induce some countries to act in a fashion that sometimes has been described as 'Finlandization.' And it can induce self-imposed restraint on the party that feels weaker and, last but not least, it can induce the party that feels that it enjoys strategic superiority to act politically in a more assertive fashion. In other words, it has the potential for political exploitation, even if in an actual warfare situation the differences may be at best, or at worst, on the margin.[9]

Vance sharply disagreed, perceiving the Soviet breakthrough as offering primarily a "theoretical" advantage. In his view, to assume that "Soviet missiles would perform with predicted accuracy and reliability and that the Soviets could actually coordinate the simultaneous arrival on widely dispersed targets of hundreds of missiles and thousands of warheads,"[10] was at best a "questionable assumption," which moreover could not be tested.

Thus Vance argued that "the theoretical vulnerability of our ICBMs would not inevitably expose the United States to nuclear coercion." This was so, he believed, because Soviet capability was not proven and American nuclear weapons were widely dispersed into land, sea, and airborne configurations. For Vance, this meant that "the ICBM vulnerability question and the suggested 'special' threat posed by Soviet heavy ICBMs were largely political problems."[11]

From these diametrically opposed positions, the president's chief advisers drew equally opposite policy conclusions. For Vance, detente remained the essential precondition for the successful execution of the strategy to restructure the global order. Therefore, it would be the secretary's policy approach to defer all major policy decisions pending completion of a SALT II treaty. In short, his approach would require detente first, and only then the resolution of issues pertaining to the United States' forward position around the Soviet periphery.

For Brzezinski, on the other hand, the Soviet technological breakthrough meant that Moscow would press its advantage in an effort to change the geopolitical balance of power. Therefore, it was most important to strengthen America's forward positions first and only afterward offer detente to Moscow. Moscow's breakthrough thus precipitated Brzezinski's deviation from the strategy agreed upon at the outset of the administration. Brezeinski, in effect, argued the case for a return to the strategy of containment against Vance's determination to carry forward efforts to construct the new international order.

It would be President Carter's fundamental inability to provide strategic guidance to harness the diverging policy recommendations of his two most important advisers that would bedevil the administration throughout. The unfortunate effect of the president's failure to establish and maintain clear lines of authority and pursue a consistent strategic course engendered policy instability, disharmony, and confusion at the highest levels within the American government, and between it and other governments. American policy appeared to be inconsistent and vacillating; and particularly during crises, appearance was reality. But what appeared to the public as presidential vacillation, indecision, and uncertainty was in reality the product of growing and fundamental disagreement within the American leadership over the proper strategy to pursue, a disagreement which the president did not, or perhaps could not, resolve.

Following his election, President-elect Carter took the position that he would promptly revive and conclude the strategic arms negotiations based on the Vladivostok accords that had stalled earlier under President Ford. This would be the SALT II agreement. Then, in negotiations to begin immediately thereafter, he would seek reductions in a SALT III accord. Shortly after his election, an indirect dialogue began between President-elect Carter and Leonid Brezhnev. In a speech in late November, Brezhnev had called for the "need to intensify" the arms control negotiations, and in a meeting with visiting Treasury Secretary William Simon had assured him that, contrary to rumors circulating abroad, he planned "no surprises" to test the new president's mettle.[12] Responding to Brezhnev's assurances, on December 3 Carter declared, "I intend to move aggressively to get the SALT talks off dead center, and maybe make an interim agreement relating to the Vladivostok terms."[13] His position was that

> after concluding the current round of negotiations, which Secretary of State Henry Kissinger has said is 90 percent completed, he would "start immediately" to seek a "more comprehensive agreement" to reduce the level of nuclear arms beneath the 2400 level.[14]

Immediately upon entering office January 20, in a wire service interview given the first week, the president reiterated his two-stage notion of the SALT negotiating process. He indicated that he wished to reach agreement quickly on the first stage and would not permit the outstanding questions of the cruise missile and the Backfire bomber to "stand in the way of some agreement."[15] By declaring that he would not permit the two issues on which negotiations had thus far foundered to stand in the way, the president was, or appeared to be, suggesting his willingness to compromise in order to reach agreement.

The Soviet leadership surely pondered the meaning of these remarks, but it was not solely the election of a new and seemingly more conciliatory American president that prompted Brezhnev to speak of the "need to intensify" the negotiations. As noted, Moscow had in the meantime made a significant breakthrough in its heavy missile guidance systems. The military significance of this development, achieved partly as a result of the transfer of Western technology that had occurred during the earlier detente period, was that it brought unexpectedly and uncomfortably nearer the day when the Soviet Union would be capable of lauching a preemptive attack against Minuteman, the land-based ICBM force, with a high damage expectancy. Ironically, the CIA's January National Intelligence Estimate predicted that the Soviet Union "would not achieve missile accuracies capable of threatening the Minuteman force before 1985."[16]

United States arms control positions, as well as planning for the development and deployment of new weapons, had been based virtually from the beginning on this and earlier estimates that assumed Moscow would not achieve the capability to strike accurately at Minuteman before the mid-eighties. It was for this reason, for example, that Kissinger had been less concerned with numbers than with the rate of MIRV deployment. He had sought "to use SALT negotiations to push the vulnerability of our land-based strategic forces as far into the future as possible; that required slowing down the rate at which the Soviets placed multiple warheads on their missiles." He noted that "sometime in the Eighties our land-based missiles would become vulnerable, depending on the rapidity with which the Soviets placed multiple warheads on their land-based missile launchers and improved their accuracy. . . ."[17]

It was also true that as of the mid-seventies, the new weapons which the United States had under development—the Trident submarine, B-1 bomber, long-range cruise missile, MX missile—were scheduled to be deployed by the mid-eighties. Subsequent decisions by the executive or Congress would accelerate or delay development and/or deployment of all of these weapons, but the lead-time planning was clear. United States weapons systems were designed to come on line in sufficient time to counterbalance anticipated advances in Soviet systems by the mid-eighties.

But Soviet weapons scientists confounded American intelligence experts by refining missile guidance systems five to eight years sooner than expected. It was on the basis of a far earlier advance in his nation's strategic weapons capability than anticipated by the American political leadership (United States intelligence had evidently warned of this possibility[18]) that Brezhnev pressed newly elected President Carter to conclude SALT II based on the Vladivostok accord "in the nearest future."[19] One may safely assume that Moscow had done its own evaluation of the American strategic position. The Soviet leadership understood and sought to capitalize on the coming shift in the strategic weapons balance by using SALT II to lock the United States into an inferior position before the shift became apparent and in this way make it very difficult to redress the imbalance when it materialized.

In the meantime, it was important not to alarm the new American leadership. Thus Brezhnev, in a speech delivered in Tula on January 18, rather disingenuously disavowed any notion of "striving for superiority in armaments with the aim of delivering 'the first strike.'"[20] Such allegations, he declared, were "totally unfounded." The Soviet Union was, he said, "prepared jointly with the new administration in the United States to accomplish a new major advance in relations between our countries."

> First of all . . . it is necessary to complete in the nearest future the drafting of the agreement on limiting strategic armaments on the basis that we had reached in Vladivostok already at the close of 1974. . . . Time will not wait and the conclusion of the agreement must not be postponed. . . . The Soviet Union, naturally, is prepared to advance further in questions of limiting strategic armaments. But at first it is necessary to consolidate what has already been achieved and to implement the accord reached in Vladivostok, the more so that the interim agreement expires this October. Then we could immediately pass on to talks on more far-reaching measures.[21]

President Carter's initial response was based on estimates that the Soviet Union would not achieve a capability to threaten Minuteman until the mid-eighties and therefore that the United States–Soviet strategic relationship would remain in essential and acceptable balance until then. In a letter to Brezhnev on January 26, the president noted with approval the Soviet leader's remarks at Tula disavowing any intention to seek nuclear superiority. The president stressed his intention to improve relations with the Soviet Union on the basis of "reciprocity, mutual respect and benefit" and identified several areas of possible cooperation.[22] First and foremost was a "rapid conclusion of SALT." Other areas included a verifiable comprehensive nuclear test ban, renewed efforts on mutual and balanced force reductions in Europe, and Soviet cooperation in the peaceful resolution of disputes in the Middle East and Southern Africa.

It would appear that it was shortly after the dispatch of the letter to Brezhnev that United States intelligence learned of the coming Soviet missile guidance tests, if the change in the president's position at this time is a fair indicator. The change in his position first became apparent in a wide-ranging discussion with Soviet Ambassador Anatoly Dobrynin a few days later, on February 1. President Carter now "called for a tangible, drastic reduction in nuclear weapons,[and] reduction of the possibility of a preemptive strike."[23] Repeating his two-stage negotiating concept, the president "clarified" his earlier statement on the cruise missile and the Backfire bomber, that he "wouldn't let these two items stand in the way of some agreement."[24] He now said for the first time that he "preferred to separate the cruise missile and Backfire issues from SALT II"—that is, leave them out altogether—and following the successful conclusion of SALT II, begin negotiations which would reduce the total number of nuclear missiles.[25]

Brezhnev replied to the president's January 26 letter on February 4, ignoring the exchange with Dobrynin. Finding Carter's letter "constructive and encouraging" the Soviet leader responded positively to the president's suggestions, including cooperation in the Middle East and Southern Africa, and even the possibility of a summit meeting. His main purpose, as National Security Adviser Brzezinski saw it, was to move to a "quick SALT agreement based on the earlier Vladivostok arrangement . . . including the Soviet version of the understanding on the cruise missile,"[26] which was to count each bomber with ten or more cruise missiles as a MIRVed launcher.

President Carter promptly responded. On February 8, he sent a letter shifting the position of the United States still further. He now set before the Soviet leader two equally (from the Soviet viewpoint) unpalatable alternatives: either a comprehensive reduction of missiles for each side, which Carter had earlier envisaged for SALT III, or a "quick agreement which would defer the questions of the cruise missile and the Soviet Backfire bomber."[27] Carter's letter also raised the issues of Berlin and human rights. The president noted "new tensions and constraints" in Berlin and expressed the hope that Moscow would "help to alleviate these tensions." On human rights, the president declared that it was "not our intention to interfere in the internal affairs of other nations," and while "we do not wish to create problems for the Soviet Union," he went on to say that "it will be necessary for our government to express publicly on occasion the sincere and deep feelings of myself and our people."

In a news conference that same day, February 8, in response to a question as to whether or not the United States should "strive for superiority," the president gave a curiously muddled answer. He declared, "I think that we are roughly equivalent, even though I think we are superior, in that either the Soviet Union or we could destroy a major part of the other nation if a major attack were made . . . ."[28] When asked if the United States was willing to restrain development of the cruise missile to "get something going in the SALT talks," the president responded with the new formulation.

> I would be willing to go ahead with the Soviet Union, conclude a quick agreement, if they think it advisable, and omit the Backfire bomber and the cruise missile from the negotiations at this stage, and then in a SALT Three talk, if necessary, put these two items back in for further discussion.[29]

Brezhnev delayed a response to the February 8 letter until the twenty-fifth, but when it came the reply was "chilling." Speaking "bluntly," the Soviet leader said that any agreement on SALT had to be based on Vladivostok and *include* the cruise missile, on which "a concrete formula . . . was practically agreed upon" in January 1976, but *exclude* Backfire entirely for the same reason. Brezhnev dismissed Carter's concern over Berlin as being "sent to the wrong address" and scathingly denounced the human rights campaign as "interference in our internal affairs." He concluded ominously, "We would not like to have our patience tested in any matter of international policy, including matters of Soviet–American relations."[30]

Brezhnev's letter jolted the top administration leadership. The president, especially, was "quite taken aback." Brzezinski saw it as "brutal, cynical, sneering, and even patronizing." He thought the letter had "a little bit of the same tone" of the first encounter between Khrushchev and Kennedy in 1961 when Khrushchev had tried to browbeat the newly elected Kennedy into concessions. Only Vance thought it "good, hard hitting, to the point."[31] In any case, Brezhnev's February 25 letter, which came hard upon the discovery by United States intelligence of Moscow's imminent advance in its missile guidance systems, set the tone and established the urgency for a major revision of American foreign policy. Over the next several weeks the president and his closest advisers hurriedly and in tightest secrecy worked out a major shift in the American arms control position, the "comprehensive proposal" which Vance would take to Moscow.

Washington Offers Moscow an Unpalatable Choice

What appears to have happened, although the evidence is understandably fragmentary, is that the Carter administration initially had been willing to conclude a SALT II agreement based largely upon the Vladivostok accord, which would have included a compromise on the cruise missile and a trade-off of some sort on the Backfire, possibly along the lines of Kissinger's January 1976 proposals.[32] This willingness was based on intelligence estimates that advances in Soviet missile accuracy were still five to eight years away. But when United States intelligence learned, probably some time immediately prior to Carter's talk with Dobrynin on February 1, that Moscow was planning to test a new, accurate guidance system for its heavy missiles later in the year (the Soviet Union would actually conduct six tests beginning in late October),[33] it changed not only the arms control picture but the entire foreign policy equation.

Soviet possession of a first-strike capability, which would be the result of a large, MIRVed, and now accurate missile force, by 1980 instead of 1982 or 1985, threw all previous calculations out the window. It meant that Moscow would have an advantageous "window of opportunity," a period of time until the United States could recover, giving the Soviet Union increased geopolitical leverage in what was already perceived as a drive to alter the correlation of forces. What this signaled for arms control was clear: under no circumstances could the United States enter into an agreement which constrained its freedom to take necessary countermeasures. This applied particularly strongly to the cruise missile, which Moscow was so energetically pressing to include in a SALT II agreement.

Of all the strategic weapons under development—Trident, MX, B-1, and the cruise missile—only the cruise missile could be deployed in time to counter the emergence of an accurate Soviet missile force, which was now predicted to appear by 1980.[34] It was imperative to have—or to be perceived as having—a countervailing force to maintain strategic stability. It was a subtle game in which no public threats needed to be issued. Both sides understood that a strategic weapons advantage possessed by one side would afford considerable political leverage and deterrence power against the other in a third-country crisis. Even if it was still true that neither country could "win" an all-out war against the other, the value of advantage lay in circumscribing Washington's willingness to contend with Moscow in other areas. This was the political utility of strategic weapons "advantage." It would free Moscow to attempt to manipulate crises in its favor, demonstrate American helplessness, and press other powers for greater accommodation to Soviet interests. This, of course, did not mean that Moscow would succeed ipso facto, but it opened up possibilities that otherwise would not arise.

Until the United States extricated itself from its strategic predicament there would be no direct contention with Moscow, no attempt "to act politically in a more assertive fashion." Indeed, "crisis avoidance" would become the major characteristic of Jimmy Carter's term in office as the American leadership grappled with what was in effect the fait accompli of a growing Soviet strategic weapons advantage. As quickly became clear, there was no short-term remedy, no quick fix, as far as the land-based ICBM balance was concerned.

The president decided that under these circumstances the most effective and rapidly deployable counterforce weapon was the long-range, air-launched cruise missile (ALCM). Because of its high accuracy, deployment of ALCM would reestablish the strategic balance at the counterforce level and have the additional advantage of not being unduly provocative. While very accurate, the cruise missile was slow. It was not, like the ICBM, a time-urgent, hard-target weapon. For that reason it could not be a first-strike weapon, which perhaps suited the president's preferences.

In order to match the anticipated deployment schedule of the Soviet Union's presumedly more accurate missiles, Carter chose to use the aging B-52 bomber as a stand-off ALCM launcher rather than the B-1, which was still in the development stage. This was a reasonable choice eliminating one potential source of delay, for time was of the essence and there was no telling what problems would arise in developing a new bomber. The B-52 was an old but proven carrier. The decision to employ the B-52 over the B-1, however, led to cancellation of the B-1, which was announced on June 30 amid a loud public outcry. By failing to explain the rationale for cancelling the B-1 beyond offering the unsatisfactory reason that it was "inordinately expensive," the Carter administration mishandled what was a logical choice. The result was that, as Vance put it, "this correct and courageous decision became a millstone around the administration's neck."[35]

The choice of weapons response made, the next problem was how to evade the arms control trap, for accession to a SALT II treaty which constrained cruise missile deployment would seal the United States into a position of strategic inferiority for several years. Here Carter employed what appeared to be the same strategem, which I term "the Jackson safeguards," used in 1973 when Moscow had unveiled four new MIRVed missiles instead of the two which had been expected.[36] In early February the president invited Henry Jackson to a breakfast meeting at the White House where the senator explained his objections to SALT I, Vladivostok, and Kissinger's January 1976 proposals. Expressing interest in his views, the president "asked him for amplification in writing."[37]

Jackson's reply, drafted by his principal aide on strategic affairs, Richard Perle, arrived on February 15. It called for equal aggregates and overall reductions, the position taken four years before. Implicitly addressing the warhead accuracy issue, Jackson proposed reopening the question of definition of the heavy missile and including the SS-19 in the heavy missile category. The senator called for a reduction in Moscow's heavy missile allowance below the 308 number established in SALT I, even though the United States had agreed to drop the heavy missile category at Vladivostok. And Senator Jackson also wanted the Backfire to be counted as a heavy bomber. The United States should be accorded the option of building heavy missiles of its own, and SALT should place no constraints on the cruise missile program, which "should continue apace."[38]

Henry Jackson's hawkish arms control positions were well known. He was the recognized Senate expert. Whether or not the president confided in him regarding the impending problem of Soviet strategic weapons superiority is unknown but beside the point. That the president used Jackson's objections to establish a baseline minimum condition of arms control acceptability within the administration, if not with the public, is undeniable. As Strobe Talbott notes, Jackson's memo, which was distributed widely in classified form throughout the upper reaches of the administration, "unquestionably reinforced the instincts of Carter, Brown, Brzezinski and Aaron to seek more than a mere consummation of the Vladivostok accord."[39]

Having thus determined an appropriate weapons response and established minimum terms for an equitable arms control agreement, the administration proceeded to formulate alternative arms control proposals which would either allow the United States to match Soviet missile deployment with the cruise missile or negate the requirement to build a countervailing system by a reduction of the threat. Here, however, sharp disagreement occurred between Vance and Brzezinski and their aides on how to proceed. Vance, insisting that the United States remain within the arms control process, argued for what was termed "Vladivostok-minus," the Vladivostok agreement minus cruise missile and Backfire, which would be deferred to SALT III.[40]

Brzezinski, as noted above, saw Minuteman vulnerability and the political benefits it conferred on Moscow as real. Although he wanted a more comprehensive approach, he says in his memoirs that he "favored modest cuts as the most attainable goal," reducing the overall ceiling to 2,000 weapons.[41] It was Brzezinski's aide, David Aaron, however, who pressed the case for deep cuts in secret meetings during the period March 10 to 19, when the critical choices were made. It is difficult to believe that Aaron could have taken the deep cuts position over a period of time without the support and encouragement of his chief. In any case, the fundamental difference between Vance and Brzezinski appeared to be over whether to remain within the arms control process as established or break out of it.

A cabinet-level Special Coordination Committee (SCC) meeting of the NSC on March 10, chaired by Brzezinski, greatly coalesced attitudes on the best means of "staving off our strategic problem." Aaron emphasized "the whole issue of Minuteman vulnerability coming up fast on the horizon," and urged deep cuts as the appropriate response.[42] Aaron's comment was implicit reference to impending Soviet missile tests which would enable Moscow to perfect missile accuracy. The tests would not begin for several more months, but it was American advance warning about them that gave meaning and urgency to the deliberations.

Secretary of Defense Harold Brown proposed limiting the number of missile tests conducted each year. This was based on a CIA estimation that it took the Soviets "at least fifteen flight tests to perfect a new missile."[43] Brown proposed that SALT II should limit Moscow to two tests per year, which would mean that it would take over seven years, practically the life of the treaty, to perfect the guidance mechanism. Otherwise, Brown believed, "an unfettered testing program would turn those Soviet missiles into 'hard-target killers.'"[44] A second idea favorably received was an ICBM freeze, which would significantly limit the "momentum of Soviet ICBM modernization."[45]

Two days later the top leadership—Carter, Mondale, Vance, Brzezinski, Brown, CIA chief Stansfield Turner, JCS Chairman George Brown, and chief arms control negotiator Paul Warnke—met in highest secrecy without deputies present.[46] There the president took the decision on the recommendation of Defense Secretary Brown to go forward with what came to be known as the "comprehensive proposal." Deep reductions and constraints on missile modernization were seen as the answer to "the impending superiority of Soviet land-based ICBMs." Of course, it was also true that the likely rejection of the American proposal would leave Washington free to take whatever countermeasures were deemed necessary. Such was the basic thrust of the decision.

That the March 10 to 12 period was decisive can be seen from a comparison of President Carter's public remarks on March 9 and 17, respectively. During a news conference on the ninth, he was still arguing for a quick "Vladivostok-minus" agreement setting aside the Backfire and cruise missile, followed immediately by discussions for SALT III. "My hope has been and is that by the exclusion of both those controversial items . . . we might move to a rapid agreement at SALT II and immediately begin to discuss, for instance, the Backfire bomber, the cruise missile, in subsequent negotiations."[47] There was no suggestion of a preference for deep reductions in SALT II.

Eight days later, however, in an address to the UN General Assembly, he revealed gingerly the broadening of his position. Noting that SALT was "extraordinarily complicated," he declared:

> My preference would be for strict controls or even a freeze on new types and new generations of weaponry and with a deep reduction in the strategic arms of both sides. . . . Alternatively, and perhaps much more easily, we could conclude a limited agreement based on those elements of the Vladivostok accord on which we can find complete consensus and set aside for prompt consideration and subsequent negotiations the more contentious issues and also the deeper reductions in modern weapons which I favor.[48]

On the nineteenth, a still more restricted circle, the president, Mondale, Vance, Brzezinski, and Brown, met to give final shape to the two-track negotiating position which had been decided upon.[49] The president subsequently indicated during a news conference on March 24 that his position had been settled earlier, by the seventeenth, at least. In response to a question whether Vance would take a "new set of proposals on SALT" to Moscow, the president answered, "Yes, substantial reductions . . . will be our first proposal. I spelled this out briefly in my UN speech. And the second fallback position will be, in effect, to ratify Vladivostok and to wait until later to solve the most difficult and contentious issues."[50]

In his opening statement before questions, President Carter had made the point of saying that he felt it "very important" to convey to Congress and the people "what is going on" regarding "issues that affect foreign policy." But it was not until his closing remarks that he gave a brief but surprising glimpse of the real objective behind the negotiations when he said, "If we're disappointed—which is a possibility—then we'll try to modify our stance." The president, in other words, was plainly inviting the Soviets to reject the proposals outright with the suggestion that they were but opening gambits.[51] In retrospect it is clear that Washington wanted no agreement unless it would satisfy what were now quite different security requirements than those which faced the nation when President Carter entered office. What Washington wanted was time, and this required drawn-out bargaining, not a quick agreement.

The Moscow Meetings and Afterwards

Secretary Vance arrived in Moscow on March 27 for three days of negotiations, holding his first meeting the next morning. The Soviet leadership, which had had some if not sufficient advance knowledge of the new United States proposals—from Vance's discussion with Dobrynin a few days before his departure, from President Carter's own public disclosures, and from the letter of February 8—showed little inclination to consider the new American position. Indeed, Brezhnev opened the first meeting with an attempt to play turnabout on human rights. Ignoring the purpose of the meeting, he launched into a "diatribe" cataloging alleged human rights abuses in the United States.[52] Finally turning to arms control, the Soviet leader dismissed the United States proposals before Vance formally presented them, insisting that the Vladivostok accord—with its cruise missile restrictions—was the "only acceptable basis for further progress."[53] This session set the tone for the impasse which ensued.

Vance presented both the comprehensive and the Vladivostok-minus proposals at a second session, on the twenty-eighth, which Brezhnev did not attend. Foreign Minister Gromyko represented the Soviet side. In the Vladivostok-minus proposal, the United States offered an agreement based on the 1974 Vladivostok accord but deferred the contentious cruise missile and Backfire bomber issues to SALT III. The comprehensive proposal, which Vance emphasized was the president's "preferred position," was more complicated and surprising.

The numbers in the comprehensive proposal were lower than in any proposal put forward during the drafting and formulation process, which explains the extreme secrecy surrounding the Vance trip.[54] The Soviets were taken aback by the sweeping reductions put forward. The proposal called for reducing overall system aggregates agreed to at Vladivostok from 2,400 to between 1,800 and 2,000, and MIRVed launchers from 1,320 to between 1,100 and 1,200. New were proposals to limit MIRVed ICBMs to 550 and to reduce the Soviet "heavy" ICBM from 308 to 150. There would be a total ban on development, testing, and deployment of *any* new ICBM; and existing ICBMs and SLBMs each could be tested only six times a year. There were no limits on the number of cruise missiles of all types with a range under 2,500 kilometers, and only those with a range greater than 2,500 kilometers were banned. The Backfire bomber would not be counted if the Soviets provided assurances that it was not a strategic bomber.[55] This, however, would also disqualify it as a cruise missile carrier.

The comprehensive proposal was clearly "loaded" in favor of the United States. The "reductions," except for Backfire, would all have to come on the Soviet side, while the United States would only have to forego the MX, which was still on the drawing board. The heart of the United States proposal was the limitation on MIRVed ICBMs to 550 and the reduction of the heavy SS-18 force from 308 to 150. The first-strike capability of the heavy MIRVed missiles was, of course, the main concern as Soviet missile accuracy grew. Assuming ten warheads on each SS-18, Moscow would be able to field only 1,500 warheads instead of the 3,080 it could have if all 308 SS-18s were MIRVed—insufficient for a first strike against Minuteman.[56]

Furthermore, the proposal—in fact, both proposals—allowed the United States to deploy unlimited numbers and types of long-range cruise missiles anywhere, including Western Europe, as long as they did not exceed 2,500 kilometers in range. Soviet leaders could no doubt conceive of a large-scale deployment of ground-launched cruise missiles (GLCM) in Western Europe with sufficient range to strike Soviet territory. Such proximity would greatly compensate for the cruise missile's slow speed.

In essence, American interests would be served regardless of which proposal the Soviets chose. Under "Vladivostok-minus" the United States would have been willing to live with higher numbers of MIRVed weapons in return for no constraints on long-range cruise missiles—its chosen method of responding to the growing ICBM threat to Minuteman. And under the comprehensive proposal, the United States sought stringent reductions in those Soviet weapons which constituted the main threat, restraints on Soviet ability to fine-tune the guidance systems on existing heavy missiles, and prohibition against development of any new ones, while similarly remaining free to deploy as many cruise missiles in land-, sea-, and air-launched modes as desired. Both proposals were transparent, inviting the brusque rejection they shortly received.

After a day of discussions and study, Vance and Brezhnev met again on March 30, when the Soviet leader delivered a "harsh" response. Vance unconvincingly says that he "expected . . . objections to specific aspects of our proposal and to our numbers" but he thought there was a possibility that the Soviets would make counterproposals. Instead, he was "angered at the vehemence and finality with which he [Brezhnev] rejected our SALT proposals. There was not even a hint of a counterproposal."[57] Brezhnev accurately called the proposals "unconstructive and one-sided," but less truthfully, "harmful to Soviet security." (Indeed, Brezhnev's comment denouncing the United States proposals suggested that the Soviet side still had no inkling of the rationale behind them. It would appear that Moscow did not realize that Washington was acting on foreknowledge of the Soviet technological breakthrough. Thus, Brezhnev struck the pose of an offended party.)

With no prospect of serious negotiations, let alone agreement, the meeting ended; but at Soviet suggestion it was agreed to meet again in May. Vance went immediately to the American ambassador's residence at Spasso House, where he held a news conference. He announced that "the Soviets told us that they had examined our two proposals and did not find either acceptable. They proposed nothing new on their side." He then explained the two proposals made by the United States.

> The first proposal was what we had called our deferral proposal. . . . The proposal is not only consistent with the agreement reached at Vladivostok, as you know, and there was no agreement reached at Vladivostok with respect to either the cruise missile or the Backfire bomber and therefore they have been and are open issues. . . . As an alternative . . . what we have referred to as the comprehensive proposal . . . was a proposal which would have really made substantive progress toward true arms control.[58]

Vance then revealed the comprehensive proposal in everything but the all-important numbers. He described the categories of reductions, the ban on modernization; the limits on flight tests; the bans on development, testing, and deployment of new weapons; the ban on intercontinental-range cruise missiles; the requested assurances on the Backfire—everything but the numbers proposed for each category. He concluded by saying, "We will leave without having achieved that general framework. I am very disappointed that we were unable to do so."[59]

When asked for the "central reason" for rejection given by the Soviets, he replied, "It was their view that the deferral proposal did not accord with Vladivostok. It is our very clear view that it does . . .

because Backfire and the cruise missile were not included in the Vladivostok accord and they remain unsettled issues." Was there a difference in interpretation of the two aides-mémoire exchanged after Vladivostok, he was asked, referring to the Soviet version, which spoke simply of "missiles," and the American version, which mentioned "ballistic missiles"? Vance replied simply, without elaboration, "There was a discussion of the aide-mémoire, yes."[60]

This was the nub of it. Vance was correct to have said that there had been no specific discussion of cruise missiles at Vladivostok.[61] It was only afterward, during the formulation of the aide-mémoire which would formally acknowledge the nature and content of the discussions, that the issue arose. President Ford and Secretary Kissinger had agreed to count each "air launched missile" with a range over 600 kilometers as a strategic nuclear delivery vehicle in the overall aggregate of 2,400. In its draft aide-mémoire, Moscow expanded the definition of "air launched missile" to include the cruise missile, to which Washington objected strenuously, declaring that the term referred to "ballistic" missiles only. This was a very clever but transparent Soviet tactic to constrain a major new weapons system, or block any agreement. It was one thing to count each air-launched ballistic missile in the overall aggregate—the United States had none and planned none—but it was quite another to count each air-launched cruise missile, which would become an important new element in the American panoply of weapons.

What was disconcerting was the way in which the dispute was resolved. Kissinger agreed to leave the term "air launched missile" unmodified in the aide-mémoire, presumably in order to avoid further embarrassment in the growing dispute over what was agreed upon at Vladivostok.[62] He did, however, seek to protect United States interests by sending a note to Gromyko stating the American understanding of the term. American domestic politics appeared to determine the issue. The Soviets, of course, emphasized the aide-mémoire and disregarded the note.

On March 30, following Vance's news conference, President Carter held one of his own, where he divulged some of the numbers associated with the comprehensive proposal but not all. The president reinforced Vance's view of Vladivostok. "One of our proposals . . . was very brief, and it was our second option."[63] Then he declared firmly, "The difference between us and the Soviet Union on this point is that the Soviets claim that Secretary Kissinger and my predecessors in the White House . . . did agree to forgo the deployment of cruise missiles. Our position is that we never agreed to any such thing."[64] Carter was engaging in a bit of verbal juggling himself. The Soviets had not objected to deployment but to how cruise missiles were counted, which, to be sure, would severely restrict deployment but not prohibit it.

The comprehensive proposal, he said, called for "substantial reductions" in the overall aggregrates and MIRV launchers well below the 2,400 and 1,320 levels established at Vladivostok. A third point was to freeze ICBMs at 550 and ban deployment of mobile missiles. The United States also proposed to "limit the number of test firings of missiles to six per year. . . ."[65] The one number the president did not divulge was that calling for reduction of the Soviet heavy missile force from 308 to 150.

Asked if he was willing to modify his human rights statements "if necessary to achieve any progress," Carter's quick reply was no. He insisted that his human rights statements were "compatible with the consciousness of the country." Besides, he said, "the Soviets have in effect ratified the rights of human beings when they adopted the United Nations Charter. The Helsinki agreement . . . also includes references to human rights. . . ."[66] Would he "hang tough" on arms control? The president's reply was an emphatic "yes."

> I think that it's important for us to take advantage of an opportunity this year to negotiate not just a superficial ratification of the rules by which we can continue the arms race, but to have a freeze on deployment and development of new missiles and an actual reduction in launchers and MIRVed missiles below what was agreed to previously. And on those items I intend to remain very strong in my positon.[67]

He went further, saying, "Obviously, if we feel at the conclusion of the discussions that the Soviets are not acting in good faith, then I would be forced to consider a much more deep commitment to the development and deployment of additional weapons." It was curious indeed. Having practically led the Soviets into an outright rejection of United States proposals before the Vance trip, when he had said that Soviet rejection would cause him to "modify" his stance, he now declared unequivocally after they had done so that he was not inclined to modify, but would remain "very strong" in his position. And if Moscow was not acting in "good faith" he would be "forced to consider" deployment of "additional weapons."

The impression conveyed by Carter and Vance was that Moscow was opposed to arms control, an impression that Soviet leaders immediately sought to alter. Shortly after seeing Vance off at the airport on April 1, Gromyko held a rare press conference of his own. He criticized the president for commenting on the talks "without even waiting for the Secretary of State's arrival in Washington,"[68] while stating the Soviet case for rejection. Reaffirming the Vladivostok accord, Gromyko declared that "there was progress after Vladivostok" and "opportunities to bring things to completion." Then, he said, "all of a sudden the question arose of the so-called cruise missiles."

> They tried to prove that the Vladivostok accord did not refer to the cruise missiles, . . . that the Vladivostok accord concerns ballistic missiles only.[69]

Gromyko then turned to the Backfire issue, saying that the American side insisted it "must be taken into consideration in the agreement." It was his view that "this question is being artifically introduced to complicate the situation along the road of concluding an agreement." He declared that Washington and Moscow had "exchanged relevant official documents which sealed the Vladivostok accords," referring to the aide-mémoire. All that remained, he said, was "to carry the matter forward to the signing of an agreement." But "all of a sudden a wall had risen and everything was frozen." Apparently, "influential forces in the U.S." were intent upon "revising the commitments taken in Vladivostok." Moscow was "categorically opposed to this."[70]

The Soviet foreign minister attacked the view "now being circulated" that the United States had put forth "some broad program for disarmament" that Moscow rejected. "This . . . is essentially false." They were asked, he said, "to liquidate half of the rockets in our possession" known as heavy missiles and to reduce the rest. This, he averred, was not the way to agreement. This approach "only damages the Vladivostok accord, breaks the balance of limitations concerning which agreement was reached in Vladivostok." What changed after Vladivostok, he asked rhetorically? "Nothing, absolutely nothing changed."[71]

Vance, he said, proposed that the two sides agree to prohibit the development of new types of weapons and give up the right to modernize existing missiles. "To put forward such demands is a dubious if not a cheap move." After an objective study of Vance's proposals the Soviet government concluded that Washington sought in its comprehensive proposal "unilateral advantages . . . to the detriment of the Soviet Union." Leonid Brezhnev said this to Secretary Vance "during the first talk . . . [and] during the last talk which was held yesterday." As far as the "narrow proposal" was concerned,

> we are offered what does not belong to the United States. A non-strategic aircraft was named a strategic one, and then they say: We are ready not to include this bomber in the agreement now, if the Soviet Union consents to give a green light for the manufacture and development of the U.S. Cruise missiles.[72]

The Soviet Union rejected the so-called "narrow proposal," too, because it would not even provide "a semblance of security." Yet, despite the unacceptability of current proposals and the fact that "substantial differences" now existed between the two countries, this did not mean that there were "insurmountable obstacles." If the United States' leadership were to "take up a more realistic stand . . . give greater consideration to the interests of the security of the Soviet Union and its allies and . . . not strive for unilateral advantages," an agreement was still possible.[73] Gromyko closed his lengthy statement by ticking off a varied list of demands, including reduction of military budgets, the non-use of force in international relations, no first use of nuclear weapons, non-transfer of strategic weapons to third countries, and, finally, liquidation of American forward bases in Europe.

Gromyko, too, had engaged in a degree of obfuscation on several points. He knew full well that it had been Moscow which was responsible for the cruise missile "issue" and that both of Washington's proposals excluded Backfire (although later in his statement he noted the United States position on Backfire correctly). He had been less than candid when he said that the two countries "had exchanged relevant official documents which sealed the Vladivostok accords" and downright deceptive in saying that all that remained was to sign the agreement. The gist of the Soviet position was clear: Moscow refused to renegotiate what it already considered negotiated. The Soviets had pocketed Washington's accession to the Soviet interpretation of "bombers" and "missiles" in the Vladivostok aide-mémoire of 1974 and would not budge—certainly not without a price. The real issue was: how much was Washington willing to pay for an agreement?

But before that issue would be addressed, Washington wished to divulge more of its concerns to the public. The day after Gromyko's press conference, but still before Secretary Vance returned to Washington, Brzezinski gave a press conference of his own, during which he laid out Washington's main concerns in reaching an equitable arms control agreement. The national security adviser stated that the United States proposals were designed to accomplish two basic purposes, to provide both sides with "political and strategic" parity and stability.[74] He stressed that "there should be no self-evident advantage in the agreement which would be either of a strategic character or which would be susceptible to political perception as an advantage." He went on to explain that a treaty had to take into account technological progress:

> If you only have certain kinds of limits but do not anticipate technologial dynamics, what may seem stable in 1977 or 1978 could become very unstable in 1980 or 1985.[75]

In these few words, Brzezinski had revealed the main concern that had driven the administration to the comprehensive proposal. The issue was not this year or next, but three to eight years from then, when the Soviet Union would have a highly accurate MIRV force and the United States no effective countervailing system. This would be particularly so if the Soviets developed their technological capabilities sooner, as Washington now expected, rather than later, and the United States was constrained in cruise missile deployment. This would indeed open up a "very unstable" situation from the point of view of the United States.

Brzezinski discussed the proposal to limit the SS-17, SS-18, and SS-19 to the Minuteman level of 550. This was not as inequitable as it seemed, he said. Although the United States had already reached that level, it would "forgo all further improvements in ICBMs, and . . . would abandon the MX program." The Soviet Union, on the other hand, "could still go up because they are below that number."[76] In trying to put together an equitable proposal Brzezinski noted that each side felt the other had weapons which were "particularly threatening." For our part, he said, "We don't want them to acquire a capability to very significantly threaten our land-based systems."[77] The United States was prepared to reciprocate by giving up MX and limiting the cruise missile. "Basically, what it would give them is the sense of security that the United States is forgoing, as a basic strategic option, the acquisition of first-strike capability against their land-based systems."[78]

In essence, what Brzezinski had explained was that Moscow had turned down the bargain the United States had offered to deny each side a first-strike capability against the other. But he also held out the hope that the Soviets would reconsider, saying, "We believe that in some respects we are in the earlier, educational part of the process in which both sides have to think through the implications both of an unchecked arms race and of the benefits of reductions and a freeze."[79]

The fact was that Moscow had turned down the United States offer and would not reconsider, which was in retrospect perhaps the principal result of the comprehensive proposal.[80] It clarified positions on both sides. No longer could Moscow hide behind the shibboleth of arms control while continuing to increase its forces—not without expecting the United States to do the same. The comprehensive proposal resolved the issue for the United States. There would not be the reductions the president had hoped for; Washington would be forced to build a countervailing threat to the emerging Soviet threat. In other words, the United States could counterbalance but could not eliminate the threat to Minuteman.

The comprehensive proposal also provided a measuring rod by which to evaluate all subsequent arms control proposals. This worked to the advantage of the administration in the short run, but once it decided—for political reasons rather than arms control reasons—to proceed with SALT II, the measuring rod would return to haunt them. The necessarily high degree of secrecy, so contrary to the professed openness of the administration, which surrounded the formulation of policy indicated the gravity of the matter, but it also confused and dismayed the bureaucracy, press, and interested public.[81] Most importantly, the March breakdown in the negotiations bought the adminstration what it needed most, and that was time. Time was required to restructure American foreign policy, to act quickly to strengthen those areas which could be expected to come under pressure from a "politically . . . more assertive" Soviet Union.

Proceeding with Arms Control—Negotiations without Agreement

The Carter administration decided to move forward with arms control negotiations, but not because it was believed that an equitable agreement could be achieved. Indeed, that was now judged to be highly unlikely.[82] The negotiations would be an important way to engage Moscow while moving actively to strengthen other positions.

Before resumption of the negotiations scheduled for mid-May, the Carter administration proceeded with a series of decisions designed to strengthen United States nuclear forces and raise the threshold for conventional conflict in Western Europe. Shortly after the realization of the impending strategic weapons shift, the president authorized an in-depth study of the overall United States–Soviet relationship, designated Presidential Review Memorandum 10 (PRM 10). Begun February 18, it was completed in June and signed as a Presidential Directive (PD 18) on August 24,1977.[83] The decision reaffirmed "essential equivalance" in strategic forces and forward defense in Europe, while maintaining a mobile deployment force "for global contingencies, particularly in the Persian Gulf region and Korea."[84]

As a step toward maintaining essential equivalance in strategic forces, Washington moved to upgrade 300 Minuteman III missiles by installing Mark 12-A warheads with the new NS-20 guidance systems.[85] This step sharply improved the counterforce capability for the weapon and for the time being kept the United States MIRVed ICBM total abreast of Moscow's ongoing MIRV program. In the course of the year, Moscow would actually deploy somewhat fewer MIRVs on SS-17s, SS-18s, and SS-19s, but the total number would eventually be much larger.[86]

In Western Europe, President Carter obtained in May reluctant consent from the allies for a 3 percent increase in NATO defense spending. At the same time, Washington hastened to reinforce American military power, increasing forces by 35,000 men, deploying two more combat brigades, and pre-positioning full sets of equipment for three additional divisions beyond the two division stocks on hand. The Supreme Allied Commander for Europe (SACEUR) was delegated added nuclear power by the substitution of three Poseidon submarines with over 400 warheads for five older Polaris submarines with 80 warheads.[87] Bomber capability was more than doubled as the mostly United Kingdom–based FB-111 bombers were increased from 80 to 164. It was also decided to proceed with development of a ground-launched intermediate-range cruise missile (GLCM) and an extended-range Pershing II.[88]

It was against the backdrop of the substantial reinforcement of the United States position in Western Europe that preparations for the next meeting between Vance and Gromyko were made. In exchanges between the two countries in early April, Washington now attempted to establish broader ties with the Soviet leadership. Following Brezhnev's public appraisal that "a reasonable accommodation is possible" if the United States altered its "one sided position," President Carter performed yet another abrupt turnabout. He now professed himself "very eager to change" any positions Moscow could "prove" were inequitable.[89]

On April 13, Brzezinski raised the idea of periodic summit meetings between the two heads of state, and two days later the president proposed meetings "on a continuing basis" at least once a year, irrespective of progress in formal arms control negotiations.[90] Toward the end of the month, in response to this proposal, Brezhnev took a position he and his successors would maintain consistently thereafter, that a visit to the United States or a summit meeting between the two leaders would only be possible in the context of a successful arms control agreement.[91] Although Washington would repeat this proposal several times both publicly and privately through mid-year, the effort to engage Moscow in a continuous dialogue lapsed following a firm restatement of the Soviet view in early July.

In the meantime, American leaders attempted to make the next arms control offer somewhat "more palatable" to the Soviets. During preliminary negotiations in late April, Vance had proposed a three-part framework for an agreement. It would consist of a treaty based on the Vladivostok numbers, to run until 1985; an interim agreement of two or three years, deferring the difficult issues; and a statement of principles regarding a commitment to deep reductions in follow-on negotiations for SALT III.[92] When the two sides met in

Geneva May 18–20, Moscow accepted the structure put forth but once again expressed dissatisfaction with the content of United States proposals.

Vance proposed and Gromyko readily accepted the three-part structure—with one change. Vance's proposal for an interim executive agreement meant that the treaty and the executive agreement would be examined separately in Congress. The Senate had sole jurisdiction over ratification of treaties, while for executive agreements simple majorities in both houses were necessary. The distribution of Washington's proposals raised an intriguing possibility. Briefly, the ICBM limits were in the treaty, while the cruise missile limits were in the executive agreement. As Gromyko quickly observed, the Senate could ratify the treaty limiting Soviet ICBMs, while the House could reject the executive agreement removing all constraints on the cruise missile. If a planned maneuver by the American side, it was clumsy and shallow. When Gromyko proposed as an alternative a protocol which would be attached to the treaty and receive identical treatment, Vance quickly assented.

Though there was agreement on structure, there was little agreement on substance. The essence of the United States proposal consisted of a trade-off between Soviet heavy missiles and American cruise missiles. Vance proposed a limit of 190 on Soviet heavy missiles (up from the 150 contained in the comprehensive proposal) in return for a limit of 250 on ALCMs. Land- and sea-based cruise missiles would be in the protocol, while the ALCM remained separate and outside. Gromyko rejected as out of order all efforts to place limits on Soviet heavy missiles, whether MIRVed or unMIRVed, and insisted that ALCMs be included in the treaty and counted in the 1,320 MIRVed launcher subceiling agreed to at Vladivostok.[93]

While Vance was prepared to accept a 600 kilometer limitation for the land- and sea-based cruise missiles for the duration of the protocol, which was agreed to run for three years (no doubt with an eye to applying pressure on the NATO allies), he would accept no such range limitation for the ALCM, or its inclusion in the treaty. "We were not prepared to accept his proposal unless the Soviets accepted a reduction in the 308 ceiling on heavy missiles."[94] Within three months, however, this negotiating approach would be discarded in the face of Soviet intransigence. Not only would Vance agree to include ALCM in the treaty, but he would also agree to no meaningful limits on Soviet heavy missiles.

For the moment, Vance attempted to put a good face on the exchange. After the last meeting on May 20, he held a news conference where he declared that "the differences between the two sides have been narrowed." But Gromyko, again not to be outmaneuvered, as after the March talks—and much to the consternation of reporters attempting to follow the deliberations—stated firmly upon departing for Moscow that "major, serious differences remain."[95] Of course, it was incorrect to say that "differences" had been narrowed; they had not. There had been no agreement on substance, only on form, but this suited the American side as Washington moved deliberately toward the Soviet position.

SALT discussions continued through the summer, mainly between the delegations assigned to Geneva. In fact, indicating the reduction in importance of the negotiations, the United States delegation was given greater latitude to explore alternatives than ever before in the talks.[96] By the summer of 1977, the essential decisions on the means to strengthen American positions around the Soviet periphery had been made and formalized in Presidential Directive 18, signed August 24, as noted above. It meant that Washington now could move forward in the effort to reach a compromise with Moscow.

As the October 3 expiration date for SALT I approached and Moscow showed no signs of budging, Vance sought to restart the high-level negotiating process. In meetings with Dobrynin on September 9 and 10, it was agreed that Gromyko would meet with the United States leadership later in September on the occasion of his attendance at the opening session of the UN General Assembly. Vance proposed that each side declare unilaterally that it would continue to observe SALT I limits as long as the other did.[97] At the same time, he asked for a response to three of Washington's concerns—reductions in the Vladivostok ceilings, limits on heavy missiles, and a new subceiling for MIRVed ICBMs.

Vance's suggestion of a sub-ceiling on MIRVed ICBMs was a new element in the United States negotiating package. Behind it lay the fear that Moscow was making an end run in its ability to threaten Minuteman. Intelligence reports indicated that the Soviet Union was attempting to improve the hard-target kill capability not only of the heavy SS-18 but of the so-called "light" SS-19 ICBM, as well.[98] The growing concern was that Moscow would *accept* the proposed heavy missile-cruise missile trade-off, thus constraining the main United

States counter weapon while leaving the SS-19 unconstrained and free to become the hard-target killer of Minuteman whose emergence American leaders were striving to prevent.

Moscow responded on September 17, dismissing out of hand the proposed trade-off between heavy missiles and ALCMs and preemptorily declaring the heavy missile issue closed. But the Soviets were silent on the idea of a MIRVed ICBM ceiling. The finality of the Soviet reply precipitated what Vance later termed an "unsatisfactory exchange" with Dobrynin during which Vance exclaimed with equal finality that further Soviet rehashing of what purportedly had been agreed to at Vladivostok "would not be productive."[99] Although Dobrynin conveyed Moscow's agreement to observe the SALT I limits as long as Washington did, there was little ground on which to expect progress when Gromyko arrived on September 22.

When Vance and Gromyko met on the twenty-second, the secretary of state once again proposed the heavy missile-cruise missile trade-off, but with a new twist. In return for a heavy missile limit of 220 (up from 190 in May and 150 in March) and a new overall sub-ceiling of 800 for MIRVed ICBMs, the United States would accept a limit of 250 on ALCM.[100] Despite the fact that Gromyko "responded dourly" and the session had been "sterile," Vance was shortly pleasantly surprised. After mulling over the United States proposal, Gromyko countered with one of his own later that same evening. If the United States would agree to "drop" demands for reductions in Soviet heavy missiles and count ALCM in the Vladivostok 1,320 sub-ceiling, the Soviet Union would be prepared to accept a new sub-ceiling of 820 on MIRVed ICBMs.[101] Furthermore, Moscow was prepared to offer written assurances outside the treaty that Backfire did not have, nor would Moscow give it, "the range to strike the United States."

Sensing Moscow's willingness to move toward an agreement and having already decided to do so themselves, the president and his aides took Gromyko's counterproposal as the basis for a new American offer. Discarding the heavy missile–cruise missile trade-off concept, the Carter leadership developed a new proposal between the end of the Vance–Gromyko meeting on the evening of the twenty-second and Gromyko's meeting with President Carter the next morning.[102] When they met on the morning of September 23, Carter proposed a four-tiered treaty which progressively narrowed the type and number of weapons possible in each tier. Employing the aggregate Vladivostok numbers as a top limit, he proposed a phased reduction in total weapons from 2,400 to 2,160 (a 10 percent reduction) over the term of the proposed treaty. He then offered the long-sought Soviet goal of including ALCM in the 1,320 limit for air-, land-, and sea-based MIRVed weapons; a 1,200 weapon limit for land- and sea-based MIRVs; and an 820 limit for land-based MIRVs.

The Carter leadership had made two major, stunning concessions, giving up the essence of what had been its bargaining position since March. First, the president had decided to exchange "reductions" in heavy missiles for a "ceiling" on all MIRVed missiles. The rationale was, according to Vance, that "we had long realized that a cutback in heavy ICBMs could not, by itself, do much to meet the issue of ICBM vulnerability."[103] Thus, they had come to the conclusion that "a ceiling on the overall Soviet MIRVed ICBM force would be strategically as advantageous to us as a subceiling on heavy missiles alone."

The assumption was that an overall ceiling on all MIRVed ICBMs would limit not only the SS-18s but the SS-19s, too. What it meant in fact, however, was that the Soviets would be free to build either or both weapons up to very threatening levels. This could not exactly be described as a brilliant proposal by the American side; the Soviets got virtually carte blanche on land-based MIRVed weapons. One is forced to conclude from this record that, despite the professed fear of Soviet development of a hard-target kill capability, Washington still preferred, first and foremost, an arms control agreement and, secondly, that the location of Moscow's capability be on land, rather than at sea.

The second major concession was ALCM. In the beginning of the negotiations in March the United States side had sought to leave ALCM free to become an unlimited counter to Soviet missiles. In May Vance proposed a limit of 250 on bombers carrying ALCMs. If each bomber carried between 12 and 20 ALCMs the United States would possess a substantial hard-target if not time-urgent kill capability of between 3,000 and 5,000 warheads. Now in September Vance offered to limit the ALCM further, cutting it by more than half to 120, which meant a reduction in the force to between 1,440 and 2,400 warheads.

This was a deal Moscow could not refuse, and the Soviets wasted no time in accepting it. Vance says that "we expected that several days would pass as the Politburo mulled over our proposals.

Instead, Gromyko asked to see the president again soon."[104] Indeed, Carter had presented the United States proposal on Friday, September 23, and on Tuesday, the twenty-seventh, Gromyko requested a meeting with the president that very evening to deliver the Soviet answer. Gromyko accepted the president's offer, proposing slightly higher numbers in three categories: 2,250 on the aggregates; 1,250 on the land- and sea-based ICBM subceiling; and 850 on the land-based, MIRVed ICBM subceiling. He proposed no change on the air-, land-, and sea-based MIRVs, whose number remained 1,320.

Except for the minor differences in the numbers, the two sides had reached agreement on "the main outlines of the treaty" by the end of September.[105] The final numbers for each category as contained in the 1979 treaty were: overall aggregates, 2,400 to be reduced to 2,250; air-, land- and sea-based MIRVed ICBMs, to 1,320; land- and sea-based MIRVed ICBMs, to 1,200; and MIRVed ICBMs, 820.

Despite the fact that the "main outlines" had been agreed upon, the treaty was not signed until June 18, 1979—over a year and a half later—and was never ratified. In part, the delay was a function of the voluminous opposition which quickly arose in Congress, among anti-SALT intellectuals, and among the allies. But there were more fundamental reasons for the delay. In essence, the delay ensued because, once the essentials had been agreed upon, the treaty became enmeshed in the diplomatic interplay between the two countries.

Each side would in its fashion attempt to use the treaty as part of its larger diplomatic approach to the other. This would become particularly evident in the second half of 1978 (see chapter 6) when the United States sought to use the end game treaty negotiations to ameliorate Moscow's very active foreign policy, and when the Soviet Union sought to hold out completion of the negotiations to keep Washington from interfering in the complex geopolitical maneuver in which Moscow was engaged.

But the agreement itself was in truth inequitable in the fundamental sense that the United States had (1) forsworn any first-strike capability while acquiescing in its attainment by the Soviet Union and (2) severely limited its counterforce retaliatory capability, at least for the life of the treaty, to ALCM and to that which could be retrofitted to Minuteman. More importantly, the Carter leadership knew and fully understood the inequitability of the treaty but supported it for a higher strategic purpose. In brief, the reason for delay in signing the SALT II treaty was that Washington was holding out the prospect of a very advantageous treaty in return for some hoped-for moderation in Soviet behavior.

In this political-strategic sense, the similarity between the 1972 United States–Soviet Trade Agreement and the arms control agreement was marked. In both instances, an American leadership dangled the prospect of very beneficial, even one-sided, agreements—one economic and the other military—in exchange for some sign that Moscow was willing to coexist peacefully with the United States, to no avail. As Soviet foreign policy aggressiveness became increasingly blatant, the prospect for congressional ratification of any agreement dimmed, triggering the congressional escape clauses contained in both agreements. The trade agreement had the Jackson–Vanik amendment, and the arms control agreement had its own internal repudiation in the equal aggregates concept (NSDM 242), which had also originated through Senator Jackson's opposition in 1973.

Short of a verified change in the Soviet policy course away from the effort to challenge United States positions, there simply was no way that such a zero-sum outcome would ever gain passage through Congress, as the Carter administration privately knew full well. The so-called "September breakthrough" was a capitulation. Of course, the administration was bound to support the treaty publicly as being in the national interest in order to give Moscow the opportunity to demonstrate its intentions. To do otherwise would compromise the strategy. At the same time, the opposition which immediately arose conveniently justified delay.

Here one wonders about the philosophy underlying American policy. The idea of offering rewards for changes in long-standing Soviet behavior and objectives cannot in theory be faulted. But for rewards to work, the disincentives must also be present and credible. The Kissingerian approach—which was what the Carter administration and particularly Secretary Vance pursued—abjured the disincentive side of the equation, insisting beyond reasonable expectation that continued supplication would bring the desired result. In fact, as the historical record amply demonstrates, it produced the opposite reaction. Soviet leaders mistakenly interpreted United States policy as being grounded either in weakness or naivete and assumed that they could have their cake and eat it too. The alternatives were not sufficiently bluntly or credibly posed.

Notes

1. Zbigniew Brzezinski, *Power and Principle* (New York: Farrar, Straus, Giroux, 1983), pp. 148–49.
2. Cyrus Vance, *Hard Choices* (New York: Simon and Schuster, 1983), p. 45.
3. Ibid., p. 46, in disagreement with Brzezinski, Vance notes that "there was considerable confusion about human rights resulting from the fact that the issue served different purposes for different groups. Some saw the issue primarily as a powerful instrument in the political offensive against the Soviet Union, whereas others saw it as having universal application. . . . I wanted to make clear . . . that it was universal in application, yet flexible enough to be adapted to individual situations." Raymond L. Garthoff, *Detente and Confrontation, American–Soviet Relations from Nixon to Reagan* (Washington, DC: The Brookings Institution, 1985) p. 573, declares that Carter "did not intend human rights to be an important element in . . . American–Soviet relations." That it was, he concludes, was due to "misjudgment."
4. For a description of the talks, see Garthoff, *Detente and Confrontation*, pp. 474–79.
5. See Brzezinski, *Power and Principle*, pp. 296–301.
6. Garthoff, *Detente and Confrontation*, pp. 568–76.
7. Juan Cameron, "Bill Perry Keeps the Pentagon's Barrels Loaded," *Fortune*, March 10, 1980, p. 60.
8. Vance, *Hard Choices*, p. 44.
9. Jonathan Power, "A Conversation with Brzezinski," *Washington Post*, October 9, 1977, p. C5
10. Vance, *Hard Choices*, p. 49.
11. Ibid., p. 50.
12. Bernard Gwertzman, "Carter, in Reaction to Brezhnev, Vows Arms Curb Action," *New York Times*, December 4, 1976, p. 1.
13. Ibid.
14. Ibid.
15. Strobe Talbott, *Endgame, the Inside Story of SALT II* (New York: Harper and Row, 1979), p. 42.
16. Jim Klurfeld, "The MX Debate," *Newsday*, February 3, 1980, p. 4R.
17. Henry Kissinger, *Years of Upheaval* (Boston: Little, Brown and Company, 1982), p. 273.
18. In 1972, the United States government permitted the export of 164 Centalign-B ball-bearing grinding machines from Bryant Chucking Grinder Company to the Soviet Union. In 1976, DIA Deputy Director Edwin Speaker reported to Congress that the grinders could "be

used in the guidance equipment of Soviet missiles," to reduce the friction of moving parts in the guidance mechanism of a MIRV warhead. It seems highly probable that the ball-bearing grinders played a critical role in enabling the Soviet Union to improve their hard-target kill capability sooner than expected. See "Technology Transfer and Export Controls," *National Security Record*, The Heritage Foundation, Washington, D.C. (September 1979), p. 2.

19. *FBIS-SU*, January 18, 1977, p. R11.
20. Ibid., p. R9.
21. Ibid., p. R11.
22. Brzezinski, *Power and Principle*, p. 152.
23. Ibid.
24. Talbott, *Endgame*, p. 42.
25. Ibid.
26. Brzezinski, *Power and Principle*, p. 153.
27. Ibid., p. 154.
28. Department of State *Bulletin*, Vol. 76, no. 1970. "President Carter's News Conference February 8," 1977, p. 158.
29. Ibid., p. 159.
30. Brzezinski, *Power and Principle*, pp. 154–55.
31. Ibid., pp.155–56.
32. See Talbott, *Endgame*, p. 44. Kissinger had offered to count each bomber carrying between 12 and 20 cruise missiles as a MIRV launcher. Cruise missile range would be set at 1,500 kilometers. On Backfire, he proposed a limit of 250 on deployment up to 1982, with no limit thereafter. Although the two sides were close to agreement, Angola got in the way of these talks.
33. The tests were held and carefully monitored. For example, Clarence A. Robinson, "Soviets Boost ICBM Accuracy," *Aviation Week & Space Technology*, April 3, 1978, pp. 14–16, noted "six recent tests [which] place the U.S. Minuteman force in jeopardy much sooner than previously anticipated by the Administration of President Jimmy Carter." William Perry, deputy secretary of defense for research and engineering, informed Secretary Brown in early November 1977, just after the tests had begun: "I think we have a problem. The preliminary information we have indicates that the Soviets have tested a new guidance system and placed it on their current systems. It will advance the threat to our land-based force. We are going to have to watch the situation very closely." Klurfeld, "The MX Debate," p. 3R. Secretary Brown, appearing on the weekly television program "Issues and Answers" November 6, declared: "Soviet ICBMs will threaten Minuteman's survival in the early 1980s, whether or not current SALT II

negotiations are concluded successfully." See John Collins, *American and Soviet Military Trends, Since the Cuban Missile Crisis* (Washington, DC: Center for Strategic and International Studies, 1978), p. 118. See also R. Jeffrey Smith, "An Upheaval in U.S. Strategic Thought," *Science*, April 2, 1982, pp. 30–34.

34. Ibid.
35. Vance, *Hard Choices*, pp. 57–58. Actually, "cancellation" was a misnomer, for development funds were continued.
36. See *The Nixon-Kissinger Years*, Chapter 9, "Detente and Tripolar Politics: 1973–1976," and the very informative article by Elizabeth Drew, "An Argument over Survival," *New Yorker*, April 4, 1977, pp. 99–106.
37. Talbott, *Endgame*, pp. 52–53.
38. Ibid., p. 53. Except for the points about the SS-19 and the Backfire, the March comprehensive proposal would look remarkably like the Jackson proposals.
39. Ibid., p. 54.
40. Vance, *Hard Choices*, p. 48.
41. Brzezinski, *Power and Principle*, p. 159.
42. Talbott, *Endgame*, pp. 54–55.
43. Ibid.
44. Ibid.
45. Brzezinski, *Power and Principle*, p. 158.
46. Talbott, *Endgame*, pp. 58–59, notes that "for at least two years, the very occurrence of that decisive meeting remained a mystery."
47. Department of State *Bulletin*, no. 1971, April 4, 1977, "President Carter's News Conference, March 9," p. 307.
48. Ibid., no. 1972, April 11, 1977, "Address to the U.N. General Assembly, March 17," p. 331.
49. Talbott, *Endgame*, p. 62, says that Vance only succeeded in gaining the inclusion of the Vladivostok-minus proposal "just before his departure" at an NSC meeting on March 24. Brzezinski, *Power and Principle*, p. 159, says that the "negotiating position . . . was finally hammered out . . . on March 19 and 22" and that the meeting of the twenty-second was "largely pro forma." Garthoff, *Detente and Confrontation*, p. 805 n.12, asserts that Talbott erred in dating the "key meeting" with the president on March 12 and cites Brzezinski to the effect that it took place on March 19. It seems evident that there were several "key" meetings, that the decision to go forward with the comprehensive approach was made on March 10 and 12, and that the final "negotiating position" was "hammered out" on the nineteenth. Vance would take yet a third proposal to Moscow, which centered on "higher

fallback numbers for . . . the comprehensive proposal." (Vance, *Hard Choices*, p. 52.) But he was not to present it unless specifically authorized by the president. Perhaps it was this third option that Vance insisted upon on the twenty-fourth.

50. Department of State *Bulletin*, no. 1973, April 18, 1977, "President Carter's News Conference of March 24," p. 357.
51. Talbott, *Endgame*, p. 67, comes to the same conclusion.
52. Vance, *Hard Choices*, p. 53.
53. Talbott, *Endgame*, p. 70.
54. Brzezinski, *Power and Principle*, pp. 159–60.
55. See Garthoff, *Detente and Confrontation*, p. 806, for discussion of the numbers.
56. Simply put, the targeting assumption is that the attacker must be able to allocate two warheads for each missile silo, plus one in reserve. Thus a preemptive strike against Minuteman's one thousand-plus launchers would require three thousand-plus warheads.
57. Vance, *Hard Choices*, p. 54. Despite his "anger," which is perhaps not the appropriate word, the vehemence of Brezhnev's denunciation induced Vance to request permission from Washington to present his third fallback option, which was denied. Brzezinski, *Power and Principle*, p. 162, noted that he "was rather surprised that Cy was so willing immediately to retreat to our fallback position" although his later assessment "was more consistent with our original expectations."
58. Department of State *Bulletin*, no. 1974, April 25, 1977, "Secretary Vance News Conference of March 30," p. 400.
59. Ibid., p. 402.
60. Ibid., p. 403.
61. See Garthoff, *Detente and Confrontation*, pp. 446f, for discussion of the dispute.
62. Ibid.
63. Vance, above, said that it was the first option. Did either man misspeak, or did Vance indeed present the deferral proposal first?
64. Ibid., "President Carter News Conference, March 30, 1977," p. 409.
65. Ibid., pp. 409–10.
66. Ibid., p. 411.
67. Ibid., p. 413.
68. *FBIS-SU*, April 1, 1977, "Andrey Gromyko's Press Conference," p. B1.
69. Ibid.
70. Ibid., p. B2.
71. Ibid., p. B3.
72. Ibid., p. B5.
73. Ibid., p. B6.

74. Department of State *Bulletin*, no. 1974, April 25, 1977, "Zbigniew Brzezinski's News Conference of April 1, 1977," pp. 414–15.
75. Ibid.
76. Ibid., pp. 415–16.
77. Ibid., p. 418.
78. Ibid., p. 421.
79. Ibid., p. 417.
80. Deputy Secretary Perry noted that "we did not realize it at the time, but the March, 1977, proposal was obsolete even before we made it. They were so far along in their guidance program that it was highly unlikely that we could have convinced them to stop." Klurfeld, "The MX Debate," p. 4R.
81. See for example, Garthoff, *Detente and Confrontation*, pp. 804–5, who notes that "most of those working on SALT did not even know about" the decision to present the comprehensive proposal and that most of the members of the delegation that went to Moscow were "still uninformed" when they got there.
82. Brzezinski, *Power and Principle*, pp. 164–65, put it this way, assessing the March breakdown: "We confronted a . . . difficult task. Were we to stand pat on our SALT proposals or, instead, begin to adjust our position so as to make it more palatable to the Soviets? . . . Finally, in this context, what response were we to generate to the continuing and growing Soviet strategic challenge?"
83. PD 18, in turn, directed the initiation of three additional studies: ICBM force modernization, a secure strategic reserve force, and nuclear targeting policy. The targeting review study would become PD 59. Titled "Nuclear Weapons Employment Policy," PD 59 shifted United States war-fighting emphasis from economic to political-military targets, including the Soviet leadership, and mandated development of the capability to fight a protracted nuclear conflict. For an extended discussion of what is publicly known of PD 59, see Jeffrey Richelson, "PD-59, NSDD-13 and the Reagan Strategic Modernization Program," *Journal of Strategic Studies*, June 1983, pp. 125–46.
84. Brzezinski, *Power and Principle*, p. 177. This and some fourteen other "reviews" were decided upon during the first NSC meeting on January 5, but PRM 10 obviously took on greater significance shortly thereafter. See p. 51.
85. Garthoff, *Detente and Confrontation*, p. 791.
86. John Collins, *U.S.–Soviet Military Balance, Concepts and Capabilities 1960–1980* (New York: McGraw-Hill, 1980), p. 443, whose figures are slightly inflated, identifies 156 MIRVed ICBMs in 1976, 270 in 1977, 456 in 1978, and 620 in 1979.
87. Garthoff, *Detente and Confrontation*, p. 850.

88. Ibid., pp. 850–51.
89. Talbott, *Endgame*, p. 82.
90. Garthoff, *Detente and Confrontation*, p. 574.
91. Ibid., p. 575.
92. Vance, *Hard Choices*, p. 56.
93. Talbott, *Endgame*, p. 86. Backfire limitations were still a part, but a less crucial part, of Washington's bargaining position. See Brzezinski, *Power and Principle*, pp. 167–68, for the list of issues discussed.
94. Vance, *Hard Choices*, p. 57.
95. Talbott, *Endgame*, p. 87.
96. Garthoff, *Detente and Confrontation*, p. 811.
97. Vance, *Hard Choices*, p. 58.
98. Talbott, *Endgame*, pp. 101–2 and 108n. Although the SS-19 carried only six warheads to the SS-18's ten, left unconstrained Moscow would simply build as many SS-19s as were needed.
99. Vance, *Hard Choices*, p. 59. Although Vance says that the Soviet response "did not raise my spirits," he must have been privately elated that Moscow had rejected the cruise missile–heavy missile trade-off. At least Washington had avoided one pitfall.
100. Ibid.
101. Ibid., pp. 59–60.
102. See Talbott, *Endgame*, pp. 125–28, for a detailed description of the late-night "frenzy of last-minute brainstorming."
103. Vance, *Hard Choices*, p. 60.
104. Ibid., p. 61. Talbott, *Endgame*, p. 120, notes that "the Americans expected it would take at least five or six days for the Politburo to digest the latest U.S. position and respond."
105. Vance, *Hard Choices*, p. 61, says that Gromyko accepted the proposed MIRV ICBM subceiling of 820 on the spot; Talbott, *Endgame*, p. 130, says that Gromyko proposed 850 and only later came down to 820.

CHAPTER 2

Reinforcing the European Flank, 1977–1979

After the March talks, President Carter and his advisers knew that in all likelihood the nation's security needs could not be met through arms control. They were forced to reach the conclusion, as had the previous administration, that Moscow was bent upon achieving a politically useful strategic weapons capability which would enable its leaders to attempt to reshape to advantage the geopolitical balance.

The problem was how to respond to Moscow's fait accompli. Even assuming popular support for a massive missile-building program, a dubious assumption at best, the United States could not embark easily upon such a course because it was too far behind in land-based systems. The scope and momentum of Moscow's program would enable it to deploy far more counterforce warheads against American silos than the United States could deploy against Soviet silos. It was simply cheaper to MIRV a heavy missile than it was to design, develop, build, and deploy a comparably large weapon from scratch.

The United States quite literally could not catch up if Moscow were determined to maintain its lead in land-based missiles. (Ironically, this was the position in reverse of the 1962–1968 period, when the United States decided not to maintain its margin of superiority in land-based systems.) Besides, it was a race no American leadership wanted to run. Aside from its political implications of a return to cold war confrontation, an arms race ran counter to American long-term strategy.

Core United States strategic weapons strategy was to shift largely to the sea even while retaining the two other legs of the "triad." The problem was that SLBM guidance capability lagged behind ICBM guidance capability and would not be ready for deployment for a decade. Therefore, if the United States were to compete with the Soviet Union in developing a counterforce weapon in the near term, it would have to do so on land. But this was a dilemma; not only would it contradict long-term strategy, it would make a "weapons sink" of the national territory in any actual nuclear exchange.

The Carter administration avoided this dilemma in the decision to move forward rapidly with the long-range cruise missile, which would serve as a bridge to the future sea-based counterforce system (Trident II). On the issue of arms control itself, the decision was to move deliberately toward an agreement, which would serve both domestic political and international ends, with the full knowledge and understanding that it would be fundamentally unsatisfactory unless Moscow had a sudden change of heart—and strategy.

There was domestic political sympathy, not to mention pressure, for an agreement—far more than for no agreement at all. Thus, negotiations would continue. At the same time, the United States would attempt to deter Soviet adventurism—to the degree possible without direct confrontation—through the talks, during which American negotiators would hold out attractive compromises in return for "cooperation." Secretary Vance was the driving force in the administration pressing for extending to the Soviet leadership the same quid pro quo which Henry Kissinger had proffered in 1973.

While the talks ensued, the United States would actively engage its allies in a broad-based effort to gain commitments from them to play greater security roles in Europe and Asia. As will be discussed in this and subsequent chapters, the Carter administration was immediately and continuously active in three areas: Western Europe, the Middle East, and Northeast Asia. Areas where the Carter administration struck a low profile, such as Iran and Central America—particularly in Nicaragua—would lead relatively rapidly to intractable problems for the Carter administration and for the Reagan administration as well.

In Western Europe, Washington urged the NATO allies to

increase defense spending (even while continuing the economic struggle for wealth and power with them), an effort that culminated after several missteps in the dual-track decision of December 1979, for which Carter had pressed. But the West European states also established the European Monetary System, which he had hoped to preclude. A major objective in both the military and economic realms was to rein in an increasingly powerful, and recalcitrant, West Germany.

In the Middle East, Washington attempted to consolidate a core relationship between Israel and Egypt which would serve as the basis for a strategic consensus in the region. This would progress in uneven fashion from 1977 through the Camp David talks to a peace treaty between the two nations in 1979. But a parallel objective, Palestinian autonomy in the West Bank and Gaza, was not achieved. Indeed, it was in fact abandoned. As a result, relations with Saudi Arabia and Jordan were strained to the breaking point.

In Northeast Asia, Washington sought to withdraw from South Korea, normalize relations with Beijing, and prompt Tokyo to increase its military capability in the hope of strengthening the region's power to resist Soviet pressure. The objective appeared to be to strengthen United States–Chinese–Japanese triangular ties. Relations with Beijing were normalized, but only—as in Europe—after several missteps. Ties with Japan eventually stabilized after a rocky beginning, at high economic cost. But the objective of promoting and channeling greater Japanese defense spending met with only marginal success; and withdrawal from South Korea was abandoned.

In all cases, friends and allies were reluctant or adamantly opposed to Washington's efforts to move them in the direction desired, forcing the Carter administration to employ subtle means to generate movement toward the desired structural solutions. Complicating the task, Moscow either was in the process of taking initiatives or took countermeasures as its leaders perceived opportunity in the fluid situations that evolved. Indeed, it would be fair to say that during the Carter years the Soviet Union embarked upon a major geopolitical offensive spanning the vast rimland of Eurasia from Ethiopia to Vietnam.

The Alliance Dilemma: Cohesion or Competition?

By the time the Carter administration entered office, the global recession precipitated by the oil crisis of 1973 was ending, and both West Germany and Japan had resumed their strong economic performances. Indeed, recovery by America's two powerful allies presented the new administration with a painful dilemma, turning the tables. The high oil price strategy, which had initially served American interests, was becoming counterproductive. While West Germany and Japan had begun to recover from the recession, almost none of the rest of the industrialized world (not to mention the less industrialized nations) had yet done so.

In truth, high oil prices—and the inflation they generated—were beginning to undermine the entire international economic system. If the United States continued its struggle with West Germany and Japan, the system would be threatened. On the other hand, if Washington gave up the struggle in order to save the system, West Germany and Japan would surge further ahead, defeating the original purpose of moderating their growth.

The Carter administration's initial choice (evidently following Schmidt's rejection of the president's offer for a "special relationship" by which the two nations would "coordinate the management of the world capitalist economy") was to attempt to accomplish both objectives.[1] Washington would persist in the effort to place economic constraints upon the West Germans and Japanese. At least through 1977, the United States continued an expansionary domestic economic policy necessitating high-volume petroleum imports which kept upward pressure on price.[2] At the same time, the expansionary domestic policy, and the larger trade deficits that accompanied it, helped to a degree the recovery of the industrialized and less industrialized nations.

As part of the effort to promote general recovery, Washington began to increase its imports to enable other countries to export more. The administration also vigorously pressed Bonn and Tokyo to reflate, that is, to import more themselves and expand their domestic economies while holding back somewhat on exports. The approach was described as the "locomotive approach," by which the three major economies would haul the rest of the system back to the healthy side of the economic ledger through domestic expansion.

Under Secretary of State for Economic Affairs Richard Cooper later explained this decision and its consequences.

> By late 1976, the world economy was in a very precarious situation. Unemployment was high in the United States; it was high and rising in Europe. Many countries, including some of the large industrialized countries as well as many developing countries, found themselves with a very large burden of external indebtedness. Those countries had to engage in economic and financial retrenchment. Yet that alone would have aggravated and prolonged the world recesssion, making corrective actions in all countries more difficult. Under these circumstances, *for both domestic and foreign policy reasons*, the United States undertook a program of economic expansion to end the recession.
>
> It would have been desirable for the world economic recovery to have been led by a balanced expansion in the leading industrial economies, and most notably in the United States, Japan, and Germany. These countries all had excess capacity and relatively strong external positions. The London economic summit in May 1977 represented an effort to achieve such a coordinated expansion by the leading countries, but it failed in that respect. The United States went ahead anyway. Largely as a consequence, the U.S. payments position deteriorated relative to that of other major countries. It was recognized at the time that vigorous economic expansion in the United States without concomitant expansion in other countries would worsen the U.S. trade position, and it could have been expected that the emerging imbalance in turn would lead to the depreciation of the dollar relative to some other currencies. A balanced expansion among the leading countries would have avoided this.
>
> Balanced expansion would certainly have been preferable to the actual development, but it was apparently unattainable at the time. Under these circumstances, I believe it was desirable for the United States to go ahead alone, even though that would predictably lead to some depreciation of the dollar. Not to have done so, in my judgment, would have courted far graver dangers for the world economy—extreme financial difficulties for a number of countries and increasing protectionist actions in most of the industrialized countries. Indeed, the highly successful international economic system which was so painstakingly established in the

preceding 25 years was in jeopardy. *The U.S. external deficit relieved the financial pressures on many countries, and it also reduced protectionist pressures abroad.*[3]

Under Secretary Cooper's reference to the London Economic Summit of May 1977, when he said that "balanced expansion would certainly have been preferable ... but ... was apparently unattainable at the time," was imprecise.[4] It was true that Chancellor Schmidt had rejected the "locomotive approach" from the very beginning, on the grounds that since German economic performance was better than American, Germany "required no lectures on economic policy from the American government."[5] In fact, however, the United States did receive promises in London from both West Germany and Japan to undertake a moderate domestic expansion, Bonn pledging to attain a growth rate of 5 percent and Tokyo 6.7 percent for the year.[6] Mr. Cooper was accurate on substance, however, for neither country came close to fulfilling its pledge. For that year German growth was actually 2.5 percent and Japan's 5 percent.

The under secretary also noted that unilateral expansion would lead to a trade imbalance which would predictably produce a depreciation of the dollar against "some other currencies." Through 1977 and most of 1978 the United States entered a period of its worst trade deficits (which are with us still) in an effort to keep the "system" intact. In the process the dollar was allowed to depreciate, particularly vis-à-vis the deutschemark and the yen. A graphic depiction of the United States trade balance during the Carter presidency makes the point.

Table 1. U.S. Trade Balance (in billions of dollars)

	1975	*1976*	*1977*	*1978*	*1979*	*1980*
Imports	103.4	132.4	160.4	186.0	222.3	256.9
Exports	107.5	115.4	121.3	143.7	182.0	220.7
	+4.1	−17.0	−39.1	−42.3	−40.3	−36.2

Source: *Direction of Trade Statistics, Yearbook—1983* (Washington, D.C.: International Monetary Fund, 1980), p. 397.

Throughout 1977 and most of 1978 the Carter administration pursued a dual policy of deliberately accepting increasing trade deficits (though depreciating the dollar to enhance exports in hopes of minimizing the deficits) and assiduously importuning Bonn and Tokyo to increase imports to assist in the effort to stabilize the international economic system—to no avail. Both Japan's and West Germany's trade balances strengthened measurably during this period. Only the Iranian crisis in 1979 produced a temporary change.

Table 2. West German and Japanese Trade Balances (in billions of dollars)

West Germany	*1976*	*1977*	*1978*	*1979*	*1980*
Exports	101.9	118.0	142.4	171.8	192.6
Imports	88.1	101.4	121.7	159.6	188.0
	+13.8	+16.6	+20.7	+12.2	+4.6
Japan					
Exports	67.3	81.0	98.3	102.2	130.4
Imports	64.8	71.3	79.9	109.8	141.2
	+2.5	+9.7	+18.4	–7.6	–10.8

Source: *Direction of Trade Statistics, Yearbook—1983*, pp. 177 and 233.

By the end of 1977 the locomotive theory had run out of steam, as neither of Washington's major partners would cooperate. German Chancellor Schmidt derisively described American policy as "naive"[7] and said that only "thrift and hard work" would produce global recovery.[8] Japanese leaders were more circumspect but equally resistant to Washington's pressure to obtain a reduction of Japan's current account surplus.[9] The United States was accused of pursuing a policy variously described as "disguised benign neglect" or "aggressive neglect" and of "talking the dollar down" as the dollar continued to depreciate.[10] In early 1978, the Federal Reserve announced that it would take action "from time to time" to support the dollar, but that the United States was not committed to supporting the dollar "at any particular level."[11]

The policy shift to large deficits had two important consequences, one foreseen and one probably unanticipated. The foreseen and intended consequence, as noted by Under Secretary Cooper, was the alleviation of the financial difficulties of several countries, whose current account balances improved substantially during 1977–78 compared with the previous two years. (See table 3.)

Table 3. Account Balances of Selected Countries (in billions of dollars)

	1974–76	*1977–78*
United Kingdom	–4.6	–0.1
Italy	–3.8	1.6
Spain	–3.7	–1.2
France	–3.9	–2.0
Brazil	–6.7	–5.6
Mexico	–3.4	–1.4
Pakistan	–1.8	–0.6
Peru	–1.1	–0.8
South Korea	–1.4	–0.3
Israel	–1.6	–0.6

Source: David Gisselquist, *Oil Prices and Trade Deficits: U.S. Conflicts with Japan and West Germany* (New York: Praeger, 1979).

It was also true, however, that the financial situation for an equally large number of countries worsened, including Canada, Norway, Sweden, Turkey, Australia, Portugal, Denmark, Austria, Belgium, and Greece, to name the largest countries.[12] This was partly because the growing United States trade deficit was the result of heavy petroleum imports, suggesting an intention to keep upward pressure on oil prices. Worse still, because the United States did not erect discriminatory barriers to German and Japanese goods, those countries profited most from the effort to hold the system together. For example, between 1976 and 1980 the United States–West German trade volume doubled, German exports to the United States doubled, and the United States ran a persistent trade deficit.

Table 4. U.S. Trade with West Germany (in billions of dollars)

	1976	1977	1978	1979	1980
Imports	5.9	7.7	10.5	11.6	12.2
Exports	5.7	5.9	6.9	8.4	10.9
	–.2	–1.8	–3.6	–3.2	–1.3

Source: *Direction of Trade Statistics, Yearbook—1983.*

The same was true but on a much larger scale with Japan. United States–Japan trade volume doubled, Japanese exports to the United States doubled, and Washington ran a persistent and large trade deficit.

Table 5. U.S. Trade with Japan (in billions of dollars)

	1976	1977	1978	1979	1980
Imports	16.9	20.2	26.4	28.1	32.9
Exports	10.1	10.5	12.8	17.5	20.7
	–6.8	–9.7	–13.6	–10.6	–12.2

Source: *Direction of Trade Statistics, Yearbook—1983.*

The unanticipated consequence of American policy was the West German decision under Chancellor Helmut Schmidt to press forward with plans to establish the European Monetary System. Recall that United States policy during the 1973 oil crisis had effectively derailed movement toward European monetary integration and Washington was acutely attuned to the possibility of a renewed West European effort.[13] Nevertheless, West European leaders under the guidance of Chancellor Schmidt, consulting with great secrecy, surprised American leaders with a decision in early 1978 to move promptly toward establishment of the European Monetary System.

United States–West German Crisis and West European Monetary Unification

As Peter Ludlow notes, "By the mid-1970s, Germany had begun to move out of the European league into a group of world economic powers of which the only other members were the United States and Japan."[14] The foundation of German resurgence was high productivity combined with relatively low production costs and an emphasis on high technology in several key industries such as steel, textiles, machinery, chemicals, and agriculture.

By 1977, the deutschemark had taken over the position previously held by sterling in the international monetary system, although West German leaders resisted American pressure to allow the deutschemark to become an international reserve currency. Despite German reluctance to play a more prominent and public financial role, there was little doubt about German dominance of any future European Monetary System. Indeed, overall economic conditions which would lead to a change in the German position appeared to be maturing. On July 1, 1977, the West European Free Trade Zone had been implemented, raising the prospects for greater integration of the West European market. In late 1977, after the failure of the "locomotive approach," Chancellor Schmidt had privately given his approval to Roy Jenkins, president of the European Commission, to press on with study of the steps which would be required for monetary union.[15]

The decision to go forward was made in early 1978, in a surprising initiative by Schmidt, in the context of a growing crisis between Washington and Bonn and rapprochement between Bonn and Paris. There were several substantive elements to German–American estrangement aside from the personal dislike that the chancellor professed to hold for the president. The German leader saw the United States human rights and security policies as impinging upon Bonn's political and economic relationships with the Soviet Union and Eastern Europe and thus undercutting *Ostpolitik*, a major element in German foreign policy.

Schmidt was also outraged by Washington's objections to the 1975 sale of German nuclear technology to Brazil.[16] The deal involved German supply of enrichment and reprocessing technology in exchange for Brazilian uranium. Washington objected to the sale on the grounds that it might open the way to the proliferation of nuclear weapons elsewhere in the hemisphere. But there was a more serious objection. Since the United States and the Soviet Union were the principal suppliers of uranium to West Germany, the German–Brazilian deal threatened to enable Bonn to develop an independent source of uranium for its own nuclear program, thereby lessening if not eventually eliminating dependence upon the United States and the Soviet Union for this essential material.

Schmidt's professed concern was that the Carter administration would destroy the German nuclear program, but there can be little doubt that the German leader fully understood the implications of the Brazilian deal. The crisis, which did not ease until the spring of 1978 and included the threat to withdraw American troops from German territory, hung over the German–American relationship as evidence of the growing divergence between the two countries and provoked several outbursts against the American leadership. On the other hand, the controversy served to strengthen Franco–German relations since France, whose nuclear program was as ambitious as Germany's, also had nuclear supply agreements with Pakistan and South Korea.

Central to the German–American crisis, however, was United States dollar policy and insistent pressure upon Bonn to reflate the German economy. Despite reassuring statements by President Carter, Federal Reserve Chairman Arthur Burns, and G. William Miller, who was appointed on December 28 to replace Burns, regarding American intentions to prevent the dollar's decline, it continued to fall. Activation of the Treasury's Exchange Stabilization Fund and the Federal Reserve's $20 billion currency swap network with other central banks in early 1978 had had only a temporary and limited effect.[17]

The main difference between the current dollar crisis and previous currency movements was that this was the first time since 1973, when floating began, that there was a serious crisis centrally involving the dollar and the mark. Moreover, not only was the dollar falling against the mark, but the currencies of West Germany's main economic partners in Europe were also falling vis-à-vis the mark. This was particularly true for the French franc, Italian lira, and the Scandinavian currencies—the Swedish, Danish, and Norwegian krone. Bonn's concern was that since over 50 percent of West Germany's foreign trade was with Western Europe, continued appreciation of the deutschemark against other West European currencies "could not be accepted without serious risks to German exports."[18]

Lastly, there was the continued issue of growth rates and American pressure upon Bonn to reflate the German economy. The collapse of the locomotive concept in late 1977 had given way in early 1978 to a new approach, the so-called "convoy" approach.[19] In this concept, the "convalescent" economies such as those in the United Kingdom, France, and Italy would expand along with the economies of the United States, West Germany, and Japan. But the Coordinated Reflation Action Program, as it was called, went the way of the locomotive concept, and for the same reason—neither Germany nor Japan would cooperate.

By early 1978 it was evident to the German leadership that the crisis with the United States was protracted and that unless action was taken continued dollar decline could upset hopes for monetary and economic stabilization in Western Europe and lead to a fundamental devaluation of the dollar vis-à-vis other currencies.[20] But if the crisis with the United States made action necessary, it was the rapprochement between Bonn and Paris which made it possible.

Franco–German Cooperation—The French Gamble

French President Giscard d'Estaing believed that France was number three militarily, behind the United States and the Soviet Union, but only number five economically, behind the two superpowers, Japan, and West Germany.[21] In an interview which appeared later in *Le Monde*, October 18, 1978, he declared that unless France were able to further develop its economic position and achieve equality with Germany, "the way would be open to the consolidation of German hegemony" over Western Europe. "It would not," he said, "be a good idea for Europe to be dominated by one country." France, in short, must undertake a necessary long-term gamble in cooperating with Germany to establish the economic conditions of stable currencies and energy prices. Stable economic conditions, in turn, would allow France to reduce inflation and concentrate on developing exports of high-technology goods and skilled labor—the keys to catching up with Germany.

Giscard's view was not unopposed, and indeed until the parliamentary elections in March President Giscard was in no position politically to undertake the sort of cooperation with West Germany that he had decided was necessary. His ruling majority was too slim to risk further fragmentation. The results of the March elections—in which the French Democratic Alliance (UDF) made a strong advance against the Gaullist party—dramatically strengthened his position, which by all accounts both inside and outside of France gave Giscard "a political freedom that he had not possessed since he became president in 1974."[22]

For Schmidt, Giscard's victory opened the way to the decision on monetary union, which West Germany could now undertake with French cooperation. Meeting on April 2 at Rambouillet, the two leaders planned the next step, which would come at the European Council meeting in Copenhagen on April 7 and 8. There, Chancellor Schmidt proposed what in Giscard's words was "a new Bretton Woods for Europe."[23] It was the chancellor's view that, due to the shortcomings of the existing international monetary system and the inadequacies of the present American administration, Europe should no longer prop up the dollar, which should be allowed to fall. There would be, he vowed, no more buying of dollars.

Instead, steps should be taken toward formation of an integrated European system. The first step should include the establishment of a European Monetary Fund, a partial pooling of reserves, increased use of European currencies in exchange intervention against the dollar, and expanded use of the EUA (European Unit of Account). General approval followed in the discussion of Schmidt's proposal, except for Prime Minister Callaghan, who remained skeptical and not a little alarmed. Although it was agreed to keep the discussions secret apart from a handful of trusted aides, it would appear that American officials shortly learned of Schmidt's proposal, probably from Mr. Callaghan, who withdrew from the secret European talks following the Copenhagen meeting.

American leaders immediately renewed a long-standing internal debate over the implications for the United States of European monetary integration. This debate, in which the Department of State invariably took a benign view and the Treasury a more suspicious one, led Treasury officials to voice their concern publicly. Anthony Solomon of the Treasury Department delivered a speech in

New York on May 15, 1978, raising the core issues of concern to the United States.[24] Solomon wanted assurances from European officials that a European monetary system would not be a closed currency bloc with restrictions on capital movements, would not result in a permanent overvaluation of the dollar vis-à-vis European currencies, would not be a new "Bretton Woods" with rigid exchange rates, would not be a threat to the IMF, would not be based on gold, and would have neither a low-growth nor inflationary bias.[25]

Publicly, Washington's attitude toward the EMS was supportive but cool. Privately, however, the period from May through October 1978 saw what could be interpreted as a determined effort by the United States to disrupt the move toward monetary union. The truce which American and West German officials had reached in March regarding the outstanding issues besetting them, particularly the questions of nuclear technology sale to Brazil and dollar depreciation, held through July. On April 12, President Carter announced a new anti-inflationary campaign, and on May 24 he declared that the United States would terminate its growth policy due to the danger of inflation from the combined effects of domestic expansion and currency depreciation.[26] Indeed, by the spring inflation in the United States had reached double digits,[27] prompting the Federal Reserve to tighten credit by, among other things, raising the discount rate a half-point in August and three-quarters of a point in September.

In the meantime, the European Council met again in Bremen on July 6 and 7, when it was decided to accept the German–French initiative and to instruct the respective finance ministers "to formulate the necessary guidelines for the competent Community bodies to elaborate by 31 October the provisions necessary for the functioning of [a European Monetary System]."[28] Curiously, the fundamental issue of EMS received only cursory public attention during the Bonn Seven Power Summit meeting July 16 and 17. The final communiqué expressed "sympathy for the ideal of European unity," although neither the United States nor Japan endorsed the European Council's decision as had been hoped.[29]

From July onward, however, even as President Carter and Chancellor Schmidt pledged improved cooperation—Carter promised to restrain American oil imports, while Schmidt promised a higher rate of growth for Germany—renewed currency unrest became apparent as the dollar began to fall against all major currencies.[30] The slide became precipitous in August, September, and October as the dollar plunged 18 percent against the mark, 17 percent against the Swiss franc, 10 percent against the French franc, 8 percent against the pound, and 6 percent against the Italian lira.[31] Ironically, the collapse of the dollar in the fall of 1978 did not disrupt, but rather facilitated progress toward union by contributing to an overall needed realignment of intra-European exchange rates.[32]

While American leaders continued to give public support to the "ideal" of monetary union, behind the scenes administration officials expressed sharp reservations. By the time of the annual meeting of the International Monetary Fund in September, United States officials were voicing concern that the EMS could become a rival "bloc" to the dollar. There were worries that the European pooling of reserves could be used to maintain an artificially high rate for the dollar by preventing or delaying appreciation of the deutschemark. There were concerns that EMS would have an overall deflationary effect on European economies, which would have adverse repercussions on the dollar. And there was apprehension that central banks, encouraged by the establishment of the EMS, would be inclined to divest dollar holdings further.[33]

If United States leaders expected or hoped that private expressions of concern and the climate of instability would dissuade European leaders from going forward with plans for monetary union, they were mistaken. West European sentiment appeared to have coalesced in favor of greater union. The decision to establish the European Monetary System was taken at the European Council meeting in Brussels, December 4 and 5, and after a three-month delay began to function on March 13, 1979. Between the fall of 1978 and the launch date for EMS, however, the United States began to implement a radical shift in monetary and international economic policy in implicit recognition of the failure to force adjustment through dollar depreciation.

By the fall of 1978 it was clear that the American strategy of dollar depreciation and heavy oil imports had failed to bring about alliance reintegration.[34] Indeed, if reserve holdings were any criterion, American strategy had been an unmitigated disaster as German and Japanese holdings reached historic highs against United States holdings. (See table 6.)

Table 6. Reserve Positions 1971–1980
(in billions of dollars, including gold)

	1971	1972	1973	1974	1975	1976	1977	1978	1979	1980
West Germany	18.7	23.6	33.3	33.1	31.5	35.9	41.3	57.8	60.4	55.5
Japan	15.3	18.3	12.2	13.5	12.8	16.6	23.2	33.4	20.6	25.7
United States	12.3	13.1	14.3	15.8	16.2	18.7	19.3	18.6	18.9	27.2

Source: *International Financial Statistics, Yearbook—1984*, pp. 287, 363, 593.

From October of 1978, in a shift which would be a year in the making, Washington moved from a depreciating to an appreciating dollar and to a reduction of oil imports. Perception of the shift would be clouded by the overthrow of the shah in Iran in early 1979 combined with a simultaneous leap in oil prices, but the tight money and reduced oil imports policies pursued so vigorously by the Reagan administration would have their antecedents in the Carter administration's decisions of October 1978.

There were three parts to the Carter administration's new course. First, on October 15, came congressional passage of the long-awaited energy package, which, however, fell short of original hopes. Despite administration promises to reduce oil imports through taxation on consumption—of domestic crude and gasoline—and through a shift to cheaper forms of energy, especially coal, the final legislation was highly disappointing. Congress rejected taxes on gasoline and domestic crude, retained price controls on natural gas until January 1, 1985, and generally emphasized conservation measures as the main means of achieving the administration's stated goal of reducing oil imports by 4.5 million barrels per day under projected usage.[35]

Second, on October 24, came the announcement of an anti-inflation program, the main elements of which were decisions (1) to limit federal spending and reduce the deficit from its current level of 23 percent of GNP to 21 percent by 1980; (2) to institute a voluntary wage and price policy whose objectives were to limit increases by 7 percent and 9.5 percent, respectively; and (3) to adjust government wage and procurement policy accordingly.[36]

Third, on November 1, the administration announced a far-reaching package of financial measures designed to halt the dollar's fall through the purchase of marks, yen, and Swiss francs. The Federal Reserve raised the discount rate again from 8.5 percent to an historic high of 9.5 percent and imposed a 2 percent supplementary reserve requirement on banks to encourage increased borrowing from abroad. The Federal Reserve also doubled the amount of currency in the swap arrangements with German, Japanese, and Swiss central banks from $7.4 to $15 billion.[37]

To acquire the funds necessary to purchase marks and Swiss francs, the U.S. Treasury, in an unprecedented step, announced its readiness to issue up to $10 billion in mark- and Swiss franc-denominated securities. Finally, the United States government drew $3 billion of its $4.1 billion allotment from the IMF, announced its intention to sell $2 billion in SDRs, and quintupled the permitted gold sales from 300,000 troy ounces per annum to 1.5 million.[38]

The November package amounted to a $30 billion intervention in the financial markets to strengthen the position of the dollar—the largest intervention in American history—and put an end to the dollar depreciation policy pursued by the Carter administration. It could not be foreseen in November 1978 just how far the United States turn would go, or what other forms it would take (a subject which will be resumed in chapter 9). The financial crisis between Bonn and Washington would parallel a security struggle of comparable magnitude: if Washington's economic strategy was a failure, the outcome of the security struggle would be quite different.

Reinforcing Western Europe—The German Question

The same impetus which had driven Washington's economic policy also drove policy in the security field. Moscow's earlier-than-expected strategic weapons advance combined with rapid German economic progress raised the prospect of major erosion of American influence over Western Europe. Worse, the Soviet breakthrough was highly complementary to long-term German strategy, which was to create conditions for the exploitation of German power in Europe. That strategy centered on the retention of the American security guarantee and the establishment of broad-based political and economic relations with the Soviet Union and Eastern Europe through detente. German strategy, in structural terms, was to employ detente and *Ostpolitik* to move in a de facto sense into the middle position between the United States and the Soviet Union while establishing an economic hegemony over Europe—a shift which was well under way when the Carter administration came into office.[39]

In terms of the United States–Soviet strategic weapons balance, the 1978 situation resembled that of the mid-fifties. Then, when American leaders feared that the Soviet Union would successfully deploy a first-generation ICBM before the United States did, they arranged to deploy intermediate-range weapons to Western Europe to compensate for an anticipated strategic weapons imbalance. As it turned out, the worst case did not occur, as the United States was able to deploy an ICBM before the Soviet Union, which had experienced technical difficulties with its first-generation system, and the United States subsequently removed the IRBM deployment from Western Europe.

In both instances, though there was a Soviet theater-level deployment—the SS-4 and SS-5 in the fifties and the SS-20 in 1977—the reason for European deployment was the United States need for a strategic counter. The difference between 1955 and 1977 was that, whereas in the former instance the United States had considerable support from its European allies to deploy intermediate-range missiles, in 1977 the Carter leadership found little support among them for deployment. Led by the West German government, the allies stressed the need for detente above all else—even though the threat was considerably more substantial.

The Carter leadership faced two problems: how to counterbalance the anticipated Soviet strategic weapons breakthrough, and how to reintegrate the European alliance, particularly West Germany's position within it. In retrospect it would appear that Washington sought to contribute to the solution of both problems through the deployment of the Pershing II extended-range ballistic missile in West Germany. That deployment alone—not counting the ground-launched cruise missile (GLCM) that eventually would be deployed along with the Pershing II—would give the United States a small but timely retaliatory (some would argue preemptive) capability against any contemplated Soviet attack. Moreover, it was hoped that the wrenching political process that would inevitably accompany any NATO decision to deploy would serve an alliance-integrating function and place a substantial constraint on Bonn's *Ostpolitik*.

Throughout the 1977–1979 period the United States pursued a

highly sophisticated political-military strategy designed to elicit from the German leadership a public commitment to NATO for the defense of Western Europe. Washington's ultimate objective was to obtain Bonn's agreement for the deployment on German territory of long-range nuclear weapons capable of striking the Soviet Union, but German and European political conditions generally—the governing coalition's extremely influential German Social-Democratic party (SPD)-left, and most importantly, the powerful antinuclear movement—dictated an oblique approach.[40]

It took no genius to perceive that any proposal to deploy additional nuclear weapons in Europe would trigger a major uproar that would perhaps defeat such a proposal outright.[41] In West Germany the SPD-left was adamantly against further deployment of nuclear weapons of any kind. In Western Europe generally, the broad-based antinuclear movement had already forced revision of plans to shift a larger percentage of electrical power generation to nuclear plants, and in 1977 it was at the peak of its strength.[42] Therefore, the Carter leadership adopted a subtle scheme designed to defuse European opposition. The tactic was to employ the enhanced radiation weapon (ERW), the so-called "neutron bomb," as a lightning rod to discharge the main force of opposition before moving forward with the desired proposal.[43]

The Carter administration set its plan in motion in the context of the reinforcement of the United States military position in Western Europe noted in the previous chapter. The centerpiece of Washington's effort was President Carter's call for a Long-Term Defense Program (LTDP) at the NATO summit in May 1977. There it was decided to estabish ten task forces, nine focusing on conventional issues and one, Task Force 10, on theater nuclear questions. The president also obtained agreement on his proposal for alliance-wide commitment to a 3 percent increase in defense expenditures. The "3 percent solution," as it was termed, was designed to serve as a lever to extract greater European commitment to NATO defense as well as a means of generating greater cooperation from Congress for increased United States support.[44]

Throughout 1977 Washington focused European attention on methods of upgrading conventional defenses, deliberately downplaying the idea of introducing long-range theater nuclear forces. Indeed, the initial approach was to reassure the allies that the increase in United States theater-designated nuclear forces—the substitution of the Poseidons for the Polaris submarines, and the doubling of the FB 111 bomber force—were sufficient to counter any Soviet theater upgrade. Secretary of State Vance made these arguments in testimony before Congress in early October, and David Aaron, Brzezinski's aide, traveled to Europe in late 1977 for this purpose.[45]

There were sound reasons for downplaying the theater nuclear issue at this stage. First, the threat—SS-20 deployment—was still in its incipient phase. Although Senator Henry Jackson had disclosed on February 23, 1977, that the Soviet Union was deploying the SS-20 in substantial numbers, the weapon had not yet become operational.[46] The first eighteen launchers became operational only in late 1977.[47] Secondly, European public opinion was not prepared for deployment of additional nuclear weapons, and it would take time to establish the proper political climate. Finally, given the West German leadership's commitment to detente, Bonn would have to be carefully maneuvered into position to accept deployment of new weapons on German soil.

The "neutron bomb" controversy broke in early June 1977 with an article written by *Washington Post* reporter Walter Pincus.[48] The Pincus article sensationalized the weapon as a "killer warhead" (as if there were any other kind) that destroyed people but left buildings intact. Followed by several other articles, it generated a firestorm of opposition, particularly in West Germany, where the weapon was to be deployed. SPD-left leader Egon Bahr described the ERW as a "symbol of mental perversion,"[49] a theme which Moscow picked up. The Soviets sought to capitalize on the controversy by mounting a massive propaganda campaign describing the weapon as the "ultimate capitalist weapon" and as a "diabolical toy."[50]

Whether the initial disclosure of congressional approval of research and development funds for the ERW was accidental, as Brzezinski implies,[51] the product of Pincus' own long-time opposition to battlefield nuclear weapons,[52] or a deliberate leak, it was the Carter administration's response that was unusual. The president could have defused the growing controversy by publicly deferring production (as he would eventually do) and then inserting the weapon into the secret "miscellaneous" budget category to continue funding. But the president showed no inclination to avoid the public dispute, turning back efforts in Congress to block funding.[53] Indeed, by his actions, the president ensured there would be controversy.

Contrary to Vance's assessment that the uproar "made production and deployment of the weapon a test of the administration's will to carry out its stated intention to strengthen NATO's defense,"[54] the reverse was true. The administration in fact adopted the opposite procedure to that normally employed for both congressional and alliance action regarding weapons decisions. Normal procedure was for the president to announce a decision, then solicit congressional funding approval. Similarly, in alliance matters, normal procedure was for the president to announce a production decision, then solicit alliance agreement for deployment. But in the case of the ERW the president did exactly the opposite.

Instead of announcing his decision to produce the ERW, the president demanded that Congress first approve funds, after which he would decide whether or not to produce. On July 12, the day before the final Senate vote, the president made his first public statement on ERW, declaring, "I have not yet decided whether to approve the neutron bomb. I do think it ought to be one of our options, however."[55] But, after "an extraordinary secret session," during which the Senate approved funding for ERW, the president then declared that he would defer a decision on production until later in the summer.[56]

Amid growing debate in West Germany over the strategic implications of the neutron weapon, President Carter pressed Chancellor Schmidt for a direct commitment to deploy ERW prior to an American production decision. Intensifying the pressure, a "leak" of Presidential Review Memorandum 10 occurred in early August.[57] In what was reported as results of a newly completed review of United States war-fighting strategy in Europe, PRM 10 advocated early withdrawal of allied forces to the Weser-Lech line, which would concede about one-third of West Germany to the Warsaw Pact at the outset of a conflict.[58]

The leak produced an immediate White House denial, and Brzezinski, who was quoted in the leak, telephoned Foreign Minister Hans Dietrich Genscher to say that the statements attributed to him were "partial, inaccurate and deal with only one aspect of the overall defense strategy."[59] Nevertheless, even implicitly calling into question the cornerstone of German defense strategy—forward defense—was a silent threat to Schmidt, who was infuriated. Worse, it stiffened his resolve on the neutron bomb issue.

Schmidt's reaction was to declare that "production of the weapon was solely an American decision. The issue of deployment would be confronted later."[60] In anticipation of the meeting of NATO's Nuclear Planning Group (NPG) on October 11 and 12 at Bari, Italy, the United States now sought to gain preliminary agreement from concerned heads of state in order to announce a consensus at the meeting. Toward this end, Brzezinski visited Chancellor Schmidt on September 27, but the chancellor raised the first of several conditions which would have to be fulfilled before Bonn would agree. He stated that he would accept deployment of neutron weapons on German soil if, first, Carter announced his intention to produce and, second, NATO as a whole determined they were necessary.[61]

Despite the fact that all prospects for agreement had evaporated when the NPG meeting convened on October 11, Secretary of Defense Harold Brown made a distinction between unanimity and consensus and insisted that, while unanimity was not required, a consensus was necessary. The ERW, he said, would not be "rammed down the throats" of the allies without it.[62] Urging that the allies share responsibility with the United States, Brown laid down an American condition, declaring that the neutron weapon "would be produced only if the Europeans made the first public commitment."[63]

Washington Shifts from Short to Long

Perhaps more importantly, at the meeting the United States side now began to move forward on the question of theater-level nuclear force modernization. Partly on the grounds that the NPG had failed to foresee the ERW controversy, Washington proposed that Task Force 10, created in May, be redesignated a High Level Group (HLG) under an American chairman. Although the High Level Group would remain formally a part of the NPG it would in fact become an independent body with greater access to allied foreign and defense ministers.[64]

By this time, West German–American relations were approaching the breaking point. When Chancellor Schmidt delivered his address to the International Institute for Strategic Studies in London two weeks later, on October 28, he used the opportunity to give vent to his growing frustration and anger.[65] Before getting to the heart of his speech—the internal considerations of Western security, specifically its "economic dimensions"—he wished first to "analyze some current strategic and political issues." Noting that there was "only a narrow divide between the hope for peace and the danger of war," he stated:

> Changed strategic conditions confront us with new problems. SALT codifies the nuclear strategic balance between the Soviet Union and the United States. To put it another way: SALT neutralizes their strategic nuclear capabilities. In Europe this magnifies the significance of the disparities between East and West in nuclear tactical and conventional weapons.

Therefore, he concluded, "because of this we must press ahead with the Vienna negotiations on mutual balanced force reductions (MBFR) as an important step toward a better balance of military power in Europe." His position was that

> strategic arms limitations confined to the United States and the Soviet Union will inevitably impair the security of the West European members of the alliance vis-à-vis Soviet military superiority in Europe if we do not succeed in removing the disparities of military power in Europe parallel to the SALT negotiations. So long as this is not the case we must maintain the balance of the full range of deterrence strategy. The alliance must, therefore, be ready to make available the means to support its present strategy, which is still the right one, and to prevent any developments that could undermine the basis of this strategy.

Nevertheless, his preference was clear: if the choice were between "a massive buildup of forces" and arms reductions, he said, "I prefer the latter." In short, without progress on MBFR, "we shall have to rely on the effectiveness of deterrence." And it is in the context of deterrence "and no other" that we must see the issue of the "neutron bomb." Is it, he asked, "of value to the alliance as an additional element of the deterrence strategy, as a means of preventing war?" Further, "what relevance and weight" does this weapon have in our efforts to achieve arms control?

Given the furor over the neutron weapon that was then consuming Western Europe, Chancellor Schmidt was clearly questioning the deterrence "relevance" of the weapon and siding with his party and those who were arguing that deployment of ERW not only made war, indeed nuclear war, more likely in Europe, it made it more likely that war would be confined to Europe. ERW was decoupling, making it less likely that the United States would automatically move to a strategic nuclear exchange with the Soviet Union in the event of an outbreak of war. Closing his remarks on the weapons question, he stressed the necessity of bringing arms control to a positive conclusion, because "failure of such negotiations can no longer be compensated for by banking on military victory."

The main thrust of Schmidt's remarks was directed toward economic renewal, "the foundation of all security." For him, "our primary task is to restabilize the economic foundations of the democratic state." In this regard he noted three problems to be solved. First, it was necessary to construct a viable world economic system, the main danger to which was protectionism. Second, it was vital to ensure access to raw material and energy supplies. Here, since the United States "uses half of the energy consumed by the Western world," he hoped that President Carter's energy conservation program succeeded. Finally, he declared, "The third major task of Western security policy in economic terms is to establish balanced and stable economic relations with the Communist state trading countries of the East."

Chancellor Schmidt had described the essence of West Germany's strategy of detente and deterrence, emphasizing the economic promise of detente and the arms control primacy of deterrence. His speech was not a call to counter the Soviet deployment of the SS-20, let alone to suggest deployment of additional nuclear weapons on German territory. Indeed, Schmidt did not mention the SS-20 at all.[66] The only weapon specifically mentioned was the neutron bomb, whose deployment he suggested would not improve deterrence and would only impair arms control negotiations.

Since Schmidt had emphasized arms control, the United States now proposed to link ERW to it. Over the winter, American policymakers devised a three-part formula which would gain European agreement on deployment.[67] First, the United States would announce a decision to produce. Second, the United States would offer to forgo deployment of ERW if the Soviet Union would forgo deployment of the SS-20. Third, NATO would announce its intent to deploy ERW in two years if arms control negotiations were unsuccessful.[68] There was undoubtedly every confidence in Washington that Moscow would refuse this patently unequal trade-off.

Schmidt welcomed negotiations but persisted in keeping his

options open if they failed. The SPD conference in mid-November produced a conflict over the issue. The SPD-left offered a resolution calling for the prohibition of ERW deployment, but after heated discussion the conference passed a resolution instructing the chancellor "to create the political and strategic prerequisites within the framework of security and disarmament policies so that storing the neutron weapon on the territory of the Federal Republic will not be necessary."[69] At the conference, Schmidt declared that "all attempts to drive a wedge between myself and my party are without purpose; they result from naive illusions. I stand in the middle of my party."[70]

The relentless American pressure for a German response, however, finally produced an official five-point position in January 1978 setting forth conditions under which deployment could occur:

> 1. The Federal Republic is not a nuclear-weapons state and therefore does not participate in decisions on the production of nuclear weapons.
>
> 2. In the event of an American decision for production, opportunities ought to be used to bring ER weapons into arms limitation negotiations.
>
> 3. The government is prepared to declare that it will allow the stationing of ER weapons on German territory, if within two years after the American President's production decision . . . arms limitation negotiations [have failed].
>
> 4. In the interests of the alliance, it would be necessary in any case not to base ER weapons only on German soil.
>
> 5. The Federal Republic must not be assigned any special position . . . at the same time, the relationship with the Soviet Union and the other neighboring European countries must be taken into consideration.[71]

Bonn's January decision opened the way for agreement on production and deployment of the neutron bomb. The compromise agreement, worked out during February and March essentially among American, British, and German negotiators, was that the United States would announce a decision to produce the neutron weapon. Deployment would take place only if the United States and the Soviet Union failed to reach an appropriate arms limitation agreement within two years. In that case, the NATO European allies would immediately declare their intention to accept deployment.[72]

Meanwhile, developments were occurring on another level which would establish the basis for President Carter's rejection of the hard-won ERW compromise. After extensive internal debate spanning January–March regarding the ominous Soviet buildup in Ethiopia, United States leaders concluded, as one of a broad set of policy decisions, that the moment had arrived to shift policy in Western Europe.[73] At the February meeting of the High Level Group in Los Alamos, New Mexico, Washington proposed a range of weapons options for consideration: (1) do nothing, (2) build a strong battlefield tactical capability, (3) make a modest addition to long-range theater nuclear weapons, and (4) develop a robust theater capability to wage nuclear war against the Soviet Union.[74]

In what was described as a "freewheeling" discussion, a "surprising consensus" evolved within the group around options three and four.[75] The consensus was that modernization of long-range theater nuclear capability (LRTNF) was necessary, that it should constitute an "evolutionary upward adjustment," and that it should include an "enhanced capability to strike targets in the Soviet Union." European reluctance to develop a serious battlefield capability, option two, conveyed a strong message to American leaders regarding the neutron bomb issue, despite just having reached agreement on a formula for deployment.

In other words, by March European leaders had declared their willingness to go forward in principle with development of a long-range theater nuclear capability and evinced a strong disinclination to upgrade NATO's tactical battlefield capability. These two choices established the fundamental basis for President Carter's decision to defer production of the neutron weapon, but there were at least two other unstated reasons as well. The United States clearly preferred the long-range over the tactical, to compensate for the anticipated shift in the strategic weapons balance with the Soviet Union. Also, as the president's preference for long-range theater weapons became apparent, it was not inconceivable that Schmidt would elect to accept ERW as the lesser of two evils and decline deployment of long-range weapons on German territory.

Therefore, while placing further progress within the High Level Group on hold (the March and April meetings of the HLG included a National Security Council representative who "waffled" on reaching a decision to proceed[76]), the president withdrew from the compromise agreement just struck with the European allies at the end of March. In what by all accounts was a personally damaging decision undermining confidence in the president's alliance leadership, Carter decided to defer production of ERW.[77] Publicly, he sought to deflect attention from Schmidt by accepting personal responsibility and declaring that the length of the deferral would ultimately be determined by "the degree to which the Soviet Union shows restraint in its conventional and nuclear arms programs and force deployments."[78]

The reason privately given for backing away from the ERW compromise was that Chancellor Schmidt had refused to give explicit commitment to deployment.[79] While it was true that Schmidt simply would not, indeed could not, take the lead in requesting deployment because of his delicate domestic position and because he clearly did not wish to be constrained by the negative implications for *Ostpolitik*, the fact was that the United States had achieved its objective in gaining agreement on a deployment formula.

It would appear that the decision to defer production of ERW was designed to shock the alliance into the realization of the necessity for theater nuclear force modernization. Clearly, if a choice was to be made, ERW was not preferable to LRTNF. As one participant and critic described it,

> the neutron weapon debacle of April 1978, viewed in retrospect, proved a critical factor in the entire decisionmaking process on the NATO LRTNF. . . . It reduced European confidence in American competence. . . . Further, the Carter administration itself felt it needed to compensate for its handling of the neutron decision. It sought to do so by responding boldly to a perceived European concern through exercising vigorous leadership in welding an alliance consensus in support of the deployment of long-range nuclear weapons, in that way generating a NATO success in the TNF field.[80]

Indeed, following the ERW decision, Washington took the lead in pressing for a NATO decision on deployment of long-range theater nuclear forces. Again, as in the ERW case, the main problem would be how to satisfy German conditions. It was clear that Bonn would have preferred no decision at all, but, since a decision in principle had already evolved, Schmidt would establish stringent conditions.

Those conditions were (1) that any NATO decision should be unanimous—no negative votes and no abstentions; (2) that a long-range theater-weapons deployment plan include at least one other Continental non-nuclear state besides the Federal Republic; (3) that since the Federal Republic had no intention of becoming a nuclear state, it was the responsibility of the United States to take the lead in nuclear decisions; and (4) that any systems capable of striking Soviet territory based in the Federal Republic be under exclusively American control.[81]

These conditions would be difficult to fulfill. Bonn would demand alliance unanimity; consensus would be insufficient. Great pressure was placed on Belgium, the Netherlands, and Italy, each of whose governments was composed of extremely fragile domestic coalitions, making their agreement problematical at best.[82] And responsibility was placed squarely with the United States, both with regard to reaching the decision and to controlling the weapons once deployed. Bonn would neither request weapons nor participate in any dual control arrangement. But that was not all. Schmidt also demanded that any deployment procedure include an arms control component.

At least partly in response to German requirements (see chapter 6) Washington undertook an extensive internal review and analysis based upon PRM 38, "Long Range Theater Nuclear Capabilities and Arms Control." Initiated in June 1978, the review was completed in October. Its principal recommendations were that NATO long-range nuclear modernization was necessary both militarily and politically to improve alliance capability as well as cohesion. Most importantly, the review concluded, without a decision to modernize there could be little hope of bringing the theater military balance under an arms control arrangement.[83]

At the same time, while making no specific recommendation, American leaders had worked out five weapons options, some combination of which would be decided upon for deployment. Ground- and sea-based cruise missiles comprised two possibilities; a longer-range variant of the FB-111, a third; an extended-range Pershing ballistic missile of the type already deployed in West Germany, a fourth; and a medium-range ballistic missile with a range of 1,500 miles, which used the same Mark 12-A warhead as Minuteman III, a fifth.

Brzezinski was sent to Europe to discuss the issue, and in the course of discussions with Chancellor Schmidt the idea of holding a small, informal meeting of United States, British, French, and West German leaders arose.[84] After further allied consultations, Giscard d'Estaing offered to host a meeting of the four leaders on the French island of Guadeloupe, January 5 and 6, 1979. Although no formal record of their meeting is available, Brzezinski's private journal entries offer a glimpse of what transpired. It would appear that at Guadeloupe Schmidt was prevailed upon to commit Bonn to deployment of long-range nuclear missiles on German soil.

German Agreement—With Reservations

There is a sense in which Schmidt was entrapped by the logic of events and his own arguments into agreeing to deployment in Germany. The High Level Group had agreed in principle to the political necessity of deploying a visible counter to the SS-20, although not so large a force as to suggest the decoupling of the United States from Western Europe. Schmidt himself had declared the necessity of maintaining the Eurostrategic balance, preferably through arms control but through a counterbalancing buildup if necessary. The issue which President Carter focused on at Guadeloupe was, would the German chancellor accept deployment of weapons on German soil?

Schmidt's preference was for deployment of sea-launched cruise missiles, which, from his point of view, would satisfy the demands of deterrence without sacrificing the German interest in detente.[85] During a comprehensive review of the security situation, the president took the lead in pressing Schmidt and the others "to define their response to the perceived threat."[86] As Brzezinski noted, both Giscard and Callaghan were "to the point," "decisive," and "vigorous." Schmidt, on the other hand, was "contentious" and ambivalent.[87] "He kept saying that he has a political problem and that he is not in a position to make any commitments."[88]

But Carter, Callaghan, and Giscard "pressed him" hard on the issue of weapons deployment in West Germany. The president turned Schmidt's own arguments against him, pointing out that he "had initiated the entire discussion of a European nuclear imbalance, and that we must have German willingness to deploy these missiles in order to negotiate successfully with the Soviets."[89] In recognition, perhaps, of the need for a "common western position," or, more likely, of the fact that being the lone holdout would damage other interests, the chancellor relented.[90]

But not entirely. Schmidt insisted that at least one other non-nuclear Continental power besides West Germany also agree to deployment and that a serious effort be made to reach an arms control settlement. Schmidt's conditions led to adoption of virtually the same three-part formula that was devised for the ERW compromise. NATO would announce its decision to deploy and offer to negotiate an agreed balance with Moscow but, failing that after four years (when the weapons would be ready), to deploy.

Brzezinski's deputy, David Aaron, led a team to Europe in late January to carry forward the Guadeloupe decision. Although officials in London and Paris continued to be supportive, Aaron encountered continued opposition in Bonn from the Social-Democratic left.[91] Positions crystallized publicly at a party meeting a few days later. Chancellor Schmidt, having made a commitment to deployment, attempted to make the case for long-range nuclear weapons by stressing the offensive political potential inherent in an imbalance favoring Moscow.

> When the Soviet Union puts into service every year 30 to 50 new SS-20 missiles, each with at least three warheads, and also puts into service 30 to 50 new Backfire bombers, one can see that in the course of the 1980s . . . the Soviet Union could theoretically be put in the position of using military intimidation for political purposes.[92]

SPD floor leader Herbert Wehner disputed the view that Soviet force modernization was offensive, arguing against the "philosophy" that Soviet military power was a threat. Soviet power should be seen as "defensive rather than aggressive," he said.[93] Defense Minister Hans Apel attempted to strike a compromise with the view that Soviet deployments should be seen as "neither aggressive nor defensive," but it was clear that the German ruling coalition was in disarray.

By spring, however, Bonn returned to its basic position that while some counter deployment might be necessary, the NATO stress must be placed on arms control. Clear sentiment in favor of the view that arms control could substitute for force modernization, especially in Germany but also in the Netherlands, prompted formation of a

NATO Special Group in April to work out an arms control approach to accompany a deployment decision.[94] Following a series of meetings through the summer, the Special Group adopted what was essentially the American position, that future theater-level arms control negotiations should take place within the framework of SALT III negotiations, safeguarding NATO Europe's interests through an appropriate consulting mechanism. Most important, it was concluded that arms control negotiations were not a substitute for force modernization.[95]

Meanwhile, on a parallel track, Washington moved forward on the actual weapons to be included in the final deployment package. The Nuclear Planning Group had met in Florida, and NATO defense ministers had concurred in principle to deployment of between 200 and 600 long-range weapons—a number neither too small to be insignificant nor too large to be provocative.[96] They also agreed that a final decision would be reached in December 1979. By mid-year, the High Level Group had developed a recommendation for deployment of a total of 572 missiles in five countries.

The deployment package would include 108 Pershing II missiles and 96 ground-launch cruise missiles (24 launchers) in the Federal Republic; 160 ground-launch cruise missiles (40 launchers) in the United Kingdom; 112 ground-launch cruise missiles (28 launchers) in Italy; and 48 ground-launch cruise missiles (12 launchers) each for Belgium and the Netherlands. The key factor governing the actual number of weapons deployed was the 108 Pershing I-a missiles already deployed in the Federal Republic. Washington's approach was to replace the 400-mile range Pershing I-a with the 1,000-mile-plus range Pershing II. The GLCM remainder would simply be a function of the highest multiple of sixteen (four missiles aboard each of four launch vehicles, which constituted a "flight"), or 29, for a total of 464.

The United States side had accepted the recommended deployment package at a meeting of the Special Coordinating Committee on July 5.[97] The decision was officially announced the following month; and on October 4, after being approved by the High Level Group, the deployment package and the Special Group report on arms control were combined into an Integrated Decision Document. This, in turn, was submitted to the North Atlantic Council in early November for final action at their Brussels meeting on December 12.

At this point in the process, Moscow returned to the fray with renewed vigor in a last-minute effort to preclude a decision for deployment. In a major speech on October 6, Brezhnev restated themes which had pervaded earlier Soviet pronouncements.[98] He declared that a balance in theater weaponry already existed, which any new NATO deployment would upset. Secondly, he asserted that the SS-20 did not change the current equilibrium. Thirdly, in announcing the withdrawal of 1,000 tanks and 20,000 troops from East Germany, he offered further reductions in theater weapons if NATO did not deploy. This would, presumably, include the SS-21, SS-22, and SS-23 missiles, with ranges of 75, 550, and 300 miles, respectively, which Moscow was also deploying, but the exact content of the reduction offer was left unclear.

Brezhnev's speech was clearly timed to maximize the disquiet regarding deployment that was present in several European capitals—not only in Bonn, but in Brussels and The Hague, as well. Chancellor Schmidt quickly responded, urging the West "to take the Soviets at their word" and "bargain" with them. A successful outcome, he argued, "could mean that new American medium-range nuclear missiles might never have to be deployed in Western Europe."[99]

Despite Schmidt's objections, it was nevertheless a case of too little, too late. The decisionmaking process was already far advanced when Brezhnev gave his speech, and the Soviet leader declined to make the one offer which could have made a difference. This was the offer to "freeze" further deployment of the SS-20. As Simon Lunn notes, "Had the Soviets made that offer, the December consensus would have been extremely unlikely."[100]

As it was, despite the fact that the December North Atlantic Council meeting approved the two-track, three-part decision, there were clearly expressed reservations. The Netherlands would withhold its final decision for over two years; Belgium reserved the right to review its approval, dragging out a final decision until 1985; and in the Federal Republic the SPD would continue to manifest hostility to deployment—indeed, though out of power, voting against deployment in 1983.

Nevertheless, in assessing American policy through the 1979 decision, the Carter administration must be accorded high marks for accomplishing a most difficult task in the face of determined allied opposition to deployment of new nuclear weapons. The Soviet breakthrough in guidance technology had a great impact upon both the timing and the content of American policy at the strategic and theater weapons levels. The breakthrough opened up the possibility of neutralizing the American strategic guarantee and concentrating a coercive preponderance of power against Western Europe.

Washington was forced to take immediate countermeasures to forestall both eventualities. To restore a degree of strategic weapons balance, the Carter administration selected the long-range cruise missile as a counterforce counter. The cruise missile was, however, not time-urgent; it required hours to reach designated targets. Another weapon would be required to provide a time-urgent capability, and it was here that the problems of European security and strategic deterrence intertwined in the calculations of American strategists.

Western Europe, as this chapter demonstrates, was in rapid transformation (or disintegration, depending upon the point of view), as West Germany succeeded in becoming an economic superpower with expansive ambitions both westward and eastward—westward in organizing the European Economic Community into a de facto separate deutschemark zone and eastward as the principal trading partner of the Soviet Union and East-bloc states. Economic success, in other words, offered West Germany the prospect of playing a new political role in Europe, that of intermediary between the United States and the Soviet Union—a role that Chancellor Schmidt was eager to play. In fact, the German chancellor actually proposed to President Carter that Bonn play the role of "secret intermediary" between the two superpowers on the occasion of his state visit to Washington in July 1977.[101]

This was, of course, one of Washington's worst fears and had to be precluded at all costs. The determination to forestall Bonn's "shift to the middle" would thus appear to explain Washington's economic and security policies. United States economic policy was designed to undercut the basis of Bonn's growing power while security policy was designed to set strict limits upon, if not preclude entirely, Bonn's shift to the middle. Economic policy suffered a severe setback in the establishment of the European Monetary System, but acceptance of conditional deployment of long-range theater weapons on German soil was at least a temporary success.

There was a certain elegance to the proposal to deploy Pershing II missiles to West Germany. Despite its name and similar appearance, the Pershing II was a different class of weapon than the Pershing I-a. The Pershing I-a was a tactical nuclear weapon with a range of 400 miles; the Pershing II was a medium-range ballistic missile with a range of 1,000 miles (the Soviets claimed 1,500 miles). It could arrive on targets in less than ten minutes, giving Washington a time-urgent counter to a potential Soviet first strike.[102] In terms of alliance politics, too, deployment of the Pershing II in West Germany would place a major obstacle in the path of Bonn's *Ostpolitik* because of the apparent German commitment to the Western alliance. But Moscow's technological demarche would have as far-reaching an effect upon Washington's Asian policy as upon European policy, a subject to which we now turn.

Notes

1. Richard J. Barnet, *The Alliance—America, Europe, Japan, Makers of the Postwar World* (New York: Simon and Schuster, 1983), p. 388.
2. U.S. total net crude imports, in millions of barrels per day, from 1973 were: 1973, 6.0; 1974, 5.8; 1975, 5.8; 1976, 7.0; 1977, 8.5; 1978, 8.0; 1979, 7.9; 1980, 6.2. Source: *Monthly Energy Review* (June 1981), p. 30.
3. Richard Cooper, "Flexible Exchange Rates after 6 Years' Experience," speech to the World Affairs Council of Philadelphia, October 31, 1979, U.S. Department of State, *Current Policy*, no. 114, November 1979. (Emphasis supplied.)
4. Ibid.
5. Robert O. Keohane, "U.S. Foreign Economic Policy toward Other Advanced Capitalist States: The Struggle to Make Others Adjust," in Kenneth Oye, Donald Rothchild, and Robert J. Lieber, eds., *Eagle Entangled, U.S. Foreign Policy in a Complex World* (New York: Longman Publishers, 1979), p. 104.
6. Ibid., p. 103.
7. Paul Lewis, "U.S. Voices Concern on Further Slowing of World Economy," *New York Times*, November 22, 1977, p. 51.
8. Paul Lewis, "European Leaders Agree to Back Loan in Common Market," *New York Times*, December 7, 1977, p. D1.
9. Keohane, "U.S. Foreign Economic Policy," pp. 104–5.
10. Peter Ludlow, *The Making of the European Monetary System* (London: Butterworth Scientific, 1982), p. 70.
11. Keohane, "U.S. Foreign Economic Policy," p. 106.
12. See *International Financial Statistics* (Washington, DC: International Monetary Fund, January 1980), passim, and David Gisselquist, *Oil Prices and Trade Deficits: U.S. Conflicts with Japan and West Germany* (New York: Praeger Books, 1979), p. 81.
13. See Thornton, *Nixon-Kissinger Years*, pp. 278–88.
14. Ludlow, *European Monetary System*, p. 8.
15. Ibid.
16. Ibid., pp. 67–68.
17. Ibid., pp. 70–71.
18. Ibid., p. 73.
18. Ibid., p. 73.
19. Paul Lewis, "Strategy to Revive Western Economies Takes a New Tack," *New York Times*, February 28, 1978, p. 41.
20. For a brief but useful discussion of the origins of EMS, see Horst Ungerer, *The European Monetary System: The Experience, 1979–1982* (Washington, DC: International Monetary Fund, 1983), pp. 1–3.

21. Ludlow, *European Monetary System*, p. 200.
22. Ibid., p. 84.
23. Ibid., pp. 91–92.
24. U.S. Treasury Press Release, B.905, May 15, 1978.
25. Ludlow, *European Monetary System*, p. 119.
26. Robert D. Putnam and Nicholas Bayne, *Hanging Together, the Seven-Power Summits* (Cambridge: Harvard University Press, 1984), p. 87, and Paul Lewis, "U.S. Shuns O.E.C.D. Growth Plan," *New York Times*, June 1, 1978, p. D1.
27. Keohane, "U.S. Foreign Economic Policy," p. 107.
28. "Extract from the Conclusions of the Presidency of the European Council of 6 and 7 July 1978 in Bremen and Annex," in Ludlow, *European Monetary System*, appendix 1A, p. 301.
29. Putnam and Bayne, *Hanging Together*, p. 94.
30. Ibid., pp. 92–93, and Ludlow, *European Monetary System*, p. 131.
31. Ibid., pp. 246–47.
32. Ibid., p. 249.
33. Ibid., p. 191.
34. See, for example, the article by IMF board member Tom De Vries, "The New Shape of U.S. Monetary Policy," *Washington Post*, September 24, 1978, p. M1.
35. For a comprehensive analysis of the bitter legislative history of the energy bill, see *Congressional Quarterly Almanac, 1978*, vol. 34 (Washington, DC: GPO, 1979), pp. 639–67.
36. Ludlow, *European Monetary System*, p. 247.
37. Council of Economic Advisers, *Economic Report of the President, January 1979* (Washington, DC: GPO, 1979), p. 157, and Ludlow, *European Monetary System*, p. 248.
38. Ibid.
39. Brzezinski, *Power and Principle*, p. 311, makes a similar point. "The Carter administration recognized that the United States and Europe had been gradually drifting apart since the 1960s. In part, this was a natural evolution as the allies fully recovered from the effects of WWII and developed a set of interests that paralleled our own but were different in important ways. But the OPEC shock of 1973 and the emergence of detente between Western and Eastern blocs on the Continent foreshadowed major points of divergence between Washington and the allies. . . . This drift was only partially arrested during the Carter years, despite our efforts to forge a more explicit consensus. . . ."
40. Barnet, *The Alliance*, pp. 379–82, succinctly discusses the power and influence of the European antinuclear movement. For a more detailed

treatment, see Dorothy Nelkin and Michael Pollak, *The Atom Besieged: Extraparliamentary Dissent in France and Germany* (Cambridge: MIT Press, 1981).

41. Simon Lunn, *The Modernization of NATO's Long-Range Theater Nuclear Forces*, Report for the Subcommittee on Europe and the Middle East, Committee on Foreign Affairs, U.S. House of Representatives, December 31, 1980 (Washington, DC: GPO, 1981), p. 26, notes: "The likelihood of strong public reaction against the deployment of additional land-based nuclear missiles indicated one of the paradoxes of the modernization proposal—while the technical experts argued that visibility was necessary in order to enhance deterrence, it was precisely this visibility that would cause the adverse public reaction."
42. Barnet, *The Alliance*, p. 381.
43. The ERW was first developed in 1958 and was part of a general evolution of nuclear technology from fission to fusion which offered reduced collateral effects from blast and heat and increased precision through smaller, more accurate warheads. The weapon's enhanced radiation effects gave it its name. ERW had been included in alliance discussions since 1975, when the United States began planning for theater modernization.
44. The contradiction between Carter's campaign pledge to reduce defense spending by $5 to $7 billion and the 3 percent increase was apparent. For a useful discussion of the role and fate of the 3 percent concept, see *The Three Per Cent Solution* (Philadelphia: Foreign Policy Research Institute, 1981).
45. Lunn, *Modernization of NATO's Forces*, p. 19, and Garthoff, *Detente and Confrontation*, p. 857.
46. Charles W. Corddry, "Soviet Said to Deploy 100 SS20s," *Baltimore Sun*, February 24, 1977, p. A5.
47. Garthoff, *Detente and Confrontation*, p. 857. By the end of 1979, 125 would be operational and by the end of 1983 there would be 378.
48. "Neutron Killer Warhead Buried in ERDA Budget," *Washington Post*, June 6, 1977, p. A1.
49. David Yost and Thomas Glad, "West German Party Politics and Theater Nuclear Modernization Since 1977," *Armed Forces and Society* (Summer 1982), p. 531.
50. "Russia Blasts U.S. on Neutron Bomb Plans," *International Herald Tribune*, August 1, 1977, p. 1.
51. Brzezinski, *Power and Principle*, p. 301, ERDA had "neglected to delete the still classified term 'enhanced radiation' from publicly released congressional testimony." General Bratton, whose testimony before the House Armed Services Committee was released publicly on April

22, stated that "systems now under development include . . . the W70 mod 3 Lance ERW . . . the W79 8-inch Artillery Fired Atomic Projectile and . . . an improved replacement for the existing W48 155 mm artillery shell . . ." as quoted in Sherri L. Wasserman, *The Neutron Bomb Controversy, a Study in Alliance Politics* (New York: Praeger, 1983), p. 33.

52. Pincus, who was a staff assistant to Senator Stuart Symington on the Joint Committee on Atomic Energy in 1973 when the issue of modernization of nuclear artillery arose, had written articles opposing nuclear artillery then. See Wasserman, *Neutron Bomb Controversy*, p. 39.
53. Vance, *Hard Choices*, p. 68.
54. Ibid.
55. "Transcript of the President's News Conference on Domestic and Foreign Affairs," *New York Times*, July 13, 1977, p. 10.
56. Richard Burt, "Neutron Bomb Controversy Strained Alliance and Caused Splits in the Administration," *New York Times*, April 9, 1978, p. 18.
57. Rowland Evans and Robert Novak, "Conceding Defeat in Europe," *Washington Post*, August 4, 1977, p. A19.
58. David N. Schwartz, *NATO's Nuclear Dilemmas* (Washington, DC: Brookings Institution, 1983), pp. 213–14.
59. Charles Mohr, "Brzezinski Assures Bonn on U.S. Strategy in a War," *New York Times*, August 4, 1977, p. A9, and Garthoff, *Detente and Confrontation*, p. 854.
60. Brzezinski, *Power and Principle*, p. 302.
61. Wasserman, *Neutron Bomb Controversy*, pp. 82–83. Brzezinski, *Power and Principle*, p. 302, in obvious reference to this episode, although he does not mention it explicitly in his account, observed: "Schmidt could not bear the wrath of the Soviets and his own domestic critics and insisted that deployment must be a collective alliance decision and not simply a bilateral agreement between West Germany and the United States."
62. David Haworth, "US Says NATO Consensus Is Needed on Neutron Bomb," *International Herald Tribune*, October 12, 1977, p. 2.
63. Ibid., "NATO Aides Fail to Agree on Neutron Bomb," and Wasserman, *Neutron Bomb Controversy*, pp. 83–84.
64. Schwartz, *NATO's Nuclear Dilemmas*, p. 217.
65. "The 1977 Alastair Buchan Memorial Lecture," *Survival*, January–February 1978, pp. 1–20.
66. Cf. Brzezinski, *Power and Principle*, p. 303, who described the address as Schmidt's speech "on the Euro-strategic balance [which] . . .

underscored the threat from the new SS-20 missiles" and, p. 307, that the chancellor "called on the Western alliance to counter this [SS-20] threat."

67. See Wasserman, *Neutron Bomb Controversy*, pp. 92–97.
68. Brzezinski, *Power and Principle*, p. 303.
69. Yost and Glad, "West German Party Politics," p. 533. Richard Burt, "US May Offer Soviet Deal Shelving Neutron Bomb," *New York Times*, November 24, 1977, p. 12, cites the same resolution, but substitutes the term "deployment" for "storing."
70. Yost and Glad, "West German Party Politics," p. 533.
71. Ibid., p. 534.
72. Wasserman, *Neutron Bomb Controversy*, p. 110.
73. See chapter 5 for discussion of the policy debate.
74. Schwartz, *NATO's Nuclear Dilemmas*, pp. 218–19.
75. Ibid. and Garthoff, *Detente and Confrontation*, p. 858.
76. Garthoff, *Detente and Confrontation*, p. 858. Garthoff notes that "some people in the U.S. government who were not yet ready to reach that decision . . . waffled."
77. Vance, *Hard Choices*, p. 94, was "startled" by Carter's decision. He felt that "the president apparently had not focused on how far down the road we were" even though he "had been kept continuously informed by the NSC staff, and checked all of the appropriate boxes on the papers that went to him." Brzezinski, *Power and Principle*, pp. 304–5, reacted with "surprise," and argued that the decision "will stamp him as weak."
78. "Carter Statement on Neutron Bomb," *New York Times*, April 8, 1978, p. 7.
79. Brzezinski, *Power and Principle*, pp. 305–6. Vance, *Hard Choices*, pp. 94–96.
80. Garthoff, *Detente and Confrontation*, p. 859. Schwartz, *NATO's Nuclear Dilemmas*, p. 224, similarly observes: "In Washington officials resolved to reaffirm American leadership in the strongest way possible. The Defense Department had been convinced of the need to proceed with LRTNF modernization ever since the February 1978 HLG consensus. Now others, particularly at State, shared this belief. . . . LRTNF modernization would now become the issue on which the United States would demonstrate firm leadership. . . ."
81. Lunn, *Modernization of NATO's Forces*, pp. 26–27.
82. Norway and Denmark barred nuclear weapons and France was excluded because it already had them.
83. Schwartz, *NATO's Nuclear Dilemmas*, pp. 224–25.
84. Brzezinski, *Power and Principle*, p. 294, attributes the idea to Schmidt, who complained that "it made him feel 'uneasy' that President Carter,

Giscard, Callaghan, and he never met together in informal, top-level discussion of political-strategic issues."

85. Schmidt's position was left ambiguous at the time, but in an interview in February 1983, he declared: "You know that at the time I defended the view . . . that sea-based systems would suit our geographical and strategic conditions better." See "Helmut Schmidt on Those Missiles," *Washington Post*, February 13, 1983, p. C7. Egon Bahr held the same position. In an article in *Vorwaerts* of February 22, 1983, Bahr urged the sea-based option because "deployment at sea is effective against the madness of wanting to limit a war to Europe." Furthermore, he argued, the Soviet Union would not be able to distinguish between theater and strategic forces, so it "would be a good thing for linking America with the fate of Europe," *FBIS-WE*, February 23, 1983, p. J1.
86. Brzezinski, *Power and Principle*, p. 295.
87. Jimmy Carter, *Keeping Faith*, pp. 234–35.
88. Brzezinski, *Power and Principle*, p. 295.
89. Carter, *Keeping Faith*, p. 235.
90. See Garthoff, *Detente and Confrontation*, pp. 859–60, who argues that Giscard and Callaghan's concurrence was "not insignificant." Helmut Schmidt, *Men and Powers, a Political Retrospective* (New York: Random House, 1989), pp. 189–91, presents a different view in which he claims to have agreed with Giscard on a deployment formula.
91. Schwartz, *NATO's Nuclear Dilemmas*, pp. 228–29.
92. Schmidt speech to the SPD Bundestagfraktion, February 6, 1979, as cited in Yost and Glad, "West German Party Politics," p. 538. Garthoff, *Detente and Confrontation*, p. 877, on the other hand, argues that "there is no evidence to support the idea that the Soviet leaders saw a political option flowing from their decision on the SS-20 or that they even considered such a political purpose in making the decision."
93. Yost and Glad, "West German Party Politics," p. 538. See also n. 43.
94. Garthoff, *Detente and Confrontation*, p. 860, Schwartz, *NATO's Nuclear Dilemmas*, p. 231, and Lunn, *Modernization of NATO's Forces*, pp. 29–31.
95. Schwartz, *NATO's Nuclear Dilemmas*, pp. 231–32.
96. Lunn, *Modernization of NATO's Forces*, p. 23.
97. Garthoff, *Detente and Confrontation*, p. 862, and Walter Pincus, "The War Game. Birth of a Euromissile: Arms Decision Stirred a Storm around NATO," *Washington Post*, November 18, 1981, p. A1.
98. L.I. Brezhnev, "Speech at the Ceremonial Meeting in Berlin on the Occasion of the Thirtieth Anniversary of the Founding of the GDR," *FBIS-SU*, October 9, 1979, pp. F1-5. See also, Garthoff, *Detente and Confrontation*, p. 864.

99. "Schmidt Bids West Accept Soviet Offer," *New York Times*, October 15, 1979, p. 5.
100. Lunn, *Modernization of NATO's Forces*, p. 29.
101. Brzezinski, *Power and Principle*, p. 307.
102. As of the spring of 1987 the United States had deployed all 108 of the Pershing II missiles to West Germany, but only 208 of the planned deployment of 464 cruise missiles.

Europe
Conic Projection
0
100
200
300
450
Miles
North Atlantic Ocean
North Sea
Baltic Sea
English Channel
Bay of Biscay
Mediterranean Sea
Tyrrhenian Sea
Adriatic Sea
Ionian Sea
Aegean Sea
Black Sea
IRELAND
UNITED KINGDOM
DENMARK
NETHERLANDS
BELGIUM
LUX.
GERMANY
(F.R.G.)
(G.D.R.)
POLAND
U.S.S.R.
CZECHOSLOVAKIA
AUSTRIA
SWITZERLAND
FRANCE
HUNGARY
ROMANIA
YUGOSLAVIA
BULGARIA
ALBANIA
GREECE
TURKEY
ITALY
ANDORRA
SPAIN
PORTUGAL
Oslo
Stockholm
Helsinki
Tallinn
Riga
Moscow
Goteborg
Copenhagen
Aberdeen
Glasgow
Edinburgh
Belfast
Dublin
Newcastle
Liverpool
Cardiff
London
Amsterdam
Hamburg
Hannover
Berlin
Rostock
Gdansk
Kaliningrad
Vilnius
Minsk
Kiev
Poznan
Warsaw
Krakow
Leipzig
Bonn
Brussels
Frankfurt
Prague
Le Havre
Paris
Strasbourg
Stuttgart
Nantes
Munich
Vienna
Bratislava
Budapest
Bern
Graz
Geneva
Bordeaux
Lyon
Zagreb
Pecs
Cluj-Napoca
Odessa
Milan
Venice
Bucharest
Constanta
Belgrade
Bilbao
Marseille
Florence
Varna
Porto
Sofia
Titograd
Macrid
Lisbon
Barcelona
Rome
Skopje
Istanbul
Tirane
Thessaloniki
Naples
Valencia
Sevilla
Cagliari
Malaga
Gibraltar
Athens

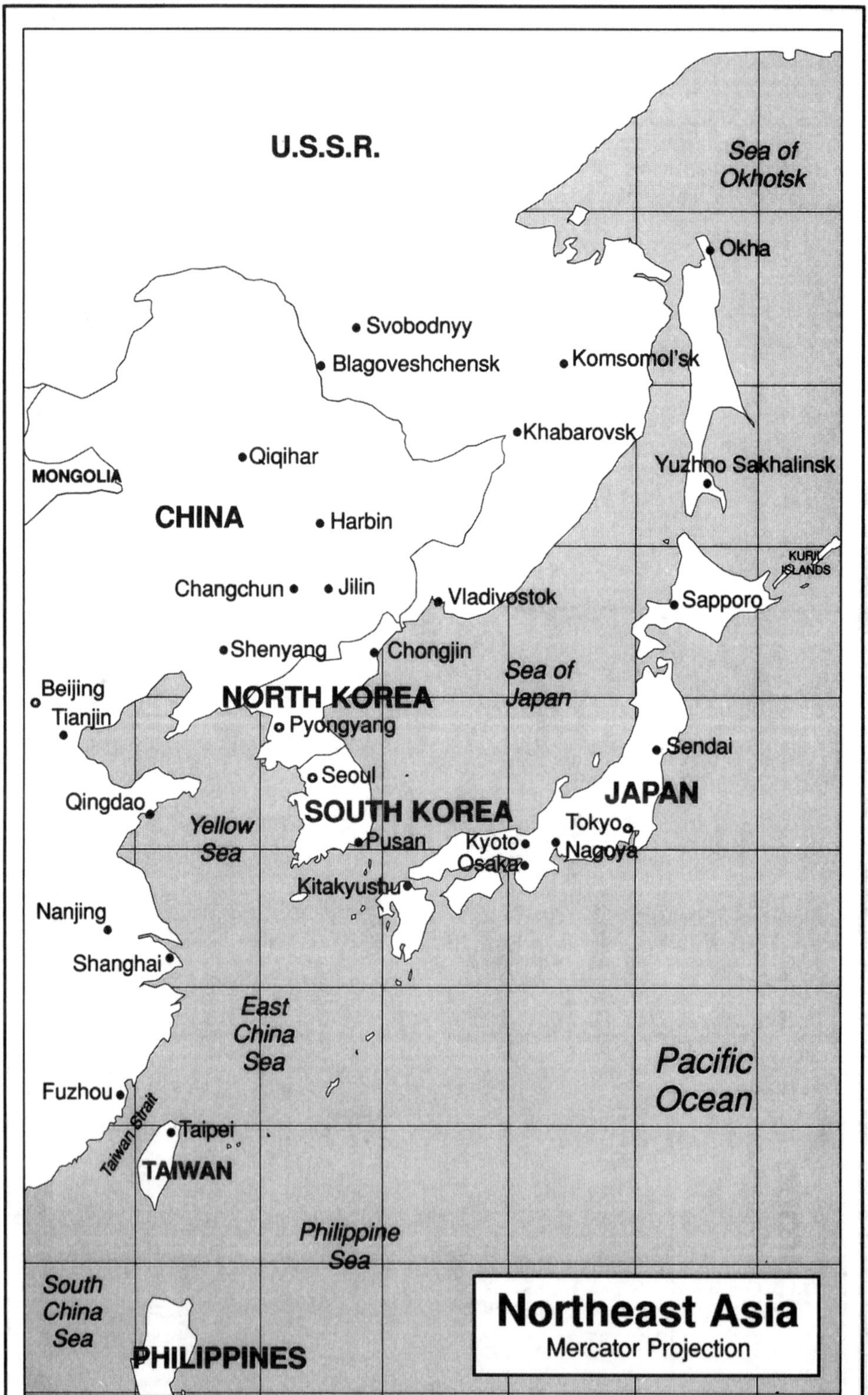
U.S.S.R.
Sea of Okhotsk
Okha
Svobodnyy
Blagoveshchensk
Komsomol'sk
Khabarovsk
Qiqihar
Yuzhno Sakhalinsk
MONGOLIA
CHINA
Harbin
KURIL ISLANDS
Changchun
Jilin
Vladivostok
Sapporo
Shenyang
Chongjin
Sea of Japan
Beijing
Tianjin
NORTH KOREA
Pyongyang
Sendai
Seoul
JAPAN
Qingdao
SOUTH KOREA
Tokyo
Yellow Sea
Pusan
Kyoto
Nagoya
Osaka
Kitakyushu
Nanjing
Shanghai
East China Sea
Pacific Ocean
Fuzhou
Taiwan Strait
Taipei
TAIWAN
Philippine Sea
South China Sea
PHILIPPINES
Northeast Asia
Mercator Projection

CHAPTER 3

Contradiction and Conflict in Asia, 1977–1979

The underlying problem American policymakers faced in Asia was similar in many respects to that confronted in Europe with West Germany. It was how to cope with the rapid rise to power of a major ally—in this case Japan. The problem was not new in either case but had become urgent of solution in both. Both countries were approaching superpower status, and it could not be assumed—and was not—that they would remain contented indefinitely with subordinate rank within the Western alliance.

In Asia, as in Europe, the United States approach was to pursue a sophisticated strategy of attempting to integrate Japan more fully into the American economic and security web, an effort which, if successful, would also lead to a moderation of Japan's rapid economic growth. The Nixon approach had been gradualistic, the Kissingerian preemptive; but neither had succeeded. Although Japan had consented to the formation of a United States–Japan Security Consultative Committee, whose subcommittee on defense cooperation began to meet from July 1976,[1] that same year Tokyo established a cap on defense spending at one percent of gross national product. Japan had continued its pattern of strong neomercantilistic growth, limiting attempts at economic and security integration while benefiting handsomely from the protection provided by the American security shield and from the wealth afforded by its market.

The Carter administration, demonstrating a marked continuity with previous efforts, sought to carry American strategy forward yet another step. That strategy called for withdrawal of American forces from the remaining military position held on the Asian mainland—South Korea. The main objective of American action was to prod Japan into playing a more prominent security role in the region as the United States shifted to a supporting position offshore. While restructuring the region, the Carter leadership sought to maintain its essential stability, increase United States maneuverability, and reduce American vulnerability.

A crucial consideration in American strategy was the impact which increased Japanese defense spending would have upon Tokyo's economic power. A defense buildup would act to curb Japan's economic resurgence in much the same way that higher energy costs were intended to do—by channeling Japan's enormous and growing financial reserves into what was in effect consumption and away from capital construction. In a very real sense the issue was not so much obtaining an increase in Japanese defense expenditures, which would be inevitable, as shaping and controlling the kind of military establishment that would result.[2]

Japan was already seeing a need to preserve vital interests, and its leaders were deep in debate over the best course to pursue. The principal American objective was to channel Japanese defense expenditures in a way which complemented and did not undermine Washington's security concerns in the region. The net effect of increased Japanese defense expenditures combined with higher energy costs would be an improvement in Northeast Asian security and significantly greater American political-economic leverage over Japan. These gains in turn would represent a step toward greater integration of "alliance" capabilities and away from any centrifugal tendencies implicit in rapid Japanese economic growth.

Moscow's technological breakthrough, which had so quickly forced the alteration of United States policy on defense expenditure,[3] on arms control negotiations, and toward Europe, forced immediate reconsideration of long-term strategy toward Northeast Asia in general and the plan to withdraw American forces from South Korea in particular. The long-term problem was that Korean withdrawal would require time (estimated at between four and five years for completion), which Moscow's earlier-than-expected technological breakthrough would deny.

If the appearance of Soviet missile accuracy was to be in 1980 instead of the original projection of 1982 or 1985, as the Carter leadership now assumed, then there would not be sufficient time to complete the restructuring of the Northeast Asia region. At the very least, it would be taking too big a risk to assume that it could be accomplished before Moscow presented a significant threat. The result could be that instead of strengthening the region against future Soviet pressure, United States policy would simply be offering Moscow a tempting opportunity to alter the geopolitical structure to its advantage.

While the scheme for Korean force withdrawal had been largely (but not completely) compromised by the Soviet technological breakthrough, American leaders believed that it was still possible to secure the principal objective of a controlled Japanese defense build-up. Therefore, Washington sought to generate maximum anxiety in the Japanese leadership in hopes of prodding them to make the desired policy changes. From March onward through the summer of 1977, United States leaders would equivocate over virtually every aspect of Carter's troop withdrawal "plan."

Washington vacillated over the very concept of "withdrawal" versus "reduction"; over the length of the plan—three, or four to five years; over what would be withdrawn—combat troops or combat and support troops; and over the timing of withdrawals—substantial early or evenly spaced withdrawals. When the bluff appeared to have had only minimal impact upon the Japanese leadership by mid-year, President Carter gambled on a scheme which could salvage the withdrawal plan—early normalization of relations with China.

Normalization of relations with China was initially low in priority but became essential once the administration perceived the imminent change in the strategic weapons balance. However, Beijing rejected early normalization and in the fall of 1977 forced the United States to abandon the scheme to withdraw forces from South Korea. Thereafter, despite President Carter's continuing public commitment, reasons would be sought and found to justify cancelling the plan, which occurred officially in early 1979.

An unexpected turn of events helped partially to extricate the United States from its dilemma. Beginning in the spring of 1978, Moscow initiated a vigorous policy of tightening the containment of China and generating greater pressure for accommodation to Soviet power in Asia. This was expressed through Soviet support for

Vietnam's conquest of Cambodia, a conflict which triggered China's invasion of Vietnam in February 1979 and which threatened to expand to Sino–Soviet hostilities. The conflict and the preparations for it enabled the United States to normalize relations with the People's Republic as Beijing sought to counterbalance Soviet pressure, but the objectives of Korean withdrawal and constraining rapid Japanese economic growth were not achieved.

The Impact of the Soviet Breakthrough on United States Asian Strategy

American strategy toward Northeast Asia was conceived and initiated at the same time as strategy toward Southeast Asia in the context of Kissinger's new international order. In both cases, the United States endeavored to shift to an offshore position from which judicious stabilizing leverage could be applied toward the mainland. If withdrawal from South Vietnam was designed to create a new Asian structure, withdrawal from South Korea was designed to generate the power to maintain it through greater Japanese security involvement. But execution of the Northeast Asian component of American strategy was interrupted and then delayed as a result of the furor over American credibility which accompanied the resignation of President Nixon and the fall of Saigon.

In accordance with the Nixon Doctrine, which called upon each ally henceforth "to assume the primary responsibility for providing the manpower for its defense," Washington began to restructure its position in Asia.[4] Aside from Vietnam troop withdrawals, which drew the most attention, the United States reduced its military personnel to varying degrees in Thailand, the Philippines, Taiwan, Okinawa, Japan, and South Korea. In the context of negotiations for the reversion of Okinawa to Japan and as the first step toward the promotion of a greater Japanese security commitment, in November 1969 President Nixon was able to elicit from Japanese Premier Eisaku Sato the view that "the security of the Republic of Korea was essential to Japan's own security."[5]

Subsequently, the United States and the Republic of Korea announced on February 6, 1971, that the Seventh Division with its full complement of 20,000 troops would be withdrawn by June of that year and that agreement had been reached on a five-year modernization program for South Korean forces.[6] Following North–South Korean talks over the next year, in July of 1972 the two states issued a communiqué which called for a peaceful unification of the peninsula that would transcend differences in ideology and system.

Sino–American rapprochement and United States–Soviet detente added additional elements of stability to the region. In the Shanghai Communiqué of February 27, 1972, both the United States and the People's Republic of China indicated their respective interests in continued peninsular stability. Beijing supported Pyongyang's program for the "peaceful unfication of Korea," while Washington supported Seoul's efforts "to seek relaxation of tension and increased communication in the Korean peninsula."[7]

As part of the May 1972 summit, Washington and Moscow signed the "Basic Principles of Relations between the United States of America and the Union of Soviet Socialist Republics." In the "principles" the two powers pledged "to do their utmost to avoid military confrontations" and recognized their "special responsibility . . . to do everything in their power so that conflicts or situations will not arise which would serve to increase international tensions." Finally, it was stressed that "recognition of the security interests of the Parties" was the prerequisite for "maintaining and strengthening peaceful relations" between them.[8] The implications for the Korean peninsula in the agreement were obvious.

By the time Jimmy Carter had announced his candidacy for the presidency in December 1974, the essential relationships comprising this structure had all frayed around the edges but still remained intact. Thus, even while Saigon's forces were crumbling before Hanoi's assault, in January 1975 Jimmy Carter declared publicly his intention—if elected president—to withdraw all United States forces immediately from South Korea.[9] By mid-year his view had evolved to the point where he believed the United States should "strengthen the air force of South Korea and withdraw U.S. troops on a rapid schedule."[10] He would also seek "guarantees" from China and the Soviet Union that North Korea would not invade.

Continued examination of the problem and a growing appreciation of the risks brought further evolution of Carter's views. Candidate Carter became increasingly concerned about a threat of conflict initiated not by the North, but by the South. During a trip to Japan for discussions with Japanese leaders, Carter "began to change his mind" about total withdrawal. Concerned that a strengthened South Korean air force "might make a preemptive strike against the north," Carter decided to retain American air power in South Korea while withdrawing ground forces. Later, he also "dropped the idea of seeking advance assurance from Peking and Moscow."[11]

Even before formally taking office, President-elect Jimmy Carter set the Korean withdrawal plan in motion. On January 5, during the first meeting of the new National Security Council-to-be, Presidential Review Memorandum (PRM) 13, the Korean withdrawal plan, was decided upon as one of the Carter administration's first fifteen policy initiatives.[12] The president-elect reaffirmed his commitment publicly a week later, on January 12. In a wide-ranging discussion of foreign policy with some fifty members of Congress held at the Smithsonian Institution, the president declared that "he had not made his campaign statements lightly."[13] Korean withdrawal would proceed, but American air power would remain, and South Korean defenses would be improved. Furthermore, the United States would be in close consultation with both South Korean and Japanese leaders as Washington's plans unfolded.

Indeed, immediately upon taking office the president dispatched Vice-President Walter Mondale on a trip to Europe and Japan (but, curiously, not to Seoul) to initiate the consultation process. However, United States plans for Korean troop withdrawal were altered before the vice-president arrived in Japan on January 31. Almost literally while Mondale was in the air, the president had learned of Soviet plans to test a new missile guidance system later in the year.[14] The implications of the Soviet breakthrough, which have already been discussed, forced reconsideration of plans for Northeast Asia just as they had for Europe, arms control, and even the defense budget.

Consequently, when the vice-president arrived in Japan, he announced a change in United States policy without acknowledging that it was indeed a change. In his news conference in Tokyo he declared that "United States ground forces will be reduced in South Korea whether or not that government objects."[15] Despite the tough-sounding language, the vice-president had subtly announced a shift in Washington's policy from "withdrawal" to "reduction." Furthermore, reduction would take place on an undetermined schedule over an unstated period of time, although the vice-president emphasized that the "phase down" would occur "only in close consultation and cooperation with the Governments of Japan and South Korea."[16]

Regarding American–Japanese relations, the vice-president pledged that "there would be no surprises in the relationship."[17] Indeed. Judging from remarks made by Japan's foreign minister, Iichiro Hatoyama, the day before Mondale arrived in Tokyo, it would appear that the Japanese government had already been reassured about United States policy toward South Korea. In a press conference on January 30, Hatoyama said that Japan was "no longer concerned" about Washington's Korea policy.[18] He observed that

> when Mr. Carter talked about withdrawing the troops in his election campaign speeches we were surprised, but later as he explained his plans we realized he was not talking about a complete withdrawal, but a gradual reduction of forces.[19]

Although the Japanese foreign minister had put up a good front, the Japanese government was of course concerned about the security implications of American withdrawal from South Korea. Following Carter's election the previous November, the Japanese vice-minister of defense had declared that "even discussing the possibility of withdrawing U.S. forces from Korea was having a 'great psychological impact.'"[20] The Japan Defense Agency had begun to study plans to strengthen defenses on the southernmost of the main islands, Kyushu, some fifty miles directly across the Tsushima Strait from South Korea. (Virtually all of Japan's meager territorial defenses were concentrated on the northernmost island of Hokkaido, adjacent to the Soviet Union.)

It was true that Carter had shifted his position from total withdrawal to withdrawal of ground troops, but up to this point there had never been any use of the term "reduction."[21] The "later explanation" to which Hatoyama referred could only have occurred a day or two earlier, for Carter had publicly reaffirmed his plan for Korean troop withdrawal on January 26 during his first press conference. In any case, thus reassured, Hatoyama declared that the issue of American forces in Korea was now "a bilateral matter between the United States and South Korea." Such questions as "the details of a timetable and the size of the reduction of forces are matters to be judged by Korea and the United States, without Japanese intervention."[22]

Hatoyama's remarks were also the first sign of Japan's policy response toward both Korea and China. While asserting that Tokyo had "no immediate plans for taking any diplomatic initiative" in the region, he said that the government "would like to see greater diplomatic efforts to increase rapprochement on the Korean peninsula."[23] Then, on February 10, Tokyo reasserted its claim to the small island of Takeshima (in Korean, Tok Do), which lies 100 miles off the Japanese coast and 54 miles off the coast of South Korea. Disputing the claim, Korean sources noted that the island had been a Korean Coast Guard "outpost" for over twenty years.[24] Japan's move, portrayed as part of an ongoing dispute with the Soviet Union over fishing rights in the sea of Japan, was undoubtedly also intended as part of a broader effort to stake a claim to future oil exploration rights on the continental shelf between Korea and Japan.[25]

During Vice-President Mondale's visit, Prime Minister Takeo Fukuda declared that Japan would no longer be opposed to inclusion of the antihegemony clause in a Sino–Japanese treaty formally terminating World War II. Japanese sensitivity to inclusion of the antihegemony clause had reflected a concern not to be seen as siding with China against the Soviet Union. The shift in position cleared the way for negotiation of the peace and friendship treaty which would be signed the following year. Undoubtedly at the urging of Vice-President Mondale, but also reflecting the Japanese government's need to play a larger role in reinforcing the diplomatic structure of the region, Tokyo now expressed its willingness to include the clause in the treaty "as long as the Chinese understand our interpretation of antihegemony."[26] Japan did not want the antihegemony principle to be interpreted as "an alliance between the two countries against any third parties," especially the Soviet Union.

Washington Bluffs to Prod Japan

The Soviet technological breakthrough had seriously compromised United States withdrawal plans, but not necessarily the reason behind them—to spur a Japanese defense buildup. So the Carter leadership moved to generate maximum pressure on Japan by bluffing on withdrawal. In order to put off abandoning the withdrawal plan for as long as possible, in early March Washington began to raise questions about the contents of the plan even while insisting that it would be carried out.

If the Japanese leadership believed that the question of withdrawal versus reduction had been settled during the vice-president's visit, they were mistaken. Two weeks before Prime Minister Fukuda's official visit to Washington on March 9 and 10, the United States government reaffirmed the withdrawal plan. During his news conference on March 9 the president declared that regarding Korean withdrawal his "commitment . . . has not changed."[27] He went on to say that he was "determined that over a period of time . . . our ground forces would be withdrawn." However,

> the schedule for withdrawal of American ground troops would have to be worked out very carefully with the South Korean government. It would also have to be done with the full understanding and, perhaps, participation of Japan.[28]

The next day, in testimony before the House Sub-Committee on Asian and Pacific Affairs, Assistant Secretary of State for East Asian and Pacific Affairs Richard Holbrooke revealed the extent of the withdrawal plan. There would be a phased but complete withdrawal of ground forces, although the United States would retain and augment its air units. Washington would earmark $5 billion in military assistance to Republic of Korea forces through 1981, and provide $275 million in military credits and $109.3 million in economic assistance for fiscal 1978.[29] (See table 1.)

Reassertion of American determination to conduct the complete withdrawal of ground forces brought an immediate outcry from Tokyo. The Japan Defense Agency saw a "strategic stone" being set in place[30] and the Liberal Democratic Party (LDP) appeared set "to oppose the withdrawal."[31] When Fukuda arrived on his state visit, March 21–23, President Carter reportedly sought to mollify the Japanese prime minister by using the term "reduction" during their talks, but Secretary Vance insisted that the term not be used in the joint communiqué issued at the end of the visit, which greatly discomfited the Japanese.[32] The president also declared that the United States would look favorably upon a Japanese effort to play "a larger political role in world affairs and particularly in Asia."[33]

On April 9 in Tokyo Congressmen Larry Wolff, chairman of the House International Relations Committee's subcommittee on Asia and the Pacific, informed Prime Minister Fukuda that "no timetable" for withdrawal had yet been formulated.[34] But less than a week later, on the fourteenth, the U.S. Eighth Army began to withdraw the Sargent surface-to-surface tactical nuclear missiles of the Fourth Missile Command and turned over to South Korea control of the

Table 1. United States Forces in South Korea—1977

Total United States Forces in South Korea	40,200
Eighth Army and Components	32,600
Combat units	15,000
Second Division	
Thirty-eighth Air Defense Artillery Brigade	
Fourth Missile Command	
Logistics units	4,800
Nineteenth Support Brigade	
Second Transportation Company	
Second Engineering Group	
Communications, intelligence units	3,500
First Signal Brigade	
Other United States Army	9,300
United States Air Force units	7,600
314th Air Division	

Sources: Charles A. Sorrels, *Planning U.S. General Purpose Forces: Asia* (Washington, DC: Congressional Budget Office, June 1977); Hubert H. Humphrey and John Glenn, *U.S. Troop Withdrawal from the Republic of Korea*, report to the Senate Committee on Foreign Relations (Washington, DC: GPO, 1978).

Nike-Hercules battery of the Thirty-eighth Air Defense Artillery Brigade.[35]

The Japanese quickly sought to probe the views of Kim Il-sung, who was noncommital. In a *Yomiuri* interview in late April, Kim pointed out that "there are discrepancies between his [Carter's] election pledge and his subsequent actions." If withdrawal is to take four or five years, he said, then "America is not intending to withdraw . . . during Carter's term of office as president."[36] Outraged that the Japanese would deal directly with Pyongyang, the Republic of Korea closed down the *Yomiuri* newspaper offices in Seoul.

The next step in the application of Washington's pressure came on May 17 with the release of a Congressional Budget Office (CBO) report on withdrawal. Authorized by the same Congressman Larry Wolff who five weeks earlier had said that there was no schedule for withdrawal, the report disclosed a timetable for the first time and called for combat and support units to be withdrawn simultaneously. The CBO timetable called for withdrawal to be completed in three years instead of four or five, for one-third of the Second Division to be withdrawn each year along with support units, and for all tactical nuclear weapons (approximately 1,000) to be withdrawn as well.[37]

Two days later, Major General John Singlaub, chief of staff of United States forces in Korea, publicly disputed the wisdom of the withdrawal plan and was immediately recalled.[38] Singlaub's recall touched off an explosion of news stories through the summer on the subject of withdrawal. Perhaps most alarming to leaders in Seoul and Tokyo were remarks by National Security Adviser Brzezinski published in *U.S. News and World Report*, which appeared on newsstands May 22. Brzezinski implied that the United States intended to seek changes in its treaty relationships with the two countries.

> We are about to engage in discussion with the South Koreans and Japanese about what kind of security arrangements would be adequate in the second half of this decade and pointing into the eighties. . . . One can certainly take a look at the situation in Korea today [compared] to that which prevailed in the 1950s when the present military arrangements were made.[39]

There can be little doubt that both Seoul and Tokyo lodged protests in Washington as soon as this issue hit the newsstands. The Japanese Foreign Ministry complained that Brzezinski's remarks suggested a change in the United States–Japan Mutual Security Treaty and had been made without prior consultation with the Japanese government.[40] The White House immediately dispatched JCS Chairman George Brown and Under Secretary of State for Asian and Pacific Affairs Philip Habib to Seoul and Tokyo, May 23 and 24, for what were described as the beginning of withdrawal consultations[41] but which were also intended to "clarify" Brzezinski's remarks and the CBO report.

Brown and Habib emphasized that there had been no change in American policy. No concrete withdrawal schedule had yet been formulated. Withdrawal would take the full four to five years, and there would be no withdrawal of support and supply units.[42] Privately, they did confirm that nuclear weapons would be removed. President Carter, during his news conference of May 26, reinforced the message of his envoys, declaring that "we will leave there adequate intelligence forces, observation forces, air forces, naval forces, and a firm, open commitment to our defense treaty."[43] The president, Chairman Brown, and Under Secretary Habib had repudiated the CBO report and reassured Seoul and Tokyo that Brzezinski's remarks had meant no change in treaty relations with Washington.

Yet, despite these reassurances, within two weeks (on June 5) Washington informed Tokyo and Seoul of its "intention" to withdraw 6,000 ground combat troops by the end of 1978.[44] Six thousand troops was almost half of the Second Division's deployment of 13,500 men and suggested an even more rapid withdrawal than called for by the just-repudiated CBO report. Hints that the United States would after all keep a nuclear deterrent in South Korea only heightened Japanese defense officials' concern that the troop withdrawal would indeed be carried out.[45] One press report described the Japanese Defense Agency as beset by a "deepening . . . sense of crisis."[46]

Later in June both Japanese and American leaders pointedly downplayed human rights concerns in South Korea as a factor inhibiting their respective relationships with Seoul. Prime Minister Fukuda, for example, in a June 22 reference to the 1973 kidnapping of South Korean opposition leader Kim Dae-jung by agents of the Seoul government in Japan, declared that no "new problems will arise with the ROK, over the Kim Dae-jung incident, in the future."[47] Similarly, Secretary of State Vance, in a major address on June 29 to the Asia Society, emphasized the need to understand Asian political culture before criticizing human rights practices.[48]

It was Secretary of Defense Harold Brown's trip to Seoul and Tokyo in late July that eased concerns of a destabilizing rapid withdrawal. Emphasizing "complementation first and withdrawal later,"[49] Secretary Brown stressed that the "bulk" of United States troops would remain in South Korea until the final year of the planned withdrawal.[50] In Tokyo, Brown obtained the concurrence of both Prime Minister Fukuda and Japanese Defense Agency head

Mihara on Washington's plans for supplementary assistance to buttress South Korean forces before withdrawal was completed.[51] Secretary Brown's trip set the stage for Washington's attempt to reach agreement with Beijing on early normalization of relations.

Early Normalization with China and Korean Withdrawal

The Soviet missile breakthrough seriously but not fatally compromised the Korean withdrawal plan. The key to the plan's success was a fundamentally stable region. If Korean withdrawal were not accomplished by the time Moscow's threat materialized, the greatest of dangers would arise. But withdrawal could be undertaken safely if the key nation determining the possibility of war on the peninsula supported Washington's plans. That nation was China.

Even though North Korea was far more powerful and militarily self-sufficient in 1977 than in 1950, the essential condition for any serious contemplation of war against South Korea remained the need to use Manchuria as a rear area for secure logistical support. Without the minimum condition of Chinese permission to allow Soviet transshipment of needed materiel across Manchuria to Pyongyang or the maximum condition of Chinese participation in such an effort, Kim Il-sung would be taking an extreme risk in launching a war against the South. Thus, even though United States–Soviet relations remained adversarial, as long as Sino-American relations were on a friendly track, Washington could proceed with its withdrawal plan and all that it implied with regard to Japan.

Early normalization of relations with China had not been one of the Carter administration's fifteen initiatives decided upon during the president-elect's first foreign policy meeting on January 5.[52] Indeed, Brzezinski notes that "the subject of China did not come up."[53] Given the assumption of continued United States strategic preeminence through the early eighties, good relations with China were not crucial to the Korean withdrawal plan. Discovery of the Soviet breakthrough brought a major change as good relations with China now became critical to a successful withdrawal from South Korea.

The Soviet breakthrough, as noted above, raised the core issue of the feasibility of continuing the strategy to build a new global order, and the ensuing internal debate sharply divided the administration on virtually every policy issue. Secretary of State Vance believed that the United States should proceed on its current course seeking detente with Moscow as the first objective and only afterward arranging for the disposition of United States positions around the Soviet periphery. National Security Adviser Brzezinski believed that the search for detente should be deferred until the United States consolidated its forward position around the Soviet periphery.

Thus, on the issue of whether or not to seek early normalization of relations with China, which would facilitate Korean withdrawal as well as strengthen containment of the Soviet Union, Brzezinski was strongly in favor. Vance opposed on the grounds that early normalization of relations with China would undercut if not prevent accomplishment of the primary objective—detente with Moscow. Thus, even though both agreed that the United States should seek to normalize relations with Beijing, they disagreed on timing. Even though early normalization would facilitate Korean withdrawal, Vance opposed it because it would worsen chances of reaching detente with Moscow, which for him was a prerequisite to all else.

In the foreign policy "briefing book" that Brzezinski delivered to the president on April 30, normalization of relations with China was now seen as the "central stabilizing element of our global policy and a keystone for peace," replacing Korean withdrawal as one of the administration's "ten goals."[54] Unfortunately, prolonged debate over the proposed terms of normalization delayed a decision to act until it was too late, which served Vance's interests.

Another reason for delay was the continuing succession struggle in Beijing over Mao's mantle.[55] Several months before his death, Mao had attempted to determine the succession through a series of moves which he hoped would decisively influence the outcome of the struggle within the leadership. He did this in the wake of Zhou Enlai's death in January 1976, by purging Deng Xiaoping a second time, naming Hua Guofeng as premier, and designating him as his political heir.

The designation of Hua split Mao's coalition into two groups, one led by Hua and the other by Mao's wife, Jiang Qing. A third group, led by Defense Minister Marshal Ye Jianying, included several of Deng's supporters and, with Deng out of power for the time being, functioned as a swing group in the succession struggle, which intensified upon Mao's death in early September 1976. In the immediate post-Mao period, the Hua and Ye groups joined forces to defeat and oust the "Gang of Four" led by Jiang Qing. The upshot of this first phase of the succession was the appointment of Hua as chairman of the party.

Part of the price that Hua was required to pay for Ye's support, however, was agreement to reinstate Deng Xiaoping. Although Hua was able to delay acting on this commitment for several months, Deng would eventually be restored to all of his previous posts in July 1977. When the Carter administration came into office in early 1977, the timing of Deng's return had yet to be decided (it would not be determined until the end of March) as Hua was stalling while attempting to strengthen his position.

In connection with this effort, Hua sought to convey to the new American leadership his interest in an early normalization of relations. Hua made plain his interest in the American connection in the context of replies to Moscow's bid for improved relations. For several months after Mao's death until the end of April 1977, Moscow stopped all public criticism of Beijing, while probing the prospects for a change in policy. In early February, the Hua leadership pointedly turned away Soviet probes, stressing continuity with Mao's position and declaring that "the basic line for China's foreign policy was developed under the personal supervision of Chairman Mao."[56]

While China opposed both superpowers, it dealt "the main blow at the U.S.S.R.," which had not given up its "ambition of subjugating China."[57] Soviet expansion was viewed as inevitable unless checked by the "joint pressure" of Western Europe, Japan, the United States, and China. Thus, opposition to the Soviet Union was "a fundamental strategic policy rather than a temporary expedient." On the other hand, the Hua leadership dismissed the Taiwan question as "a small matter" which should not impede the improvement of relations with Washington. "The Taiwan issue is a small matter compared with the many common objectives the United States and China have."[58]

The Hua leadership's pro–United States stance offered the possibility of the successful execution of Washington's Asian policy—if rhetoric could be translated into actual political agreements. The questions were: would the new American administration act quickly and decisively, and was Hua politically strong enough to reach an agreement? As it turned out the answer to both questions was no, and a major opportunity to establish the foundation-stone of overall Asian policy was lost.

The initial discussions in Washington spanned the period from late January to mid-April and centered on the nature of the relationship to be established. National Security Adviser Brzezinski "felt strongly that we should open a dialogue with the Chinese that would stress the strategic aspects of the relationship, especially as they bore on the Soviet Union," but he "did not have a clear notion of when to seek normalization as such." Indeed, he "wondered if we could not promote a strategic connection even without normalization."[59]

Normalization would be time consuming, and since time was of the essence, Brzezinski advocated a more direct approach. He divided the question into three "tracks"—bilateral contacts, common strategic interests, and the normalization process. Contacts "should be expanded as much as possible"; common interests "could be furthered by quiet consultations"; and normalization "should be moved forward whenever opportune."[60] It was this formulation of the question which enabled Brzezinski to argue the case for immediate action in the form of a "strategic connection . . . without normalization."

Secretary of State Vance took the opposite position against those who "were arguing that we should forge a de facto security relationship with the PRC before, or instead of, diplomatic relations."[61] Moreover, he saw no need for haste, insisting that the administration "review the overall political-military situation in Asia and . . . analyze how U.S.–China relations would weigh in the strategic and regional balances." Vance believed that the Chinese leadership, "still preoccupied with an internal political realignment, would also want to proceed with caution. . . ."[62]

Vance's April 15 memorandum to the president settled the question of the nature of the relationship Washington would seek. The United States did not want to suggest that relations with China were "one dimensional," that is, simply anti-Soviet. Therefore an early strategic connection, which Brzezinski advocated, was ruled out in favor of normalization, which Washington viewed in a broader context. In short, there would be no immediate action. Vance's memo concluded that he did "not believe we should feel so compelled to establish diplomatic relations with Beijing that we jeopardize the well-being and security of the people of Taiwan. Neither should we place ourselves under artificial deadlines."[63]

Vance's arguments reflected obsequiousness toward the Soviet Union and arrogance toward China. His professed intent was to maintain the "fragile equilibrium" between Moscow and Beijing—meaning he intended the United States to have better relations with each than either had with the other. He opposed security ties with Beijing on the grounds that "because of the Soviets' excessive fear of China, any U.S. security cooperation with Peking would have serious repercussions on U.S.–Soviet relations."[64] But Vance went further, using the "fear of China" argument against security ties to argue against taking any early action at all.

Coming at a time when Moscow was making strenuous efforts to reach an understanding with Beijing, Vance's position was inconsistent with the concept of "fragile equilibrium" but perfectly consistent with the strategy he was pursuing. As recounted above, the new global order Vance pursued required prior establishment of detente with the Soviet Union before completing new arrangements around the Soviet periphery as the United States moved to relocate its power to more secure positions. Brzezinski, also acting consistently with the strategy of containment, sought to conclude security arrangements around the Soviet periphery before reaching detente. China, of course, was a major, if not the major, piece on the diplomatic chessboard to be disposed of, for Moscow would read the evolution of Sino–American relations as a barometer of Washington's broader strategic intent.

Vance and his advisers appeared either to misunderstand the signals emanating from the Hua leadership regarding Beijing's intense interest in an early connection or, more likely, to understand them too well. The Hua leadership's description of Taiwan as "a small matter" could hardly have been missed. Could Vance have misunderstood the impact early normalization would have on Hua's position? Was Vance's solicitousness for the "people of Taiwan" in reality an attempt to play hard ball on the assumption that Hua would be forced to make concessions in order to stay in power?

The Vance memorandum's phrase rejecting "artificial deadlines" appeared to convey the same message: that it was Hua who was operating under the deadline, not Washington. It would seem that Washington understood only too well that the internal political balance in Beijing was shifting rapidly. Vance's only concession in this regard was to arrange on April 11 to have his trip to China, originally scheduled for November, moved up to August.

Between mid-April and the end of July several developments occurred. First, Moscow broke off further attempts to reach an understanding with the Chinese leadership, persuading the president that an opportunity existed to seek early normalization after all. Unfortunately, the political situation inside China also changed, constraining Hua's freedom of action, and making early normalization impossible.

The crucial development was Moscow's decision to break off further efforts to improve relations with Beijing. Moscow first signaled this decision, breaking a self-imposed seven-month silence, on April 20 in a *New Times* article which charged the Hua leadership with "anti-Soviet hysteria." Five days later, on April 25, came a major attack in which the Soviets charged the Hua leadership with "damaging the cause of peace" and hindering the "anti-imperialist struggle."[65] A broader-gauged analysis of United States–China relations followed a few weeks later in *Pravda.* Indicating that Soviet Asian policy was being reassessed, Moscow warned the United States against "arming China" and against the dangerous development that Beijing might draw Washington into an "anti-Soviet alliance."[66]

Meanwhile, the Hua leadership, having agreed in late March to a timetable for Deng Xiaoping's return, was racing against time in an effort to prod Washington into action. At the end of April an unnamed "senior Chinese official" was highly critical of American policy on normalization. The official expressed "deep dissatisfaction with president Jimmy Carter's failure so far to open serious negotiations on the establishment of full diplomatic ties with China."[67] He declared that "we haven't yet found any sign on the part of the United States that they have made up their minds to discuss normalization of relations." Apparently hoping to generate some reaction from Washington, the official said that "war with Taiwan might be inevitable *after normalization* if the Nationalist regime continued to stockpile weapons."[68]

If the Chinese hoped that the remark about the possibility of war with Taiwan after normalization would spark a dialogue they were disappointed. Asked during a news conference two weeks later, on May 12, whether he had a "target date . . . for full diplomatic recognition," Carter's response was simply that he "would like to see progress made toward normalization of relationships."[69] The president saw Taiwan as "the one obstacle—major obstacle. . . . We don't want to see the Taiwanese people punished or attacked. And if we can resolve that major difficulty I would move expeditiously to normalizing relationships with China. But I can't put a time limit on it."

At this point, the Hua leadership made its last bid to provoke a dialogue with the Carter administration. It came a week later in the form of an interview by Hua's ally and Politburo member Ji Dengkui given to the Japanese newspaper *Yomiuri*. Referring to Carter's news conference, Ji asserted that the president said he hoped for peaceful reunification. "Peaceful settlement" of the Taiwan question, Ji declared, violated the Shanghai Communiqué and was an additional condition which China could not accept. China would not compromise on matters of principle.[70]

This sounded like standard fare from Beijing, except for two things: Carter had said nothing about peaceful reunification, and the phrase "peaceful settlement" was not an additional condition violating the Shanghai Communiqué but the very phrase used in it. The communiqué reads specifically that the United States "reaffirms its interest in a peaceful settlement of the Taiwan question by the Chinese themselves."[71] Quite clearly, Ji knew what he was doing; he hoped to precipitate a response which would "clarify" Carter's remarks and move the dialogue forward more expeditiously.

He succeeded. As the Carter administration began to reappraise its initial approach, the president publicly conveyed the change in his thinking. In his speech at Notre Dame University four days later, he stated at the urging of Brzezinski that "we see the American–Chinese relationship as a central element of our global policy, and China as a key force for global peace. We wish to cooperate closely with the creative Chinese people on the problems that confront all mankind, and we hope to find a formula which can bridge some of the difficulties that still separate us."[72] The Carter administration had for the first time in its references to China gone beyond a simple reaffirmation of the Shanghai Communiqué to a declaration that Sino–American relations were a "central element" in Washington's global policy.

The change in the United States position came in the context of discussion over the draft of PRM-24, the policy paper on China which had been in progress since the spring. PRM-24, as Vance notes, "reflected the judgments"[73] of his April memorandum regarding the security ties issue and on the terms of the future "link" to Taiwan, but not on the timing of normalization. Where the April memo had cautioned against haste, the Policy Review Committee decided on June 27 to recommend to the president that the United States "seek normalization in the 'near term' . . . if it would not damage Taiwan's security."[74] PRM-24's conclusion was that "full diplomatic recognition of Peking would reinforce positive trends in Asia and would improve the environment for achieving our goals in South Korea and Southeast Asia."[75]

As the decision was being reached, the administration sought to address Moscow's main concern and signal its intention to Beijing. In response to Moscow's May 14 warning against arming China, part of PRM-24 was "leaked" to the *New York Times* June 24 disclaiming any intent to seek a security relationship with Beijing. Then, in a major address on June 29, Secretary Vance reaffirmed American interest in "full normalizaton of relations" guided by the principles of the Shanghai Communiqué. The United States, he declared, considered friendly relations a "central part" of American foreign policy and would "not enter into any agreements with others that are directed against the People's Republic of China."[76]

Vance also said that "we . . . place importance on the peaceful settlement of the Taiwan question by the Chinese themselves," a phrase which was a direct quote from the Shanghai Communiqué. The Chinese responded in early July, reiterating their long-held position. Politburo member Li Xiannian, in an interview with visiting former Chief of Naval Operations Elmo Zumwalt, declared that before normalization could take place Washington must sever diplomatic relations with Taiwan, withdraw its troops, and abrogate the defense treaty. Fastening upon the single word "peaceful" with regard to Taiwan, Li said it was for Beijing to decide how to proceed on unification. "As to when and in what way the Chinese people are to liberate their sacred territory of Taiwan . . . that is entirely China's internal affair, which brooks no interference."[77]

No Normalization and No Withdrawal

After further hesitation generated by second thoughts (and continued dispute between Brzezinski and Brown versus Vance regarding the security aspect of the proposed relationship), at the end of July the president decided to make an attempt at early normalization. Unfortunately for the United States, Washington's decision for early normalization came at precisely the same time that a reorganized Chinese leadership arrived at the opposite conclusion.

The Chinese Communist party held its Third Plenum July 16–21, in which the formation of an enlarged Politburo was announced. While the plenum formally designated Hua Guofeng chairman and expelled the Gang of Four from the party, it also rehabilitated Deng Xiaoping to all of his former party, state, and military posts.[78] From this position of strength Deng was able to block early normalization, although he was not yet strong enough to undertake any of his own initiatives. The plenum also decided to hold the Eleventh Congress of the CCP early, scheduling it to conclude just before Vance arrived for his visit.

Meanwhile, on July 30, during a discussion in preparation for the Vance trip, perhaps sensing that the situation in Beijing had changed, "the President decided quite abruptly to go for normalization."[79] He instructed Vance "to go directly to the issues and to move as rapidly as is possible." He said: "Cy, lay it all out on the line. I've never gained anything from procrastinating. Describe our full position."[80] Instructing Vance to prepare a draft communiqué on normalization which he would take to Beijing, the president said he "wanted to complete normalization and he was prepared to face the political criticism of those who would claim we were abandoning Taiwan."[81]

Brzezinski, perhaps also sensing the change in Beijing, "was pleased but also worried" that the Chinese would not go for it and urged that "alternative arrangements . . . short of normalization" be made.[82] On the eve of Vance's trip it appeared that the president was out in front of his advisers. Brzezinski, after several pirouettes, seemed to agree with Vance that early normalization was now unlikely. Vance then decided "for political reasons" to "represent a maximum position to the Chinese on the Taiwan issue," which would effectively foreclose early action.[83] Then, after Vance had arrived in Beijing but before beginning talks, "the President, warned by Mondale, started developing second thoughts on how hard we should push for normalization, and on August 22 . . . he pulled back."[84]

What had happened? Each of the president's principal advisers asserts that the reason for the shift to "a somewhat slower, more deliberate pace" was the impending Senate ratification process for the Panama Canal treaty.[85] While it is quite possible that, as the president said, "it would be asking the Senate too much to handle this and Panama all at once," it is highly unlikely Panama was the main reason. After all, workload considerations—physical or political—did not deter the administration from attempting to complete *three* major agreements simultaneously the following year: normalization with China, SALT II with the Soviet Union, and the Egyptian–Israeli peace treaty. Finally, the Panama ratification schedule had been known for some time and had not prevented the decision to go for normalization in the first place.

The reason Carter "pulled back" had to be related to the rather major shift that had just taken place in Beijing, which the president belatedly recognized. The Eleventh Party Congress had concluded four days before Vance's arrival, but its decisions had not been made public. Chairman Hua's political report to the congress, in fact, was only released on the day of Vance's arrival.[86] In it, he declared that both the United States and the Soviet Union are "beset with difficulties," but this "was particularly true of Soviet social-imperialism." Nevertheless, in the current strategic situation, "Soviet social-imperialism is on the offensive and U.S. imperialism is on the defensive." Hua saw "a trend towards appeasement" as some "try to divert the peril of the new tsars toward the East." But most important was the major realignment of the Politburo which had taken place, in which Deng now moved into a strong position.

Indeed, the reason for the administration's last-minute pullback was the realization that normalization could not be accomplished under the new circumstances. The obstacle was not Panama, Taiwan, or the proposed terms of normalization. It was not Hua Guofeng, with whom Vance did not negotiate. It was Deng Xiaoping. Deng's return had put him into position to block any movement toward early normalization. Perhaps Deng had interpreted United States strategy correctly, persuaded the Chinese leadership that Washington needed normalization more than Beijing did, and decided to drive a hard bargain. More likely, normalization would represent a "tilt" toward the United States which Deng would not accept at this time; the newly returned leader stressed a policy of equidistance once again, as he had done following his return in 1973. Whatever his reasons, Deng, as Michael Oksenberg notes, rejected Vance's proposals "even before hearing the Secretary's presentation on Taiwan and on the prospects for normalization."[87]

Vance's proposals thus fell on deaf ears. The secretary of state declared that, "provided we can find a basis that will not lessen the prospects for a peaceful settlement of the Taiwan question by the Chinese themselves," the United States "was prepared to recognize the PRC as the sole legal government of China . . . , [the] defense treaty with Taiwan would 'lapse' . . . and we would complete the withdrawal of our military forces and installations from Taiwan."[88] To enable the American people to continue to have contact with the people of Taiwan, however, "it would be necessary for U.S. Government personnel to remain on Taiwan under an informal arrangement." Finally, "at the appropriate time" Washington would publicly state its interest in a "peaceful settlement" of the Taiwan question. Vance "stressed" that Beijing neither "contradict such a statement or make any new statements about liberation by force."[89]

Deng Xiaoping rejected Vance's proposal as "a retreat from the Shanghai Communiqué." He read portions of memoranda of conversations he had held with Kissinger and Ford in 1975 in which he claimed that both men had agreed recognition would occur "in conformity with Chinese . . . conditions" and "in accordance with the so-called Japanese formula," without, however, noting that these were promises qualified by Ford's reelection and a satisfactory settlement of the Taiwan question.[90] He described Vance's proposed unofficial office for Taiwan "as an embassy that would not have a sign or a flag at its door," but an embassy nonetheless. That, he could not accept. Deng's clear predisposition against acceptance of Washington's terms explains Vance's decision not to raise the even more troublesome question of arms sales to Taiwan after normalization.

Despite the administration's efforts to put a good face on Vance's trip, it was in fact a major blow to those who sought to reinforce containment as well as to facilitate Korean withdrawal. Indeed, from the perspective of early September 1977 it seemed that there would be no normalization in the foreseeable future, which suited Vance's purposes perfectly. Although early newspaper reports from Beijing described American and Chinese officials as "jovial" and discussions as "useful," Vance stopped short of saying the two sides had "moved toward normalization." He did say that the talks represented "an important step toward progress along that road."[91] "Whatever happens," he maintained, "relations will remain amicable."

Upon Secretary Vance's return to the United States on August 27, President Carter personally contributed to the impression of "progress." In his welcoming remarks at Andrews Air Force Base, he said that Vance's trip had been "a very important step forward in our ultimate goal of normalizing relations."[92] The president stated that although the secretary's trip had been "exploratory," his reports from Beijing had been "very encouraging." Then, in comments evidently designed to assuage leaders in Taipei, he said: "When we do make a decision about China, if we make one of recognition, it is undoubtedly going to be well into the future and it will be based on what I consider to be the best interest of our country."[93]

The administration's attempts to mask the failure of the Vance visit prompted Deng himself a few days later to clarify what had transpired in Beijing. In an interview with a group of editors and executives of the Associated Press visiting China, Deng declared that Vance's trip had been a "setback" to normalization.[94] Deng reiterated China's three conditions for normalization, declared that former President Ford and Secretary of State Kissinger had both "promised" to normalize relations on these terms, but that Vance proposed simply "to reverse the present situation" by "establishing full diplomatic relations with China . . . [and] a diplomatic liaison office on Taiwan." The Chinese leader declared that "the reverse liaison proposal was unacceptable . . . because it would mean continued diplomatic links between the United States and Taiwan."

Deng stressed that the meetings with Vance had been "cordial and useful for the exchange of views but that reports of progress were wrong." He said that the "American side had been responsible for creating an impression after Mr. Vance's visit that the Chinese would be flexible about promising not to take Taiwan by force if the United States withdrew." While emphasizing that "there was no such flexibility on the part of the Chinese," Deng went on to demonstrate the very opposite! In finding a solution to the Taiwan problem, he said, the Chinese would in fact take into consideration the special conditions on the island. Leaving the door open to eventual normalization, Deng observed, "If the United States did not interfere, the Chinese would not rule out the possibility of solving the problem peacefully."

For President Carter's immediate policy needs, eventual normalization was not good enough. It meant that for the time being, at least, the United States could not count on a "benign China," which in turn spelled the end of the Korean withdrawal scheme.[95] On the other hand, deferral of normalization kept intact Vance's larger strategy of detente with Moscow first. Curiously, just as Vance's meetings were taking place, State Department officials conveyed concern that relations with China be strengthened to "preserve those parallel foreign-policy attitudes that the U.S. finds so helpful," particularly the "joint interest in preventing war on the Korean peninsula."[96]

Within days of Vance's trip Washington began to prepare the ground for a change in its Korean withdrawal policy. At the end of August, a high United States government official disclosed to a Japanese reporter that the Korean withdrawal scheme would be "reversed 180 degrees" if an abnormal situation were to arise on the peninsula.[97] In early September, the administration "leaked" an additional portion of PRM-10, the global assessment which had first been leaked in August regarding the European military balance.[98] This time it revealed that in the event of a North Korean surprise attack, and even with the presence of United States ground forces, "Seoul could not be held."[99]

On September 9, as Korean lobbyist Tong Sun Park was being indicted in absentia on thirty counts of bribing congressmen, the administration announced that it would defer bills approving plans to leave behind $500 to $600 million in equipment following withdrawal.[100] Despite concurrent statements that President Carter remained "strongly committed" to withdrawal plans, the plain fact was that the withdrawal plan was dead in the water. To make intentions clear, in a meeting with visiting Japan Defense Agency head Mihara, National Security Chief Brzezinski described the Korean plan as "a gradual reduction rather than a withdrawal."[101]

Finally, in mid-December, the eventual rationale for entirely cancelling the scheme surfaced in an administration report to Congress regarding the withdrawal plan. It noted that North Korea's "major long-term buildup" gave it a sizable advantage over South Korea, but that withdrawal would not endanger Seoul's security if accompanied by additional military assistance and force modernization.[102] It would, of course, be the sudden discovery of a much larger than believed North Korean force buildup that would justify the complete cancellation of the Korean withdrawal plan in early 1979.[103]

In short, Vance's foreign policy in Asia by the end of 1977 had kept open the possibility of detente with Moscow first, but failed totally to address major regional issues. The failure to reach agreement for normalization of relations with China in the summer of 1977 and the abandonment of Korean withdrawal resulted in the loss of extremely important policy leverage on Japan. The failure to achieve the long-term objective of curbing Japanese economic power by generating greater defense expenditures to compensate for withdrawal from South Korea, in turn, ensured that an economically unconstrained Japan would soon become a major area of concern for American policymakers.

Moscow Takes the Geopolitical Offensive

The period from the spring of 1977 through the spring of 1978 saw the Soviet leadership reach a multifaceted decision—undoubtedly based upon the leverage expected to accrue from the strategic weapons advance as well as the successes already registered in the face of American passivity—to make a major effort to alter the geopolitical balance. The main impact of Soviet policy was felt across the vast region stretching from Africa to the Far East. As will be discussed in the next chapter, Moscow's turn to the offensive began in Africa in the spring of 1977, building upon the successful Angolan operation, with the Cuban-led offensive against Zaire and agreement to supply Ethiopian forces in their struggle with Somalia.

In Asia the turn came somewhat later, following Moscow's reappraisal of the initial outcome of the Chinese succession struggle. Soviet leaders had hoped that Deng Xiaoping, having consistently opposed Mao since the mid-fifties, having been instrumental in shifting Chinese policy away from the United States during 1973–1976, and having blocked Hua's efforts to move toward normalization after his return in 1977, was the one leader with whom they could reach an understanding. But in ensuing months, despite his return to all previous posts, Deng failed to advance further as both Chairman Hua and Defense Minister Ye strengthened their positions.

Indeed, it appeared that a combined effort by Hua and Ye was responsible for thwarting Deng's further advance.[104] Along with Deng, both Hua and Ye gained power at the Eleventh Party Congress. Hua had been confirmed as chairman of the party, and Ye had succeeded in placing several supporters onto the Politburo. Each leader seemed to have the support of roughly a third of the twenty-three member Politburo, which together gave them sufficient power to contain Deng.

But on the eve of the Fifth National People's Congress, which opened on February 26, 1978, the situation seemed to be changing. As the jockeying for position continued, it appeared that Deng would be appointed to a top state post at the Fifth National People's Congress after all.[105] Deng was judged most likely to be appointed to either the reestablished "presidency" of the Chinese People's Republic, which had been abolished during the Cultural Revolution; the premiership, currently being held by Hua Guofeng; or as the head of the Defense Ministry, currently Ye Jianying.

Contrary to expectations, however, Deng suffered a startling and unexpected reversal, as neither he nor any of his supporters was appointed to a high state office. It was decided not to reestablish the presidency. Instead, Marshal Ye was named chairman of the Standing Committee of the National People's Congress, the ceremonial head-of-state post. In assuming his new office, Ye relinquished the Ministry of Defense portfolio to his ally, Marshal Su Xiangjian. In a major development, Hua retained the premiership, giving him command of both party and state apparatuses, a position of great power.

The prospect of Hua's continuing in power and Deng's failure to dislodge him, particularly as evidenced in the Fifth National People's Congress outcome (but perhaps earlier), brought the period of Moscow's "reappraisal" to an end. Indeed, in their unusual reply to the Soviet note of February 24 delivered on the eve of the Fifth National People's Congress, the Chinese leadership made plain that no improvement in relations would be possible. The Soviet note called upon the two countries to agree to a "joint statement on the principles of mutual relations" as a means to "advance the cause of normalization of our relations."[106] Rejecting the Soviet offer, the Chinese leadership published the full text of the note at the end of March "so that all who are interested in Sino–Soviet relations may know the truth." Terming Moscow's request a "vain attempt to make us alter the revolutionary line of Chairman Mao," the Chinese reply concluded that the Soviet move was "a propaganda stunt."

For Moscow the die was cast. Soviet leaders no doubt were under few illusions about the prospect for an improvement in relations with Beijing as long as Hua remained party chairman, so the Chinese reply was not unexpected. In any case Moscow was prepared to tighten the vise around China. The spring of 1978 saw Moscow strengthen its position in the Soviet Far East along the Chinese border, commence a buildup for the first time on the Northern Islands adjacent to Japan, support the overthrow of the Daoud regime in Afghanistan (which will be discussed in the context of Middle East–Southwest Asian events in chapter 5) and, most importantly, to support Hanoi in ongoing military efforts to bring Kampuchea under its control.

In the spring Moscow set up a major military command structure for the Far East, the Far Eastern TVD (theater of operations), the first time the Soviets had formed such a war-fighting command in the Soviet Far East since the Korean War. In conjunction with the establishment of the new command structure, Moscow also made substantial qualitative and quantitative improvements in its force posture for the region, including deployment of SS-20 missiles and the Backfire bomber. At the same time, unexpectedly, the Soviets began a deployment which would eventually reach division size on the largest of the four Northern Islands located off the coast of Hokkaido. Japanese intelligence identified 13,000 men, 260 medium tanks, and 300 armored personnel carriers, the normal complement of a Category I motorized rifle division.[107] These developments were accompanied by an increasingly vigorous long-range aerial reconnaissance effort in the Western Pacific which ranged as far south as Indochina, where Moscow had landing and refueling rights.

Most important was the Soviet decision to support Hanoi in a major effort to conquer the Chinese-supported regime in Kampuchea. Earlier in Indochina, as both the Kampuchean and Vietnamese states had moved to consolidate their respective territories after coming to power in 1975, initially cool relations between the two countries had soon deteriorated; and by the spring of 1976 border clashes had become commonplace. Hanoi's forces had mounted two large but inconclusive punitive expeditions against Kampuchea in 1977, the first in April and the second, larger, in December, carrying over into January of 1978. Simultaneously, Hanoi's leaders had sought through diplomacy to gain Chinese acquiescence in its domination of the region, but with little success.

By the early spring of 1978 it was clear to the leaders in Hanoi that although the Socialist Republic of Vietnam had succeeded in establishing a dominant influence in Laos—a treaty of peace and friendship had been signed the previous July—incorporation of

Kampuchea into Hanoi's sphere of influence would be impossible without recourse to a significant increase in the use of force. It was also clearly understood that adoption of such a course of action would inevitably provoke Chinese counteraction. This, in turn, would necessitate Soviet assistance to deter Beijing from frustrating Hanoi's designs. By the spring of 1978, then, a coincidence of interest had evolved between Hanoi and Moscow.

Moscow's decision to support Hanoi in a major drive to conquer Beijing's client state, Kampuchea, threatened to defeat China's long-term strategy toward Indochina. For a quarter of a century Chinese strategy consistently had been to maintain the fragmentation of the region in order to preserve Chinese influence there. A Vietnamese invasion of Kampuchea would leave Beijing no choice but to intervene militarily to protect its client. The unacceptable alternative would be to stand idly by and witness the emergence of a Hanoi-dominated Indochina closely allied to Moscow, a region in which Beijing would have little influence and which would constitute a continuing threat to China's southern flank.

Hanoi's determination to pursue a military solution in Kampuchea offered Moscow an unparalleled opportunity to accomplish broader goals. Hanoi's success would alter the geopolitical structure of Asia and mark the defeat of China's—particularly Mao's—long-term strategy. If this did not lead to a change in Chinese leadership as a result, it would in any case lock China into a vastly more threatening two-front conflict situation, which in turn would increase pressures on Beijing to reach an accommodation with Moscow.

In retrospect, Moscow's decision was signaled in March by Hanoi's sudden crackdown on the Chinese community in Vietnam. Deportation of several hundred thousand Chinese residents from the cities to rural "new economic zones," or labor camps, and the "nationalization" or seizure of all Chinese property in May led directly to a sharp deterioration of already strained relations with Beijing. Beginning in July, Vietnam moved to upgrade air defense capabilities in the northern part of Vietnam, fortifying the border and conducting a campaign of active defense.[108] Later in the summer both sides called their respective ambassadors home, and Beijing shut its side of the border to all but official traffic.

While securing the internal front, from early April and continuing through the summer Hanoi carried out its largest military operations thus far against Kampuchea, conducting sweeps across the border as deep as twenty miles.[109] Vietnamese cadre also began openly training ethnic Khmer soldiers as part of what would be a Hanoi-imposed government—the Kampuchean United National Front for National Salvation. In June, Hanoi joined the Soviet-controlled Council for Mutual Economic Assistance, reportedly to bolster its sagging economy. By late summer of 1978, Vietnam's preparations for a large-scale invasion of Kampuchea were well under way even as Hanoi's forces were stepping up operations—bolstered by an infusion of supplies through a massive Soviet airlift.[110]

War in Indochina and Sino–American Normalization

There can be little doubt that Chinese leaders closely followed the evolving situation and early on began to debate among themselves the possible course of events, the implications for Chinese security, and the range of countermeasures that could be adopted. Moreover, it would appear that American leaders, also closely following the events, concluded that the tightening Soviet–Vietnamese vise and the likelihood of Sino–Vietnamese armed conflict revived the prospects for normalization. The evidence suggests that the Chinese reached the conclusion that normalization should go forward for strategic reasons some months before the Carter leadership came to the same conclusion.[111]

When Vietnamese forces embarked upon major military operations in Kampuchea in December 1977, Chinese forces commenced action on the Sino–Vietnamese border in what would essentially be an unpublicized dress rehearsal of the Chinese invasion of Vietnam in February 1979.[112] Beijing's determination to prevent Hanoi's conquest of Kampuchea drove the decision-making process in both Hanoi and Beijing. In Hanoi, as described above, it produced the need to gain Moscow's support to deter Beijing when Hanoi mounted its main effort. In Beijing, it produced the decision to seek the normalization of relations with Washington in the hope that the United States could neutralize the Soviet Union, thus permitting China to prevent Vietnam's conquest of Kampuchea.

Some in the administration, notably Brzezinski, saw the need to maintain contact with the Chinese leadership following the August rejection of Vance. But Brzezinski's object, as before, was "to focus more on a politically consultative relationship and less on normalization."[113] Toward this end, in early November, the national security adviser solicited an invitation to visit China from the departing head of the liaison office. The Chinese were more than willing to extend the invitation in order to move the normalization process along, for Vietnamese preparations for the December drive were already under way.

It was not until the time of the Fifth National People's Congress, February 26 to March 5, 1978, that the Carter leadership came to realize the active Chinese interest in normalization and seek to reciprocate. As soon as the congress ended it was clear not only that Hua had retained his position in the Chinese leadership, but that he was hinting broadly for the resumption of contacts with Washington. In a portion of his speech to the congress released immediately afterward, Hua said that while fundamental differences, such as Taiwan, remained between the United States and China, "the two countries have quite a few points in common on some issues in the present international situation."[114] On the other hand, Hua condemned Moscow's unremitting "policy of hostility" as a failure and harshly castigated Soviet leaders as "these pygmies [who] go on ranting and raving."

No doubt the Carter leadership understood the significance of Hua's remarks.[115] Brzezinski, according to his own account, "badgered the President enormously" for permission to accept the invitation extended in November. The president agreed on March 12 that he was now "inclined toward sending a mission to China."[116] Vance, however, opposed a trip by Brzezinski because it would suggest too much of an interest in security ties, and he suggested that the vice-president make the trip instead.

The upshot of the dispute between the president's advisers was Carter's decision to send Brzezinski and convert what had originally been planned as a "consultative" trip into a substantive one which would get the normalization process going. The president's decision reflected a growing realization on his part that the Soviet Union was much more interested in using its military power than it was in detente, and that the United States would have to be prepared to respond.

As planning got under way for Brzezinski's trip, scheduled for late May, the president delivered his first major address on national defense since taking office. Speaking at Wake Forest University on

March 17, he took a hard-line stance on relations with the Soviet Union, asserting that the massive Soviet military buildup left the United States no recourse but to match it. The United States, he said, "will not allow any other nation to gain military superiority over us" and will "counter any threats to our allies and our vital interests in Asia, the Middle East and other regions of the world."[117]

In words clearly calculated to imply American support for China versus the Soviet–Vietnamese axis, but without specifically mentioning it, the president observed that there has been "an ominous inclination on the part of the Soviet Union to use its military power to intervene in local conflicts with advisers, with equipment and with full logistical support and encouragement for mercenaries from other Communist countries, as we can observe today in Africa."[118] Of course, as knowledgeable observers understood, his words applied equally to the developing crisis in Southeast Asia.

Brzezinski's instructions were to indicate to the Chinese leadership that the United States was "serious" about normalization and that its interest was "strategic" and not tactical.[119] The president "would like to move rapidly" on normalization if the Chinese were prepared to meet two minimum conditions with respect to Taiwan: the first was that Beijing not contradict Washington's public expression of interest in a peaceful settlement, and the second was that Beijing not object to continued United States arms sales after normalization.[120]

The national security adviser was instructed to discuss overall American strategy and to emphasize that it was "designed to shape an international system not subject to hegemony by a single power." With regard to the Soviet Union he was to explain that even while offering "genuine detente" the United States was "determined to respond" to Soviet adventurism around the globe. If the Chinese leadership found the United States position satisfactory, Brzezinski was instructed to convey the president's decision to begin normalization negotiations immediately, in early June.[121]

At this point, the American leadership assumed—and all indications were—that Hua had survived the challenge by Deng and was in command, although Deng was in a strong position.[122] Indeed, President Carter was asked to address a handwritten note to Chairman Hua which Brzezinski would hand to him together with a piece of moon rock brought back by United States astronauts. The rock was meant to symbolize the two countries' "joint quest for a better future,"[123] although the symbolism was at best murky and certainly potentially demeaning.

On May 8, several days before Brzezinski arrived in Beijing, Moscow, probably suspecting the purpose of his visit, precipitated the largest military clash on the Sino–Soviet border since 1969. A thirty-man Soviet raiding party, supported by eighteen naval craft and a helicopter, penetrated two and a half miles into Chinese territory across the Ussuri river.[124] The Chinese protest note condemned the incident as a deliberate "military provocation" and accused the Soviets of seizing, beating, and kicking fourteen Chinese inhabitants, shooting and wounding several, before releasing them and retreating back across the river.

Moscow expressed "regrets" for what it termed a mistaken landing on Chinese territory by a Soviet border patrol pursuing "a dangerous, armed criminal."[125] The Chinese expressed dissatisfaction with the Soviet explanation but dropped the matter. A few days later, however, they raised the issue of future Sino–Soviet relations in a way that established a favorable context for Brzezinski's visit. Declaring that war with the Soviet Union was "inevitable," the Chinese Communist party called upon the People's Liberation Army to "intensify preparations against an aggressive war."[126]

Arriving on May 20, Brzezinski was surprised by what he encountered in Beijing—not only the strong attitude toward the Soviet Union, but also "the vehemence with which the Chinese denounced Vietnamese perfidy."[127] Informing the Chinese that the "United States has made up its mind" on normalization, a reference to the April 29, 1977, comment by a high Chinese official noted above, Brzezinski found Deng skeptical and Hua receptive. While describing Deng as "a political leader who knew what he wanted and with whom one could deal," Brzezinski was clearly put off by the Chinese leader's persistent questioning of whether the United States had, in fact, made up its mind. After a "final dig," along this line, Brzezinski "shot back, 'I have told you before, President Carter has made up his mind.'"[128]

Adhering to his skeptical attitude, Deng expressed China's interest in obtaining American technology, but doubted Washington's willingness to extend it. "Perhaps," he said, "you have a fear of offending the Soviet Union. Is that right?" To Brzezinski's explanation that arms control negotiations with Moscow were designed to obtain strategic stability, Deng observed: "To be candid with you, whenever you are about to conclude an agreement with the Soviet Union, it is the product of a concession on the U.S. side."[129] Despite being "somewhat irritated" by Deng's barbs, Brzezinski characterized his meeting with him as "positive" and not "polemical" in its general thrust.

If Deng was "blunt and forthright," Hua seemed "somewhat effeminate," exhibiting the mannerisms and bearing that "the Chinese Emperor is supposed to possess." [130] Nevertheless, Hua spoke of the need for action, connecting China's war preparations ("so that one is not at a disadvantage if it breaks out") with the "urgency of upsetting the strategic deployment of Soviet aggression."[131] In this regard, Hua complained that Japan was holding back on concluding the peace and friendship treaty because of the antihegemony clause. Brzezinski promised to urge the Japanese to conclude the treaty, which they did on August 19.

Hua's remark about Japan was disingenuous. The two countries had resumed treaty discussions in April, but a "sudden and mysterious" Chinese move to lay claim to the Senkaku (Tiaoyu) Islands at a delicate moment in the negotiations in late April brought them to a standstill. It seems that several armed Chinese fishing boats sailed to the islands sporting large blackboards on which was written, "Tiaoyutai is the territory of the People's Republic of China."[132] The Chinese Foreign Ministry downplayed the incident as trivial, but press speculation was that the fishermen had been sent "by some Chinese faction opposed to improving relations with Japan or determined to embarrass the new administration of Chairman Hua Kuo-feng."[133]

Discussing Taiwan, Brzezinski raised the issues of peaceful settlement directly and arms sales indirectly, in the context of ensuring that "an insecure Taiwan" not turn to the Soviet Union. Hua, however, was well prepared and offered Washington a choice between the two. The United States could either continue arms sales to Taiwan after normalization, without receiving a Chinese statement of peaceful intent, or discontinue arms sales and receive a Chinese declaration of peaceful intent. "As Hua put it, for us to sell arms and request China to commit itself to a peaceful resolution of the issue would clearly lead to a 'two Chinas' solution."[134]

While agreeing to begin normalization negotiations the next month, Hua had subtly offered an enormous concession if only the Carter leadership had the wit to grasp it. In short, Hua was willing to accept continued arms sales to Taiwan after normalization as long as the United States did not insist on the public humiliation of a formal declaration of peaceful intent. Implicit in Beijing's offer to agree to continued arms sales was the recognition that no invasion of the island would succeed and therefore would not be attempted. Just as Mao had done six years before, Hua had finessed the Taiwan question, opening the door to normalization. It was up to President Carter to walk through it.

United States Negotiating Strategy and Chinese Domestic Politics

Following Brzezinski's return, the administration worked out its negotiating strategy. In agreeing to normalization, Hua Guofeng had offered to grant the United States the substance of its demands on Taiwan—arms sales after normalization—provided that Washington was willing to live without public reassurance of Beijing's future attitude toward the island. But the Carter leadership decided, presumably to neutralize any domestic opposition that might arise, that it could have both the form and the substance of its conditions. This led the administration, on June 20, to adopt a strategy of prolonging the negotiations until the end of the year. The agreed target date for the announcement of normalization of relations was December 15 but was to be kept secret.[135]

The Carter leadership interpreted the international situation in precisely the same way everyone else had, namely, that for China to succeed in preventing Hanoi's conquest of Kampuchea United States support to deter the Soviet Union was required. They calculated that as negotiations dragged on and the war drew nearer in Southeast Asia, the pressure would build on the Chinese to accept Washington's demand for a public commitment to a peaceful settlement of the Taiwan question in return for United States support. Unfortunately, what American leaders did not understand was the impact that prolonging the negotiations would have on the fundamentally unstable internal political balance in Beijing.[136]

Leonard Woodcock, head of the United States liaison office in Beijing, began his formal and exasperatingly deliberate presentations of the American position on July 5 and continued them as planned at roughly ten-day intervals thereafter. As the summer wore on, the

Chinese became increasingly anxious to conclude the process. On August 17, for example, during Brzczinski's first meeting with the new head of the Chinese liaison office in Washington, Chai Zemin, Chinese concern was apparent. Chai declared:

> No doubt, in the final analysis we will come to a successful conclusion. But judging from the current international situation, the earlier that normalization would be realized, the better. But the U.S. bears the major role in reaching a successful conclusion.[137]

Chai's concern was well founded. In the first week of August Vietnamese military operations against Kampuchea intensified, reinforced by a massive new Soviet airlift of supplies and advisers, and despite additional Chinese support for Cambodian forces.[138] A Soviet commentator noted with satisfaction that Soviet–Vietnamese relations were "becoming filled with new content," while the Chinese charged that Moscow was "pushing" Hanoi into a "large-scale invasion of Kampuchea."[139]

September saw the Chinese leadership reach the decision to begin preparations in earnest for armed conflict on both the Soviet and Vietnamese fronts. Deng Xiaoping, for example, traveled to Pyongyang in hopes of ensuring Korean neutrality in any conflict with the Soviet Union and on the same trip inspected Manchurian defenses, which were being strengthened. At the same time the Chinese began deploying the first of twenty-seven divisions and over five hundred combat aircraft to the Sino–Vietnamese border area. The September deployment indicated that the decision to prepare for intervention had already been made, and its size suggested a major military campaign. Whether a strike would actually occur and what its exact nature and timing would be, however, would ultimately depend upon Beijing's ability, alone or in concert with allies, to neutralize the Soviet Union.

While the Chinese were in the process of positioning their forces, the Carter leadership took the opportunity to press its demands on both arms sales and a peaceful settlement. President Carter, marking his first personal involvement in the negotiations with the Chinese, met with Ambassador Chai on September 19. He "hit the Chinese hard on our right to sell arms to Taiwan and on the importance of a noncontradicted statement by the United States . . . [on] a peaceful resolution of the issue of Taiwan."[140]

President Carter's hard-hitting (or callous) rejection of Hua's offer to Brzezinski of either arms sales or a declaration of peaceful intent—but not both—combined with a simultaneous Washington move to agree "in principle" to normalization of relations with Hanoi, brought the normalization negotiations to the verge of collapse in early October. Consistent with the Vietnamese reading of the international situation, Hanoi had sought to neutralize the United States by offering to normalize relations. In Washington, Secretary Vance evidently perceived in the Vietnamese offer the possibility of dissuading Hanoi from proceeding with its plans for conquest in return for normalization.

On October 11, realizing the contradiction in attempting to normalize relations simultaneously with both Hanoi and Beijing, the president decided against a move toward Vietnam and, in an effort to avert a breakdown in negotiations with the Chinese, to submit a draft communiqué on normalization setting January 1 as the date.[141] Submission of a draft communiqué conveyed the president's resolution, but to drive the point home that time was running out, Brzezinski met with Ambassador Chai in mid-October to declare that "if we missed this opportunity we would have to delay normalization until far into 1979," citing as reasons the ever-convenient congressional schedule, but more importantly, that SALT and a Carter–Brezhnev summit would take precedence.[142]

Indeed, over the next two months persistent rumors surfaced in the press regarding a possible Soviet–American summit meeting in January or February 1979.[143] The summit rumors were designed to generate pressure on the Chinese to come to an agreement by the end of the year. Chinese calculations for conflict against Vietnam were affected significantly by the monsoon weather pattern in Indochina—in much the same way that seven years earlier Hanoi's calculations had been affected for the Easter Offensive against South Vietnam. The dry season would extend from late in the year to the following spring; thus, the optimum time to initiate hostilities was early in the year. Furthermore, a Soviet–American summit when Beijing began hostilities threatened to take the United States out of any hoped-for deterrent role.

Moscow's decision to sign a peace and friendship treaty with Hanoi on November 3 also had a positive effect on the normalization negotiations, perhaps contrary to Soviet intent. Soviet leaders hoped that the treaty, with its threat of Soviet support for Hanoi, would deter Chinese counteraction in the same way that the Soviet–Indian treaty had done in 1971. Indeed, key language in the two treaties was identical and the situations analogous.[144]

Both treaties said that if either country were attacked the two parties "shall immediately consult . . . with a view to eliminating that threat and shall take appropriate and effective measures to safeguard peace and security." Similarly, in both instances the Soviets acted to counter the impact of a prospective improvement in Sino–American ties, which in fact, however, had the effect of driving Beijing closer to Washington. Nevertheless, the Chinese were momentarily stunned, rushing Politburo member Wang Dongxing to Phnom Penh immediately after the treaty was announced to reassure Pol Pot that it would have no effect on China's support.

The Soviet move may have had, however, an undetermined impact on the Chinese leadership equation, which began to undergo substantial change from mid-November. American reporters noted the upsurge in wall poster commentary critical of Hua Guofeng, his supporters, and even of Mao Zedong himself.[145] Soviet analysts saw events as a "power bid by Deng," anticipating that "a major reshuffling of personnel will probably take place in the supreme organ of the CCP. It is most likely that some of Hua's faction will be removed to the benefit of Deng's faction." It was the Soviet view that "the outcome of the Hua-Deng conflict . . . could arrive at any moment."[146] President Carter, too, observed during his news conference on November 30 that "the attitude of China, the domestic situation in China, has changed, and we watch it with great interest."[147]

There were undoubtedly grounds for apprehension when on December 4 Ambassador Woodcock completed his extended presentation of the American position, including the final draft of the revised joint normalization communiqué. The Carter leadership, although apprehensive, expected a prompt and affirmative reply. To their mounting concern there was only silence. When a week had passed without a reply, the United States side became anxious, and on December 11 Brzezinski called in the Chinese ambassador to urge that "we should move rapidly on normalization" now.[148] He also told Chai that Beijing "should consider favorably an invitation either to Deng or to Hua to visit Washington in the course of January." This visit, he said, dropping all pretense, would come "before any meeting between Carter and Brezhnev on SALT."

The delay in the Chinese response occurred, as American leaders surmised, because the Chinese leadership struggle had reached a critical stage. Brzezinski's inability to specify to whom an invitation should be extended ("either to Deng or to Hua") further indicated that Washington still was not certain who was in charge as of December 11 despite earlier hints that Deng had gained the upper hand. The outcome became clear the next day, when Deng Xiaoping met with Woodcock to confirm Beijing's agreement on normalization and his acceptance of the invitation to visit the United States.[149]

Woodcock's cable reporting Deng's acceptance prompted the president to propose that the decision to normalize be announced immediately, on December 15. The president's advisers have explained his decision to propose December 15 as the announcement date in various ways: Brzezinski asserted that he wanted simply to "move promptly"; Oksenberg that he wanted to prevent "leaks" and loss of initiative "in presenting the case . . . to the public"; and Vance that "the negotiations might become unraveled."[150]

It would appear that Vance's explanation comes closest to the truth, for Deng's victory over Hua led to a dramatic change in the Chinese terms for normalization. Earlier, immediately after resolution of the conflict with Hua, Deng had flatly rejected one of the two minimum demands for normalization: Chinese acceptance of a United States statement in favor of the peaceful settlement of the Taiwan question. "Under no condition will China enter into any pledge to refrain from the use of force," he said. Furthermore, the "maximum concession" China could make would be to allow the United States to emulate the "Japanese model," whereby Washington could deal with Taiwan "through the continuation of people-to-people and business contacts," but no official government contacts.[151]

Now, in the meeting with Woodcock on December 14, during which the ambassador conveyed President Carter's proposal that normalization be announced the next day, Deng raised the crucial issue of arms sales, demanding that the United States terminate arms sales immediately upon normalization.[152] Woodcock attempted to strike a compromise by conveying Carter's "willingness to forgo new obligations for arms sales in 1979," except for those already contracted, but the meeting came to an unsatisfactory conclusion.[153]

After hurried consultation with Washington, Woodcock was instructed to see Deng again immediately the same day to reassert the president's formulation of September 19 on the United States "right to sell arms to Taiwan and on the importance of a noncontradicted statement . . . that we expected a peaceful resolution. . . ." Deng's response was equally firm: "Arms sales to Taiwan infringed on Chinese sovereignty and could not be accepted." Woodcock replied that arms sales to Taiwan "will continue after a one-year pause during which the treaty is abrogated."[154]

The United States, in Brzezinski's words, was "faced with the prospect of a last-minute fiasco . . . and the situation called for fast action." Without consulting Secretary Vance, who was on his way home from Jerusalem, the national security adviser called in the Chinese ambassador to emphasize that arms sales "will go on after 1979, that they can disagree with this, but since we are going ahead with normalization we should try to minimize the difference."[155] He also overrode Woodcock's objections and instructed him to tell Deng that on the subject of arms sales domestic American politics made it "impossible for the United States not to reaffirm its position on this subject."

Deng's last-minute attempt to extract a vital concession—the essence of Washington's demands for normalization—failed. The two sides reached no agreement on arms sales, except to defer their differences in the interest of proceeding with normalization. The Chinese, as Oksenberg notes, "reserved the right to raise the issue again"[156] and would do so after the conflict with Vietnam had ended early in the Reagan administration. Indeed, had it not been for Beijing's need to range the United States on China's side in the impending conflict in hopes of neutralizing the Soviet Union, normalization might not have taken place at this time.

It was, of course, as the Carter leadership probably guessed, imperative for Beijing to proceed. The announcement to establish diplomatic relations was duly made on December 15, but Hua, the loser in the struggle with Deng, was required publicly to reiterate Deng's position that the Chinese "can absolutely not agree" to arms sales.[157] The joint communiqué had a larger purpose, being all but explicitly directed at Moscow and Hanoi. In that regard, it emphasized two points: that both the United States and the People's Republic of China "wish to reduce the danger of international military conflict," and that "neither should seek hegemony in the Asia-Pacific region or in any other region of the world, and each is opposed to efforts by any other country or group of countries to establish such hegemony."[158]

The timing of Sino–American normalization was clearly a triumph for Brzezinski. He strengthened containment while outmaneuvering Secretary Vance and his preferred sequence requiring that SALT take precedence. Indeed, SALT would be delayed until mid-1979, and it would never serve the intended role as steppingstone to detente. Nevertheless, neither China nor the United States got what it wanted from normalization beyond the formal establishment of diplomatic relations.

If the Chinese hoped that the United States would provide even minimal support permitting China to dislodge Vietnam from Kampuchea, they would be disappointed. The failure to force Vietnam's withdrawal in turn would lead to the collapse of a decades-long Chinese strategy toward Indochina. Indeed, United States behavior, which more closely resembled that of a weak nation than that of a superpower, undermined the arguments of those Chinese leaders inclined to favor long-term cooperation with Washington and strengthened the arguments of those, like Deng, who argued that equidistance was the correct strategy to pursue.

The United States leadership, in seeking normalization of relations with China, overreached itself. In declining the bird in the hand in May of 1978—of Chinese acceptance of continued arms sales to Taiwan—in favor of pursuing two in the bush—which promised arms sales and a peaceful settlement—the Carter leadership got neither. The question of arms sales would arise as a major stumbling block in the early Reagan administration. Moreover, American policy probably contributed to the eclipse of Hua Guofeng in the bargain.

Perhaps explaining but not justifying American policy behavior toward Beijing was the explosion of events occurring in Southeast Asia and the Middle East at the same time. The laborious American effort to knit together an Egyptian–Israeli peace treaty was on the verge of success but stalled. In Iran the shah had collapsed, and Khomeini's return on February 1 presaged more, not less, chaos. Finally, while the Chinese invasion was in progress South Yemen had attacked North Yemen under what was widely believed to be Soviet instigation. It is therefore to an analysis of United States Middle East strategy that we now turn.

Notes

1. Japan Defense Agency, *Defense of Japan 1977* (Tokyo), pp. 122–23.
2. Despite the one percent cap, Japanese defense expenditures doubled during the period 1976–1979, from $5 billion to $10 billion. See the International Institute for Strategic Studies, *The Military Balance 1979–1980* (London, 1979), p. 95.
3. Carter had promised during the campaign to reduce defense spending by $5 to $7 billion, but, on February 22, he asked Congress to cut only $315 million from former President Ford's fiscal 1978 budget. Indeed, according to Secretary of Defense Brown, the president's proposal to spend $111.9 billion compared to Ford's projected $112.2 billion represented "substantial real growth" in defense spending. See Jim Coates, "Only $315 Million Cut from Defense Budget," *Chicago Tribune*, February 23, 1977, p. 6.
4. Richard Nixon, *U.S. Foreign Policy for the 1970's: Building for Peace*, February 25, 1971, vol. II (Washington, DC: GPO, 1971), p. 14.
5. Richard Nixon and Eisaku Sato, "Text of Joint Communiqué," November 21, 1969, Department of State *Bulletin*, December 15, 1969, p. 555.
6. The original plan was to withdraw the Second Division from its deployment on the DMZ. See U.S. Congress, *Investigation of Korean–American Relations*, Report of the Subcommittee on International Organizations of the House Committee on International Relations, October 31, 1978 (Washington, DC: GPO, 1978), pp. 63ff. For a discussion of the rancorous withdrawal "negotiations," see Robert Boettcher, *Gifts of Deceit* (New York: Holt, Rinehart and Winston, 1980).
7. *New York Times*, February 28, 1972, p. 1.
8. "Text of the 'Basic Principles of Relations between the United States of America and the Union of Soviet Socialist Republics,' May 29, 1972," *Weekly Compilation of Presidential Documents*, vol. 8 (June 5, 1972), pp. 943–44.
9. Don Oberdorfer, "Carter's Decision on Korea Traced to Early 1975," *Washington Post*, June 12, 1977, p. A15.
10. Ibid.
11. Ibid.
12. Brzezinski, *Power and Principle*, p. 52.
13. Don Oberdorfer and Edward Walsh, "Carter to Press Liberalizing of Korea, Withdrawal of GIs," *Washington Post*, January 14, 1977, p. 5.
14. See chapter 1 above.
15. Henry L. Trewhitt, "Mondale Says U.S. Will Reduce Forces in Korea," *Baltimore Sun*, February 1, 1977, p. 4.

16. Walter Mondale, "Tokyo News Conference, February 1, 1977," Department of State *Bulletin*, March 7, 1977, pp. 190–91.
17. Ibid.
18. "Japan Shifts Policy on U.S. Pullout," *Baltimore Sun*, January 31, 1977, p. 2.
19. Ibid.
20. Ivan P. Hall, "A Carter Proposal Stirs Fears among the Japanese," *Washington Star*, January 13, 1977, p. 1.
21. Vance, *Hard Choices*, pp. 128–29, suggests that the origin of the Korean withdrawal scheme was Carter's campaign pledge and gives the impression that the policy remained unchanged, because the president was "dug in," until 1979 when "an opportunity to reargue the case" arose.
22. "Japan Shifts Policy on U.S. Pullout," p. 2.
23. Ibid.
24. Matthew J. Seiden, "Tokyo Reasserts Ownership of Island Claimed by Seoul," *Baltimore Sun*, February 11, 1977, p. 2.
25. In fact, the Japanese parliament approved an agreement for joint oil exploration of the continental shelf in early June. See John Saar, "After Three Years, Tokyo Ratifies Seoul Oil Pact," *Washington Post*, June 9, 1977, p. 17.
26. Matthew J. Seiden, "Japan Offers China Treaty Compromise," *Baltimore Sun*, February 5, 1977, p. 2.
27. "President's Press Conference, March 9, 1977," *Public Papers of the Presidents of the United States, Jimmy Carter*, vol. 1 (Washington, DC: GPO, 1977), p. 343.
28. Ibid.
29. Department of State *Bulletin*, no. 1971, April 4, 1977, pp. 322–26.
30. *Yomiuri*, March 11, 1977, p. 2. Japanese press citations are from the *Daily Summary of the Japanese Press*, United States Embassy, Tokyo.
31. Ibid., March 18, 1977, p. 1.
32. *Mainichi*, March 22, 1977, p. 2, revealed Carter's use of the term "reduction" and *Asahi*, June 30, 1977, p. 1, Vance's role.
33. Don Oberdorfer, "Fukuda Reassured on U.S. Presence," *Washington Post*, March 22, 1977, p. 1.
34. *Nihon Keizai*, April 10, 1977, p. 2.
35. *New York Times*, April 15,1977, p. 12. The Honest John surface-to-surface missiles remained for the time being with the Fourth Missile Command, and the Thirty-eighth Air Defense Brigade retained control of the three remaining Hawk surface-to-air missile batteries.
36. *Yomiuri*, April 28, 1977, p. 1.
37. *Yomiuri*, May 19, 1977, p. 2.
38. See *Washington Post*, May 19, 1977, for his criticism.

39. *U.S. News and World Report,* May 30, 1977, pp. 36–38.
40. *Mainichi,* May 28, 1977, p. 2.
41. John Saar, "U.S. Team in Truce Talks Faces a Skeptical South Korea," *Washington Post,* May 24, 1977, p. A17.
42. *Yomiuri,* May 24, 1977, p. 2.
43. "President's News Conference of March 26," *Public Papers of the Presidents of the United States, Jimmy Carter,* vol. 1 (Washington, DC: GPO, 1977), p. 1018.
44. Bernard Gwertzman, "6000 Ground Troops in Korea Will Leave by End of Next Year," *New York Times,* June 6, 1977, p. 1.
45. *Nihon Keizai,* June 6, 1977.
46. *Nihon Kenzai,* June 8, 1977.
47. *Mainichi,* June 23, 1977, p. 2.
48. Cyrus Vance, "America's Role in Consolidating a Peaceful Balance and Promoting Economic Growth in Asia," Department of State *Bulletin,* no. 1988, August 1, 1977, pp. 141–43.
49. *Tokyo Shimbun,* July 27, 1977, p. 1.
50. Bernard Weinraub, "U.S. Will Keep Bulk of Combat Forces in Korea until 1982," *New York Times,* July 27, 1977, p. 1.
51. *Yomiuri,* July 28, 1977, p. 2.
52. Brzezinski, *Power and Principle,* pp. 51–52.
53. Ibid., p. 197.
54. Ibid., pp. 53–54.
55. For a full account of the succession, see the author's *China: A Political History, 1917–1980* (Boulder: Westview Press, 1982), chapter 15.
56. *FBIS-PRC,* NCNA Peking, February 9, 1977, p. A5.
57. "Moscow Warns U.S. on Ties to China," *International Bulletin,* no. 4, May 23, 1977, p. 1.
58. Ibid. For an early analysis of this issue, see Banning Garrett, "China Policy and the Strategic Triangle," in Oye, Rothchild and Lieber, *Eagle Entangled,* pp. 235–37.
59. Brzezinski, *Power and Principle,* pp. 197–98.
60. Ibid., p. 199.
61. Vance, *Hard Choices,* p. 76.
62. Ibid., p. 75.
63. Ibid., p. 76.
64. Ibid., pp. 76–78.
65. *FBIS-PRC,* April 25, 1977, p. A6.
66. *Pravda,* May 14, 1977; Christopher Wren, "Harsh Soviet Attack Says China Prepares for Full-Scale War," *New York Times,* May 15, 1977, p. A1. For an alarmist interpretation of the May 14 article, see Henry Bradsher, "Increased Soviet Threats to China Could Adversely Affect Arms Talks," *Washington Star,* May 31, 1977, p. 9.

67. *FBIS-PRC*, Agence France Presse, Hong Kong, April 29, 1977, pp. A1 2.
68. Ibid.(Emphasis supplied.)
69. "Transcript of the President's News Conference on Foreign and Domestic Matters," *New York Times*, May 13, 1977, pp. A12–13.
70. *FBIS-PRC*, Hsin Wan Pao, Hong Kong, May 18, 1977, pp. N2–3.
71. For the complete text, see Henry Kissinger, *White House Years* (Boston: Little, Brown and Co., 1979), pp. 1490–92.
72. Brzezinski, *Power and Principle*, p. 199. The phrase describing China as a "central element" in United States foreign policy was taken almost literally from the April 30 "briefing book" description. Administration officials also attempted to foster the impression that it did not understand these signals. See for example, Ross H. Munro, "U.S.–China Formal Ties Less Likely," *Christian Science Monitor*, June 1, 1977, p. 1.
73. Vance, *Hard Choices*, p. 77.
74. Ibid., p. 78. Brzezinski's treatment of the late June PRM-24 discussion is curious. He declares that he "came out strongly for a commitment to normalization when Cy goes to China, as well as collateral measures de-emphasizing our links with Taiwan." He concludes that he was "relatively isolated" as most felt that "we could not move that rapidly." Brzezinski, *Power and Principle*, p. 200.
75. Vance, *Hard Choices*, p. 77.
76. Cyrus Vance, "America's Role in Consolidating a Peaceful Balance and Promoting Economic Growth in Asia," Department of State *Bulletin*, no. 1988, August 1, 1977, p. 142.
77. Ross Munro, "Peking Takes Hard-line Tone on Status of Taiwan," *Christian Science Monitor*, July 6, 1977, p. 7.
78. See Thornton, *China: A Political History*, pp. 396–98.
79. Brzezinski, *Power and Principle*, p. 201.
80. Michael Oksenberg, "A Decade of Sino–American Relations," *Foreign Affairs*, Fall 1982, p. 182.
81. Vance, *Hard Choices*, p. 79.
82. Brzezinski, *Power and Principle*, p. 201.
83. Vance, *Hard Choices*, p. 79. The maximum position was the reverse liaison proposal whereby Washington would move its embassy to Beijing and the liaison office to Taipei.
84. Brzezinski, *Power and Principle*, p. 201.
85. Ibid. Vance, *Hard Choices*, p. 79; Oksenberg, "A Decade of Sino–American Relations," p. 182.
86. *FBIS-PRC*, NCNA August 22, 1977, pp. D28ff. Vance's description of the Chinese political scene at this point was terribly inaccurate. See *Hard Choices*, pp. 79–80. For example, what he described as the "Eleventh National People's Congress" in fact was the Eleventh Party

Congress, a major difference. Although he referred subsequently to it as the party congress he compounded his error by stating it was the meeting "at which Chairman Hua Guofeng was elected premier." Hua, of course, had been named premier in April of 1976, over a year before; the Eleventh Party Congress had reconfirmed his position as chairman of the party. Even less informed was the secretary's description of the congress as "the final spasm of Maoism and the consolidation of the pragmatists." Whatever this phrase means, no "spasm" of Maoism occurred, nor was there any "consolidation" of pragmatists.

87. Oksenberg, "A Decade of Sino–American Relations," pp. 182–83. Vance met Hua Guofeng, but he presented United States proposals first to Foreign Minister Huang Hua and then to Deng. Only Deng exhibited the authority actually to negotiate with the secretary of state. See Vance, *Hard Choices*, pp. 81–82.
88. Ibid., p. 81.
89. Ibid., p. 82.
90. Ibid. The "Japanese formula" would involve only an unofficial presence on Taiwan with no United States government personnel.
91. "Vance, Teng Talks Yield 'Progress,'" *Baltimore Sun*, August 25, 1977, p. 1. Vance, *Hard Choices*, p. 83, denied that he had "reported" progress in the talks in his cables to Washington and insinuated that Brzezinski leaked the idea to the press.
92. Bill Peterson, "Full China Ties Are Still Distant, President Asserts," *Washington Post*, August 28, 1977, p. 1.
93. Ibid.
94. Louis D. Boccardi, "Teng Says Vance's Talks in China Set Back Prospect of Normal Ties," *New York Times*, September 7, 1977, p. 1.
95. Robert Keatley, "Vance to Sound Out China's New Leaders on Normalized Ties during Peking Visit," *Wall Street Journal*, August 22, 1977, p. 4.
96. Ibid.
97. *Sankei*, September 3, 1977, p. 2.
98. See chapter 2 above.
99. Rowland Evans and Robert Novak, "PRM-10 and the Korean Pullout," *Washington Post*, September 7, 1977, p. 15.
100. *Washington Post*, September 10, 1977, p. 12.
101. *Sankei*, September 17, 1977, p. 1.
102. "Administration Says North Korea Is Building Up Military Forces," *New York Times*, December 13, 1977, p. 4.
103. Senator John Glenn, *U.S. Troop Withdrawal from the Republic of Korea: An Update, 1979*, Report of the Committee on Foreign Relations, United States Senate (Washington, DC: GPO, June 1979). Senator Glenn concluded, p. 1, that based on this new information of consid-

erably stronger North Korean forces, "the risks involved in continuing the troop withdrawal demand that we reverse our policy and maintain the 2nd Infantry Division in Korea."

104. See Thornton, *China: A Political History*, pp. 396–403.
105. See Henry Bradsher, "Post-Mao Power Struggle Nears Climax in China," *Washington Star*, February 24, 1978, p. 1.
106. "Real Deeds, Yes; Hollow Statements, No!" *Peking Review*, March 31, 1978, pp. 14–18.
107. Patrick Garrity, "Soviet Policy in the Far East," *Military Review*, December 1982, pp. 30–36.
108. Marquis Childs, "China's Wary Watch over Hanoi's Ambitions," *Washington Post*, August 1, 1978, p. A15.
109. Don Oberdorfer, "Hanoi Is Massing Troops at Border with Cambodia," *Washington Post*, April 8, 1978, p. A1.
110. Michael Parks, "Vietnam Threatens War in Dispute with China," *Baltimore Sun*, September 1, 1978, p. 8.
111. The historian must take strong exception to Brzezinski's account of the normalization process, *Power and Principle*, pp. 202–31. Despite emphasizing his sense of "obligation to inform the citizen . . . of how the major decisions . . . were made," of claiming to "provide a more systematic analysis of how policy was made," of offering to set forth both "a narrative account . . . and, equally importantly, to explore in depth those central issues of American foreign policy which were my main concern," p. xiii, in the case of Sino–American normalization, at least, his account, while useful, is seriously misleading. The principal shortcoming is the absence of context, that is, the Soviet turn to the offensive and the impact of the looming Sino–Vietnamese conflict on the negotiating positions of Washington and Beijing. This is even more striking because Brzezinski's chief aide on China policy, Michael Oksenberg, included these very factors in an account written a year before Brzezinski's memoir appeared. See Oksenberg, "A Decade of Sino–American Relations," p. 186.
112. Frederic A. Moritz, "China–Viet Conflict: More than Border Spats," *Christian Science Monitor*, April 21, 1978, p. 4. Beijing also shipped tanks and long-range artillery to Kampuchean forces at this time. See Henry Kamm, "Indochina Fighting Breaks Out Again," *New York Times*, May 18, 1978, p. 9.
113. Brzezinski, *Power and Principle*, pp. 202–3.
114. Jay Mathews, "Common Interests with U.S. Stressed by Chinese Leader," *Washington Post*, March 7, 1978, p. 1.
115. Oksenberg, "A Decade of Sino–American Relations," p. 184, suggests that it was the Senate ratification of the Panama Canal treaty that determined the timing on the United States side.

116. Brzezinski, *Power and Principle*, pp. 205–6. See chapter 5 for a discussion of the broader policy debate, of which the China decision was a part.
117. "Excerpts From Carter's Speech on Defense Policy and Soviet Ties," *New York Times*, March 18, 1978, p. 9.
118. Ibid.
119. Brzezinski, *Power and Principle*, Annex I.
120. Ibid., p. 207.
121. Ibid., Annex I.
122. Both Brzezinski, subtly, and Oksenberg, less so, insinuate that Deng was in command at this time, which is not supported by United States actions. Brzezinski's account of his meetings with Deng and Hua, *Power and Principle*, pp. 212–18, leaves the impression that Deng was in charge without explicitly stating it. Oksenberg, on the other hand, argues in one place, "A Decade of Sino–American Relations," p. 185, that "by May, Deng Xiaoping had gained considerable initiative within the Politburo, though not until the end of the year did he achieve a totally dominant position"; and in another place on the same page he speaks of "Deng's consolidated position." This is a case of modern revisionism, or whiggism. Deng would eventually defeat Hua, but in placing his "victory" in May it minimized the impact American policy had on the Chinese leadership struggle as normalization negotiations reached the decisive point.
123. Brzezinski, *Power and Principle*, p. 208.
124. Jay Mathews, "Peking Accuses Soviets of Raid across Border," *Washington Post*, May 12, 1978, p. 1.
125. David K. Shipler, "Soviet Union Apologizes to China for Patrol That Crossed Border," *New York Times*, May 13, 1978, p. 5.
126. "Chinese Term War with Soviet 'Inevitable,'" *Baltimore Sun*, May 15, 1978, p. 2.
127. Oksenberg, "A Decade of Sino–American Relations," p. 185. Brzezinski omits all reference to the impending Sino–Vietnamese conflict.
128. Brzezinski, *Power and Principle*, p. 214.
129. Ibid., pp. 214–15.
130. Ibid., p. 215.
131. Ibid., p. 216.
132. Jay Mathews, "China's Row with Japan May Peril Ties to U.S." *Washington Post*, April 22, 1978, p. 20.
133. Ibid.
134. Brzezinski, *Power and Principle*, pp. 218–19.
135. Ibid., pp. 223–24; Oksenberg, "A Decade of Sino–American Relations," p. 186, notes that "the idea was to unfold the American

position at a deliberate speed, and to prolong the negotiations if it became clear the Chinese would not meet the minimum terms."

136. Ibid., p. 186. Oksenberg states it in the following way: "The discussions proceeded as the top leaders on both sides kept their eyes on three related developments: their relations with Vietnam, the SALT talks with the Soviet Union, and their domestic standing."
137. Brzezinski, *Power and Principle*, p. 227.
138. Don Oberdorfer, "Soviet Union Completes Vietnam Airlift," *Washington Post*, September 2, 1978, p. 1.
139. *Pravda*, September 2, 1978, and *People's Daily*, September 17, 1978.
140. Brzezinski, *Power and Principle*, p. 229.
141. Ibid., p. 229. Oksenberg, "A Decade of Sino–American Relations," p. 187, says the January 1 date was not communicated until November 2.
142. Brzezinski, *Power and Principle*, p. 229.
143. Oksenberg, "A Decade of Sino–American Relations," p. 187.
144. Henry Bradsher, "China Hurries to Side of Cambodia in Wake of Hanoi–Moscow Pact," *Washington Star*, November 7, 1978, p. 3.
145. See for example, Michael Parks, "New China Policy Spells Trouble for Radicals," *Baltimore Sun*, November 17, 1978, p. A2.
146. *FBIS-SU*, November 28, 1978, pp. C1–2.
147. *U.S. Policy toward China, July 15, 1971–January 15, 1979*, Selected Documents no.9 (Washington, DC: GPO, January 1979), p. 44.
148. Brzezinski, *Power and Principle*, p. 230.
149. Ibid., p. 230. For a detailed analysis of the Chinese internal struggle, see Thornton, *China: A Political History*, pp. 405–10.
150. Brzezinski, *Power and Principle*, p. 230; Oksenberg, "A Decade of Sino–American Relations," p. 188; Vance, *Hard Choices*, p. 110.
151. A.T. Steele, "China Would Consider Special Taiwan Status," *Washington Star*, December 4, 1978, p. 3.
152. The sequence of events is evident when Brzezinski's (*Power and Principle*, p. 231) and Oksenberg's ("A Decade of Sino–American Relations," p. 188) accounts are joined.
153. Oksenberg, "A Decade of Sino–American Relations," p. 188.
154. Brzezinski, *Power and Principle*, p. 231.
155. Ibid.
156. Oksenberg, "A Decade of Sino–American Relations," p. 188.
157. Fox Butterfield, "Peking Concession on Arms to Taipei Led to U.S. Accord," *New York Times*, December 17, 1978, p. 1.
158. "Text of Communiqué," *Baltimore Sun*, December 16, 1978, p. 2.

CHAPTER 4

The Middle East to the Horn of Africa: From Whipsaw to Backlash, 1977

In the Middle East and the Horn of Africa the United States faced two extremely complicated, interrelated problems. The gradual shift of Ethiopia from the American to the Soviet orbit raised the prospect of Soviet control of the entire Horn—an accomplishment which could provide Moscow with tremendous leverage against the Middle East in general and Saudi Arabia in particular, as well as becoming a steppingstone for further Soviet penetration into Africa. The problem of the Horn therefore required the immediate attention of the Carter administration.

In the Middle East, the United States faced potentially the most explosive problem of all, a structural stalemate resulting from a geopolitical shift which had been halted midway and which was thus unstable and reversible. The breaking of the Arab encirclement of Israel and Egypt's shift into the American camp after the Yom Kippur War were not yet permanent; they were secured only by separation of forces agreements. Furthermore, the agreements did not address the fundamental issues of peace, security, and the Palestinian question.[1]

The two areas of tension were interrelated in that all of the Middle East principals were deeply concerned about Ethiopia's shift into Moscow's camp and were directly involved in efforts to forestall it. From Washington's perspective the problems of the Middle East and the Horn were made more urgent by the Soviet Union's impending strategic weapons breakthrough. Assuming that it faced "a prolonged period of widespread, turbulent upheaval,"[2] as Moscow sought to manipulate the geopolitical balance to its advantage, the Carter administration placed undue reliance upon guile and indirection in efforts to secure its own position.

The Carter administration's main objective was to consolidate the gains made after the Yom Kippur War by securing an Egyptian–Israeli peace treaty and at least a procedural accord on resolution of the Palestinian issue. A peace treaty would establish the foundation of regional security which had been left unfinished when Israel decided not to go beyond the initial separation of forces agreements reached after the war. A Palestinian framework, in turn, would strengthen American influence with the moderate Arab states and defuse the appeal of the radical Arabs, thus undercutting the Soviet Union's main political entrée into the region.

The problem was that the positions of Israel and the Arabs seemed unbridgeable. Israel felt no compelling need to make additional concessions, particularly since the United States remained committed to its support. It was unthinkable to the Israeli leadership that the Carter administration—or any American administration, for that matter—would compromise the tangible benefits of relations with Israel for the ephemeral promises of Middle East peace. Washington's fundamental commitment to Israel, it was assumed, constituted a bottom line beyond which pressure for compromise would cease.

The position of the Arabs was less realistic but equally rigid—although there were shades of differences among them. Except for Egypt, the Arab principals refused to concede Israel's right to exist, let alone agree to compromise on the territorial issues or the question of the Palestinians. As Secretary Vance discovered during his trip to the region in February, the Arabs remained divided and "still psychologically unready to accept real peace."[3]

American strategy through 1977 would be to generate different kinds of pressure on both sides in order to bring about a basis for an agreement. Toward Israel, the Carter administration would in effect support the fundamental Arab position of Israeli withdrawal to the 1967 lines and the estabishment of a Palestinian homeland or entity. Toward the Arabs, on the other hand, in addition to direct diplomatic approaches, Washington would pursue a broader scheme, attempting to employ Soviet penetration of the Horn to increase the general, regionwide threat level in hopes of making compromise with Israel seem more acceptable.

By the end of the year, the Carter administration's policy in both the Middle East and the Horn of Africa had failed. Washington's attempt to combine an Egyptian–Israeli peace treaty with a Palestinian resolution had fallen prey to skillful if short-sighted Israeli diplomacy, which had brought Anwar Sadat to the verge of a separate peace whose terms would have shattered the larger United States position in the region. It required personal intervention by President Carter to dissuade Sadat from accepting the Israeli offer in favor of a renewed effort to reach the broader settlement which the United States preferred.

In the Horn of Africa, American policy produced an unexpected backlash as the attempt to intensify the threat to the Arabs got out of hand. The Soviet response to the Ethiopia–Somalia conflict was to mount a major threat to American interests beyond the immediate question of the Horn, forcing a substantial adjustment of Washington's strategy for the next three years. Indeed, United States policy in the greater Middle East after 1977 was executed under the shadow of growing Soviet military pressure throughout the region.

Initial Decisions: The February 23 NSC Meeting

Reflecting the priority accorded to the Middle East, on February 14 Secretary of State Vance departed on a fact-finding trip to Israel, Egypt, Syria, Jordan, and Saudi Arabia to assess the positions of the principal participants.[4] On February 23, the day after Vance's return, the president convened an NSC meeting to determine the administration's policy course. Vance had not been surprised by what he had found. Neither the Israelis nor the Arabs saw any reason to change—the Israelis because they were stronger than ever (the IDF had "doubled in strength" since Yom Kippur)[5] and the Arabs because no Arab leader, with the exception of Anwar Sadat, would break ranks to negotiate directly with Israel.

Vance's talks in Israel convinced him that the structural freeze which the Rabin cabinet embodied had not changed since it took office in 1974. Israel's main concern was security. Although willing to make minor territorial concessions, the Israelis would not compromise on security to achieve full peace with the Arabs. Israel was willing to resume negotiations at Geneva if the United States insisted, but Rabin made plain that there could be neither a return to the 1967 lines nor any agreement for the establishment of a separate Palestinian state in the West Bank and Gaza. Israel would refuse to accept the PLO at Geneva (although Palestinians could be included in the Jordanian delegation), and Jerusalem was non-negotiable.[6]

Vance's discussions with the Arab leaders also convinced him that they remained divided and incapable of pursuing a united course of action. All wished to see progress made on the Palestinian issue, although Saudi Arabia alone demanded establishment of an independent Palestinian state; yet all were at odds in one way or another with the PLO. All wished to prevent Egypt from further negotiations with Israel, yet they would not negotiate with Israel themselves. Sadat expected, indeed needed, relations to develop with Israel, but in deference to Arab sensitivities he would make no advance commitments to full peace. Syria's Assad opposed full peace and would accept only "peaceful coexistence" indefinitely. Jordan's Hussein was ambivalent and would take no initiative whatsoever.[7]

Thus, the central question facing the American leadership at the February 23 meeting was how to break the stalemate. The decision was to increase the pressure on both sides to negotiate while raising the level of threat in the region. The administration decided to revive the idea of reaching a comprehensive settlement at a Geneva conference, which, paradoxically, was itself a prescription for stalemate. Everyone understood that for Geneva to succeed, agreements would have to be reached beforehand, not at the conference itself. Nevertheless, the essential point of the decision to seek a comprehensive settlement at Geneva was that it enabled the United States to engage the participants in discussion of a broad agenda. Thus, Geneva was not so much an end as it was a means to restart the stalled negotiation process.

The issue of how to use the Geneva format engendered disagreement between Vance and Brzezinski. Vance wished to make a strong negotiating effort at Geneva, reasoning that "attempting to reach a comprehensive peace would not, of course, rule out falling back to additional partial agreements if that was all that appeared possible."[8]

This meant that as cochairman of the conference the Soviet Union "should be accorded a role in negotiations." Vance saw inclusion of the Soviets as a way to "dissuade [Moscow] from undermining our efforts."[9] The secretary appeared to believe that Washington could coopt Moscow in support of United States objectives.

Brzezinski saw danger in this procedure. He did not believe the Soviets could be coopted since their interests were intrinsically opposed to those of the United States. He argued that the Soviets should be kept out of the negotiations just as Kissinger had done. He advocated that "we keep the Soviets informed . . . but that we not involve them prematurely." They "should not be involved substantively in the negotiations." He was concerned that "if we only resolve procedural questions before going to Geneva, Geneva will break down and the Soviets will try to exploit the situation."[10]

It was his view that "Geneva should not be used for negotiations as such but should be held to legitimize any agreement previously reached by the parties through U.S. efforts."[11] Moreover, "the prospect of a Geneva Conference . . . should be used as a form of pressure on the Israelis and inducement for the Arabs, though not as an end in itself." In other words, "We should hold out the promise of a Geneva conference this fall and work toward it but stop short of being committed to holding it."[12]

The decision on the Middle East which came out of the February 23 NSC meeting was to "target" September 1977 for convening the Geneva conference without being unalterably committed to it if conditions were unfavorable. The short timetable meant that Washington would have to move rapidly to reach agreement among the participants on procedure and at the same time "seek some agreement on principles" dealing with the basic issues of peace, borders, and the Palestinians.[13] The short timetable also related to the conflict then reaching the boiling point in the Horn of Africa.

Accelerating the Pace of Conflict in the Horn

The day after the NSC meeting, Secretary Vance announced before the Senate Appropriations Subcommittee on Foreign Operations that because of human rights considerations the United States had decided "to reduce foreign aid to Argentina, Uruguay and

Ethiopia."[14] As far as Ethiopia was concerned, even though the actual dollar figure was small (the cutback related only to grant aid, amounting to $6 million; regular arms sales in much larger amounts continued), the impact in Addis Ababa was far reaching.

The context for Washington's decision on foreign aid was the fundamental turn in Ethiopian politics dating back to 1974 and the involvement of the Soviet Union. The outbreak of rebellion in the Ethiopian coastal province of Eritrea in early 1974 had sparked strikes, first in the army and then throughout the rest of the country.[15] The aging emperor, Haile Selassie, was unable either to quell the rebellion or to retain control of his own army and in June was forced to relinquish command to a military coordinating council known as the Dergue.

Within three months the Dergue grew strong enough to force the emperor to abdicate, and on September 12 the Ethiopian Provisional Military Government was established. Turning to the left in March of 1975, the new military leadership proclaimed a "Socialist Ethiopia" as a one-party state[16] and nationalized all land, industry, and property. The regime then proceeded, in the name of the revolution, to exterminate large numbers of the "capitalist classes," including former government officials, military officers, clergy, and Western-educated students.[17]

At the same time, the Dergue stepped up efforts to extinguish the Eritrean rebellion, which was supported by Saudi Arabia, Egypt, Sudan, Somalia, Iraq, and Syria.[18] When the Dergue asked the United States to provide additional arms, the Ford administration procrastinated, concerned about the leftward bent of the regime. Eventually, in an unsuccessful effort to retain influence with the Dergue, the Ford administration agreed to the largest arms sale ever to Ethiopia, over $135 million; but by then the Dergue had begun secret talks with Moscow regarding its political reorientation as well as arms supply.[19]

By early 1976 the Dergue had established a communist state structure, but without a unified communist party. A politburo, created in March, became Mengistu Haile's power base, while General Atnafu Abate commanded the People's Militia and General Teferi Bante controlled the government apparatus as head of state. Throughout the year the three men and their supporters maneuvered for dominance. General Teferi made a temporarily successful bid for power in December through a reorganization of the government which stripped power from Mengistu; but his strategy quickly backfired.

On February 3, 1977, Mengistu, supported by Atnafu, took control by assassinating General Teferi and his supporters in a shootout at the Grand Palace. Mengistu's ascension to power occurred in the context of a public turn to the Soviet Union as Moscow signed its first arms supply agreement with Addis Ababa in December.[20] Sending its congratulations on the outcome of the coup, Moscow quickly ferried thirty tanks from stocks in Aden to support the new regime, supplementing them over the next two months with delivery from the Soviet Union of a hundred tanks and armored personnel carriers.[21]

Moscow threw its support to Mengistu against the People's Revolutionary party (PRP), a doctrinaire Marxist-Leninist organization vehemently opposed to Mengistu's military rule, which it described as fascist.[22] In the spring the PRP mounted a major challenge to the regime from within, carrying on urban guerrilla warfare operations inside Addis Ababa. Shootings, sabotage, and assassinations drenched the capital and were countered by neighborhood revolutionary defense squads authorized by the government to conduct "hunt down" drives against "counterrevolutionary outlaws."

Mengistu's rise also triggered reaction from Ethiopia's neighbors.[23] The prospect of a substantial increase in Ethiopia's military power thoroughly alarmed the leaders of surrounding states, but particularly General Siad Barre in neighboring Somalia. To Siad Barre, also a Soviet client, Moscow's decision to supply arms to Ethiopia threatened to eliminate any possibility of recovering the Ogaden, an Ethiopian province, ethnically Somalian, to which Somalia laid claim. Siad quickly increased support to the anti-government guerrilla forces he was sponsoring in the Ogaden, the West Somalia Liberation Front (WSLF), hoping to gain control over the province before Soviet arms precluded that possibility.

It was at this point that Washington entered with the decision to cut aid to Ethiopia. The aid cut, which amounted to an announcement that Washington was shifting away from Ethiopia, nudged Mengistu further toward Moscow and opened the door to better United States relations with Somalia. Its effect was to accelerate an ongoing trend toward conflict in the region, which the Carter leadership hoped would make the Arabs more receptive to reaching an agreement with Israel. It was against the backdrop of rapidly developing conflict in the Horn that Washington executed its Middle East strategy.

Building the Conditions for Israeli–Egyptian Negotiations

The first step in the administration's "political strategy [was] to get the parties to engage in the negotiating process."[24] Under no circumstances could it be allowed to appear that the United States and Israel were in collusion. On the contrary, Washington had to demonstrate genuine interest in resolving the Palestinian question to allay suspicions, never far below the surface in Moscow and Arab capitals, that the United States was simply using the negotiations as a cover for arranging a separate peace between Israel and Egypt.

Over the next several months the administration attempted to put its political strategy into effect, beginning with President Carter's personal meetings with each of the principals in the Middle East drama. Yitzhak Rabin came first, March 7 and 8. During talks on the first day, Rabin elaborated Israel's position. Israel, he said, was willing to relinquish "the bulk of Sinai" to Egypt in return for full peace.[25] The Israeli Defense Force (IDF) would like to control a few key points, like Sharm el Sheikh at the tip of the Sinai Peninsula, but felt no need to exercise sovereignty over them. Israel wanted to retain the Golan Heights as a buffer against Syrian attack; but on the West Bank, which Rabin termed the "most delicate issue," there could be compromise, though not total withdrawal.

Turning to the Palestinian issue, Rabin said that Israel no longer ignored the problem, but while it "should be solved in an honorable way," it was "not the heart of the matter."[26] Ruling out the possibility of a "third state" between Israel and Jordan, Rabin spoke of a "Jordanian–Palestinian state," in which the Palestinian identity would be an internal matter of no concern to Israel. As to the Geneva conference, Rabin cautioned against haste, urging the president to make careful preparations beforehand. Finally, he urged Carter not to insist on a unified Arab delegation at Geneva.

The initial encounter was "cordial" and the exchange promising.[27] In fact, the Camp David accords would look remarkably similar in content to the position developed during the first day of talks. The second day, however, brought surprises from both sides.

Rabin set forth what was from Washington's perspective a preposterous proposal for Israeli–American collusion which would have destroyed American strategy in the Middle East. "Pointing to the moderate Arabs' need for progress, he argued that the United States and Israel had an opportunity to extract concessions if we would take a tough stand together."[28] Rabin was alluding chiefly to Sadat and the Egyptian leader's need to make concessions in order to demonstrate the validity of his peaceful approach.

Rabin also sought to turn the Geneva conference into a forum for interminable negotiation resolving little. He proposed that Washington "seek advance Arab agreement that the principal purpose of the Geneva conference would be to negotiate 'real' peace and normalization, with the 'sequence' for implementing that peace to be the subject of detailed negotiations." Finally, the Israeli leader "dismissed" all offers of UN, United States, or United States–Soviet guarantees as "meaningless," asserting that the "only commitment Israel wanted from [the United States] was to supply arms."[29]

Rabin's completely unacceptable and indeed outrageous ploy actually made it easier for the president to take a tough line. Responding to the Israeli prime minister in a manner that was "direct without being aggressive," Carter declared that he favored "rapid negotiations . . . minimum border changes, and that the Palestinians (including the PLO) . . . be somehow included in the discussions."[30] Elaborating, the president insisted that there could be only "minor modifications of the 1967 borders," to which Israel must withdraw.[31] Raising for the first time the issue of Israeli settlements in the occupied territories, the president flatly termed them "illegal."

Turning to the Palestinian question, the president expressed the hope that Israel would permit PLO leaders "in an Arab delegation." Warning of the consequences of continued refusal, he said, "it would be a blow to U.S. support for Israel if you refused to participate in the Geneva talks over the technicality of the PLO being in the negotiations."[32] Carter's words were a thinly veiled ultimatum threatening a cutoff of United States support, which presented the Israeli leader with a Hobson's choice. To refuse Carter's proposals threatened the loss of American support, but to accept them would mean the undoing of all Israel's gains over the previous decade. The prospect clearly stunned Rabin, who "was taken aback,"[33] and he "pleaded with Carter not to reveal the differences of opinion between them over borders and the Palestinian question."[34]

It was no surprise that the American side concluded that the meetings with Rabin had gone badly; there had been little rapport between the president and the Israeli prime minister.[35] But the discussions had in fact served their purpose of stimulating the Israeli leadership into thinking about what hitherto had been unthinkable—reaching an actual settlement. This in itself was an important step forward. The alternatives implicit in the Carter–Rabin meetings were also plain, if unpalatable. Israel could either go to Geneva for a comprehensive negotiation, which would undoubtedly require far-reaching concessions, or reach a separate agreement beforehand with Egypt in which concessions would still have to be made, but would be more limited.

What happened next should have come as no surprise, as the Israeli leadership turned to the American Jewish community for help in reversing the Carter leadership's policy. Thereafter the president and others in the administration were subjected to a steady drumbeat of attacks over Middle East policy.[36] The Israelis, moreover, as feared, attempted to build the public image of cooperation with Washington, an impression the president himself immediately and repeatedly strove to dispel.

For example, in comments to the press after the second meeting, Rabin pointed to an earlier Carter reference to defensible borders as meaning that Israel "should never be expected to return to the 1967 lines."[37] Carter held a news conference the next day to contradict him, thus beginning a tattoo of commentary to show United States opposition to Israel in virtually all aspects of the negotiations. Although he could not predict the exact lines to which Israel would withdraw as part of a final peace agreement, the president said, "I would guess it [*sic*] would be some minor adjustments in the 1967 borders."[38]

Then, a week later, in a public forum, Carter delivered a second, major blow to the Israeli position and to Rabin personally when he declared that "there has to be a homeland provided for the Palestinian refugees." Carter's statement greatly increased the pressures on the Israeli leadership in general on the eve of its national elections and severely undercut Rabin's political standing. The lack of confidence which Carter publicly indicated in Rabin was undoubtedly an important factor contributing to his decision to resign in early April.

In the meantime, President Carter met with the Arab leaders, starting with Anwar Sadat, April 4 and 5. The president was predisposed to be friendly with all of the Arabs but with none more than Sadat, who played a crucial part in American strategy. The United States objective was to prod Sadat into an independent negotiation with Israel, but the problem was the Egyptian leader's insecurity vis-á-vis the Israelis and his dependence upon the United States for support. The extremely difficult task for the president was to nudge Sadat forward without seriously alienating him.

Sadat believed that unless the United States played a central role, further progress was unlikely. Thus, Sadat sought to employ the same tactic he had used after the Yom Kippur War by insisting upon an "American plan" on the grounds that Washington held 99 percent of the cards. In effect, Sadat's scheme was to have Washington negotiate with Israel on Egypt's behalf. Indeed, it was the Egyptian leader's view that "peace in the Middle East should be made under American auspices."[39]

This meant that the parties should make every effort to reach agreement before Geneva, which was the place to go "simply to sign the agreements." Sadat would be willing to go to Geneva to negotiate with the Israelis if the United States insisted, but he believed "that process would take ten years and Egypt would get nothing."[40] Sadat also opposed the proposal for a unified Arab delegation, which he saw as Assad's attempt to reduce his room for maneuver. Nevertheless, he would accept if the president insisted. He preferred separate delegations.

Responding to the president's main concerns, Sadat agreed there could be "slight modifications in the 1967 lines" but not in Sinai; and any Palestinian state or entity "should have some link to Jordan." The Egyptian leader was clearly interested in reaching agreement quickly, primarily in recovering Egyptian territory and without undue participation, or interference, from other Arab states or the Soviet Union. Carter candidly agreed with Sadat, saying:

> If we can get your advice and support at the crucial moments, I think we might be able to go to Geneva only for the signing ceremony. That would be the best possible outcome. If we go to Geneva with lots of loose ends and with the Soviets present, there is little chance of reaching harmony there.[41]

In attempting to impress upon Sadat the urgent need to act now in establishing full diplomatic relations with Israel, the president held out the prospect of long-term American military and economic largess and political support. Carter spoke of the United States' future relationship with Egypt. "Ten years from now," he mused, America's ties to Egypt "will be just as strong as the ties we now have with Israel." But it "would require a strong Egyptian–Israeli relationship" to make that possible.[42] Sadat's reaction was to suggest that full normalization of relations with Israel could be achieved within five years, a major change in position. Up to this point, Sadat had been adamant against the establishment of "full peace," saying that it was something for the next generation to achieve.

Following Sadat's visit, the president and his advisers held another policy review meeting on April 19 to assess the state of play. The administration had taken different approaches with the two countries. After all, any negotiating initiative would necessarily have to come from Israel, the party which would make the larger concessions. Thus, Washington's approach had been to demand that Israel go to Geneva to negotiate in the hope that it would galvanize the Israelis into action beforehand. With Sadat, on the other hand, in the hope of increasing his receptivity to an Israeli offer, Carter had said that agreements should be reached before going to Geneva.[43]

There were clear grounds for optimism that this strategy was working. Rabin's resignation suggested that Israel's period of immobility was over and that his interim replacement, Shimon Peres, whose election seemed assured, would display more initiative. The talks with Sadat had also been encouraging. Not only was the Egyptian leader willing to enter into another round of negotiations, he appeared to be eager to establish—within five years—full diplomatic relations with Israel. It was also obvious that neither Israel nor Egypt wished to go to Geneva for actual negotiations, and neither was excessively committed to the Palestinian cause. Given this assessment, the president concluded that Washington must keep up the pressure for convening a Geneva conference in 1977. This would give both parties incentive to move toward each other to avoid what both considered to be an undesirable forum.

To add to the incentive, the Carter leadership also decided that "after June" Washington "would consider the option of direct contacts with the PLO."[44] To open the door to contact, it was proposed that the PLO be asked to accept UN Resolution 242 with the reservation that it did not deal adequately with the Palestinian question (its sole reference to the Palestinians was as a refugee problem).[45] Through the summer United States leaders explored several alternative formulations aimed at obtaining PLO acceptance of UN Resolution 242, but in the end they were unable to do so.

Conflict Erupts in the Horn of Africa

Meanwhile, the Soviets, hoping to forestall a major conflict between Ethiopia and Somalia, which would force a choice between clients, unsuccessfully attempted to mediate—first indirectly, through Castro, then directly, through Politburo member Nikolai Podgorny. In early March Castro visited both Addis Ababa and Mogadishu and, at a secret meeting in Aden, proposed that Ethiopia and Somalia dissolve their differences in a "socialist" federation to include South Yemen and Djibouti (Afars and Issas), which would receive independence from France in June.[46] Siad Barre rejected both Castro's proposal and the efforts later in the month by Podgorny to bring about a compromise.[47]

Failing to resolve the differences between the two countries, Moscow chose to strengthen military ties with Ethiopia, including the dispatch of Cuban advisers. Mengistu, in turn, moved to sever ties with the United States. Having been advised that Washington planned to close down the Kagnew communications center in Asmara before the September date originally planned, on April 23 Mengistu demanded the immediate closing of Kagnew and several other United States facilities in Ethiopia within four days and expelled an American correspondent.[48]

A few days later Mengistu went to Moscow for a state visit, where on May 1 he signed a second, major arms agreement. As Mengistu strengthened relations with Moscow, Siad Barre sought to open channels to Washington, at first through intermediaries, especially Egypt, Saudi Arabia, and Iran. Indeed, Sadat had raised the subject of American support for Somalia during his visit to Washington, but he received no commitments.[49] The rapid warming of Soviet–Ethiopian relations and cooling of Soviet–Somali ties prompted Siad in May to make "a direct and urgent request" to the United States for arms and economic aid.[50]

Secretary Vance asserts that he "recommended . . . that we refuse to supply even defensive military equipment or to permit our allies and friends to transfer U.S. arms to Somalia until the Ogaden affair was settled."[51] The president, however, after almost two months of deliberations, made a contrary decision, secretly notifying the Somalis in mid July that the United States, in conjunction with Great Britain and France, was in principle prepared to "help other countries to meet Somalia's needs for defensive equipment."[52] Moreover, the Saudis reportedly assured Siad Barre during his visit to Riyadh earlier that month that if Mogadishu broke completely with Moscow, the United States would supply and they would pay for a major arms package worth $460 million.[53]

The upshot of these representations was the launch of a full-scale Somali offensive into the Ogaden on July 23.[54] Clearly acting on the assumption that he had secured an alternate supply of arms, Siad Barre committed the majority of his army, some 40,000 troops, in an invasion of the Ogaden, although publicly he denied any of his regular forces were involved. Moscow, which had not yet terminated its arms supply to Somalia, attempted to persuade Siad to desist, while increasing the flow of weapons to Ethiopia as well as several thousand Cuban troops to employ them. By the end of July, Somali and Ethiopian forces were fully engaged in a major conflict, which Somalia was winning.

Menachem Begin Visits Washington

The big surprise in the Middle East had occurred in Israel with the election on May 17 of Menachem Begin as prime minister. Few had expected the hard-line Begin to succeed in his bid for the prime ministership against Peres and the Labor party, which had held power in Israel since 1948. Begin's election represented a change in Israel's strategy from immobility to engagement. The Israeli leadership had decided to seize the initiative and entered into interminable negotiations which would resolve nothing and leave the Israeli position intact. In effect, under Begin, Israel would carry out what Rabin had proposed to Carter in Washington earlier in the year.

The initial reaction in Washington to Begin's election was surprise, even shock, but upon reflection the view (or rationalization) began to take hold in the administration that an extremist like Begin could do what a labor leader could not—make the compromises necessary to reach peace. Indeed, Brzezinski went so far as to argue that Begin would enable Carter to mobilize "a significant portion of the American Jewish community" in favor of a settlement.[55]

Inviting the new prime minister for an official state visit July 19 and 20, the administration set about preparing for his arrival. The concern was that Begin would either derail the negotiating process openly or attempt to appear conciliatory, express a willingness to go to Geneva without preconditions, and then blame the Arabs for demanding preconditions. To counter the latter maneuver, which was considered the more dangerous, the administration placed on the public record its conception of the essential ingredients for a comprehensive settlement.

In the "U.S. Statement on the Middle East" of June 28, Washington declared its adherence to UN Resolutions 242 and 338 and its interpretation of the kind of settlement they provided.[56] Negotiations among the parties must lead to "security arrangements on all fronts satisfactory to all" and include "steps toward normalization of relations with Israel." In return for full peace, Israel must be prepared to withdraw "from all three fronts" and "deal with the Palestinian issue." The statement threw down the gauntlet to Israel, which had adamantly refused withdrawal on all three fronts and rejected any suggestion of an independent Palestinian state. Indeed, the Begin government complained that Washington was "trying to box it in before the prime minister and his advisers had fully developed their positions."[57]

A few days later, on July 5, the Carter leadership also decided on a private strategem which would drive even an intransigent Begin into negotiation with Egypt.[58] This was the concept of the "five draft principles," which was nothing more than a reformulation of the June 28 statement. The procedure would be to invite all of the parties to respond to the principles, revise them so as to obtain general agreement, then issue the invitations to Geneva. This would establish a presumptive timetable and a negotiating framework as a penultimate step to Geneva.

All parties, but particularly the Israelis, would understand that time was running out and that fundamental decisions would have to be made. The administration was indeed trying to box in the Begin government, leaving but one avenue for escape: an independent move to Egypt. The degree of Israeli concern could be measured in the intensity of attacks by American Jewish community leaders on the Carter administration in the days leading up to the Begin visit.[59]

The Carter–Begin meetings, July 19 and 20, produced surprises on both sides. As expected, the president and Secretary Vance strove to gain Begin's acceptance of the five draft principles. The first three principles were acceptable: a comprehensive settlement, compliance with UN Resolutions 242 and 338, and full normalization of relations among the parties. It was the remaining two principles which created the difficulty for the Israelis. They required withdrawal on all three fronts, with minor modifications, to the 1967 lines and agreement on the establishment of a Palestinian homeland.[60]

Although the president insisted that the United States would confine itself to the role of mediator and would not impose an American plan,[61] the fact was that Israeli acceptance of the five draft principles would amount to prior commitment to an American-defined settlement. Begin's response, as expected, was to wriggle out of any prior commitments while declaring Israel's readiness to enter into negotiations without preconditions to sign peace treaties with each of the Arab states. While heatedly rejecting any possibility of a "Palestinian state, entity, or homeland on the West Bank"[62] during the first meeting, Begin said that he would reserve comments on the border issue for his private conversation with the president.

After responding to the "draft principles," Begin now produced his own formula for convening, or rather scuttling, the Geneva conference, for it was a formula designed to be unacceptable either to the Arabs or to the United States. He declared Israel's readiness to attend the Geneva conference any time after October 10, 1977.[63] But only sovereign states could attend—no Arab delegation and no PLO. There could be no prior conditions as the price of Arab attendance. Negotiations would be bilateral between Israel and each of the Arab states without either American or Soviet participaton. The two superpowers' roles would be simply to open the conference and then to reconvene it when the peace treaties were ready for signing.[64]

Despite the cordiality of their discussions, it would be incorrect to say that any progress was made during the first session. That evening after dinner, however, the president and Prime Minister Begin held a private meeting which produced two major developments. Begin's first bombshell was to tell Carter "that he was making tentative plans for direct meetings with Sadat."[65] This, of course, was precisely that for which the administration had been striving. Begin's second eye-opener was the revelation that Israel was, in fact, prepared to negotiate new territorial arrangements on all three fronts as Washington demanded.[66]

Within the framework of a peace treaty with Egypt, Begin said, Israel was prepared "to make a significant withdrawal of her forces in Sinai." On the Syrian front, he continued, Israel would remain on the Golan Heights, "but within the framework of a peace treaty, we shall be prepared to withdraw our forces from their present lines and redeploy them along a line to be established as the permanent boundary." Finally, with regard to Jordan, he declared that "Israel will not transfer Judea, Samaria and the Gaza District to any foreign sovereign authority."[67]

While Begin's last statement on the West Bank and Gaza appeared to be inflexible it was in fact a change of position, particularly in Begin's own personal view. As Moshe Dayan notes, while "there was no surrender of Judea, Samaria and Gaza to a foreign sovereignty . . . neither was there the claim for Israeli sovereignty."[68] This did not mean that Israel would relinquish control, but it did mean that other solutions would be considered. In short, Begin was declaring that all subjects were open to discussion without preconditions, including areas which he had previously declared to be non-negotiable, such as West Bank/Gaza and even Jerusalem.

In return, the president agreed—at the prime minister's request—that he "would not speak publicly anymore about Israeli withdrawals to the 1967 borders with minor modifications, and that he would refrain from using the formula 'a Palestinian homeland.'"[69] Brzezinski claims that Begin "exacted" this pledge from Carter, but the evidence suggests that the president willingly agreed to withhold comment on the two issues while Begin arranged for the secret meetings with Sadat. Otherwise, Carter would hardly have said of Begin that he had been "pleased with our discussions."[70] Nor would the president have approved, immediately after Begin's departure, a substantial arms sale to Israel, which included the unprecedented provision of American foreign military sales credits for Israel to build its own tanks.[71]

Crisis in the Horn, Breakthrough in the Middle East

With Prime Minister Begin attempting to make contact with Sadat, Washington acted to put off the Geneva conference and to increase Arab, particularly Sadat's (and Saudi King Khalid's) receptivity to an Israeli bid. The latter involved a maneuver in the Horn which greatly alarmed the Arabs and encouraged Moscow to become even more deeply involved in Ethiopia. Since it was the very object of American strategy to promote an Israeli–Egyptian settlement as the first step toward a broader one, it was not surprising that "impediments" now arose between Washington and Jerusalem which served to put off the projected opening of the Geneva conference.

Thus Israel continued to build settlements on the West Bank, take a hard line against PLO involvement, and even begin to equivocate on terminology. For example, Begin, who was renowned for his semantic abilities, noted following his talks with Carter that while he had agreed that UN Resolution 242's call for withdrawal *applied* to all three fronts, that did not necessarily mean that withdrawal had to be *executed* on all three fronts.[72]

While this understandably exasperated the American side, Washington raised impediments of its own. Vance, for example, chose to interpret Israeli agreement to accept Palestinians in the Jordanian delegation to mean that PLO representatives could be in the delegation—even though the Israelis had made a clear distinction betweeen PLO and Palestinians. Washington also continued to press for Israeli adherence to the five draft principles even though Begin had clearly delineated between the acceptable and the unacceptable during his visit.

In the meantime, on August 1 Secretary Vance set off on another trip to the Middle East. His itinerary took him to Alexandria, Damascus, Amman, Taif, Jerusalem, and back to Alexandria just as a major decision regarding policy toward the Horn occurred. The United States move was to reverse policy toward Somalia and appeal to Moscow to join Washington in exercising restraint to resolve the conflict. The president and Vance in news conferences of July 28 and 29 set the new policy in motion, emphasizing restraint but as yet giving no hint of the reversal toward Somalia.

When asked whether recent decisions on arms transfers to Egypt, the Sudan, Somalia, Israel, and Iran contradicted his pledge to restrain arms sales, the president replied: "These proposals are compatible with my new arms sales policy, which is to reduce the level of arms sales in each succeeding year." He declared that he was "trying to get our own allies, France, England . . . and also the Soviet Union, to join us in this effort." Denying that this was "setting up a competition with the Soviet Union in Africa," he cited the Ethiopia–Somalia conflict as an example where the United

States was attempting "to deal . . . on a multilateral basis to reduce the competition between ourselves and the Soviet Union."[73]

The next day Secretary Vance continued in a similar vein. Asked whether there was intensified competition with the Soviet Union in the Horn of Africa, the secretary insisted firmly that there was no competition. Citing Somalia, he declared that "we have indicated that, in principle, we would be prepared to consider the furnishing of some military assistance for defensive arms—and I underscore that, for defensive arms." While also willing to provide "additional assistance" to the Sudan, this was because of "pressure from countries on their borders," but, he emphasized, "this is in no way to be construed as an attempt to enter into an arms race with the Soviet Union."[74]

A few days later, while Vance was in the Middle East, Washington executed the second part of its policy. On August 4, the Department of State notified Siad Barre that "although our agreement in principle to provide defensive arms to Somalia still stood, their [*sic*] involvement in the Ogaden prevented its implementation."[75] What had happened? Less than a week before, both the president and the secretary of state had publicly reaffirmed United States support for Somalia. The decision to reverse policy toward Mogadishu was devastating, cutting off supply for Siad Barre in midstream, just after he had committed most of his army to an invasion of the Ogaden.

To the consternation of Anwar Sadat, Gaafar Numayri of the Sudan, King Khalid of Saudi Arabia, and the shah of Iran, not to mention Siad Barre, the United States explained its reversal in terms of an unwillingness to support a violation of the principle of African territorial integrity. Was the Carter administration suddenly struck by a pang of conscience, belatedly realizing that it had agreed to support Somalia's invasion of Ethiopia? Had Washington's assurances not been "of such a nature that a prudent man would have mounted an offensive on the basis of them," as an administration spokesman later averred?[76] Did Washington ever really make "any firm commitments" as one author has questioned?[77] What was the explanation for the baffling reversal of policy?

The Carter administration's commitment to Somalia was made with a clear understanding of Siad Barre's purpose. There were too many public and private assurances for there to be any doubt.[78] Siad Barre's request for weapons was specifically to enable Somalia to move decisively into the Ogaden. Furthermore, although publicly ambiguous at the time, the United States commitment was not primarily to provide American weapons. In his news conference Vance had left the impression that the United States would consider the "furnishing of some military assistance for defensive arms,"[79] which could, of course, include American weapons. But in his memoir Vance cites the actual commitment, which was to "help other countries to meet Somalia's needs for defensive equipment."[80] Given the ongoing conflict with Ethiopia, the qualification about "defensive equipment" was meaningless to Somalia and an escape clause offering plausible deniability for the United States.

In other words, the operational phrase was to "help other countries . . . meet Somalia's needs." It was this which the Carter administration, in conjunction with Britain and France, had committed itself to do. What other countries? Given the fact that Somalia possessed an army which had been well armed and trained by the Soviet Union for the previous eight years, what Washington had committed itself to do was to help Somalia obtain Soviet equipment from third parties. The obvious third parties were Egypt, the Sudan, and even Iran, with Saudi Arabia as financier. But as long as the United States declined to resupply them with American arms, they were reluctant to part with the Soviet equipment they had, although some was transferred by Egypt.[81]

With Washington's cutoff in effect, at the end of August Siad flew to Moscow in a last-ditch attempt to restore Soviet military support, to no avail. Brezhnev would not receive him, and Moscow, too, terminated its arms supply to Somalia.[82] Washington's action placed Siad Barre in a quandary. His forces were already in control of substantial portions of the Ogaden. Over a hundred towns reportedly were flying the flag of the WSLF.[83] If Siad pulled back he would have nothing to show for his effort and might suffer a political crisis at home. If he pressed forward it would only be a matter of time before his forces exhausted their ammunition and supplies and he would be defeated on the battlefield—a fact which all involved understood.

Siad Barre's fateful choice was to press the offensive forward (see pp. 166ff), but it was the United States decision in early August to abrogate its commitment that formed the backdrop to Secretary Vance's Middle East trip. At each stop the secretary discussed Begin's procedural ideas for convening Geneva, the five draft principles, and his idea of a trusteeship for West Bank/Gaza. As expected, none of the Arabs thought much of Begin's proposals or the idea of a trusteeship, although all of the Arabs (but not the Israelis) believed there was merit in the concept of a transitional regime. Indeed, the origin of the Camp David framework of a transitional regime for West Bank/Gaza seems to have originated at this time.

An underlying purpose of Vance's trip was to assess Sadat's receptivity to an Israeli bid. Perhaps to the secretary's surprise, little pressure was needed. Sadat was more than ready, indeed impatient, to move forward. One can only assume that part of the reason for the Egyptian leader's eagerness to begin negotiations was the growing fear of a Somali collapse as a result of the just-announced United States decision to cut off support. Sadat did not relish the prospect of seeing a Soviet-dominated Horn with substantial forces of his own tied down on an unsecured front facing Israel.

Whatever the reason, the thrust of Anwar Sadat's comments to Secretary Vance was to urge strongly that Geneva be delayed until everything was prepared and that Washington sponsor "discreet" negotiations between Egypt and Israel along the lines of Kissinger's first disengagement agreement.[84] Sadat minimized the roles of Syria and Jordan, said that the PLO need not take part at all, suggested that in effect Egypt could negotiate for the Palestinians, and reassured Vance that once Egypt signed a treaty with Israel the others would follow.

The Egyptian leader told Secretary Vance that he was now ready to meet Begin.[85] Then, urging the secretary "not to tell anyone but the president," Sadat handed him the text of a draft peace treaty with Israel, which, he said, "Egypt would be prepared to sign."[86] Pursuing the strategy he had advocated from the start, Sadat wanted Vance to elicit draft treaties from Israel and the other Arab participants and then shape them into an acceptable compromise. In short, the basis for a breakthrough was at hand. Sadat was determined to move forward with or without his fellow Arabs, whose choice it would be to participate or not.

As it turned out, Vance's visits to Syria, Jordan, and Saudi Arabia led to nothing. Vance's request for draft treaties was met with little enthusiasm, and the PLO declined yet another offer to adhere to Resolution 242. In effect, the Arabs were determined to sit firmly on the sidelines to watch and criticize the unfolding drama of Egyptian–

Israeli rapprochement. And unfold it did. Although Vance's visit with Begin was publicly marred by the Israeli leader's sharp criticism of Washington's professed intention to deal with the PLO, the news of Sadat's readiness to deal directly and secretly with Israel was privately considered a very auspicious development.[87] Vance then returned briefly to Alexandria to reassure Sadat that Begin was indeed "sincere" about peace. In retrospect, there can be little doubt that Vance's "shuttle" between Alexandria and Jerusalem opened the door for the secret exchanges that followed.[88]

The Israeli government wasted no time, sending Foreign Minister Moshe Dayan to London to meet secretly with King Hussein of Jordan on August 22.[89] The Israelis believed that the chances for a peace settlement with Egypt were quite good; the trip to London was designed to explore the same prospect with King Hussein. Indeed, even though highly unlikely, a peace agreement with Jordan would open the door to the best of all possible outcomes from Israel's point of view, so it was worth a try. Indeed, it would lift any responsibility from Egypt for the Palestinian issue. Thus, Dayan raised the prospect of reaching a peace treaty with Jordan based on the partition of the West Bank, but King Hussein refused. Declining any involvement at all on behalf of the Palestinians, the king's position was that the only solution was full Israeli withdrawal to the 1967 lines.

With no prospect for negotiation with Jordan, the only remaining alternative was for Israel to deal directly with Egypt. Thus, a few days after Dayan's return from London, Prime Minister Begin made a trip to Bucharest, Romania. His purpose was to initiate secret contacts with President Sadat through Nicolae Ceausescu.[90] Ceausescu sent Begin's message to Sadat by an unknown means. Sadat, however, responded through yet another intermediary, King Hassan of Morocco. It was King Hassan who invited Dayan for a visit, which occurred on September 4, in Fez, Morocco.

Arriving secretly and in disguise, Dayan expressed Israel's desire for a meeting "at the highest level" of the Egyptian leadership. Dayan explained the complex situation in which the Israeli government found itself. A comprehensive settlement was impossibly complicated and Egypt was unwilling openly to reach a separate peace. Dayan's scheme for breaking this vicious circle was a series of steps, the first of which would be a secret agreement with Egypt. As Dayan described it,

> The form of this first step would be a kind of gentleman's agreement, accompanied by an exchange of letters with the Americans. These letters, addressed to the President of the United States, would commit the parties to fulfill the agreement between them.[91]

Then, if this process could be repeated with other Arab states "gradually," over time they could "meet the other problems one by one until we reached open, comprehensive peace treaties with all." The king, intrigued by the possibilities, promised a reply from Cairo within five days.

A reply came on the ninth. Sadat would be willing to meet personally with Begin or his trusted emissary as soon as possible. The Israelis opted for a Begin–Sadat meeting, but Sadat had second thoughts, preferring a secret meeting "at a lower level," which was agreed.[92] Once again Dayan, while on his way to Washington for talks with the Carter administration, slipped off for a secret meeting in Morocco, this time in Rabat, on September 16, with Sadat's secret emissary, Hassan Tuhami.

The two men probed each other's positions over a marathon, four-hour "working dinner," which lasted until two o'clock on the morning of the seventeenth. Although Tuhami stressed that their meeting must be held in the highest secrecy ("not even the Americans were to be told") the upshot of their talks specifically involved the United States. Tuhami proposed that "we each draw up peace documents, show them to the United States, study them carefully, meet again and discuss them."[93] Dayan agreed. They would exchange peace documents, which would be "shown to the United States," then meet again within two weeks.[94]

Dayan returned immediately to Jerusalem, meeting early that morning with Begin. The prime minister agreed to exchange "proposals for a peace treaty for mutual study, . . . notify the Americans," and that Dayan should "meet Tuhami in a fortnight."[95] There would be no rest for the Israeli foreign minister; he departed later that same day for Washington. On September 19, in discussions with Secretary Vance, Dayan informed the secretary of the secret meeting with Tuhami and of the decision to exchange draft peace treaties.[96] This would complete the circle; each country had a draft of the other's treaty and the United States had both. But if Dayan thought the president would be pleased, he was in for a rude awakening.

Closing Off the Geneva Track and Going Public

Now that the secret exchanges between Egypt and Israel had begun, Washington sought to do two things—bring them into the public light and dispense with the Geneva format. The two steps were interrelated. Thus, in the meeting with Dayan and one a few days later with Egyptian Foreign Minister Ismail Fahmy, Carter took the same tack as he had with Rabin and Sadat in the spring. On the one hand the president took a tough stand with Dayan, while on the other, in talks with Fahmi, he portrayed the United States and himself as practically helpless. The idea, of course, was to prod Israel into making an acceptable proposal and to persuade Egypt not only to be receptive, but to move independently.

In his meeting with President Carter, Dayan said that he was "made to feel like the accused in a court of law facing the prosecuting attorney" as the president and "even more so" Vice-President Mondale "launched charge after charge against Israel."[97] The focus of criticism was the recent Israeli military operations in Lebanon, the continuing construction of settlements in the occupied territories, and the Palestinian issue. The president declared, "You are more stubborn than the Arabs, and you put obstacles on the path to peace." Indeed, the president "had doubts about Israel's desire for peace."[98]

Without confirming his actions with Begin, Dayan bent enough on each of these issues—operations in Lebanon would be curtailed, settlements would not inhibit negotiations, and Geneva could open with a unified Arab delegation—for the president to say that their meeting had been "surprisingly productive," but Dayan left resentful of the way he had been treated, and he aired his views to the press.[99] Despite efforts of the president's staff to persuade Dayan to limit his personal criticism of the president, the foreign minister refused, declining to be mollified.[100]

Two days later, September 21, the president met with Egyptian Foreign Minister Fahmy. In an abrupt reversal of form Carter displayed extraordinary flaccidity and weakness during his conversations with Fahmy. During his private meeting with him, Carter said, regarding his ability to exert pressure on Israel, "I want you to know that I simply cannot do it because it would be a personal political suicide for me."[101] On relations with Moscow, he said, "I want you to understand that I can neither provoke the Soviet Union nor bear [*sic*] pressure on them. . . . I simply cannot bear pressure on Moscow because this would be a second political suicide for me."

If Fahmy was "dismayed to find President Carter so hesitant" in their private meeting, it was nothing compared to his performance in the presence of the entire Egyptian delegation. The president "shocked" them by his "candid confession of U.S. impotence."[102]

> It is important that you do not forget that my influence on Israel is proportionally related to the scope of support which I get from American public opinion, Congress and the Jewish circles in this country. . . . In the absence of such a triangular support my ability to influence Israel is minimal.[103]

Shocking the Egyptians still further, Carter said that since the Soviets were cochairmen at Geneva "we should get their approval" on the agreements and understandings thus far reached between the Arabs and Israelis.[104]

After the meetings, Fahmy drew the conclusions the United States side had hoped he would draw. Conveying his impressions to Sadat, Fahmy urged that he reevaluate America's role in the peace process. It was his view that "after Carter had personally admitted his limitations, President Sadat should never have continued to depend entirely on the United States as his major partner."[105] There was a sense that Carter was preaching to the choir in attempting to convince Fahmy that Egypt should draw away from the United States. That was his preference. It did, however, have some impact on Sadat.

In discussions with Dayan a week later, on September 26 and 29, Secretary Vance attempted to give the Israelis still another shove in the direction of peace talks with Egypt. The secretary hammered on the theme that "Egypt was the exception among the Arab states. Her representatives had said they were opposed to a united Arab delegation, and were prepared to start negotiations . . . even before the Geneva Conference. . . . The Egyptians were sincerely anxious to make peace with [Israel]."[106] But Washington's pressure was backfiring. Dayan was becoming extremely irritated. He said of American leaders: "What annoyed me was their show of innocence, and their repeated excuse that they had wrongly interpreted what we had said, and we had misunderstood their intentions."[107]

At this point, Washington played its last card in attempting to push the Israelis into negotiations. It was also the step which led to the breakdown of the Geneva track. Ironically, it involved bringing the Soviet Union into the negotiating process. This was the United States–Soviet joint statement on the Middle East issued on October 1.[108] The statement itself was bland enough, calling for the start of Geneva before the end of the year. It was the fact that Washington solicited Soviet involvement and associated itself with Moscow's position on the terms of a peace conference that was anathema to Israel's interests.

Moscow's long-held position was that full normalization of relations among the states of the Middle East could occur only after Israel's withdrawal to the May 1967 lines. The outcome of negotiations must see the establishment of a Palestinian state. There must be a united Arab delegation in the negotiations, which should take place along functional and not territorial lines. Upon being shown a preliminary draft of the joint statement by Vance, Dayan asked the secretary why Washington felt a statement was needed. Vance's reply—"to reach a coordinated policy on the Middle East with the Russians"—was the last straw for the Israeli government.[109] No conference based on a coordination of views with Moscow could possibly result, from Israel's view, in a fair outcome.

Amid the resultant uproar both in Israel and the United States over the United States–Soviet joint statement, the Carter administration acted to close off the Geneva track and give the final push to Israel and Egypt toward direct negotiations. The American leadership accomplished this delicate task in New York meetings with Israeli Foreign Minister Dayan and Egyptian Foreign Minister Fahmy on October 4 and 5. The meeting with Dayan was designed to show that the United States and Israel were once again cooperating, while the meeting with Fahmy was more subtly orchestrated to scuttle Geneva.

Dayan came prepared for a confrontation with Washington over the United States–Soviet statement. That the Israeli leadership believed it was in a serious crisis was evident in Dayan's threat to blackmail the president by making public all previous secret agreements.[110] He was surprised to find that Carter wished no confrontation and was instead extraordinarily conciliatory, declaring that he wanted the "world to see that the United States and Israel were working together."[111] Indeed, the upshot of a long and tendentious meeting was issuance of a joint communiqué which released Israel from adherence to the United States–Soviet statement as a condition of going to Geneva, agreement on a confidential "working paper" which ostensibly cleared away all Israeli objections for attendance, and an agreed "minute" regarding a procedure by which Israel could prohibit objectionable Palestinians from attending.[112]

There can be little doubt that domestic considerations played some part in Carter's decision to avoid a showdown with Israel, but the main objective was to push Israel into direct negotiations with Egypt, which clearing the way to Geneva would certainly do. Israel, for the reasons already cited, would not negotiate in Geneva under *any* circumstances. The meeting also had a dramatic impact on the Arabs, who interpreted it as Washington's capitulation to Israeli pressure and a portent of United States–Israeli collusion to their detriment.[113] And Washington encouraged this impression by circulating the presumably confidential "working paper" to Arab capitals for comment.

The next day, October 5, President Carter stunned Egyptian Foreign Minister Fahmy with the request that he agree to meet secretly with Dayan at Camp David.[114] Clearly, a meeting between Fahmy and Dayan, no matter how secret, would leak; and once it became public it would alienate the other Arabs, who would conclude that Egypt and Israel were signing a separate peace. That would be the end of the Geneva track. Moreover, a meeting would discredit Fahmy, who was in sharp disagreement with Sadat over a separate peace with Israel.

During their meeting, the president remarked to Fahmy, "It would be my dream if I could arrange a meeting between you and Dayan. This would represent the climax of my career."[115] Fahmy, "completely taken by surprise," concluded that the Israelis had put Carter up to it, for it was obvious to him that it "would have destroyed the American effort to reconvene the Geneva Conference because of the extreme negative Arab reaction to a private meeting between me and Dayan."[116]

Uncertain how to respond and noticing that the "other members of the American delegation . . . appeared as bewildered as I was by their President's brainchild," Fahmy declared, "Mr. President, I am ready . . . I have no problem." Now it was the president who appeared to be taken aback. Unable to "hide his excitement," he "grinned, looked at his colleagues and asked in disbelief, 'Are you serious? This would really be fantastic.'" Proposing a secret meeting at Camp David, he asked, "Do you think we could do this next weekend?" At this point, Fahmy deflated the president's hopes with the reply: "When I come to Camp David, Mr. President, I shall bring with me Yasser Arafat." At this, Carter got "really upset and screamed, 'Oh my God, it's impossible.'"[117]

That the effort to lure Fahmy into a "secret meeting" with Dayan was deliberate policy and not a thoughtless, spur-of-the-moment suggestion is clear from the fact that a second attempt was made after the initial failure. Two days later, attending a luncheon in his honor given by the board of directors of NBC, Fahmy was approached by Henry Kissinger. Offering to become involved, the former secretary of state declared that "he was sure . . . that he could convince Dayan to agree to a third disengagement along the El Arish–Ras Muhammed line without any political concessions from the Egyptian side." Although Fahmy was tempted by this proposal, he demurred, whereupon Kissinger then offered "to arrange a top secret meeting between Dayan and myself during the weekend at the Rockefeller estate outside New York City."[118]

It was Fahmy's view that this was an "Israeli trap," to which President Carter was not consciously a party. But whatever the origin of the Fahmy–Dayan secret meeting idea, it had the effect of persuading Sadat at last to "search for alternatives to heavy reliance on the United States to produce the breakthrough he was seeking."[119] Sadat had initially seen the United States–Soviet statement as a "master stroke" putting pressure on Syria, but "he was then shaken by the manner in which the United States retreated" in the face of Israeli pressure.[120]

By the end of October, in other words, it would be fair to conclude that Sadat believed a Washington-sponsored Geneva conference would not convene and that he was prepared to move independently. At this point, the president acted to confirm the Egyptian leader's conclusions in an exchange of letters. Sadat had responded on October 19 to the United States–Israeli "working paper" by saying that he preferred an earlier version. But the president now moved to cut off further negotiation with two notes, October 21 and 28. The first was a handwritten missive beseeching the Egyptian leader for the public support Sadat had earlier promised the president he would give when the "crucial moment" arrived.[121] The second stated more firmly that the preliminaries were over. Additional agreements were neither possible nor necessary. "Remaining problems," President Carter said, "could be worked out at Geneva."[122]

The October 28 message was timed to arrive as Sadat and Fahmy set off on state visits to Romania, Iran, and Saudi Arabia. In Romania, Ceausescu told Sadat that he had invited him after Begin's earlier visit to Bucharest and that he wished to mediate between Egypt and Israel.[123] Indeed, Ceausescu may have said more. It may have been the Romanian leader who suggested to Sadat a trip to Jerusalem, although the evidence is only circumstantial. According to Fahmy, Sadat's first mention of the Jerusalem trip was the evening immediately after the meeting with Ceausescu "in the guest house in Sinaia" outside Bucharest, when Sadat "suddenly announced the completely new idea of going to Jerusalem."[124]

The correspondence with Carter had predisposed Sadat to be receptive to a bold maneuver, which a trip to Jerusalem would be. Fahmy says that Sadat's later claim of credit for the idea, which ostensibly occurred to him at the end of the trip while he was aloft en route from Saudi Arabia to Egypt, was "simply not true" and "just a diversion."[125] The fact is that Sadat and Fahmy argued about the wisdom of such a trip that evening in Sinaia, and the foreign minister opposed it as a "publicity stunt," proposing instead an international summit in East Jerusalem as a prelude to Geneva.[126]

Before he had arrived in Riyadh on October 31, Sadat cabled Carter promising an unspecified "bold step," but the proposal that arrived in Washington three days later was Fahmy's East Jerusalem summit idea. While Vance described this proposal as "far-fetched" and Brzezinski saw it as "somewhat droll," its significance was that it revealed a deep cleavage between Sadat and his foreign minister, which threatened to stymie further progress.[127] President Carter's November 5 reply discouraging the proposal for an East Jerusalem summit effectively undercut Fahmy and opened the door to Sadat's preferred option of the bold move to Jerusalem.[128]

It was during a speech to the Egyptian national assembly on November 9 that Sadat, departing from the prepared text, declared that he would "go anywhere in the world, even to Jerusalem," for peace.[129] Sadat's electrifying offer stunned observers around the world. Washington, meanwhile, acted quickly to facilitate the exchange of correspondence between Cairo and Jerusalem, resulting in the extension of Begin's invitation to Sadat to speak before the Israeli Knesset on November 20. The Egyptian–Israeli breakthrough was at last publicly at hand, making the Geneva track irrelevant.

Policy Failure in the Middle East

President Carter and his advisers believed that they had finally cleared the way for negotiation of an Egyptian–Israeli peace treaty and a framework for solution of the Palestinian problem. But after a brief, promising start they realized that the Begin leadership had maneuvered Washington and Cairo into a corner, from which the only way out seemed to be Israel's preferred outcome of a separate peace with Egypt and nothing more. Simultaneously, an unexpectedly ominous Soviet decision with regard to events in Africa prompted the Carter administration to abruptly shift gears, adopting a policy of delay in hopes that the growing Soviet threat combined with continued American pressure would persuade the Israeli leadership to accept a broader solution.

Sadat had assumed, or had been led to assume, that his trip to Jerusalem would be reciprocated with an equally magnanimous gesture by Begin. Washington, too, appeared to believe that the two leaders would now reach a mutually acceptable accommodation.[130] What Cairo and Washington expected was a general statement of principles from Begin regarding withdrawal and Palestinian self-determination. This would justify Egypt's entry into a separate agreement and provide a basis for future negotiation by the other Arab states with Israel. It would also reduce if not eliminate the need for any specific resolution of the Palestinian issue. In short, the more said on withdrawal, the less needed to be said about the Palestinian issue.

During Secretary Vance's trip to the Middle East, December 10 through 14, it became clear that Begin had in mind a different approach. "Begin understood that it was up to him to respond to Sadat's initiative, but despite a personal plea from President Carter . . . he was unwilling to make a clear statement on withdrawal."[131] The Israeli prime minister explained to Vance that his response to Sadat would be an offer on withdrawal from the Sinai and a plan for Palestinian "home rule." But before advancing it, he wanted to go to Washington to discuss it with President Carter.[132]

The Carter administration decided to take whatever proposal Begin made for West Bank/Gaza and "turn it into an interim arrangement," which would also attenuate the linkage between the Egyptian–Israeli treaty negotiations and the Palestinian question.[133] During his visit to Washington, December 16 and 17, Begin offered two proposals. The first called for establishment of full diplomatic relations with Egypt in return for Israeli withdrawal from Sinai. The withdrawal would take place in two stages, but for three to five years after normalization Israel would maintain "some military positions" along the El Arish–Ras Muhammud line in the Sinai.[134]

Begin's second proposal was a self-rule plan for the West Bank/Gaza. According to it an elected administrative council would "deal with the problems of daily life" for the Palestinian inhabitants, but not for Israeli settlers. Israel would maintain military camps in the area, and a military governor would be responsible for public order and security.[135] Israel would withhold any claim of sovereignty over the area for five years, after which time this arrangement would be reviewed, leading possibly to permanent local autonomy.

From the United States point of view the principal deficiencies in the plan were Israel's refusal to withdraw its forces or even commit to withdrawal in principle; the absence of any role for other Arabs, particularly Jordan; and the absence of any procedure whereby the issue of sovereignty would ultimately be resolved. The plan's strengths included the fact of an autonomy proposal itself indicating Israeli recognition of a Palestinian problem, concurrence that Palestinian Arabs should participate in governing themselves, and acceptance of the 1967 borders as the extent of Israeli sovereignty—even though the "security border" was the Jordan River.

After the meeting, Carter telephoned Sadat, who thought Begin's proposals "seemed promising."[136] The Egyptian leader's main objection to the Sinai proposal was that neither Israeli troops nor even settlers could remain on Egyptian territory after diplomatic relations were established. On self-rule, Sadat liked the idea of leaving sovereignty open but felt that after five years the Palestinians "should be able to exercise their right of self-determination." He did not agree with the idea of Israeli responsibility for security. On the basis of Sadat's not unfavorable reaction, Carter met Begin again on the morning of the seventeenth and said that his proposals were "constructive" and that Sadat would probably react well to the Sinai proposal. Finally, responding to Begin's repeated entreaties for an expression of support, Carter agreed that the proposals "could be a fair basis for negotiations."[137]

Following his meeting with President Carter, Begin met with Sadat on Christmas Day at Ismailiya, located on the Suez Canal. The formal United States record of their meeting is sparse and what transpired unclear. Brzezinski, for example, omits all mention of the meeting; Quandt declares that the talks were a "failure."[138] Only Vance makes substantive comment, noting that Begin's Sinai proposal was "well received" but that the self-rule plan "received little attention," as the two leaders "spent much of their time discussing a profound disagreement stemming from Sadat's demand for an Israeli declaration on withdrawal and Palestinian self-determination."[139]

But the Ismailiya meeting appears to have been far more significant than acknowledged by the American side. Reconstructing from fragmentary data, what appears to have happened is the following: Sadat believed, and Washington encouraged him to believe,[140] that he and Begin would "deal with general principles at Ismailiya," leaving their respective foreign and defense ministers to negotiate details afterward.[141] Consistent with this agreement, the first order of business conducted was the establishment of political and military committees, which were scheduled to begin meeting in mid-January.

Then Prime Minister Begin dropped his bombshell, presenting a plan which surprised Sadat by its specificity. Sadat declared that it was "the first time since the establishment of Israel that the Jews presented something specific. . . . They went further than one could imagine."[142] Sources differ over what occurred next. Vance says that Sadat "received with satisfaction" Begin's Sinai plan but rejected "any continuing Israeli presence . . . after withdrawal."[143] Columnists Elmo Zumwalt and Worth Bagley, providing an informed account of the negotiations from the Israeli side on the eve of the Camp David talks, imply that Sadat accepted "a continuing Israeli presence in the border area."[144] Vance declares that "Begin's West Bank–Gaza self-rule plan received little attention,"[145] while Zumwalt-Bagley assert that "Sadat accepted the [self-rule] plan in principle and made the statement: 'This is definitely a plan the Egyptians can accept.'"[146]

There can be little doubt that to obtain Sadat's acceptance of his plans Begin invoked Carter's earlier statement, made in Washington, that his proposals "could be a fair basis for negotiations."[147] Perhaps unwittingly, President Carter may have added to the pressure on Sadat. As the two leaders were beginning their discussions, the president telephoned them from Plains, Georgia, to say that the United States "did not have strong views on what the parties should accept. Anything they could agree on would be all right with him."[148]

Whatever promise the Ismailiya talks may have held dissipated when Begin refused, as Vance notes, to agree to the general principles of "withdrawal and Palestinian self-determination."[149] As a result, Sadat postponed a final decision on both plans. In his formal statement afterwards, Sadat declared that "we have made progress" on the question of Israeli withdrawal from Sinai, "but not on the Palestinian question."[150] The expectations which the administration had built up in the days before Ismailiya had been so tremendous that Carter and his aides were quite concerned that Sadat, if only to save face, would accept Begin's offer of an Egyptian–Israeli peace treaty and the Basutoland figleaf as a substitute for Palestinian self-determination.[151]

While this would result in the recovery of Egyptian territory, it would not only have a dramatic impact upon Sadat's political position, but it would severely damage the United States position regionwide. Acceptance of Begin's limited self-rule plan would be seen by the other Arabs as capitulation, producing a long-term estrangement of Saudi Arabia and Jordan. Sadat was already denouncing his Arab critics as "dwarfs," "pygmies," and "ignoramuses" for attacking his efforts as "peace at any price."[152] For the United States, the estrangement of Saudi Arabia in particular would mean a repolarization of the Middle East between Egypt–Israel on the one side and the radical Arabs on the other—with the moderate Arabs inevitably forced over to the radical side. Plainly, the Carter administration's year-long effort to produce a viable settlement in the Middle East had crumbled before the Israeli leadership's intransigence over the Palestinian issue. Worse, what had apparently produced Sadat's compliant attitude was a major United States failure on another front—in the Horn.

Soviet Backlash in the Horn of Africa

Following the aid cutoff to Somalia in early August, Carter administration officials pleaded with Moscow to join in a cooperative approach to settlement of the conflict. The latest instance of Washington's approach was an appeal by Anthony Lake, director of policy planning in the Department of State. In a speech on November 7 entitled "Africa in a Global Perspective,"[153] Lake hoped that "the Soviet Union will recognize that it, as well as the United States, would benefit from cooperating fully with African efforts to mediate conflicts. If both superpowers would exercise restraint in supplying arms and would use their influence for peace, both would enhance their relations in Africa."

Lake cited the March invasion of Shaba by Angola as an instance of restraint by Washington. "The fact that Shaba did not evolve into a major crisis is evidence that our policy was mature and correct." But, he went on,

> We face a still more complicated problem in the Horn. In early July, before the conflict in the Ogaden escalated so severely, we agreed in principle that we would consider favorably requests by Somalia for arms that could be used in defense of Somalia's internationally recognized borders. The Ogaden fighting has raised both political and legal barriers to our doing so. As the conflict continues, it is clear that a policy of restraint is the wisest course.[154]

Lake proposed that Moscow and Washington refuse to supply arms to either side, support diplomatic initiatives by the Africans themselves, and be willing to provide economic and humanitarian assistance to both sides. Lake's plea for restraint from Moscow in the Horn could not be faulted in the abstract, but it obscured the dilemma which the United States had created for Soviet policymakers. Indeed, it was already too late for "restraint," for the problem which Moscow faced was how to avert defeat for its ally in Addis Ababa.

Siad Barre had plunged ahead in his attempt to conquer the Ogaden despite Washington's aid cutoff, and through mid-September his forces had been highly successful. The fall of Jijiga, a major tank and radar base, left only two major fortified towns—Harar and Diredawa—to conquer. Throughout October and November, Somali forces concentrated their assault on Harar, the walled medieval capital of ancient Ethiopia, as the Mengistu regime mobilized its people for the decisive struggle.[155] In short, the outcome of the war would turn on the battle for Harar.

Washington's plea for Soviet restraint, if heeded, would simply have meant victory for Somalia, the probable fall of Mengistu, and victory by the Eritrean separatists as well, whose struggle continued. In other words, Soviet "restraint" would in all likelihood have led to the elimination of Soviet influence in the Horn of Africa. On the other hand, a Soviet effort to support Mengistu would place Moscow in the position of repudiating Washington's offer of cooperation and being labeled the aggressor. Indeed, it would free Washington from any commitment to cooperate with Moscow on other fronts, most notably the October 1 United States–Soviet joint statement regarding the Geneva negotiations.

The evidence suggests that by mid-November, when Siad Barre denounced the Somalia–Soviet friendship treaty of 1974, expelled all Soviet advisers, and broke diplomatic relations with Cuba, the Soviet leadership had already reached a major decision whose main thrust was to seize the geopolitical initiative. While Moscow responded to the issue of the Horn, the nature of its response transcended the immediate question of Ethiopia, posing a major threat to United States interests throughout what can be termed the great triangle—the Middle East–Southwest Asia–African Horn region. Indeed, in retrospect, it seems clear that the Soviet response in the Horn was the beginning of a sustained effort to alter the geopolitical balance of power in and beyond the region to Moscow's advantage.

As Somali forces breached the walls of Harar and began fighting the city's defenders in the streets, Moscow mounted a massive emergency airlift to avert Ethiopian defeat.[156] Somali commando units had penetrated the defenses of the ancient fortress on November 23, and early reports suggested a quick victory.[157] But literally at the moment that Somali spokesmen were declaring that WSLF held "absolute control of Harar and the surrounding area" and that their forces "have never had it so good" the Soviet airlift, in the third week of November, was already beginning to change the balance.[158]

The Soviet effort to strengthen Ethiopia's military forces had been under way for several months—since March—but it was primarily a sealift. Indeed, 75 percent of the more than $1 billion in equipment ultimately delivered arrived by boat, but what now occurred, from late November through mid-December, was in the nature of an emergency airlift to prevent defeat in the Ogaden. Launching communications satellites to facilitate coordination and ignoring protests of several countries for violating international overflight rules, Soviet air transports (mainly An-22 and Ilyushin-76 types) made 225 flights to Ethiopia with refueling stops in Tripoli and Aden.[159]

Decisive for the battle at Harar, in addition to ammunition, were battle tanks, armored personnel carriers, anti-tank missiles, MI-6 helicopters—and the trained personnel to use them. During these weeks Moscow and Havana "more than doubled their military personnel" to what was conservatively estimated to be over a thousand men.[160] Siad Barre, in a press conference on November 24, claimed that there were 20,000 Cubans in Ethiopia and criticized the Carter administration "for failing to disclose the facts of Cuban involvement in the Horn of Africa."[161] Siad's claim was only a few weeks premature. By January, the Cuban troop presence in Ethiopia would exceed 15,000 men.

The Soviet airlift, deployment of Cuban troops, and use of Soviet "advisers" stemmed the Somali threat to Harar, gradually turning the tide of the battle for the Ogaden. As the Soviet–Cuban buildup continued, the question became, where would the Ethiopian counteroffensive be directed? Would Mengistu be content to drive Somali forces out of the Ogaden and restore the status quo ante, or was there now a more ominous prospect? The dispatch to Ethiopia of General Vladimir I. Petrov, commander in chief of Soviet ground forces, along with General G. Barisov, the former chief of the Soviet military mission to Somalia, suggested a larger mission. Would Ethiopian forces under Soviet command and direction attempt to detach northern Somalia, recapturing the naval base at Berbera, from which Moscow had just been expelled?

This issue in particular was very much on the minds of American policymakers as Washington now moved to reasses.[162] Not only had Moscow turned the tables on Washington in the Horn, transforming imminent Ethiopian defeat into probable victory, but the Israelis, too, had skillfully maneuvered around Washington's position and had brought Sadat to the point of accepting an agreement which was against his better interest. Reassessment of American policy was clearly necessary in the light of the twin failures. Therefore, the president acted to avoid the separate peace-Palestinian figleaf outcome in the Middle East by personally persuading Sadat to suspend the negotiations and resume them later with American support. Presumably, the two nations working in concert could succeed in obtaining a broader solution which would serve the objectives of both Egypt and the United States.

While on his trip to Poland, Iran, India, Saudi Arabia, France, and Belgium, President Carter personally undertook the task of persuading Sadat to accept Washington's new plan. The trip also made clear Washington's concern over the reactions of the moderate Arabs. Carter met with both King Khalid of Saudi Arabia and King

Hussein of Jordan. Hussein adamantly refused to support the Egyptian–Israeli negotiations so long as the Israelis refused to accept the principles of full withdrawal and Palestinian self-determination.[163]

In Riyadh on January 3, King Khalid continued to insist that the Palestinians must have the right to an independent state and urged that Sadat "not be allowed to fail in his initiative."[164] The king and President Carter agreed that the key to success was Israeli acceptance of the principles of withdrawal and self-determination, which the president declared he "would do his utmost to get Begin to accept." Pleased with what Carter believed was the king's positive attitude, the president promised to proceed with the sale of F-15s to Saudi Arabia.

Armed with the categorical views of Kings Hussein and Khalid that the principles of withdrawal and self-determination were the essence of the negotiations, Carter stopped off at Aswan for an unscheduled hour-and-a-half meeting with Anwar Sadat on January 4.[165] There is no record of the meeting between the two men, but their actions immediately afterward suggest some of what transpired. At the end of the meeting President Carter made a public statement calling for a commitment to the estabishment of full peace between Egypt and Israel, and urging Israel's agreement in principle to full withdrawal and to Palestinian participation in the "determination of their own future."[166]

This brought to an end the president's earlier pledge to Prime Minister Begin not to speak publicly about the issues of Israeli withdrawal and a Palestinian homeland and signaled that the United States was changing policy. The next day Sadat, too, signaled that he had changed his mind. Speaking of the political talks scheduled to begin on January 14, the Egyptian president declared that they were "doomed in advance because of Begin's . . . intransigence."[167] Conveying a signal of their own, indicating that they understood the meaning of Aswan and objected to it, the Israelis immediately announced the construction of four new settlements in the Sinai.

American policy, after a grueling year-long effort, had failed to achieve its goals. The Israelis had not budged beyond their opening position of willingness to reach a separate peace with Egypt. At virtually the eleventh hour, the president had averted that outcome, and persuaded Sadat to give negotiations another chance, this time with the United States as a principal participant in the "peace process." Those negotiations would take place in a rapidly disintegrating political-military environment, much of it the result of a massive Soviet effort to alter to their advantage the greater Middle East–Southwest Asian–African Horn geopolitical balance. That an Egyptian–Israeli peace treaty was eventually signed in March of 1979 was testimony to the courage and tenacity of the Carter administration, but the price in terms of the region's overall stability was extremely high.

Notes

1. For an analysis of the agreements, see my *Nixon-Kissinger Years*, pp. 253–78.
2. Cyrus Vance, *Hard Choices*, p. 164.
3. Ibid., p. 166.
4. The Middle East was a top priority. PRM 3 was to be completed by January 31, 1977, barely a week into the new administration. The timetable implied that the new American leadership had already worked out its objectives, as indeed it had. Initial Middle East policy (as was true for initial policy regarding withdrawal from South Korea), was based on a Brookings study, *Toward Peace in the Middle East* (Washington, DC, 1975). Brzezinski, *Power and Principle*, pp. 85–86, who had participated in the study, gives a summary of its conclusions.
5. Yitzhak Rabin, *The Rabin Memoirs* (Boston: Little, Brown and Co., 1979), p. 290.
6. Vance, *Hard Choices*, pp. 168–69.
7. Ibid., pp. 168–71.
8. Ibid., p. 166.
9. Ibid., p. 164.
10. Brzezinski, *Power and Principle*, p. 87.
11. Ibid.
12 Ibid., p. 88.
13. Ibid., p. 89.
14. Bernard Gwertzman, "U.S. Cuts Foreign Aid in Rights Violations: South Korea Exempt," *New York Times*, February 25, 1977, p. 1.
15. For an analysis of the revolution, see Haggai Erlich, *Ethiopia and the Challenge of Independence* (Boulder, CO: Lynne Rienner Publishers, 1986), pp. 225–48.
16. The Dergue, contrary to Soviet urging, did not in fact form a one-party structure.
17. See Colin Legum, "Angola and the Horn of Africa," in Stephen S. Kaplan, ed., *Diplomacy of Power* (Washington, DC: Brookings Institution, 1981), p. 612.
18. The two main resistance groups were the Muslim-based Eritrean Liberation Front (ELF) and the quasi-Marxist Eritrean Popular Liberation Front (EPLF). Each commanded between 20,000 and 25,000 troops. A third group, which had splintered off from EPLF, was the Eritrean Liberation Front-Peoples Liberation Front (ELF-PLF), which commanded 5,000 to 6,000 men. See U.S. House of Representatives, Committee on International Relations, *War in the Horn of Africa: A Firsthand Report on the Challenges for United States Policy*, report of a factfinding mission to Egypt, Sudan, Ethiopia, Somalia and

Kenya, December 12 to 22, 1977 (Washington, DC: GPO, February 3,1978), p. 8. (Hereafter referred to as the Bonker–Tsongas report.)

19. Bruce D. Porter, *The USSR in Third World Conflicts: Soviet Arms and Diplomacy in Local Wars, 1945–1980* (London: Cambridge University Press, 1984), pp. 192–93, 207.
20. Vance, *Hard Choices*, p. 72. For a detailed account of the events in 1977, see Colin Legum and Bill Lee, *The Horn of Africa in Continuing Crisis*, (New York: Africana Publishing Company, 1979), pp. 18ff.
21. Porter, *USSR in Third World Conflicts*, p. 201. David B. Ottaway, "Soviet Weapons Begin Flowing to Ethiopians," *Washington Post*, April 16, 1977, p. 1, mentions only thirty tanks and forty armored personnel carriers—all from stocks in South Yemen—but adds that the tanks were the older-style T-34 medium tank, which was no match for the more than one hundred T-54 and T-55 tanks Moscow had sent to Somalia.
22. David Ottaway, "Fighting Up Sharply in Ethiopia," *Washington Post*, March 14, 1977, p. 20, and the Bonker–Tsongas report, pp. 12–13.
23. Although beyond the scope of this chapter, it seems to this author that the invasion of Zaire, which began March 8, should not be understood in isolation but in the context of the internal strife in Ethiopia.
24. Brzezinski, *Power and Principle*, p. 121.
25. William B. Quandt, *Camp David: Peacemaking and Politics* (Washington, DC: Brookings Institution, 1986), pp. 292–95.
26. Ibid.
27. Ibid.
28. Vance, *Hard Choices*, p. 173.
29. Ibid.
30. Brzezinski, *Power and Principle*, p. 91.
31. Quandt, *Camp David*, pp. 45–46.
32. Ibid., p. 46. Rabin, *Memoirs*, p. 297, says Carter used the phrase "sharp reaction" by the American people, which the Israeli leader described as "tough talk."
33. Brzezinski, *Power and Principle*, p. 91.
34. Quandt, *Camp David*, p. 46.
35. Vance, *Hard Choices*, p. 173; Brzezinski, *Power and Principle*, p. 90; see also Jimmy Carter, *Keeping Faith* (New York: Bantam, 1982), p. 280.
36. See Brzezinski, *Power and Principle*, pp. 96–98, for discussion of this issue and the administration's response.
37. Quandt, *Camp David*, p. 47.
38. Ibid.
39. Ibid., p. 51.
40. Ibid. Both Vance, *Hard Choices*, pp. 174–75, and Brzezinski, *Power and Principle*, p. 93, assert without reservations, or evidence, that Sadat

wished to go to Geneva. For them to do otherwise, of course, would make it difficult to explain why the United States persisted in attempting to convene the conference.

41. Quandt, *Camp David*, p. 52.
42. Ibid., p. 52.
43. Carter took the same tack with Jordan's King Hussein, pressing for an agreement before Geneva to keep the Soviets out. See Quandt, *Camp David*, pp. 55–56.
44. Ibid., p. 54.
45. See Brzezinski, *Power and Principle*, p. 94; Quandt, *Camp David*, p. 54; Vance, *Hard Choices*, p. 175, for accounts of the April 19 meeting.
46. Garthoff, *Detente and Confrontation*, pp. 630–53, provides a detailed discussion of the Horn events. See also Porter, *USSR in Third World Conflicts*, p. 195, and Michael T. Kaufman, "Castro in Ethiopia after Somalia Visit," *New York Times*, March 16, 1977, p. 11.
47. For a description of the Soviet diplomatic campaign, see David Ottoway, "Soviets Try to Keep Close Ties with Somalia, South Yemen," *Washington Post*, May 26, 1977, p. A28.
48. The government also closed down the Military Assistance Advisory Group, the USIA office, a naval medical research unit, and the consulate in Asmara. See Henry Trewhitt, "U.S. Pledges Orderly Withdrawal from 5 Installations in Ethiopia," *Baltimore Sun*, April 26, 1977, p. 4, and John Darnton, "Ethiopian Move Breaking Old Link with U.S.," *New York Times*, April 25, 1977, p. 3.
49. Legum, "Angola and the Horn of Africa," p. 619.
50. Vance, *Hard Choices*, p. 72.
51. Ibid., p. 73.
52. Ibid., and Garthoff, *Detente and Confrontation*, p. 634.
53. Neil Matheson, *The "Rules of the Game" of Superpower Military Intervention in the Third World, 1975–1980* (Washington, DC: University Press of America, 1982), p. 91.
54. Somali forces already held a strong position in the region prior to the invasion. See David Ottoway, "Somalia Said to Hold Most of Ethiopia's Ogaden Region," *Washington Post*, May 24, 1977, p. A15.
55. Brzezinski, *Power and Principle*, p. 96.
56. Bernard Gwertzman, "U.S. Calls on Israel to Quit Some Lands in All the Sectors," *New York Times*, June 28, 1977, p. A1.
57. Vance, *Hard Choices*, p. 180.
58. Vance, *Hard Choices*, pp. 179–80; Quandt, *Camp David*, p. 80.
59. Brzezinski, *Power and Principle*, p. 98.
60. See Quandt, *Camp David*, p. 80, for a clear description of the draft principles.
61. Vance, *Hard Choices*, p. 181.

62. Ibid., pp. 181–82.
63. Moshe Dayan, *Breakthrough, a Personal Account of the Egypt–Israel Peace Negotiations* (New York: Alfred A. Knopf, 1981), p. 19.
64. Vance, *Hard Choices*, p. 182.
65. Carter, *Keeping Faith*, p. 291.
66. Dayan, *Breakthrough*, pp. 19–20, and Quandt, *Camp David*, pp. 81–82.
67. Dayan, *Breakthrough*, p. 20. For Carter's notes of this discussion, see Quandt, *Camp David*, pp. 81–82.
68. Dayan, *Breakthrough*, p. 20.
69. Brzezinski, *Power and Principle*, p. 100.
70. Carter, *Keeping Faith*, p. 291. Brzezinski, *Power and Principle*, p. 100, states that Begin told Carter that "he plans to meet with some of the top Arab leaders," but Carter actually says Begin spoke only of plans for "direct meetings with Sadat." See Carter, *Keeping Faith*, p. 291. If Brzezinski is misleading, Quandt, *Camp David*, p. 78, makes excuses for the president and says that he "did not always listen" to what Begin said and wished to "avoid sharp controversy" and the "constant bickering" that attended sessions with the Israelis.
71. Quandt, *Camp David*, p. 83.
72. Vance, *Hard Choices*, pp. 185–86.
73. "Jimmy Carter News Conference, July 28," Department of State *Bulletin*, no. 1991, vol. 77, August 22, 1977, pp. 221–22.
74. "Secretary Vance's News Conference of July 29," ibid., p. 229.
75. Vance, *Hard Choices*, p. 73. On August 18, Washington also informed the Somalis that the United States would not permit the transfer of American-manufactured arms in the hands of third parties while Mogadishu was engaged in the Ogaden. This meant that the arrangement made earlier for the shah of Iran to airlift United States equipment to Somalia on a contingency basis was cancelled. See William Lewis and Michael Ledeen, *Debacle: The American Failure in Iran* (New York: Vintage Books, 1982), pp. 91–93.
76. Remark by Richard Moose, assistant secretary of state for African affairs, as quoted in Porter, *USSR in Third World Conflicts*, p. 208 n. 62.
77. Garthoff, *Detente and Confrontation*, p. 637.
78. Ibid., pp. 633–37.
79. "Secretary Vance's News Conference of July 29," p. 229.
80. Vance, *Hard Choices*, p. 73.
81. See the Bonker–Tsongas report, pp. 39–40.
82. Garthoff, *Detente and Confrontation*, p. 636.
83. Legum and Lee, *Horn of Africa*, p. 69.
84. Quandt, *Camp David*, pp. 88–90.
85. Carter, *Keeping Faith*, p. 296.
86. Quandt, *Camp David*, p. 90.

87. Ibid., p. 92, and Carter, *Keeping Faith*, p. 296.
88. Vance, *Hard Choices*, p. 190, notes simply that "we had reached a turning point in our strategy."
89. Dayan, *Breakthrough*, pp. 35–37.
90. Eitan Haber, Ze'ev Schiff, Ehod Ya'ari, *Year of the Dove* (New York: Bantam Books, 1979), pp. 3–4.
91. Dayan, *Breakthrough*, p. 41. Cf. Quandt, *Camp David*, p. 109, who says that Dayan proposed "informal understandings."
92. Dayan, *Breakthrough*, p. 42.
93. Ibid., p. 48. Cf. Quandt, *Camp David*, p. 110, who says that "Tuhamy said the Americans should not be informed, though once the parties reached agreement the Americans should be allowed to take the credit."
94. Dayan, *Breakthrough*, p. 50.
95. Ibid., p. 52. The meeting would not actually take place until December 2.
96. Vance disclosure to Quandt in interview on March 1, 1984, in Quandt, *Camp David*, p. 111.
97. Dayan, *Breakthrough*, p. 59.
98. Ibid. and p. 62.
99. Carter, *Keeping Faith*, p. 293, and Quandt, *Camp David*, p. 114.
100. Dayan, *Breakthrough*, p. 64.
101. Ismail Fahmy, *Negotiating for Peace in the Middle East* (Baltimore: Johns Hopkins Press, 1983), p. 196.
102. Ibid., p. 199.
103. Ibid., p. 198.
104. Ibid., p. 200.
105. Ibid., p. 197.
106. Dayan, *Breakthrough*, p. 65.
107. Ibid., p. 66.
108. The statement can be found in Quandt, *Camp David*, pp. 343–44.
109. Dayan, *Breakthrough*, p. 65.
110. Quandt, *Camp David*, p. 127, and Brzezinski, *Power and Principle*, p. 108.
111. Quandt, *Camp David*, p. 129.
112. See Dayan, *Breakthrough*, pp. 70–71; Quandt, *Camp David*, p. 130; and Vance, *Hard Choices*, pp. 193–94.
113. Brzezinski, *Power and Principle*, pp. 109–10, notes, "The impression was now created by these statements that we were prepared to collaborate more closely with the Israelis on matters involving Geneva, and this, in turn, generated increasing skepticism among the Arabs as to the likelihood of Geneva producing any constructive result."
114. Fahmy, *Negotiating for Peace*, pp. 236–39.

115. Ibid., pp. 236–37.
116. Ibid., p. 237.
117. Ibid., pp. 237–38.
118. Ibid., pp. 239–40.
119. Quandt, *Camp David*, p. 131.
120. Brzezinski, *Power and Principle*, p. 110.
121. See Quandt, *Camp David*, pp. 139–41, for a photocopy of the note. Brzezinski, *Power and Principle*, p. 110, says that "Sadat apparently read this [note] as an admission of the President's domestic weakness and thus as a plea for an Egyptian initiative to break the stalemate." Vance, *Hard Choices*, p. 194, claims that Carter had "asked" Sadat "how he thought the deadlock might be broken."
122. Quandt, *Camp David*, p. 143.
123. Fahmy, *Negotiating for Peace*, p. 253.
124. Ibid., p. 255.
125. Ibid. Sadat's account came in the context of a response to Dayan's inquiry; see *Breakthrough*, p. 87.
126. Fahmy, *Negotiating for Peace*, pp. 256–59.
127. Brzezinski, *Power and Principle*, p. 111, and Vance, *Hard Choices*, p. 194.
128. Quandt, *Camp David*, p. 145, claims that Sadat was "disappointed" by Carter's negative response, but this seems hardly likely since it was not his preference, but Fahmy's. Indeed, three pages later Quandt quotes Sadat as confirming that Carter's rejection of the East Jerusalem summit cleared the way for his trip to Jerusalem.
129. Fahmy, *Negotiating for Peace*, p. 265. The decision to go to Jerusalem precipitated the resignation of the foreign minister.
130. As late as December 30 Carter declared that "any agreement which can be reached between Israel and her Arab neighbors would be acceptable to us." *Public Papers of the Presidents: Jimmy Carter, 1977*, vol.2, p. 2206.
131. Vance, *Hard Choices*, p. 197.
132. Sadat had called for a pre-Geneva meeting in Cairo in mid-December. It was a failure. Only Egypt, Israel, and the United States sent representatives; Begin authorized his representative to only listen, not negotiate.
133. Brzezinski, *Power and Principle*, p. 115, vaguely describes it as a means of "breaking the logjam" of "conflicting Israeli and Palestinian aspirations."
134. Vance, *Hard Choices*, p. 198.
135. Ibid., pp. 198–99.
136. Quandt, *Camp David*, p. 156. See also Brzezinski, *Power and Principle*, pp. 115–20.

137. Quandt, *Camp David*, p. 157. Begin immediately went public with Carter's comment. See Bernard Gwertzman, "Begin Says Carter Views Israeli Plan As 'Fair' Approach," *New York Times*, December 19, 1977, p. 1.
138. Quandt, *Camp David*, p. 160.
139. Vance, *Hard Choices*, p. 200.
140. Henry Tanner, "Cairo Expects Israel to Relax Its Stand on Palestinian Issue," *New York Times*, December 23, 1977, p. 1.
141. Clayton Fritchey, "What Derailed the Mideast Talks Last January?" *Washington Post*, July 8, 1978, p. 13.
142. Ibid.
143. Vance, *Hard Choices*, p. 200.
144. Elmo Zumwalt and Worth Bagley, "U.S. Spoiled Secret Pact Reached by Begin, Sadat," *Washington Post*, August 20, 1978, p. 15.
145. Vance, *Hard Choices*, p. 200.
146. Zumwalt and Bagley, "U.S. Spoiled Secret Pact."
147. In fact, Carter, *Keeping Faith*, p. 300, charged that Begin significantly revised the plans he had shown the president in Washington.
148. "Plains, Georgia: Informal Exchange with Reporters Prior to Visiting Allie Smith, December 25, 1977," *Public Papers of U.S. Presidents: Jimmy Carter, 1977*, vol. 2, pp. 2172–74. See also Quandt, *Camp David*, p. 158.
149. Vance, *Hard Choices*, p. 200.
150. "Texts of Statements by Sadat and Begin and Their News Conference in Ismailia," *The New York Times*, December 27, 1977, p. 16.
151. See, for example, Thomas W. Lippman, "Despite Feeling of Letdown in Egypt, Sadat Sees Accord in 2 or 3 Months," *Washington Post*, December 28, 1977, p. 1.
152. Michael Parks, "Sadat Labels Peace Critics as 'Dwarfs,'" *Baltimore Sun*, December 9, 1977, p. 1.
153. Department of State *Bulletin*, no. 2007, vol. 77, December 12, 1977, pp. 842–46.
154. Ibid., p. 845.
155. Legum and Lee, *Horn of Africa*, p. 71.
156. Porter, *USSR in Third World Conflicts*, p. 201.
157. Legum and Lee, *Horn of Africa*, p. 72. See also "Combat Said to Be Heavy in Harar," *Baltimore Sun*, November 27, 1977, p. 2.
158. Porter, *USSR in Third World Conflicts*, p. 201, says the airlift began on November 26, but it probably began a few days earlier. See also "Somali Claim of Victory in Harar is Disputed," *Baltimore Sun*, November 29, 1977, p. 2.
159. Porter, *USSR in Third World Conflicts*, pp. 201–5 and "The Soviets

Exercise Their Airlift Capability," *Air Force Magazine*, March 1978, p. 27.

160. Dusko Doder and Jay Ross, "Soviets, Cuba Double Ethiopia Force," *Washington Post*, December 17, 1977, p. 1.
161. Bruce Loudon, "Soviet Plot Seen in Somalia Battle," *Boston Globe*, November 25, 1977, p. 10. Loudon noted unconfirmed reports that Ethiopian defenders at Harar were "reinforced with recently acquired Russian armor and Cuban advisers." Porter, *USSR in Third World Conflicts*, pp. 203–4, cites the deployment of a thousand-man Cuban expeditionary force to the Ogaden front but dates it in late December, by which time he estimates the total number of Cubans in Ethiopia to have been 2,000.
162. In their interview with Mengistu, Congressmen Bonker and Tsongas asked, "Do you intend to advance into Somalia?" Mengistu replied: "We have no objective of crossing once we have thrown the Somalis out—we do not intend to repeat the same mistake as the Somalis." Bonker–Tsongas report, p. 11.
163. Vance, *Hard Choices*, p. 201. Carter also met with the shah of Iran, whom he unfortunately described as an island of stability in a turbulent corner of the world.
164. Quandt, *Camp David*, p. 160.
165. The stopover in Egypt was not part of the president's itinerary. See James T. Wooten, "Carter Leaves Today on Tour of 6 Nations," *New York Times*, December 29, 1977, p. 14.
166. Carter, *Keeping Faith*, p. 303. Vance, *Hard Choices*, p. 201, says that this phrase "was meant to come close to support for Palestinian self-determination without using the phrase itself."
167. Fritchey, "What Derailed the Mideast Talks," p. 13. Quandt, *Camp David*, p. 161, notes in understatement that the Aswan Declaration "was not well received by the Israelis."

CHAPTER 5

Growing Strategic Doubt and Policy Vacillation: 1978

The Soviet military buildup in Ethiopia precipitated a major reassessment of policy through the spring. The fundamental issue was whether Soviet action constituted a challenge to the United States or was an attempt to exploit targets of opportunity. If a challenge, the basic thrust of American strategy—which sought an early SALT II agreement followed by the establishment of new collective security arrangements around the Soviet periphery—would have to be changed, or certainly deferred. The attempt to construct a new geopolitical order could not proceed in the context of a major Soviet challenge to United States positions. If, on the other hand, Soviet policy was simply the exploitation of targets of opportunity and posed no threat to American strategy, then Washington could proceed on its present course.

Soviet leaders, perceiving opportunity in the instability created by Washington's new course and bolstered by the belief that their own strategic and intermediate-range missile power would deter any countermove, seemed to be sponsoring a massive, multifaceted, Eurasia-wide thrust which included SS-20 deployments combined with a strengthening of Soviet command, control, and communications capability; client military action in places as widely dispersed as Syria, Ethiopia, and Vietnam; and successful coup attempts in Yemen and Afghanistan. The objective appeared to be to alter the geopolitical balance to advantage all along the vast rim of the Eurasian landmass.

Ankara
TURKEY
Tabriz
Caspian Sea
U.S.S.R.
CYPRUS
SYRIA
Kirkuk
Tehran
Mediterranean Sea
LEBANON
Beriut
Damascus
Baghdad
Qom
ISREAL
Jerusalem
Amman
IRAQ
IRAN
Alexandria
JORDAN
Al Basrah
Abadan
Cairo
Suez
KUWAIT
Iraq-Saudi Arabia Neutral Zone
Kuwait
Strait of Hormuz
EGYPT
BAHRAIN
Persian Gulf
QATAR
Riyadh
Aswan
UNITED ARAB EMRATES
SAUDI ARABIA
Jiddah
Mecca
Bur Sudan
Red Sea
OMAN
SUDAN
Sana
YEMEN
Khartoum
Asmera
Aden
Gulf of Aden
DJIBOUTI
Djibouti
Berbera
Addis Ababa
SOMALIA
ETHIOPIA
Juba
Lake Rudolf
ZAIRE
UGANDA
Middle East and the Horn of Africa
Conic Projection
0 50 100 200 300 450
Miles
Mogadishu
KENYA
Indian Ocean
Mombasa

Beijing
Tianjin
Taiyuan
Qingdao
Lanzhou
Yellow Sea
Xi'an
CHINA
Nanjing
Qamdo
Chengdu
Shanghai
Wuhan
Chongqing
Changsha
INDIA
Fuzhou
Kunming
Taiwan Strait
Taipei
Guangzhou
TAIWAN
Mandalay
VIETNAM
Victoria
HONG KONG
(U.K.)
BURMA
Hanoi
LAOS
Haikou
Gulf of Tonkin
Vientiane
Rangoon
South China Sea
PHILIPPINES
THAILAND
Manila
Bangkok
CAMBODIA
Da Nang
Andaman Sea
Phnom Penh
Ho Chi Minh City
Iloilo
Gulf of Thailand
Sulu Sea
Bandar Seri Begawan
BRUNEI
MALAYSIA
Celebes Sea
Medan
Kuala Lumpur
MALAYSIA
Singapore
SINGAPORE
INDONESIA
Indian Ocean
Southeast Asia
Mercator Projection

The growing scale of Soviet geopolitical activity produced increasing policy vacillation and strategic doubt; the president in fact changed course on two occasions in three months. In the spring, President Carter decided to reverse priorities and emphasize the strengthening of United States positions around the Soviet periphery in advance of concluding a SALT II agreement. Then, in mid-year, he reversed course once again, moving the SALT II agreement to the forefront even as he concluded new collective security arrangements around the Soviet periphery. In this latter context, Washington sought to negotiate a Middle East settlement, the Camp David accords.

Carter Sides with Brzezinski: The Decision to Ride the Whirlwind

The Soviet airlift to Ethiopia had ended in mid-December, bringing something of a pause in Cuban and Soviet force levels at about three thousand men. In January, however, Soviet troop and materiel deliveries to Ethiopia abruptly increased, raising the Cuban troop presence to close to fifteen thousand and Soviet and other East-bloc advisory personnel to over one thousand.[1] The Soviet buildup in Ethiopia, now far beyond what was necessary for Ethiopian defense, combined with other disquieting developments in and beyond the region, raised fundamental questions in the minds of the Carter leadership about Soviet objectives.

The substantial increase in Soviet activity in Ethiopia was accompanied by a buildup in South Yemen, over and above replenishment of stocks shipped earlier from Aden to Addis Ababa. At the same time there occurred sharp upswings of terrorist activity in Turkey, Pakistan, and Western Europe. In Asia, since December Moscow had been materially assisting Vietnam in a substantial though not well publicized effort to subdue Kampuchea. Beijing, in turn, was lending support to Kampuchea and conducting military probes along the Sino–Vietnamese border. In February, the Soviets also established a Far Eastern TVD (theater of operations) strengthening positions in the region of the Sino–Soviet border, began initial deployments of ground and air units into prepared bases on the northern islands adjacent to Japan, and also commenced deployment of SS-20 intermediate-range missiles in the western USSR.

These unfolding events formed the immediate backdrop for an

extensive review of American policy.[2] Even the most benign interpretation of these developments as all locally inspired and unconnected raised troubling questions about the future stability of the vast rimland from the Middle East to the Horn of Africa across to East and Southeast Asia. The problem was not tidy and neatly defined. As discussion proceeded, information was at best sketchy and incomplete—and open to different interpretations. The Carter leadership strained to grasp the meaning of events: To what extent were disparate events interconnected? How much and to what end was the Soviet Union involved? What should the United States do? Ambiguity muddied every issue.

While it was the Soviet buildup in Ethiopia that precipitated the policy review, the review itself focused on the broader issue of overall United States–Soviet relations. Indeed, the underlying question which was raised by this welter of events was whether the United States should proceed with its strategy or defer it in order to contend with what some were interpreting as a Soviet challenge. The central policy question, whether or not to proceed on SALT, provoked a familiar split in the administration.

To Brzezinski, Moscow's objectives were "a favorable SALT treaty, a flexible and one-sided detente, and a regional condominium in the Middle East."[3] Brzezinski argued that Soviet involvement in the Horn was part of a grand strategy whose main objective was Saudi Arabia, Suez, and the oil pipelines.[4] He worried that Moscow had turned the tables on Washington and was using the Horn for a broader purpose. Thus he "was concerned not only about the foreign implications of perceived U.S. passivity in this strategic area, but also about the effect it would have on domestic politics and what that would mean for SALT."[5] What if, he queried, a "Soviet–Cuban offensive could coincide with the signing of SALT"? In that case, Moscow would have harnessed the United States in support of its foreign policy objectives. Failure to counter Soviet actions would mean acceptance of one-sided detente.

He believed that "it was the responsibility of the United States" to give its allies confidence in repelling Soviet aggression. Toward this end, he proposed a show of force in deployment of a carrier task force to the area of the Horn. When pressed by Vance and Brown about the wisdom of such a move, he suggested a joint United States–French carrier deployment.[6] When neither Vance nor Brown was prepared to "engage in a bluffing game," Brzezinski was reduced to arguing that "just placing the carrier in the area did not mean that we were going to war."[7]

Explicit in the national security adviser's argument was the view that Washington should counter Moscow's thrust, and implicit was the suggestion that United States objectives, particularly SALT, be deferred if necessary. Brzezinski also argued successfully that the United States upgrade intermediate-range forces in Europe and proceed to normalize relations with China, two related decisions which were made during the January–March time frame.[8]

Secretary Vance, on the other hand, rejected the thesis of a Soviet challenge. He "did not believe Soviet actions in Africa were part of a grand Soviet plan, but rather attempts to exploit targets of opportunity." For him "the central question was what politically and militarily feasible strategy would most effectively counter Soviet actions while advancing our overall interests."[9] By "overall interests" Vance meant first and foremost detente with the Soviet Union, and that meant SALT. Indeed, SALT was central to the success of Vance's strategy, and he therefore refused to countenance any proposal which would undercut it. He pressed for an early summit, as early as mid-year, during which a SALT treaty would be signed.[10]

His prescription for Ethiopia was for the United States to pursue a "diplomatic strategy," emphasizing allied and African peace-keeping efforts combined with remonstration with Moscow. He recognized that such a strategy would take time and that in the meantime political pressures would grow "to counter Soviet and Cuban assistance to Ethiopia by calling into play other aspects of the U.S.–Soviet global relationship."[11] He suggests that Brzezinski was the main source of pressure but that there were also others, "both inside and outside the administration," who pressed for a slowdown of SALT negotiations, a limitation on economic relations, and a curtailing of high-level exchanges.[12]

Since in his view Soviet activity was not part of a coordinated effort, Vance adamantly opposed any "linkage" of Soviet geopolitical actions to United States–Soviet bilateral relations. The upshot of the policy debate was that Secretary Vance's view on linkage prevailed, but not his strategic preference. The public course decided upon was that "there should be no direct linkage between Soviet and Cuban actions in the Horn and bilateral activities involving either country and the United States."[13] In actuality, however, Brzezinski's arguments carried, as Carter decided to place relations with Moscow on hold—and with them SALT II.

The Soviet surge had thrown American strategy out of synchronization. Washington, under Secretary Vance's leadership, had hoped to coordinate a SALT agreement with arrangements strengthening collective security structures in Europe, the Middle East, and the Far East. Instead, Moscow's geopolitical moves threatened to turn American strategy inside out, using a SALT agreement to reinforce Soviet geopolitical successes, which would undermine the very collective security structures Washington had hoped to build. It was imperative that Soviet action not divert the United States from its purposes. Therefore, the essential decision was to slow the policy pace across the board and attempt to utilize the Soviet surge to prod reluctant allies into acceptance of Washington's proposals.

The United States would attempt to ride the whirlwind of the growing Soviet proxy presence as leverage for its policies. The Carter administration would be in no hurry to complete its initiatives, including and especially SALT, or to seek an early detente with the Soviet Union. The fundamental decision was to delay seeking fulfillment of United States objectives until the Soviet threat grew more ominous, thus producing greater pressure when Washington did decide to wrap things up. In practice, this meant a negotiating slowdown of several months, depending upon the speed with which the Soviet threat grew in various areas, combined with a persistent public relations campaign highlighting Soviet intervention in Africa and human rights abuses at home.

Thus, through the spring of 1978 Washington pressed for a diplomatic solution in the Horn, stalled in the Middle East negotiations, shifted emphasis in Western Europe from deployment of ERW to deployment of long-range theater nuclear weapons,[14] and began cautiously readdressing the question of improving relations with Beijing.[15] Ambivalence would characterize the initial attitude toward Iran, for it is unclear precisely how—or whether—already visible initial upheavals were incorporated into the policy choices made at this time.[16]

Three developments, behind each of which was discerned a Soviet hand, would have substantial impact on American policy resulting in its abrogation by mid-year: Afghanistan, where a communist coup would greatly increase Soviet leverage on both the regional and global balance; Lebanon, where direct and increasing Syrian and Israeli involvement threatened to upset the delicate negotiations with Egypt; and Kampuchea, where the makings of a Sino–Soviet conflict were brewing.

President Carter, in what he described as "a serious and a sober talk" at Wake Forest University on March 17, revealed the shift in American policy toward the Soviet Union. He acknowledged that the United States government had "recently completed a major reassessment of our national defense strategy" prompted by the "challenge" of an "excessive Soviet buildup" and "an ominous inclination on the part of the Soviet Union to use its military power—to intervene in local conflicts. . . ."[17] The president stressed the determination of the United States to match any Soviet buildup and "not allow" Moscow "to gain military superiority over us." The Soviets, he said, "will never be able to use their nuclear forces to threaten, to coerce, or to blackmail us or our friends."

While offering to cooperate with the Soviet Union in areas of common interest, Carter declared that Moscow's failures "to demonstrate restraint in missile programs" and to curtail the "projection of Soviet or proxy forces into other lands and continents" would inevitably mean the erosion of "popular support in the United States for such cooperation."[18] Although "we are making good progress," on SALT, the president declared, "before I sign any SALT agreement . . . I will make sure that it preserves the strategic balance, that we can independently verify Soviet compliance, and that we will be at least as strong, relative to the Soviet Union, as we would be without any agreement."

Not once in his speech did the president use the word "detente," a fact which Soviet commentators immediately picked up.[19] American affairs specialist Georgi Arbatov noted in a *Pravda* article that the Carter administration was split between those who wished to develop detente and those who wished to retard it. The result, he said, was that Soviet–American relations were "at a turning point."[20] Regarding the SALT negotiations, he said, it is now time for the United States "to decide whether the agreement is to be, or not to be." Brezhnev himself, in a speech on April 7, also argued the point that it was time to fish or cut bait, lamenting American "indecision, [and] inconsistency." Detente was a reality, he affirmed, but unless a SALT accord were concluded soon, the opportunity might be lost.[21]

Although Brzezinski represented the January–March decisions

as a tactical adjustment and not a change in strategy, if fully carried out they would have reversed the strategic course laid out by Secretary Vance. In any case, the Brzezinski line continued only through early June of 1978 when Secretary Vance, who plainly did not agree with the decision, effected its reversal. But through the spring a slowdown in United States–Soviet relations occurred as SALT negotiations were allowed to languish. In sum, for the short term, the United States would neither cooperate with Moscow in arms control negotiations nor contend with the Soviets in the third world. Instead, the United States would persistently emphasize the growing Soviet threat—particularly in Africa, even though the conflict with Somalia was essentially over by mid-March—to lend force to its plans to put into place collective security structures around the Soviet periphery.

SALT II Delay, Afghan Coup, and China Card

President Carter's Wake Forest speech had put Moscow on notice that there would be no early conclusion of an arms control agreement. Indeed, Washington now moved to protract the negotiations, a task made relatively easier given the continuing decline in United States–Soviet relations. Thus, the meetings between Vance and Gromyko in late April did not wrap up the few remaining details on SALT, despite Gromyko's effort to be conciliatory, but led to an increase of issues to be resolved.

Secretary Vance, who was opposed to the decision to ride the whirlwind, offers a unique insight into the policy process during these months. His brief account is curiously contradictory, for while asserting that he had "hoped to use the April talks to pave the way to resolving the remaining issues in the SALT negotiations,"[22] his description of what took place belies his claim that "important progress was made" and glosses over the reasons for failure.

Vance noted that Moscow agreed to a MIRVed missile launcher ceiling of 1,200, down from their original proposal of 1,250, and that Washington agreed to 2,250 for the aggregate number of strategic nuclear delivery vehicles, up from the original United States proposal of 2,160. Vance also claims that Moscow agreed to the resolution of the noncircumvention issue "on our terms," but here he indulges in semantic obfuscation. The United States sought to preserve the right to transfer cruise missile technology to its allies, which Moscow strove to prohibit. The "terms" Vance refers to were the terms of American agreement to prohibit circumvention of the obligations of the treaty "through any other state or states." While this preserved the legal right to transfer cruise missile technology to Washington's allies, it in fact prohibited such transfer for the life of the treaty.

The secretary's explanation of why the April talks "did not produce a major breakthrough" is exceedingly vague; he says only that "escalating public rhetoric and the talk about linkage were having a political impact on the negotiating climate."[23] He, of course, does not mention the actual reason no breakthough occurred, which was primarily because of United States insistence on a resolution of several issues, the most important of which was the Backfire bomber.[24] Although Vance does not mention the Backfire issue in his memoir, he was instructed to raise the question during the talks—resurrrecting it for the first time in over a year.[25] Washington would use the Backfire as a device to stall the negotiations, in much the same way that the Soviet side used the issue of forward-based systems.

Thus, when Vance forced the Soviet leadership to go over the same ground already traversed a year earlier, much of which properly belonged to the technical experts in Geneva, and particularly when he insisted on Soviet written assurances that Backfire was not a strategic bomber, they no doubt understood that Vance had not come to settle the "remaining issues." The joint communiqué issued after the talks pointedly referred only to "a narrowing" of the two sides' positions on "some" of the remaining unresolved issues, as what transpired in Moscow was quickly shrouded in secrecy.[26]

In his Moscow departure statement, Vance declined to say when a treaty would be signed but implied that it would not be soon. Emphasizing Washington's "new realism," the secretary declared that the structure of peace had to be built slowly, "brick by brick, with workmanlike and realistic steps."[27] Then, on the plane en route to London before returning to Washington, Vance refused to discuss the negotiations with the reporters accompanying him—contrary to practice—on the grounds of "jeopardizing future progress."[28]

No sooner had Vance returned to Washington than additional evidence of Moscow's geopolitical offensive appeared—the communist coup in Afghanistan. A brief survey of recent Afghan history makes plain that the coup was a preemptive blow designed to prevent Kabul's shift out of Moscow's orbit. Mohammed Daoud had taken power five years before in a bloodless seizure of power overthrowing King Zehir. Initially, Daoud had maintained close ties with the Soviet Union, with which he had had friendly contacts for many years, and extensively employed the services of the People's Democratic Party of Afghanistan (PDPA).[29]

From 1974, at the urging and with the support of the United States, the shah of Iran had begun, as Selig Harrison observes, "a determined effort to draw Kabul into a Western-tilted, Tehran-centered regional economic and security sphere. . . ."[30] As part of a growing entente with Egypt and Saudi Arabia, the shah had entered into economic and military agreements with several neighboring states, including Afghanistan. In 1974, Iran signed a $2 billion, ten-year economic agreement, through which, had the coup not occurred, Iran would have eventually supplanted the Soviet Union as Kabul's largest donor. As part of the economic agreement, planning began for construction of a rail network linking Afghanistan to Persian Gulf ports—a development which would also have ended Afghanistan's land-locked status and dependency upon Soviet trade and transport outlets.

In the course of 1975 and 1976, Iranian–Afghani relations improved to the point that Daoud moved to lessen his dependence upon Moscow, and he broke with the domestic communist groups which had been instrumental in bringing him to power.[31] In the fall of 1975, he terminated officer-training arrangements with Moscow, dismissing forty Soviet-trained officers, and concluded new officer-training agreements with Egypt and India. He also announced the formation of a National Revolutionary party and banned all other parties, including the communist PDPA. Moscow responded to these steps by promoting the unification of the Parcham and Khalq wings of the PDPA under Khalq leader Noor Mohammed Taraki, a merger which was accomplished with some difficulty by May 1977.

Meanwhile, in February 1977, Daoud had promulgated a new one-party constitution and appointed Abdul Qadir Nuristani as interior minister to enforce it. From the spring of 1977, therefore, efforts to suppress communist and other opposition elements intensified as Daoud sought to strengthen Kabul's relations with the West. (Soviet intelligence had immediately recognized the shift. During a meeting between Daoud and Brezhnev in Moscow, April

12–15, 1977, the Soviet leader directly demanded that Daoud reduce Western influence, but the Afghan leader heatedly refused.)[32]

By early 1978 Daoud's policy of reducing Soviet and PDPA influence appeared to be succeeding. In March, Daoud concluded a peace agreement with Pakistan, pledging to oust Baluch and Pathan guerrillas from Afghan territory. Pakistan, in turn, agreed to provide additional training for Afghan officers. In early April, Daoud visited Egypt and Saudi Arabia, and was scheduled to receive the shah of Iran in June and President Carter in September.[33]

The coup of April 27, the so-called "Saur revolution," abruptly halted Kabul's shift. The immediate trigger for the coup was Daoud's arrest of the top Communist party leadership on April 19 following their show of defiance during a funeral procession honoring recently assassinated Parcham party leader Mir Akbar Khyber. Fearing that Daoud would move next to arrest the party's sympathizers in the military, the party hurriedly put long-developed plans into action.[34] The timing of the coup was therefore precipitated by Daoud himself, but the Communists were preparing to strike in any case.[35] Their plans originally had called for an insurrection in August.[36]

There can be little doubt that Moscow gave the green light for action, just as there can be little doubt that had Moscow opposed it no coup would have taken place. Given the clear adverse trend of the previous few years in Afghanistan, the fact that Moscow was willing to countenance a coup testified to growing Soviet boldness based upon a perception of the favorable change in the overall "correlation of forces."

The coup in Afghanistan was a severe and unexpected blow to American policy, removing a buffer state between, as Vance put it, "the Soviets and areas of U.S. interest to the south," namely, Iran and Pakistan.[37] In his zeal to deny a Soviet role, or even that local communists were involved, the secretary initially described the perpetrators as "officers . . . from the far Left . . . [with] no evidence of Soviet complicity."[38] Within days, however, that argument was punctured by the assumption of power by Taraki, Amin, and other leaders of the Afghan Communist party, and the rapid escalation of Soviet political and military presence in Afghanistan to unprecedented levels.

Indeed, in the White House the question quickly became how long it would be "before the Soviet influence in Afghanistan's internal affairs would become irreversible."[39] And beyond that, what impact would a Soviet-controlled Afghanistan have in the region? Although Vance believed that Kabul's first priority would be to "consolidate its own position," he recognized that there were "substantial risks" regarding the impact of a Soviet-controlled Afghanistan upon its neighbors. Curiously, Vance professed to believe that the main threat was to Pakistan, rather than to Iran.[40] Nevertheless, a national intelligence estimate was commissioned to reassess the situation in Iran.[41]

There was also the larger issue of the strategic impact of the coup on Moscow's global position. Here, it would appear, Washington sought to counter the Soviet advance in Afghanistan by an improvement in relations with Beijing. The Carter leadership had decided in mid-March to resume "consultations" with the Chinese leadership following the Fifth National People's Congress.[42] The Afghan coup, in conjunction with other developments, quickly persuaded President Carter to accelerate the timetable for China.

The Afghan coup, combined with the strengthening of Soviet forces on the Chinese border, including creation of the Far Eastern TVD, deployment of additional forces on the northern islands adjacent to Japan, and the heavy reinforcement of Hanoi's effort to subdue Kampuchea, all pointed unmistakably toward a near-term crisis in Sino–Soviet relations.[43] In this context, the Afghan coup persuaded the president to advance the policy timetable toward China on the assumption that Beijing would be more willing to compromise on outstanding issues between the United States and China in order to gain American support against the Soviet Union.

Thus, Brzezinski's planned May trip was now converted from one seeking the resumption of consultations to one in which the president authorized him to "move rapidly" on normalization—if the Chinese were willing to compromise.[44] Brzezinski was authorized to tell the Chinese that the United States was determined "to respond assertively to the Soviet military buildup and to Soviet proxy expansion around the world." Indeed, if the Chinese agreed, Brzezinski was instructed to authorize the beginning of normalization negotiations in June.[45] The United States had decided to counter the Soviet geopolitical drive with an early move toward China. Or so it appeared until Secretary Vance moved to reverse the drift toward confrontation with Moscow.

Secretary Vance Regains Control

By the end of May Vance had become thoroughly alarmed at the course of American policy and quickly moved to reestablish his preeminence. On May 25, although denying linkage between SALT II and Soviet policy elsewhere, the president proceeded once again, as he had all spring, to decry Soviet human rights abuses and African policy as factors which would reduce chances for ratification of the SALT II treaty.[46] A few days later, in an unproductive meeting with Gromyko, the president criticized the Soviet role in the Angola-based rebel invasion of Zaire, which Gromyko rebutted as being "fantastic."[47] The Soviet foreign minister in turn, in a meeting with Vance, strongly protested Brzezinski's trip to Beijing and his briefing of the Chinese on SALT. Following the meetings with Gromyko, the president announced his decision to delay any summit with Brezhnev until fall "at the earliest" and to discourage all "non-essential" travel to the Soviet Union.[48]

De facto linkage combined with Brzezinski's trip to Beijing, with its strident anti-Soviet tone (especially his remarks during a TV interview upon his return), brought United States–Soviet relations to a low point. In his appearance on "Meet the Press" on May 28, Brzezinski accused the Soviets of behavior incompatible with the "code of detente." Commenting on the SALT negotiations, he declared that the United States had made "very proper, balanced . . . proposals. If they are accepted, we could have an agreement within days. If they are not accepted, we will wait until they are accepted."[49]

Brzezinski's highly charged comments appear to have been the last straw for Vance, who on May 29 went "outside the regular bureaucratic channels" to make a direct appeal to the president to change policy. Vance "urged the president not to accept the counsel of those who wanted to intensify the tensions for domestic political reasons or for transitory foreign policy gains."[50] There was nothing to gain, he said, from a "renewal of cold war tensions," which was where current policy would inevitably lead. Instead, he recommended a reversal of the present course of growing confrontation with the Soviet Union.

The essence of Vance's proposal was a plea to the president to reinstate a conciliatory, non-provocative approach toward the Soviet Union. While agreeing to a "prudent increase" in defense spending and continued efforts to strengthen NATO, Vance urged immediate conclusion of a SALT II treaty "to stabilize the strategic competition."[51] He believed that "we should accept the fact of competition with the Soviets" and not link Soviet third world policy "to issues in which we had so fundamental an interest as SALT." The United States, he said, should not directly confront the Soviet Union and Cuba in Africa. Rather, we should employ "our many instruments of influence," such as diplomatic pressure, economic and military aid, and better relations with African states.

Vance cautioned the president to "be careful" in management of the triangular relationship with Beijing and to "avoid trying to play China off against the Soviets."[52] Furthermore, he called for a review of the application of human rights policy toward the Soviet Union on the grounds that there was a point beyond which criticism was counterproductive. Finally, he recommended that either he or the president deliver a major speech on United States–Soviet relations "realistically" describing Washington's policy for regulating the relationship.

Meanwhile, Brzezinski, believing that he had won the battle for Carter's ear, strove to ensure that the president held to the "tough" course he proposed. Brzezinski discussed the matter with the president's aide, Hamilton Jordan. The two men sought to arrange the proper forum for a presidential determination. They rejected a big meeting of advisers on two grounds: "First of all, suppose the consequence of the meeting is that the president decides to go for the soft line. It will be harder to deter him in a larger meeting. Secondly, suppose he decides to go for the hard line and publicly or semipublicly in a group meeting has to reject the advice that Vance is giving. This would really undercut Vance." Therefore, at Brzezinski's urging, they decided upon a small meeting "with Carter being encouraged to define his line himself, preferably the one that Jordan and I favor, and then simply impose it by edict . . . giving us the order to stick to the line as he has expressed it."[53]

Upon learning of Vance's letter to the president and realizing that Carter was persuaded by his arguments, Brzezinski became alarmed and overplayed his hand. In early June a story appeared in the *Washington Post* which, its authors claimed, was based on "authoritative government sources" and sources "close to Carter." They asserted that the president had decided to "freeze" the SALT talks for the time being.[54] The principal source for the story was undoubtedly Brzezinski, which infuriated the president. In an unprecedented step, an angry President Carter summoned the Washington press corps to the Oval Office and issued a firm denial. The president declared that his policy was "to proceed aggressively with SALT discussions, to conclude a treaty as early as possible and without delay because of political considerations."[55]

Brzezinski's attempt to lock the president into an anti-Soviet stance backfired. The president's speech at the Naval Academy on June 7 marked the end of Brzezinski's provocative approach. In his speech, Carter challenged the Soviet Union to "choose either confrontation or cooperation," declaring that "the United States is adequately prepared to meet either choice." The speech, which the president had "stitched together"[56] from drafts submitted by Brzezinski and Vance, was badly received in Washington and Moscow and led quickly to a decision to change course.[57]

Two days later, on June 9, in a small meeting with his top advisers, Carter designated Secretary Vance as his "chief foreign policy spokesman."[58] Although Brzezinski's "close working relationship" with the president remained unchanged, his role thereafter was as Carter's "inside adviser and not [as] a spokesman for foreign policy."[59] The national security adviser plainly had lost the struggle regarding policy toward the Soviet Union. Indeed, he dropped out of the public view, for the time being making no public speeches or appearances on television. Despite denials, Brzezinski had been muzzled—but he had not been silenced.[60]

The issue was more than a personality clash and involved infinitely more than the question of who would be "spokesman." The two men espoused radically different strategic approaches to the Soviet Union.[61] To reiterate, Brzezinski wanted to consolidate the United States position around the Soviet periphery before improving relations with Moscow. The policy pursued over the previous several months—delaying action while calling attention to the growing Soviet threat—was designed to accomplish this objective.

Vance, on the other hand, wanted to estabish the Soviet connection first through SALT II and other measures before consolidating the United States position around the periphery. Indeed, the two men were not in complete agreement on what should be "consolidated." Brzezinski's approach would tend to reinforce the existing structure of containment; Vance's would facilitate a greater disengagement of the United States security presence from around the Soviet periphery.

The danger in Vance's approach was that it risked putting American policy at the service of Soviet strategy. Vance undoubtedly understood this danger but deemed it more important to establish the link with Moscow—even if that occurred within the context of a Soviet design—because of its centrality to the strategy of building a new global order. Brzezinski, too, understood that delaying establishment of the Soviet link would certainly complicate Vance's strategy if not make it impossible. Indeed, Brzezinski demonstrated his opposition to Vance's strategy at every opportunity, specifically during the Yemeni and Iranian crises.

In any case, having regained control, Secretary Vance quickly proceeded to effect sweeping decisions in virtually all areas of American foreign policy in order to redirect its course in a manner which was consistent with his strategy. Its essence would be an extremely non-provocative approach, which the secretary hoped would reopen the door to a greatly improved relationship with the Soviet Union. Once the new relationship was established in the form of SALT II and renewed detente, the United States would proceed to forge the desired security relationships in Europe, the Middle East, and Asia.

It is appropriate to restate the rationale of those who advocated the new order strategy. At its core lay a specific view of the fundamental change that had taken place in the strategic weapons relationship with the Soviet Union. The growth of Soviet strategic weapons power to parity with, if not ascendency over, the United States made containment an increasingly costly and unviable strategy—first, because the United States would not risk a war of annihilation to maintain it, and secondly because American allies had long since abandoned all pretense of dedicated opposition to the Soviet Union and were major competitors with the United States. Thus the need to change strategy.

The ultimate objective of the strategy was the gradual withdrawal of American power from mainland Eurasia, as time and circumstance permitted, and the substitution of stable collective security structures for American presence. The central assumption in this strategy was that it could succeed only within the context of a coooperative relationship with the Soviet Union. The corollary was that the Soviet Union would welcome Washington's efforts to adjust, and not attempt to disrupt American strategy. That was why Vance chose to interpret the Soviet geopolitical advances, whether in Africa, Afghanistan, Yemen, or anywhere else, as an uncoordinated drive to secure targets of opportunity rather than as a grand strategy directed against the United States.

It was fundamentally inconceivable to Vance and his supporters that the Soviet Union would attempt to defeat the execution of an American strategy which also served long-term Soviet interests—the withdrawal of American power from threatening positions close to the Soviet Union. That was why the Soviet invasion of Afghanistan was such a crushing blow. It represented Moscow's repudiation of any cooperation with Washington in the adjustment of superpower positions and indicated the reassertion of a traditional foreign policy approach based upon raw power. In short, Washington offered a mini-max approach where both sides could benefit, but Moscow's preference was for zero-sum.

In June of 1978, however, Secretary Vance had no inkling of such a Soviet response as he proceeded to forge a more accommodating policy. Vance signaled the shift in his testimony to the House International Relations Committee on June 19.[62] In his opening statement, which was a positive reinterpretation of the president's Naval Academy speech, he indicated that the United States would temper its criticism of Soviet human rights abuses, henceforth treat African problems "in their own terms, and not as an arena for East-West differences," and "persist in our efforts to negotiate a sound SALT II agreement."[63] At the same time, Vance arranged for a three-day "summit" meeting in mid-July with Soviet Foreign Minister Gromyko "to review the entire spectrum of East-West issues."[64]

Vance also moved in June to recast American policy elsewhere to avoid any conceivable provocation of Moscow. First, he delayed normalization with Beijing so as not to appear to be playing a "China card," even though Brzezinski had authorized the beginning of fast-track negotiations during his May trip. In a memo of June 13, the secretary recommended mid-December as the target date for the announcement of normalization, hoping to coordinate it with a SALT II agreement, which he hoped would be signed before then.[65]

The secretary of state deferred any decision by NATO on the selection of actual weapons to deploy as part of the long-range theater nuclear force upgrade already decided upon in principle. The deferral decision came in the context of a response to West German insistence upon an arms control component to any deployment of new weapons. It came in the form of PRM 38, a study begun in June to review "Long Range Theater Nuclear Capabilities and Arms Control."[66] Washington's internal review effectively put off the actual choice of weapons to deploy until 1979, which in Vance's calculations would place it after negotiation of a SALT II agreement.

It would be in the Middle East–Southwest Asia area that Vance would direct United States policy onto its most difficult path. There he would oversee a policy that witnessed extraordinary involvement in one area and equally extraordinary *non*involvement in another. These opposite courses of action would be pursued in the Egyptian–Israeli talks, on the one hand, and the Iranian revolution, on the other hand. The secretary's objective, in this interpretation, was to relocate the fulcrum of United States power in the region, from Iran to Egypt and Israel. He undoubtedly believed that the ultimate outcome of the repositioning of American power to a point further removed from the direct Soviet periphery would be the establishment of a more stable region, contrary to what actually occurred.

Secretary Vance shifted policy in the Middle East in June, taking control of the negotiations, as a brief review will confirm. When Anwar Sadat arrived for a state visit in Washington February 3 through 8, 1978, Carter had already decided upon Brzezinski's delay strategy.[67] Sadat, of course, was prepared to sign a separate peace with Israel, despite his apparent unhappiness with Israeli negotiating techniques, but the Carter leadership persuaded him instead to engage in a "secret strategy," that is, collusion with the United States, ostensibly to obtain concessions from Israel on the West Bank/Gaza question.[68] In reality, the agreement with Sadat was a double deception by the United States resulting from its general strategic decision to delay action until the Soviet threat grew more ominous.

On the one hand, the "secret strategy" to put pressure on Israel *never* went beyond words—tough words, to be sure, but words nonetheless—and was discarded in June when Vance regained policy control.[69] On the other hand, the secret strategy meant a de facto delay in direct American involvement in negotiations between Egypt and Israel, a development which was related to the Soviet thrust in Africa. The Soviet thrust in the Horn presented an obvious threat to

Saudi Arabia and required an adjustment in United States strategy to include strengthening of relations with the desert kingdom.

Thus, the general decision to delay action while the Soviet threat grew would, it was hoped, make the Saudis more willing to compromise on the Palestinian issue in return for improved military relations with the United States. To maintain the confidence of the principals, in mid-February Washington offered a multiple-fighter aircraft deal to Saudi Arabia, Egypt, and Israel. Sixty F-16s were to go to Riyadh, fifty F-5Es to Cairo, and seventy-five F-16s and fifteen F-15s to Jerusalem. While this assuaged the Arabs, it alarmed the Israelis, whom Carter sought to mollify by indicating his readiness to "consider a bilateral security arrangement with Israel."[70] At any rate, the effort to secure passage of the plane deal through Congress preoccupied the administration through mid-May, when the Senate voted in favor of the president.

At this point, Secretary Vance moved to prepare for a change of approach by establishing a secret planning group.[71] Both internal and external developments no doubt prompted this shift. Internally, there appeared signs of growing frustration with what one NSC staffer called "paper exercises" and "negotiation by questionnaire."[72] Through the spring, as part of the collusion strategy, Washington pressed the Israelis to commit themselves in principle to withdrawal from the West Bank and Gaza, hoping to elicit a declaration by secretly dangling before them a treaty with Egypt which was already negotiated but not signed.[73] The action throughout this period consisted primarily of repetitive requests and counter-requests to define terms and explain conditions, hence the reference to "questionnaire diplomacy."

While the internal exercises were becoming increasingly tedious, it was the external pressures on both Sadat and the Israelis which prompted the change. Both from inside Egypt and from other Arab capitals came calls for Sadat to admit that his "initiative" had failed and for him to rejoin the other Arab nations.[74] There was increasing talk of an Arab "mini-summit," which, if held, could produce a graceful way for Sadat to terminate his initiative. Domestically, too, Sadat's "open door economic policy" was not attracting the volume of foreign capital needed for the creation of new industry and jobs.

Lastly, events in Lebanon were escalating. Sizable incursions by both Israeli and Syrian forces effectively fragmented the country.

Sadat's visit to Jerusalem, which indicated that a basic shift in the overall structure of the Arab–Israeli conflict was under way, removed Israel from the Arab pincer. Sadat's trip also foreshadowed the isolation of Syria, which repaired its relations with Moscow but also sought to strengthen its position in northern Lebanon. Dropping all pretense of disarming the Palestinians in Lebanon, Syrian forces moved from February 1978 through the summer to create a defense in-depth in the northern part of the country.[75]

The Syrian move was matched by an Israeli invasion of south Lebanon in mid-March (Operation Litani) to create a similar defense in-depth. Although Israeli forces eventually gave way to a United Nations Interim Force (UNIFIL), they left a six-mile-wide strip along the Israeli border under the control of friendly Christian militia forces commanded by the pro-Israeli Christian, Major Saad Haddad.[76] Lebanese unity, always tenuous at best in the modern era, increasingly became a contradiction in terms. Secretary Vance's fear that the looming prospect of larger conflict in Lebanon would undermine the Egyptian–Israeli negotiations prompted him to try to get the two parties back together under American auspices in early June.

The United States would now become, in Sadat's words, a "full partner" in the Middle East negotiating process. On June 11, Ambassador to Egypt Herman Eilts quietly conveyed the president's request for a meeting of the foreign ministers of Egypt and Israel together with Secretary of State Vance in London.[77] Ambassador Samuel Lewis made the same request to the Israeli government. With these moves Secretary Vance completed the reversal of Brzezinski's hard-line strategic course set earlier in the year. But in tragic irony, while the United States was shifting to a more accommodative course, the Soviet Union was moving in the opposite direction.

Moscow Presses the Geopolitical Offensive

During Secretary Vance's appearance before the House Committee on International Relations June 19, he noted that "within the last few days, there has appeared a lengthy article in *Pravda* which we are studying with careful attention." He went on to express the view that "the most constructive course for both countries . . . would be to concentrate on the concrete actions we both can take to reduce tensions and to reach agreement on the critical issues now under negotiation."[78]

The article to which Vance referred was a harsh condemnation of American policy combined with a pious denial of Soviet wrongdoing and advice on how to improve relations. Describing the "acute struggle" between those who "would like to undermine detente and return the world to the cold war, to new confrontations and unrestrained military rivalry" and those in favor of detente and peaceful coexistence, the article declared that the hard-liners "are beginning to take the upper hand." In words and deeds, the United States government was seen to be seeking "the deliberate worsening of bilateral relations with the U.S.S.R. . . . [and] a common language with the aggressive anti-Sovietism of the Chinese. . . ."[79]

The president's Annapolis speech, which "was read in the Soviet Union with attention and was objectively assessed," was an unsuccessful attempt "to reconcile the unreconcilable." Declared intentions of improving relations with the Soviet Union were juxtaposed by "so preconceived and distorted a descripton of Soviet realities as one has not encountered even in the most ill-wishing American papers since the times of the cold war." Far from dispelling them, "it increased the doubts about the course taken by the U.S.A."

Denouncing those who, "whipping up the arms race," charged the Soviet Union with seeking strategic superiority, the article claimed that it was Moscow which had grounds for concern. Washington, after all, was pressing the long-term modernization plan for NATO, exporting arms in ever-larger quantities ($11.3 billion in 1977 and $13.2 billion planned for 1978) and expressing doubts about Senate ratification of a SALT II agreement. "What grounds in the light of all these facts does the United States have to sound the alarm about the Soviet Union's desire to achieve 'military superiority'?"

Charging that American hard-liners really feared "equality" and hoped to establish "military superiority by means of new lunges in the arms race and by putting a brake on the negotiations," the article averred that this ran counter to the "principle of equality and equal security of sides, agreed upon by the U.S.S.R and the United States." To avoid the further erosion of the "modest foundation of mutual confidence, which was created through much work, effort and patience," would require considerable "political courage" in opposing the hard-liners. The article concluded with the view that relations could improve if Washington were able "to outline and consistently implement a principled political course . . . [to] display restraint without fearing the heckling of political opportunists and not fall for the advice of adventurers."

Did the Soviet leadership misread the changes that had just taken place in United States policy or, more likely, did they read them too well? Certainly Vance wasted no time in communicating the new policy to them, to no avail. The record suggests that the Soviets saw Washington's move toward restraint as a timely opportunity to press forward toward their own objectives, using earlier United States hardline rhetoric as justification.

Over the course of the next several months, while bitterly assailing aggressive American moves and attempts to play the China card, Moscow moved boldly in two broad areas. One was Southeast Asia, where Moscow provided extensive support for the Vietnamese attempt to conquer Kampuchea. The other was what I have termed the great triangle—the Middle East–African Horn–Southwest Asia. It was here, in the center of the triangle, indeed on the very day of one of Brezhnev's bitterest attacks on United States policy, that both Moscow's and Cuba's hands were evident in the bizarre turn of events in the Yemens.[80]

The last week of June in Yemen saw the culmination of a long-standing power struggle between South Yemen President Salim Rubaya Ali and Central Committee chief Abdel Fattah Ismail, which Ismail won. The triggering event was the assassination of North Yemen President Ahmed Hussain al-Ghashmy by a package bomb carried in the briefcase of President Ali's unsuspecting personal envoy, who also perished. The struggle between the two men and their supporters, however, had recently entered a new stage, centering on Aden's geopolitical orientation between East and West and the country's deepening economic difficulties.

In their geopolitical aspect, the circumstances in Yemen resembled those in Afghanistan the previous April. In both cases an internal coup cut short an attempted move toward the West and consolidated the Soviet hold. The split in the Aden leadership occurred in early 1975 in the context of a United States-sponsored Saudi Arabian attempt to develop better relations with the People's Democratic Republic of Yemen (PDRY) and the Yemen Arab Republic (YAR).[81] In PDRY (South Yemen), the deteriorating economy combined with the collapse of the Dhofar rebellion in neighboring Oman, which Aden had been supporting, prompted President Ali to respond favorably to Saudi entreaties, particularly as Moscow then showed little interest in providing needed assistance.[82]

In short, in the absence of Soviet support, Ali's arguments in favor of South Yemen's rapprochement with Saudi Arabia carried the day over the objections of Ismail's advocacy of continued strict reliance upon Moscow. In March 1976 diplomatic relations were established, followed by a Saudi pledge to provide $400 million in aid to South Yemen.[83] Improved Saudi–PDRY ties paralleled improving Saudi ties with North Yemen. Indeed, the Sana regime publicly drew away from Moscow, agreeing to accept arms from the United States in a package to be financed by Saudi Arabia.[84] By the end of the year both North and South Yemen were moving quietly into a comfortable relationship with Riyadh—a development which agitated Soviet commentators. Moscow warned Saudi Arabia against its strategy of attempting to draw "progressive" Yemen into its "conservative" camp.[85]

The growing conflict in the Horn and Moscow's increasing role in it created the circumstances for the reversal of Aden's move into the Saudi camp. Moscow's need for reliable logistical access to Ethiopia sharply raised the value of Aden to Soviet planners and led to renewed interest in the South Yemeni regime's affairs. In March 1977 Moscow had attempted unsuccessfully to forestall the conflict between Ethiopia and Somalia with a proposal for a federation which included the Aden regime.[86] The ensuing Somali–Ethiopian conflict raised once again the issue of Aden's geopolitical orientation within the leadership. This time, the stakes were much higher for Moscow, and accordingly so was its interest.

Moscow's shift from Somalia to Ethiopia in the summer of 1977 presented a dilemma for the Aden leadership, whose closest ally had been Siad Barre of Somalia. Moreover, Aden's principal supporters were now aligned on opposite sides, as Saudi Arabia supported Somalia. It was thus in a complex and intensifying political milieu that the Ali–Ismail leadership conflict moved toward a resolution which would also determine Aden's geopolitical orientation. President Ali's trip to Riyadh in the summer occurred concurrently with the visit to Moscow of Ismail's ally, Prime Minister Ali Nasir. Aden's critical role as staging and transshipping point for Soviet support of Ethiopia persuaded Soviet leaders to make an attractive offer, tipping the balance within the leadership back to Ismail.[87]

The August decision to reinforce ties to Moscow led to the suspension of relations with Saudi Arabia in November.[88] Large-scale Soviet and Cuban involvement in Ethiopia had beneficial consequences for the Aden regime. A new economic agreement was signed in February,[89] and by spring of 1978 there were by some reports five thousand Soviet and four thousand Cuban troops, advisers, and technicians in the People's Democratic Republic of Yemen, in addition to an undetermined number of East German advisers.[90] By the spring, in other words, it seemed that Moscow had weathered a difficult period, repelling the Saudi challenge and strengthening its relationship with the Aden regime in the context of policy toward the Horn. Moreover, it also appeared that Ismail had emerged victorious over his rival, Ali.

But in the spring of 1978, President Ali made another attempt to align South Yemen more closely to the West and to undercut Moscow's hold. In May he ordered South Yemeni forces—some 1,000 pilots and soldiers—in Eritrea to end their involvement in that conflict.[91] He had arranged for Chinese assistance in building Aden's armed forces to counter the roles of the Soviet, Cuban, and East German advisers.[92] More importantly, he moved to improve relations with North Yemen, restore diplomatic relations with Saudi Arabia, and establish ties to the United States.[93] Indeed, a high-ranking Department of State team, led by Director of Arabian Peninsular Affairs Joseph W. Twinam, was scheduled to arrive in Aden on June 27, 1978.[94]

It was as part of the effort to improve relations with the Sana regime that President Ali had sent his personal envoy to President al-Ghashmy on June 24, with his deadly baggage. Ismail denied complicity in the assassination and attempted to place the blame on North Yemeni exiles living in Aden.[95] While the exiles certainly had motive, they appeared to have had little opportunity to execute a complicated plot. Ismail also attempted to blame Ali posthumously; but that charge, too, rang hollow.[96] On the other hand, Saudi Arabia, North Yemen, and China charged Ismail with responsibility for the plot; and indeed events immediately following the assassination seemed consistent with the thesis of a preemptive inside job.[97]

The evening after the assassination, Ismail convened a meeting of the Central Committee, which decided to suspend the president, who had not attended, pending an investigation into his role in the assassination. Responding to the challenge, President Ali immediately called upon loyal army troops for support. There followed brief but furious fighting through June 26, in which Ismail, supported by Cuban-trained forces, prevailed.[98] Ali surrendered and was promptly executed by firing squad. Reports from Aden claimed that Cuban troops "spearheaded the attack against Robaya Ali at the presidential palace and that it was Cuban pilots who flew the MiG fighters which pounded the palace where Robaya Ali and his supporters were entrenched."[99]

Other sources said Soviet warships also shelled the palace.[100] Whether Moscow was directly involved or not, Ali's death resolved the long-standing factional struggle within the Aden leadership and in very timely fashion the issue of the geopolitical orientation of the People's Democratic Republic of Yemen. There would be no shift toward the West. Moscow now had firm grip on a key staging area from which to exert leverage on the Horn as well as on Saudi Arabia.

Washington immediately recognized that its plans for improving relations with South Yemen had failed—and thereby its objective of undercutting the basis of Moscow's power projection capability in the region. The Department of State diverted the high-level delegation, which was already en route, from Aden to Sana, where discussions were held regarding the upgrading of North Yemen's defenses. Indeed, United States military sales to North Yemen sharply increased. For example, in 1977 and 1978 military sales were estimated at $2.6 and $5 million. Planned sales for fiscal 1979 were $150 million.[101] The coup in Aden had policy repercussions beyond the region, precipitating another reappraisal by the Carter leadership of Soviet "provocative behavior," a reappraisal which resulted in yet another reversal of policy toward Moscow.[102]

Soviet Policy, SALT II, and American Strategy

The Aden coup strengthened Moscow's influence in the Horn and the Arabian peninsula, raising anew the issue of Soviet intentions. Moreover, by mid-year there was no longer any doubt that a major confrontation between Beijing and Hanoi was looming as Vietnamese forces enlarged their military operations in Kampuchea.[103] In short, the intensity of Moscow's broad-based geopolitical surge sensitized the president and his aides to both the content and timing of SALT II on Washington's overall geopolitical position. As

American leaders engaged in discussions among themselves during the last few days of June, arguments focused upon two important implications in Moscow's provocative behavior.

The first was that Soviet leaders appeared to be signaling their determination to pursue objectives in blatant disregard of, if not disdain for, Washington. The Aden events coincided with trials of prominent Soviet dissidents and the Soviet arrest of two American journalists and a businessman on what appeared to be trumped-up charges (the journalists were accused of "slander").[104] The most outrageous trial was that of Anatoly Scharansky, whom Moscow had charged with working for the Central Intelligence Agency and whom President Carter had publicly defended. The trial appeared to be "a deliberate slap in Mr. Carter's face" on the eve of the scheduled meeting between Secretary Vance and Foreign Minister Gromyko.[105] Senator Jackson, among others, urged postponement of Vance's trip "to show our disapproval," but Vance insisted that the meeting should not be delayed.[106]

The second implication was the apparent belief in Moscow that the "correlation of forces" continued to evolve in the Soviet Union's favor. This, of course, related to ongoing developments in the field of missile accuracy and explained the abrupt turnabout by the Carter administration on SALT. After much heated debate during the last few days of June, the president, deciding against the view put forth by Vance and arms control chief Paul Warnke and in favor of Brzezinski and Defense Secretary Harold Brown, determined that the United States should in effect delay conclusion of the treaty negotiations and take steps to ensure survivability of Minuteman. Given the expected increase in the accuracy of Soviet heavy missiles, the only way to ensure invulnerability of land-based missiles was to make them mobile.

Thus, in early July Paul Warnke was instructed to inform Soviet Ambassador Dobrynin that nothing in the proposed treaty denied the United States the option to deploy a mobile missile during the life of the treaty.[107] This, of course, flew directly in the face of the decision just made in early June to adopt Secretary Vance's view that SALT II must be negotiated as quickly as possible. Indeed, the concealed purpose behind the Brzezinski–Brown argument to inform the Soviets that the United States retained the option of deploying a mobile missile was to place an obstacle in the path of early conclusion of the negotiations.

Deployment of a mobile missile was prohibited in the treaty protocol, but not in the treaty itself. Vance and Warnke argued therefore that there was no legal bar to deployment and the issue should simply not be raised. Furthermore, since the administration had not yet decided upon a mobile missile or a basing plan, raising the issue would be premature. Brzezinski and Brown, on the other hand, insisted that it would be better to "face the issue head-on" now, rather than wait until the Senate ratification process began and opponents raised potentially paralyzing objections.[108] The president agreed.

But it was the manner in which the decision was conveyed to Moscow that disclosed the larger purpose. United States representatives declared themselves to be "under instructions" to make clear that Washington's new position was a unilateral step which required no Soviet response.[109] This, of course, ensured a Soviet response—and respond they did. During the Vance–Gromyko talks July 12 and 13, Soviet arms control negotiator Vladimir Semyenov told Warnke that he, too, was "under instructions" to express "grave reservations" about whether Washington's proposed mobile aim point system (MAPS) would be "valid and permissible" under the verification provisions of the treaty.[110]

In other words, nothing could have been better calculated to throw a monkey wrench into the negotiating process, which was precisely the objective. Washington wished neither to be locked into a treaty which prevented a free response to a Soviet technological surprise—although what was anticipated was already bad enough—nor to be maneuvered into signing an arms control treaty at a moment when Moscow shifted its geopolitical offensive into high gear.

Oddly enough, the Soviets, too, wished to delay—but not break off—the negotiations. Thus, at Geneva while Semyenov raised formal objections to Washington's mobile missile declaration, Gromyko refused to be drawn into commenting on the dissidents' trials or the arrest of the journalists, and in fact he offered a partial but substantial compromise on the issue of missile modernization.

In May 1977, the United States had proposed to ban testing of any new ICBM for the three years of the protocol.[111] Moscow sought an exception for a non-MIRVed ICBM to replace old types. In April 1978, Washington countered with a ban on any new ICBM for the protocol period but allowed an exception, MIRVed or unMIRVed, for the treaty period through 1985. This would have left open the possibility of deployment of MX, then under development.

Seizing the opportunity to attempt to close off not only the United States MX program but also the Trident II SLBM program just getting under way, in May Gromyko proposed either a test and deployment ban on any new ICBMs or a ban with one exception for an unMIRVed ICBM—*for the life of the treaty*. Either of these proposals would have effectively thwarted the MX and Trident II programs, which were designed to provide the United States with both land- and sea-based counterforce capability.[112] Of course, Washington rejected the Soviet proposals.

In the July meetings, Gromyko now offered his partial but substantial compromise. The Soviet negotiator now melded his previous proposals together, offering a test and deployment ban for all new ICBMs during the treaty period with one exception, MIRVed or unMIRVed. It was a substantive concession in that it would have permitted Washington to proceed with MX (and Moscow with its planned unMIRVed missile). It was partial in that his proposal would still have blocked Trident II. The Soviets wanted Trident I, which was on the verge of deployment, to be the exempted weapon, disallowing Trident II, while their exemption would be the rough equivalent of Trident II. In Vance's words, "we could not agree" and "decided to give up on trying to negotiate a similar ban . . . with one exemption for each side" for SLBMs.[113]

Nevertheless, Vance was encouraged, despite Gromyko's publicly stated caution after the meetings had ended that the new proposals introduced on both sides "requires the sun to rise more than twice," and that "decisions aren't taken with the suddenness of a cloudburst."[114] Nor did a stinging criticism of American policy on human rights, which Moscow threatened "was opening the way to a Soviet–United States confrontation" dampen Vance's enthusiasm.[115] He believed that Gromyko's offer of a compromise was "the first clear signal" that the Soviets "were prepared to go into the endgame."[116]

Belief that the Soviets were now ready to reach agreement reinforced Vance's view that this important stage in the strategy of establishing the Soviet connection first with a SALT II agreement, followed promptly by arrangements with allies and friends in Western Europe, the Middle East, and the Far East, was moving forward according to plan. The secretary, in fact, would make a strong bid to complete the SALT agreement in September following the Camp David talks, only to find to his "disappointment" that Moscow was inexplicably not yet ready. But that takes us slightly ahead of the story. The July talks occurred just as Washington was preparing to enter the Middle East negotiations as a "full partner" and crisis erupted in Iran.

The Camp David Summit

By mid-year it had become obvious that the United States could delay action in the Middle East no longer. The events in Afghanistan, Yemen, and the Horn threatened to undercut United States efforts to construct the new foundation of regional collective security—the Egyptian–Israeli nexus. Sadat was clearly feeling increased pressure from within and without Egypt to turn away from his "initiative," which meant that time was rapidly running out for Washington. Nor were the Israelis showing any inclination to budge from Begin's offer of the previous December.

It seemed clear that, left to themselves, Sadat and Begin would either not reach any agreement, or, if they did, it would not be satisfactory to the United States. The president had sent Vice-President Mondale to the Middle East in early July to make a final attempt to assess the chances for an unbrokered compromise. The issue continued to be West Bank/Gaza, the satisfactory resolution of which would establish the basis for a comprehensive settlement in the region. In Israel the vice-president proposed applying the same formula to the West Bank/Gaza that Israel had proposed to Egypt for Sinai, namely, withdrawal from territory in return for peace and security. But Prime Minister Begin angrily rejected the analogy and the proposal.

The vice-president had more luck in Cairo. The strengthening circle of Soviet-sponsored regimes appears to have increased Sadat's anxiety. He was now anxious to move forward, dropping an earlier demand for Palestinian self-determination and proposing that Gaza be returned to Egypt and the West Bank to Jordan. After five years the Palestinians could "participate" in the resolution of both questions. If this were unacceptable, Sadat said, then the United States "should come up with some other proposal."[117] In brief, Sadat demanded that the president introduce an American plan.

Following a friendly but unproductive meeting of Egyptian and Israeli foreign ministers and Secretary of State Vance, July 18 and 19 at Leeds Castle outside London, President Carter decided to hold what came to be known as the Camp David summit. In an unprecedented step in American diplomatic history, Washington became directly involved as a participant in an effort to broker a settlement in the Middle East. Camp David was an ambitious effort not simply to reach agreement between Egypt and Israel, but to devise a peace formula which would be acceptable to the other involved parties.[118]

The stakes were high. Complete failure would mean repolarization of the region as it had been following the Six Day War and United States estrangement from the Arabs. Even though it was Israel's preferred outcome, such an extreme development was unlikely if only because the United States would proceed to develop a relationship with Egypt, with or without Israel. Israel's optimum position was to be the sole American ally in the region—even at the cost of being completely surrounded by hostile states. Despite the fact that Israel's ideal structure had become less and less feasible following the Yom Kippur War, the Israelis doggedly attempted to move toward that structural objective at every opportunity.

Sadat was bent upon continuing Egypt's shift into the United States camp; therefore the Egyptian leader accepted minimum terms consistent with his larger national purposes. Central among those purposes was negotiated recovery of the territory lost in war with Israel. As self-proclaimed leader of the Arab world, however, Sadat had to demonstrate Egypt's concern for and ability to deliver on broader issues, especially the Palestinian question. Therefore, he could not cavalierly dismiss this bedeviling problem and enter into an undisguised separate peace with Israel. For Sadat the question was how to finesse the Palestinian obstacle and recover Sinai.

For the United States the Camp David summit represented the decision to enter the final phase of the Carter administration's Middle East initiative. There seemed little question that a peace treaty between Egypt and Israel was well within grasp—and had been since the previous December. The core objective now was to establish the formula which would provide a hopeful basis for resolving the Palestinian question in the long run and thereby neutralizing the radical Arabs in the short run. Thus the central dynamic at Camp David was not negotiations between Egypt and Israel but those between the United States and Israel. Washington would press the

Israelis hard to go beyond Begin's autonomy plan to a commitment "in principle" to withdraw from the West Bank, but ultimately the United States would settle for what was attainable. Indeed, the fundamental meaning of Camp David was that the United States was now prepared to settle on the best terms available.

Unquestionably, the United States did not wish to see establishment of a Palestinian state in the West Bank even though Washington pressed for Israeli commitment to the principle of at least partial withdrawal from it. What the Carter administration sought at Camp David was time. An Israeli promise to settle the Palestinian question on honorable terms in the foreseeable future based on the implementation of Begin's autonomy plan would provide at minimum five years. In other words, Carter sought to devise a formula[119] which he hoped would mollify if not satisfy the Palestinians and persuade the Saudis and Jordanians to adhere in one form or another to the collective security structure the United States was building.[120] No effort was made to bring in Syria or Lebanon.

The meeting at Camp David, September 5 through 17, produced several surprises, not the least of which was a sustained Israeli attempt to precipitate a breakdown of the negotiations. But there were others as well. During head-to-head meetings on the second day, for example, Sadat attempted to turn the tables on Begin. Recall that the previous December at Ismailia, Sadat had expected the Jewish leader to discuss general principles. Instead, Begin produced specific terms for a treaty and the autonomy plan for West Bank/Gaza. Now at Camp David, Begin expected Sadat to discuss general principles, but the Egyptian leader presented a very elaborate, comprehensive proposal which stressed linkage of the major issues: Sinai, West Bank/Gaza, and the Palestinian problem.

Sadat had presented a maximalist position for the record, to satisfy his own advisers as well as other Arab leaders who would eventually learn what had transpired at Camp David. But he was fully prepared to accept far less than a maximal settlement, as he privately informed Carter.[121] Whether Begin understood Sadat's opening gambit as a self-protective tactic or not, his response was to take the opportunity to attempt to scuttle the talks. Replying the next day, Begin took the surprising position that, although he was willing to reach agreement on a treaty with Egypt and withdraw from Sinai, he would never agree to dismantle the Israeli settlements there. As Carter described the scene,

> There seemed an absolute deadlock on the Sinai settlements. Within a few minutes Sadat announced angrily that a stalemate had been reached. He saw no reason for the discussions to continue. As far as he was concerned, they were over. Sadat then ignored Begin, stood up, and looked at me.[122]

Although Carter managed to persuade the two leaders "not to break off their talks," Begin held to the Sinai settlements "bargaining chip" (indeed, adding to it three airfields which the Israelis had constructed in Sinai) until the very last negotiating session with Carter, when he finally agreed to put the issue to a vote in the Knesset.[123] But that evening "the word had spread like wildfire through Camp David that the talks had broken down."[124]

After averting the first of what would eventually be seven major Israeli attempts to provoke a breakdown, Carter dropped all pretense of mediating and prepared to introduce an American plan. Begin vehemently objected and tried to dissuade the president from introducing an American proposal, which he termed "a bad idea." Instead, he insisted that he and Carter first reach agreement between themselves, after which Israel and Egypt would negotiate an agreement. Begin "wanted the world to know that there were no serious differences between Israel and the United States."[125]

Carter, of course, was not taken in by these rather blatant attempts to cut the United States out of the negotiations, isolate Egypt, and place Israel in a controlling position. On the contrary, Carter himself assumed direct control. The decision was made at this point to split the negotiations into two "frameworks," one dealing with a Sinai agreement, which would lay the ground work for an Egyptian–Israeli treaty, and a second dealing with the West Bank/Gaza question. Henceforth, from the third day until the last, there would be no further face-to-face meetings between Begin and Sadat. Instead, the procedure followed would be negotiation of United States texts, first with Egypt, then with Israel, back and forth until agreement was reached on a point-by-point basis.

In a meeting with Begin on Sunday evening, September 10, the president conveyed to the Israeli leader the decision to split the negotiations and to specify precisely what the United States wished to accomplish while at Camp David. First and foremost, the president wanted an agreement on Sinai which would lead to a final peace treaty between Israel and Egypt.

> An agreement between Israel and Egypt would preclude any successful attack against your country by other Arab countries. Without Egypt, they could not successfuly challenge you. This in itself would be a major source of security, but, of course, it should be seen only as a first step on the way to agreement with the other Arab states.[126]

The president said that he also wanted to resolve the issue of Israeli settlements in the West Bank, although "they will need to be treated separately." The issue of sovereignty over the West Bank and Gaza, however, was "not to be resolved here at Camp David."[127] Nor would the status of Jerusalem—which everyone recognized to be a "no-win" issue—be resolved.

Begin's response to the American proposal was to dispute its very basis and applicability to the West Bank. He flatly rejected UN Resolution 242, particularly the phrase "inadmissibility of acquisition of territory by war," which the United States side had included as a preamble in its draft, producing another near-collapse of the negotiations. Begin asserted that "this language applies only to wars of aggression; therefore we cannot base our negotiations on it. The war of 1967 gives Israel the right to change frontiers." Carter responded incredulously, "Do you reject United Nations Resolution 242? . . . To delete this phrase would mean that we have no basis for negotiation now or in the future."[128]

Begin's fourth challenge hung over the negotiations until the next to last day and was met only by agreeing to remove the offending phrase from the body of the agreement, appending the entire UN resolution as an annex to the "Framework for Peace in the Middle East," and declaring that the "principles" of 242 applied to the negotiations, without specifying what that meant.[129] This carefully hedged implicit and indirect association of UN Resolution 242 with the framework agreement would be as close as Sadat and Carter would come to an Israeli commitment to the principle of withdrawal from the West Bank and Gaza.

By Thursday evening, September 14, although the two framework agreements on Sinai and the West Bank had been negotiated, the Israelis remained rigid on the issues of Sinai settlements and airfields and on the commitment to eventual withdrawal from the West Bank and settlements there. There appeared to be no means of resolving these few remaining issues. "We could go no further," the president believed, and he sent notes to Sadat and Begin informing them that he planned to bring the talks to an end on Sunday.

Carter also instructed his staff to begin drafting what he termed "failure plans," which included a speech the president would deliver to Congress "explaining what we had attempted during the two weeks at Camp David and why we had not been successful."[130] The president intended to precipitate a public confrontation with the Israeli leadership. He would side publicly with Sadat and appeal directly to American Jews and the Israeli people to urge the Israeli leadership "not to miss the chance for peace."[131]

Learning of the president's intentions and hoping to avoid the heavy onus of responsibility for the failure of the talks, the Israeli leadership decided to provoke Sadat into breaking up the negotiations. On Friday morning, the fifteenth, Foreign Minister Dayan dropped in to Carter's quarters to say that he had just had "an unsatisfactory meeting" with Sadat, whom he had gone to see that morning "in hopes that the two men might find some basis for continuing the talks."[132] In reality Dayan had gone to see Sadat for a quite different purpose. According to Sadat's account to Carter, Dayan had visited him to declare that "Israel would not sign any agreements." Infuriated, Sadat "accused Dayan of wasting our time by coming to Camp David in the first place."[133]

The result of the exchange was Sadat's decision to leave Camp David immediately. The president learned of the Egyptian leader's decision shortly afterward, when a shaken Secretary Vance burst into the president's room to say, "Sadat is leaving. He and his aides are already packed. He asked me to order him a helicopter!"[134] Deeply concerned, Carter went over to Sadat's cabin to dissuade him from giving up. According to Carter,

> I explained to him the extremely serious consequences of his unilaterally breaking off the negotiations: that his action would harm the relationship between Egypt and the United States, he would be violating his personal promise to me, *and the onus for failure would be on him*.[135]

Dayan had been convincing. Sadat concluded that if Egypt signed an agreement with the United States alone, and if direct discussions were ever resumed with the Israelis, the points to which Egypt had already agreed would become the "basis for all future negotiations." Carter acknowledged that this was "a telling argument" but replied, "We would have a complete understanding that if any nation rejected *any* part of the agreements, *none* of the proposals would stay in effect." The president's response swayed Sadat, who promised, "If you give me this statement, I will stick with you to the end."[136]

The president's quick thinking had averted a collapse of the negotiations and seemingly left the Israelis with no recourse but to reach agreement or be themselves responsible for the collapse of the negotiations. In the latter instance, the president was of course still prepared for the public confrontation with Begin. Thus hedged, the Israeli leadership decided to reach agreement, yet even while doing so, they made one last attempt to scuttle the summit.

Friday and Saturday, September 15 and 16, were devoted to ironing out remaining differences. On the two problems in the Sinai framework, the United States agreed to assist Israel in construction of two airbases in the Negev to compensate for three which Israel would relinquish in Sinai, and Begin agreed to have the Knesset vote on withdrawal of settlements from Sinai. On the West Bank/Gaza framework, as noted above, in return for language calling for recognition of the "legitimate rights of the Palestinian people," Carter agreed to remove the text of UN Resolution 242 from the framework, appending it as an annex, and referring only to the "provisions and principles" of the resolution in the framework itself. This meant, among other things, that there would be no mention of the term "withdrawal" in the framework and that only the negotiations, not necessarily their results, would be based on UN Resolutions 242 and 338.[137]

It was over the last issues, settlements in the West Bank/Gaza and the Jerusalem question, that the Israeli leadership made its sixth and seventh attempts to evade agreement. It was understood from the beginning that the question of Jerusalem would not be resolved at Camp David, and it was decided that each side would append a letter to the framework on the Middle East restating its position. But when Begin saw the text of the United States letter, which declared that "East Jerusalem should be considered occupied territory," he threatened to walk out of the negotiations. Begin refused to sign any document which included criticism of Israel. It was not until Carter agreed to remove the offending language that Begin agreed to accept the letter.[138]

Begin refused to budge at all over the issue of Israeli settlements in the West Bank/Gaza. During a late Saturday night session which spilled over into Sunday morning, Carter insisted that Israel agree to a freeze on establishment of new settlements during the negotiations to create the self-government structure in the West Bank/Gaza. Begin and Dayan rejected this proposal on the grounds that if negotiations were prolonged it could mean a ban on new settlements "for at least five years."[139] The most they would agree to was a moratorium on settlement activity for three months, which could be extended beyond that.

The two sides were at an impasse. Finally, after much haggling, they agreed to remove this point from the agreement and append it as a letter to the text. Begin was to send the letter later that day. (It was already Sunday morning, September 17.) Carter claims Begin agreed to a settlements freeze and cites Vance, the only other American present, in support.[140] Begin claims he agreed only to think the matter over and cites Dayan and legal adviser Aharon Barak, the only other Israelis present, in support of his view.

It was a difficult moment. Whether the Camp David accords would be signed at all was in question and what actually happened next will probably never be known. Clearly, the two sides had not reached agreement on the duration of a settlements freeze, despite what Carter and Vance have said. If they had agreed there would have been no point in removing it from the text. That they removed it is evidence enough that there was no agreement. It would appear that the president decided to finesse the Israeli objection in order to obtain Sadat's signature on the accords.

That was the function of the Begin letter, to be delivered later on Sunday afternoon. In the meantime, President Carter hurried over to inform Sadat that everything was completed, including Begin's supposed acceptance of a settlement freeze in West Bank/Gaza during the negotiations to establish self-government there.[141] That afternoon Barak brought over the texts of two letters, one containing the question to be addressed to the Knesset regarding withdrawal of settlers from the Sinai and the other regarding the duration of the moratorium on settlement construction in West Bank/Gaza.

Both were unacceptable, but the way Carter dealt with each letter reinforces the view that he sought to finesse an unbridgeable disagreement over the West Bank settlements. The president personally redrafted the Sinai letter for inclusion in the papers to be signed later that evening at the White House.[142] The West Bank settlements letter was another matter. Begin restated his willingness to suspend construction for only three months, the position he had taken the night before, but he left out the possibility of extension beyond three months and further muddied the issue by tying the moratorium to the negotiation of the Egyptian–Israeli peace treaty.

President Carter did not redraft this letter. Instead, he "read to Barak from my detailed notes what we had mutually decided,"[143] instructing him to tell Begin to redraft the letter and deliver it the next day. Rather than attempt to resolve the issue on the spot, Carter determined that Begin's letter would not arrive until the day after the Camp David accords were signed. As William Quandt noted, "it was an act of faith, to say the least, to think that Begin would change his mind."[144] It also bears noting that once the Egyptian–Israeli treaty negotiations had begun in mid-October the president would drop the subject altogether.[145]

In retrospect, the reason for Carter's West Bank finesse was straightforward enough. The only substantive concessions which the Egyptians believed they had obtained from Begin were the removal of the Sinai settlements and the freeze on West Bank settlements. Even with these concessions the Egyptians feared they would have an extremely difficult time selling the agreement to the rest of the Arab world.[146] For Carter to have acknowledged beforehand that he had not in fact obtained the West Bank settlements freeze, or had attempted to do so and failed, would have been to jeopardize the entire negotiation. The outcome then would have been simply a separate peace, which Sadat could not have signed.[147]

But there was a deeper consideration. The plain fact was that a West Bank settlements freeze would have opened the door to Jordanian–Israeli negotiations, negotiations which neither Israel, Jordan, nor the United States wished. Jordan occupied the fourth chair at Camp David.[148] A delicate if somewhat antagonistic symbiosis existed between Amman and Jerusalem, which grew out of the fact of Israel's occupation of the West Bank. Israel's occupation and control of some 800,000 Palestinians there and close to half a million more in Gaza played a very important, if unacknowledged, role in the evolution of a stable and prosperous Jordan since 1967. This was especially true after King Hussein's destruction of PLO military power in the civil war of 1970–1971, known as Black September.

Israeli control of the West Bank forestalled the emergence of a Palestinian majority in Jordan which could pose a political threat to

King Hussein. Hashemite rule was after all a minority regime based on an alliance between the Transjordan families and the Bedouin tribes. On the other hand, Israeli occupation justified the king's decision to postpone parliamentary elections until the West Bank was returned, freezing the Palestinians out of the political process. Thus, even though King Hussein adopted the stance of an Arab loyalist, there were serious concerns of national self-interest which prompted him to avoid participation in any effort to alter the status quo. In a very real sense, and contrary to public perception of the issue, any change in the status of the West Bank would weaken both states. The West Bank was territory which Israel could not do without and which Jordan did not want. It was therefore no surprise that King Hussein declined to participate in the negotiations.

The "Framework for Peace in the Middle East," while proposing a negotiated means of settling the "final status" of the West Bank and Gaza, was in actuality a prescription for stalemate and the status quo. Although the framework stipulated a three-stage transitional arrangement, there were actually four stages. First, Israel, Egypt, and Jordan (if Hussein decided to participate) were to negotiate the "modalities" of a transitional arrangement "not exceeding five years," in which a freely elected self-governing authority would replace the Israeli military government and its civilian administration.[149] Second, the election of the self-governing authority would be followed by the withdrawal of Israeli military forces into "specified security locations" and the establishment of a "strong local police force." Then,

> as soon as possible but not later than the third year after the beginning of the transition period, negotiations will take place to determine the final status of the West Bank and Gaza and its relationship with its neighbors and to conclude a peace treaty between Israel and Jordan by the end of the transitional period.

This oddly worded paragraph called for two separate sets of negotiations, covering different time periods. One was a negotiation between Israel and Jordan to conclude a peace treaty "by the end of the transitional period." The other was a negotiation among Egypt, Israel, Jordan, and elected representatives from the West Bank and Gaza to "determine the final status of the West Bank and Gaza." Although stipulating Palestinian participation in all but the first stage of the negotiations, the fundamental shortcoming of the framework was the failure to establish a starting point for the beginning of the five-year transition period and a deadline for negotiating the final status of West Bank and Gaza. The "final status" negotiations were open-ended and the term itself undefined.

For a brief moment after the signing of the Camp David accords, it appeared as if President Carter's "all or nothing gamble"[150] on a Middle East settlement had an even chance of success. Israel and Egypt had agreed to normalize their relationship by treaty, and Israel appeared ready to negotiate equitable arrangements with Jordan over the West Bank. Furthermore, three other sets of negotiations—with Moscow, with Beijing, and with NATO—all appeared to be heading for completion according to Secretary Vance's plans.

Indeed, the fifteen months following Camp David would witness several apparent policy successes: relations with China would be normalized, an Egyptian–Israeli treaty would be signed, SALT II would be signed, and NATO would reach a decision regarding the deployment of new weapons to defend Western Europe. The picture, however, was quite misleading. The approaching conflict in Southeast Asia, rapid disintegration of order in Iran, the early beginnings of political strain in Nicaragua and El Salvador, evidence of Soviet support for renewed Cuban activism in the Western Hemisphere, and the Soviet invasion of Afghanistan would all have substantial negative impact on Vance's strategy. One might well argue that the Camp David accords—with their shortcomings—were the high point of the Carter presidency and that the agreements with Moscow, Beijing, and NATO represented major efforts to hold together a rapidly disintegrating policy framework.

The irony was that policy success would not translate into strategic success. On the contrary, the Soviet invasion of Afghanistan in December 1979 signified the collapse of the strategy the Carter administration had been pursuing fitfully since it came into office. Moreover, the failure to construct the new order did not mean a return to containment. By the time the Carter administration left office, American strategy was in disarray and the question of America's strategic course an election issue. It is to the collapse of United States strategy that we now turn.

Notes

1. See "Soviet Arms for Ethiopia Jam Sealanes," *Washington Post*, January 20, 1978, p. A30. Estimates on troop strength varied from ten to twenty thousand, depending on the source. Siad Barre, as noted above, claimed there were twenty thousand Cubans in Ethiopia as early as November. Brzezinski, *Power and Principle*, p. 184, on the other hand, indicates ten or eleven thousand.
2. Brzezinski, *Power and Principle*, p. 316, notes that "by the spring of 1978, U.S.–Soviet relations were stalemated. The SALT talks were at best creeping forward. The Soviets were steadily increasing their military presence by proxy near the strategically vital Arabian peninsula (notably in Ethiopia and South Yemen).... There were first hints of a Soviet military presence in Vietnam, and the beginnings of development of a new Soviet weapons system targeted on Western Europe (the SS-20)."
3. Brzezinski, *Power and Principle*, p. 187.
4. Ibid., p. 181.
5. Ibid., p. 182.
6. Ibid., pp. 182–83.
7. Ibid., p. 183, and Vance, *Hard Choices*, p. 87.
8. See chapters 2 and 3 for the January–March discussions and decisions.
9. Vance, *Hard Choices*, p. 84.
10. Ibid., p. 99. See also, Marquis Childs, "A Quiet, Confident Aproach to SALT II," *Washington Post*, March 21, 1978, p. 17.
11. Vance, *Hard Choices*, p. 85.
12. Ibid.
13. See Brzezinski, *Power and Principle*, p. 184, and Vance, *Hard Choices*, pp. 87–88, for the scrap which immediately ensued over the president's public linkage of Africa and SALT following this decision.
14. See chapter 2.
15. See chapter 3.
16. Gary Sick, *All Fall Down* (New York: Penguin Books, 1986), pp. 40–41. Sick, who was the NSC staff member with responsibility for Iranian affairs, noted in a memo to Brzezinski analyzing the February 18 riots in Tabriz that the "reactionary Muslim right wing" represented a "formidable" opposition and "may be the true threat to the shah's regime."
17. "The President: National Security Interests," Department of State *Bulletin*, vol. 78, no. 2013 (April 1978), pp. 17–19.
18. Ibid.
19. See Murray Marder, "Diplomatic Signals Show U.S., Soviets at a Vital Juncture," *Washington Post*, March 26, 1978, p. 1.

20. "Georgi Arbatov, The Soviet View of Our SALT Policy," *Long Island Newsday*, April 6, 1978, p. 96, a translation from "Soviet–American Relations: A Time for Crucial Decisions," *Pravda*, March 28, 1978, p. 2. See also Garthoff, *Detente and Confrontation*, pp. 594–95.
21. "Excerpts from Brezhnev's Address on Disarmament," *New York Times*, April 8, 1978, p. 6, and Kevin Klose, "Brezhnev Assails U.S. for Stalling on Arms Talks," *Washington Post*, April 8, 1978, p. A1.
22. Vance, *Hard Choices*, p. 99.
23. Ibid.
24. There were seven other issues which Vance raised in addition to Backfire: the definition of new types of ICBMs to be restricted, the definition of cruise missile range, total numerical limits on all systems, the principles for SALT III, the expansion of the data base, the question of MIRV verification, and the issue of how to distinguish among different planes of the same type capable of carrying cruise missiles. See "Eight Issues Remain to Be Resolved in Salt II," *Defense/Space Daily*, April 12, 1978, p. 247. See also William Beecher, "US Says SALT-2 Must Limit Warheads," *Boston Globe*, May 5, 1978, p. 1.
25. Vance, *Hard Choices*, p. 100, and Bernard Gwertzman, "U.S. and Soviet Said to Resolve a Key Issue Blocking Arms Pact," *New York Times*, April 25, 1978, p. 1.
26. Daniel Southerland, "Vance–Gromyko Talks: Tough Bargaining Ahead," *Christian Science Monitor*, April 24, 1978, p. 1.
27. Ibid.
28. Gwertzman, "U.S. and Soviet Said to Resolve a Key Issue." Talbott, *Endgame*, p. 152, explains the imposition of secrecy as a result of Vance's embarrassment in Moscow. It seems that the secretary had authorized one of his aides to provide an outline of the talks to two reporters from *Time* and *Newsweek*. Soviet intelligence intercepted their cabled report and confronted Vance with the charge that the United States side was already leaking the results of the confidential negotiations. "As a result," says Talbott, Vance refused to disclose any further details.
29. For balanced treatments, see Henry S. Bradsher, *Afghanistan and the Soviet Union* (Durham: Duke University Press, 1983), and Thomas T. Hammond, *Red Flag over Afghanistan*, (Boulder, CO: Westview Press, 1984).
30. Selig Harrison, "The Shah, Not Kremlin, Touched Off Afghan Coup," *Washington Post*, May 13, 1979, p. C1.
31. Ibid.
32. See Abdul Samad Ghaus, *The Fall of Afghanistan, an Insider's Account* (New York: Pergamon-Brassey, 1988), p. 179. Ghaus was deputy foreign minister.

33. For further discussion of Kabul's growing ties with Iran and Pakistan during 1976–78, see former Ambassador Theodore Eliot's "Afghanistan after the 1978 Revolution," *Strategic Review*, (Spring 1979).
34. See Hammond, *Red Flag*, p. 51, and Ralph Joseph, "Military, Leftists Cooperated in Afghan Coup," *Washington Star*, May 29, 1978, p. D13.
35. The shah of Iran reportedly warned the Carter administration of the impending coup in mid-April. See Rowland Evans and Robert Novak, "Ignoring the Dangers of the Afghan Coup," *Washington Post*, May 8, 1978, p. 23.
36. Ghaus, *Fall of Afghanistan*, p. 195.
37. Vance, *Hard Choices*, p. 384.
38. Ibid. Ghaus, *Fall of Afghanistan*, p. 206, says: "There is no need to speculate whether the Soviets were aware of the planned coup. Without equivocation it can be said that the Soviets, for a variety of reasons, had decided on Daoud's elimination."
39. Sick, *All Fall Down*, p. 42.
40. Vance, *Hard Choices*, p. 385.
41. Sick, *All Fall Down*, p. 43.
42. Brzezinski, *Power and Principle*, p. 205.
43. See chapter 3 above.
44. Brzezinski, *Power and Principle*, pp. 204, 206–7.
45. Ibid., Annex I.
46. Transcript of President's News Conference on Domestic and Foreign Affairs," *New York Times*, May 26, 1978, p. 9.
47. Vance, *Hard Choices*, p. 103. Vance claimed that Gromyko's visit in fact produced "one of their most important concessions in SALT II," the agreement to limit the number of MIRV warheads to ten on existing ICBMs. For an account of their meeting, see "Carter and Gromyko Report Some Gains on Strategic Arms," *New York Times*, May 28, 1978, p. 1.
48. John F. Wallach, "Carter Delays Soviet Summit, Aims to Pressure Cuba," *Baltimore News American*, May 31, 1978, p. 2.
49. See Robert Kaiser and Walter Pincus, "U.S. Reportedly Will Freeze Strategic Arms Talks," *Washington Post*, June 2, 1978, p. 1.
50. Vance, *Hard Choices*, p. 101. See Brzezinski, *Power and Principle*, pp. 319–20, for his reaction.
51. Vance, *Hard Choices*, p. 101.
52. Ibid., p. 102.
53. Brzezinski, *Power and Principle*, pp. 222–23.
54. Kaiser and Pincus, "U.S. Will Reportedly Freeze Strategic Arms Talks."
55. "President: 'This Story . . . Is Totally Inaccurate,'" *Washington Post*, June 3, 1978, p. 8.

56. Vance, *Hard Choices*, p. 102, and Brzezinski, *Power and Principle*, p. 320.
57. See Murray Marder, "Which of Two Speeches Did the Kremlin Hear?" *Washington Post* June 8, 1978, p. 1, and Kevin Klose, "Pravda Hits 'Cold War' Tone of Carter's Annapolis Speech," *Washington Post*, June 12, 1978, p. 1. A few weeks later Carter said that it was a speech "I very carefully wrote myself and . . . went over with my advisers, almost every word in it." See "Transcript of President's News Conference," *New York Times*, June 27, 1978, p. 12.
58. Martin Schram, "The Ascendancy of Cyrus Vance: Dominant Voice Is His," *Washington Post*, August 6, 1978, p. 1. Brzezinski, *Power and Principle*, p. 320, says it happened on June 2.
59. Schram, "Ascendancy of Cyrus Vance," p. 1.
60. For his denial, see Brzezinski, *Power and Principle*, pp. 320–22.
61. Brzezinski, *Power and Principle*, p. 319, subtitled his account of these events "The Policy Conflict Surfaces," suggesting that the two men had no substantive differences earlier.
62. "Text of Vance's Opening Statement to House Committee," *New York Times*, June 20, 1978, p. 12.
63. Vance amplified on United States policy toward Africa the following day. See "Excerpts from Secretary Vance's Address on U.S. Policy toward Africa," *New York Times*, June 21, 1978, p. 6.
64. John P. Wallach, "U.S., Soviets Plan July Summit," *Baltimore News American*, June 21, 1978, p. 1.
65. Brzezinski, *Power and Principle*, p. 223, and chapter 3, p. 119.
66. See chapter 2, p. 71.
67. The president initially had been determined to bring both Sadat and Begin to Washington for three-way negotiations until persuaded to shift pace by Brzezinski and Mondale. At a meeting on January 23 attended by Mondale, Brzezinski, Vance, Jordan, Powell, and his wife Rosalynn, the president was prevailed upon to meet Sadat and Begin separately. See Brzezinski, *Power and Principle*, pp. 240–41.
68. Ibid., pp. 239f.
69. Ibid., p. 249. On p. 252, he says it was dropped because it "was too complicated to execute."
70. Ibid., p. 249.
71. Quandt, *Camp David*, p. 194.
72. See the memo by Quandt to Brzezinski of May 17, pp. 192–96.
73. See Muhammad Ibrahim Kamil, *The Lost Peace in the Camp David Accords* (in Arabic), pp. 145–51, as cited in Quandt, *Camp David*, pp. 176–77, n. 9.
74. See Karen Elliot House, "Sadat: Is Time Running Out?" *Wall Street Journal*, May 25, 1978, p. 4.

75. See the highly informative article by John J. Donohue, "From Nation to Factions," *Commonweal*, June 8, 1979, pp. 335–38.
76. Jim Markham, "Israeli Raid in Lebanon: Keeping Palestinians off Balance," *New York Times*, August 21, 1980, p. A3.
77. Quandt, *Camp David*, p. 195.
78. "Text of Vance's Opening Statement to House Committee," *New York Times*, June 20, 1978, p. 12.
79. "Excerpts from Pravda Commentary on Relations between Soviet and the United States," *New York Times*, June 18, 1978, p. 10.
80. "Brezhnev Attacks United States for Trying 'to Play Chinese Card,'" *New York Times*, June 26, 1978, p. 1.
81. See the "Prepared Statement of Lt. Col. John J. Ruszkiewicz," U.S. military attache to the YAR, April 1978–January 1980, in *U.S. Interests in, and Policies toward, the Persian Gulf, 1980.* Hearings before the Subcommittee on Europe and the Middle East of the House Committee on Foreign Affairs (Washington, DC: GPO, 1980), pp. 103–7.
82. See Haim Shaked and Tamar Yegnes, "The People's Democratic Republic of Yemen," in Colin Legum and Haim Shaked, eds., *Middle East Contemporary Survey, 1976–1977*, vol. 1 (New York: Holmes and Meier Publishers, Inc., 1978), p. 549.
83. For the announcements, see *FBIS-MEA*, March 11 and 12, 1976, pp. C4-5 and C6, respectively. For the Saudi aid report, see *Middle East Economic Digest, Annual Review*, December 31, 1976, p. 63.
84. *FBIS-MEA*, June 17, 1976, p. C2. See also Ruszkiewcz' prepared statement cited above.
85. A. Feoktistov, "Saudi Arabia and the Arab World," *International Affairs* (Moscow), no. 7 (July 1977), pp. 104–7.
86. See chapter 4.
87. For a broader discussion, see "Loss of Gulf States' Aid May Be Price of Foreign Policy," *Middle East Economic Digest, Annual Review*, December 31, 1976, pp. 100–101.
88. Shaked and Yegnes, "People's Democratic Republic of Yemen," vol. II, pp. 661–62. See also Nimrod Novik, *On the Shores of Bab Al-Mandeb: Soviet Diplomacy and Regional Dynamics* (Philadelphia: Foreign Policy Research Institute, 1979), pp. 37–38.
89. *FBIS-MEA*, February 7, 1978, p. C5.
90. Admiral Gorshkov, chief of the Soviet navy, went to South Yemen in May 1978 undoubtedly to evaluate Aden's facilities. *FBIS-SU*, May 24, 1978, p. F4. For troop reports, see "Soviet Appears to Gain from Aden Executions," *Baltimore Sun*, June 28, 1978, p. 1.
91. Robert Manning, "Yemen: More Conflict Ahead," *International Bulletin*, July 17, 1978, p. 5.

92. Sources differ over which of Aden's armed forces were controlled by whom. Charles T. Creekman, Jr., "Sino–Soviet Competition in the Yemens," *Naval War College Review*, July–August 1979, pp. 78–79, argues that Ali controlled the people's militia, which was being trained by the Chinese. Another source argues that Ismail controlled the people's militia and that it was being trained by Cuba. See "The Yemens: Important Changes," *Defense and Foreign Affairs Digest*, July 1978, p. 40.
93. "Improved Relations Sought with Neighbors," *Middle East Economic Digest*, June 16, 1978, p. 52.
94. David Binder, "U.S. Putting Off Bid to Southern Yemen," *New York Times*, August 6, 1978, p. 11. See also Paul Findley (congressman from Illinois), "A Bungled Opening in South Yemen," *Washington Post*, July 7, 1978, p. 19.
95. "Southern Yemenis Deny Role in Killing," *New York Times*, June 26, 1978, p. A5.
96. Ali evidently learned of the plot and attempted to warn al-Ghashmy by telephone but was too late. See *FBIS-MEA*, June 28, 1978, p. C1.
97. *FBIS-MEA*, June 27, 1978, p. C1; *FBIS-PRC*, July 11, 1978, p. A-6. See also the account by Robin Bidwell, *The Two Yemens* (Singapore: Longman/Westview Press, 1983), pp. 284–85.
98. For an account of the fighting, see *FBIS-MEA*, June 26 and 27, 1978, pp. C3–5 and C2, respectively.
99. "Cubans Turned the Tide in Aden Coup, Leftist Newspaper in Beirut Contends," *Washington Star*, June 28, 1978, p. 10.
100. J.B. Kelly, *Arabia, the Gulf and the West* (New York: Basic Books, 1980), p. 472. Kelly claims that five thousand Cuban troops had been flown in to Aden the previous week, presumably for this purpose.
101. Henry Bradsher, "U.S. Steps up Military Aid to North Yemen," *Washington Star*, July 25, 1978, p. A1. *World Military Expenditures and Arms Transfers, 1972–1982* (Washington, DC: U.S. Arms Control and Disarmament Agency, 1984), p. 93, shows a total increase of imported arms of $360 million, from $90 million in 1978 to $450 million in 1979. The difference can probably be accounted for in terms of French arms imports.
102. Talbott, *Endgame*, p. 155.
103. See chapter 3, pp. 55ff, and also Richard Burt, "Asia's 'Great Game' Moves with a Vengeance," *New York Times*, July 9, 1978, p. E3, and Frederic A. Moritz, "China–Vietnam Confrontation Grows," *Christian Science Monitor*, July 11, 1978, p. 4.
104. See "2 U.S. Reporters Accused of 'Denigrating' Soviet TV," *Baltimore Sun*, June 29, 1978, p. 1; David K. Shipler, "Soviet Judge Rules U.S.

Reporters Libeled TV and Orders Retraction," *New York Times*, July 19, 1978, p. 1, and "U.S. to Warn Soviet on Newsmen Ruling," *New York Times*, July 19, 1978, p. 4.

105. David K. Shipler, "Portent of Soviet Dissident's Trial," *New York Times*, July 10, 1978, p. 1.
106. Vance, *Hard Choices*, p. 103. The secretary initially professed the hopeful view that the Soviets were simply attempting to clear the deck of unpleasant matters "in order to assure a more favorable political ambience for SALT the following spring." See Talbott, *Endgame*, pp. 154–55.
107. See Talbott, *Endgame*, pp. 171–77; Richard Burt, "U.S. to Insist on Mobile Missiles in a Soviet Pact," *New York Times*, July 9, 1978, p. 4; and William Beecher, "Vance Vows No Letup in Push for SALT 2," *Boston Globe*, July 11, 1978, p. 6. The mobile missile concept then in vogue was the multiple aim point system (MAPS), or "shell game," in which 200 ICBMs would be moved among 4,000 empty launching sites in random fashion.
108. Talbott, *Endgame*, p. 172.
109. Ibid., p. 173.
110. Ibid. Vance, *Hard Choices*, p. 104, softens it, saying that Semyenov "made an ambiguous statement that suggested Soviet reservations about our position." The irony here was that it had been the Carter administration which had insisted upon stringent verification procedures in the first place and was now faced with the problem of how to maneuver around its own provision.
111. Garthoff, *Detente and Confrontation*, pp. 816–17.
112. Vance, *Hard Choices*, pp. 103–4, indicates that the Soviet proposal was meant to apply to both MX and Trident II. So does Talbott, *Endgame*, pp. 161–63. Garthoff, *Detente and Confrontation*, pp. 816–17, skirts the issue.
113. Vance, *Hard Choices*, p. 104.
114. Karen Elliott House, "Geneva Arms Talks End with No Signs of Gains or Relieved U.S.–Soviet Strains," *Wall Street Journal*, July 14, 1978, p. 1.
115. "Soviet Warns U.S. of Showdown," *New York Times*, July 16, 1978, p. 3.
116. Talbott, *Endgame*, p. 161.
117. Quandt, *Camp David*, p. 197.
118. The scholarly world is indebted to William Quandt for publication of his memoir-analysis of this most intricate problem.
119. Dayan, *Breakthrough*, p. 134, believed that "the Americans were looking for semantic compromises."

120. Brzezinski, *Power and Principle*, p. 235, makes this point in a similar way. "We wanted a peace process that would engage the moderate Arabs in such a way that the American position in the region would be strengthened. . . . We were prepared to work with Begin and Sadat, provided we could create opportunities in the process for engaging other moderate Arabs. That goal meant that some clashes between the United States and Israel were inevitable. The Israelis clearly preferred to confine the peace process to a separate Israeli–Egyptian agreement, which would split the Arabs while letting Israel continue its occupation of the West Bank and Gaza."
121. Carter, *Keeping Faith*, p. 342. "Sadat wanted a strong initial proposal on the record, to appease his fellow Egyptians and the Arab world, but during the negotiations he would be willing to make major concessions (within carefuly prescribed limits), so that his final proposal would prove to everyone the reasonableness of his approach."
122. Carter, *Keeping Faith*, p. 359.
123. Quandt, *Camp David*, p. 245. The United States would eventually agree to help build two new airfields in the Negev to compensate for Israeli withdrawal from the Sinai bases.
124. Carter, *Keeping Faith*, p. 360.
125. Ibid., pp. 366–67.
126. Ibid., p. 373. Quandt, *Camp David*, p. 228, notes that the afternoon before, Carter had told the Americans: "If there are any delays in negotiation of the West Bank/Gaza agreement, that is somebody else's problem. He said that he hoped both agreements could move in parallel, but it was clear that the Egyptian–Israeli one took priority, and if nothing happened in the West Bank for ten years he would not really care very much."
127. Carter, *Keeping Faith*, p. 373.
128. Ibid., p. 374.
129. Quandt, *Camp David*, pp. 243–45. See also Vance, *Hard Choices*, pp. 464–68. The resolution, recall, called generally for "withdrawal of Israeli armed forces from territories occupied in the recent conflict."
130. Carter, *Keeping Faith*, pp. 390–93.
131. Quandt, *Camp David*, p. 240.
132. Carter, *Keeping Faith*, p. 391.
133. Ibid., p. 392.
134. Ibid., p. 391. Vance, *Hard Choices*, p. 224, gives a more restrained account.
135. Carter, *Keeping Faith*, p. 392. Brzezinski, *Power and Principle*, pp. 271–72, who was not informed of the incident by the president until two days later, offers an embellished version of the president's

remarks which leaves out the main point, that the onus for failure would have been on Sadat. Quandt, *Camp David*, p. 239, curiously cites Brzezinski's second-hand account instead of Carter's.

136. Carter, *Keeping Faith*, p. 393 (emphasis in original).
137. Quandt, *Camp David*, pp. 241–46.
138. Ibid., p. 252, and Carter, *Keeping Faith*, p. 398. Why Carter permitted inclusion of a letter restating the long-standing United States position on Jerusalem is unclear, unless he wished to use it to create a delay which he could easily resolve when he desired. See n. 143 below.
139. Quandt, *Camp David*, p. 247.
140. Carter, *Keeping Faith*, p. 397. Vance, *Hard Choices*, pp. 228–29, does say in his memoir that "it is difficult to understand how Begin could have so totally misinterpreted what the president was asking," but in his remarks to the American team immediately after the meeting he acknowledged that Begin had insisted on a three-month moratorium, agreeing only that it *could* be extended, but not that it *would* be extended. See Quandt, *Camp David*, pp. 249–50, for his notes of Vance's remarks.
141. Carter, *Keeping Faith*, p. 397, "I was eager to meet with President Sadat, and he and I quickly went over the proposals for the final language." Ambassador to Egypt Herman Eilts, who was present at Camp David, confirmed that "Sadat . . . was told of Begin's alleged agreement, signed the Camp David accords that Sunday night believing U.S. assurances that a protracted settlements freeze, even if not inscribed into the accords, constituted part of the Camp David package and would be confirmed by letter the following day." See Hermann Eilts, "Improve the Framework," *Foreign Policy*, Winter 1980–81, p. 8. See also Quandt, *Camp David*, p. 251.
142. Quandt, *Camp David*, p. 252.
143. Carter, *Keeping Faith*, p. 400. Vance, *Hard Choices*, p. 225, says that "because of the Jerusalem issue, which consumed much of the next day, we were unable to get the settlements letter signed at Camp David."
144. Quandt, *Camp David*, p. 253, also says that Carter's failure to get Begin's signature on the letter was Washington's "most serious technical mistake." But, of course, there was no letter to sign, at least not one acceptable to the president.
145. Quandt, *Camp David*, p. 267.
146. Ibid., p. 251.
147. Dayan, *Breakthrough*, p. 229, noted that "if the U.S. President wanted clear and specific commitments . . . he should have demanded and tried to get them before the signing of the Camp David accords."
148. For an enlightening analysis of Israeli–Jordanian relations, see Ian S.

Lustick, "Kill the Autonomy Talks," *Foreign Policy*, Winter 1980–1981, pp. 21–43.

149. For the Framework, see Quandt, *Camp David*, pp. 378–79.
150. Carter, *Keeping Faith*, p. 318.

PART II

Strategic Disintegration and Collapse

CHAPTER 6

The Unraveling of American Strategy: SALT II and Iran

In the fall of 1978 American foreign policy entered a very delicate and complicated phase. Policies pursued by the United States and the Soviet Union clashed in climax at several points as the superpowers sought to neutralize each other through deterrence diplomacy, to enable achievement of geopolitical ends without provocation of superpower confrontation. For the United States, the result was partial geopolitical success at the cost of strategic failure.

Five main policy trends converged in the fall of 1978, four in two interrelated theaters—the Middle East–Southwest Asia and East–Southeast Asia—and one of global significance, the SALT II negotiations. In the Middle East–Southwest Asian theater, what was expected to be a three-month treaty negotiation between Egypt and Israel following Camp David dragged on for six months, finally requiring a virtual capitulation by the United States to Israel to reach conclusion. In Iran, on the other hand, Washington's attempt to guide the shah through a transition from autocracy to constitutional monarchy failed utterly, opening an opportunity for the Soviet Union to make its most significant geopolitical advance since World War II.

In Asia, Washington sought to employ the looming conflict between Vietnam and Kampuchea—in which Beijing was determined to intervene on Phnom Penh's behalf—as leverage in the normalization negotiations to establish diplomatic relations between the United States and the People's Republic of China. In providing the materiel and diplomatic support for Hanoi's invasion of Kampuchea, Moscow sought to strengthen its containment of China as well as to build a counterweight to the Sino–American–Japanese entente which appeared to be evolving at that time.

Straddling these two geopolitical crisis areas, but very much a part of them, was the American–Soviet relationship itself and particularly the course of SALT II negotiations. In a classic example of the attempted use of deterrence diplomacy during a pre-conflict period, Washington pressed for conclusion of a SALT treaty in hopes of building a positive relationship with the Soviets and thereby dissuading Moscow from becoming involved either in the Sino–Vietnamese war against China or in Iran as political stability disintegrated.

Ironically, the Soviet Union sought to employ the very same strategem against the United States, but in reverse. The Soviets held out the prospect of reaching a SALT II agreement in the hope of delaying Sino–American normalization beyond the imminent outbreak of the Sino–Vietnamese war. Had this tactic succeeded, Beijing would have been left isolated in the conflict and Moscow free to exert pressure on both China and the United States.

The Carter administration briefly confounded Soviet plans through the normalization of diplomatic relations with China before the outbreak of the Sino–Vietnamese war. This established a diplomatic structure for the conflict which placed each superpower in position to support its respective ally. Unfortunately, while the United States was in position to neutralize Moscow, it took no action in support of Beijing except to give moral support.

SALT As Deterrence Diplomacy

In late summer of 1978 the SALT II negotiations became increasingly governed by geopolitics. Under Secretary Vance's direction, but disputed vigorously by Brzezinski, Washington's policy plans called for resolution of the four major policy issues—signing of the Egyptian–Israeli peace treaty, completion of the Iranian transition, normalization of relations with China, and SALT II—by the end of the year, or shortly thereafter, with SALT II coming first. The precedence of SALT II was particularly important as far as China normalization was concerned because of the obvious and repeated alarm that Soviet leaders expressed over the prospect of a hostile Sino American nexus.[1]

The essential concept governing both American and Soviet negotiating tactics from the fall of 1978 was deterrence diplomacy, the idea that one's adversary could be deterred by diplomatic means from taking undesired action. Theoretically, a SALT II agreement prior to the outbreak of a Sino–Vietnamese conflict would tend to neutralize Moscow with regard to support for Hanoi. On the other hand, Sino–American normalization prior to the outbreak of conflict would tend to range the United States on China's side, protestations of noninvolvement notwithstanding.

For Vance, aside from the fact that SALT II was the centerpiece around which all else was arranged for the success of his strategy, it was particularly important in crafting the diplomatic structure of the impending Sino–Vietnamese conflict. Indeed, the secretary feared that there might be no SALT II accord should normalization precede SALT. In that case, the structure of the conflict would see Moscow and Washington lined up in presumed support of their respective partners, Hanoi and Beijing, respectively. This structure carried within it the basis for a superpower confrontation, should the conflict escalate.

Vance sought to avoid such an evolution by seeking an agreement on SALT II, to be followed by normalization.[2] A major arms control agreement supplemented by promises of increased trade, extension of credits, and technology transfer in the context of a greatly improved superpower relationship offered the best prospect of neutralizing Moscow in the coming conflict and avoiding a superpower confrontation. The secretary would go to extraordinary lengths to secure a SALT II agreement prior to the outbreak of the conflict.

What Vance apparently failed to comprehend, or chose to ignore, was that Moscow was pursuing its own agenda—which dictated that as the conflict approached, Moscow would under no circumstances make agreement on SALT II. Moscow wished no agreement for precisely the same reasons that Washington wanted agreement—it would inhibit the Soviets' freedom of action in the coming conflict. Thus, Moscow's optimum diplomatic structure was to have neither SALT II nor Sino–American normalization by the time war broke out. This would not only leave Moscow free to deter

China, but leave Beijing isolated and without even formal United States support. Indeed, without at least the appearance of American support, the Chinese leadership might be deterred from taking any action to prevent Hanoi's conquest of Kampuchea.

Soviet negotiating tactics from the fall of 1978 therefore were to hold out the *prospect* of a SALT II agreement in hopes of *delaying* Sino–American normalization until *after* the war. Needless to say, this maneuver did not succeed, and Moscow's optimum outcome was not realized, but the tactic illuminates otherwise inexplicable Soviet behavior regarding the SALT II negotiations. Moscow's tactical maneuver did not succeed primarily because the American leadership (except for Secretary Vance, for whom SALT II remained overriding) belatedly recognized the move for what it was and went forward with Sino–American normalization.

Two developments beginning in early August, in retrospect, prompted the Carter leadership to attempt to bring continuing negotiations on both SALT II and normalization with China to fruition. First, there was accumulating evidence that Soviet modifications to the guidance systems of the SS-18 and SS-19 missiles "were making our Minuteman III increasingly vulnerable."[3] Second, the massive Soviet airlift of materiel and advisers to Vietnam began in early August.[4] Up to this point, Washington had procrastinated. It was decided to use Gromyko's annual trip to New York City for the opening of the United Nations session in late September to begin the final phase of the SALT II negotiations.

On September 1, the Special Coordination Committee (SCC) convened to formulate a series of proposals which would "resolve virtually all the remaining major issues" and move the SALT II negotiations to the final stage.[5] Paul Warnke, chief arms control negotiator, was sent to Moscow on September 7 to "tell the Soviets we were ready for what negotiators call the 'endgame.'"[6] To emphasize United States intent, the administration approved a "long-stalled" license for high-technology oil drilling equipment, gave permission for resumption of Soviet trade delegations to the United States, and cleared the trip of Treasury Secretary Blumenthal to Moscow in December.[7] Meanwhile, seeking to accelerate the pace of Sino–American normalization, President Carter became personally involved for the first time in the negotiations with the Chinese and met on September 19 with Ambassador Chai Zemin.[8]

In the weeks prior to Gromyko's visit the Soviet press began to refer to SALT as a "task of supreme urgency" saying that both sides faced their last chance to reach agreement.[9] This seemingly positive press position prompted Vance to observe that the Soviets had "taken several steps" indicating "there were modest grounds for hope that the erosion in U.S.–Soviet relations could be halted."[10] Indeed, after Gromyko's meetings with Vance in New York, September 27 and 28, the secretary was persuaded that "the Soviets were ready to resolve most of the remaining problems and complete a SALT II agreement."[11]

Gromyko had offered a major compromise on cruise missiles, proposing to remove the range limit on ALCM (the pending limit was 2,500 kilometers) in return for a strict 600-kilometer range limit for ground- and sea-launched cruise missiles.[12] During his meeting with Gromyko, the president in turn indicated United States willingness to compromise on the number of ALCM allowed per bomber if the Soviet Union agreed to the American proposal of ten warheads on MX.[13] Carter also sought to dispose of the Backfire issue by simply saying that in the absence of formal Soviet assurances not to upgrade the bomber the United States would reserve the right to deploy a "comparable aircraft."[14]

The president termed his meeting with Gromyko "our most productive one," going so far as to rate it as "one of the best meetings I've ever had with any foreign leader."[15] Brzezinski noted that after the president's meeting with Gromyko "we could all sense that the end was in sight."[16] Vance believed that he and Gromyko "might be able to tie up the loose ends on SALT in a matter of days."[17] Carter "considered the SALT II negotiations to be about over. . . . Now the details could be wrapped up without further delay."[18]

In part, the Carter leadership's optimism was fueled by one of Gromyko's proposals which was not made public at the time. The Soviet foreign minister had proposed that the SALT II treaty "go into effect by next March 31—signing by Presidents Carter and Leonid I. Brezhnev, Senate ratification and all."[19] Gromyko's proposal was clearly designed to suggest, as "some" American officials thought, that "the Kremlin might be eager to complete the treaty."[20] For a March 31 effective date, the implied timetable for completion of negotiations was the end of the year.

But the American side's optimism was shortly deflated. Instead of extending his stay for a few extra days to wrap up the negotiations, Gromyko abruptly departed, arranging for Vance to visit Moscow the following month for what he intimated would be the final negotiating session. When the president learned about Gromyko's sudden departure he "was taken aback" and then irritated to learn that Vance had agreed to go to Moscow without his approval.[21] He felt that "this was a negotiating error, because it implied that we were still open to further discussion on the positions that had just been covered with Gromyko." The president "finally relented" and agreed to Vance's trip only "when he assured me that its primary purpose was to arrange for a summit meeting."[22] Privately, however, Carter began to doubt Soviet sincerity, observing to his staff that "the Soviets seemed to be 'dragging it out.'"[23]

Moscow Eludes Commitment

Thus began a cat-and-mouse game with Washington pressing to conclude the SALT II accord as soon as possible and Moscow "dragging it out," making concessions, raising old issues, retreating on issues already resolved, but always suggesting that agreement would probably be reached in just one more meeting. The American side, and particularly Secretary Vance, so far as the record indicates, professed to believe that the reasons for Soviet delay were contained within the negotiations themselves, that there continued to be legitimate arms control issues which needed resolution.

So Secretary Vance persisted, traveling to Moscow in late October. The atmosphere seemed promising. President Carter noted, "The Soviets seemed quite eager to conclude an agreement on SALT II, and were also more friendly and cooperative in their attitude toward other nonrelated issues."[24] In a note to Carter, Brezhnev promised to provide "maximum assistance" in pressing Syrian President Hafez Assad to agree to a cease-fire in Lebanon, prompting Carter to muse "how fine it would be if we could cooperate like this more often."[25]

The day before Secretary Vance departed for Moscow a story appeared in the *Wall Street Journal* raising doubt that a treaty could be signed before the end of the year. "Neither side," it said, quoting outgoing negotiator Paul Warnke, "wants to appear to be giving last-minute concessions to get a treaty."[26] The argument was that "any hint of hasty U.S. compromises would imperil chances for ratification by the Senate." It would appear that the newspaper story was designed to generate pressure on the Soviets to wrap things up.

Hoping for "SALT by Christmas," Vance made every effort in Moscow to convey American eagerness to conclude the agreement, "bluntly" telling Gromyko that "the Soviets had missed an opportunity to conclude a SALT treaty" in September.[27] Indeed, the secretary seemed genuinely perplexed, believing that "the Russians did not seem to understand that Carter had made a serious attempt . . . to make an agreement possible." Referring to the compromise on ALCM ranges, he declared that they "should have understood the importance of this move."[28]

In the meetings, Gromyko offered a symbolic concession on ICBM testing, agreeing to give advance notice on all extraterritorial and multiple-missile launches.[29] The two sides also came closer on the number of ALCMs permitted per bomber, Vance moving to thirty from the original United States position of thirty-five and Gromyko moving to twenty-five from the original Soviet position of twenty, bringing them within range of agreement. But, in what one participant characterized as "one good news/bad news joke after another," Gromyko began to retreat on issues which seemed to have been resolved.[30]

First, Gromyko reversed position on the number of warheads permitted on new ICBMs, or what was termed "fractionation." He insisted that the SS-17, SS-19, and MX should all be permitted to have six warheads, instead of the current uneven distribution of, respectively, four, six and ten. After prolonged haggling Vance gave in, agreeing to the principle of even distribution but at sharply higher levels. The secretary succeeded in preserving ten warheads for MX, but at the high price of allowing ten each for the SS-17 and SS-19, too.[31]

Gromyko's major step backward came on the issue of encryption, the encoding of missile-test telemetry, which had prevented United States intelligence from deciphering test data to verify Soviet compliance with the proposed treaty. A few days prior to Vance's trip, American negotiators in Geneva had insisted that the treaty must spell out a "common understanding" that telemetry should be banned "whenever it impedes verification."[32] After lengthy discussion, the Soviet negotiator Vladimir Semyenov agreed.[33]

When Vance sought to confirm the "common understanding" with Gromyko and Semyenov, who was also present, Gromyko denied any relevance of missile-test telemetry to the provisions of SALT, "sharply" repudiating Semyenov, who, it was said, had not "understood" the Soviet position.[34] Vance professed to believe that "Moscow did not understand what we were proposing."[35] Despite repeated efforts to explain that the United States simply wished to "ban only encryption . . . that impeded verification," he thought the Soviets suspected that Washington wanted a formulation which would enable a challenge of all encryption.[36] At any rate, the encryption issue was "wide open again."

Then, in a meeting with Brezhnev just prior to his departure, Vance conveyed President Carter's interest in an early summit meeting. But Brezhnev's reply was that "a summit was not possible until Gromyko and I had settled all the remaining issues on SALT."[37] Despite the neat maze which the Soviets had contrived for the secretary, from which the only exit was through Moscow, he continued to believe "that there was a chance we could resolve most of the remaining 'big' issues by the end of the year and hold a summmit early in 1979."[38] President Carter took a different view. He saw the Moscow meeting as accomplishing "nothing," saying that "the Soviets seemed to reverse themselves. . . ."[39] To him "it was now obvious that although the Soviets could accept our remaining proposals, they were holding back on one or two. . . ."[40]

While the Carter leadership puzzled over the reasons for Moscow's backtracking—Secretary Vance and the arms control team persisted in explaining Soviet inflexibility in terms of the negotiations themselves—Moscow took a major step in Southeast Asia. On November 3, the Soviet Union signed a "peace and friendship treaty" with Vietnam. Aside from signalling the imminence of conflict, the treaty—combined with continuing Soviet arms shipments—clearly conveyed Moscow's intention to support Hanoi and served as a warning to Beijing, and also to Washington.

The immediate result was a slowdown in the SALT negotiations as United States officials expressed doubt that "a new agreement . . . can be achieved, as they had once anticipated, by the end of the year."[41] Another report, based on interviews with East-bloc officials, noted that the "Kremlin's concern over China has a lot to do with the lack of progress. . . ."[42] The Russians, one said, wanted to see a more balanced approach to the USSR. "They do not . . . see that balance in President Carter's recently accelerated drive to normalize

US relations with China, or, even more, in his acquiescence in his NATO allies supplying arms to China."[43]

But over the course of the next week, the president reversed himself, as Moscow evidently eased the American leadership's concerns. At a breakfast meeting with reporters on November 16, the president asserted that "U.S. relations with the Soviet Union are improving," and that he "expects to meet with Soviet leader Leonid I. Brezhnev for a 'quite broad' discussion of overall Soviet–American relations."[44] Asked by reporters to explain the sudden turnabout over the past few weeks Carter declared that he couldn't say why there had been a recent improvement in relations.

Although it is unknown precisely what had transpired, it obviously involved private Soviet reaffirmation of interest in, if not commitment to, SALT and the summit; and it galvanized the Carter leadership into renewed efforts to bring the treaty negotiations to conclusion. Over the second half of November a package of inducements was put together in hopes of finally concluding the negotiations. In effect, the Carter leadership tried to strike the same quid pro quo that the Nixon adminstration had attempted to arrange in 1972–73: trade and advanced technology in return for strategic weapons restraint, that is, an arms agreement.

In addition to Treasury Secretary Blumenthal's already scheduled trip, the United States government now encouraged some four hundred American business leaders to attend the seventh annual meeting of the Joint Commercial Commission, first established in 1972. The attendance of such a large and prominent "blue-chip" group was clearly intended to suggest a readiness to do business with Moscow. Nor was the quid pro quo left ambiguous. Although "a White House official" denied any "linkage" between SALT and trade, saying that it was a "question of atmosphere," he conceded that "any major increase in the scope of U.S.–Soviet trade," that is, "any serious attempt to remove legislative trade barriers would depend on a successful treaty resolution."[45] An arms control treaty would provide, he said, "the atmosphere for transfer of advanced technology."

Secretary Vance also publicly declared that "relations with the Soviet Union are improving and there is still a possibility of a stategic arms limitation treaty this year."[46] Placing an arms accord "at the top of the list of priorities," he said he was "hopeful things are now in a more stable condition than they were in the past." Asked why he believed this, Vance, too, fudged, saying simply that it was the result of "numerous discussions that I've had with senior officials in the Soviet government. It is based upon their statements. . . ." The secretary declared that his next session with Gromyko in late December "would not be a negotiating session." In fact, he said, "it would be held only if the arms issues were settled, allowing both men to focus on preparing the way for a meeting in the United States between President Carter and Leonid I. Brezhnev."[47]

The secretary's discussions with Soviet officials persuaded him to sweeten the arms control pot with "an outright American concession."[48] He had come to the conclusion that it was the United States position on cruise missile definition that was the reason for Soviet procrastination and that a unilateral concession would produce the desired breakthrough. The United States position was that during the three-year protocol period any plane carrying a cruise missile would be counted as a heavy bomber against the 1,320 subceiling.[49] Once the protocol expired, however, only heavy bombers carrying cruise missiles would count against the subceiling. Other aircraft would then be free to carry cruise missiles, as long as they were conventionally armed. How to distinguish between nuclear- and conventionally-armed cruise missiles was not specified.

After a protracted and extensive internal deliberation, the Carter leadership reached agreement on the issue of cruise missile definition. It was decided to withdraw the proposed exemption for conventionally armed cruise missiles on aircraft other than heavy bombers.[50] A few days later, in early December, Secretary Vance conveyed the decision to Dobrynin, making it clear that he expected this concession to finally produce an agreement. Dobrynin indicated, without committing Moscow beforehand, that the next Vance–Gromyko meeting in Geneva just before Christmas "should be productive and might permit the two sides to announce a date for a summit meeting."[51]

As if in response, Brezhnev told the four hundred visiting American business executives that "the Soviet Union wanted to complete a new treaty on the limitation of strategic arms 'without further procrastination' and to expand trade with the United States."[52] Brezhnev declared: "If the American side has the desire and is prepared to rectify the situation in Soviet–American relations, it will find the Soviet Union to be a reliable partner."[53]

Vance's euphoria over finally nailing down the treaty lasted only a few days until Victor Karpov, Semyenov's replacement in Geneva, told Ralph Earle, who had replaced Warnke, that the Soviet Union was backing away from yet another agreement which they had already accepted. It involved the issue of defining new types of ICBMs.[54] As so far agreed, each side could test and deploy one new light ICBM during the life of the treaty. One of the agreed rules distinguishing a new ICBM from modification of an existing one was that any ICBM with a 5 percent, plus or minus, difference in size from existing types would be considered a new ICBM.

Karpov accepted the upper 5 percent limit, but wanted no limit on "downsizing" ICBMs, a patently transparent ploy which would have allowed the Soviet Union to build and test any number of smaller ICBMs instead of being restricted to the one which had been agreed upon. Needless to say, exasperated American negotiators objected to the Soviet proposal in the strongest terms. Had the Soviets simply miscalculated, agreeing to the 5 percent rule before analyzing its implications, as one author suggests?[55] Given the clear evidence of the previous three months' deliberate foot-dragging by the Soviets, this seems unlikely.

More likely, it seems, the "downsizing" ploy was yet another attempt to hold out the prospect of an agreement in hopes of delaying Sino–American normalization, now reaching its critical point. Indeed, Ambassador Woodcock had just completed presentation of the United States position on December 4, and Washington was anxiously awaiting the Chinese leadership's reply. After some tense moments and last-minute haggling, President Carter decided to announce the agreement to normalize Sino–American relations on December 15 along with Deng Xiaoping's acceptance of the president's invitation to visit the United States in late January.[56]

The Failure of SALT As Deterrence Diplomacy

Moscow's tactic had partially failed. The imminence of conflict between Hanoi and Phnom Penh had after all governed the timing of Sino–American normalization. On the surface at least, the United States was now linked to and in support of China. Although the Soviets had failed to establish the optimum structure of no SALT and no normalization, Moscow could and would ensure that it retained the freedom to support Hanoi, to exert pressure on Beijing, and to attempt to neutralize Washington. This, of course, required that the Soviet Union abjure agreement on the SALT treaty.

President Carter "was sure that our announcement . . . of plans to normalize diplomatic relations with China would cool the Soviets' willingness to conclude the SALT agreement,"[57] but he claimed to be pleasantly surprised by the "very positive" message received from Brezhnev a few days later. The president said in disclosing the note that the Soviet leader expressed "his understanding" that the entirely "proper" decision to establish diplomatic relations with China "will contribute to world peace."[58]

Nevertheless, Secretary Vance departed for his Geneva meetings, December 21 to 23, "with mixed feelings of hope and concern."[59] Earlier, the Soviets had assured the secretary, and he had duly made public, that the coming meeting with Gromyko would be held "only if the arms issues were settled" and would "not be a negotiating session."[60] The focus was to be the coming summit in Washington. But the Vance–Gromyko meetings concentrated entirely upon the "arms issues," and while progress was made on some, more were dredged up to delay agreement—and the United States side now participated in this procedure.

On the first day, Vance offered a draft of the common understanding on the encryption issue, and Gromyko countered with a Soviet draft; the United States draft emphasized the impermissibility of encryption when it impeded verification, and the Soviet draft emphasized its permissibility when it did not. Gromyko "wanted to remand the two proposals to the expert level for resolution," but Vance opposed that, concerned that "the issue would then drag on indefinitely."[61] Hoping to "crack this nut then and there," Vance said he wanted to reflect on it overnight and discuss it again the next day.

That afternoon the Soviet intent became unmistakable, even to Secretary Vance, as Gromyko raised a series of "trivial" issues, including multiple-warhead cruise missiles and unarmed cruise missile drones. As Vance put it, "when Gromyko raised for the first time in the negotiations the question of including remote pilotless vehicles (drones) in the treaty, my colleagues and I became uneasy. This was clearly a red herring."[62]

While Vance and Gromyko were meeting, Tass released details of Brezhnev's message to President Carter of three days before, claiming that the president had "distorted" it.[63] The president, Tass said, had failed to mention the "deep reservations" which Brezhnev had expressed regarding both Beijing's intentions and the anti-hegemony clause contained in the communiqué. Emphasizing Soviet concerns, policy adviser Georgi Arbatov declared that if Washington and Beijing formed "even an informal alliance," there would be "no place for detente" between Washington and Moscow.[64]

The Tass release set the stage for Vance's meeting of December 22 with Gromyko. Although further progress was made on several issues—including narrowing the gap on the number of ALCMs per bomber to a difference of one (Vance moving from 30 to 28 and Gromyko from 25 to 27), reverting to their earlier agreement on the number of MIRVs (four for the SS-17, six for the SS-19, and ten for MX), and the 5 percent limit for downsizing—Gromyko made the reason for Soviet displeasure over the negotiations plain.[65] It was the timing of Sino–American normalization.

Gromyko was "angry" that the announcement on normalization came "at this time," which resembled to Soviet leaders "some sort of political game on the broadest possible scale."[66] Vance's profuse declarations that normalization was "not aimed at the Soviet Union or anyone else" allowed the two men to set their difference aside and return to the remaining major arms control issue—encryption. Overnight the United States side had produced a "marriage" of the Soviet and American proposals, in effect the inclusion of both positions in the common understanding. The resulting common understanding specified that telemetry "would be banned whenever it impeded verification" but that it "would be permitted as long as it did not impede verification."[67]

Feeling that "we were about to break the back of the single biggest issue remaining," Vance cabled home the proposed compromise.[68] Anticipating a favorable reply, he authorized spokesman Hodding Carter to say that "we are close to the end of the road," prompting dispatch of several wire service stories suggesting that "SALT was at hand."[69] In Washington, however, Vance's cable precipitated concern that the proposed understanding was too vague and would permit every kind of encryption.[70] After several hours of deliberation and discussion with the president, who was in Plains, Secretary Vance was instructed to seek Moscow's agreement against encryption of the sort employed in a missile test earlier in the year, on July 29.

Vance was extremely upset. He felt that to press the issue would "jeopardize SALT" and insisted that Brzezinski "review the situation with the President."[71] After considering the issue a second time, the president reaffirmed the instructions. When Vance raised the issue with Gromyko, the Soviet foreign minister "refused to respond," seeing it as an "attempt to apply retroactively a provision of a treaty that was not yet concluded, much less in force."[72]

Whatever valid concerns the United States had, taking a tough stance on encryption facilitated Gromyko's stall. He replied that the Soviet leadership, as it had repeatedly declared, could not commit itself to a summit until all outstanding treaty issues were resolved. He then listed cruise missile drones, multiple-warhead cruise missiles, bomber definition, the expiration date for the protocol, and the dismantling schedule for weapons currently over the limit imposed by the treaty. These, he declared, were issues which could not be remanded to the delegations and must be decided upon by the principals.[73]

Thus, the talks ended with no agreement for a summit. Vance stated in his press conference afterward that the two sides had "agreed in principle" to a summit, but Gromyko said in a separate statement that "there were still too many issues to resolve to set a date."[74] The plain fact was that Moscow did not want an agreement because it would tie Soviet hands in the coming conflict. Vance blamed the failure to reach agreement in December on the "manner and timing" of the announcement of Sino–American normalization.[75] But the argument that a SALT agreement would have been reached had normalization not preempted it ignores Soviet stalling tactics of several months designed precisely to delay normalization.

Moscow wanted no SALT agreement and no entrapment in American largess before the outbreak of the Sino–Vietnamese conflict in order to be free to attempt to influence its outcome. No agreement—SALT or otherwise—could paper over the very real and growing geopolitical differences between Moscow and Washington. The imminent Southeast Asian conflict was crucial, but of growing importance was the collapsing American position in Iran, a situation which Moscow also hoped to exploit, and to which we now turn.

The United States and Iran

In analyzing the extremely complex issue of Iran, the reader must keep in mind two distinct though interacting processes. One was the self-destruction of the Pahlavi dynasty, commonly referred to as the

Iranian revolution, and the other was the United States government's response to it. Under the containment strategy, Iran clearly played a crucial role along with Turkey, Pakistan, and Afghanistan as the "northern tier" of containment. Under containment, Washington's relationship to Tehran was equally clearly a patron-client relationship.

The shift in American strategy in 1973 as the United States moved to restructure its forward position around the Soviet periphery meant a gradual but inevitable change in Iran's role and in Washington's relationship to Tehran. Iran, after all, having a fifteen-hundred-mile border with the Soviet Union, occupied the forward-most position in the containment structure. President Nixon's policy to employ Iran (and Saudi Arabia) as substitutes for a departed Great Britain and a weakened Pakistan after 1971 was made in the context of reinforcing containment, hence the decision to supply military weaponry in great volume to Tehran. From 1973 onward, however, the emphasis broadened to include economic modernization and political liberalization as well as military construction, as the United States sought to strengthen Iran to play a more prominent and independent regional role.

Given the change in American strategy, it was only a matter of time and circumstance before the United States would seek to change the patron-client relationship with Tehran to more equitable, balanced ties. Under the Carter administration, the form which this change took was an American effort to promote the culmination of the transition from autocracy to constitutional monarchy. Unfortunately, while the purpose of American policy was to assist in the evolution of more democratic government in Iran, its effect was to hasten the collapse of the regime, which was already in an advanced state of decay by the time the Carter administration took office.

The crisis of regime in Iran was essentially the product of three long-range decisions: the strategic bargain struck with President Nixon for Iran to become the "protector of the Gulf"; the shah's decision to embark upon a rapid modernization program in the wake of the windfall of high oil prices in 1973; and the shah's determination to promote political liberalization leading to constitutional government. Perhaps the most critical factor was the quadrupling of oil prices, which persuaded the shah that he would have the revenues necessary to transform his backward nation into a "great civilization" and the world's fifth-largest industrial power by the end of the century.[76]

Discarding the gradual approach in force since the fifties and opting for a "big push" strategy, in 1974 the shah decided—against the advice of his planners and most of his political advisers—upon a massive and rapid modernization drive. Infrastructural bottlenecks—such as a primitive communications system, inadequate port capacity, absence of a heavy industrial base, limited water and power supply, and, most of all, a severe lack of an educated population, let alone technical expertise—could not be overcome quickly through infusion of money alone.

The shah's decision was premature. As a society, Iran had simply not yet reached the takeoff point. By the end of 1975, the hyperboom generated by the big push strategy quickly sent the economy out of control. The infusion of large amounts of money, beyond the capacity of the economy to absorb, triggered an inflationary spiral which had a most profound and debilitating impact on the nation. The cost of everything from the largest developmental project to daily necessities skyrocketed.

The shah's initial response was to attempt to impose price controls, rather than to cut back on expenditures and slow the pace of his programs. He exhorted his people to exert "more effort" to overcome problems. The result was that producers simply stopped producing at controlled prices, a black market became rampant, and the economy stagnated. It was not until October of 1976, partly owing to the global recession which reduced revenues, that the shah reversed course, cut back expenditures, and gradualized his programs.

By then, virtually every sector of Iranian society had become alienated from the regime, which the cutback now exacerbated. The shah had decreed land reform, giving land to the tiller only to snatch it away in an unsuccessful attempt to establish an agribusiness system on the American model. Iran's urban population grew rapidly as peasants drifted to cities, where wages were higher; but housing was inadequate and, after retrenchment began, work scarce. Some success had occurred in the attempt to establish a heavy industrial base, but at the price of large-scale importation of much-resented foreign expertise.

The attempt to develop a modern secular state also involved repudiation of the tacit alliance with the Islamic clergy, as traditional state subsidies to religious leaders were terminated. The growing economic pressure on the mosques inflamed the already alienated mullahs. Subsidization of student education abroad brought little benefit in the short run, and it generated considerable disaffection as educated Iranians became imbued with Western values. The gap between expectation and reality grew.

The armed forces appeared to be the principal beneficiary of the shah's modernization drive as massive amounts were spent on importation of the most modern equipment available. In the twenty-year period preceding 1971, Iran purchased less than one billion dollars in arms from the United States. However, in the seven-year period which followed, the shah ticketed nineteen billion dollars for arms purchases.[77] The rapid expansion of the armed forces, however, meant that there was insufficient time to develop the necessary loyalties to unit, service, and nation which would have occurred over a longer period—let alone time to acquire the technical expertise needed to operate and maintain highly sophisticated weaponry.

The irony was that at the moment the shah had decided to transform his nation he also learned of the cancer which virtually ensured that he would not live to see the fruit of his efforts. Sometime in 1974, if not earlier, the shah's French physicians diagnosed that he was suffering from a form of cancer which had caused the death of other members of his family.[78] Although the shah kept this knowledge from everyone, the discovery of his disease coming when it did invites speculation regarding his choice of an accelerated modernization program. In retrospect it seems undeniable that his subsequent decisions, particularly the way he dealt with or failed to deal with the challenge to his regime, were profoundly affected by his advancing illness.

Politically, Pahlavi rule was characterized by extreme institutional compartmentalization, with all decisionmaking centered in the person of the shah himself. Despite the perhaps genuine intent to move toward the political liberalization of Iranian politics, the shah never permitted real power to be held by any other individual, group, or institution. In the army, for example, all senior officers reported directly to the shah. Indeed, no two generals could meet without the shah's permission.[79] Since he was literally the central and indispensable element of his regime, revolution in one form or another would be the inevitable consequence of the shah's departure.

By the time Jimmy Carter became president of the United States the classic conditions for turmoil and instability, if not revolution, were already well developed and evident in Iran. The early thrust of American policies, under the direction of Secretary of State Vance, was without question aimed at furthering the process of political liberalization and the gradual reduction of the United States "profile" in Iran. Washington's emphasis on human rights, professed American intentions to reduce arms sales, and the supine United States reaction to Soviet geopolitical moves in Ethiopia, Yemen, and especially Afghanistan—all had the effect of diminishing United States reliability in the shah's eyes.

The shah's uncertainty regarding Iran's role in United States strategy clearly affected him. He expressed the view to both American and foreign leaders that the United States had made "a drastic change in strategy" and questioned whether Washington had decided to withdraw its support.[80] In May, just after the coup in Afghanistan, he queried visiting former Vice-President Nelson Rockefeller "point-blank" whether the United States and the Soviet Union were colluding in an effort to divide the world between them—which, of course, would place Iran in Moscow's sphere.[81] American denials of a change in strategy or of collusion with Moscow were unconvincing. The shah's suspicions that the United States–Iran relationship had changed clearly added to his uncertainty and confusion as the domestic situation in Iran worsened.

Although it is common to date the beginning of the Iranian revolution from the riots in Qum in January 1978, it was not until much later in the year that a cohesive, well-directed opposition to the regime coalesced. Until mid-year, urban disturbances appeared to be well under the control of the regime and actually diminishing.[82] But the mid-year quiescence was misleading. By the end of July clashes between a now more unified opposition and the government resumed, but with a new twist. Up to this point, the opposition's demand had not been for the end of the monarchy, but only for adherence to the 1906 constitution and for state respect for Islam. From this point onward, however, exiled religious leader Ayatollah Khomeini's call for the end of the Pahlavi regime and establishment of an Islamic republic began to drown out the voices of the more moderate opposition.

The shah was sufficiently attentive to this shift to attempt to counter it. On August 5, the anniversary of the 1906 constitution—and also the beginning of the fasting month of Ramadan—he announced that in the context of continuing his program of political liberalization there would be completely free elections in June 1979 which would exclude only the communists. This carrot was accompanied by greater application of the stick as police and army units used increasingly harsh methods, including firing on and killing demonstrators, in an effort to suppress the dissidence.

But the increased use of the "stick" served only to inflame opposition to the regime. The violence, beginning in the city of Isfahan on August 10 and 11, where over a hundred people were killed, quickly spread.[83] A government curfew imposed to discourage demonstrations and riots against the regime was defied all over the country. Culminating this phase of violence was the burning of the Rex Cinema in the city of Abadan where some 477 people perished. The government accused "Islamic fundamentalists" of the crime, but it was widely believed to have been the work of the Iranian secret police, SAVAK.[84]

The shah's response was an attempt at the end of August to split the religious from the lay opposition with the appointment of a "reform" government of national reconciliation under Ja'far Sharif-Emami, a former prime minister with contacts in the Islamic community and the grandson of a well-known religious figure.[85] Sharif-Emami made an outright appeal to the religious community for support, by advocating a return to the Islamic calendar, which had been discarded two years earlier, and promising a greater response to the opposition's concerns. His attempt at reconciliation failed. Khomeini, who in the meantime had moved to the forefront of the opposition, called openly for the overthrow of the shah.[86]

The level of violence jumped alarmingly in September with the Jaleh Square massacre on the eighth. Peaceful, large-scale demonstrations of over a hundred thousand people had occurred in Tehran on September 4 and 5 celebrating the end of Ramadan. Having successfullly organized these demonstrations against government wishes, the opposition now called for a general strike. The government immediately responded with a declaration of martial law in a dozen major cities.[87] On September 8, some 20,000 people congregated at Jaleh Square in Tehran and refused to disperse when ordered to do so. Army troops under the command of martial law administrator General Gholam Ali Oveissi opened fire, killing between three and four hundred people and wounding over three thousand more.

The bloody incident appalled and politicized the public, marking the beginning of general public alienation from the shah, who was believed to have been directly responsible for the decision to shoot.[88] Within two weeks, the impact of "Black Friday," as the Jaleh Square massacre was called, had spread and shops began to close down and workers to strike. By the end of September workers in some eighty trade unions had walked off their jobs, despite government prohibition against strikes.[89] Incredibly, the government continued to pay the salaries of striking workers, which only increased their incentive to stay off their jobs.

The shah's attempt to defuse worker discontent in October through generous wage settlements and announcement of several development projects in housing, education, and agriculture had little effect. Indeed, October saw the beginning of widespread strikes and work stoppages in the oil fields, and petroleum output began to drop rapidly.[90] By the end of the month, as Secretary Vance noted, "the Shah was at a crossroads."[91] It was only at this point, after ten months of civil disturbance, that the White House held its first high-level policy meeting on Iran.[92]

Containment and Disengagement in Iran

After the Sharif-Emami government's conciliatory measures failed, the shah sought Washington's support for the establishment of a military government under himself.[93] In what had become an almost daily occurrence, the shah met with Ambassador William Sullivan and British Ambassador Anthony Parsons on October 24. Careful not to reveal his preference, indeed expressing doubt that military government would work, the shah proposed two options: a military government, or a coalition which would include some members of the opposition.

He appeared to be operating on the assumption that the United States would prefer a military government and that the threat to install a coalition would prod Washington into a public commitment. Perhaps to the shah's surprise, Ambassadors Sullivan and Parsons argued against the military option, urging a broadening of the Sharif-Emami government into a coalition with members of the opposition.[94] A week later the shah increased the pressure on Washington for a commitment by raising the prospect of his abdication, a threat which generated a flurry of activity in Washington.

The shah's postulation of the alternatives divided the Carter leadership, bringing to a head fundamental differences of strategy between Brzezinski and Vance. Up to this point, so long as the shah had appeared to retain control, there had been few discernible differences between the two men regarding assisting the shah in his widely proclaimed modernization program, as it included making a political transition from autocracy to constitutional government. Brzezinski and Vance agreed on the need to promote political liberalization and economic modernization while moderating Tehran's military buildup.

When the crisis of the regime arose and it became apparent that the shah might abdicate, the two men split over the proper policy course to pursue. It was at this point, in late October, that the internal conflict surfaced between the advocates of containment and the advocates of the new order in the administration. The president, though he supported the shah and "did not want him to abdicate,"[95] vacillated between them.

Each man pressed for policies consistent with his strategic conception. Vance's policy position implied an outcome under which Iran would occupy a neutral, independent position between East and West and no longer be an American instrument of pressure against the Soviet Union. Brzezinski, on the other hand, argued for an outcome which would retain Iran as an important American ally within a containment structure. The strategic question was containment versus disengagement, but the policy issue was: What role for the shah?

Thus, when constitutional monarchy in Iran appeared infeasible, Secretary Vance pressed for a coalition government of major claimants to power—first including the shah, then later without him. Brzezinski, on the other hand, argued for a military government under the shah, then, when that possibility vanished, sought his removal and a military coup to preserve a pro-American regime.[96] The record indicates rather clearly that until very late in the day President Carter understood neither the strategic conception which underlay Secretary Vance's policy positions, which he initially endorsed, nor the implications in them for America's relations with Iran. Until very near the end, the president appears to have believed that close relations between the United States and Iran would be an integral part of whatever political arrangement evolved there.

In truth, Vance and his representative in Iran, Ambassador

William Sullivan, did not wish to see the collapse of Iran into chaos and/or the emergence of an anti-American regime. Secretary Vance's proposals for fostering a transition in Iran from autocracy to Western-style government—first constitutional monarchy and then coalition government—were the policy manifestation of the strategy of constructing a new global order, as described in this volume. As Vance put it, "We believed that over time U.S. and Iranian interests in a strong, stable, non-Communist Iran should permit a cooperative, if far less intimate, relationship to emerge."[97]

In the Special Coordinating Committee meeting of November 2, it was decided—after the president's intervention—to convey support to the shah "without reservation" and "confidence" in his judgment, but also to urge the "need for decisive action and leadership."[98] Regarding the shah's "options," the message stated, "our position is that this is up to the Shah." Once "order and authority" have been restored, the message concluded, Washington hoped that he would "resume prudent efforts to promote liberalization and to eradicate corruption."

In a telephone call to the shah the next day, in which he conveyed the gist of the November 2 decision, Brzezinski attempted to place the emphasis on the need to "demonstrate effective authority." During their conversation, the shah requested that Brzezinski repeat the point that "concessions alone are likely to produce a more explosive situation." He then asked, "Is your ambassador briefed?" indicating that the concessions approach, that is, coalition government, was being urged on him by Sullivan.[99]

Brzezinski was satisfied with the November 2 decision because it placed the United States on record as favoring the need for decisive action, even though it left vague precisely what "decisive" meant. Vance agreed with it because, aside from the fact that the president had decided the policy issue, he still saw the shah as the critical political figure in managing any transition to constitutional monarchy. Vance's concern was to hold together what was perceived to be the only cohesive institution, the army. Thus, "If the shah's decision was to turn to the military we would strongly prefer a military government with the shah to one without him. Without his unifying presence as a focus for its loyalty, the army might rapidly splinter into warring factions."[100]

The shah, however, was agitated over Washington's refusal to take a strong stand. The United States government would support "whichever route" he chose, but would not make the decision for him.[101] Since Washington had declined to support his preferred option, the shah moved to make Washington's commitment in favor of military government unavoidable. On November 4 and for the next two days, it is now known, on the shah's orders SAVAK carried out a wave of violence in Tehran, which included the burning of the British embassy and a number of other buildings identified as representing Western influence.[102]

On the fourth, while much of the city was in flames and tanks surrounded the palace, the shah called Sullivan in to say that he now "felt he had no choice but to establish a military government."[103] To his inquiry as to whether Washington would support him, Sullivan replied that he had "already anticipated this request and had received Washington's assurance that he would be supported in this action." The shah, "enormously relieved, . . . ordered a whiskey" for the ambassador. When Sullivan asked the shah whether rumors he had heard "that the burnings were an action by professional arson squads of SAVAK, who were using this means to provoke the shah into a drastic reaction that would install a military government," the shah replied, "Who knows? These days I am prepared to believe anything."[104]

Sullivan had been closer to the mark than he knew. While expressing extreme reluctance to Sullivan and Parsons regarding the employment of force against his own people, the shah showed a radically different face to his military chiefs. In fact, he specifically ordered martial law chief General Oveissi to "prevent his soldiers from stopping the fires set by SAVAK incendiaries."[105] He explained that "all they're doing is burning tires—for the most part. . . . Tires make a lot of smoke. People get scared. That will help you when you want to fire on them." To Oveissi's response that the situation was already out of control, the shah declared, "Our machine guns will keep everyone quiet."[106]

On November 6 the shah replaced the Sharif-Emami government with a military government headed by General Reza Gholam Azhari, chief of staff of the armed forces.[107] Brzezinski mistakenly interpreted this step as "a welcome sign that the Shah had finally faced up to the crisis and was prepared to assert effective leadership."[108] The reverse was true. The Azhari government was military in name only, as most ministries continued to be manned by civilians. Moreover, the shah's speech announcing the new government was unexpectedly mild and apologetic as he declared his determination "to make up for" past "mistakes, unlawful acts, oppression and corruption."[109]

Indeed, rather than crush the revolution, the shah attempted to align himself with it. Over the next several weeks as the Azhari government attempted to restore order, scores of current and former high officials were arrested, including the head of SAVAK, General Namatollah Nassiri, and former Prime Minister Amir Hoveyda, men who had loyally served the shah for many years.[110] The shah also announced the institution of several measures against government corruption and an investigation into the finances of the royal family. The shah's shift, however, failed to placate the opposition, with whom he attempted to reach a negotiated solution, and alarmed his supporters, who concluded that it was now every man for himself.[111]

Furthermore, the shah's ploy to gain United States support for a military government boomeranged. On November 9, Ambassador Sullivan sent a cable to Washington entitled "Thinking the Unthinkable"—that is, the future of Iran without the shah.[112] For the first time the issue was raised of an alternative to the United States policy of working with and through the shah. It was an extremely sensitive subject. Sullivan sought to ease the concern of those who believed that the fall of the shah would have negative consequences for the American position in Iran.

In a carefully hedged analysis, Sullivan saw virtually every conceivable outcome, even a future government dominated by Khomeini, as inevitably pro-Western and anti-Soviet. Iran would become a "Kuwait writ large," and while "U.S. involvement would be less intimate than with the shah . . . it could be an essentially satisfactory one, particularly if the military leadership preserved its integrity."[113] The only change in orientation he foresaw was "a shift on Iran's part from a pro-Israeli to an anti-Zionist position, and a certain aloofness in our overall dealings."[114]

Whatever the impact of Sullivan's cable—and opinions vary[115]—by mid-November the deteriorating situation in Iran had clearly polarized the Carter leadership. Vance began to lean toward the view that change was "certain and imminent" and that the United States should begin cautiously to adjust to an Iran without the shah, but he was not yet ready to drop him. "I did not believe that we should abandon the shah or promote an arrangement between the generals and the religous hard-liners while there was still a chance that the shah might succeed in reaching an agreement with responsible members of the opposition on an orderly transition to a constitutional monarchy."[116]

Brzezinski, on the other hand, began to intensify his efforts to "encourage the shah to use the army to smash the opposition."[117] Indeed, at this point, he evidently was the inspiration behind the scene for a military coup under martial-law commander General Oveissi, whose object was to save the throne for the shah.[118] The "plan," if it can be called such, was to spirit the shah away to a safe haven, perhaps on the Iranian island of Kish in the Persian Gulf, restore order and authority, then bring him back. Two separate approaches, one by several high-ranking Iranian generals and another by agents of the Central Intelligence Agency, brought firm rejections from General Oveissi, who adamantly refused "to do anything against the shah."[119]

Moscow, too, saw collapse coming and sought to deter Washington from any direct effort to forestall it. On November 18, Brezhnev sent a letter to President Carter, (which *Pravda* published simultaneously) warning the United States against intervening in Iranian affairs.[120] "It must be clear," he said, "that any interference, especially military interference in the affairs of Iran—a state which directly borders on the Soviet Union—would be regarded by the U.S.S.R. as a matter affecting its security interests." The letter did not say what the Soviets would do in case of Western military intervention, but it contained the strong hint of "possible military moves by the Soviet Union to counter any western military effort on behalf of the shah."[121]

Brezhnev's letter came only five days after President Carter had declared in a news conference that there was no "evidence that the Soviets . . . are trying to disrupt the existing government structure in Iran."[122] He averred that it was in Soviet interest to have a "stable government there no matter who its leaders might be." Contradicting Carter, Brezhnev saw the eradication of American influence as paramount, and turmoil as preferable to continuation of Iran's close ties to the United States. In a policy change, Moscow appeared to be positioning itself as the "protector" of the revolutionary forces. On cue, the National Voice of Iran (NVOI), Moscow's clandestine radio station, stepped up its incendiary broadcast chant that Moscow stood firmly in support of those in "the battle to oust imperialism, particularly U.S. imperialism."[123]

Concerned that the Soviet Union was planning to use claims of Western intervention in Iran as a pretext for intervention of its own, Carter sent back a sharply worded reply. "We have no intention of permitting others to interfere in the internal affairs of Iran."[124] Additionally, determined to rebut what was interpreted as embarrassing, gratuitous criticism of the president, a formal public rejoinder was issued in Secretary Vance's name (but was actually a collective effort by Brzezinski, Brown, and Vance made after a series of unusual high-level meetings at the White House).[125]

The Carter Leadership in Disarray

The Brezhnev letter, as Brzezinski notes, introduced a "more ominous international dimension"[126] just as it became painfully evident that the Azhari government would fail to restore order, Khomeini's forces were preparing to step up their offensive, and the shah began to withdraw into inaction.[127] The burgeoning crisis, in turn, increased the pressure upon the Carter leadership; and at this point Vance and Brzezinski moved with a growing sense of urgency onto sharply divergent policy paths, which the president found ever more difficult to reconcile.

Vance sought to push the shah into jettisoning the military government and forming a civilian coalition. On November 22 he "cabled Sullivan that we must offer the shah our frank advice in helping him try to put together a new civilian government."[128] At the same time, he sought to repair relations with Moscow, claiming (without citable evidence) that ties were improving. In an interview with the *New York Times* a week after Brezhnev's warning letter, the secretary declared, "We've had difficult and rough spots during the past year, but I'm hopeful things are now in a more stable condition than they were in the past."[129] He asserted that the Soviets "believe that if we can achieve a SALT agreement, it will be then easier to lessen tensions and to seek parallel interests and improve relations not only bilaterally but also internationally."

Finally, in early December, the secretary attempted unsuccessfully to cut Brzezinski entirely out of the policy process on Iran. Brzezinski had arranged for Ambassador Zahedi to meet with President Carter on November 21, the eve of his return to Tehran. Zahedi's intent was to stiffen the shah's resolve; perhaps he even entertained visions of playing a role similar to the one which his father had played in 1953 in managing the shah's restoration. President Carter told Zahedi to "keep in touch with" Brzezinski, and the national security adviser had "four or five telephone conversations" with him before his return to Washington in mid-January.[130]

At any rate, Brzezinski's contacts were the stimulus behind Secretary Vance's attempt to muzzle the national security adviser in much the same way he had done earlier in the year,[131] but this time he had different results. Vance claimed that "Brzezinski had opened up his own direct channels to Tehran and had carried on discussions with Ardeshir Zahedi without the knowledge of anyone in the State Department."[132] When Vance confronted him with this accusation, Brzezinski denied it, whereupon Vance insisted that he "come with me to see the president. The president met with us and I told him what I had learned. He asked Zbig if this was true. Zbig denied it. The president then asked that he be supplied with copies of all communications between the White House and Tehran. That was the last I heard of the matter, but the back-channel communications stopped."[133]

It is not clear from the record that Vance in fact stopped Brzezinski's back-channel contacts. According to Brzezinski, in early December "the president approved my calling Zahedi in Tehran to reassure him."[134] Nor did Vance succeed in ending Brzezinski's policy involvement. The national security adviser continued to play a prominent, even though largely ineffectual, role in opposition to Vance on Iranian policy. Brzezinski had reached the point in early December where he believed that "the Shah was becoming an obstacle to any resolution of the issue" and had "moved gradually and reluctantly to the view that a military government without the Shah was our only viable option."[135]

Indeed, at this point, Brzezinski was preparing the ground for direct American military involvement, requesting that the Department of Defense formulate "contingency plans for the deployment of U.S. forces . . . in southern Iran so as to secure the oil fields."[136] Upon being briefed on this question on December 5, the president authorized Defense Secretary Brown to "move expeditiously on this matter." Of course, as Brzezinski understood, a direct United States military presence in Iran would also serve to buttress an Iranian military regime. But on another of Brzezinski's ideas—the dispatch to Tehran of a cabinet-level presidential emissary, either himself or

Energy Secretary Schlesinger—Carter was noncommittal and eventually negative.[137]

December was the month of Moharram, when for the entire month there would be religious demonstrations and ceremonies to honor the martyrdoms of the two nephews of Mohammed. (Shiites believe Mohammed's son-in-law and his heirs to be the true successors to the Prophet.) The ceremonies took the traditional form of public processions, services at mosques, passion plays, and special rites involving self-flagellation with chains. Moharram was perceived by all parties to be the true crisis period for the shah, when Khomeini was expected to make a decisive bid for power. Indeed, on November 23, Khomeini had issued a call from Paris (where he had gone after a fourteen-year exile in Iraq) for Iranians "to go into the streets," and he described the coming mourning period of Moharram as "a month of blood and vengeance."[138]

The shah himself understood that Moharram would be "a true test of strength" and had prohibited demonstrations, ordering his troops to break them up before they got started.[139] But from early in December large numbers of people gathered in the mosques for religious observances, disregarding the government's prohibitions and curfew.[140] President Carter contributed to the turmoil and growing uncertainty about the shah with an infelicitous remark to reporters on December 7. During a breakfast meeting at the White House, the president said, "We personally prefer that the Shah maintain a major role, but that is a decision for the Iranian people to make."[141] The president's statement created a sensation in Tehran, for it implied that the shah's fate would be decided in the streets.

The president tried to undo the damage caused by his remark by issuing an immediate clarification; but a week later during a news conference, he stirred further confusion. Asked about the repercussions "if the Shah fails to maintain power," Carter answered:

> I fully expect the Shah to maintain power in Iran and for the present problems. . . to be resolved. . . . I think the predictions of gloom and disaster . . . have certainly not been realized at all. The Shah has our support and he also has our confidence. We have no intention of interfering in the internal affairs of Iran and we have no intention of permitting others to interfere. . . . I think it's good to point out that the Iranian people for 2,500 years . . . have had the ability for stable self-government. There have been changes in

> the government, yes, sometimes violence, but they have a history of an ability to to govern themselves.[142]

Contrary to the president's contention that "predictions of gloom and disaster" had not been realized, as he spoke the Iranian people in "waves of demonstrations" were rocking Tehran.[143] It was against the tense background of increasing and widespread demonstrations and an accelerating exodus of American personnel from Iran that the Carter leadership gathered to consider the recommendations of former Under Secretary of State George Ball.[144] In late November, the administration had agreed to task Ball with preparing a comprehensive policy review, and on December 13 the Special Coordinating Commmittee met to hear his recommendations.

Upon reflection, the Ball episode appears to have been a quite clever and sophisticated attempt to bring the president around to Vance's view. It was clever because the initiative to propose Ball in the first place came from Treasury Secretary Blumenthal to Brzezinski, who "liked the idea."[145] Belatedly, however, Brzezinski "came to regret" this bureaucratic initiative when he realized that Ball was Vance's "good friend"[146] and that the advice of the former under secretary would not conform to his own views.

Indeed, the presentation of Ball's report on December 13 to the Special Coordinating Committee resembled nothing so much as a bureaucratic squeeze play. Although Vance was in the Middle East when the meeting took place, his absence should not be interpreted as noninvolvement. In the two weeks in which Ball prepared his report, he "drew heavily" on relevant State Department officials for information, particularly Vance's chief aide, Assistant Secretary of State for Near East and South Asian Affairs Harold Saunders, and his proposals were forwarded to Sullivan in Tehran for comment and, it seems, coordination.[147] The same day that the SCC met, a cable arrived from Ambassador Sullivan. Sullivan's cable and Ball's report converged on the same policy recommendation—a civilian coalition government.

Sullivan reported that the shah had set out three options: a national coalition in which the shah would become a titular monarch; his departure and the formation of a regency council which would turn political control over to the opposition; or a military junta, which would restore order and enable the shah to continue in power.[148] The shah expressed preference for the first idea, but noted that his military advisers were advocating the last. He believed that capitulating to Khomeini would lead to disintegration of the country. The ambassador "urged the shah to continue with his negotiations and even suggested that he might form a Council of Notables that could act as a guarantor for whatever agreement was reached."[149]

Sullivan's cable meshed perfectly with George Ball's proposal to bring about a coalition government within a constitutional monarchy. Ball proposed that the shah make a dramatic announcement of the creation of a Council of Notables, which would stand between him as constitutional monarch and a new government.[150] Brzezinski, who chaired and controlled the SCC deliberations, opposed Ball's suggestion as simply "transferring power to the other side." He argued instead in favor of formation of a military government by coup d'etat, "which in time can become increasingly civilianized, as in Turkey or Brazil."[151]

The national security adviser's opposition and President Carter's disinclination to insist bluntly that the shah relinquish power defeated this bureaucratic maneuver, but it had an important consequence. It brought the president to the recognition "that we had passed the point of unreservedly supporting the shah," as he began to consider a compromise solution.[152] Toward this end, Vance proposed, and Carter agreed, to send a message to Sullivan which contained a number of pointed questions designed to elicit the shah's "considered judgement" on the crucial choices facing him, particularly on the feasibility of "any solution short of a military government."[153]

Brzezinski had "great reservations about the message," fearing the shah would conclude that "the United States was pressing for a coalition government."[154] He went along with it for two reasons: first, because he decided that the "best way to establish the case" for a military coup was "to exhaust all alternative avenues," but mainly because he "had no choice."[155] The fact was, the president had sided with Vance, who "strongly advocated a political solution with the shah remaining as constitutional monarch if possible, but without him if necessary, coupled with efforts to preserve the Iranian military as an institution."[156]

Ambassador Sullivan met with the shah on December 18, and the monarch's answers to the presidential questionnaire were not encouraging. Although the shah had asked the aging Social Democratic National Front leader Gholam Hossein Sadiqi to form a government of national unity to replace the military government, he did not think he would succeed because "most opposition politicians would not dare offend Khomeini."[157] In that case, the shah said he would turn to Shapour Bakhtiar, also of the National Front; and if he, too, should fail he would then form a regency council.

The shah accepted the role of constitutional monarch, in which he would remain as commander-in-chief of the armed forces, but he was vague about relinquishing control over the budget, a question that would have to be "worked out." In short, it was clear to Secretary Vance, particularly when Sadiqi failed to form a government a few days later, that the shah was "still unwilling to share enough power with a coalition government to split the moderate nationalists off from the Khomeini followers."[158]

The secretary faced a quandary. Neither President Carter nor the shah wanted to act. Carter would not ask the shah to relinquish power, and the shah would not move unless Carter asked. Vance believed that the shah was maneuvering to have the United States take the responsibility for the decision to use the iron fist. While the secretary "did not rule out eventual support for a military government whose purpose would be to restore order and end the bloodshed, [Vance] did not believe the United States should make such a fundamental decision for Iran, which is precisely what the shah was attempting to get us to do"[159] and what Brzezinski was also urging at every opportunity.

When a few days later, on the twenty-sixth, "the shah asked point-blank what the United States wanted him to do"[160] and whether we would "support a policy of brutal repression," it "brought matters to a head" between Brzezinski and Vance.[161] Vance hastened to draft a telegram "instructing Sullivan to tell the shah unequivocally that the United States would not support the iron fist option and that we believed he must move swiftly to establish a new civilian government to replace General Azhari."[162]

With no hope that a constitutional monarchy could be realized, Secretary Vance now "wanted . . . to authorize Sullivan to talk immediately with responsible political elements in the government, the opposition, and the military . . . to urge establishment of a civilian government with firm military support."[163] Vance believed a cohesive and united army "would be needed for the dangerous transition to a new Iran without the shah."

Meeting on December 28, Brzezinski, Vance, Brown, Deputy

Secretary of Defense Charles Duncan, and Director of Central Intelligence Stansfield Turner attempted to compose instructions for Ambassador Sullivan.[164] Vance found that "there was no support for my draft cable" authorizing immediate contacts with "responsible political elements" and establishment of a coalition government.[165] After much discussion the others "prevailed on Vance to agree to a strongly worded telegram which would have the effect of giving the Shah the needed reinforcement."[166] But while the draft Vance agreed to was strongly worded, he subsequently succeeded in persuading the president to make a crucial alteration.

The original compromise cable called upon the shah to "terminate the continued uncertainty," which was "destructive of Army morale and of political confidence."[167] The "preferred alternative" would be a civilian coalition "that is moderate and can work with the United States and with the Shah and maintain order." But, the message continued, "if there is uncertainty" about the orientation of such a regime or its capacity to govern or if the army is "in danger of becoming more fragmented," then "a firm military government under the Shah may be unavoidable."

Afterward, Vance "went alone to Camp David that afternoon to discuss with the president the message [they] had prepared."[168] There he persuaded the president that the shah's continued "presence in Iran would prevent any understanding between the moderate opposition and the military leaders." He and Vance then "worked out" a change in the draft, which was added after the reference to the army's "becoming more fragmented." It read: "Then the Shah should choose without delay a firm military government which would end the disorder, violence and bloodshed. If in his judgment the Shah believes these alternatives to be infeasible, then a regency council supervising the military government might be considered by him."

Brzezinski professed to believe that "this message represented the clearest and most direct effort to get the Shah to do what needed to be done, without the United States assuming, in effect, the responsibility of governing Iran on his behalf."[169] But this is misleading. In fact, as he must have known, the message left out the two key points which Brzezinski had insisted upon—"a firm military government under the Shah may be unavoidable,"[170] stipulating that the shah should remain and rule through a military regime.

The Carter–Vance emendation removed both elements. As

Vance noted, "The shah could not fail to see from this message that we would support a military government only to end bloodshed, but not to apply the iron fist to retain his throne."[171] In other words, the small but significant change in wording brought the essence of the message back to the thrust of Vance's original draft cable—moving toward a coalition government without the shah. Vance, who was in direct contact with Sullivan by secure telephone and teletype, now moved to give approval for the ambassador to press forward with contacts to opposition leaders, including the religious opposition. None of this, however, was "shared with the White House."[172]

The shah correctly interpreted the December 28 message to mean that Washington had withdrawn its support for him, that he was in fact, though very carefully, being asked to leave.[173] Discussing the message with Sullivan, the shah noted that Shahpour Bakhtiar's chances of forming a civilian coalition were slim. (Bakhtiar had accepted the mission on condition that the shah leave the country.[174]) The shah "did not have the heart" for and "would not wish to be associated with" a military government. Indeed, "if it were to be tried," he would leave the country. Finally, he said, a regency council would "normally act only in the monarch's absence." All of the options, in other words, involved the shah's departure and led him to the obvious question of where he would go, prompting Sullivan to ask whether he should "seek an invitation" for him to go to the United States."[175]

Still, the shah temporized, even as the Azhari government fell at the end of December. On January 2, he said to Sullivan that he hoped to swear Bakhtiar in by the fourth or sixth, after which he intended to "leave the country for a rest," but would not indicate a date of departure.[176] The shah's continued vacillation precipitated another round of meetings by the Carter leadership the next day to ponder the best means of effecting the shah's departure. Although all now agreed that the shah should leave, there was disagreement over how to convey that message. The main concern was that if the United States were openly "to tell the Shah to step aside," such a recommendation, no matter how subtly conveyed, would be read in Iran as "U.S. disengagement" and even "seeming U.S. disengagement . . . could plunge the country into anarchy and even civil war."[177]

The Failure of Vance's Attempt to "Broaden the Base"

After lengthy deliberation, two decisions were reached on January 3. The first was "intended to end the shah's hesitation and to strengthen the chances of Bakhtiar being able to broaden his cabinet."[178] A message to the shah stated American support for the "decision to establish a civilian government under Bakhtiar. . . . It also said that the president concurred in the shah's intention to leave Iran under a regency council, and assured him that he would be welcome in the United States. The message concluded by stressing the importance of the military leadership remaining united and in control of the armed forces."[179]

The second decision was to send a high-ranking military emissary to Iran to show continuing support for the Iranian armed forces and to maintain their cohesion. The officer, General Robert E. Huyser, who had worked closely with the Iranian military for many years and knew personally many of the high command, arrived January 4 with instructions to convey United States support for the military. He was explicitly enjoined to ensure Iranian military support for the civilian government. "It is extremely important for the Iranian military to do all it can to remain strong and intact in order to help a responsible civilian government function effectively." Moreover, his instructions stated, "No Iranian military leaders should leave the country now."[180]

Brzezinski was disappointed with the message, declaring to the president that they "should have encouraged the military to stage a coup."[181] To the president's acerbic reply that there was "no military leader we could identify who would lead . . . a coup," Brzezinski responded, "We do not need to identify a leader. What we need to do is give a clearer signal and a leader will emerge." His "hope" was that Huyser's instructions "will be interpreted by the Iranian military as encouragement to take firm action when the moment of truth arrives."[182]

But upon Huyser's arrival in Tehran, Sullivan "angrily demanded that Huyser be instructed to coordinate with him."[183] Secretary Vance immediately sent Huyser a hold order based on Ambassador Sullivan's report that the military was about to execute a coup.[184] Huyser recalls that Vance ordered him to "ignore all previous instructions. . . . I was not to make contact with the Iranian military leaders as originally instructed. I was to do nothing until I received further word from Washington."[185] Sullivan, who conveyed the message to Huyser, "expressed no opinion about the sudden change of plan, but it did not seem to upset him."[186]

With Huyser on hold, Vance called the president, who had gone to Guadeloupe with Brzezinski for meetings with British, French, and German leaders. Vance also used the report of a coup in his plea to Carter for a change in Huyser's orders to say "to the Iranian military that we will not support this."[187] He told the president that we should "stay away from both the military and the Shah."[188] But Carter, egged on by Brzezinski, "told Cy that he did not wish to change General Huyser's instructions in order to water them down, that Ambassador Sullivan should ascertain the Shah's attitude regarding the coup, [and] that he should not deliver the last message to the Shah, which was urging him to leave the country."[189]

It was the president's view that "our relationships with the Shah and with the military [were] our only two ties to future sound relationships with Iran, since we didn't know the form of government it [*sic*] might take if the military was eliminated as a major factor."[190] Indeed, the president's instructions to Secretary Vance represented a 180-degree turn in policy from the decision of the day before. As Brzezinski noted, regarding the coup report, "Unless the Shah completely disowns this effort, this would mean that we would be prepared to back it."[191]

Any prospects for a coup were quickly dashed. When Sullivan met with the shah later that same evening (January 5), the monarch explained that the "coup scenario" was of his own making, designed "to put pressure on Bakhtiar," about whose chances he remained pessimistic.[192] Huyser, after talking with several armed forces commanders, concluded that no planning had been done, which meant that, at this point at least, no coup was feasible.[193] Indeed, the Iranian high command opposed the shah's departure, and if it occurred, they wanted to leave with him.

What explains the president's turnaround? For some weeks, certainly since early November when he had issued a presidential criticism of the overall intelligence effort,[194] the president had grown increasingly dissatisfied with the policy being urged upon him by Secretary Vance, even though he had supported it up to this point. Carter had sent Huyser to Iran "because Sullivan seemed unable to provide us with adequate reports from the military, which was a crucial source of information and advice."[195]

But the turn in the president's attitude occurred when he began to realize that what Vance meant by a broad-based civilian coalition government was not merely the government of Shapour Bakhtiar, but one which included Khomeini as well, which the president adamantly opposed. Indeed, on January 7, while the president was still in Guadeloupe, Vance called recommending that he "be authorized to open a direct channel to Khomeini in Paris."[196] The secretary hastened to assure the president that "the purpose in contacting Khomeini was not to negotiate, but to convey a message that unless he allowed Bakhtiar time to form a viable government, the Commmunists might seize the leadership of the radical Left."[197]

President Carter plainly was not spooked by the "threat" of a communist seizure, nor taken in by Vance's assurances. He did not wish to deal directly with Khomeini and realized that Vance's proposal was essentially an opening gambit, which could lead to Khomeini's victory. So the president stalled. First, he said that he feared it would signal that the United States had abandoned the shah "and [was] prepared to go outside the constitutional process to reach an understanding with Khomeini."[198] He believed that "such a perception would destroy Bakhtiar's slender chances and possibly split the military leadership as well." When Vance said that the shah had approved of the approach to Khomeini, Carter was taken aback but on Brzezinski's suggestion put off a decision until his return to Washington.[199]

The Carter leadership convened to discuss Iranian policy on January 10, following the president's return from Guadeloupe. Vance reiterated the argument he had made before in favor of opening a "direct channel to Khomeini," and Brzezinski repeated his opposition. Carter refused to authorize direct American contacts. Finally, after the discussion had "raged back and forth,"[200] the president decided to ask French President Valery Giscard d'Estaing to initiate discreet contacts on behalf of the United States to "urge Khomeini to give Bakhtiar an opportunity to restore order."[201]

The policy decision of January 10 was to continue to allow Iran's constitutional processes to operate, seeking parliamentary approval of Bakhtiar's cabinet, and pressing for military cohesion and support for the civilian government. Toward this end, Sullivan was instructed to reaffirm United States support for Bakhtiar and to advise the shah to leave promptly following creation of a regency council. Huyser was also ordered to stay on to keep the military together through contingency planning for a military government in case Bakhtiar failed.[202]

Carter's decision precipitated an hysterical cable from Sullivan, who said it was "insane."[203] In his memoir the president treated Sullivan's cable with considerably more restraint than he undoubtedly did at the time he received it, describing it as "bordering on insolence, condemning our asking the French President to contact Khomeini instead of doing it ourselves. He used such phrases as 'gross and perhaps irretrievable mistake,' 'plea for sanity,' and 'incomprehensible.'"[204]

Carter had had enough. Declaring that Sullivan's "activities and statements cost him much of the confidence he had previously enjoyed . . . from me," he "told the Secretary of State to get Sullivan out of Iran."[205] But Vance refused! "Cy insisted that it would be a mistake to put a new man in the country in the midst of the succession crisis we probably faced." Carter "reluctantly agreed, but from then on . . . relied primarily on General Huyser. . . . He always sent back balanced views." There can be little doubt that Vance's defense of his ambassador also cost him in the eyes of the president, who now moved firmly away from Vance's broad-based coalition scheme which had envisaged the inclusion of Khomeini.[206]

Both Vance and Brzezinski, seeing the denouement rapidly approaching in Tehran, persisted in their respective strategies. On January 12 Sullivan reported that he had carried out his instructions; the shah would depart on the sixteenth, after Bakhtiar was formally installed as prime minister. He then "recommended urgently that we attempt to bring about an accommodation between the military and Khomeini."[207] Brzezinski, meanwhile, according to Sullivan, "was trying to get General Huyser to push the military into a coup attempt."[208] Vance "told Sullivan that he and Huyser should understand clearly that a military coup should be discouraged, and that neither he nor Huyser should be misled by any unauthorized communication," that is, from Brzezinski.[209]

Huyser's long hours of discussion with the top military leadership persuaded him that they were not prepared to back Bakhtiar unreservedly.[210] They would support him if he succeeded but were hedging their bets if he failed, conducting "secret, but so far unproductive, meetings with Ayatollah Mohammed Beheshti, Khomeini's main representative in Tehran."[211] The military high command was moving toward a position of neutral guarantor of public order, not active participant in the succession. At this point, at any rate, it was neither capable of executing a coup nor willing to do so. Furthermore, the high command possessed almost none of the managerial skills necessary to run the country, even if they came to power.

Reporting to Secretary Brown on January 12, Huyser averred that "Bakhtiar could use the military in three ways. First, with their support, he could succeed in exercising constitutional rule. Second, if that collapsed he could introduce martial law, plus military control of essential services. Third, if that looked unworkable he could invite an outright military takeover."[212] These were referred to as options A, B, and C over the next few weeks. The only other options Huyser saw were an Islamic republic under Khomeini and a communist takeover.

The shah departed on January 16 amid rumors of Khomeini's impending arrival in Tehran. He did not fly to the United States as agreed but flew instead to Cairo, inspiring thoughts that he might after all be planning a military coup following which he would return to Tehran. The prospect of widespread bloodshed following a possible coup, prompted Vance to insist once again that Washington facilitate "an understanding between Khomeini and the military."[213]

The president finally relented, essentially because the French had proved unwilling to act as intermediaries. The chief of the embassy political section in Paris, Warren Zimmerman, held several meetings over the next few days with Ibrahim Yazdi, who acted as Khomeini's interlocutor.[214] The gist of their exchanges was as follows: Zimmerman cautioned against action which would undermine the Bakhtiar government and Iran's constitutional processes. He urged Khomeini's support for the meetings between military and clergy then getting underway in Tehran and warned against Khomeini's sudden return, which could produce a confrontation with the "unpredictable" military.

Yazdi claimed that Khomeini had no plans for an "imminent return" to Tehran and wanted no confrontation with the military. Khomeini, he said, wanted a new constitution proclaiming an Islamic republic, not a rewrite of the existing one, which he considered bankrupt. Iran would pursue a policy of strict, peaceful nonalignment, turn inward, and not attempt to foment revolution in neighboring countries. Tehran would seek friendly relations with

Moscow, and, once "America stopped interfering in Iran's affairs," with Washington too.[215]

These expressions of Khomeini's seemingly peaceful intent formed in part the background for yet another crucial series of meetings of the Carter leadership beginning on January 19. In discussions regarding the advisabiity of further contact with Khomeini, the president declared, "We should tell Bakhtiar that we will not accommodate any more to the left; we support the military in their position and in their effort to maintain stability, but we are not in favor of bringing Khomeini and his people into the government."[216] To Vance's astonished query, "Does it mean we don't broaden the political base?" the president declared that the United States "had only the military and the remnants of the Shah's supporters on our side left in Iran and we could no longer undermine them."

Vance countered with the argument that "this might imply that we were encouraging the military to move," but the president "snapped, with unusual sharpness," saying that "if the word got back to Iran that we did not support the military, the effect would be to undermine the military's morale."[217] Vice-President Mondale weighed in on Vance's side, arguing that "Bakhtiar had to broaden his base and we had to recognize the fact that Khomeini represented the most powerful force." At this point, the president exploded, "We never agreed among ourselves to a coalition government. Yet all people hear abroad is the implication that we favor a coalition government. We will back the military in their support of Bakhtiar but we don't want it to slide any further to the left. The threat of a military coup is the best way to prevent Khomeini from sliding into power."

The next day in Tehran Bakhtiar stated publicly that "he would either succeed or would turn the country over to the military."[218] Surprisingly, his statement's greatest impact was upon the military chief of staff, General Abbas Gharabaghi, who declared that he would not be part of any military takeover and was submitting his resignation! Only after hurried meetings with Bakhtiar, Huyser, and Sullivan, who pleaded with him to remain, did he consent to stay on. Gharabaghi, the nephew of Ayatollah Shariatmadari's wife, was in close contact with the religious opposition,[219] making his reliability in a confrontation with Khomeini's forces questionable at best.[220]

In response to renewed rumors of Khomeini's imminent return,

Bakhtiar disclosed to Huyser his intention to divert Khomeini's plane and arrest him, prompting yet another dispute within the American leadership. In meetings of January 23 and 24 the question of whether the United States should support Bakhtiar was thrashed out. President Carter's initial reaction to Bakhtiar's plan was to say, "Great!" But Vance "argued strenuously that the result would be massive disorders and that Khomeini might even get killed in the process, setting in motion altogether unforeseeable consequences."[221] Brzezinski argued that "if Bakhtiar wished to arrest Khomeini he should be encouraged to do so."

In the end, Carter decided to send a message which gave Bakhtiar the "green light" to arrest Khomeini upon his arrival.[222] Bakhtiar thereupon closed the airports and let word out that he planned to confront Khomeini and his supporters.[223] Khomeini, however, put off his return and thwarted Bakhtiar's plans, a decision in which Secretary Vance seems to have played a part. The context was ostensibly a joint request by Sullivan and Huyser for a "reexamination of U.S. policy."[224]

Sullivan and Huyser had sent a joint report through Department of State channels, in which, according to Vance, Huyser "in particular" asked that he "be authorized to inform the military that the United States would not support a coup and that should Bakhtiar fail, the army should maintain its integrity and attempt to negotiate an understanding with Khomeini."[225] There is a serious problem with Vance's statement, for it badly misrepresents Huyser's position. According to Brzezinski, Huyser requested a change in instructions "to permit the possibility of a coalition between the military and the religious elements" in Iran, but not with Khomeini.[226]

Huyser himself, discussing the joint report, says nothing of this request.[227] He notes simply that he strongly disagreed with Sullivan, that he thought "much more highly" of the military's capability than Sullivan did, but that both agreed "if there was to be any military action, it should be taken under Prime Minister Bahktiar's leadership if at all possible. I did not rule out the possibility that it might be necessary [for the military] to do it on their own should Bakhtiar fail."[228] In response to the question of whether the military were capable of taking action, he now gave "an unqualified Yes."

In any case, after a "tense discussion," on January 24 the president authorized Vance to send a message to Khomeini through the Zimmerman–Yazdi channel advising the ayatollah that it would be "premature"[229] for him to return and "to allow his representatives in Tehran to reach an understanding with the military and the Bakhtiar government on a process in which all could participate in reshaping the Iranian political system."[230] The president remained opposed to direct dealings with Khomeini and hoped that the threat of a coup would keep him away. Thus, Huyser was instructed "to continue to advise the military on contingency planning [for a coup], but also to make clear that Khomeini's return was not in itself a cause for implementing the contingency plans."

Neither Coalition, Military Coup, nor Bakhtiar

United States policy at this point resembled nothing so much as a three-headed dog, with each head pulling in a different direction. The president insisted upon a civilian government led by Bakhtiar but without Khomeini, Vance sought to "broaden the base" of the coalition with the inclusion of Khomeini, and Brzezinski pressed for a military coup with neither. Within three weeks, by the middle of February, American Iran policy would suffer complete collapse. Khomeini would refuse to participate in a coalition, Bakhtiar would flee into hiding, the army would disintegrate, and Ayatollah Khomeini would emerge as the preeminent power figure in Iranian politics.

On January 27 Khomeini rejected Vance's proposal to agree "on a process in which all could participate." On the other hand, the ayatollah suggested that Washington's "concerns about his attitude toward relations with the United States would be resolved when we saw the provisional government he intended to name to guide Iran to an Islamic republic."[231] Khomeini's nominee as provisional prime minister, Mehdi Bazargan, a highly respected pro-Western political figure, combined with intelligence that his intent was to establish a moderate secular government "with the Islamic clergy remaining in the background as the guiding political and spiritual force of the revolution," completely satisfied Secretary Vance.[232]

Vance now moved as hastily as he could away from Bakhtiar in order to accommodate to Khomeini, believing that "we were tying ourselves to the Bakhtiar experiment beyond the point where there was any chance of his participating in a new regime."[233] As the secretary put it, "Despite our continuing public pronouncements of support, it was obvious that Bakhtiar had little time left." Vance's efforts to "press harder for an understanding between the military and the religious and secular opposition forces arrayed around Khomeini," however, was hampered by "Brzezinski's determined opposition to direct contacts with the ayatollah."[234] What the secretary neglected to mention, however, was that this was also the position of President Carter.

On January 29, Bakhtiar, having failed to persuade Khomeini to give him time to stabilize the government, decided to permit the ayatollah to return, hoping beyond hope that his presence would either precipitate division among his supporters or a willingness to negotiate. Neither happened, contrary to press reports.[235] Khomeini's arrival on February 1 and his appointment of Mehdi Bazargan as provisional prime minister created a situation of divided power, which clearly sapped whatever vigor was left in the Bakhtiar government.

Under the circumstances, while reiterating American support for Bakhtiar as the legal head of government, on February 6 Secretary Vance authorized Sulllivan "to work informally with Bazargan on such matters as the safety of Americans and arrangements for evacuation of U.S. personnel."[236] At this point, for Vance, "our only sensible course was to attempt to come to terms with the revolution."[237] General Huyser, meanwhile, was ordered to return to Washington.

Within days, the collapse of the military became evident. On February 9 air force units at bases outside Tehran rebelled, declaring allegiance to Khomeini. When the Imperial Guard, the most loyal and disciplined unit of the army, was sent to quell the rebellion, heavy fighting ensued and the guard began to dissolve.[238] Defections accelerated, and fighting spread rapidly. Within two days the military disintegrated, and the military high command decided to return their troops to barracks, adopting a position of neutrality which, of course, favored Khomeini. When the military deserted him, Bakhtiar resigned and went into hiding; his government quickly evaporated.[239] The collapse of the former regime was now complete, and Ayatollah Ruhollah Khomeini was now ascendant.

At this point, February 11, Brzezinski attempted to drum up support within the Carter leadership for a military coup, "option C," but with no success. Clearly, at this late date, the chances of a successful coup were nonexistent. Although military preparations had progressed to the point where action could have been taken, even the optimistic General Huyser believed that a military coup would only be feasible in the context of a massive American military commitment. The Iranian high command, Brzezinski finally concluded, "did not have the will to act."[240] In the final analysis, as Sullivan had been insisting since the shah's departure, the Iranian military was "a paper tiger."[241]

Secretary Vance believed that the "cooperative attitude" of Bazargan's government was indicative not only of the "political moderates' strong desire to continue a military relationship with the United States," but also of Khomeini's. So on February 16 he announced that the United States would maintain normal diplomatic relations with the new regime. "We believed that over time U.S. and Iranian interests in a strong, stable, non-Communist Iran should permit a cooperative, if far less intimate, relationship to emerge."[242] This was, of course, the strategic objective toward which Secretary Vance had been working throughout the crisis, but it was not to be realized.

Over the course of the next several months and despite virtually constant provocation, the secretary went to great lengths to establish "a cooperative . . . relationship" with the new regime—even to the extent of denying the shah entry into the United States. As the secretary put it, "U.S. interests in establishing a modus vivendi with the new Iranian government and the safety of the Americans in Iran dictated that the shah should not be allowed into the United States at this time."[243] In his extraordinary zeal to dissociate the United States from the shah, Secretary Vance went so far as to oppose the entry of the empress into the United States for medical treatment on the grounds that "we would be skirting dangerously close to confirming suspicions in Iran that the United States still supported the shah."[244]

However objectionable Vance's management of policy was, the fall of the shah of Iran was not created by the failure of American policy. The shah himself is responsible; his choices over a period of many years produced his fall. The failure of American policy was the inability to help effect the transition from autocracy to constitutional government in Iran. There was nothing to support the American belief that Khomeini was a democrat, or that if only Washington "came to terms with the revolution" United States relations with Iran would not skip a beat. Indeed, the effort to cooperate simply compounded failure, for it led directly to worsened relations.

The attempt to establish a new relationship with Khomeini's Iran came in the context of an explosion of oil prices, which the revolution had precipitated; war in Southeast Asia, with China's invasion of Vietnam; and Washington's renewed efforts to bring stalled treaty negotiations between the United States and the Soviet Union as well as between Egypt and Israel to a satisfactory conclusion. It is to these events—the prelude to the Soviet invasion of Afghanistan and the collapse of American strategy—that the focus now shifts.

Notes

1. Brzezinski, *Power and Principle*, p. 330, attempting to show that Vance was in support of his own view, says that "the decision to proceed on normalization with China was made on the basis of consensus within the U.S. government, with Vance proposing in a memorandum that ratification of SALT be *preceded* by normalization of the U.S.–China relationship" (emphasis supplied). The decision on normalization undoubtedly was "made on the basis of consensus," but Brzezinski's assertion that Vance wished normalization to precede SALT is disputed by Vance himself, *Hard Choices*, p. 116. The memo Brzezinski refers to was Vance's May 10 memorandum to the president, signed also by Brzezinski and Brown. In it the three stated that "we did not want SALT and normalization to come to Congress at the same time. . . . At that time we considered it too early to foresee which would be concluded first." Indeed, *at that time* Brzezinski was in the ascendancy, but even so the position taken in the memo does not support Brzezinski's assertion that Sino–American normalization should precede SALT. Later, however, when Vance had regained control of American foreign policy direction, his position was unequivocally that SALT must come first. Thus, Vance, *Hard Choices*, pp. 109–10, discussing Sino–American normalization in December 1978, says, "before I had left for the Middle East, we [Vance and the president] had agreed that if the negotiations in Peking were successful—as we were confident they would be—the announcement would be made on January 1, that is, one week *after* my discussions with Gromyko in Geneva," where he expected to reach a final agreement on SALT. Indeed, *Hard Choices*, pp. 118–19, Vance says when the president called him in Jerusalem to say he would announce normalization within forty-eight hours on December 15, instead of January 1 as agreed, "the news came as a shock. At a critical moment, Brzezinski had blacked Christopher and Holbrook out of the decision-making for about six hours, and they had been unable to inform me of what was taking place."
2. Vance, *Hard Choices*, p. 113, says in justifying pursuit of SALT and normalization "at about the same time" that "accomplishing these two fundamental objectives in close juxtaposition could have greatly strengthened both foreign and domestic perceptions that the administration was managing a balanced and stable triangular relationship. . . . The problem arose from announcing normalization on the eve of a critical SALT meeting and the backgrounding which accompanied it."
3. Brzezinski, *Power and Principle*, p. 333.

4. Don Oberdorfer, "Soviet Union Completes Vietnam Airlift," *Washington Post*, September 2, 1978, p. 1.
5. Brzezinski, *Power and Principle*, pp. 326–27, and Vance, *Hard Choices*, p. 105.
6. Vance, *Hard Choices*, p. 105.
7. Ibid., p. 106.
8. Brzezinski, *Power and Principle*, p. 229.
9. Talbott, *Endgame*, p. 209.
10. Vance, *Hard Choices*, p. 105.
11. Ibid., p. 107.
12. For accounts of the September meetings, see Carter, *Keeping Faith*, pp. 231–33; Vance, *Hard Choices*, pp. 106–7; Brzezinski, *Power and Principle*, p. 327; and Talbott, *Endgame*, pp. 213–15.
13. The United States position on ALCMs was thirty-five per bomber, the Soviets' was twenty, both negotiable.
14. Talbott, *Endgame*, p. 214.
15. Carter, *Keeping Faith*, pp. 231–32.
16. Brzezinski, *Power and Principle*, p. 327.
17. Talbott, *Endgame*, p. 214.
18. Carter, *Keeping Faith*, p. 232.
19. Henry S. Bradsher, "Soviets Seek Wrap-up of New SALT Treaty by March 31; U.S. Cool," *Washington Star*, November 9, 1978, p. 3.
20. Ibid.
21. Carter, *Keeping Faith*, p. 232. Talbott, *Endgame*, pp. 214–15, notes that Carter was "disappointed and angry," the American side "annoyed as hell." All felt that Gromyko "should have stayed and seen it through."
22. Carter, *Keeping Faith*, p. 232. Vance also argued that "proximity . . . to the Politburo might make it easier to get quick and favorable Soviet decisions . . .," Talbott, *Endgame*, p. 217.
23. Talbott, *Endgame*, p. 215.
24. Carter, *Keeping Faith*, p. 233.
25. Ibid. No cease-fire materialized.
26. Kenneth H. Bacon, "Issues Blocking SALT Pact Are Unlikely to Be Resolved during Talks in Moscow," *Wall Street Journal*, October 20, 1978, p. 8.
27. Vance, *Hard Choices*, p. 107.
28. Ibid.
29. Talbott, *Endgame*, pp. 217–18.
30. Ibid., p. 219.
31. Ibid. Vance, *Hard Choices*, pp. 107–8, for obvious reasons omits all reference to the fractionation issue.
32. The imprecise language was carefully crafted to avoid revealing to the

Soviets exactly which kinds of encryption American intelligence had difficulty deciphering.

33. Talbott, *Endgame*, pp. 221–22; Vance, *Hard Choices*, p. 108.
34. Talbott, *Endgame*, p. 222; Vance, *Hard Choices*, p. 109. Semyenov was shortly removed from his post, but reassigned to the prestigious position of ambassador to West Germany. He had not after all been sacked but promoted. This suggests in hindsight that the episode may have been part of Moscow's way of protracting the negotiations. It would seem that Semyenov was due for reassignment in any case following Warnke's resignation.
35. Vance, *Hard Choices*, p. 109.
36. Ibid.
37. Ibid.
38. Ibid.
39. Carter, *Keeping Faith*, p. 233.
40. Ibid.
41. David K. Willis, "SALT Standoff: US, Soviets Slow the Dance," *Christian Science Monitor*, November 8, 1978, p. 1.
42. Eric Bourse, "Anti-China Bias Creeps into SALT," *Christian Science Monitor*, November 8, 1978, p. 6.
43. Ibid.
44. Edward Walsh, "Carter Expects Wider Agenda in SALT Talks with Brezhnev," *Washington Post*, November 17, 1978, p. 8.
45. Vernon A. Guidry, "Trade, SALT Linked, U.S. Experts Believe," *Washington Star*, November 26, 1978, p. 3.
46. Bernard Gwertzman, "Vance Says Ties with Russians Have Improved," *New York Times*, November 26, 1978, p. 1.
47. Ibid.
48. Talbott, *Endgame*, p. 223.
49. See Talbott, *Endgame*, pp. 187–89.
50. Ibid., pp. 224–25.
51. Ibid.
52. Craig R. Whitney, "Brezhnev Supports Prompt Arms Pact and U.S. Trade Rise," *New York Times*, December 7, 1978, p. 1.
53. Ibid.
54. Talbott, *Endgame*, pp. 226–27.
55. Ibid., pp. 227–28.
56. Cf. chapter 3, pp. 66ff, and see n.1 above.
57. Carter, *Keeping Faith*, pp. 233–34.
58. Edward Walsh and Robert Kaiser, "U.S.–Peking Ties Backed By Brezhnev," *Washington Post*, December 20, 1978, p. 1.
59. Vance, *Hard Choices*, p. 110.

60. Bernard Gwertzman, "Vance Says Ties with Russians Have Improved."
61. Vance, *Hard Choices*, p. 110.
62. Ibid. See also Richard Burt, "Arms Snag Linked to Demands by Soviet on New U.S. Missiles," *New York Times*, December 28, 1978, p. 2, who reported that "the fact that Moscow introduced the new issues on the last day had led some officials to conclude that the Russians were looking for an excuse to delay an accord."
63. Kevin Klose, "Soviets Dispute Carter Version of Brezhnev Note," *Washington Post*, December 22, 1978, p. 1.
64. David K. Shipler, "Soviet, Citing Its Note to Carter, Indicates Concern on China Ties," *New York Times*, December 22, 1978, p. 1. See Carter, *Keeping Faith*, p. 234, who claims that Brezhnev "reversed some of these private assurances through the Soviet news media."
65. Talbott, *Endgame*, pp. 234–37.
66. Vance, *Hard Choices*, p. 111.
67. Talbott, *Endgame*, p. 238. Brzezinski, *Power and Principle*, p. 329, reversed the order: "Encryption . . . not relevant to verification would be permitted, but encryption . . . relevant to verification would be banned."
68. Vance, *Hard Choices*, p. 111.
69. Talbott, *Endgame*, p. 240. Cf. Vance, *Hard Choices*, p. 111, who claims that "in our own contacts with reporters in Geneva we tried to curb any excessive optimism, but press reports from Washington reflected high-level backgrounding that agreement was near," implying that the inspiration for these stories was Brzezinski.
70. Brzezinski, *Power and Principle*, p. 329.
71. Ibid.
72. Vance, *Hard Choices*, p. 112, and Talbott, *Endgame*, p. 244.
73. Talbott, *Endgame*, p. 244.
74. Vance, *Hard Choices*, p. 112.
75. Ibid.
76. Hossein Razavi and Firouz Vakil, *The Political Environment of Economic Planning in Iran, 1971–1983* (Boulder, CO: Westview Press, 1984), p. 74.
77. Fereydoun Hoveyda, *The Fall of the Shah* (New York: Wyndham Books, 1979), p. 99.
78. Gary Sick, *All Fall Down, America's Tragic Encounter with Iran* (New York: Penguin Books, 1986), p. 15.
79. Simon Henderson, "The Generals Consider Their Options," *Financial Times*, February 12, 1979, p. 14.
80. See the analysis by Michael Ledeen and William Lewis, *Debacle: The*

American Failure in Iran (New York: Vintage Books, 1982), pp. 120–22.

81. Mohammad Reza Pahlavi, *Answer to History* (New York: Stein and Day, 1980), p. 155, and Sick, *All Fall Down*, pp. 39, 42. He also sent a letter to President Carter to this effect.
82. See, for example, "Nobody Can Overthrow Me—I Have the Power," interview with the shah of Iran, *U.S. News and World Report*, June 26, 1978, p. 20.
83. Hoveyda, *Fall of the Shah*, pp. 40–41.
84. Sick, *All Fall Down*, p. 55.
85. Robert Graham, *Iran, the Illusion of Power* (New York: St. Martin's Press, 1980), p. 231.
86. By this time the troubles in Iran were being reflected in the American press. See, for example, James O. Jackson, "Rebellion in Iran Threatens West," *Chicago Tribune*, August 27, 1978, p. 10.
87. John Stempel, *Inside the Iranian Revolution*, (Bloomington: Indiana University Press, 1981), pp. 114–18.
88. See "An Interview with the Shah," *Time*, September 18, 1978, p. 43, for the shah's attempt to explain the shooting.
89. Stempel, *Inside the Iranian Revolution*, pp. 121–22. See Walter Laqueur, "Trouble for the Shah," *The New Republic*, September 23, 1978, pp. 18–21, for a useful analysis of the domestic Iranian situation.
90. Nicholas Cumming-Bruce, "Iran's Oil Production Exports Hit by Strike," *Washington Post*, November 1, 1978, p. 1.
91. Vance, *Hard Choices*, p. 327, and Jonathan C. Randal, "Iran: 'Situation Is out of Control,'" *Washington Post*, October 29, 1978, p. 1.
92. Sick, *All Fall Down*, p. 70.
93. Vance, *Hard Choices*, p. 327.
94. Sick, *All Fall Down*, p. 68, and Anthony Parsons, *The Pride and the Fall, Iran 1974–1979* (London: Jonathan Cape, 1984), pp. 85–86, who asserts that the shah was "implacably opposed to a military takeover."
95. Carter, *Keeping Faith*, p. 439.
96. Brzezinski, *Power and Principle*, p. 371.
97. Vance, *Hard Choices*, p. 343.
98. Brzezinski, *Power and Principle*, p. 364.
99. And also the British ambassador. See Parsons, *Pride and the Fall*, p. 85. Not surprisingly, the shah, *Answer to History*, pp. 169–70, saw the messages as "confusing and contradictory."
100. Vance, *Hard Choices*, p. 329.
101. Brzezinski, *Power and Principle*, p. 364, and Vance, *Hard Choices*, pp. 328–89, who paraphrases the November 2 decision without either identifying or dating it. Curiously, he also asserts that the shah called

the White House on November 3, rather than acknowledging Brzezinski's call to the shah of that date. The reason for this appears to be Vance's attempt to portray Brzezinski's direct communications to Tehran as "intolerable" and conducted "without the knowledge of anyone in the State Department." The fact is, however, that Brzezinski's communication was authorized by the president. See Brzezinski, *Power and Principle*, p. 365, and Sick, *All Fall Down*, pp. 80, 85. See below, p. 257.

102. See Mansur Rafizadeh, *Witness, from the Shah to the Secret Arms Deal* (New York: William Morrow and Co., 1987), pp. 281–82. Rafizadeh was head of SAVAK in the United States.
103. William H. Sullivan, *Mission to Iran* (New York: W.W. Norton, 1981), p. 178.
104. Ibid., p. 179.
105. Rafizadeh, *Witness*, p. 282.
106. This is not inconsistent with the shah's remark to Sullivan two weeks later in response to Brzezinski's messages urging him to be tough. He heard that "he was getting old, that he was no longer able to make decisions and that he was lacking in 'guts.'" The shah asked Sullivan "to tell these people that he had guts, but he also had a heart and a brain. He did not intend to murder the youth of his nation in order to rule it." Sick, *All Fall Down*, p. 109.
107. "Premier Resigns in Iran," *Baltimore Sun*, November 6, 1978, p. 1.
108. Brzezinski, *Power and Principle*, p. 366.
109. Sick, *All Fall Down*, p. 89. For a brief moment this tactic appeared to be working. See Ray Vicker and Peter Roche, "Iran Oil Workers Are Ending Walkout; Many Other Industries, Offices Start Up," *Wall Street Journal*, November 15, 1978, p. 4.
110. Nicholas Gage, "Shah Orders the Arrest of Former Prime Minister," *New York Times*, November 9, 1978, p. 1. Fifty-four former public officials and businessmen were indicted on charges of "corruption and abuse of power."
111. Sullivan, *Mission to Iran*, pp. 181–88, and Sick, *All Fall Down*, p. 90.
112. Sick, *All Fall Down*, pp. 94–101; Brzezinski, *Power and Principle*, pp. 367–68; Vance, *Hard Choices*, p. 329.
113. Sick, *All Fall Down*, p. 96.
114. Sullivan, *Mission to Iran*, p. 203. How Ambassador Sullivan could assert that Khomeini would be pro-Western is difficult to understand, for the aging cleric had made no secret of his opposition to the shah as an American puppet. See Hamid Algar, trans., *Islam and Revolution, Writings and Declarations of Imam Khomeini* (Berkeley: Mizan Press, 1981).
115. Sick, *All Fall Down*, pp. 408–9, minimizes its impact; Vance, *Hard*

Choices, p. 329, says that it "caused consternation in the White House."

116. Vance, *Hard Choices*, p. 330. The disagreement between Vance and Sullivan here was one of timing not substance. Sullivan had already reached the conclusion that the shah had "abandoned his imperial role," while Vance thought "there was still a chance" that the shah could arrange for "an orderly transition."
117. Ibid., p. 330.
118. Rafizadeh, *Witness*, p. 277.
119. Ibid., pp. 278–80. Cf. Sick, *All Fall Down*, p. 115, who asserts that Oveissi was part of the group that "wanted to form a military government . . . to use force against the opposition."
120. Kevin Klose, "Brezhnev Admonishes U.S. on Iran," *Washington Post*, November 20, 1978, p. 1.
121. Ibid.
122. President Carter "Interview for 'Bill Moyers Journal,'" November 13, 1978, in Department of State *Bulletin* (December 1978), p. 15.
123. Sick, *All Fall Down*, p. 111. See also Michael K. Burns, "Americans in Iran Growing Edgy," *Baltimore Sun*, November 16, 1978, p. 1.
124. "Carter Acknowledges Warning Brezhnev on Interfering in Iran," *Baltimore Sun*, December 15, 1978, p. 2.
125. See Brzezinski, *Power and Principle*, p. 369, for the national security adviser's efforts to strengthen a proposed State Department reply which was "almost apologetic in tone." Vance omits all discussion of the Brezhnev November 18 letter.
126. Brzezinski, *Power and Principle*, p. 368, and Cord Meyer, "The Kremlin's Work in Iran," *Washington Star*, February 10, 1979, p. 9.
127. William Branigin, "Shah's Days As Absolute Ruler Seem Numbered," *Washington Post*, November 17, 1978, p. 22.
128. Vance, *Hard Choices*, p. 330. See also Don Oberdorfer, "U.S. Makes Contacts with Shah's Foes," *Washington Post*, November 28, 1978, p. 1.
129. Bernard Gwertzman, "Vance Says Ties with Russians Have Improved."
130. Brzezinski, *Power and Principle*, p. 370. William Sullivan, "Envoy's Version of the Collapse," *Washington Star*, September 7, 1980, p. G4, believed that Zahedi "reported daily . . . to Brzezinski."
131. See chapter 5, the section "Secretary Vance Regains Control."
132. Vance, *Hard Choices*, p. 328. There was some irony here. The shah, *Answer to History*, p. 165, believed that he was "ill-served by Ardeshir Zahedi's inaccurate reporting. . . . He pretended to have access to the highest authorities but his reports could never be confirmed."

133. Vance, *Hard Choices*, p. 328.
134. Brzezinski, *Power and Principle*, p. 372.
135. Ibid., p. 371, claims that both he and Vance had reached that conclusion at this time, but the record indicates that the secretary still sought a solution with the shah until late December.
136. Ibid., p. 372.
137. See Ledeen and Lewis, *Debacle*, pp. 171–73, for Schlesinger's role in the emissary idea.
138. Parsons, *Pride and the Fall*, p. 107. For Khomeini's speech, see Algar, *Islam and Revolution*, pp. 242–45.
139. Sick, *All Fall Down*, p. 109, and Youssef M. Ibrahim, "Iran Acts to Prevent Riots during Moslem Holy Month," *New York Times*, November 29, 1978, p. 3.
140. R.W. Apple, "Outbreaks in Iran Growing As Rioters Defy Curfew Order," *New York Times*, December 3, 1978, p. 1.
141. "Excerpts from President's Meeting with Reporters," *New York Times*, December 8, 1978, p. 14.
142. "Transcript of President's News Conference," *New York Times*, December 13, 1978, p. 20.
143. Vance, *Hard Choices*, p. 331, and Jonathan C. Randal, "Iranians Harden Protest Tone," *Washington Post*, December 12, 1978, p. 1.
144. Douglas Watson, "Americans Line Up for Planes Out of Iran," *Baltimore Sun*, December 8, 1978, p. 2. By this time over 10,000 of the estimated 42,000 Americans in Iran had already departed.
145. Brzezinski, *Power and Principle*, pp. 370–71.
146. Vance, *Hard Choices*, p. 330. Indeed, the shah, *Answer to History*, p. 170, counted Ball as "among those Americans who wanted to abandon me and ultimately my country."
147. Ibid., and Sick, *All Fall Down*, pp. 125–27. Sullivan, *Mission to Iran*, p. 221, claims that he "was only generally aware of what Ball's thinking was, because he had the Department of State address a number of cabled inquiries to the embassy. . . ."
148. Brzezinski, *Power and Principle*, p. 373; Vance, *Hard Choices*, p. 331; Sick, *All Fall Down*, p. 130. Brzezinski for some reason dates the Sullivan cable December 12.
149. Sick, *All Fall Down*, p. 130, notes that the Council of Notables suggestion was "surprising in view of Sullivan's expressed opposition to the concept only a few days earlier."
150. Vance, *Hard Choices*, p. 330, and Sick, *All Fall Down*, p. 135. The shah would retain command of the armed forces. The main problem with Ball's formulation was that the National Front, from whom the majority of the "Notables" would come, like Khomeini also demanded

that the shah must go, refused to support any prime minister he chose, and insisted upon a national referendum to decide whether Iran would become a constitutional monarchy or a republic. See Douglas Watson, "Foe of Shah Sets Forth 3 Demands," *Baltimore Sun*, December 7, 1978, p. 2.

151. Brzezinski, *Power and Principle*, p. 373.
152. Vance, *Hard Choices*, p. 331.
153. See Sick, *All Fall Down*, pp. 137–39.
154. Brzezinski, *Power and Principle*, p. 374.
155. Ibid. and Jonathan C. Randal, "Military Shows Signs It Is Uneasy with Shah's Rule," *Washington Post*, December 14, 1978, p. 18.
156. Vance, *Hard Choices*, p. 331.
157. Sick, *All Fall Down*, pp. 138–39, and Nicholas Gage, "New Strife Erupts in Many Iran Cities; Shah Presses Talks," *New York Times*, December 15, 1978, p. 1.
158. Vance, *Hard Choices*, p. 331.
159. Ibid.
160. Brzezinski, *Power and Principle*, p. 374.
161. Vance, *Hard Choices*, p. 332.
162. Ibid.
163. Ibid.
164. Ibid. Vance confuses the meeting of December 27 when both Schlesinger and Aaron were present but Duncan was not, with that of the twenty-eighth, when Duncan was there but Schlesinger and Aaron were not. See Brzezinski, *Power and Principle*, p. 375, and Sick, *All Fall Down*, p. 147.
165. Vance, *Hard Choices*, p. 332.
166. Brzezinski, *Power and Principle*, p. 375.
167. See Ibid. for the final, approved and amended wording, but not the original. Vance, *Hard Choices*, p. 333, includes both the original wording and the amendment which he and the president added.
168. Vance, *Hard Choices*, p. 333.
169. Brzezinski, *Power and Principle*, p. 375.
170. Ironically, Vance, *Hard Choices*, p. 333, includes this while Brzezinski doesn't.
171. Ibid. Sick, *All Fall Down*, p. 148, claims that "both Brzezinski and Vance . . . saw it as a victory for their respective positions," but the former surely knew better.
172. Ibid., p. 155, who also notes that "the first stage of the plan that had resulted from these contacts was worked out with the Department of State," by which he presumably means Secretary Vance, although he does not say so.

173. See Ibid., pp. 148–49 for the shah's reaction, which was based on Sullivan's report. Ambassador Sullivan, however, omits this meeting with the shah in his account.
174. Brzezinski, *Power and Principle*, p. 376.
175. Sullivan, *Mission to Iran*, p. 231. Cf. Sick, *All Fall Down*, p. 149.
176. Ibid., p. 153, and Brzezinski, *Power and Principle*, p. 376.
177. Brzezinski, *Power and Principle*, p. 376.
178. Vance, *Hard Choices*, p. 335, unaccountably dates the meeting January 4.
179. Ibid. Brzezinski, p. 377, makes the same point, but omits reference to the regency council: "We support his decision to leave the country when the civilian government is confirmed and that he will have hospitality here." See also Sick, *All Fall Down*, p. 154.
180. Gen. Robert E. Huyser, *Mission to Tehran* (New York: Harper and Row, 1986), p. 18.
181. Brzezinski, *Power and Principle*, p. 377.
182. Ibid., p. 378.
183. Vance, *Hard Choices*, p. 336. Sullivan, *Mission to Iran*, p. 229, claims that he did "not register any objections to his coming to Tehran at this juncture."
184. Sick, *All Fall Down*, p. 154. The ambassador's report turned out to be false. In retrospect his "coup" report provided Vance with an excuse for delay. Sullivan himself did not believe the military capable of executing a coup. He had told Huyser upon his arrival that "the military had already decayed to the point where they were incapable of doing anything." Huyser, *Mission to Tehran*, p. 24.
185. Ibid., p. 23, and Sick, *All Fall Down*, p. 154.
186. Huyser, *Mission to Tehran*, p. 24.
187. Brzezinski, *Power and Principle*, p. 380.
188. Carter, *Keeping Faith*, p. 445.
189. Brzezinski, *Power and Principle*, p. 380. Vance immediately cabled Huyser to proceed "as previously instructed." See Huyser, *Mission to Tehran*, p. 25.
190. Carter, *Keeping Faith*, p. 445.
191. Brzezinski, *Power and Principle*, p. 380.
192. Ibid.
193. Huyser, *Mission to Tehran*, p. 52.
194. Brzezinski, *Power and Principle*, p. 367.
195. Carter, *Keeping Faith*, pp. 443–44. The president had become "increasingly troubled by the attitude of Ambassador Sullivan, who seemed obsessed with the need for the Shah to abdicate without further delay."
196. Vance, *Hard Choices*, pp. 335–36.

197. Ibid., p. 336. The secretary had already arranged for retired former ambassador Theodore Eliot to go to Paris to see Khomeini "to urge the ayatollah to give Bakhtiar time to restore order before he returned to Iran."
198. Ibid., p. 337.
199. Brzezinski, *Power and Principle*, p. 380. Vance thereupon cancelled the Eliot mission. Sick, *All Fall Down*, pp. 155–57, portrays this as "Sullivan's plan," but such a "tail wags the dog" interpretation strains credulity. This was Secretary Vance's plan, as the evidence clearly and voluminously attests, which Sullivan faithfully attempted to execute.
200. Brzezinski, *Power and Principle*, p. 381.
201. Vance, *Hard Choices*, p. 337.
202. Ibid., and Sick, *All Fall Down*, p. 161.
203. Sick, *All Fall Down*, p. 161.
204. Carter, *Keeping Faith*, p. 446.
205. Ibid.
206. See Brzezinski, *Power and Principle*, p. 381, whose relations with Vance also "became more strained."
207. Vance, *Hard Choices*, p. 337.
208. Ibid., pp. 337–38.
209. Ibid., p. 338.
210. Huyser, *Mission to Tehran*, p. 72. The shah, *Answer to History*, p. 172, thought that Huyser's unannounced arrival was ominous, concluding that his mission was "to neutralize the Iranian army."
211. Vance, *Hard Choices*, p. 338. Sick, *All Fall Down*, pp. 163–64, says these were known to both the shah and Bakhtiar and encouraged by Huyser as a means of developing a line of communication.
212. Huyser, *Mission to Tehran*, p. 97.
213. Vance, *Hard Choices*, p. 338.
214. Sick, *All Fall Down*, pp. 166–68.
215. Ibid., p. 169.
216. Brzezinski, *Power and Principle*, p. 387.
217. Ibid.
218. Sick, *All Fall Down*, p. 171.
219. Ledeen and Lewis, *Debacle*, p. 167.
220. For Huyser's reservations about him, see *Mission to Tehran*, pp. 277, 283, and 285.
221. Brzezinski, *Power and Principle*, p. 388.
222. Ibid.
223. Sick, *All Fall Down*, p. 171.
224. Vance, *Hard Choices*, pp. 338–39.
225. Ibid., p. 339.
226. Brzezinski, *Power and Principle*, p. 388.

227. The failure of Huyser to mention the issue raises an intriguing question. Did Sullivan alter the joint report without Huyser's knowledge prior to sending it, or did Vance simply misinterpret what Huyser had said?
228. Huyser, *Mission to Tehran*, p. 178.
229. Sick, *All Fall Down*, p. 171.
230. Vance, *Hard Choices*, p. 339.
231. Ibid.
232. Ibid., p. 340.
233. Ibid., p. 341.
234. Ibid., p. 340.
235. James M. Markham, "2 Sides in Iran Take Conciliatory Steps; Contacts Reported," *New York Times*, February 5, 1979, p. 1.
236. Vance, *Hard Choices*, p. 341.
237. Ibid., p. 347.
238. Paul Lewis, "Iran's Elite Army Guard Was Routed by Civilians," *New York Times*, February 13, 1979, p. 8.
239. Bill Paul, "Iran's Government Collapses As Many Troops Defect," *Wall Street Journal*, February 12, 1979, p. 2.
240. Brzezinski, *Power and Principle*, p. 393.
241. Vance, *Hard Choices*, p. 338.
242. Ibid., p. 343. Even so, the remaining 7,000 Americans in Iran were being urged to leave. See William Claiborne, "Embassy in Iran Urges Americans to Flee Violence," *Washington Post*, February 16, 1979, p. 11.
243. Vance, *Hard Choices*, p. 344.
244. Ibid., p. 345.

CHAPTER 7

Crisis and Failure in Asia and the Middle East: 1979

The course of American foreign policy under President Carter moved erratically from crisis to crisis in 1979 before reaching its denouement in the Soviet invasion of Afghanistan in December. Secretary Vance had planned four major foreign policy goals to be achieved by late 1978–early 1979: completion of the SALT II treaty with the Soviet Union at a summit meeting in Washington, normalization of relations with China, conclusion of the Egyptian–Israeli peace treaty, and a successful transition to a constitution-based regime in Iran. These accomplishments would cap over two years of virtually constant negotiation and involvement and were to establish the basic contours of the new international order Vance hoped to create.

Secretary Vance not only failed, however, to achieve his desired structure, but American foreign policy was turned inside out. SALT II did not come first as Vance had planned, but last as Moscow wished. Normalization of relations with China did not follow but preceded SALT II. The Egyptian–Israeli peace treaty was not signed in December 1978 as scheduled, but the following March—and then only after President Carter had backed completely away from the Camp David formulas. And in Iran, as we have seen, the attempt to bring about a transition to constitutional government failed utterly.

SALT II, aside from its centrality in Vance's strategy, also functioned as a deterrent to Moscow in the coming Sino–Vietnamese conflict. In Vance's calculations, a SALT II–detente relationship with

Moscow would effectively dissuade the Soviets from threatening military action against China; and he hoped normalization of relations with China would serve to limit Beijing's punishment of Vietnam. But this would be true only if normalization followed SALT II, which would remove any Soviet concern about Sino–American collusion. However, in Vance's absence, Zbigniew Brzezinski persuaded the president that normalization with China should precede SALT II, which was then delayed. As a result, eventual Sino–Vietnamese conflict saw each of the protagonists supported by a superpower, the classic structure for confrontation.

The Struggle to Construct a Foundation in the Middle East

The crisis in United States–Israeli relations was inevitable. The two nations were pursuing divergent strategies, which had been only superficially papered over by the Camp David accords. The United States sought to continue along the path to a broadly based security structure in the Middle East built upon an Egyptian–Israeli peace and eventual resolution of the Palestinian problem. This was the course set in 1973 and toward which the United States sought to move as opportunity arose.

Israel, on the other hand, was pursuing a much narrower objective—maximization of its own security by holding the territory acquired in 1967 and by being the United States' chief ally in the Middle East. This strategy, of course, had been partially compromised by the United States–sponsored rapprochement with Egypt following the Yom Kippur War—even as it marked the starting point for the new American approach. Since that time, successive Israeli leaders had conducted a protracted, rear-guard action to prevent further territorial and political erosion, with some success.[1]

On the surface the Camp David accords had moved Israel toward the American objective of a comprehensive peace. But Camp David was a temporary compromise. Israel had resisted all efforts to link the Egyptian–Israeli peace treaty and the Palestinian problem on the grounds that the peace treaty must come first and stand on its own. As a result Washington had decided to split apart the two problems in the hope of facilitating negotiation of a peace treaty first and establishing a negotiating procedure by which the Palestinian question could be addressed over time. The two-framework approach had made agreement at Camp David possible and, if implemented, the arrangements would have resulted in the establishment of diplomatic relations between Egypt and Israel and the election of a Palestinian self-governing body in the West Bank and Gaza. There had been, however, no formal requirement to conduct simultaneous negotiations.

Now, after Camp David, as the negotiations for the Egyptian–Israeli peace treaty got under way, Washington attempted to reconnect the two issues—for good reason. To negotiate the peace treaty without reference to the Palestinian question would smack of a separate peace, which would alienate Saudi Arabia and Jordan, not to mention the Palestinians. It would spell the end of any effort to build a strategic consensus in the region. So the United States and Egypt sought to gain Israeli agreement to begin negotiations on the self-governing authority for the West Bank/Gaza at the same time that the peace treaty negotiations were occurring. As Secretary Vance put it, the treaty negotiators "were to conduct parallel discussions on a joint Egyptian–Israeli 'side letter' defining arrangements for negotiating autonomy for the inhabitants of the West Bank and Gaza."[2]

The Begin government would have none of it. Before the ink was dry on the Camp David accords, Begin was declaring that what he had agreed to for the West Bank and Gaza was nothing more than administrative autonomy for the Palestinians, which he said was entirely consistent with his self-rule plan of December 1977.[3] Moreover, Foreign Minister Moshe Dayan insisted that what Israel had agreed to at Camp David was "to reach a peace treaty with Egypt, and only after that . . . discuss the question of the West Bank and the Palestinians."[4]

While the United States believed that negotiations for a peace treaty between Egypt and Israel and for the autonomy process should proceed simultaneously, Begin was willing to agree only to the peace treaty, and indeed he used every opportunity to stifle, not simply to delay, the autonomy process. His apparent purpose was at least to dissuade Jordan from participating in the autonomy talks and at most to precipitate the collapse of both agreements, which would force a return to the pre-1973 situation, the preferred Israeli position. His alternative was an undisguised separate peace treaty with

Egypt that would alienate the other Arabs and obviate any necessity to withdraw from the West Bank and Gaza—as President Carter and his national security adviser soon concluded.[5]

In other words, as the negotiations for the peace treaty began in mid-October, the United States and Israel were as far apart as ever, and their differences were not minor but fundamental. Under these circumstances, for President Carter to say that the peace treaty negotiations would not last "more than two or three weeks," given his insistence that the autonomy talks should parallel them, was either a self-deception or a weak attempt to put pressure on the Israelis.[6] It would be more than five months before a peace treaty would be signed, and then only after Washington had capitulated on the West Bank/Gaza question and reaffirmed its strategic partnership with Israel.

Negotiations got under way at Blair House in Washington on October 12. The procedure was the same as that used at Camp David, where the United States had provided the basic negotiating draft. By October 21 the two sides had reached tentative agreement on the treaty but not on the side letter. At this point the treaty was referred to the respective governments for consideration. In the meantime, on October 18, the United States had formulated its response to fourteen questions which Jordan's King Hussein had posed about the Camp David accords. Washington's answers were clearly designed to gain the king's participation in the autonomy talks and to reassure the Saudis, but they shocked the Israelis.

To Secretary Vance, the king's questions offered an opportunity to spell out "the American interpretation of what had been agreed, particularly on the meaning of full autonomy, and our view of the strategy for resolving the ultimate status of the West Bank and Gaza."[7] But to Dayan, "The replies distorted what had been agreed upon at Camp David; were hostile to Israel's security needs, and to the position taken by every Israeli Government; and even contradicted President Carter's own declarations."[8] To make matters worse, Washington's response to Hussein failed to persuade him to take part in the negotiations, though the Saudis promised to take a neutral attitude.

The Israeli response came on October 26, and it was designed to precipitate a breakoff of negotiations. Prime Minister Begin announced cabinet acceptance of the treaty draft but accompanied this announcement with another—the government's decision to "thicken" the West Bank settlements. Carter was outraged and wrote to Begin that "no step . . . could be more damaging" to the West Bank negotiations.[9] But Begin replied in mock innocence that, while he had agreed at Camp David to refrain from establishing new settlements for three months, he had said nothing about enlarging existing settlements.[10] White House insistence that what Begin had actually told Carter was that "the only new settlers that would be invited to the West Bank would be family members of people already there"[11] could not undo the damage.

Predictably, Sadat threatened to withdraw from the negotiations; but after remonstrating with him, Secretary Vance got the talks going again, focusing discussions on the side letter. Sadat, hoping to coordinate completion of the peace treaty with the election of the self-governing authority—and no doubt with one eye on the Arab summit set to convene in Baghdad early in November—wanted a timetable for completion of the autonomy negotiations, and he proposed implementation of the autonomy process first in Gaza.

Begin, however, meeting with Secretary Vance in New York City on November 2 while on his way to Canada, opposed a timetable or any special status for Gaza and, moreover, wanted to weaken language in the treaty preamble regarding commitment to a comprehensive peace—that is, the linkage between the treaty and the autonomy talks.[12] During their meeting Begin also reinforced a line of argument Dayan had initiated a few days earlier regarding the payment of additional money to Israel for the agreement and formal assurances of support.

In a very negative discussion with Vance on October 30, the foreign minister had taken a tough stand on Egypt's proposals for the West Bank and Gaza. Dayan declared that only the procedures for electing the self-governing authority should be negotiated now, not its "powers and responsibilities,"[13] which could be dealt with later. Furthermore, he said, not only would the Israeli military government remain after election of the self-governing authority, the government would retain at least 20 percent of all public lands for its own use, and would construct eighteen to twenty more settlements in the Jordan Valley. On top of all this, Dayan had demanded that the administration "revise and update" all previous agreements, generally referred to as memorandums of understanding (MOU), between the United States and Israel.[14]

In his talk with Vance, Begin reinforced Dayan's remarks on United States guarantees to Israel and also said that Israel wanted a twenty-five-year low-interest loan of $3.37 billion to help pay the costs of the Sinai withdrawal. The cabinet, he said, "would never approve the treaty . . . unless the question of aid was solved first."[15] In short, in response to American and Egyptian insistence that Israel be more forthcoming on coordination of the autonomy issue with the treaty, the Israelis had increased their demands, especially financial demands, for completing the peace treaty.

While American leaders fumed over Begin's obstructionist tactics, Arab leaders had gathered in Baghdad on November 2 and called on President Sadat to refuse to sign a treaty with Israel; and they threatened an economic boycott of Egypt if he signed. Privately, they offered Sadat a bribe of $5 billion, nearly twice what Egypt received annually from Saudi Arabia and other Persian Gulf states, if he would abandon the Camp David process and seek a comprehensive settlement at Geneva.[16] Washington's gamble that the Camp David arrangement would facilitate rapid movement toward an Egyptian–Israeli peace treaty before the Arab world mobilized against it had failed.

Although Sadat was publicly unmoved, according to his aides he was "terribly shaken" by the Baghdad meeting, primarily because King Hussein and the Saudis, who had promised to stay neutral, had sided with the radicals, or rejectionists.[17] Sadat was convinced that Prince Fahd of Saudi Arabia had "gone over to the other side."[18] Indeed, the Saudis now informed Sadat that they would pay only half (instead of all) the cost of the F-5 jets that Washington had sold to Egypt. Moreover, Kuwait refused to pay Egypt the $250 million fourth-quarter installment of a ten-year-old, billion-dollar-a-year subsidy arrangement.[19]

Sadat's concern prompted him to write to President Carter on November 8 that "there must be unequivocal agreement on what was to take place on the West Bank and Gaza. Otherwise he would be accused of making a separate deal with the Israelis and abandoning the Palestinians."[20] Sadat's message combined with one from the American ambassador to Israel, Samuel Lewis, regarding "increasingly firm Israeli demands for money," persuaded the president immediately to convene his top advisers—Vance, Mondale, Brzezinski, and Ham Jordan—"to review where we stood."[21]

As President Carter saw it, "The negotiations [were] going backwards."[22] The Israelis wanted "a separate peace, then U.S. payments, and finally a free hand in the West Bank."[23] He adamantly insisted that "any aid-loan program if agreed must be predicated on Israeli compliance with [the] Camp David agreements" and, furthermore, that there would be no decisions on aid "until Begin accepted a target date for elections." [24] On the settlements question, the president declared, "We do not intend to subsidize illegal settlements and we will so inform Congress." Finally, it was his view that the "thickening" of existing settlements was "deliberately done to prevent Jordan and the Palestinians from joining the negotiations."[25]

To alleviate the pressure on Sadat the president and his advisers now decided to "pin down" Israeli agreement on the West Bank and Gaza, "even if it meant delaying the signing of an Egyptian–Israeli treaty."[26] Indeed, Brzezinski believed delay was necessary because "once . . . a treaty is signed we will have less leverage."[27] The president agreed and instructed Secretary Vance "to withdraw from the negotiations at the end of this week, to let the technicians take over, and let the leadership in Israel and Egypt know that we are through devoting full time to this nonproductive effort."[28]

A hint of this decision surfaced in the president's news conference on November 10. When asked if the peace treaty and the West Bank/Gaza issues "have to be linked in some way," the president answered:

> Well, there's never been any doubt in my mind, nor President Sadat's nor Prime Minister Begin's that one of the premises for the Camp David negotiations was a comprehensive peace settlement, that includes not just an isolated peace treaty between Israel and Egypt, but includes continuation of a solution for the West Bank, Gaza Strip and ultimately for the Golan Heights as well.[29]

Indeed, the president continued, "I have heard President [*sic*] Begin say in my presence that he did not desire a separate peace treaty with Egypt."

But the Israeli leadership was now in less of a mood to compromise than before. Evidently assuming that Rabat had put as much pressure on Carter as on Sadat, Begin took a tougher line.[30] Carter had sent Begin a compromise proposal requesting that he accept the peace treaty with the side letter, "which committed Israel to begin negotiations one month after ratification of the peace treaty, with a target date of not later than the end of 1979 for holding an election for the self-governing authority."[31]

Meeting with Vance in New York City on November 12, on his way back from Canada to Israel, Begin flatly rejected the American compromise. He refused to agree to any fixed target date or to accelerated withdrawal. Furthermore, he told the secretary, his earlier request for a loan had been "a mistake."[32] What he had meant to ask for was a grant, not a loan. Finally, on the subject of oil supplies, the prime minister wanted to know "how America could help."[33] An exasperated Secretary Vance replied noncommittally to both queries with the standard diplomatic evasion: the administration would have to "study" the matter. In response to Begin's intransigence, Washington was closing off discussion on financial aid or petroleum supply until the Israelis became more cooperative.

The following evening, in a nationally televised interview with Bill Moyers, President Carter gave vent to his frustration. Without singling out the Israelis, but clearly addressing his remarks to them, Carter called on both parties to put aside "little, tiny technicalities" and to reach agreement.[34] If the talks broke down, Carter warned,

> Our children, our grandchildren, future generations (will) look back and say these little, tiny technicalities, phrases, phrasing of ideas, legalisms, which at that time semed to be paramount in the eyes of the Egyptian and Israeli governments, have absolutely no historical significance. That is basically what the problems are.[35]

Sadat's position now appeared to soften on the peace treaty even as it hardened on the question of linkage; he made public the "Gaza first" idea that he had raised earlier.[36] Over the next few days in messages to Carter and in talks with Ambassador Eilts, Sadat laid out his views. In essence, his position was that "Egypt would not agree to peace with Israel without having reached an agreement at the same time on the West Bank and Gaza. Even if the interim withdrawal had to be delayed until November 1979, he said, that could be done if by then the Palestinians had their self government, at least in Gaza."[37]

To reinforce this position, Sadat sent his vice-president, Hosni Mubarak, to Washington on November 16. Mubarak insisted that linkage must be explicit, otherwise "the positions of both Egypt and the United States in the Arab world would deteriorate."[38] On the main sticking point of a fixed timetable for establishment of the self-governing authority, Mubarak "agreed to accept the looser American language of [a] 'target date' rather than a fixed time."[39] With a major hurdle passed, Mubarak then declared that only two key points remained to be agreed upon: the autonomy side letter with the Gaza-first proposal, and article 6 of the treaty concerning the priority of obligations. On the former, Mubarak argued that it would be easier to reach agreement because the issue of Jerusalem would not arise. On the latter, it had to be made clear that if Israel attacked another Arab nation Egypt would be free to assist that nation.[40]

The Israeli leadership had painted itself into a corner, adopting an indefensible position at a time when its leverage was diminishing. The key factors were, on the one hand, the agreement between Egypt and the United States, and on the other, the rapidly collapsing situation in Iran, which was impacting on petroleum supplies. Refusal to accept what after all was a general statement on linkage in the treaty preamble had boomeranged. Egypt had responded, at Washington's urging, with specific demands for a fixed timetable coordinating withdrawal from Sinai and establishment of the self-governing authority and for a "police presence" in Gaza. On top of this the United States now declined to discuss financial aid or economic assistance. Foreign Minister Dayan described Israel's predicament:

> The Prime Minister had come back empty-handed. He had been able to get nothing from his meeting with Vance and his telephone talks with President Carter. The treaty changes our Government had asked for had been turned down. No progress had been registered in the areas of economic aid and oil supplies. The Egyptians were putting up new demands, and there was now no certainty that the United States would maintain her reservations about them.[41]

The negotiations had reached the point where Israel would have to accept some form of linkage. Begin's obvious preference was for a more general formulation than the specific timetable Sadat was now demanding. The problem was how to return to the more general compromise formulation he himself had already rejected. After assurances from legal advisers Meir Rosenne and Aharan Barak that the phrasing of linkage in the draft treaty preamble was "not a legal pitfall at all but a statement of intent," the way was open for a decision.[42] Begin's plan was that "all proposals put forward since the compromise treaty draft should be withdrawn in return for Israel's agreeing to drop its earlier objections to the draft treaty." In other words, to avoid commitment to a specific timetable, Begin proposed to "agree to the draft treaty as it was at the end of October, and exclude everything that has happened since then."[43]

On November 21, Begin called Carter to say that the cabinet after all would accept the United States draft treaty—providing that Egypt also accepted it—but would not accept a specific date for completing the autonomy negotiations or for holding elections for the self-governing authority.[44] Before formalizing the cabinet decision, Begin wanted to resolve the questions of a financial grant and oil supply, which was increasingly becoming a problem as a result of the growing turmoil in Iran.[45] Israel received the bulk of its petroleum imports from Iran, whose production had dropped sharply in November due to oil field workers' strikes. But Carter declined to make commitments on either question, just as Vance had done earlier.[46]

The president's firm position now produced some give. In a press statement the next day, Foreign Minister Dayan declared that, as far as the Israelis were concerned, the treaty negotiations were concluded. Egypt should "take it or leave it."[47] Although the statement suggested total inflexibility and although Israel continued to oppose formal linkage and a timetable, Dayan went on to say that Israel was "ready to begin negotiations on the West Bank–Gaza civil autonomy plan immediately after a peace treaty had been signed." Israel would not object to opening negotiations within a month. Indeed, "it [might] be shorter than a month." In other words, the Israeli government had now embraced the essence of the American compromise proposal regarding the beginning of autonomy negotiations, but not that regarding their conclusion.

Begin's reversal, combined with Dayan's indicated willingness to promptly commence West Bank/Gaza negotiations, persuaded the president to change positions, too. In early November Israeli intransigence had led Carter, at Brzezinski's suggestion, to delay conclusion of the peace treaty on the grounds that to complete the treaty first would reduce American leverage on the West Bank/Gaza issue.

That approach had produced the Israeli reversal on the preamble, but not on a West Bank/Gaza timetable, although Dayan's statement suggested de facto if not de jure linkage. The Israeli shift now prompted the president to swing to the opposite view: that completion of a treaty first would increase Washington's leverage on the West Bank/Gaza issue.[48] He would give negotiations another try.

Vance was dispatched to the Middle East on December 9, hoping beyond hope to reach agreement by the December 17 deadline established at Camp David. During a breakfast meeting with reporters two days before the secretary's departure, President Carter emphasized the importance of the deadline. "If, because of mutual lack of agreement, we go past December 17, it would cast doubt on whether the Egyptians and Israelis would carry out the difficult terms of the upcoming peace treaty, and it would set a precedent that would have far-reaching, adverse effects."[49] His instructions to Vance were to complete the negotiations on the text of the treaty and to ensure that the side letter mentioned as a target date the end of 1979—if not for the establishment of the self-governing authority, then at least for conclusion of the negotiations prior to elections.[50]

Vance also went armed with an idea for breaking the linkage impasse. The United States proposal derived from the Camp David accords, which called for the establishment of diplomatic relations after the interim Israeli withdrawal from Sinai, but mentioned nothing about the timing of the exchange of ambassadors. Vance proposed that Sadat agree to "establish diplomatic relations after the interim withdrawal, but that the actual exchange of ambassadors . . . not take place until the self-governing authority in the West Bank and Gaza had actually been established."[51]

As anticipated, Sadat readily agreed to this proposal, cheerfully predicting that it would produce a confrontation in Israel. Despite objections from his advisers over several points, American willingness to add interpretive notes clarifying the remaining contentious but not major issues[52] persuaded Sadat to pronounce himself willing to accept the entire package. But he warned Secretary Vance that he had reached the limit on the concessions he could make. "There was," he said, "no further room for compromise."[53]

In Jerusalem, on December 13 and 14, Vance presented the compromise proposals worked out with Sadat. Hoping to give the Israelis a sense of Washington's broader perspective, the secretary warned that the "political conditions for peace . . . were eroding";

and, referring to Iran, he spoke of the "growing dangers of instability in the entire Middle East."[54] Vance reported that he had persuaded Sadat to drop his demands for altering the treaty and mentioned the idea of the two parties' agreeing to a good-faith target date instead of to a fixed timetable for establishment of the self-governing authority by the end of 1979. He said that the United States would resolve technical disagreements in articles 4 and 6 through interpretive notes. Finally, the secretary set forth Sadat's Gaza-first proposal and his new position on "not exchanging ambassadors until after the self-governing authority was established."[55]

Begin angrily rejected the entire package. He accused Sadat of "deviating from Camp David" on the exchange of ambassadors and on Gaza. Israel, he said, would never accept a target date. Nor did he like the idea of interpretive notes, which would only open loopholes through which Egypt could avoid carrying out the treaty. Then Begin accused the United States of "unfairly siding with Egypt when it should instead be supporting Israel."[56] Begin's assessment was that Vance's proposals "did not bring a peace treaty closer."[57] That was also the view of the Israeli cabinet, with which Vance met after his talks with Begin.

Whether anything could have come of further negotiations became moot when President Carter instructed Vance to return home immediately to be present for his announcement of the agreement between Washington and Beijing on establishment of diplomatic relations. En route home the secretary learned that the Israeli cabinet had issued a statement rejecting "the attitude and the interpretation of the U.S. government with regard to the Egyptian proposals."[58] Venting his anger, Vance "told the traveling press that it was the government of Israel that had prevented us from meeting the December 17 deadline."[59]

President Carter, expressing his "acute frustration" with Begin, declared that "it now was up to Israel to accept or reject the projected treaty."[60] The United States, he said, had spent too much time on the Middle East, to the detriment of "other pressing international problems." State Department spokesman Hodding Carter echoed the president, saying, "in our judgment, the time has come for a pause, not a breakdown but a pause," in the mediation effort.[61] The "pause" would last a month, until the second half of January 1979, and in that time the American leadership entered a protracted crisis of strategy.

One of the "other pressing international problems" to which the president referred became obvious later that same day.

Sino–American Normalization and the Road to War

Secretary Vance's Middle East trip concealed a far greater failure than his inability to persuade the Israelis to conclude the treaty with Egypt. In his absence the president had made a major policy decision regarding China that crippled the strategy the secretary had been pursuing. Ironically, Vance had not wanted to make the Middle East trip, perhaps realizing the potential policy damage which could occur in his absence.[62]

In any case, in an effort to ensure that the SALT agreement would precede all else, he had reached an agreement with the president that "if the negotiations in Peking were successful—as we were confident they would be—the annnouncement would be made on January 1, that is, one week after my discussions with Gromyko in Geneva."[63] The secretary "wanted the announcement of normalization to come after my Geneva meeting with Gromyko."[64] Having obtained the president's word, Vance proceeded to the Middle East "not at that point overly concerned about leaving Washington, for I assumed then that there would be more than two weeks to take critical preparatory steps after I got back."

When Carter called Vance in Jerusalem to tell him that he intended to announce normalization on December 15 instead of January 1, Vance was stunned. He "asked the president if it would be possible to hold up the announcement until January 1, as we had planned," but Carter said no, explaining that "he was concerned that the negotiations might become unraveled."[65] It was, of course, Secretary Vance's strategy which was unraveling as a result of the China-first decision. Vance complained that "at a critical moment, Brzezinski had blacked Christopher and Holbrooke out of the decision making for about six hours, and they had been unable to inform me of what was taking place."[66]

But if President Carter had been persuaded by Brzezinski that the announcement to normalize relations with China would deter Hanoi, he, too, miscalculated. If anything, it simply advanced the timetable for the invasion of Kampuchea. Vietnam invaded Kampuchea with

100,000 men, including elements of fourteen infantry divisions and an armored division on December 25, 1978, one week before formal normalization between Washington and Beijing occurred.[67] On the day of the invasion the *People's Daily* carried the ominous headline, "Hanoi Has Gone Far Enough . . . Don't Complain That We Didn't Warn You in Advance."

The Vietnamese invasion, with the prominent involvement of Soviet and Cuban advisers, was a multi-pronged effort carrying along all of the major routes of access into Kampuchea. Within two weeks, by January 7, Phnom Penh had fallen to the invaders and the west coast port of Kompong Som (formerly Sihanoukville) was under heavy attack.[68] In the east, by January 19, Hanoi's forces had secured control of the Mekong River between Phnom Penh and the Vietnamese border.[69]

Hanoi's armies had overrun much of Kampuchea in a blitzkrieg-like operation lasting less than a month, but the rapidity of advance had left units overextended and vulnerable at many points. Despite Hanoi's and Moscow's insistent claims of victory and the initial staggering losses suffered by Pol Pot's forces, Kampuchean troops quickly reverted to guerrilla warfare tactics, avoiding direct engagement while concentrating on cutting Hanoi's supply lines.[70] By late January, Pol Pot's scattered forces were still actively engaging the enemy, although they were clearly on the defensive and in danger of total collapse.[71]

Against the background of Vietnam's invasion of Kampuchea, Washington, Moscow, and Beijing maneuvered in a three-cornered game of deterrence diplomacy to occupy an optimum position when, as expected, Beijing attacked Vietnam in an effort to prevent its ally's defeat.[72] The United States pressed for completion of the arms treaty with the Soviet Union, Moscow continued to elude commitment, and Beijing sought to align Washington on its side. In seeking to complete the arms control negotiation with Moscow, Washington hoped to be able to restrain both sides in the coming conflict. The Soviets, on the other hand, dragged out commitment, even while assuring Washington that the treaty would soon be signed, in order to be free to exert pressure against China. Beijing sought to range the United States on its side to neutralize Moscow and to be free to accomplish its objectives against Vietnam.

Soviet leader Leonid Brezhnev continued the demurral tactic in an interview with *Time* magazine's senior editors in mid-January.

Responding to a question about "the progress toward SALT II and a possible summit meeting," Brezhnev said that conclusion of negotiations was not imminent. "Work on a new agreement on the limitation of offensive strategic arms is drawing to a close, although it will obviously take some more time for the positions to be finally agreed."[73] Declining to elaborate on the second part of the question, which implied setting the date for a Washington summit, Brezhnev deftly avoided reference to either a date or a place, saying simply that he hoped "President Carter and I will be able in the near future to affix our signatures to the accord."

A few days later, in attempting to explain the delay in concluding SALT, President Carter said that the "impression we got" at Geneva the previous month was that "the Soviet Union may have stalled completion of a strategic arms limitation treaty . . . because of concern about U.S.–China ties."[74] Carter thought that the Soviets might have wished to put off the visit by Brezhnev to Washington for the signing ceremony "so it would not be so close in time" to Deng's scheduled trip at the end of January. The president said that "we have almost concluded the SALT negotiations" with "some minor but important issues to be agreed. . . . And my hope is that they will be concluded without undue delay."

Hoping to encourage the Soviets, Vance gained acceptance for a policy of "evenhandedness," the essence of which appeared in a story a few days before Deng's arrival. It said that "President Carter has decided that even though the United States and China are entering a new and potentially close relationship, everything possible must be done to seek improvement at the same time in American ties with the Soviet Union."[75] The secretary specified that "an arms treaty with the Soviet Union and a visit to this country by Leonid I. Brezhnev . . . are crucial goals of American foreign policy." The president reinforced that view in his State of the Union address, saying that "nothing is more important" than completing the arms control agreement with the Soviet Union.[76]

Administration spokesman Hodding Carter, referring to a sharp increase in Jewish emigration over the previous year, noted that "Soviet policies, in American eyes, had improved." Finally, as part of the so-called policy of evenhandedness, it had been decided to send a large scientific mission headed by the president's chief science adviser, Dr. Frank Press, to Moscow in early February to explore "new areas of scientific cooperation."[77]

Washington officials put forth the hopeful view that following a "decent interval" after Deng's visit, word would come from Moscow "clearing the way for a SALT treaty."[78] Estimates on when a summit would be held ranged "from late next month through March." It was argued that the reason for Soviet procrastination was simply that Brezhnev "would not be upstaged" by Deng and that once he had departed the treaty would be signed. Finally, congressional leaders noted that the timing of the ratification process would not be affected by election-year politics "as long as we get it [the treaty] by spring."[79]

But it was Deng Xiaoping who made the boldest play in the deterrence game, attempting to range the United States on China's side. His bid came during his visit to the United States following the normalization of diplomatic relations on January 1, 1979. His trip, spanning the week of January 28 to February 5, 1979, was intended, at least in part, to elicit from the American leadership the extent of support that China could expect to receive when its forces moved into action against Vietnam. Vance notes, "Even before he arrived in the United States, Deng was calling for greater Sino–American efforts to oppose the Soviet Union and was issuing warnings to Vietnam."[80]

Deng did considerably more than call for "greater Sino–American efforts." As part of his advance preparation for the trip, the Chinese leader had also given an interview with *Time* magazine four days before his departure, which appeared on the newsstands the day of his arrival. It was a blockbuster. As *Time*'s editors phrased it, "The point [Deng] made most emphatically was a dramatic one—and one that Moscow expected, and feared, would be his main messsage to President Carter: that Sino–American rapprochement should be turned into an explicit anti-Soviet alliance."[81]

Responding to a question about the evolving Sino–American–Japanese relationship, Deng replied: "After setting up this relationship between China, Japan and the U.S. we must further develop the relationship in a deepening way. If we really want to be able to place curbs on the polar bear, the only realistic thing for us is to unite."[82] Deng's assertion that Chinese strategy was based on a "united front against hegemonism . . . and this united front includes the U.S." was a thinly disguised attempt to associate Washington with China's coming strike against Vietnam. The Chinese leader repeated the same theme in his arrival speech on the White House lawn, declaring that the threat of war was growing and that "our two countries are duty bound to work together" to maintain peace.[83]

It is difficult to believe that Deng genuinely harbored any illusions about the prospect of a formal alliance with the United States. Brzezinski's views aside, neither Chinese policy under Deng nor American policy under Carter gave much hope for that. Deng's objective appears to have been the subtler one of creating the public impression of Sino–American cooperation—even if no cooperation in fact existed—in hopes of playing the "American card" against Moscow in the three-cornered diplomatic deterrence game under way.[84]

The prospect of being drawn into the coming conflict on China's side precipitated another of the seemingly interminable disputes within the Carter administration over the proper policy course. For Brzezinski, continuing Soviet adventurism transformed Deng's trip "from what initially was conceived of as a formal diplomatic act into a summit meeting of global geopolitical significance."[85] For the national security adviser "the very fact of Deng's visit . . . brought to a head the question of how far the United States should go in developing the new relationship with China," and he saw it as "a strategic opportunity . . . to offset the Soviet military buildup."[86]

Secretary Vance, as on most issues, strongly disagreed with the national security adviser. While Deng's visit would be "an extravaganza" celebrating the attainment of the long-cherished goal of normalized relations between the two countries, it should not be allowed to spill over to influence broader strategic issues. Perceiving that Deng was attempting to play the "American card," Vance recommended to the president that "he make it clear to Deng that we would not permit any disruption of our policy toward the Soviet Union." The Chinese must not be allowed, said Vance, "to influence us to take a harder public line against the Soviets."[87]

For Deng the most important question was, would Washington act to neutralize Moscow when Chinese forces struck Vietnam? Of course, he would not put the question bluntly. First, he wanted to learn just what the United States was willing to do in the context of the newly established relationship. This issue arose during the first meeting between Deng and the president on January 29, the morning after the Chinese leader's arrival. During a lengthy, "very frank" discussion focusing largely on world issues, in which Deng "minced no words," he "urged joint American–Chinese cooperation against the Soviets, though carefully adding that he was not proposing at this stage a formal alliance."[88]

The president replied cautiously, agreeing that "close consultations between our two countries were necessary to stem Soviet expansionism," but avoided any reference to cooperation. "Worried that Deng might feel somewhat rebuffed," Brzezinski urged the president to identify those areas where the two nations could "co-operate and consult." In recapitulating the day's discussions, the president restated Deng's position that the relationship was "not a formal alliance," and listed the following areas for cooperation: Africa (Zambia, Somalia), Pakistan–India, the Middle East (possible Sino–Israeli relations), Korea, and the non-aligned movement.[89]

The answer to Deng lay in what the president had not listed, namely, Vietnam! Clearly, if indirectly, the president had conveyed to the Chinese leader the answer he sought: the United States would not cooperate over Vietnam and therefore would take no action to deter the Soviet Union. Brzezinski, describing this performance, less than candidly declared that he was "greatly encouraged that the basis for enhancing our relationship had been laid," but the plain fact was that the United States would not cooperate with China in the area most immediately necessary.

Still, Deng persisted, requesting a private meeting with the president, which he received the next afternoon, January 30. Here Deng set forth the Chinese decision to strike Vietnam, discussing "various possible Soviet responses, indicating how China would respond to them." His analysis included "the worst possibility" of a Soviet invasion of China; he said that "even in such a case China would hold out."[90] Having already been told that cooperation on Vietnam had been ruled out, all Deng asked of the United States was "moral support." Whatever Chinese leaders might have planned for Vietnam, the failure to obtain the cooperation of the United States forced a downgrading of the effort from a major strike to a "lesson." Deng declared that "China would undertake a limited action and then withdraw its troops quickly," as in the Sino–Indian border conflict of 1962.[91]

President Carter put off an immediate response to Deng's request for "moral support," instead "pointing out that this was a serious issue which he would like to discuss with his advisers before giving his reaction" and noting that "the Chinese action could be highly destabilizing and that restraint was desirable in such a difficult situation."[92] The president and his advisers, including Brzezinski, all agreed that the United States "could not collude formally with the Chinese in sponsoring what was tantamount to overt military aggression." The president drafted a personal letter to Deng to this effect.

The next day, while Brzezinski was meeting separately with Foreign Minister Huang Hua, sharing his "concern" that China "might be forced to withdraw by a Soviet nuclear threat," the president met privately with Deng. He urged him to "reconsider," saying that "he wanted Deng to understand that our position was not based on fear of the Soviet Union," although it was impossible for the Chinese leader not to draw that conclusion. As to "moral support," the president's decision was that if Beijing went forward with the attack the United States would criticize both China and Vietnam, calling upon both countries to withdraw. This "would provide a partial diplomatic umbrella for the Chinese action without associating the United States with it."[93] The president also agreed to provide satellite intelligence, particularly of Soviet troop movements along the Sino–Soviet border, which would give Beijing ample warning of any Soviet attack.[94]

Despite the setback, Deng strove to obtain as great a degree of association between American and Chinese policy as possible. In negotiation of the joint press communiqué, the Chinese insisted upon insertion of the term "hegemony," the code word for Soviet adventurism. To avoid that problem, before Deng arrived Secretary Vance had lobbied against issuance of a communiqué, but he was overruled.[95] Having lost the argument over the communiqué, he "was adamantly against using that term [hegemony], viewing it as a concession to the Chinese and a provocation to the Soviets."[96] But Vance readily agreed to a qualified formulation. The final wording retained the word "hegemony," followed by "or domination over others."[97]

Vance's willingness to accept "hegemony" in the communiqué undoubtedly stemmed from the fact that the term had been used in the joint communiqué signed in Shanghai during President Nixon's 1972 visit and again in the joint announcement in December of the normalization of relations. But he also had a countermove in mind. The next day the secretary proposed that the government issue a statement upon Deng's departure reemphasizing evenhandedness. The president reached out to take the prepared statement from Vance, but "even before reading it muttered, 'Is it another apology?'"[98] Although taken aback, Vance pressed strongly for a statement reemphasizing evenhandedness. However, in a heated discussion among Vance, Brzezinski, and the president, the chief executive decided against issuing Vance's statement on the grounds that it would contribute to the impression that the United States was once again "weak and zigzagging."

Deng Xiaoping undoubtedly hoped for a greater degree of association with Chinese policy than the United States was willing to give, and after leaving Washington he expressed his dissatisfaction. In Tokyo, en route to Beijing, Deng was highly critical of American policy. He said that he could not complain while a guest in the United States but having left could say what he thought. "The Soviet Union," he remarked with characteristic acerbity, "will never be impressed by half-way positions."[99] The United States, he said, "is allowing the Soviet Union to place a lot of pawns on the world's chessboard . . . things cannot be allowed to go on this way."[100]

Chinese strategy in Indochina for a generation had been to promote fragmentation in order to preserve influence in the region. Given the imminent prospect of the utter failure of that strategy in the Soviet-supported Vietnamese invasion of Kampuchea, the last remaining area of any significant Chinese influence, the only type of "lesson" that would have been consistent with long-term strategy was one powerful enough to force Vietnam to withdraw from Kampuchea. Yet such a lesson would only have been possible with Washington's support in deterrence of Moscow, which would not be forthcoming.

In any case, Beijing would claim that whatever happened was the intended "lesson." The simple fact was that Chinese war policy ultimately would be dictated by Moscow's response. The Chinese would go as far and for as long as the Soviet Union would permit, hoping that the impression of Sino–American cooperation generated by Deng Xiaoping's trip to Washington would delay a Soviet response long enough to give Chinese forces sufficient time to bring about Vietnamese redeployments from Cambodia.

Moscow Probes Washington's Intentions

Moscow, of course, did not know whether or not the United States and China had reached an accord on the coming conflict, and Soviet commentary seemed designed to elicit information on the precise nature of the emerging relationship. What had President Carter meant when he said that the United States and China had "charted a new and irreversible course toward a firmer, more constructive, and a more hopeful relationship"?[101] The president acknowledged that the two countries' security concerns "do not coincide completely" but said, "while we pursue independent foreign policies, our separate actions in many places can contribute to similar goals."[102] Toward that end the president said that he and Deng had "agreed to consult regularly on matters of common global interest."

Similarly, what lay behind Deng's statement that, aside from the agreements signed on scientific and cultural exchanges, there were "many more areas of bilateral cooperation, and many more channels waiting for us to develop"? Deng's comments came in the context of several statements denouncing Soviet adventurism, declaring China's readiness to take military action against Vietnam, and expressing warm friendship for the United States. For example, in a television interview on the same day the agreements were signed, Deng said, "If you don't teach them [the Vietnamese] some necessary lessons, it just won't do" and remarked that "the honeymoon will continue" between Washington and Beijing.[103]

Soviet leaders were also acutely conscious of the fact that President Carter's warm words of a new and irreversible course with China came in the context of stepped-up criticism of the Soviet Union. The United States chose the day of the signing ceremonies with Deng to issue sharp criticisms of Moscow's continued encoding of missile telemetry data as well as long-range cruise missile tests which could "complicate arms control negotiations" between the two countries.[104]

Soviet Ambassador Anatoly Dobrynin called on Secretary of State Vance the next day, February 1, to express concern over Deng's "incendiary" attacks and to request "clarification" of American China policy.[105] *Pravda* followed with an attack on the Carter administration for giving Deng a "platform" for "slandering the U.S.S.R." in the presence of American officials. Nor was *Pravda* mollified by the attempt to dilute the antihegemony clause with the word "domination"; the editors asked, "Well, really, can anyone be deceived by such tricks?"[106]

Georgi Arbatov, Moscow's Americanologist, criticized Deng's "great act of seduction" because it created "the impression that China is trying to involve the United States, maybe the West in general, including Japan, into some sort of military-political alliance directed against the Soviet Union."[107] Deng, he said, had "attempted to create . . . an illusion that . . . a military-political alliance with China can be a sound alternative to detente, to arms control." This illusion, he went on, "is dangerous, even in the era of conventional warfare. It becomes tremendously dangerous in the era of nuclear warfare."

Washington's protestations that there was nothing more to the Sino–American relationship than was already known was undercut by other high-level administration statements regarding American intentions to counter Soviet expansionism. For example, Defense Secretary Harold Brown, testifying before the House Appropriations Defense Subcommittee on February 7, declared that the United States "must 'find a way' to help other countries fight off Soviet surrogate forces like the Cuban troops deployed in Africa."[108] Although Brown's remarks came the day before his trip to the Middle East and were generally interpreted to apply to conditions there, he had also discussed Vietnam, which Deng had called "the Cuba of the Orient."

In the final days leading up to the outbreak of the war, in response to increased Soviet criticism of United States policy,[109] including indications that SALT II negotiations would be delayed further and that the summit was in jeopardy, the Carter administration began to waffle on support for China. Amid complaints from Moscow that Washington had "completely spoiled the atmosphere" came Soviet objections on SALT.[110] First was an objection to the administration's proposed plan to deploy the MX missile in an underground random-basing scheme.[111] The Soviets claimed that such a scheme was barred by the SALT II treaty, which bans construction of additional fixed launchers. The United States position was that the missile contained its own launcher in a transporter-erector-launcher (TEL) vehicle, and the launch-points to which it moved were simply "holes in the ground."

The second Soviet objection occurred a few days later regarding the major sticking point—encryption—which the United States side had thought resolved with the marriage of Soviet and American proposals at the December meeting. On February 14, Soviet negotiator Victor Karpov declared that his government believed the previously agreed common understanding was adequate and that there was "no need for further interpretation."[112] In short, Moscow had dismissed the December understanding and reverted to the interpretation on encryption that emphasized its permissibility. Moscow's move sent American negotiators scrambling to devise still another formula which would resolve the issue to mutual satisfaction.

These essentially semantic disputes were followed by the far more serious questions of whether there would be a SALT treaty or a summit meeting between Carter and Brezhnev at all. Citing Brezhnev's poor health, "officials . . . closely familiar with contacts between Washington and Moscow" said that the Soviets first suggested that there be no summit meeting and that Secretary Vance and Foreign Minister Gromyko sign the treaty in Geneva.[113] Then, in the face of "adamant" White House insistence that the summit be held, and in Washington as agreed, the Soviets agreed to hold the summit, but in Moscow.[114] Although Brezhnev's "poor health" was used to justify Soviet suggestions, it was made plain that the real reason for raising the issue was Soviet refusal to follow Deng to the United States and a concern that the United States was seeking to coopt Soviet policy.

In any case, Soviet recalcitrance brought results as Washington began to edge away from the earlier appearance of support for China. On February 9, the State Department warned Beijing that "the United States would regard any military move by China with the same disapproval that it had viewed Vietnam's actions in Cambodia."[115] A few days later, on the thirteenth, Secretary Vance met with Dobrynin to offer an explicit trade-off on SALT in hopes of removing any remaining obstacles. Hoping to retain the 5 percent, plus or minus, parameter in defining new types of missiles under the treaty, Vance offered to "ban the testing of MIRVed ALCMs in exchange for getting our way on the new-types definition."[116] He also accepted the Soviet proposal to apply the cruise missile range limitations to unarmed pilotless reconnaissance drones.

Before any response could be made, however, events occurred in Iran and Afghanistan which shelved the talks for the time being. In Tehran, on February 14, armed guerrillas attacked the American embassy, trapping Ambassador William Sullivan and about a hundred staff members inside for over two hours before they were freed by Khomeini's forces.[117] Two embassy guards were wounded and two attackers killed. Khomeini accused the Communist Tudeh party of responsibility, but reports from Washington identified a group with ties to the Tudeh, the left-wing Charik group, as the guerrillas.[118]

At the same time, in Kabul three or four men seized Ambassador Adolph Dubs and held him hostage in the Hotel Kabul.[119] A few hours later the ambassador was caught in a crossfire when the Afghan police charged into the room with guns blazing, killing both the abductors and the ambassador. The Afghan police, ignoring pleas from American embassy officials for caution, evidently had heeded the advice of three Soviet police advisers and a Soviet embassy security official who were on the scene and "involved in preparations for the assault." Washington protested to Moscow in the strongest possible terms declaring that "the refusal by the Soviet advisers to consult on the spot is impossible to justify, given the fact that the life of the American ambassador was in jeopardy."[120]

Whatever motives drove the Afghan police in Kabul and Tudeh-related guerrillas in Tehran, it was plain to many in the administration that the United States presence in those countries was being challenged in a most brutish manner and that the Soviet Union was associated with, if it had not instigated, the challenge. No doubt Washington would have made more of the embassy attack and the killing of its ambassador in Afghanistan had not an even more serious occurrence overshadowed these events. This was the long-awaited Chinese invasion of Vietnam, which commenced on February 17.

War, and Wider War, but No Deterrence

Although Beijing had mobilized over 300,000 troops and deployed more than 500 planes for the invasion, only a small fraction of the total force, some 30,000 men, carried out the initial attacks, crossing the border at twenty-six points along a 450-mile front.[121] At the end of the first day of fighting, Chinese forces had penetrated only five to six miles. While the main points of attack were as yet unclear, operations appeared to be developing along both railroad lines connecting the two countries, toward Lao Cai in the northwest and Lang Son in the northeast. The latter, a key rail junction, lay twelve miles from the border and eighty miles northeast of Hanoi.

The Soviet Union immediately warned China to stop its invasion "before it is too late" and affirmed its intention to "honor its obligations" under the treaty of friendship and cooperation signed with Vietnam the previous November.[122] Washington also responded, but to stress that the United States "would not become involved"; it would intervene only diplomatically, in bringing the conflict to an end and in "persuading the Soviet Union not to intervene."[123] Top officials in Washington expressed uncertainty over how far Chinese forces would attempt to penetrate into Vietnam and as to "what kind of military response, if any, the Soviet Union might make against China on behalf of its ally."

After the first day, a brief lull occurred in the fighting as Lao Cai fell and Chinese forces were reinforced with two more divisions. They were positioned for the main thrust of the attack on Lang Son in the northeast, the gateway to Hanoi.[124] A French reporter on the scene described the rapid evacuation of Lang Son, a city of 46,000 people, in preparation for the coming battle and the Chinese and Vietnamese buildups on the hills surrounding and overlooking the city.[125] Meanwhile, reports from Moscow and Beijing revealed that the two communist giants were girding for confrontation along their mutual border. Moscow placed its troops on alert, cancelling all military leaves, and Beijing did the same in the provinces along the Sino–Soviet border, even while declaring that its forces would withdraw soon from Vietnam.[126]

While acknowledging that relations with the Soviet Union were "a mixture of cooperation and competition," President Carter declared in a major speech that nevertheless SALT II was "in the national interest to pursue . . . even as we continue competition with the Soviet Union elsewhere in the world." Indeed, discussing the Middle East and Southeast Asia situations, the president took a strong stand, declaring, "We will stand by our friends—we will honor our commitments—and we will protect the vital interests of the United States." There "must be no doubt that the people of the United States are fully prepared to meet its commitments, and to back up those commitments with military strength."[127]

Pravda immediately charged that during Deng's visit to the United States Washington had given Beijing the "green light" to invade and that China should be "punished" for its attack.[128] A Moscow television commentator declared, "These aren't the days of Chinese feudalism, and such a war won't remain unpunished."[129] Washington's reaction was publicly muted, but privately officials were concerned that the war might escalate. State Department officials declared that there were as yet "no indications" of Soviet military preparations for action against China, but they "did not rule out a countermove if China moves deeper into Vietnam."[130] Some officials feared that "a border clash could escalate into a nuclear exchange. 'It's a very dangerous situation.'"[131]

As Chinese and Vietnamese forces prepared for a major battle at Lang Son, the Soviets orchestrated a series of moves designed to exert pressure on Beijing, dissuade Washington from becoming involved, and support Hanoi. Moscow initiated an airlift to Hanoi, continued to augment its naval squadron in the South China Sea, and began to ready military units in Outer Mongolia to put pressure on Beijing.[132] On February 23, American intelligence noted that "rapid changes over the preceding 48 hours had generated an intense new scrutiny of Chinese and Russian intentions" and had produced a new estimate that the war might "last for a month or longer instead of a few days."[133] The chances for Sino–Soviet confrontation were now very good.

Soviet uncertainty of the role Washington might play in a Sino–Soviet confrontation led Moscow to attempt to create a dilemma in the event the United States sought to support Beijing. Thus, at the critical moment in the Sino–Vietnamese conflict, on February 23, the Soviet Union triggered an attack by South Yemeni forces on North Yemen. The attack, which will be discussed in greater detail below, raised the specter of a potentially major setback for the United States in the Middle East, if Washington chose to become entangled in support of China in Indochina.

At this moment the Middle East was exploding. The Israelis were stalling on completion of the peace treaty, which was to have been signed in mid-December 1978; Iran was in chaos following the resignation of Prime Minister Shahpour Bakhtiar; and American relations with Saudi Arabia were on the verge of collapse because of Washington's failure to produce an acceptable Palestinian settlement. The South Yemeni attack appeared to threaten the unification of Yemen and the establishment of a major Soviet position on Saudi Arabia's flank, precisely the fear expressed within the administration two years earlier during the Ethiopia–Somalia battle over the Ogaden. In short, moving the South Yemeni pawn raised the prospect of the encirclement of Saudi Arabia and perhaps the eleventh-hour derailment of the Egyptian–Israeli peace treaty.

Finally, just before the Chinese attack on Lang Son began, Moscow sought to neutralize the United States by indicating its interest in finalizing the SALT negotiations and by warning against further support of China. On February 26, Ambassador Dobrynin met with President Carter and Secretary Vance to offer "new ideas on the few outstanding issues that substantially narrowed the differences" on SALT II.[134] The next day Foreign Minister Gromyko issued a harsh criticism of American efforts to play the "China card," declaring that "if this is being done in order to pressure the Soviet Union, such attempts are futile and can only yield the opposite effect."[135] It was the Chinese who were "striving with particular eagerness to set the Soviet Union and the United States at loggerheads," he said. "The development of Soviet–American relations is being obstructed under their influence, and also under the influence of certain internal forces in the United States."

Gromyko's speech reinforced "dark hints," to use Strobe Talbott's phrase, "in back-channel conversation both in Washington and Moscow . . . that the Soviet leadership might be undertaking a fundamental reassessment of its policy toward the U.S., including a reassessment of the desirabiity of concluding a SALT agreement at all."[136] Even allowing for the possibility that the Soviets were engaging in a bit of psychological warfare as the critical point in the Sino–Vietnamese conflict was reached, the SALT threat seems to have galvanized the Carter administration to clarify its position. Secretary Vance was particularly concerned that the United States "avoid any misinterpretation by Peking that we supported their adventure or by Moscow that we were colluding with the Chinese."[137]

In a television interview on February 25, Defense Secretary Brown declared that "Soviet intervention in Southeast Asia would be a matter of important concern to the United States" but said that "the United States had no interest in intervening" in "a war on China's northern border."[138] This view was reinforced by a "source close to official American thinking," who declared that a Soviet strike on China's northern border "would not be of direct concern to the United States."[139]

Treasury Secretary Michael Blumenthal arrived in China on February 26 on a previously scheduled visit to discuss commercial matters. During a two-hour meeting with Deng he delivered a personal letter from President Carter calling for China's prompt withdrawal from Vietnam.[140] Before meeting with Blumenthal, Deng met with American reporters and, no doubt anticipating the message the secretary was carrying, declared that "both the Cuba of the Orient and the Cuba of the West seem to be emboldened by the so-called tremendous backing force behind them. Now, some people of the world are afraid of offending them. Even if they do something terrible, these people wouldn't dare to take action against them. It's a question of being afraid of them."[141]

During his news conference on February 27, in answering criticism that his foreign policy exhibited "weakness and impotency," President Carter insisted that the United States was "adequately protecting" its interests. "An exercise of prudence in trying to contain regional disputes and combat among other nations is in the best interests of our own country."[142] It would be, he said, "completely improper . . . to inject ourselves in any active way into the combat that's presently taking place among Communist Asian nations." The United States, he said, had expressed "strong disapproval" to Beijing and Moscow over the Vietnam events, but it would be "counterproductive" to terminate bilateral relations simply because a country does "something contrary to our desires."

Clear statements that the United States would not support China in a conflict with the Soviet Union brought an immediate response from Deng Xiaoping, who declared, "China might withdraw its forces in about ten days. . . . We'll pull out as soon as our objective is attained."[143] The Chinese leader now endorsed Washington's position calling for mutual withdrawal of Chinese troops from Vietnam and Vietnamese troops from Cambodia. "We would welcome it," he said, but "the problem is that Vietnam won't withdraw its forces from Cambodia."

Then, just as Lang Son was falling to Chinese forces on March 2,[144] Brezhnev, in a wide-ranging address on foreign and domestic policy, repeated the same theme connecting SALT and China. He "took a conciliatory stance toward the United States, forsaking the harsh anti-American language that [had] been appearing in the official press and describing a treaty on strategic arms as virtually concluded."[145] Toward China, on the other hand, though not threatening military action, Brezhnev demanded the "immediate end of the Chinese aggression against Vietnam—the withdrawal of all the troops of the interventionists to the last soldier." After alluding to past Soviet support in the war with the United States ("our friendship with fraternal Vietnam has been tested in practice over many years"), he concluded with a veiled threat: "Nobody should have any doubts: the Soviet Union is true to the treaty of friendship and cooperation binding our countries together."[146]

Brezhnev's relatively restrained comments contrasted sharply with a Soviet government statement issued two hours after his speech claiming that Chinese forces were concentrating for an attack on Laos. The government warned that "the Chinese aggressors must know that the more crimes they commit, the more severe will be the retribution for them."[147] The day after Brezhnev's speech Moscow "denied rumors . . . that it had been engaged in secret negotiations with China and the United States to end the fighting in Vietnam."[148] It was impossible to glean from this what message Moscow sought to convey, but "French sources in Moscow quoted officials as having said that the Chinese had 48 hours to get out of Vietnam," which implied that the Soviet Union had issued a secret ultimatum.[149]

The breakthrough at Lang Son after a fierce week-long battle in which Beijing employed six divisions—approximately 72,000 men[150]—opened the door to a direct attack on Hanoi and forced the redeployment of at least two and perhaps three main-force divisions for defense of the capital.[151] It appeared that the Chinese would accomplish their objective of forcing Vietnam's withdrawal from Kampuchea. Yet, at this moment, on March 4, the Beijing leadership declared that its military objectives had already been met and announced that the beginning of withdrawal from Vietnamese territory would take place "shortly."[152] In fact, Chinese forces would substantially complete their withdrawal from Vietnamese territory by March 16.

Despite Chinese protestations that they had accomplished their objectives, the Chinese offensive against Vietnam, February 17 to March 16, 1979, did not come remotely close to forcing Hanoi's forces to withdraw from Cambodia.[153] Despite the mobilization of over 300,000 troops and 500 aircraft, no objective commensurate with either Beijing's long-term strategy or the size of the military buildup was achieved. If the Chinese objective was simply a spoiling action containing no other "lesson" than a demonstration of the capability to inflict punishment, as some have suggested, then it was extremely costly and produced a worse situation than had existed prior to the attack.

In less than a month of actual fighting the Chinese absorbed combat losses of some 28,000 killed and 43,000 wounded and exacted perhaps double that combined figure against Vietnam. Nevertheless, Beijing's forces failed to engage, let alone destroy, a single main-force Vietnamese division, encountering only well-armed regional forces during the month-long campaign. Worst of all from

Beijing's point of view, the Soviet Union moved quickly to reinforce Hanoi as well as to increase its own presence in Vietnam with expanded air and naval facilities at the American-built base at Cam Ranh Bay.

Clearly, the Chinese leadership under Deng Xiaoping deliberately chose not to continue the offensive even when the main objective of the invasion had come within grasp. What had happened, the record strongly suggests, was that in the absence of any countervailing United States pressure on the Soviet Union, Moscow's subtle saber rattling proved sufficient to deter Beijing's further advance. The Chinese would not tempt a Soviet strike and involvement in a two-front conflict and so withdrew. Beijing's claims that their military objectives had already been met and that Vietnam had been taught a "lesson" were simply face-saving gestures.

Even more startling, Deng's reaction to the reverse in Vietnam was to offer to normalize relations with Moscow! In the context of giving formal notice of the Chinese government's intention not to extend the 1950 Sino–Soviet treaty, Foreign Minister Huang Hua proposed that the two countries open negotiations for "the solution of outstanding issues and the improvement of relations between the two countries."[154] Deng was attempting to pursue an evenhanded policy toward the two superpowers, a sharp blow to the Carter administration's proclaimed objective of envisaging China as a "central element" in American strategy.

Regarding the Sino–Vietnamese conflict, American leaders obviously did not wish to be placed in the position of supporting China against the Soviet Union and then having the bluff called, given what was perceived to be an unfavorable strategic equation. This was the crucial difference between events in 1979 and those of 1969, when the United States had acted to deter the Soviet Union from taking action against China. Yet there appears to have existed a preferable course of action to the one chosen. Washington could have opted for normalization earlier and then negotiated with Moscow over Southeast Asia in the context of SALT II negotiations. That after all had been the sequence in 1972. But that was under the Nixon strategy of modified containment. Under the Kissinger–Vance strategy, detente with Moscow was judged to be central and had to come prior to geopolitical adjustments around Moscow's periphery.

Thus, not only did the Carter administration abjure support for China against the Soviet Union to avoid a superpower confrontation, it did so because such support would have contradicted the general strategy. Finally, the Carter administration declined involvement also because its highest priority area, the Middle East, needed immediate attention. Treaty negotiations between Israel and Egypt had foundered in acrimony, the decades-long relationship with Iran had collapsed, relations with Saudi Arabia were rapidly deteriorating, and the two Yemens were in conflict. The region had reached a flash point.

The Erosion of Washington's Leverage in the Middle East

By early 1979 the rapidly collapsing situation in Iran had had a dramatic, fissile impact on the Middle East negotiations. It was now clear to all that the United States was powerless to prevent the collapse of the shah and that its own position in Iran would also be lost. Consequently, all of the participants in the Egyptian–Israeli negotiations realized that they now possessed greater leverage vis-à-vis the United States than before, since Washington now more desperately than ever needed to reach a successful conclusion, lest its position unravel in the region.

Sadat saw Washington's predicament as an opportunity for Egypt to replace Iran as the stabilizing force in the region.[155] This possible advantage strengthened his resolve against any suggestion of a separate peace treaty that would alienate the very moderate Arabs he hoped to protect. Begin, on the other hand, recognizing Washington's growing desperation, believed that a separate peace was more likely than ever and refused to budge from his position of December. He also proposed that Israel replace Iran as the United States' pillar in the region. Finally, the Saudis, although deeply concerned about American inaction in Iran and urging greater regional involvement, also believed their leverage on the negotiations had strengthened; they insisted that Washington drop the whole idea of a treaty and intensified their demands for complete Israeli withdrawal.[156]

In short, by early January 1979, when the Carter leadership began to reassess the state of play, the negotiations were "falling apart."[157] In highly secret deliberations, it was decided to proceed firmly along two policy paths to resolve the Middle East issues as quickly as possible. First, with regard to Egypt and Israel, the United

States would restart the treaty negotiations, diluting the terms of the Camp David agreements to the degree necessary to obtain Israel's adherence to the treaty. Above all, the United States wished to conclude treaty negotiations between Egypt and Israel, even though Jordan would probably not participate and the Palestinian framework would suffer.

Secondly, hoping to counterbalance the adverse effect which dilution of the Palestinian agreement would have on the Saudis, Washington sought to increase pressure on Riyadh to gain at least tacit acceptance of the peace treaty.[158] The Carter leadership attempted to accomplish this objective through a traditional means—by emphasizing the Soviet threat over local and regional disputes. In short, Carter sought to persuade the Saudis that concern about the Soviet threat should take precedence over resolution of the Palestinian issue and the Zionist threat. The president and his advisers calculated that demonstrated American support for Saudi security would allay fears that the United States was an unreliable ally.

In an effort to maximize American leverage on all of the parties, it was decided to send Secretary of Defense Harold Brown to the Middle East February 9 through 19, 1979. His mission was to explore the possibility of establishing an American military presence in the Persian Gulf region, specifically in Saudi Arabia, as well as to offer incentives in the form of military hardware to Egypt, Israel, and Jordan prior to restarting the treaty negotiations. Although carefully phrased, the quid pro quo to each was increased weapons supply in return for support of Camp David.

In Saudi Arabia, declaring that he had come with "ideas for a broad strategy" on regional cooperation, the secretary went to some lengths to emphasize American readiness to assist in Riyadh's defense against the growing Soviet threat, particularly in South Yemen.[159] In this regard, he confirmed a weapons package for North Yemen negotiated earlier as well as one for the Sudan. Pledging that the United States would do its part, Brown proposed joint military cooperation with Saudi Arabia and establishment of an American military base, presumably at Dhahran, a former World War II American base next to Ras Tanura on the Persian Gulf.[160]

In return for American assistance, Brown pressed the Saudis to support the Camp David process. The Saudi leadership listened attentively to the secretary's presentation, applauding American intentions to play a greater role in the region, for which, after all, they had called. But aside from expressing a desire to acquire the F-14s sold to Iran and reaffirming their own willingness to finance the weapons packages for North Yemen and the Sudan, the Saudis dismayed the secretary by their response to his proposals.

Indeed, Washington's approach came up hard against a radically different Saudi interpretation of events. Paradoxically, the fall of the shah seemed to offer the Saudi leadership a way out of a growing dilemma. On the one hand, in the face of increasing regional instability, the Saudis demanded greater American commitment to Saudi security. On the other hand, the Saudis rejected the Camp David formulas, which Washington urged Riyadh to support. The Saudi leadership came to the conclusion that even though the collapse in Iran increased Saudi security concerns, the loss of access to Iranian oil increased American reliance upon Saudi Arabia. Hence, their confidence in increased Saudi political leverage on Washington enabled them to take a stronger stand in opposition to Camp David.

Saudi leaders had decided that they could bring the United States around to their position through subtle execution of petroleum diplomacy. The pattern was to be publicly conciliatory, but to edge oil prices upward. For example, the Saudis had promised visiting Treasury Secretary Michael Blumenthal in December 1978 that they would oppose an oil price increase, but in January they agreed to the first OPEC price rise in eighteen months, from $12.70 (which had prevailed since July 1977) to $13.34.[161] Similarly, the Saudis informed visiting Commerce Secretary Juanita Kreps in January 1979 that they would continue production in the 10 to 10.5 million b/d range "for some time," yet a week after her departure they cut production to 9.5 million b/d.[162] After the signing of the Egyptian–Israeli peace treaty, of course, the price of oil would skyrocket.

While the Saudis exerted economic leverage, Washington sought to demonstrate strong support for Saudi security against the Soviet threat. The focus of Washington's effort was the Arabian peninsula and developing hostilities between North and South Yemen. The evolving conflict between the Yemens was, of course, of immediate concern to Saudi Arabia. South Yemen already represented a Soviet foothold on Saudi Arabia's doorstep, and unification of the Yemens under Aden's leadership would present a major threat.

Through mid-1978, Saudi strategy toward the peninsula had been to win over North Yemen through the supply of arms purchased from the United States. The United States had acquiesced in this strategy for obvious reasons. Moreover, it was succeeding. But the assassination of North Yemen's president in June 1978 (see chapter 5 above), led to increasing demands by the new North Yemeni leadership for disengagement from the Saudi arms tie and a direct arms relationship with the United States. The Saudis were decidedly ambivalent about a stronger, independent North Yemen, which would provide more security against the South but would also represent a potential threat to Riyadh itself.[163] Their reaction was simply to stall.

The fall of the shah forced the Saudis to act. The deployment of Iranian military power to contain unrest in Oman had been a welcome counterweight to neighboring South Yemen. With the withdrawal of the Iranian counterweight, the Saudis were left with no alternative but to increase North Yemeni power, and by January 1979, after lengthy negotiations, Saudi Arabia concluded a major arms package of $300 million for North Yemen from the United States.[164] The Saudis, it seemed, now were not only willing to accept an American support presence in Sana, they even urged Washington to play a greater role in the region. It was this situation which had offered some encouragement to the Carter leadership and had been the reasoning behind Brown's proposal to establish an American base and joint defense arrangements with the Saudis.

But the Saudi leadership spurned Brown's proposal of a United States military presence, rejecting the very logic on which it was offered, and denounced Camp David. After Brown's visit, Saudi Foreign Minister Prince Saud expressed the leadership's outlook in an interview with the London-based Arabic-language newspaper *Al Hawadith*. Saud said that "the Americans feel that the Soviet Union is trying to benefit from the changing situation in the area and believe that the Soviets are trying to deepen disputes and encourage violence." Then he said:

> We have explained to the U.S. secretary and his aides that we have nothing to do with international strategies. The domain in which we work is the Arab and Islamic domain. We believe that the Zionist danger is a threat to the Arab area and its stability. The only way to restore balance, calm and stability to the area is for Israel to accept a withdrawal from the occupied Arab territories, to return Jerusalem and to recognize the Palestinian people's right to self-determination.[165]

With regard to the proposal for joint defense arrangements, Saud declared that he saw no threat to the Gulf's security and therefore no need for any defense arrangements with the United States. "U.S. and Soviet plans are found in Washington and Moscow. As far as we are concerned, we have no such plans. The kingdom's security and stability depend on its own people."[166] Saudi Arabia, he concluded, "believes in the good neighbor policy regardless of the type of regime involved," and is prepared to have good relations with both South Yemen and Ethiopia. The Saudis also let it be understood that they were entertaining an offer from Moscow to establish diplomatic relations.

Although Washington attempted to put a good face on Brown's visit, the first and most important consultations on his trip had not gone well.[167] Events at the next stop, Jordan, went no better. King Hussein wished to replace his F-5 jets with more powerful F-16s, to acquire the Stinger, a newly developed hand-held anti-aircraft weapon; and to purchase additional armored personnel carriers. But Brown reportedly informed the king that "until Jordan concludes a peace pact with Israel, the prospect of more modern arms being sold to Amman is not rated high."[168]

From Amman Brown went to Tel Aviv, where he encountered an Israeli leadership which very skillfully attempted to turn the tables on him. Defense Minister Ezer Weizman told Brown that "Israel planned to reduce its military requirements by about 25 percent over the next 10 years because the Government expected to sign a peace treaty with Egypt soon."[169] But he also argued that the Iranian revolution and the coming Egyptian–Israeli peace treaty created a new situation which the United States and Israel should meet by becoming "full strategic partners" for defense of the region.[170]

Brown's response was to agree to accelerate arms deliveries to Israel, but he declined to designate Israel as a full partner.[171] Moreover, Brown explored the possibility of Israeli participation in a broad regional grouping with the Arabs, an idea which the Israeli leadership vigorously opposed.[172] Indeed, the Israeli leadership was concerned over American willingness to provide arms to any of the Arabs, but especially to Egypt, which they feared would now become the main Middle East recipient of United States arms.

When Secretary Brown arrived in Cairo on the last stop of his trip, Sadat proposed precisely what Israel feared. If the United States agreed to modernize Egyptian forces, he told Brown, Egypt would take on the responsibility for "ensuring stability in a region stretching from Algeria east to Afghanistan and from the Mediterranean south into sub-Sahara Africa to Somalia or beyond."[173] The secretary, no doubt privately skeptical of so ambitious a claim, promised that the Carter administration would "consider Sadat's arms requests seriously," without attaching any political preconditions.

He added, however, that "the realities of U.S. politics mean there would be little likelihood of Egypt receiving massive infusions of American weapons unless the Camp David talks lead to a peace treaty."[174] Reacting animatedly to what was a rather unsubtle attempt to pressure him into making more concessions, Sadat "categorically" declared that he had made all the concessions he was going to make. "It was now up to the Israelis."[175]

If the purpose of the Brown trip was to prepare the way for a greater American role in the region and to demand as a quid pro quo support for Camp David, then the secretary failed in his mission. He had been rebuffed at every stop. As Secretary Vance delicately phrased Brown's view, "There was neither panic nor any willingness to suppress local disputes . . . in the interests of greater regional security cooperation." The United States would have to "find a way to enhance our military capabilities in the area without the necessity of establishing local American bases."[176]

The Retreat from Camp David

While Secretary Brown was still in the Middle East, the global and regional situations abruptly began to change. On February 17, China attacked Vietnam, raising the issues of Soviet and American involvement in support of their respective allies and potential confrontation should the conflict escalate. This situation combined with the Iranian collapse, the SALT II impasse, and the Egyptian–Israeli deadlock, made the United States position a shambles. It was in this context, recall, that Moscow triggered the South Yemeni attack on North Yemen, February 23, creating the additional dilemma for the Carter administration of simultaneous crises in the Middle East and the Far East.

Two widely separated and simultaneous conflicts placed great strain upon Washington's ability to respond. Given the deployment pattern of American power in 1979, whatever military response the United States made would have to come from the Seventh Fleet, whose area of operational responsibility stretched from the northern Pacific to the Horn of Africa. Indeed, there was little possibility of responding to both crises with equal force. If Washington chose to act in the Middle East it would leave Beijing vulnerable and undoubtedly have an adverse effect upon the just-normalized Sino–American relationship. On the other hand, if Washington acted in support of Beijing in Asia it would leave the Middle East exposed. The South Yemeni attack threatened the unification of Yemen and establishment of a major Soviet client position on Saudi Arabia's doorstep, as well as derailment of the still unsigned Egyptian–Israeli peace treaty.

But at the outset the dilemma was only potential, not real. The Carter administration had already decided to give only diplomatic support to Beijing, and the Yemeni events merely reconfirmed the decision to concentrate efforts on the Middle East. Indeed, in a perverse way the South Yemeni attack opened up an opportunity for the United States to advance its strategy of demonstrating support for Saudi Arabia. Over the next several weeks, the Carter administration would in fact exaggerate the magnitude of the South Yemeni attacks in order to demonstrate its ability to move American military power quickly into position for Saudi defense.

At the same time, the president had decided to establish a deadline for conclusion of the treaty negotiations. Earlier, Carter had invited Egyptian Foreign Minister Mustafa Khalil and Israeli Foreign Minister Moshe Dayan to meet with Secretary Vance at Camp David on February 21. Since Prime Minister Begin strictly limited Dayan's authority to negotiate, no substantive progress was made; and the talks concluded four days later on February 24. Carter invited both men to meet with him privately the next afternoon; the only other participants were Vance and Brzezinski.

Gravely emphasizing the need to complete the negotiations quickly, Carter said that "he, as President of the United States, had to determine America's policy in the Middle East, and he proposed to do that within the next ten days,"[177] by the end of the first week in March. Toward this end, he continued, he proposed to invite Prime Minister Begin and President Sadat to Washington to conclude the negotiations. It was arranged that the Israeli leader would come to Washington for private discussions with the president on March 2, with Sadat to follow.[178]

Meeting with his top advisers on February 28 to prepare for the meetings with Begin, the president called for recommendations. Vice-President Mondale urged him not to press Begin, and "simply let things go on their own," on the grounds that another blowup would be "politically counterproductive."[179] Brzezinski, on the other hand, startled the president with his blunt assessment that the Israelis sought to undermine the president's reelection and that "this objective was influencing their current tactics." Their strategy all along, he said, had been "to stall the negotiations so that in the end we would pay them for a separate peace with Egypt."[180]

When Begin and Carter met on March 2 it seemed that Brzezinski's evaluation had been an underestimate. Begin stonewalled, demanding "massive American help" and reiterating the proposals made to Brown for an American–Israeli strategic partnership. In this connection he offered the use of the huge airfield at Etzion in the Sinai that was already ticketed for reversion to Egypt.[181] The thrust of Begin's remarks was that the United States should abandon the comprehensive peace process and rely solely upon Israel in the region. "Only Israel stood in the path of a Soviet takeover of the whole Middle East," he said.[182]

On Camp David, calculating that Carter was desperate, Begin took an even more rigid position, rejecting every facet of the compromise package that had been negotiated over the previous several months. "I will not sign it under any conditions," he said repeatedly.[183] The treaty, Begin insisted, must stand unchanged; no interpretive notes were acceptable. The target date in the side letter was a deviation from Camp David and was also unacceptable. Finally, Israel needed a firm guarantee from Egypt on oil, without which Israel would not relinquish the Sinai oil fields. After this performance by Begin, a "frustrated" and "angry" President Carter was "convinced the peace effort was at an end."[184] The Camp David accords appeared doomed.

The March 2 meeting was Begin's response to Carter's ultimatum of February 25. The fact of the matter was that President Carter had attempted to bluff the Israeli leader into compliance and had failed. Begin had correctly calculated that Carter was bluffing and called his hand. Carter had made a serious mistake in issuing his February 25 ultimatum to "determine America's policy . . . within the next ten days," to *both* parties, in each other's presence. Begin knew that was a bluff, for Carter had threatened to turn away from the only two options available.

Worse, the Israeli leader had not only called Carter's bluff, but had also turned it to his own advantage. On the day of Begin's arrival in Washington the story of Carter's "10-day ultimatum for a settlement with Egypt" was leaked to the press and radio and confirmed by Israeli Foreign Ministry officials.[185] When asked upon departure for Washington how he would respond if Carter tried to apply pressure, Begin declared, "If pressure is used against us, we shall reject it."[186] Although White House spokesmen denied the ultimatum story and the Israeli Foreign Ministry subsequently also repudiated it, Begin had said nothing, generating great pressure on the president.[187]

Immediately following the morning's meetings with Begin, Carter, Brzezinski, Jody Powell, and Bill Quandt huddled together over lunch to discuss "how [they] should react to the overall collapse of the Camp David Accords,"[188] and began work on the fallback formula decided upon earlier. Joined the next day by Vance, Brown, and Jordan, the Carter leadership formulated what Brzezinski termed "a major Presidential initiative," but which in fact was a decision to cave in completely to Israeli demands.

The United States would attempt to purchase Israel's agreement with a "security treaty in the context of larger progress toward peace in the Middle East, involving implementation of the Camp David Accords."[189] However, what this meant in reality was that Carter would not only accede to the demand for a strategic partnership, he would capitulate on the target date for holding elections to the self-governing authority. In short, the accords were virtually gutted of their central content in order to make them acceptable to the Israelis.

All along, President Carter had stipulated that any decision on aid would come only after Israel had complied with the accords reached at Camp David. Secondly, since resumption of the negotiations, Washington and Cairo had insisted on a timetable, that is, a target date for election of the self-governing authority by the end of 1979. However, the new "scenario" dropped both the condition for aid and the entire idea of a target date for elections by the end of 1979.[190]

In the new proposal the word "goal" was substituted for "target date" and it applied to completion of the negotiations defining the self-governing authority rather than to the elections. Elections to the self-governing authority would then follow "as expeditiously as possible." This formula offered Begin a means to put off elections for the West Bank/Gaza self-governing authority indefinitely, for the goal was not fixed; nor were negotiations tied to elections, but only to the body to which Palestinians would be elected.

Watering down the West Bank/Gaza formula and offering a security treaty to Israel reflected a crucial decision, no doubt born of the multiple crises then facing the Carter administration, to nail down the treaty as soon as possible. President Carter accurately described the changed situation.

> Now, at best, we could have a bilateral peace treaty followed by extended negotiations on the West Bank and on Palestinian rights. At worst, the Egyptians and Israelis would break off relations, Egypt would rejoin the other Arabs as enemies of Israel, and the Palestinians on the West Bank and in Israel itself would increasingly demonstrate for full citizenship rights, causing a bloody confrontation which might arouse the entire world against Israel.[191]

It was to prevent the worst case that Sadat would have to be convinced that this change—at least as much of it as would be divulged to him—was in his interests. He had called on March 3 to arrange his trip to Washington, but the president put him off, telling him "to stay cool for forty-eight hours and let the pressure build up on Begin."[192]

On the next day, March 4, the president presented the new proposals to Begin. After making a few minor modifications, in a remarkable turnaround from the first meeting, the Israeli prime minisister quickly accepted them. And no wonder—he had gotten more than he had hoped for, particularly the delinkage of the security relationship from the West Bank/Gaza question. Begin described the change on the target date as a "serious" proposal, and now deemed acceptable the new interpretation of article 6 on the priority of obligations.[193] On the remaining problems of oil supplies and the exchange of ambassadors President Carter indicated that he would deal directly with Sadat. Begin then agreed to cable the new compromise back to the Israeli cabinet for an urgent decision; and after a single "day of debate," the cabinet approved the new proposals.[194]

With cabinet approval of the new package on the fifth, the president had every reason to feel that "success was at hand"[195]—if Sadat could be persuaded to take the long view and make the necessary "concessions."[196] He thereupon called Sadat to say, "without giving him any details," that the Israelis had accepted the treaty text.[197] Sadat was overjoyed, but insisted on seeing the text. Here the president demurred, deciding that only his personal involvement "stood a chance"[198] of gaining Sadat's approval. Rather than cable the text by itself, he arranged to send Brzezinski on ahead with it "to explain some of the more difficult parts and to review the strategic considerations which might help to ease Sadat's anticipated objections to the wording."[199]

Brzezinski, who says he was sent to "make sure that Sadat would not do anything rash" before the president got there, took with him a personal message from Carter appealing for Sadat's support.[200] It stated in part that even though "the language may not be exactly what you want . . . the target date issue and the 'priority of obligations' issue are such that you can accept them and legitimately claim a victory."[201] Privately, Brzezinski expressed the concern that "Begin might even wish to see the President defeated."[202] But Sadat would not be told of the decision to offer Israel a new security relationship.

When Carter called Sadat on March 5 to tell him Brzezinski was coming immediately and that he would follow a day later, the Egyptian president replied: "Great! Your trip will be a wonderful event, and a complete success." Carter's feeling now was that he "had a guarantee from President Sadat that my mission would not fail, or at least, that a failure would not be caused by differences between him and me."[203] Earlier the president had considered a trip to the Middle East an "act of desperation."[204] Although Carter's trip would pubicly still be depicted as a "gamble,"[205] privately he was now reasonably certain that it would produce a treaty and give his sagging domestic position "a much needed political boost."[206]

The Failure to Win Over Saudi Arabia

There was yet another Middle East problem needing urgent attention, which would also be addressed in the context of the president's trip. This was the problem of Saudi Arabia. Although

President Carter was reasonably confident that Sadat would go along with a watered-down West Bank/Gaza formula because he was after all recovering Egypt's conquered territories, he knew the Saudis would not. Indeed, since the Palestinians would now receive not even the figleaf guarantee of elections to the self-governing authority, the Saudis would inevitably be even more opposed to the Camp David framework than before.

The Carter administration's response was to act along lines charted earlier, hoping to persuade the Saudi leadership that the Soviet threat should take precedence over the Zionist danger. The added twist was that Washington itself would accentuate the Soviet threat. In a highly secret decision worked out following the South Yemeni (PDRY) attack on February 23, the Carter administration moved to exaggerate the extent of hostilities between the two Yemens in order to raise the threat level and demonstate United States responsiveness. In short, Washington had decided to increase the pressure on the Saudis for the same quid quo pro posited earlier—United States defense of Saudi Arabia against the Soviet threat in return for Saudi support for Camp David.

In retrospect, it would appear that the North Yemen leadership, too, saw the South Yemeni attack as an opportunity to extricate Sana from Saudi domination and obtain a direct relationship to the United States—a strategem whose odds were much improved by Washington's search for more access points in the Middle East. Thus, on February 23, YAR president Ali Abdulah Saleh called in the American ambassador to state that South Yemeni forces were attacking his country with Soviet assistance; he asked for United States support.[207]

Over the next three days YAR officials provided "increasingly grave accounts of a deteriorating military situation which suggested South Yemen would soon occupy the southern third of North Yemen."[208] Though no one in the United States embassy was able to confirm these reports, they were nevertheless promptly sent on to Washington, where American intelligence moved immediately to assess the nature of the hostilities, using every means at its disposal, including satellite reconnaissance. By March 2 at the latest, but more likely by February 27, which is when reports of the conflict first appeared in the American press, the Carter leadership had concluded that while some fighting was indeed occurring, "the situation was not at all serious."[209]

South Yemen had attacked with about three thousand men and

a dozen tanks, drawn from its small army of ten brigades, and a small group of North Yemeni defectors named the National Democratic Front.[210] When the attack began, North Yemeni border units slowed advancing PDRY forces with delaying tactics while pulling back to defensible positions in the mountains astride the main roads through the passes. Consequently, the border towns of Qatabah, Al Bayda, and a few others fell without much of a struggle; but extremely rough terrain beyond the immediate border area made off-road tank movement impossible and wheeled transport along the unpaved roads torturously slow.[211]

Indeed, the mountainous terrain defined and limited the scope of the attack. The main communications route was along the dirt road from Qatabah to Ibb through mountain passes controlled by YAR forces. South Yemeni tanks (T-54s and T-55s) moved as far as the terrain permitted, about twenty miles, then stopped several miles short of the passes, remaining there for the duration of the hostilities. Six truck-mounted rocket launchers (BM 21s) armed with standard and short-range rockets capable of firing 12.7 and 6.8 miles were able to accompany ground forces somewhat further; but, unable to operate effectively off-road, they also failed to get close enough to support the skirmishing in the passes.[212] As the U.S. Army military attache's after-action report put it,

> Since the mountain ridgelines along the road from Qatabah to Ibb are too rugged to move a herd of mountain goats, much less permit the movement of tanks and artillery, and since no signs of fighting could be found within 38km of Ibb, I concluded that the Sana-Taiz highway was never threatened by PDRY forces advancing from Qatabah toward Ibb.[213]

Precisely because the situation "was not at all serious," the Carter leadership decided that with minimal risk it could use the South Yemeni attack to forward its own objective of emphasizing the Soviet threat to Saudi Arabia. Hence, from February 27 and for the next three weeks, spanning the president's crucial trip to the Middle East, United States intelligence began to send reports greatly exaggerating the level of conflict. These reports then became the basis for a series of newspaper articles repeating the same theme and stressing the Soviet threat.[214]

The general interpretation of events was that "the PDRY attacks, if pressed, could succeed in gaining radical control over the southern parts of the YAR or toppling the government in Sana. Thus, the invasion seemed . . . to present a threat not only to the YAR but also to the peninsula as a whole."[215] CIA reports described the battlefield situation even more dramatically.

> YAR forces by the 27th of February were exhausted from a week of intense fighting. PDRY forces were advancing along mountain ridgelines toward Ibb. They were advancing with tanks and artillery, employing rolling artillery barrages and tank thrusts which the YAR could not match. The PDRY strategy was to move on top of the mountains rather than up the valleys. At their present rate of advance they would soon be in Ibb . . . cutting the main north-south highway and the southern third of the country off from the remainder.[216]

CIA reports also claimed that the hospital at Al Bayda had been "shelled to rubble,"[217] and that the entire town of "Qatabah itself had changed hands so many times during the course of the fighting that it had been reduced to rubble." Finally, it was said, upon withdrawal following the cease-fire, PDRY forces employed a scorched earth policy "ripping door frames and windows out of homes and making off with generators and whatever else they could get their hands on."[218]

None of it was true. Photographs taken of the two towns by the military attache showed the "unrubbled town of Qatabah, the passes where YAR forces defended, and the countryside through which no sane tank commander would even attempt to maneuver tanks."[219] He also had photographs of "the newly constructed Al Bayda hospital."[220] Asked to explain the discrepancy between the intelligence reports and the photographs, embassy personnel declared, "We were hoodwinked, that's what it means."[221]

Indeed, after the fact, the Department of State acknowledged as much in its message of May 1, 1979, transmitted to all diplomatic posts. "The YAR's apparent exaggeration of the battle conditions at Qatabah (similar to its exaggeration of the fighting around Bayda) may have been, in part, due to faulty communications and poor command and control procedures. It is probable, however, that the YAR'S gloomy reports were also aimed at obtaining maximum U.S. and Saudi sympathy . . . which would explain the reason the YAR steadily refused to allow our Defense Attache in the battle areas until long after fighting ceased."[222]

The Department of State's message acknowledged that the situation had been exaggerated, but placed the blame entirely on the YAR, which, to be sure, had portrayed the events as a major crisis. But American intelligence had conducted its own analysis, knew that there was never a danger of toppling the Sana government, yet even further exaggerated the YAR version of events. It would appear that, as one officer noted afterward, "if Yemen had not happened at that particular time, it would have been invented."[223]

The Carter administration's portrayal of a Soviet-inspired invasion of North Yemen was the basis for expediting shipment of the previously negotiated, Saudi-financed arms package for North Yemen, which was now in the amount of $400 million. The package included twelve F-5 jet fighters, sixty-four M-60 tanks, fifty armored personnel carriers, thirty antiaircraft guns, seven thousand shoulder-fired antitank rockets, and a dozen recoilless rifles.[224] In addition, several mobile training teams with about seventy instructors were sent to North Yemen to help Yemeni personnel familiarize themselves with United States equipment.[225] Finally, the president ordered the deployment of a carrier task force from Subic Bay to the Arabian Sea and two AWACS battle-management planes to Saudi Arabia from Okinawa.[226]

To expedite delivery, and also to avoid congressional certification that a genuine emergency existed on the Arabian peninsula, on March 7 President Carter invoked for the first time a provision of the 1976 Arms Export Control Act empowering him to waive the thirty-day congressional review period for arms sales in excess of $7 million.[227] The waiver, an administration official declared, was intended to be "a political signal, to the South Yemenis and the Russians not to push any further, and to the Saudis that we won't let this be pushed any further."[228]

Riyadh did not get the "signal" Washington hoped to send. After a brief panic, the Saudi leadership decided that the threat to the peninsula was not as great as the Carter administration was making it out to be. When the fighting first erupted, the Saudis called for an immediate cease-fire and negotiations between the two Yemens. At the same time they cancelled all leave for their own small army, made plans to withdraw their small peacekeeping force from Lebanon, and requested permission from Washington to transfer weapons purchased from the United States to North Yemen.[229]

Following prolonged discussions with the South Yemeni leadership, however, the Saudis decided the "Soviet threat" was not what Washington claimed. Saudi Crown Prince Fahd had been scheduled to visit Washington on March 13 but cancelled his trip when the fighting broke out. Instead, he received South Yemeni Foreign Minister Mohammed Saleh Motel in Riyadh.[230] The South Yemeni foreign minister in fact went twice to Riyadh, first on February 24 and then three days later, to confer with the secretary-general of the Arab League. The outcome of his second visit was an announcement that both Yemens had accepted a mediation attempt by the Arab League Council.[231]

Believing that the conflict was under control, the Saudis backed away from their early request to transfer arms to Sana.[232] Under pressure from Washington, however, the Saudis agreed as part of the United States' arms package to North Yemen to deliver from its own stocks twelve F-5s, thirty-two M-60 tanks, and sundry small arms, which Washington would then replace. But while delivering the small arms, the Saudis delayed delivery of the planes, sending only four of the twelve in mid-May, long after the fighting had ended, and the remaining eight only in September. They also sent the tanks, but provided only a token amount of ammunition for them.[233] Clearly, the leaders in Riyadh did not believe that the fighting was serious. If anything, their evident desire to keep the weapons on a short leash indicated some concern that they could be used against Saudi Arabia. In short, the use of Yemen as a ploy to persuade the Saudis to support Camp David failed ignominiously, with fateful consequences, as we shall see.

The Egyptian–Israeli Treaty and Its Costs

In the meantime, indeed, on March 7, the day he invoked the congressional waiver for arms deliveries to North Yemen, President Carter was bound for the Middle East anticipating quickly wrapping up a peace treaty between Egypt and Israel. The first stop, Cairo, was believed to be crucial. Even before the president arrived, there were grounds for optimism, for Brzezinski had cabled to Carter the results of his talks with Sadat. Hearing that "Sadat could not have been more cooperative," the president was "extremely pleased."[234]

The essence of the discussions between Carter and Sadat on March 8 was that, despite objections to the changes worked out with

Begin, particularly those concerning the West Bank/Gaza timetable and the interpretive note on the priority of obligations, Sadat realized that the time had come to conclude the negotiations. The "most important consideration was to get the treaty signed and the autonomy negotiations started. His mind was very much on Iran and the general threat to Middle East stability,"[235] as punctuated by the conflict in Yemen. As Carter noted, "Over the opposition of some of his close advisers, Sadat accepted the troublesome texts, and within an hour he and I resolved all the questions which still had not been decided after all these months."[236]

There can be little doubt that Sadat was swayed by several extravagant promises which Carter made. First, he promised Sadat "massive" American military and economic aid and expressed hope for large-scale Western private investment in Egypt.[237] The president also promised Sadat that the United States would "participate directly in the negotiations between Egypt and Israel aimed at bringing Palestinian home rule to the West Bank and Gaza."[238] And he promised to exert "maximum influence" to gain Jordanian and Saudi Arabian support for the treaty.

At the conclusion of the meetings with Sadat, "an American–Egyptian formula had emerged" and Sadat had given Carter "carte blanche for his subsequent negotiations with the Israelis."[239] The last hurdle had been cleared. The president could now proceed to Israel and wrap up the treaty. To disguise their jubilation, Carter, Vance, Brzezinski, and their entourage "agreed among [themselves] to arrive in Tel Aviv with a somber demeanor, so that the Israelis would not feel that an Egyptian–American deal had been cooked up, though privately [they] were quite cheerful and hopeful."[240]

Indeed, President Carter "felt confident of success as we approached the Tel Aviv airport."[241] Proceeding directly to Begin's home for dinner, the president still "felt confident that we would finally have a peace treaty." After dinner, Carter proposed that the two of them go into the study, where the president could give his report on the meeting with Sadat. Carter hoped to "expedite his acceptance of the treaty terms, arrange for the signing ceremonies, and have a conclusion of my trip to the Mideast without any further interruptions."

But Begin "seemed to show little interest in my conversations with Sadat." After the president made his presentation, Begin declared that "he could not sign or initial any agreement; that I would have to conclude my talks with him, let him submit the proposals to the cabinet, let the Knesset have an extended debate, going into all the issues . . . and then only after all that would he sign the documents."[242] The entire procedure would consume two weeks or more and meant that the president would have to depart without a signed treaty.

President Carter was dumbfounded. He "couldn't believe it." He demanded to know whether Begin "actually wanted a peace treaty, because my impression was that everything he could do to obstruct it, he did with apparent relish." For almost an hour the two men argued with each other "on our feet in his study," before the president departed around midnight. He felt that it had been "an extremely unsatisfactory meeting, equivalent to what we'd had the previous Saturday night at the White House."[243]

This was closer to the mark than the president realized, for what Begin was doing was related directly to his meeting at the White House a week earlier. At that time Begin's refusal to budge had produced major concessions from Carter; now he was repeating the same tactic. According to Dayan, "When Carter spoke to Begin in Washington about his visits to Cairo and Jerusalem, it was indicated that in the course of his stay there would also be a ceremonial signing of the treaty. If Begin had it in mind to hold discussions in the Cabinet and the Knesset before the signing, he should have told Carter in Washington, and not surprised him in Jerusalem."[244] In short, Begin had set the president up, leading him to believe agreement was at hand. Once Carter had decided on the highly risky course of a presidential trip to bring the negotiations to an end, Begin correctly concluded that rather than accept failure, with its attendant domestic political consequences, the president would make additional concessions. So he stonewalled.

Immediately upon leaving Begin's home, President Carter called his top aides to his room at the King David Hotel. Furious, Carter was now "convinced that Begin would do everything possible to block a treaty." After lengthy discussion, the president and his aides decided that their "only hope was to present the facts to the Israeli cabinet the next day."[245] The next morning, March 11, before the cabinet meeting, Vance met with Dayan to go over the outstanding issues: the MOU between Israel and the United States, the autonomy letter, the question of oil, and article 6 of the treaty.

But most importantly, Vance sought to persuade Dayan that Israel should sign the treaty first and debate it in the Knesset later, as the United States had done regarding the Panama Canal treaty. Vance warned that "no one could predict what speeches woud be made, what the impact of those speeches would be, and what the reaction to them in Egypt might mean for the treaty negotiations."[246] In short, he said, "a Knesset debate in advance of signing might produce a negative result." Dayan acknowledged that Carter had come "expressly to get the treaty signed. If he were now to return to Washington without it, it would affect him adversely."[247]

When the president and his aides met with the Israeli cabinet, he declared that after these many months of negotiations, if we failed now "to conclude all the required conditions for the signing of the treaty," it would "be very difficult to do so later," for Sadat was under heavy pressure from the Arab states opposed to the treaty to change course. The president's pleas fell on deaf ears, as Begin interrupted him several times in a manner which was "tough, dominating, almost antagonistic."[248] When he had finished, the prime minister held fast to his position: before signing anything "the Cabinet had to hold basic deliberations on the autonomy programme, and the Knesset had to debate the peace treaty."[249]

Although Begin focused at length on a change in the note to article 6 of the peace treaty regarding the priority of obligations (the Egyptians had changed the words "does not derogate from" to "is not inconsistent with"), the principal Israeli objections were to having Egyptian liaison officers in Gaza and to starting the autonomy process there first. They also wanted to insert the words "administrative council" in brackets after the term "self governing authority" to make clear that it had only limited power.[250] The meeting adjourned at one-thirty for lunch, to reconvene again at three.

When the two delegations met again, President Carter spoke to the question of United States–Israeli relations, declaring that Israel was a strategic asset and that the two countries were "equal partners." To alleviate Israeli concerns that Egypt might violate the treaty, he offered to sign an MOU making the United States the treaty's de facto guarantor.[251] He also promised to guarantee Israel's oil supply and ensure an exchange of ambassadors after initial Israeli withdrawal, if only words could be found to bridge the differences on the note to article 6.

The meeting then adjourned to search for language which would satisfy Israeli concerns. The delegations reconvened for a third time that afternoon at five. The result was the phrase "is not to be construed as contravening the provisions of Article 6," which both sides accepted. Begin then announced that the Knesset would meet that very evening to begin its deliberations and that in about two weeks the treaty would be ready for signing if all proceeded smoothly. In the meantime, Vance could go to Cairo and Carter could go home.[252] President Carter objected, declaring that Vance would not go to Cairo for there was no point to it. Furthermore, he insisted that they continue until all the problems were solved and the treaty was signed. Begin replied that he was tired and that anyway "the sky would not fall if agreement was not reached," and he concluded the meeting.[253]

At the state dinner that evening, Begin said publicly what he had told the president privately. Rising to give his toast, the prime minister declared, "It is my duty to say that we have serious problems to solve before we can sign this peace treaty."[254] As some of the guests gasped aloud, "Carter's face turned grim and ashen. He looked as pained as if he had been struck." A government official close to Begin explained to a reporter that Israel needed "a real agreement, not a wishy-washy one." When asked if Begin was going to send the president back to Washington without an agreement, the official replied without a smile: "There's been some discussion about whether to send him back to Washington or back to Atlanta."[255]

After the dinner the Israeli cabinet met, deliberating all night, until five the next morning, March 12. A few hours later, at ten-thirty, Carter and his aides met with the entire cabinet for a full discussion. But on the two remaining obstacles, Egyptian liaison officers in Gaza and oil supplies, there was no give. The Israelis claimed that the Camp David accords had made no mention of stationing liaison officers in Gaza and, on that ground, rejected the proposal. On the oil question, the cabinet also rejected Vance's proposal that Israel receive Egyptian oil through an American company, because it would perpetuate the Arab boycott against Israel.[256]

Despite the fact that oil supplies had not been mentioned in the Camp David agreement, the United States side did not turn the argument against the Israelis. Instead, President Carter promised to be "even more forthcoming on aid if the peace treaty were concluded."[257] The cabinet confirmed the new formulation for the note to article 6, warned against any United States role in the West Bank/Gaza negotiations, and advised the president that more settlements would be built there, as well as on the Golan Heights.

After an hour, the meeting adjourned so that Carter and Begin could address the Knesset. There both leaders sprinkled ad hominem remarks in their speeches reflecting their mutual feelings and testiness. Carter declared that the "people of the two nations were ready now for peace. The leaders have not yet proven that we are also ready for peace, enough to take a chance."[258] Begin replied, "We no longer have to prove our desire for peace, our love of peace and our readiness to assume risks and make sacrifices for peace. We have done this." The Israeli leader then conveyed to the president that his mission had failed and that he would go home empty-handed. He said, "We have undertaken before the Knesset not to sign the peace treaty before we bring it for its debate and approval."[259]

After the Knesset addresses the cabinet convened again and was joined later by Vance, Brzezinski, and their aides. The meeting continued until six-thirty in the evening. Vance made a last attempt to produce agreement by suggesting that both the Gaza and oil questions be dropped from the agreement, since they had not been included in the Camp David formula, but Begin refused on the grounds that oil was a "matter of life and death and could not be left out of the agreement."[260] Begin then surprised the Americans, declaring that the "talks were over." As the meeting was breaking up he handed Vance a draft communiqué which he wanted to issue. As Vance described it, "It tried to paper over the harsh reality that . . . we had failed to bridge the last narrow gap."[261]

Immediately informed of the outcome, Carter was "bitterly disappointed." He decided that there was no longer any reason to stay and ordered his plane readied for immediate departure to Washington.[262] Cooler heads prevailed, however, persuading the president to adhere to his itinerary, which scheduled departure for the next morning, and the president agreed to spend the night in Jerusalem.

Later that evening Dayan called Vance, and the two ministers worked out an acceptable compromise, which, it was agreed, would be presented by Carter to Begin the next morning at breakfast as a new American proposal. Dayan proposed that the Gaza-first issue and stationing of liaison officers be dropped from the autonomy letter but stressed that the Egyptians could, if they wished, raise the matter during the ensuing autonomy negotiations. Finally, on the issue of oil, Dayan admitted that they could not expect Egypt "to sell Israel oil on a long-term basis and at a preferred price"[263] and accepted a United States guarantee should the Sinai supply be interrupted.

Dayan says, "During our talk, Vance was on the telephone to President Carter several times"; Vance says he called the president only afterward; Carter claims that Vance and Dayan "met while Rosalynn and I accompanied the archaeologist, Professor Yigael Yadin, to see the remarkable Dead Sea scrolls," and mentions nothing about discussions with Vance during or after his talks with Dayan.[264] The explanation for the discrepancy may lie in what happened next.

Both ministers believed that they had succeeded, but at breakfast the next morning, before Vance and Dayan joined them, Carter tried to salvage something of his agreement with Sadat. So he put forth everything of the compromise worked out the night before, except the issue of Egyptian access to Gaza. Begin, however, had been fully informed of what had been decided the night before, and he held back. The result was that the breakfast meeting broke up with agreement on all but the issue of Egyptian access to Gaza. Then, at the very last moment, Carter changed his mind. "In the lobby, as we were preparing to leave, I asked Begin if he would accept our proposals provided the Gaza language was deleted. When he said he would, I believed I could get Sadat to accept the entire proposal. We had a good chance for an agreement!"[265]

Indeed, in Cairo, Sadat once again overrode the objections of his advisers and accepted the entire package. Informed of Sadat's acceptance, Begin agreed to submit the treaty to the Israeli cabinet the next day, and the positive outcome was no longer in doubt. Nevertheless, the negotiation had left a bitter aftertaste. Sadat refused to go to Jerusalem as originally planned for the treaty signing, after which Begin would have gone to Cairo for a duplicate signing.[266] Instead, a joint signing ceremony was arranged, perhaps befitting the enormous American broker effort, in Washington. The treaty ceremony, as well as the signing of the MOU between the United States and Israel, took place in Washington, March 26, 1979.

The Egyptian–Israeli peace treaty clearly served American interests in some ways but not in others, and it was of mixed utility to Egypt and Israel. First and foremost, the treaty fundamentally altered the geopolitical structure of the region, relocating the fulcrum of American power from Iran and formally removing Israel from Arab encirclement. Henceforth, there would be no conflict along the lines of 1967 or 1973, with the attendant possibility of superpower confrontation.

Paradoxically, however, the treaty did not reduce the prospects for conflict in the region. Indeed, it promoted further conflict for two reasons: First, with their mutual border secure, both Israel and Egypt moved to consolidate other geopolitical positions. Israel continued to build a forward position in Lebanon where Syria, with Soviet backing, was doing the same. In short, one geopolitical effect of the treaty was to make Lebanon a permanent battleground. Egypt in turn moved to deal with an increasingly assertive Soviet-supported Libya.

Secondly, future conflict was ensured because of the failure to make headway on the Palestinian issue. The West Bank/Gaza autonomy agreement remained a dead letter.[267] This failure split the Arab world, creating openings for Soviet diplomacy among the "rejectionists" and "moderates" alike, not to mention among the Palestinians, who, behind PLO leadership, became increasingly radicalized. The irony was that in all likelihood there would have been an Egyptian–Israeli peace treaty a year earlier had not the Carter administration persuaded Sadat to delay on the grounds that the United States could obtain a better deal for the West Bank and Gaza. The lengthy and futile attempt to gain autonomy for the Palestinians simply deepened Egypt's isolation from the Arab world.

Secretary Vance, noting the centrality of American participation, argued that the reason the autonomy process did not lead to elections and a self-governing authority was primarily because the Carter administration's attention was diverted elsewhere by the hostage crisis and election-year politics.[268] But progress on the autonomy process was not Washington's responsibility. Vance's excuses notwithstanding, surely Israel's strategy also came into play here.

The Israeli leadership had decided to retreat from agreeing to full autonomy because they had no interest in furthering the creation of Washington's strategic consensus in the region and were content to consolidate a one-front situation, which ensured their security. In the short run, at least, the increase in terrorist attacks—which accompanied the realization that the autonomy process had stalled—was an acceptable price to pay for an improved strategic position.

The treaty did not move the region toward the American objective of a strategic consensus. Indeed, one is struck by the negative impact which the treaty had on the "moderate" Arabs. Jordan simply refused to participate. More significant was the steady deterioration of relations with Saudi Arabia. The Saudi leadership denounced the Carter administration's decision, against Riyadh's wishes, to press forward with the treaty between Israel and Egypt. Despite maintaining formally correct relations with the United States, which after all was an important source of revenue as well as of technology and weapons, the Saudis quietly decided to make Washington pay, literally, for the consequences of its policy.[269]

From April 1, 1979, following the signing of the treaty, through the next year until the outbreak of the Iran–Iraq war on September 22, 1980, and despite a growing worldwide oil surplus estimated to be 2.5 million b/d over demand, Saudi Arabia more than doubled the price of oil, from the January 1979 price of $13.34 to $28.00 by June 1980.[270] The Saudi price was lower than the OPEC average and gave rise to the notion that Riyadh was a price "moderate," but the fact was that Saudi Arabia restrained production, which allowed higher overall prices. Nor was there anything moderate about Saudi representations to OPEC for adoption of a long-term plan for "systematic but gradual price increases" of $2.00 per year beyond the $28.00 price level, a plan which was shelved once the Iran–Iraq war broke out.[271]

The Saudis made no secret of their displeasure with the "Israeli orientation" of United States policy. Prince Fahd, for example, denouncing the treaty in May 1979, called it "an invitation to war rather than peace" because it only pushed the region toward greater violence and radicalism.[272] Even the Soviet invasion of Afghanistan in December 1979 failed to change the Saudi position. In January 1980 Prince Fahd declared that "there are many doors open to us and we can replace the Americans any time we want."[273] It was time, he said, for the "few wise men in the United States who realize the importance of their interests with Saudi Arabia . . . [to] ask themselves if the American line is identical to that of Israel."[274]

The Saudi leadership went to some lengths to set forth its opposition to American policy on the Palestinian question. Responding to press reports that the Carter administration was soft-pedaling differences with Riyadh during the coming election campaign, on May 27, 1980, Prince Fahd declared unequivocally that certain governments

> were trying to portray Saudi Arabia as a supporter of the negotiations of the current peace process. . . . What is certain is that the attitude of the Kingdom of Saudi Arabia to the Middle East problem and the issue of Palestine is firm, clear and known. It derives from the Arabs' unanimous attitude that the issue of Palestine is the core of the Middle East problem, and that a just and comprehensive solution cannot be achieved unless Israel withdraws from all the Arab territories occupied in 1967, including, first and foremost, Holy Jerusalem, to which Arab sovereignty must be restored. No solution of the Palestinian issue can achieve peace unless it is based on recognition of the Palestinian people's legitimate rights to return and to self-determination, including the setting up of an independent state on their territory.[275]

The Carter administration had invested an enormous amount of time, energy, and money to produce a result of dubious benefit.[276] The president himself had doubts about its worth. In retrospect, as he reflected upon it, its value had "not always been the same," and he concluded that ultimately whether his efforts had been of value or not would "depend on the wisdom and dedication of the leaders of the future."[277] In short, President Carter's framework for peace in the Middle East had produced continuing regional instability, a sharp deterioration of United States–Saudi and United States–Jordanian relations, and an explosion in petroleum prices.

Notes

1. For the early stage, see Thornton, *Nixon-Kissinger Years*, chapter 8.
2. Vance, *Hard Choices*, p. 232.
3. Carter, *Keeping Faith*, pp. 405–6.
4. Dayan, *Breakthrough*, p. 201.
5. Carter, *Keeping Faith*, p. 409, and Brzezinski, *Power and Principle*, p. 276.
6. Dayan, *Breakthrough*, p. 199.
7. Vance, *Hard Choices*, p. 237.
8. Dayan, *Breakthrough*, p. 202.
9. Quandt, *Camp David*, p. 277.
10. Vance, *Hard Choices*, p. 236.
11. Bernard Gwertzman, "Carter Cold Shoulder Awaits Begin in First Post-Summit Visit Here," *Washington Star*, November 1, 1978, p. 1.
12. Ibid.
13. Quandt, *Camp David*, p. 278.
14. Ibid., p. 277. Dayan omits all reference to discussion about the MOUs here.
15. Quandt, *Camp David*, p. 279.
16. William Beecher, "What's behind the Holdup in Mideast Peace Treaty," *Boston Globe*, December 22, 1978, p. 21. See also Jonathan C. Randal, "Arabs Approve Multi-Billion War Chest, Anti-Sadat Steps," *Washington Post*, November 6, 1978, p. 21.
17. Beecher, "What's behind the Holdup," p. 21.
18. Joseph Kraft, "Mideast: The Trouble with One-Man Shows," *Washington Post*, November 12, 1978, p. B7. Christopher S. Wren, "Sadat Seems Bitter at Arab Moderates," *New York Times*, November 21, 1978, p. 11, noted that the editor of Cairo's *October* magazine, Anis Mansour, a confidant of Sadat's, asked pointedly whether Saudi Arabia under Prince Fahd had "turned to the Soviets to become a member of the Warsaw Pact," and the Cairo daily *Al Akhbar* labeled Kuwaiti Emir Sheik Jaber al Ahmad al Sabah "a new marxist leader."
19. Beecher, "What's behind the Holdup," p. 21.
20. Quandt, *Camp David*, p. 280. Vance, *Hard Choices*, p. 238, erroneously dates this letter November 9, evidently to remove it as the precipitating factor for the assessment that followed, but Sadat's position had been clear for days. See "Egypt to Seek Strong Link in Peace Treaty to Solution of Palestinian Question," *Baltimore Sun*, November 6, 1978, p. 1.
21. Brzezinski, *Power and Principle*, p. 276.
22. Carter, *Keeping Faith*, p. 409.

23. Brzezinski, *Power and Principle*, p. 276.
24. Quandt, *Camp David*, p. 280.
25. Ibid., and Carter, *Keeping Faith*, p. 409.
26. Quandt, *Camp David*, p. 281.
27. Brzezinski, *Power and Principle*, p. 276.
28. Carter, *Keeping Faith*, p. 409.
29. "Transcript of President's News Conference," *New York Times*, November 10, 1978, p. 20.
30. Charles W. Corddry, "New Israeli Anti-linkage Effort Begun," *Baltimore Sun*, November 9, 1978, p. 2, and John Goshko, "Israel Asks Treaty Changes; Doubts on Early Accord Grow," *Washington Post*, November 9, 1978, p. 28.
31. Vance, *Hard Choices*, p. 238.
32. Quandt, *Camp David*, pp. 281–82.
33. Dayan, *Breakthrough*, p. 245.
34. Edward Walsh, "Pace of Peace Talks Irritates Carter," *Washington Post*, November 14, 1978, p. 1.
35. Ibid.
36. Thomas W. Lippman, "Sadat Reportedly Signals Softening on West Bank Linkage in Peace Pact," *Washington Post*, November 15, 1978, p. 26.
37. Quandt, *Camp David*, p. 283. There were, of course, implications for King Hussein in the "Gaza first" proposal and some interpreted Sadat's shift to signal displeasure with Hussein's reluctance to join the talks. See William Claiborne, "Israel Halts Debate to Await Sadat's Linkage Proposals," *Washington Post*, November 16, 1978, p. 29.
38. Vance, *Hard Choices*, p. 239.
39. William E. Farrell, "U.S. Officials Optimistic on Draft," *New York Times*, November 21, 1978, p. 10.
40. Quandt, *Camp David*, p. 283.
41. Dayan, *Breakthrough*, p. 248.
42. William E. Farrell, "Begin to Ask Cabinet to Approve Treaty Draft It Rejected 2 Weeks Ago," *New York Times*, November 21, 1978, p. 10.
43. William Claiborne, "Israel Reported Ready to Accept U.S. Draft," *Washington Post*, November 21, 1978, p. 1.
44. Vance, *Hard Choices*, p. 239.
45. Douglas Watson, "Israel Seeking New Oil Suppliers to Supplement Iranian Exports," *Baltimore Sun*, November 17, 1978, p. 2, reporting from Tel Aviv noted that Iranian oilfield strikes had "greatly reduced petroleum production . . . and briefly shut off shipments to Israel." Israel imported 98 percent of its petroleum needs. Of an estimated 156,000 barrels per day, 60 percent came from Iran.

46. Dayan, *Breakthrough*, p. 248.
47. William E. Farrell, "'Take It or Leave It,' Israeli Says of Pact," *New York Times*, November 23, 1978, p. 5.
48. Quandt, *Camp David*, p. 286.
49. "Excerpts from President's Meeting with Reporters," *New York Times*, December 8, 1978, p. 14.
50. Quandt, *Camp David*, p. 286.
51. Ibid. Vance, *Hard Choices*, p. 241, portrays this as Sadat's idea, saying, "Sadat would not yield on the exchange of resident ambassadors, which he now said would take place one month after inauguration of the self-governing authority."
52. For the details, see Vance, *Hard Choices*, p. 241.
53. Quandt, *Camp David*, p. 287.
54. Vance, *Hard Choices*, p. 241.
55. Quandt, *Camp David*, p. 287.
56. Ibid., p. 288.
57. Vance, *Hard Choices*, p. 242.
58. Quandt, *Camp David*, p. 289.
59. Vance, *Hard Choices*, p. 242.
60. Terence Smith, "Carter Says Treaty Is Up to Israel Now; U.S. May Curb Role," *New York Times*, December 15, 1978, p. 1.
61. Ibid.
62. Quandt, *Camp David*, p. 285, and Bernard Gwertzman, "Vance to Make Trip to Egypt and Israel on Peace Deadlock," *New York Times*, December 6, 1978, p. 1.
63. Vance, *Hard Choices*, p. 109.
64. Ibid., p. 118.
65. Ibid., pp. 109–10.
66. Ibid., pp. 118–19.
67. Edward K. Wu, "New Regime Installed in Cambodia," *Baltimore Sun*, Janury 9, 1979, p. 1.
68. Elizabeth Becker, "Vietnam-Backed Insurgents Claim Capture of Phnom Penh," *Washington Post*, January 8, 1979, p. 1.
69. Henry Kamm, "Vietnam Said to Gain Its Major Goals in Cambodia," *New York Times*, January 24, 1979, p. 8.
70. For the Soviet position, see Peter Osnos, "Cambodian Takeover Pleases Moscow," *Washington Post*, January 9, 1979, p. 16; Hal Piper, "Soviet Supports New Cambodian Regime," *Baltimore Sun*, January 10, 1979, p. 2; and Elizabeth Becker, "Soviets Block U.N. Demand for Withdrawal from Cambodia," *Washington Post*, January 16, 1979, p. 12.
71. Richard Nations, "Pol Pot Forces Regroup, Harass Vietnamese in Cambodian Countryside," *Washington Post*, January 26, 1979, p. 20.

72. George C. Wilson, "Chinese Beef Up Forces Near Soviet, Viet Borders after Fall of Cambodia," *Washington Post*, January 9, 1979, p. 16.
73. "An Interview with Brezhnev," *Time*, January 22, 1979, p. 20.
74. Don Oberdorfer, "Carter Explains SALT Delay," *Washington Post*, January 19, 1979, p. 8.
75. Bernard Gwertzman, "U.S. Tries Balancing Moscow and Peking," *New York Times*, January 24, 1979, p. 1.
76. Hedrick Smith, "Carter Pushes for Arms Pact and Curb on Inflation to Set a New Foundation for Peace," *New York Times*, January 24, 1979, p. 1.
77. William Beecher, "A Strategic Move by US to Soviets," *Boston Globe*, January 25, 1979, p. 10.
78. Vernon A. Guidry, "U.S. Expects Nod on SALT Accord after Teng Visit," *Washington Star*, January 25, 1979, p. 6.
79. Ibid.
80. Vance, *Hard Choices*, p. 121.
81. "An Interview with Teng Hsiao-p'ing," *Time*, February 5, 1979, p. 32.
82. Ibid.
83. Karen Elliott House, "Teng Says the U.S. and China Must Unite to Counter Soviet Threat to World Peace," *Wall Street Journal*, January 30, 1979, p. 2.
84. High American officials were "agitated" over Deng's tactics. One complained that "he may be sucking us into his attack, hoping for at least an aroma of collusion." See Don Oberdorfer, "Reds vs. Reds in Indochina: A New, Confusing Kind of War," *Washington Post*, April 1, 1979, p. B1.
85. Brzezinski, *Power and Principle*, p. 403.
86. Ibid., pp. 403–4.
87. Vance, *Hard Choices*, pp. 120–21.
88. Brzezinski, *Power and Principle*, p. 406. For the president's version of the visit, see Carter, *Keeping Faith*, pp. 202–11.
89. Brzezinski, *Power and Principle*, pp. 406–7.
90. Ibid., pp. 408–9.
91. Ibid., p. 409.
92. Ibid., p. 410.
93. Ibid., pp. 410–11.
94. Brzezinski disclosed United States intelligence support during a trip to China in July, 1986. See "Between Friends," *Washington Times*, July 31, 1986, p. 3.
95. Joseph Kraft, "Teng's Progress," *Washington Post*, February 8, 1979, p. 25.
96. Brzezinski, *Power and Principle*, p. 407.

97. Terrence Smith, "U.S.–China Communiqué Contains Softened Criticism of Soviet Union," *New York Times*, February 2, 1979, p. 9.
98. Brzezinski, *Power and Principle*, p. 408.
99. Henry Scott-Stokes, "Teng Criticizes the U.S. for a Lack of Firmness in Iran," *New York Times*, February 8, 1979, p. 12.
100. William Chapman, "Teng Scores U.S. Policy on Iran," *Washington Star*, February 8, 1979, p. A1.
101. "Transcript of Statements at Ceremony," *New York Times* February 1, 1979, p. 16.
102. The word "completely" in the phrase "do not coincide completely" was not in the original text and was inserted by the president when he delivered the statement. The insertion suggested that there "was at least some coincidence of strategic outlook" between them. See Joseph Kraft, "Teng's Progress," p. 25. It was Kraft's view that "if China does take any action against Cambodia, the world—and especially the Russians—will assume a green light from the United States."
103. Fox Butterfield, "Teng Again Says Chinese May Move against Vietnam," *New York Times*, February 1, 1979, p. 16.
104. Richard Burt, "U.S. Warns Russians to Stop Encoding Missile Data," *New York Times*, February 1, 1979, p. 6, and Charles Corddry, "New Soviet Tests Called Cloud on Arms Limitation," *Baltimore Sun*, February 1, 1979, p. 1.
105. Kevin Klose, "Soviets Ask U.S. to Clarify China Policy," *Washington Post*, February 2, 1979, p. 1.
106. "Pravda Attacks U.S. for Allowing Teng to 'Slander' Soviets on Visit," *Washington Post*, February 5, 1979, p. 13.
107. "Kremlin's Expert Labels Teng Message 'Dangerous,'" *Washington Star*, February 3, 1979, p. 5.
108. George C. Wilson, "Brown Backs Countering Soviet Surrogate Forces," *Washington Post*, February 8, 1979, p. 14.
109. Craig Whitney, "Kosygin Complains to Americans on Teng's Remarks," *New York Times*, February 10, 1979, p. 3. Kosygin called Deng's remarks "a declaration of war and expressed disappointment and surprise the United States had not commented on or refuted them."
110. Ibid.
111. Charles Corddry, "Soviet Says SALT Would Ban U.S. MX Missile," *Baltimore Sun*, February 9, 1979, p. 1.
112. Talbott, *Endgame*, p. 257.
113. Henry Bradsher, "Sticky Times with Soviets Imperils Summit Hopes," *Washington Star*, February 13, 1979, p. 3. See also Talbott, *Endgame*, p. 251.
114. Bernard Gwertzman, "Soviet Hints It Now Favors Moscow As Site

for Brezhnev–Carter Parley," *New York Times*, February 11, 1979, p. 1.

115. Bernard Gwertzman, "U.S. Warns Chinese against an Attack on the Vietnamese," *New York Times*, February 10, 1979, p. 1.
116. Talbott, *Endgame*, p. 261, and "Vance Offers Gromyko 3 New SALT Proposals," *Washington Post*, February 14, 1979, p. 6.
117. Nicholas Gage, "Guerrillas in Teheran Attack U.S. Embassy; Khomeini Forces Free Staff," *New York Times*, February 15, 1979, p. 1.
118. David K. Willis, "Washington, Moscow in a Sharp Exchange, "*Christian Science Monitor*, February 16, 1979, p. 1.
119. Henry Trewhitt, "U.S. Scores Soviet Role in Ambassador's Death," *Baltimore Sun*, Feburary 15, 1979, p. 1.
120. Henry Bradsher, "State Dept. Protests U.S.S.R. Role in Envoy's Death," *Washington Star*, February 15, 1979, p. 1.
121. Drew Middleton, "China's Drive in Vietnam Reflects Classic Military Tactics," *New York Times*, February 18, 1979, p. 1.
122. Craig Whitney, "Soviet Warns China to Pull Out Forces," *New York Times*, February 19, 1979, p. 1. The text of the declaration is on p. 11.
123. Bernard Gwertzman, "U.S. Emphasizes That It Will Shun Involvement in the Fighting in Asia," *New York Times*, February 19, 1979, p. 1.
124. Barry Kramer, "China, Vietnam Battle Resumes; Casualties Heavy," *Wall Street Journal*, February 21, 1979, p. 2; Drew Middleton, "China Renews Push; Hanoi Said to Call Regulars to Front," *New York Times*, February 22, 1979, p. 1, and Drew Middleton, "Questions Persist on China's Military Goal," *New York Times*, February 21, 1979, p. 8.
125. Jean-Pierre Gallois, "Major Vietnamese Force Moving toward Border," *Washington Post*, February 21, 1979, p. 6.
126. Kramer, "China, Vietnam Battle Resumes," p. 2.
127. "Text of Speech by President Carter at Georgia Tech," *New York Times*, February 21, 1979, p. 4.
128. "Soviet Contends U.S. Knew Peking's Intent and Remained Silent," *New York Times*, February 21, 1979, p. 9.
129. Kramer, "China, Vietnam Battle Resumes," p. 2.
130. Don Oberdorfer, "U.S. Sees Little Likelihood of Soviet Invasion of China," *Washington Post*, February 22, 1979, p. 1.
131. Barry Kramer, "Regulars of China, Vietnam May Clash, Raising Specter of War Involving Soviets," *Wall Street Journal*, February 22, 1979, p. 3. Secretary Vance, *Hard Choices*, p. 122, complained that there was "no evidence" to support White House briefings to reporters about "a Soviet buildup taking place on the Sino–Soviet border." He insisted that "there was no extraordinary military movement on the Soviet side of the border."

132. Charles Corddry, "New China Attack Due, U.S. Says," *Baltimore Sun*, February 24, 1979, p. 1; Henry Kamm, "Soviet Arms Airlift to Vietnam Hinted as Combat Goes On," *New York Times*, February 23, 1979, p. 1; and Barry Kramer, "Soviet Troops Reportedly Closer to China's Border as Major Battle Brews in Vietnam," *Wall Street Journal*, February 23, 1979, p. 2. Although United States officials denied Japanese reports that "some of Russia's three divisions stationed in Mongolia . . . had moved south toward the Chinese border," Zbigniew Brzezinski has since confirmed the troop movements and United States intelligence cooperation with Beijing. See "Between Friends," *Washington Times*, July 31, 1986, p. 3. See also Garthoff, *Detente and Confrontation*, p. 726, who notes that "in February–March the Soviet Union carried out military exercises in the area north of China in a major show of force that was readily picked up by Chinese (and American) intelligence, although not publicized. In these exercises the Soviets reportedly moved tanks firing blank rounds right up to the border, illuminated Chinese positions with floodlights, and flew tactical air sorties along, and in some cases over, the frontier." See also Michael Weisskopf and Howard Simmons, "Armed Monglian Herdsmen Ready to Defend Border Village," *Washington Post*, February 9, 1981, p. A10.
133. Jim Hoagland, "U.S. Policy: A Worried Reassessment," *Washington Post*, February 24, 1979, p. 1.
134. Robert Kaiser, "Soviets Take Significant SALT Step," *Washington Post*, March 2, 1979, p. 1. In response to American insistence that any change in missile size by 5 percent, plus or minus, would constitute a new missile, Dobrynin proposed to define a new type of missile as one 5 percent larger or 10 percent smaller than existing missiles, bringing the two sides close to agreement on that issue. The one major remaining roadblock, encryption, was not resolved, nor was the location of a summit.
135. Craig Whitney, "Gromyko Says China Obstructs Improved U.S.–Soviet Relations," *New York Times*, February 27, 1979, p. 10. See also "Speech of A. A. Gromyko," *FBIS-SU*, March 1, 1979, p. R3.
136. Talbott, *Endgame*, p. 251.
137. Vance, *Hard Choices*, p. 122.
138. Frederic A. Moritz, "Hanoi Hits Back at Peking Foe," *Christian Science Monitor*, February 28, 1979, p. 1.
139. Ibid.
140. Edward Cowan, "President, Seeing 'Risks,' Bids China Quit Vietnam," *New York Times*, February 28, 1979, p. 1.
141. Ibid.

142. "Transcript of President's News Conference," *New York Times*, February 28, 1979, p. 16.
143. Barry Kramer, "Teng Says That China Might Withdraw Troops from Vietnam in About 10 Days," *Wall Street Journal*, February 27, 1979, p. 10.
144. Henry Kamm, "Lull Is Reported in Asian Fighting As Peking Awaits Hanoi Regulars," *New York Times*, March 2, 1979, p. 6; Edward K. Wu, "Chinese Troop Withdrawal Appears to Be Imminent," *Baltimore Sun*, March 4, 1979, p. 1; Drew Middleton, "Fighting at Lang Son, a Key Chinese Goal, Now Reported Intense," *New York Times*, March 1, 1979, p. 1; and Drew Middleton, "Peking Warns Hanoi against Any Attack during Withdrawal," *New York Times*, March 5, 1979, p. 1.
145. "Brezhnev Condemns Chinese, but Voices No Military Threat," *New York Times*, March 3, 1979, p. 1.
146. Ibid.
147. Ibid.
148. Craig Whitney, "Secret Peace Talks Denied by Russians," *New York Times*, March 4, 1979, p. 15.
149. Drew Middleton, "Fighting at Lang Son," p. 1.
150. Drew Middleton, "Peking Warns Hanoi," p. 1.
151. Charles Corddry, "Hanoi Said to Move Up Troops," *Baltimore Sun*, March 1, 1979, p. 1, reported movement of elements of the 308th and 312th Divisions as well as heavy artillery from Hanoi toward Lang Son.
152. Lee Lescaze, "China Repeats Pledge to Leave Vietnam Soon," *Washington Post*, March 5, 1979, p. 14.
153. "Text of China's Statement on Withdrawal of Troops," *New York Times*, March 6, 1979, p. 10.
154. Xinhua (China News Agency), April 3, 1979.
155. John Goshko, "Sadat Seeking Arms, Broader Pro-West Role," *Washington Post*, February 21, 1979, p. 1.
156. Norman Kempster, "U.S. to Remain a Reliable Ally, Visiting Defense Secretary Tells Saudi Arabians," *Los Angeles Times*, February 11, 1979, p. 5.
157. Quandt, *Camp David*, p. 293.
158. Carter evidently was not overly concerned about the Saudis, assuming that they "would have nowhere else to go after the treaty was signed. They have to work with the United States and Egypt." Quandt, *Camp David*, p. 297.
159. Don Sider, "Brown Reassures Saudis of America's Intentions," *Washington Star*, February 11, 1979, p. 3, and Bernard Weinraub, "Brown

Pledges Aid to Saudis' Defense," *New York Times*, February 11, 1979, p. 17.

160. Richard Burt, "Saudis Reject Idea of a U.S. Base," *New York Times*, February 27, 1979, p. 2, and Henry Bradsher, "Saudi Quoted as Saying Defense Won't Be a Joint Effort with U.S.," *Washington Star*, March 3, 1979, p. 5.
161. Joseph Albright, "Self-interest and Saudi Oil," *Washington Star*, March 11, 1979, p. D1. For the price data, see the Report of the Subcommittee on Europe and the Middle East of the House Committee on Foreign Affairs, *Saudi Arabia and the United States, the New Context in an Evolving "Special Relationship"* (Washington, DC: GPO, August 1981), p. 28.
162. Joseph Albright, "Self-interest and Saudi Oil," p. D1.
163. Saudi Arabia had annexed two Yemeni provinces in 1934, and Saudi money had perpetuated the 1962–1969 civil war which resulted in the division of Yemen. Although Sana's relations with the Saudis were correct, resentment smoldered under the surface. The YAR, the most populous country on the Arabian peninsula, also supplied over a million and a half workers to Saudi Arabia.
164. House Committee on Foreign Affairs, Hearings before the Subcommittee on Europe and the Middle East, *U.S. Interests in, and Policies toward, the Persian Gulf, 1980* (Washington, DC: GPO, 1980), pp. 109–11. (Hereafter referred to as Persian Gulf Hearings.) The United States also sought to strengthen Oman. See Bruce Ingersoll, "U.S. Weighs Military Aid for Oman," *Chicago Sun Times*, March 15, 1979, p. 23.
165. Ibid. For Prince Sultan's similar remarks, see Kempster, "U.S. to Remain a Reliable Ally."
166. Bradsher, "Saudi Quoted as Saying."
167. See Bernard Weinraub, "U.S. Links to Saudis Taking a New Turn," *New York Times*, February 13, 1979, p. 10, who described Brown as "exultant about his meetings in Saudi Arabia," and reported "defense officials'" claims that "the trip had laid the groundwork for broader, perhaps significant, American involvement in the region."
168. William Beecher, "Egypt Reportedly Trying to Buy $1B Worth of Arms from US," *Boston Globe*, February 14, 1979, p. 3.
169. Bernard Weinraub, "Israelis, Looking to Egyptian Pact, Weigh a 25% Cut in Arms Outlay," *New York Times*, February 14, 1979, p. 1.
170. John K. Cooley, "Israelis Rethinking Position," *Christian Science Monitor*, February 15, 1979, p. 6.
171. Kenneth H. Bacon, "Brown, in U.S. Arms Pledge, Stops Short of Making Israel Dominant Peace Force," *Wall Street Journal*, February 16, 1979, p. 24.

172. Jay Bushinsky, "Brown Faces Stiff Grilling in Israel," *Chicago Sun Times*, February 13, 1979, p. 15.
173. John Goshko, "Sadat Seeking Arms," p. 1.
174. Ibid.
175. Bernard Weinraub, "Sadat Sees Brown; Bars a Compromise," *New York Times*, February 18, 1979, p. 9.
176. Vance, *Hard Choices*, p. 243.
177. Dayan, *Breakthrough*, p. 264. Cf. Carter, *Keeping Faith*, p. 413, Vance, *Hard Choices*, p. 243, Brzezinski, *Power and Principle*, p. 279, and Quandt, *Camp David*, pp. 297–98. None refers to this meeting.
178. Carter, *Keeping Faith*, p. 413.
179. Brzezinski, *Power and Principle*, p. 279.
180. Ibid.
181. Ibid., p. 280, and John P. Wallach, "Carter's Secret Plan for Peace in the Mideast," *Baltimore News American*, March 7, 1979, p. 1. Begin reportedly also offered the port of Haifa for use as a United States naval facility.
182. Quandt, *Camp David*, p. 298.
183. Brzezinski, *Power and Principle*, p. 280, and Quandt, *Camp David*, pp. 298–99.
184. Vance, *Hard Choices*, p. 243, and Carter, *Keeping Faith*, p. 415.
185. William Claiborne, "Israelis Allege U.S. Ultimatum on Mideast Pact," *Washington Post*, March 1, 1979, p. 1.
186. Ibid.
187. Jonathan Randell, "As the Pressure Grows, Israel Acts to Mold Opinion," *New York Times*, March 2, 1979, p. 7. A Foreign Ministry official "was at a loss to explain why the Government's usually smooth-functioning public-information machinery had failed to quash the report as soon as it came out."
188. Brzezinski, *Power and Principle*, p. 280.
189. Ibid.
190. Vance, *Hard Choices*, p. 244, and Quandt, *Camp David*, p. 300.
191. Carter, *Keeping Faith*, pp. 413–14. His words were indeed prophetic.
192. Ibid., p. 416.
193. Quandt, *Camp David*, pp. 300–1. Dayan, *Breakthrough*, p. 268, cites Begin's report that "there had been a complete turnabout in the American position." Vance, *Hard Choices*, p. 244, had dropped the legal opinion on the priority of obligations in favor of an interpretive minute, which declared, contradictorily, that for Egypt the treaty did not prevail over its other treaty obligations, and for Israel that this interpretation "did not contravene" the binding nature of the treaty.
194. Vance, *Hard Choices*, p. 245.
195. Quandt, *Camp David*, p. 301.

196. Brzezinski, *Power and Principle*, p. 281.
197. Carter, *Keeping Faith*, p. 416.
198. Vance, *Hard Choices*, p. 245.
199. Carter, *Keeping Faith*, p. 417.
200. Brzezinski, *Power and Principle*, p. 282.
201. Carter, *Keeping Faith*, p. 417.
202. Quandt, *Camp David*, p. 301.
203. Carter, *Keeping Faith*, p. 417. According to Senator Henry Jackson, who was visiting Begin at Blair House, after talking with Sadat Carter called Begin, who returned from the call "a jubilant man." See Hedrick Smith, "Carter's Bold Stroke: Risk and High Hopes," *New York Times*, March 6, 1979, p. 1.
204. Carter, *Keeping Faith*, p. 416.
205. See Edward Walsh and Martin Schram, "Mideast Trip: Major Gamble for Carter," *Washington Post*, March 6, 1979, p. 10, and Henry L. Trewhitt, "Stakes Are High As Carter Sets Out on His Middle East 'Gamble' Today," *Baltimore Sun*, March 7, 1979, p. 1. Vance, *Hard Choices*, p. 245, also called it a "breathtaking gamble."
206. Quandt, *Camp David*, p. 301.
207. Persian Gulf Hearings. The following account is drawn largely from the testimony of Lt. Col. John Ruszkiewicz, the United States Army military attache to Sana, North Yemen, from April 1978 to January 1980; the reply of the State Department; and Lt. Col. Ruszkiewicz's rebuttal.
208. Persian Gulf Hearings, Ruszkiewicz's "testimony," p. 112.
209. Ibid., p. 117. The first press account was that of Edward Cody, "Hostilities in Yemen Pit Marxist Regime against Ally of West," *Washington Post*, February 27, 1979, p. 9.
210. Persian Gulf Hearings, Department of State reply, p. 418.
211. Ibid., Ruszkiewicz rebuttal, pp. 423–24.
212. *Jane's Armor and Artillery, 1987–1988* (London: Jane's Publishing Co., 1989), pp. 787–88.
213. Persian Gulf Hearings, Ruszkiewicz rebuttal, p. 424.
214. For a sample, see Henry L. Trewhitt, "U.S. Set to Rush Arms to North in Yemeni Clash," *Baltimore Sun*, March 1, 1979, p. 1; Richard Burt, "Saudis Said to Ask U.S. for Help in Yemen War, " *New York Times*, March 6, 1979, p. 8; Richard Burt, "U.S. Sends Ships to Arabian Sea in Yemen Crisis," *New York Times*, March 7, 1979, p. 1; Charles W. Corddry, "U.S. Sends Task Force to Yemen," *Baltimore Sun*, March 7, 1979, p. 1; "Soviet Said to Enter Yemen Conflict," *New York Times*, March 9, 1979, p. 8; Kenneth H. Bacon, "Carter Speeds Arms Flow to North Yemen to Confront Soviets and Comfort Saudis," *Wall Street Journal*, March 12, 1979, p. 7.

215. Persian Gulf Hearings, Department of State reply, pp. 418–19.
216. Ibid., Ruszkiewicz rebuttal, pp. 422–23.
217. Ibid., p. 427.
218. Ibid., p. 423.
219. Ibid., p. 424.
220. Ibid., p. 427.
221. Ibid.
222. Ibid., p. 424.
223. Ibid., Ruszkiewicz testimony, p. 120.
224. Jim Hoagland and Dan Morgan, "U.S. Speeds Arms for N. Yemen," *Washington Post,* March 7, 1979, p. 1, and Richard Burt, "Carter Will Speed Arms to Yemen, Bypassing Any Review by Congress," *New York Times,* March 10, 1979, p. 1.
225. Bernard Weinraub, "U.S. Says Its Instructors in Yemen Will Avoid Combat," *New York Times,* March 14, 1979, p. 3.
226. Charles W. Corddry, "U.S. Sends Task Force to Yemen," p. 1, and Kenneth H. Bacon, "Carter Speeds Arms Flow to North Yemen" p. 7.
227. Richard Burt, "Carter Will Speed Arms to Yemen," p. 1, and Jim Hoagland, "U.S.–Saudi Relations Seen Strained by Treaty," *Washington Post,* March 15, 1979, p. 20.
228. Ibid. Washington also advised the forty American citizens in southern North Yemen, including thirteen Peace Corps volunteers, to move out of the southern portion of the country and go to Sana. See Richard Burt, "Saudis Said to Ask U.S. for Help in Yemen War," *New York Times,* March 6, 1979, p. 8.
229. Henry L. Trewhitt, "U.S. Set to Rush Arms to North in Yemeni Clash," p. 1, and Jim Hoagland and Dan Morgan, "U.S. Speeds Arms for N. Yemen," p. 1.
230. Edward Cody, "Hostilities in Yemen Pit Marxist Regime against Ally of West," p. 9.
231. Ibid.
232. Hoagland and Morgan, "U.S. Speeds Arms for N. Yemen," p. 1.
233. Persian Gulf Hearings, Ruszkiewicz testimony, p. 168. Each M-60 carried forty-three shells for its cannon; the Saudis provided six shells per tank.
234. Brzezinski, *Power and Principle,* pp. 282–83.
235. Vance, *Hard Choices,* p. 246.
236. Carter, *Keeping Faith,* p. 417.
237. Quandt, *Camp David,* pp. 302–3.
238. Christopher S. Wren, "U.S. Agrees to Take a Direct Role in Talks on Palestinian Home Rule," *New York Times,* March 15, 1979, p. 16.
239. Brzezinski, *Power and Principle,* p. 283.
240. Ibid.

241. Carter, *Keeping Faith*, p. 420.
242. Ibid., pp. 420–21.
243. Ibid.
244. Dayan, *Breakthrough*, p. 272.
245. Carter, *Keeping Faith*, p. 421.
246. Vance, *Hard Choices*, p. 247.
247. Dayan, *Breakthrough*, p. 270.
248. Brzezinski, *Power and Principle*, p. 284.
249. Dayan, *Breakthrough*, p. 271.
250. Ibid., pp. 271–72.
251. Quandt, *Camp David*, pp. 305–6.
252. Ibid., p. 306.
253. Ibid., p. 307.
254. Hedrick Smith, "Begin, with a Dinner Comment, Turns a Smiling Carter Ashen," *New York Times*, March 12, 1979, p. 1.
255. Ibid.
256. Dayan, *Breakthrough*, p. 274.
257. Quandt, *Camp David*, p. 307.
258. "Text of the President's Address and Excerpts from the Prime Minister's Reply," *New York Times*, March 13, 1979, p. 10.
259. Ibid.
260. Quandt, *Camp David*, p. 309.
261. Vance, *Hard Choices*, p. 249.
262. Quandt, *Camp David*, p. 309.
263. Vance, *Hard Choices*, p. 249.
264. Dayan, *Breakthrough*, p. 276, Vance, *Hard Choices*, p. 250, and Carter, *Keeping Faith*, p. 423.
265. Ibid., p. 425. Brzezinski's absence from this breakfast may explain why, in *Power and Principle*, p. 285, he claimed that "we left Jerusalem concluding that Begin did not want to reach an agreement."
266. Dayan, *Breakthrough*, p. 278.
267. Quandt, *Camp David*, p. 315.
268. Vance, *Hard Choices*, p. 254.
269. See Karen Elliott House, "The Anger in Saudi Arabia," *Wall Street Journal*, June 11, 1979, p. 14.
270. *Saudi Arabia and the United States, the New Context in an Evolving "Special Relationship,"* Report of the Subcommittee on Europe and the Middle East, House Foreign Affairs Committee (Washington, DC: GPO, 1981), p. 28.
271. Ibid., pp. 28–29.
272. See his interview in *Le Monde*, May 14, 1979. See also "Vance Sees Decline in U.S.–Saudi Links," *New York Times*, May 9, 1979, p. 1, and

Jim Hoagland and J.P. Smith, "U.S. Moving to Repair Saudi Ties," *Washington Post*, June 12, 1979, p. 1.

273. *Middle East Economic Digest*, January 18, 1980, p. 37.
274. Ibid.
275. *Saudi Arabia and the United States*, p. 35.
276. Charles W. Corddry, "U.S. Committed to $5 Billion Aid Package after Egypt, Israel Sign Pact," *Baltimore Sun*, March 16, 1979, p. 2.
277. Carter, *Keeping Faith*, p. 429.

CHAPTER 8

SALT II, Cuba, and Central America: The Pursuit of Illusion

When SALT II was finally signed in mid-1979, prospects for ratification were fragile, as evidence mounted of extensive Soviet proxy involvement through Cuba in Central America, particularly in Nicaragua, and in the Carribean. The possibility of SALT II's failing to be ratified because of Soviet involvement in the promotion of revolution in the Western Hemisphere, in blatant disregard of American interests, was a stark challenge to the strategy Secretary Vance was pursuing. It prompted him to pose explicitly to Moscow the question of whether relations with the United States would be based on cooperation and detente, or on competition and confrontation.

This was the significance of the seemingly arcane dispute over the Soviet brigade in Cuba, which occurred midway through the Senate Foreign Relations Committee's consideration of SALT II. A successful resolution of this issue would have demonstrated Moscow's interest in cooperation with the United States, thus facilitating ratification of SALT II. Soviet rejection of cooperation, however, left no alternative to continued competition between the two superpowers, a position made unmistakable by the Soviet invasion of Afghanistan, which sounded the death knell for the strategy Secretary Vance had been pursuing.

Iraq and Iran
Conic Projection
0 50 100 200 300 400
Miles
TURKEY
U.S.S.R.
U.S.S.R.
Caspian Sea
SYRIA
CYPRUS
LEBANON
Beirut
Damascus
ISRAEL
Amman
Jerusalem
JORDAN
IRAQ
Al Mawsil
Irbil
Kirkuk
Baghdad
Karbala
An Najaf
An Nasiriyah
Al Basrah
SAUDI ARABIA
Iraq-Saudi Arabia Neutral Zone
KUWAIT
Kuwait
Riyadh
IRAN
Tabriz
Rasht
Zanjan
Tehran
Qom
Bakhtaran
Esfahan
Dezful
Ahvaz
Abadan
Yazd
Shiraz
Bushehr
Mashhad
Qayen
Kerman
Zahedan
Bandar Abbas
AFGHANISTAN
PAKISTAN
Persian Gulf
BAHRAIN
Al Manamah
QATAR
Ad Dawhah
UNITED ARAB EMIRATES
Abu Zaby
Strait of Hormuz
OMAN
OMAN
Gulf of Oman
Red Sea

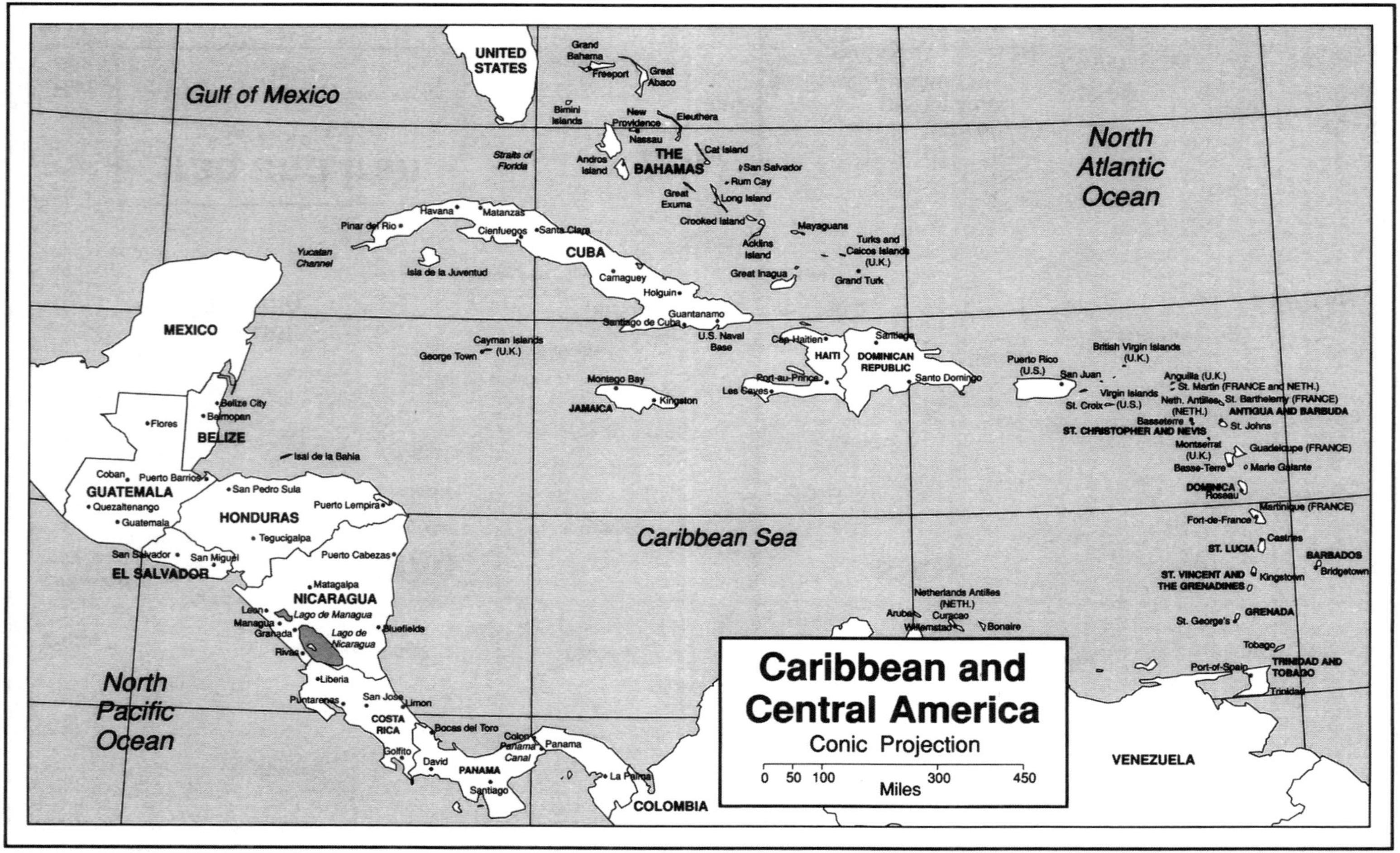

Caribbean and Central America
Conic Projection
0 50 100 300 450
Miles
Gulf of Mexico
North Atlantic Ocean
Caribbean Sea
North Pacific Ocean
UNITED STATES
MEXICO
BELIZE
Belize City
Belmopan
Flores
GUATEMALA
Coban
Puerto Barrios
Quezaltenango
Guatemala
HONDURAS
San Pedro Sula
Puerto Lempira
Tegucigalpa
Isal de la Bahia
EL SALVADOR
San Salvador
San Miguel
NICARAGUA
Puerto Cabezas
Matagalpa
Lago de Managua
Lago de Nicaragua
Leon
Managua
Granada
Rivas
Bluefields
COSTA RICA
Liberia
Puntarenas
San Jose
Limon
Golfito
PANAMA
Bocas del Toro
David
Santiago
Colon
Panama Canal
Panama
La Palma
COLOMBIA
VENEZUELA
CUBA
Havana
Matanzas
Pinar del Rio
Cienfuegos
Santa Clara
Camaguey
Holguin
Guantanamo
Santiago de Cuba
U.S. Naval Base
Isla de la Juventud
Yucatan Channel
Straits of Florida
Cayman Islands (U.K.)
George Town
THE BAHAMAS
Grand Bahama
Freeport
Great Abaco
Bimini Islands
New Providence
Nassau
Eleuthera
Andros Island
Cat Island
San Salvador
Rum Cay
Great Exuma
Long Island
Crooked Island
Acklins Island
Mayaguana
Great Inagua
Turks and Caicos Islands (U.K.)
Grand Turk
JAMAICA
Montego Bay
Kingston
HAITI
Cap-Haitien
Port-au-Prince
Les Cayes
DOMINICAN REPUBLIC
Santiago
Santo Domingo
Puerto Rico (U.S.)
San Juan
British Virgin Islands (U.K.)
Virgin Islands
St. Croix (U.S.)
Anguilla (U.K.)
St. Martin (FRANCE and NETH.)
Neth. Antilles (NETH.)
St. Barthelemy (FRANCE)
ANTIGUA AND BARBUDA
Basseterre
St. Johns
ST. CHRISTOPHER AND NEVIS
Montserrat (U.K.)
Guadeloupe (FRANCE)
Basse-Terre
Marie Galante
DOMINICA
Roseau
Martinique (FRANCE)
Fort-de-France
Castries
ST. LUCIA
BARBADOS
Bridgetown
ST. VINCENT AND THE GRENADINES
Kingstown
GRENADA
St. George's
Tobago
TRINIDAD AND TOBAGO
Port-of-Spain
Trinidad
Netherlands Antilles (NETH.)
Aruba
Curacao
Willemstad
Bonaire

The United States and Central America

Although the Carter administration declared its intention to change the former hegemonic and paternalistic "Yanqui" approach to all of the nations of Latin America in hopes of building "more mature relationships based on mutual respect," the means chosen to move toward these ends were contradictory and unsuccessful.[1] In Central America, four policies, one general and three specific, constituted the administration's approach. These were the general policy of human rights, the effort to normalize relations with Cuba, the negotiation of the Panama Canal treaties, and the attempt to promote democracy in Nicaragua.

The human rights policy was applied selectively and inconsistently, and results were as unsatisfactory in the Western Hemisphere as in the Eastern. In a structural sense, the policy established new criteria by which to evaluate traditional relationships.[2] In most cases, the human rights policy amounted to little more than the issuance of critical reports on the repressive internal conditions in Latin nations, which justified adoption of new, unfriendly policies toward them and often engendered bitterly hostile reactions.

Condemnation of large, independent countries like Argentina, Brazil, and Chile for violation of the basic human rights of their citizenry, however justified, clearly did not further the Carter administration's declared objective of developing more "mature" relationships with them. Indeed, it had the opposite effect, and Washington's relations with the governments in Buenos Aires, Rio de Janeiro, and Santiago stagnated during the Carter years. Though the human rights policy was little more than an irritant to the larger Latin American countries, it had a destabilizing impact on smaller ones like Nicaragua, where the United States possessed greater leverage and had a different agenda.

Human rights, however, was not a major component of United States policy toward Cuba, where attempts to improve relations had reached an impasse by the mid-seventies. The policy of isolating the island regime in place since the early sixties, following the Cuban missile crisis, had become ineffective, partly as a result of Havana's own change of policy and partly because of American efforts to wean Havana away from Moscow.

Castro had abandoned the open promotion of revolution in the hemisphere following Che Guevara's death in Bolivia in 1967. But even while seeking to establish normal state-to-state relations with Latin nations, he turned to organizing a new clandestine apparatus for conducting subversive operations in the region, which came to be headed by the America Department, formed in 1974.[3] By the mid-seventies, and despite its increasing involvement in Africa, Cuba had largely erased its former image and had diplomatic relations with most of the states in the hemisphere, including Argentina, Costa Rica, Ecuador, Mexico, Panama, Peru, Venezuela, and Colombia.

Under Henry Kissinger's direction in the spring of 1975, the United States assisted in this process. Seeking to dissuade Castro from involvement in Angola, Kissinger offered to normalize relations with Cuba in return for Havana's foreign policy restraint. Kissinger's gambit failed, but his efforts encouraged other Latin nations to believe that the door was open to improved relations with Havana. Thus, in late July 1975, with Washington's blessing, the OAS passed a resolution eliminating mandatory sanctions and allowing member nations to normalize relations with Cuba if they wished.

The Carter administration repeated Kissinger's normalization ploy, for the same reasons and with the same results. The new administration attempted to open a dialogue with the Castro regime in early 1977, discontinuing overflight intelligence operations as a show of good faith. Formal talks in the spring led to agreements on fisheries and maritime boundaries, and later in the year interests sections were opened in both capitals. But Cuba's heavy involvement in Ethiopia in late 1977 brought Washington's initiative to a standstill. Castro had simply pocketed American concessions and proceeded with his own policies.

United States relations with Panama were also in serious disrepair by the time Carter took office. Negotiations to replace the 1903 treaty giving the United States control in perpetuity over the Panama Canal and canal zone had begun in 1964 following large-scale riots against the United States' imperial presence. Within three years a draft treaty placing the canal under joint control had been negotiated. In 1968, however, a military coup in Panama saw the rise to power of General Omar Torrijos, who rejected the draft and demanded full sovereignty and control for Panama.

Negotiations stagnated until 1974, when Kissinger reached agreement with Torrijos on principles that would guide future negotiations. These included an agreement to return control of the canal to Panama after a fixed period, in return for the United States retaining the right to operate and defend the canal during the life of the treaty.[4] No progress was made beyond an agreement in principle, however, leaving it to the next administration to conclude the negotiations.

President Carter, concerned that failure to resolve the Panamanian dispute was alienating Latin nations from the United States, pressed forward with treaty negotiations. Despite significant domestic opposition,[5] following a favorable report on human rights practices in Panama two treaties were negotiated. One established joint operation of the canal until the year 2000, at which time Panama would assume complete control. The other guaranteed the canal's permanent neutrality and the United States' right to defend it. The president signed both treaties on September 7, 1977, and the United States Senate ratified them on March 16 and April 18, 1978. Reflecting domestic opposition to the treaties, the House delayed completion of implementing legislation for seventeen months, until September 27, 1979, four days before the treaties took effect.[6]

The new, human rights approach to foreign policy, steps toward the normalization of relations with Cuba, and negotiation of the Panama Canal treaties were the highly visible aspects of the Carter administration's policy toward Central America. Each was important in its own right, but each also contributed to the execution of the unheralded policy of promoting the democratization of Nicaragua.

Nicaragua had been ruled by the Somoza family—father succeeded by son in 1956, both named Anastasio—for over forty years. Although cloaked in constitutional forms, Somozan rule was in fact dictatorship, or, more precisely, caudillo—rule by virtue of control over military power. The Somozas' command of the National Guard, a combined national army and police force, ensured their political rule over the nation.

By the middle seventies, before the Carter administration came to office, significant opposition to Somoza had nevertheless begun to grow both inside and outside Nicaragua. Internally, the Somoza family's accumulation of vast wealth and control over the country's economy combined with repression of dissent had progressively alienated virtually all segments of the population—businessmen, peasants, clergy, and intellectuals alike. Externally, perhaps as a mark of the low esteem in which Somoza was held, several countries not identified with the Soviet bloc supported a left-wing insurgency in Nicaragua. Venezuela, Panama, Costa Rica, and Colombia (and also

Cuba) had begun to cooperate loosely in support of low-level guerrilla operations against the Somoza regime.[7]

Castro's essential involvement in the effort to subvert Somoza was very low-key and circumspect until 1978.[8] Castro was extremely cautious in his approach to political activities in the hemisphere and reluctant to take steps that could precipitate American intervention, for which there was ample hemispheric precedent, most recently in Chile. Thus, Cuban participation was confined to training, advisory, and some logistical support channeled through indirect means. At this point, Cuba was still in the early stages of constructing the organizational infrastructure necessary to play a more prominent regional role and was also heavily involved in Angola.

In early 1977, with no imminent danger to Nicaragua on the horizon, there seemed to be ample time for the United States to pursue a long-term strategy of neutralizing the left, while moving to transform a repressive regime and eliminate a major focus of regional instability. The attempt to normalize relations with Cuba and the negotiation of the Panama Canal treaties served the additional purposes of holding in abeyance the main external threats to Somoza. The Carter administration's efforts to develop good relations with Venezuela carried the same thrust.

Despite growing political opposition to Somoza, the internal security situation appeared to be reasonably stable, with little near-term likelihood of a revolutionary upheaval. At this point, there was no visible threat to the regime, and the powerful National Guard was in control of the country. The only potential threat, represented by the Marxist Frente Sandinista de Liberacion Nacional (FSLN), or the Sandinistas, was too weak and fragmented to be a danger, the result of an effective counterinsurgency campaign carried out by the Guard since 1974.[9]

In early 1977, the FSLN was split into three factions, the Proletarios, who were urban-based and the most ideologically orthodox; the Guerrilla faction, based in the countryside, who espoused Mao Zedong's guerrilla warfare concepts; and the Terceristas, or third force, which had split from the other two and was the least ideologically doctrinaire.[10] Overall FSLN strength was estimated to be but fifty men. Somoza's National Guard, of 5,000 men, on the other hand, was believed to be strong enough to defeat any foreseeable challenge.

It is literally correct to say, as Robert Pastor, former National

Security Council director for Latin American and Caribbean affairs during the Carter administration, has argued, "There was no specific policy toward Nicaragua early in the Carter presidency, there were only human rights policies that applied to Nicaragua."[11] But this begs the question. The human rights policy was, after all, a policy. Indeed, Pastor's assertion avoids the key questions. The Carter administration had sought from the outset to move Nicaragua away from dictatorship and toward democracy. The key questions were how to change the decades-long relationship based specifically upon an anticommunist rationale, how to transform dictatorship into constitutional democracy, and how to foster the emergence of the necessary political groupings capable of governing after Somoza.

Obviously, such an ambitious undertaking would take time. It would be necessary, first of all, to distance the United States from being generally perceived as supporting the Somoza regime and to promote the emergence in Nicaragua of a reasonably cohesive and moderate political opposition—as the object and the vehicle of any democratization effort. In the instance of American policy toward Nicaragua, it seems, the principal instrument stimulating change was precisely the policy of human rights, which served these ends. The human rights criticism raised implicit questions about the moral and ethical bases of Somoza's power and about United States support for such a regime, and it stimulated the emergence of domestic opposition, providing it with a focus. Initial American policy toward Nicaragua, as Under Secretary Anthony Lake has noted, was in fact one of "distancing" Washington from Managua.[12]

Through the fall of 1977, the main thrust of American policy was the redefinition of United States–Nicaragua relations in the context of a human rights reassessment. Somoza, who clearly understood the implications of the American policy shift (not least from his many friends in the United States), sought to satisfy Washington's concerns.[13] Refusing suggestions to consider relinquishing power following his recovery from a heart attack in July 1977, Somoza took steps to broaden his government and improve political conditions in Managua. In September 1977, he enlarged his cabinet and made several changes. At the same time he ended press censorship and terminated the state of siege which had been in effect since a Sandinista raid in December 1974.

Before these changes could influence popular attitudes, however, the FSLN reemerged from several years of dormancy and stepped up its attacks on the regime. On October 13, 1977, several small bands under Eden Pastora carried out raids from Costa Rican territory on the towns of San Carlos, Masaya, and Ocotal. At the same time, the Terceristas, the self-proclaimed "moderate" faction of the FSLN led by the Ortega brothers, Humberto and Daniel, proclaimed that their objective was to overthrow Somoza and establish democracy through free elections—not to install a communist regime. In retrospect, the upsurge in guerrilla attacks reflected the FSLN concern that Somoza's policy shift could succeed in eroding the popular base for revolution in Nicaragua.[14]

The key event crystallizing domestic and regional opposition to Somoza occurred on January 10, 1978, with the assassination of Pedro Joaquin Chamorro. Chamorro was widely recognized to be the one member of the emerging "moderate" opposition most qualified to succeed Somoza. Ironically, although Somoza was probably not responsible for Chamorro's death and Somoza's opponents clearly benefited from it, Somoza was tagged with the blame, which severely damaged his legitimacy.[15] Not only did the assassination energize domestic opposition to Somoza, it also pushed Carlos Perez of Venezuela, Omar Torrijos of Panama, and Daniel Oduber of Costa Rica into greater coordination of their efforts to topple Somoza.

The surprising vitality of the opposition, marked by huge demonstrations against "Somocismo," led to renewed and more straightforward efforts by the United States to persuade Somoza to agree to a peaceful transition to constitutional rule. But he rebuffed Washington's suggestions, insisting that he complete his term of office, which was to expire in 1981. By the spring of 1978, an active if highly disorganized moderate opposition movement, the Broad Opposition Front (FAO), had coalesced. The FAO was an umbrella organization embracing some sixteen groups of the left and right in opposition to Somoza's ruling Liberal Nationalist party (PLN).[16]

The summer of 1978 saw two key developments. The first was the unexpectedly rapid evolution of the FAO into a significant political force with greater cohesion. The second was the alacrity with which the FSLN moved to the forefront of the opposition. The key to their prominence was the increase of hit-and-run attacks against the National Guard culminating in a daring raid by Eden Pastora, who with thirteen men attacked the National Palace on the morning of August 22. A focal point of the government, the palace was the seat of the Nicaraguan Senate and Congress, the Ministries of Finance and the Interior, and the office of the Comptroller General.[17]

Pastora and his men held some fifteen hundred people hostage for two days before negotiating their release. In exchange for release of fifty-nine prisoners, half a million dollars, safe passage out of the country—to Panama—and publication of a "manifesto," the hostages were set free.[18] Unable to retaliate directly against the FSLN, Somoza reacted by attempting to undercut support for the guerrillas, and he arrested large numbers of leaders and members of the opposition. He incarcerated those even suspected of supporting and financing the opposition, eventually imprisoning between six hundred and eight hundred people.[19] But the use of harsh methods in attempting to stem growing opposition backfired, and it quickly became evident that Nicaragua was entering a period of growing political crisis.

America's Failure in Nicaragua

Nicaragua's crisis was also a crisis of a different sort for American policy. A fundamental assumption governing United States policy—Cuban noninvolvement—was rapidly proving false. During Carter's visit to Panama in June to exchange the official Panama Canal treaty transfer documents, the president had raised the subject of Cuban, and implicitly Soviet, involvement in Nicaragua. In discussions with the heads of state of Mexico, Costa Rica, Colombia, Venezuela, and Jamaica, Carter "talked about how to constrain Cuban and other communist intrusion in the internal affairs of Caribbean and Latin American countries, and how to encourage freedom and democracy in Nicaragua."[20]

In late July, during the World Youth Festival in Cuba, Castro publicly announced the unification of the three factions of the FSLN, the first of three occasions on which he would do so, and urged all Latin American radicals to demonstrate solidarity with the Sandinista cause. Stepped-up Cuban involvement could only have followed from Havana's decision that the prospects for revolutionary upheaval had markedly improved because of the weakened position of Somoza and the continued United States refusal to support him.

Indeed, by early September evidence began to accumulate of indirect Cuban involvement in weapons shipments to the FSLN. As the CIA reconstructed the Cuban effort,

> In preparation for the first FSLN offensive in the fall of 1978, arms were flown from Cuba to Panama, transshipped to Costa Rica on smaller planes, and supplied to Nicaraguan guerillas based in northern Costa Rica. To monitor and assist the flow, the America Department established a secret operations center in San Jose.[21]

Cuban–Panamanian cooperation, if publicized, would impact negatively upon the very delicate Panama Canal treaty negotiations. By the fall of 1978 the treaties had been ratified, but implementing legislation had not yet been passed. Nor would the implications for United States–Soviet relations of increased Cuban involvement in the hemisphere be missed. Just as Cuba was then being criticized for its role as a surrogate for Moscow in Angola and Ethiopia, Soviet support for Cuban subversive activity in Central America would inevitably fuel arguments against SALT II. So the administration downplayed Cuba's role in the hemisphere.[22]

Of more immediate importance, greater Cuban involvement meant that Washington no longer had the luxury of time to help bring about a gradual transition to constitutional rule in Nicaragua but would have to move quickly to dislodge Somoza and speed the democratization process. The accelerated pace of events in turn placed great pressure on the administration's loudly proclaimed principle of nonintervention in Latin American affairs. A failure to become involved, however, risked leaving the issue to be determined on the battlefield and by the possible victory of the FSLN.[23]

As the Carter administration's policymakers pondered this conundrum, Rodrigo Carazo Odio, who succeeded Daniel Oduber as president of Costa Rica in May, unexpectedly offered a possible solution. In early September, Carazo informed President Carter of his willingness to mediate the conflict between Somoza and the moderate opposition. The administration welcomed but was puzzled by Carazo's offer, for the Costa Rican president was deeply involved in support of the FSLN cause.[24]

As noted above, Carazo in fact was permitting FSLN to use Costa Rican territory as a staging area for attacks on Nicaragua, though he publicly denied involvement. Occasionally bowing to Nicaraguan pressure, the Costa Rican government "periodically rounds up Sandinistas in staging camps there . . . [and] deports them to Panama, where they are fed and housed and quickly sent back to the same camps."[25] Costa Rica was also the logistical base to which

Cuba, Panama, Venezuela, Colombia, and other countries were shipping weapons and supplies.

Why, then, offer to mediate the conflict? Carazo's offer came a few days before the outbreak, on September 9, of the first major FSLN offensive against the Somoza regime. There can be no doubt that Carazo was aware of the large logistical buildup in the Costa Rican staging areas in preparation for the offensive. His concern, therefore, must have been to preempt any decision by Somoza, once the conflict began, to adopt a policy of hot pursuit of the rebels into their staging areas over the lightly guarded Costa Rican border—a pursuit that had occurred on many occasions.[26] In other words, in hopes of protecting the FSLN's base areas and confining the conflict to Nicaragua, Carazo offered to mediate.

President Carter quickly accepted Carazo's offer, on September 5. Indeed, the Costa Rican president's proposal was important from Washington's point of view for two reasons. If a multilateral effort could be put together behind Costa Rica, the United States would be spared the choice of intervention. Secondly, precisely because Costa Rica was the main conduit through which arms were reaching the FSLN, Carazo would presumably suspend his support role for the duration of the mediation effort. Therefore, to buy time, maintain the integrity of the administration's nonintervention pledge, and perhaps staunch the flow of weapons from other sources as well, President Carter not only agreed to support Carazo's mediation, he sought to build on the offer, instructing that efforts be made to obtain Venezuelan, Colombian, and Mexican support for it.[27]

Before Washington could pull together a multilateral mediation effort, however, on September 9 the FSLN began its most sustained attacks against the Somoza regime. FSLN forces, which had in previous months grown to comprise some 1,200 well-armed men, attacked National Guard outposts in several cities and towns. Their proclaimed political objective was to forestall a military coup, which they professed to believe would only rid the country of Somoza while preserving Somocismo.[28] Their primary military objective was to provoke reprisals against the populace and further alienate them, not to topple Somoza, whose forces were still too powerful to engage in direct combat. Paralleling the offensive, the FAO led a countrywide general strike.

Fighting spread—much of it spontaneously—to Leon, Esteli,

and Chinandega north of Managua, and to Masaya, Rivas, Diriamba, and Penas Blancas in the south. Somoza responded to the FSLN attacks in the same way he had responded to Pastora's raid on the National Palace, but even more harshly. He ordered the Guard to retaliate against real and suspected supporters of the FSLN among the populace. The result was that thousands of innocent civilians were killed, almost totally alienating the people from the regime.

On September 12, Nicaraguan aircraft strafed and bombed the Costa Rican frontier in an effort to cut off the Sandinista forces from their source of supplies in Costa Rica. Immediately afterward, Carazo withdrew his offer to mediate (since it had not deterred Somoza anyway) and came out openly in support of the FSLN. After the fact, Carazo attempted to attribute a high motive to his reversal. He claimed that the Nicaraguan air attack had injured Costa Rican "students, who were celebrating independence day there," and that their suffering the attack "was the reason . . . I backed away from the mediation initiative. We were no longer completely neutral."[29]

Considering the extensive support that Costa Rica had been giving the FSLN, Carazo's explanation was less than candid. Radio Sandino broadcast from the Costa Rican capital, in which also lived 60,000 expatriate anti-Somoza Nicaraguans. Anti-Somoza sentiment had been evident in the very streets of San Jose for years, and particularly so after the government of Rodrigo Carazo broke diplomatic relations with Nicaragua on October 23, 1978. No clandestine apparatus was required to see Costa Rican support for the Sandinistas; it was undeniable.

The collapse of the Central American initiative accompanied the realization that the Sandinistas were far stronger than anyone had believed. Left to run its course, the only outcome of the Nicaraguan unrest would be a Sandinista victory. Indeed, the Carter leadership believed that "the choice between Somoza and the Sandinistas was a false one; the longer Somoza stayed in power, the more likely it was that the Sandinistas would replace him."[30] Washington's course, based on this logic, was clear: Somoza must be removed as soon as possible in order for a democratic solution to have a chance of succeeding.

On September 19, President Carter authorized United States participation in a mediation effort. Exploring alternatives over the next few days, it was decided that Guatemala and the Dominican Republic would join the United States in a multilateral approach.

Mediation, of course, was a misnomer, as was its nominally multilateral character. The mediation was simply a disguised political intervention by the United States, whose objective was to negotiate Somoza's expeditious departure from Nicaragua. In the process, Washington planned to preserve the National Guard—overlooking its complete identification with Somoza and alienation from the people—through which the United States hoped to ensure a peaceful transition to a post-Somoza constitutional regime.

Herein lay the fundamental contradiction in United States policy. It was the wholly erroneous assumption that Somoza and the National Guard were separable. Thus, Washington looked the other way during the mediation effort over the next four months (October 6 to February 8) as Somoza expanded his Guard from 7,000 to 11,000 men, while concentrating on negotiating a scheme that would, with Somoza's agreement, result in the dictator's departure, create a transition government, and establish the basis for consitutional rule. The fact was, however, that the stronger Somoza's armed forces became, the less inclined he was to consider relinquishing power.

Somoza accepted the United States–proposed mediation, at the same time announcing his intention to expand the Guard. Although the United States sent no military equipment to Nicaragua, Somoza received arms from Guatemala, Argentina, Spain, and Israel. The FSLN offensive as well as the general strike had ended in late September, and the Guard had regained control of the country; but the damage was extensive. Several thousand people had been killed (Red Cross estimates were between 1,500 and 3,000 killed), and thousands more rendered homeless (some 30,000). The devastation was compared to that resulting from the 1972 earthquake.[31]

The mediation began on October 6. After five weeks of unproductive negotiation, Somoza countered with an alternative proposal of his own. In response to the FAO's demand for his immediate resignation, on November 12 Somoza proposed a plebiscite. He was, of course, under no illusions about the outcome of a genuinely fair plebiscite, for his popularity was at its lowest point. Somoza's purpose was to protract the negotiations further in order to buy the time necessary to expand, train, and re-equip his forces for the next round of struggle, as Carter's advisers realized.

The United States accepted Somoza's idea of a plebiscite but artfully turned it against him, reformulating it as a vote for or against the dictator. Thus, it appeared that the United States could achieve its ends in a free election without directly demanding Somoza's departure, to which in any case the Carter leadership was averse. If Somoza lost he "would stand aside in favor of a new government."[32] In early December Somoza and the FAO met to negotiate the specifics of the plebiscite.

Of course, if the plebiscite actually occurred and the FAO won, it would spell defeat not only for Somoza, but also for the FSLN, which they and their respective supporters fully realized. As the negotiations over the plebiscite got under way, the leaders of the three Sandinista factions repaired to Havana, where on December 9 they denounced the mediation and announced their unity for the second time; and once again Castro promised to provide assistance.[33] Indeed, Cuba now began direct arms shipments to Costa Rica as well as continuing those through Panama; and Cuban advisers were dispatched to San Jose, where a secret operations center had been established, to train and equip FSLN forces.[34] The Soviet Union, coincidentally, also greatly enlarged the size of its embassy in San Jose.

From November 1978 until the Sandinista victory the following July, weapons poured into Costa Rica from Venezuela, Panama, and Cuba, as the FSLN expanded its forces. According to a special Costa Rican legislative commission report of 1981, President Carazo had secretly authorized as many as sixty flights from all sources, including Colombia, carrying "approximately one million pounds of arms and ammunition" (but which may have amounted to closer to two million because haphazard recordkeeping procedures made an accurate count impossible).[35] The CIA, too, had identified the Cuba–Panama–Costa Rica supply route for the Sandinistas, though apparently underestimating the quantity of arms transported.[36]

On December 20 the mediators produced their final proposal for the plebiscite and presented it to both sides. It called for an internationally supervised election on February 25, 1979. If Somoza lost he would leave the country; if he won, then the FAO would constitute itself as a peaceful opposition. The FAO accepted the terms of the plebiscite, but Somoza did not. He objected to the election procedures, which would have made it impossible for him to manipulate the vote. So he attempted to gain control of the electoral process by insisting on substituting a national plebiscitary authority for an international one.

The Carter leadership responded with a counterproposal that called for both levels to be represented, but for the international authority to have the power to "monitor, mediate, and arbitrate" problems. At the same time, the president agreed to establish a deadline against continued stalling by Somoza and approved a set of phased sanctions to persuade the Nicaraguan leader to accept the plebiscite. Somoza complained that Washington was openly orchestrating his removal, saying, "If I turn right, I hit the wall, if I go forward, I hit the wall, if I turn left, I hit the wall."[37] Only in withdrawal was there a way out.

After being accepted once again by the FAO, this final proposal was delivered to Somoza on January 12. Receiving the proposal with disdain, the Nicaraguan leader left no doubt that he had finished with negotiations. He declared to the American mediator, William Bowdler, "You [the Carter administration] have been threatening me since January 1977" and you've failed.[38] He insisted that he was strong and the FAO was weak. The United States, he said, should be supporting him, not his enemies. Bowdler replied that "this was out of the question" and insisted that Somoza accept the final plebiscite proposal.

When Somoza's negotiators replied a few days later by proposing additional changes, Washington concluded that it was a stalling tactic and drew the line. The mediation was over. On February 8 the State Department formally announced the end of the mediation, publicly accusing Somoza of "blocking all peace efforts" and creating an impasse that "could not be broken by further negotiation."[39] At the same time, Washington decided to impose some sanctions, including termination of the military advisory group, a freeze on all additional aid programs, withdrawal of all Peace Corps volunteers, and the halving of its embassy staff. Diplomatic relations would be maintained at the "bare-bones" level, to keep the door open in case of a change of heart.

The February 8 announcement marked the effective end of any constructive United States involvement in—and ability to shape the desired outcome of—the Nicaraguan revolution. Washington's withdrawal dealt a fatal blow to any possibility that the moderate opposition, the only hope for a democratic future for Nicaragua, could prevail. The FAO leadership signaled recognition of their loss of influence as a result of Washington's withdrawal by promptly aligning with the United People's Movement (UPM), a Sandinista front organization established the previous fall. The FAO harbored no illusions regarding the communist danger but had no alternative. As one moderate opposition leader put it, "The longer Somoza stays in power, the greater the mess will be after he leaves. . . . As far as I'm concerned the sooner the insurrection comes, the better."[40] Together, the FAO and the UPM formed a new united front, the National Patriotic Front.[41]

The Promise of Detente and Nicaragua Policy

The United States had done nothing to prevent either side from rearming during the mediation, which predetermined a military solution in Nicaragua (and which may also have doomed the mediation from the start). In a related development, in mid-February Venezuelan President Carlos Perez was defeated in his bid for reelection by Luis Herrera Campins. Thereafter, Venezuelan involvement and influence with the FSLN declined, even though Herrera continued to provide some arms.

The reduction in Caracas' role left Havana as the principal supplier of the Sandinistas. In early March the leaders of the three FSLN factions met with Castro in Havana. The Cuban leader "spent nearly 48 hours over a four-day period helping to hammer out a basis for cooperation."[42] On March 9, the FSLN announced the establishment of a nine-man directorate, with three leaders from each faction. Proclaiming FSLN unity (for the third time), Castro once again promised to increase his support of "money, arms, and ammunition."[43]

The Cuban leader was as good as his word. By late April, Carazo and Torrijos had "opened the door to Fidel Castro,"[44] who responded with a substantial airlift of war materiel to Costa Rica. "An estimated 1 million pounds of arms and ammunition entered the country, based on an estimated minimum of 30 flights with a capacity of 30,000 to 35,000 pounds of cargo on each."[45] The timely Soviet delivery of a fourth IL-62 long-range transport to Cubana Airlines and a squadron of medium-range transport planes greatly assisted Castro in this effort.[46]

By any standard, a million pounds of arms was a major intervention. At the same time, Castro was openly organizing and transporting a so-called "international brigade" to fight alongside the

Sandinistas in their struggle, and he also dispatched Cuban military specialists to "help coordinate" the war effort.[47] Finally, on March 13, when a leftist group under Maurice Bishop took power on the tiny island of Grenada, Castro immediately responded to the new regime's call for assistance. There was considerable indication that he had provided guidance and arms for the takeover.[48]

Thus, from early spring of 1979, Cuban involvement in Central American and Caribbean affairs had sharply escalated, presenting the Carter leadership with a dilemma whether or not to publicly identify the growing Cuban role. There can be no doubt that United States intelligence was fully aware of Cuban activities.[49] After the fall of 1978, the United States had intensified its intelligence coverage of Cuba, first in connection with Soviet deployment of reportedly nuclear-capable MiG-23s and later with regard to the presence of a Soviet "brigade" on the island.[50] Under the circumstances of the intensified intelligence coverage, it would appear highly unlikely that the United States government would have missed the extensive Cuban supply effort to Costa Rica, Panama, or anywhere else.

Thus, the administration's dilemma: Identifying the Cuban role would raise troubling questions about Soviet support for Cuba in the Western Hemisphere, which, in turn, would raise serious questions about entering into an arms control treaty with Moscow. In short, Cuban involvement in Nicaragua threatened to destroy SALT II, whose essence went beyond arms control to the basic issue of mutual respect of the superpowers for each other's vital interests. The Carter administration's most sought-after objective, which Secretary Vance in particular had pursued so doggedly from the beginning, was in danger of being thwarted at the eleventh hour.

On the other horn of this dilemma was the issue of Panamanian cooperation with Cuba against Somoza, which, if publicized, would threaten yet another of the president's most cherished objectives, the Panama Canal treaties. For this very reason, since the previous September Washington had been exerting almost continuous pressure on Torrijos to stay out of the Nicaraguan conflict. According to a Carter administration official, "nothing would defeat" the Panama Canal legislation faster than "Panama's entry into a Central American conflict between Nicaragua and Costa Rica, or evidence that Torrijos was supplying Nicaragua's Sandinista guerrillas with guns." Such a discovery "would be absolutely devastating for both Torrijos and us."[51]

Finally, identification of a communist effort in Nicaragua would make it virtually impossible for the United States to deny assistance to Somoza, and the intent to dislodge him and move forward with the democratization of Nicaragua would be defeated. In strategic terms, identifying a communist challenge would also undercut the strategy of moving toward a new global order and would reinforce anticommunist containment.

Thus, contrary to Pastor's claim that until "late June [Washington] never suspected that the arms flow was very large or that both the Cuban and Costa Rican governments were directly involved," the facts tell a quite different story.[52] Cuban, Panamanian, and Costa Rican support for the FSLN, in particular, was evident from the beginning and only increased after the failure of the mediation. The assertions that the Carter administration "never suspected" a large arms flow, or that Cuba and Costa Rica were not "directly involved" are—to put it kindly—the very opposite of the truth. Pastor's dissemblance, however, conceals the larger quandary facing the Carter administration.

The United States leadership was clearly neither ignorant of nor surprised by the events in Nicaragua. It was simply that other issues received priority. The Carter leadership was preoccupied with SALT II, the collapse of the shah's government in Iran, the conflicts in Southeast Asia and the Middle East—all of which reached critical points in early 1979. SALT II, the cornerstone of the administration's strategy, received the highest priority. Indeed, it would not be too strong to say that the drive to secure the arms control treaty dictated the policy reaction toward Nicaragua.

In view of the issues at stake, the president's decision, one no doubt strongly recommended by Secretary of State Vance, was to adopt a policy of studied indifference to the Nicaraguan revolution, at least until it was clear that there would in fact be a SALT II treaty. The main objective was to buy time and hope that the Nicaraguan revolution would not explode and take SALT II with it. This decision implicitly accepted the victory of the Sandinistas. The moderate democratic elements possessed no military force; therefore, without American support they would not be a decisive factor in the outcome.

Thus, following the mediation, "the United States withdrew from the crisis."[53] The administration would neither confirm nor deny Cuban, Panamanian, or Costa Rican involvement in the conflict, nor even identify the Sandinistas as Marxists.[54] Indeed, the administration portrayed the conflict as a standoff between "anti-Somoza guerrillas" and the National Guard. On the other hand, consistent with the objective of hoping to delay Somoza's collapse until after SALT II, the United States made no attempt to deny him access to arms supplies until mid-June, when the signing of the SALT II treaty was assured.[55]

By then the conflict was essentially over, and only then did the United States make a half-hearted effort to facilitate a transition to post-Somoza rule by appealing to the OAS. Washington's effort, however, was primarily "for the record," because the issue had already been decided on the battlefield. There would be no American military intervention to install a moderate regime. The end of the Somoza dynasty came quickly thereafter as Latin American support coalesced behind the Sandinistas.

In mid-May, Fidel Castro traveled to Mexico City to meet with President Lopez-Portillo. Amid fulsome mutual praise between the two leaders, Castro accused the United States of intervention in Nicaragua and, naturally, denied Cuban intervention. On May 18, President Carazo also visited the Mexican president to urge him to give support to the Sandinistas, who were, he said, "within a month of coming to power."[56] Carazo's concern was that with Venezuela's diminished role, Mexico's support was needed to provide balance. He feared that if Washington saw Cuba as the only major supporter of the Sandinistas, the United States "might intervene."[57]

President Lopez-Portillo, who was more than willing to help the Sandinistas, agreed with Carazo's analysis. On May 20, Mexico broke diplomatic relations with Nicaragua and urged other countries to do the same in order to isolate Somoza.[58] The Mexican president in effect provided diplomatic cover for Cuba, while flatly rejecting Washington's repeated efforts to gain his cooperation in facilitating the emergence of a moderate regime in Managua. Lopez-Portillo had told President Carter earlier in the year that "both Nicaragua's old and current troubles were wholly of U.S. manufacture."[59]

Through the spring, Sandinista military strength grew from 1,200 to 5,000.[60] The acquisition of more sophisticated weaponry and increased firepower, in turn, produced bolder tactics and willingness to enter into longer engagements with the Guard. The FSLN increasingly went beyond its former hit-and-run tactics, adopting attack-and-hold operations, sometimes battling the Guard for days at a time. On April 9, for example, the FSLN attacked Esteli, a town with a population of 35,000 located ninety miles north of Managua. Erecting barricades, they held the town for five days before retreating in the face of a heavily armed counterattack by the Guard.[61]

Tactically, the attack on Esteli, like later attacks on Leon, Ocotal, Chinandega, Jinotega, Potosi, and others, were designed to draw Guard forces to the north and away from the main attack, which began on May 29 from staging areas in Costa Rica. Three hundred men under Eden Pastora attempted to take control of the town of Rivas, located in the narrow strip of land between the Pacific Ocean and Lake Nicaragua, and establish a "liberated zone" with Rivas as provisional government capital. (The plan never succeeded, despite later commitment of an additional four-hundred-man force, so the FSLN established a provisional government in San Jose, Costa Rica, instead.)

Thomas Borge, the doctrinaire Marxist on the FSLN directorate, declared on May 29 that "the offensive has begun," vowing that it would "soon spread to nationwide insurrection" and overthrow Somoza.[62] He insisted that the Sandinistas "do not propose a socialistic scenario, but rather a democratic one," with early elections. Guerrilla attacks combined with strikes in the major cities, including Managua, quickly confirmed what Sandinista spokesmen were proclaiming: "This is what we've been preparing for .... We're throwing everything we have into the final offensive. Somoza's days are numbered."[63]

By the beginning of the second week of June, while failing to take Rivas, the FSLN had gained control of several key towns, including the provincial capitals of Leon and Matagalpa, and commenced attacks in Managua itself, investing the sprawling slum areas surrounding the capital.[64] Fighting in the streets of the capital set the stage for Washington's effort to bring the conflict to an end. At this point, it was clear, certainly to the Carter leadership—which was preparing to depart for Vienna to sign the SALT II treaty—even if not to the American public, that Somoza's days were indeed numbered.

On June 11, Warren Christopher, Secretary Vance's deputy, convened a Policy Review Committee meeting to assess overall Central America policy. The occasion was completion of a presidential review memorandum (PRM) on the subject. In what can only be described as an extraordinary, self-serving analysis, "The general assessment on Nicaragua was that the war was a standoff and the Guard would probably survive this round of violence, but that Somoza would not likely be able to serve out his term."[65] With fighting in the streets of Managua within a few blocks of Somoza's headquarters—the infamous "bunker"—and the United States Embassy, it was an optimistic interpretation to say that the war was a "standoff."[66] Furthermore, it continued the flawed assumptions that Somoza and the Guard were separable and that the Guard would be a factor in post-Somoza Nicaragua.

Nevertheless, on the basis of this assessment the administration decided on a three-point plan that looked reasonable on the surface but that, if successful, would facilitate the FSLN assumption of power. First, the United States would issue a statement calling for an end to the violence and for Nicaraguan self-determination. Second, Washington would explore Latin American attitudes regarding the establishment of a multilateral force to keep the peace following Somoza's departure. Finally, the United States would issue public and private warnings that the flow of arms to both sides must cease.[67]

This plan made sense only if, in fact, its underlying premises were true. The premises would come under challenge from within the administration itself within twenty-four hours. The very next day the CIA contested the Policy Review Committee's "assessment" of the Nicaraguan conflict. On June 12, the agency issued an analysis repudiating the "standoff" thesis, saying that the Sandinistas were stronger and the Guard weaker than the administration believed and that Somoza would only be able to hold onto power "for a short time."[68]

With the battle clearly moving in favor of the Sandinistas, it was unrealistic to believe they would heed a call for a cease-fire before victory was certain. For the same reason, it was unrealistic to believe the FSLN would share power with the moderates, which was implicit in the United States call for Nicaraguan self-determination. Subsequent United States efforts to find a place for the moderate opposition were half-hearted, at best, reflecting both the administration's lack of leverage and a disinclination to become involved.

The peace-keeping force was a complete non-starter. No other country would agree to the invitation of a United States military force in Nicaragua, or anywhere else in Latin America, however disguised as a "multilateral" force. In truth, the Carter administration was not prepared to send one. Finally, since Washington would do nothing to upset the delicate relationships with Cuba and Panama, "warnings" against continued arms supply meant efforts to stop the arms flow to Somoza, not to the Sandinistas. In fact, on June 14, the United States effected the return of an Israeli ship in mid-passage loaded with weapons bound for Nicaragua.[69] As the Guard's weapons supply began to dry up, arms continued to flow to the Sandinistas, accelerating the end of the Somoza dynasty, which occurred on July 17 with the dictator's departure.

The Cuban Impediment to Detente

By the spring of 1979 it was clear that a SALT treaty would be signed. Against a background of suggestions that completion of an arms control treaty would lead to changes in the United States posture on trade and technology transfer with the Soviet Union, the remaining important arms control issues were worked out in the month and a half following the end of the Sino–Vietnamese conflict. In other words, the administration, under Secretary Vance's lead, was carefully formulating the same quid pro quo put to Moscow in the early seventies, of increased trade and technology in return for Soviet geopolitical and strategic weapons restraint.

In March, Secretary Vance and Treasury Secretary Blumenthal proposed to approach Congress in an effort to extend most-favored-nation status to the Soviet Union before the treaty was signed, but the president said no.[70] At the end of April, however, because of a sharp upsurge in Jewish emigration (31,000, or almost double the previous average of 16,000) and "Soviet cooperation in the SALT negotiations," the two men met with Dobrynin to "explore the possibilities of changing or circumventing the Jackson–Vanik amendment that ties the granting of most favored nation trade status for the Soviet Union to relaxation of Soviet emigration policy for Jews."[71]

Vance had also attempted to gain the president's approval for Treasury Secretary Blumenthal and Commerce Secretary Kreps to attend the Vienna summit, but Brzezinski "succeeded in thwarting" this plan on grounds that it would generate inappropriate expectations of a trade agreement.[72] Earlier in the year, Congressman Charles Vanik had stated publicly that he might be willing to support removal of legislative restrictions on trade. And Senator Adlai Stevenson III, author of the 1974 amendment that restricted the level of credit the Export-Import Bank could extend to Moscow, proposed raising the credit limit from its original level of $300 million to $2 billion.

Senator Jackson, however, remained obdurate, continuing to oppose MFN status for the Soviet Union, raising the level of available credit, and legislative changes to enhance trade. Indeed, on the eve of the president's departure for the Vienna summit, Jackson formally declared his opposition to the SALT II treaty and accused the Carter administration of following the same policy of appeasement toward the Soviet Union that Kissinger had followed. Nevertheless, despite growing opposition, the treaty negotiations themselves moved forward.

In the negotiations, the Soviet Union finally accepted the 5 percent rule on changes of key elements of existing ICBMs, while the United States agreed not to test multiple warheads on ALCM during the treaty period, and on GLCM and SLCM during the term of the protocol.[73] The two sides recognized in an exchange of letters that encryption should not deny information relevant to verification. (CIA chief Stansfield Turner, however, remained dissatisfied with this arrangement; and it was decided that the president would raise the issue with Brezhnev at the summit in order to obtain an on-the-record statement confirming the Soviet commitment.)

Finally, since the Soviets simply refused to divulge formally the production rate of the Backfire bomber, which was publicly known to be thirty per year, Vance and Dobrynin agreed to employ the device of the non-contradicted statement to get around the problem. It was agreed that at the summit President Carter would state the United States understanding of the Backfire production rate and Brezhnev would not contradict it.[74] This would ensure inclusion of the production rate as a part of the treaty's negotiating record.

The negotiations were concluded on May 7, and four days later it was announced that the summit would take place in Vienna June 15 through 18. That the treaty would now be signed was a foregone conclusion. The chief question, however, was, would it be ratified? Had events, and especially improvements in weapons technology, overtaken it? By the spring of 1979, it was clear to the American leadership that the "strategic nuclear balance was deteriorating faster than we had expected two years ago and would continue to do so into the early eighties."[75] This was in large part because Soviet improvements in the SS-18 and SS-19 missiles "were making our Minuteman III increasingly vulnerable."

Furthermore, the Soviet Union's geopolitical offensive—spearheaded by Cuban military involvement in Angola, Ethiopia, and South Yemen—was apparent to the most casual observer of the international scene. Worse, but less apparent to the average citizen, were ominous signs that the Soviet–Cuban offensive was being extended into the Western Hemisphere.

Although several thousand Soviet ground-force personnel had been stationed in Cuba since the 1962 missile crisis, the character of the Soviet presence on the island began to change in late 1975 in the context of extensive deployment of Cuban troops to Angola. In conjunction with the dispatch of 20,000 Cuban troops to save the embattled pro-Soviet MPLA, which was on the verge of defeat in civil war, the initial insertion into Cuba of what came to be known as the Soviet "combat brigade" evidently occurred.[76]

When an additional 20,000 troops were dispatched to Ethiopia in 1977–78, a further change occurred in the Soviet presence on the island. The Soviets began to upgrade their intelligence facility at Lourdes, a few miles southwest of Havana, making it one of the largest in the world and giving it a very impressive communications and interception capability. Expansion of the submarine port at Cienfuegos began, with construction of a second, large, deep-water pier and extensive shore-side facilities, much of which was completed in the spring of 1979.[77] Turning the port over to the Cuban navy, Moscow delivered one diesel-powered Foxtrot class attack submarine in February 1979 and a second one later in the year.

Moscow had delivered a squadron of MiG-23 fighter planes the previous fall, causing concern that they might be nuclear-capable and thus violate the United States–Soviet 1962 understanding prohibiting the introduction of nuclear weapons into Cuba. (After assurances from Moscow, however, the United States officially expressed its satisfaction but declared that it would continue to monitor the aircraft to ensure compliance.) While upgrading Cuba's ground-attack capability with the MiG-23s, the Soviet Union also moved to improve Cuban air defenses with deployment of modern air-defense missiles and also began construction of a military airfield.[78] From Cuba, Soviet reconnaissance aircraft increased the frequency of long-range patrols along the east and west coasts of the United States.

In the spring of 1979, the Soviet Union also delivered a squadron of medium-range AN-26 transport planes, bringing the Cuban inventory of that aircraft to twenty.[79] The AN-26, with a range of almost 700 miles, is capable of transporting five tons of cargo or thirty-eight passengers. These were used in addition to ten older Il-14s with similar range and cargo capacity, which Havana already had, and evidently also the four Il-62 airliners of Cuba's civilian airline, Cubana, in the Cuban airlift of war materiel to Nicaragua mentioned above. They augmented Cuba's capability for intervention thoughout Central America and the Caribbean.

In the context of this overall buildup, Moscow stealthily deployed what later would be described as a "combat brigade" of some 2,600 men with full complement of equipment, including tanks, rockets, and artillery. This deployment was over and above the several thousand Soviet personnel assigned to Cuba in an advisory status since 1962. While the deployment of the brigade had not been confirmed by the spring of 1979, what was already clear was the Soviet Union's buildup of Cuba into an island fortress for expanded Soviet intelligence, training, naval, air, and ground presence, and the enhancement of Cuba's global proxy role, now even including the Western Hemisphere.

Moscow's activities in Cuba and Cuba's growing involvement in Central America and the Caribbean were clearly incompatible with the kind of broad-ranging detente envisaged by Secretary Vance. The Cuban role in the final phase of the Nicaraguan revolution was of particular concern to the Carter leadership, for it was in full swing just as the ratification campaign for SALT II began.[80] Worse, intelligence began to appear showing increased Cuban support for communist guerrilla movements in El Salvador, Honduras, and Guatemala.[81] At the very least, there were grounds for serious concern that the Soviet Union was supporting an ambitious Cuban effort to promote revolutionary change in Central America and the Caribbean.

Ratification of SALT II meant public debate, and the subject of Soviet support for Cuba in Central America and the Caribbean would inevitably arise. It was conceivable, even if improbable, that the American public could be persuaded to accept a degree of independent Cuban sponsorship of revolutionary activity in the hemisphere. In that case the ratification of SALT II would not be endangered. But if the Soviet Union was perceived to be actively supporting Cuba as its surrogate in the Western Hemisphere, as it was so clearly doing in Africa and the Middle East, there was simply no possibility that the American public would accept an arms control agreement with the Soviet Union—not to mention the expanded economic relationship that would accompany it.

It was an inevitable linkage and one which would doom SALT II. This chain of logic was clearly understood by Brzezinski and Vance, but each reacted differently to the increasingly visible Soviet–Cuban role in Central America and the Caribbean.[82] Brzezinski supported SALT II, but on condition that Moscow in fact agree to geopolitical as well as strategic weapons restraint. This explained his and the president's insistence on engaging Moscow in a broad-ranging dialogue regarding each power's interests in the third world, particularly in the Western Hemisphere. Vance, on the other hand, wished to rush the SALT II treaty through the signing and ratification process, establishing the basic framework for detente before Soviet–Cuban activism could ruin it. Thus, Vance and his supporters in the administration downplayed growing Soviet and Cuban involvement in the Western Hemisphere, characterizing it as nothing unusual.[83]

In March, possibly spurred by Castro's renewed commitment to support the FSLN and the Soviet transfer to Cuba of the capability to do it, but perhaps also influenced by the coming summit, Brzezinski moved to bring together the evidence on the "size, location, capabilities, and purposes of Soviet forces in Cuba," ordering an intelligence assessment.[84] He was supported by Defense Secretary Brown, who had also "begun to express concern about stepped-up Soviet military activity in the Caribbean and had urged that we consider a broad range of political, military, and diplomatic countermeasures."[85]

A stepped-up intelligence effort over the next two and a half months produced additional information, including evidence of the presence of a Soviet "brigada" located at two sites southwest of Havana. Based on this information, a search of NSA files formed the basis for a study, completed in mid-June, which concluded that "at a minimum, a Soviet brigade headquarters had been estabished in Cuba" separate from the pre-existing advisory unit.[86] The study, which had obvious implications for American policy toward the Soviet Union, immediately engendered heated debate among the intelligence agencies. While the dispute raged, the president departed for Vienna to sign the SALT II treaty.

The Vienna Summit

The Vienna summit, June 15 through 18, 1979, was a major disappointment for President Carter and Secretary Vance. They had wanted the treaty signing ceremony to take place in conjunction with a visit by Leonid Brezhnev to Washington. They had hoped that their meeting would be the starting point for a major dialogue and increased understanding between the two countries, if not for detente. They had hoped to gain agreement for proceeding with SALT III. None of these occurred. In fact, the Carter–Brezhnev "summit" was probably the least productive meeting ever held between Soviet and American leaders, and certainly one of the most disheartening.

The summit was held in Vienna, not in Washington as originally planned, or as protocol required. The previous meeting had been in Vladivostok, November 23 and 24, 1974. (Indeed, the Vladivostok visit itself violated diplomatic protocol, the meeting before that having been the Nixon–Brezhnev summit in Moscow, June 27 to July 3, 1974.) The Vienna meetings were relatively brief and heavily scripted in advance, with little room left for spontaneity and free-wheeling discussion. The reason given by the Soviets for both the change in venue and the rigidly controlled agenda was Brezhnev's debilitated health.[87] Nevertheless, the president did find opportunities to raise the central issue that concerned American leaders: Would Moscow in fact agree to strategic weapons and geopolitical restraint?

In his first statement, President Carter made a plea for both, urging the Soviet Union to maintain a "peaceful relationship in spite of serious differences."[88] It was imperative, he said, "to move immediately to SALT III." The president insisted that "neither country can dominate the other. Each nation is too powerful to permit this to happen." Furthermore, he continued, referring obliquely to Cuba, "We should avoid confrontation by refraining from intrusions into troubled areas, either directly or indirectly through proxies."

Brezhnev, however, was extremely ambiguous on the issues of both strategic and geopolitical restraint. On the strategic weapons issue, Brezhnev was preoccupied with ways of holding the United States to the letter of the treaty while leaving Moscow's hands as free as possible. He insisted, for example, that the treaty would not go into effect until ratified, warned that the Soviets would accept no unilateral amendments, and, disputing the MX mobile-basing scheme, said that the Soviets could not accept any plan in which there would be more than one silo per missile.[89] And on the prearranged exchange regarding the Backfire bomber, the Soviet leader initially refused to say his lines, trying to avoid commitment.[90] (Carter subsequently obtained Brezhnev's reluctant concurrence.)

Despite the fact that the essence of the treaty was to establish a nuclear balance between the two powers, Brezhnev expressed "concern about any Soviet promise to maintain permanent equivalency of nuclear power with [the United States] which did not take into account additional French, British, and Chinese arsenals."[91] Finally, throwing cold water on any hope for prompt movement to SALT III, he said that "there was a definite limit on how much further they could go with arms control without counting all the medium-range and tactical weapons systems in Europe."

Carter attempted to rebut each point, either with the argument that the Soviet view was "a departure from international custom" (regarding when the treaty would take effect) or that "we had already covered this point" (regarding MX basing), but the Soviet leader would not budge.[92] The next day the president pressed Brezhnev again to agree to commence SALT III negotiations, listing a dozen proposals, but he could elicit no response. The only glint of hope here was that after the session Brezhnev asked for a written copy of the president's proposals, to which he presumably would give some consideration.[93]

Despite Carter's pleas, however, the Soviet leadership ultimately remained unmoved. Responding to the president's arms proposals, Brezhnev took a hard line, saying, "If we proceed on SALT III, other countries will have to be involved. American forward-based (medium-range) systems must be included, and SALT II must be implemented first. All strategic factors, some of which are very complicated, must be considered, and a simple 5 per cent annual reduction [one of Carter's twelve proposals] would not be advisable."[94]

If Brezhnev's response on the future of arms control was disappointing, his reaction to the issue of geopolitical restraint was even more so. In their first meeting, while declaring that "the Soviets have no hostile designs against the United States," he went on to say that "the Soviet Union is dedicated to support the struggle for emancipation and solidarity. Revolutions, which the Soviets do support, emerge only within other nations. The instigation for them never originates with us."[95]

In what had become a ritual at Soviet–American summits, Brezhnev embarked on a lengthy peroration about China, saying that Moscow had "no objections to normal relations between your two countries," that indeed the Soviet Union sought to improve relations with China, too, but that the Soviets would view with great concern "anything beyond the present line."[96] Carter replied that "we would not use our new friendship with China to the detriment of the Soviet Union, and would like the Soviet leaders to keep us informed about their own relations with China."[97]

Then, during the session covering "trouble spots around the world," the two leaders exchanged standard restatements of long-held positions. Included as part of his statement of the American position, however, according to senior members of the SALT delegation, President Carter told Brezhnev that "a Soviet buildup of arms in Cuba would adversely affect the relationship of the two countries."[98] (In his memoir, Carter omitted the remark about the problem of a "Soviet buildup" in Cuba, referring only to Cuban military activities.[99]) The relevant passage reads:

> The military activities of Cuba are of deep concern to us. They now have more than 40,000 troops in Africa, constantly embroiled in every trouble spot, and now they are becoming more active in the Caribbean and in Central America.[100]

Brezhnev's response was to say blandly, "We are strictly observing a 1962 agreement not to build up any forces in Cuba which might be considered a threat to the United States."[101] He went on to say that regarding Cuban military activities, Moscow did not "control these decisions, which are made by the Cuban leaders themselves." Brezhnev's answer was a crude and unsatisfactory evasion. He said that the Soviet Union was observing "a 1962 agreement," but not the 1970 understanding on submarine bases. He, in fact, had not denied a Soviet buildup in Cuba, but only a buildup which might be considered a threat to the United States. And this, of course, was not for him to decide.

In fact, Washington had consistently voiced its concern over Soviet naval and air activities in Cuba. Development of the submarine base at Cienfuegos, particularly construction of the new, deep-water pier, which Soviet missile-carrying submarines could use, was hardly consistent with either the 1962 agreement or its 1970 clarification. That clarification, in fact, included the definition of what constituted a Soviet naval base in Cuba. On October 9, 1970, Henry Kissinger had transmitted a "president's note" to the Soviet government that stated:

> The US Government understands that the USSR will not establish, utilize, or permit the establishment of any facility in Cuba that can be employed to support or repair Soviet naval ships capable of carrying offensive weapons, i.e. submarines, or surface ships armed with nuclear-capable, surface to surface missiles.[102]

Thus, construction at Cienfuegos would be a violation of the 1970 understanding whether the base was formally under Cuban control or not. The deep-water piers were large enough to accommodate several vessels in addition to the two diesel submarines Cuba currently possessed. Nor was the deployment of potentially nuclear-capable MiG-23s of any less concern because the currently deployed models were not fitted with the bomb racks that would make them nuclear-capable. The new airfield construction only heightened apprehension.

The Carter leadership was thoroughly discouraged by the Soviet performance in Vienna, despite the public hoopla that accompanied the signing of the SALT II treaty. Aside from Brezhnev's clear disinclination to proceed with SALT III, his evasions about Cuba must have been particularly distressing for what they portended regarding SALT ratification. The fact of the matter was that the only area in which the Soviets were then "strictly observing" the 1962 agreement on Cuba was in the nondeployment of ballistic missiles. It was only a matter of time before the Soviet buildup in Cuba and the Cuban role in Nicaragua and elsewhere in Central America and the Caribbean would begin to have a public impact.

The Soviet "Combat" Brigade in Cuba

Meanwhile, disagreement continued within the intelligence community over whether or not the evidence confirmed the presence of a Soviet combat brigade in Cuba. This led, on July 12, to issuance of a coordinated interim report, a compromise assessment engineered by CIA chief Turner that "a Soviet force was present as a separate unit, not part of an advisory group. But there was no agreement on the size, organization or mission of the Soviet force."[103] Army intelligence had insisted on including the possibility that the Soviet unit's mission was "to guard existing or potential nuclear weapons," but Turner "ordered them to cave in" on the grounds that it was simply "gratuitous speculation."[104]

Issuance of the report did not end the controversy. Indeed, there were two immediate consequences. The first was that the president promptly ordered stepped-up surveillance to resolve the issue; the second was a series of leaks to members of Congress and the news media. The most serious leak was to Senator Richard Stone, a Florida Democrat and member of the Senate Foreign Relations Committee, who was staunchly opposed to the SALT II treaty. Sensitized by his large Cuban consituency to Soviet and Cuban activities in the Caribbean, he was convinced that the Carter administration was downplaying the Soviet threat in the Western Hemisphere to promote the treaty.

Stone had been concerned about Soviet activities in the Caribbean for some time. During the Panama Canal treaty ratification process, in January 1978 he had pressed President Carter for assurances that the treaty would not signal the beginning of an American "retreat" in the hemisphere.[105] Carter had written to him declaring that "it has been and will continue to be the policy of the United States to oppose any efforts, direct or indirect, by the Soviet Union to establish military bases in the Western Hemisphere."[106]

Nevertheless, Senator Stone's concerns had led him to persistently prod the intelligence community for information on Soviet and Cuban activities, and he obtained periodic briefings on the subject. On the morning of July 17, 1979, while he was on his way to a hearing on the SALT treaty (and coincidentally the same day that Anastasio Somoza left Nicaragua), Stone was informed by one of his aides about the CIA finding of the twelfth.[107] The senator immediately asked the witnesses at the hearing, Admirals Elmo Zumwalt and Thomas Moorer, whether "the introduction of a large number of combat troops of the Soviet Union into Cuba" would be a "direct or indirect effort to establish a military base."[108]

Later, in the afternoon's closed session, Stone insisted that CIA chief Stansfield Turner and NSA chief Robert Inman "confirm or deny" his information. Turner "denied that the intelligence community had found anything new in Cuba," but Inman "did not deny

Stone's charge."[109] Secretary of Defense Harold Brown, however, supported Turner and offered to put his position in writing. Committee chairman Frank Church promptly released Brown's statement, hoping to counteract the impact of any public remarks Stone might make, particularly affecting SALT. Brown declared,

> There is no evidence of any substantial increase in the size of the Soviet military presence in Cuba over the past several years. Apart from a military group that has been advising the Cuban Armed Forces for 15 years or more, our intelligence does not warrant the conclusion that there are any other significant Soviet military forces in Cuba.[110]

Stone was not satisfied. He called upon the administration to intensify its surveillance effort and made several statements attempting to publicize the issue. The *Washington Star* carried a brief account of his remarks in the Senate Foreign Relations Committee the next day.[111] On July 20, Ted Koppel of ABC's "Nightline" picked up and exaggerated the issue, reporting that "a brigade of Soviet troops, possibly as many as 6,000 combat-ready men, has been moved into Cuba within recent weeks."[112] Television newscaster John Scali made similar comments on July 24.

In between these telecasts, two press accounts appeared that further elaborated the Soviet–Cuban collaboration. The first reported remarks by Ramon Sanchez-Parodi, Cuban interest section envoy, who bluntly proclaimed Cuba's intention "to support guerrilla insurrections [in other Latin American countries] just as it did in Nicaragua."[113] Responding to a question about Soviet troops in Cuba, he said that Cuban–Soviet ties "will continue to increase in all fields, including military collaboration." The second account was the leak of the CIA's May 2 intelligence report (cited above), detailing Cuban support for Central American guerrilla groups.[114]

Remarkably, these reports attracted little public attention. A few days later, on July 24, Stone requested and was given a detailed classified intelligence briefing.[115] That same day, just as Brzezinski was alerting the president to the "serious repercussions" the issue could have for SALT,[116] Stone wrote to President Carter requesting his comments on reports that the Soviet Union had established a brigade command structure in Cuba.

Secretary Vance replied on behalf of the president three days later, basing his remarks on a CIA finding of the nineteenth, which reaffirmed Turner's position of the twelfth. The finding concluded that "there was a Soviet ground force unit in Cuba. . . . [but] intelligence analysts were not prepared to say whether it was a combat force, a training structure for Cuban forces, or a facility for Soviet development and testing of tropical combat tactics."[117]

Vance reaffirmed the president's January 1978 commitment to Senator Stone that "it is the policy of the United States to oppose any efforts, direct or indirect, by the Soviet Union to establish military bases in the Western Hemisphere."[118] He closely paraphrased Brown's statement of July 17, saying that there was "no evidence of any substantial increase of the Soviet military presence in Cuba over the past several years," adding, "or the presence of a Soviet military base."

Vance said that United States intelligence was closely monitoring the situation and confirmed that Carter had "raised the question of the Soviet presence in Cuba with President Brezhnev in Vienna and made clear to him that a Soviet buildup would adversely affect our relationship."[119] Vance then reviewed the United States–Soviet "understandings" of 1962 and 1970 regarding the prohibitions against introducing nuclear weapons and submarine bases into Cuba and concluded that "we have no evidence that the Soviets are in violation of this understanding."

Senator Stone immediately labeled Vance's letter "a whitewash."[120] If it was not a whitewash it certainly was an evasion. Vance acknowledged that at least the structure of a Soviet brigade headquarters was present in Cuba separate from other advisory organizations,[121] but he believed that neither the 1962 understanding banning offensive nuclear weapons nor the 1970 prohibition on submarine bases "covered Soviet ground forces."[122] Therefore, the secretary could reply truthfully, even if not to the point, that the Soviets had not violated their understandings with the United States.[123]

Once again, on August 10, Senator Stone wrote to the president requesting more intense intelligence coverage. And the president responded by ordering "the highest priority" of reconnaissance.[124] The intensified effort paid off almost immediately. On August 14, Brzezinski informed the president that the Soviet brigade would be holding firing exercises within a week and that this was "an extremely serious development which could most adversely affect SALT."[125] Meeting with Brown and Vance later that same day, Brzezinski attempted to get them to agree to "put more pressure on Cuba," but

Vance demurred, consenting only to discuss the issue further "if harder evidence becomes available."[126]

As it turned out, "harder evidence" became available within days, forcing Secretary Vance to take a risky gamble in his effort to save the SALT II treaty. On August 17, satellite reconnaissance observed the Soviet brigade "on maneuver" at the San Pedro maneuver grounds a few miles west of Jose Marti International Airport.[127] The composition of the brigade included a rocket battalion, a tank battalion, and two infantry battalions. Further observation three days later showed the equipment stowed at two military camps near Lourdes, the Soviet communications complex. The weapons, reconnaissance conclusively showed, belonged to the Soviets.

Based on the new evidence, the CIA's National Foreign Assessment Center (NFAC) issued a coordinated intelligence finding on August 22 confirming the Soviet presence as a "Soviet combat brigade."[128] The finding used the term "combat brigade" for the first time to distinguish the unit from a training outfit, despite the absence of any indication that it had actually engaged in combat. It was the term "combat" more than anything else that would finally alarm the public and raise the issue of the Soviet presence in Cuba to a crisis in United States–Soviet relations, as well as in American domestic politics.

President Carter was informed of the finding the next day, August 23. He, Vice-President Mondale, Vance, Brzezinski, Brown, and most of Congress were out of town for the Labor Day recess, which lasted until September 4. Carter and his wife were on a Mississippi riverboat cruise and had stopped off at Hannibal, Missouri, where he was informed of the NFAC finding. He "sent word back to Brzezinski" to assemble all of the information on Soviet ground forces in Cuba and hold an interagency meeting to discuss the matter.[129] The interagency group promptly convened and concluded that the issue did not have a "short time fuse"; they decided that any "major action could be delayed until after Labor Day."[130]

Brzezinski was still on vacation in Vermont, and was not due in Washington until September 4, the day before Congress reconvened. In Brzezinski's absence Secretary Vance, who had returned from his own vacation on August 28, seized the issue of the brigade rather than allowing it to spiral out of control into the broader issue of Soviet support for Cuban revolutionary activity in the Western Hemisphere, which would surely sink SALT. Indeed, the key fact about the brigade crisis, which then unfolded from this point, is Vance's controlling role.

Posing the Question to Moscow

Vance was determined to keep the issue focused narrowly on the brigade so that, in the event the Soviets responded negatively, the larger questions of SALT II and detente would not also be foreclosed. In essence, Vance used the issue of the brigade to pose the question to Moscow of whether relations with the United States would be based on cooperation or confrontation. Moscow's reaction to the brigade crisis would indicate whether or not the Soviet Union was willing to exercise geopolitical as well as strategic weapons restraint, the essential preconditions for detente.

Vance appears to have believed that the Soviets would react to the brigade issue in much the same way they had reacted earlier to the 1962 Cuban missile crisis, the 1970 submarine base dispute, and the 1978 flap over the MiG-23s.[131] In each of the previous cases, "the Soviets had taken seriously the U.S. appproach. The Soviets had reaffirmed that an understanding existed. They had responded, without public commitment, by limiting their deployment and activities." Undoubtedly, Vance hoped that "if the Soviets were approached in a similar vein on the brigade, the pattern would repeat itself."[132]

Vance's plan, which he says was developed on August 28, was "to brief by telephone key members of Congress. We would outline the recent intelligence and tell them that we had lodged a strong protest with the Soviets underlining our serious concern."[133] He and his staff had drafted a position statement.

> We have recently confirmed the presence in Cuba of what appears to be a Soviet combat unit. This is the first time we have been able to confirm the presence of a Soviet ground forces unit on the island.
>
> Elements of the unit appear to have been there since at least 1976. We estimate that it consists of some two thousand to three thousand men. The unit includes armored, artillery and infantry elements. In addition, we estimate that the Soviet Union maintains between 1,500 and 2,000 military advisory and technical personnel in Cuba.

> As currently configured and supported the unit poses no threat to the United States.
>
> Ground forces per se did not figure in our bilateral understandings with the Soviets which were directed toward offensive weapons systems.
>
> Nonetheless we are concerned about the presence of Soviet combat troops in Cuba.
>
> We have in recent months raised with the Soviets the issue of the Soviet–Cuban military relationship. On August 29 we called in the Soviet Charge to express our concerns about this Soviet ground force unit. We will continue our discussions with them on this subject.
>
> We will of course continue to monitor all aspects of Soviet military activities in Cuba to ensure there is no threat to the United States.[134]

On the morning of August 29, the Special Coordinating Committee (SCC) convened. Brzezinski was still in Vermont; David Aaron, his deputy, apparently chaired the meeting.[135] According to Brzezinski's account, "The State Department proposed a demarche to the Soviets on the alleged Soviet brigade in Cuba." Brzezinski's "staff objected on the grounds that this course of action could immediately precipitate a Soviet denial, thereby making it more difficult for the Soviets to change their position later on."

After considerable discussion leading only to an impasse, "the group decided that Secretary Vance would be asked to discuss this issue by telephone with [Brzezinski] and with Acting Secretary of Defense Graham Claytor."[136] Aaron, meanwhile, called his chief, Brzezinski, in Vermont, and Brzezinski "asked him to defer any action on this issue until [he] had returned to Washington around Labor Day, so that Vance, Brown, and [he] could consult with the President."[137] Brzezinski, too, like the interagency group earlier, believed that no immediate action was required.

But Vance, instead of calling Brzezinski and Claytor, moved quickly to put his own plan, the demarche to the Soviets, into action.[138] The justification for taking immediate action, rather than waiting until the senior leaders of the administration could convene to discuss it, was the ostensible fear that the NFAC report would become public. The *National Intelligence Daily* (NID), a classified publication with limited circulation, carried the story of the brigade in its August 28 issue. The NID report was promptly leaked to Clarence Robinson, staff writer for *Aviation Week and Space Technology*, who called Newsom's office the next morning to confirm the intelligence report.[139]

That afternoon, the twenty-ninth, Newsom went over to the Soviet embassy for a meeting with Vladillian Vasev, the Soviet chargé d'affaires (Dobrynin was away in Moscow). Newsom conveyed the information that a "brigade equipped with combat weapons was present in Cuba."[140] Because of the importance of good relations and "continued understanding" between the two countries, and particularly at a time when the SALT II treaty was before Congress, he "hoped that the Soviet Union might provide an explanation that would assist the administration in dealing with the expected inquiry" from Congress.

The next day, August 30, as Vance had planned but much to Brzezinski's "amazement," Newsom telephoned key members of Congress, including the chairman and ranking minority members of the Senate Foreign Relations Committee and the House Foreign Affairs Committee.[141] When Newsom called Senator Frank Church, chairman of the Foreign Relations Committee, at his home in Boise, Idaho, Church's first words were, "That will sink SALT."[142] He asked whether the State Department intended to release this information and "was told that that was not the intention." Newsom emphasized that there was no threat and that the department was seeking an explanation.

Church promptly called Secretary Vance and reportedly insisted that "someone in authority make the information public immediately, before it was leaked in some distorted form."[143] Vance replied that "we did not intend to make any statement until we had more information." Asked what would happen if Church himself made a statement, Vance said "it would be harmful, but . . . acknowledged to him that he was the only one who could make the decision." Vance claims that he believed "Church would say nothing, and that there would be no public discussion."[144]

But this is hardly satisfactory. As Brzezinski noted, failing "to instruct Church [on] how to deal with the matter in public" was disastrous.[145] Failure to instruct him, in light of the senator's obvious desire to go public with the information, ensured that he would do so. Yet, from Vance's point of view, no one could represent the connection between Soviet geopolitical and strategic weapons restraint better or more appropriately than the very chairman of the Senate Foreign Relations Committee, which was at that moment considering the SALT II treaty. The point could hardly be clearer: without Soviet geopolitical restraint there could be no treaty.

Hastily convening a press conference at his home, Church announced the presence of the Soviet brigade and called on the president to insist on the "immediate withdrawal of all Russian combat troops from Cuba."[146] Although acknowledging that the presence of the unit did not threaten the United States in the same way that the 1962 missile deployment had, Church declared that "Russian combat units do not belong in Cuba. The president must make it clear, we draw the line on Russian penetration of this hemisphere."[147] At this press conference, Church made no comment on the linkage between the brigade and SALT II.[148]

On the same day that Church's remarks appeared in the press, Hodding Carter, assistant secretary of state for public affairs, released the statement Vance and his staff had prepared previously (see above) acknowledging the presence of a Soviet ground force on the island.[149] Senator Stone immediately declared that "the Soviet presence in Cuba should become part of the debate over the [SALT II] treaty." Senators Robert Dole of Kansas and Harry Byrd of Virginia both went further, calling for "suspension of the debate pending removal of the Soviet combat forces." But Senate Majority Leader Robert Byrd of West Virginia said that there was "ample time" to explore the Cuban issue before the treaty debate resumed.[150]

Amid the growing furor over the brigade, the Carter leadership, now returned from vacation, met on the evening of September 4. Brzezinski told the president that he saw "no immediate strategic threat, [and] that we should work quietly but firmly to resolve the issue with the Soviets."[151] But Carter sided with Vance, who, much to Brzezinski's surprise, wanted "to [publicly] demand a withdrawal of the brigade."

Indeed, at this meeting the group devised the phrase that Vance was supposed to put forward the next day, "the status quo is unacceptable."[152] The president also gave Vance the unprecedented authority to manage the crisis through the Department of State Policy Review Committee, rather than permitting Brzezinski to do so through the normal crisis-management mechanism of the National Security Council's Special Coordinating Committee (SCC).[153]

In his memoir, Vance claims that his intention was to "defuse the issue before it became a 'crisis,'" but that Senator Church's public demand for removal of the brigade and linkage of it to passage of the SALT II treaty precipitated the crisis "before we had a chance to pursue quiet diplomacy."[154] To make the claim that Senator Church brought about the crisis, however, Secretary Vance was forced to reverse the chronology of events.

The truth of the matter was that, as noted above, the decision to make a public issue of the brigade came on September 4, and the initiative for it was Vance's. Up to that point, Senator Church had not yet publicly linked SALT II and the brigade. He would not make that connection until *after* Secretary Vance had done so in a news conference on the morning of September 5, and until *after* Vance's closed-door testimony later that same day before the Senate Foreign Relations Committee!

Vance also claims that his press conference of September 5 was a "regularly scheduled" event.[155] But his deputy, David Newsom, disclosed that it was not a regularly scheduled event at all, but one designed specifically to highlight the brigade issue. According to Newsom, Vance had decided that "a higher-level statement than that issued by Hodding Carter on August 31 was needed. He decided to hold a press conference on September 5, the day Congress reconvened."[156]

At the press conference, Secretary Vance made a brief opening statement repeating the gist of the August 31 press release and emphasizing that "we regard [the presence of a Soviet combat unit in Cuba] as a very serious matter affecting our relations with the Soviet Union."[157] Following his statement, he asked for questions. The first two questions put to Vance linked the brigade to SALT II. They were: "Will you ask the Soviets to remove those troops? And how do you think this all will affect the national debate on SALT?"

In reply, the secretary declared that "the discussions with the Soviets will affect the action which we will take." But instead of putting forth the formulation devised the night before that the "status quo is unacceptable," Vance softened it, saying, "I will not be satisfied with the maintenance of the status quo." The secretary carefully phrased his response to the query about SALT, saying that SALT was a matter of "fundamental importance" and that the hearings should proceed. He intimated, however, that the administration would not object if the hearings were held up pending resolution of the brigade issue, saying that "we will be keeping in close touch with the Senate Committee and the members of the Senate as we proceed in our discussions with the Soviets."[158]

Following Vance's (and Stansfield Turner's) closed-door session with the Senate Foreign Relations Committee that afternoon, Senator Church emerged to declare that, while the committee would continue its hearings on the SALT II treaty, there was "no likelihood whatsoever" that the Senate would approve it as long as Soviet combat troops remained in Cuba.[159] It is, of course, hardly likely that he would have reached the conclusion to link the issues of the treaty and the brigade against the testimony of Secretary Vance, for Church's position "all along" had been that "the SALT agreement should stand on its own merits."[160]

Now "a parade of senators made that link . . . with some of them demanding that Carter put SALT II and everything else on the line to get the Soviet troops out of Cuba."[161] Senate Minority Leader Howard H. Baker, of Tennessee, said that unless Carter showed "substantial resolve" and told the Russians that the brigade was "inimical to our interests," the United States "will in effect be letting the Soviet Union thumb their noses at us [*sic*]." Senator Stone reiterated his insistence that SALT II "and everything else the Soviets are interested in should be 'put on the table' to get the Soviet troops out." There should be "total linkage," he said.

Two days later, on September 7, President Carter gave a televised address cautioning the nation that "this is a time for firm diplomacy, not panic and not exaggeraton."[162] Carter put forth the agreed formulation—correcting Vance—that the "status quo is not acceptable," and declared that the core of the issue is "the stationing of Soviet combat troops here in the Western Hemisphere, in a country which acts as a Soviet proxy in military adventures in other areas of the world. . . . We do have the right to insist that the Soviet Union respect our interests and our concerns if the Soviet Union expects us to respect their sensibilities and their concerns. Otherwise, relations between our two countries will inevitably be adversely affected." Brzezinski, in a meeting with out-of-town editors the same day, reemphasized the point that "Castro is a puppet of the Soviet Union and we view him as such."[163]

Soviet Ambassador Dobrynin returned to Washington the next day, and on September 10 he and Secretary Vance held their first meeting. No results of the meeting were announced and no public statements were made, but the following day's news carried the story that the United States had "formally urged the Soviet Union . . . to remove its combat troops from Cuba, warning of the consequences for the SALT treaty, but received no encouragement."[164] Anticipating Vance's request, Moscow had prepared its reply. Within minutes of the conclusion of the meeting between Vance and Dobrynin, the Soviet news agency Tass began distributing a translation of what would be the next day's lead editorial in *Pravda*.[165]

Claiming to present "the true state of affairs of Soviet military personnel in Cuba," the editorial asserted that "for 17 years there has been in Cuba a training center at which Soviet military personnel help Cuban servicemen master the Soviet military equipment used by the Cuban Army."[166] The editorial went on to say that "neither the number nor the function of the said Soviet personnel has changed throughout all these years [and] all contentions about the arrival in Cuba of 'organized Soviet combat units' are totally groundless."

In any case, the editorial continued, longstanding Soviet–Cuban cooperation "comprises an inalienable right of two sovereign states" and Soviet military personnel were in Cuba "at the request of the Cuban government." The editorial's writers saw the purposes of those "fanning up this hullabaloo" to "undermine the prestige of Cuba," which was then hosting the sixth conference of so-called non-aligned nations, and to "prevent the ratification of the SALT II treaty and in any case to complicate the process of its ratification."

Moscow's Rejection and Secretary Vance's Response

If, as Vance says, he sought to obtain agreement on "unilateral Soviet measures that would alter the status quo and resolve our concerns," Moscow's private and public answer was a firm no.[167] After this first meeting Vance immediately altered his approach, seeking a compromise formulation that would not require withdrawal of the brigade. Prior to his second meeting with Dobrynin on the twelfth, Vance was already reportedly "examining the possibility that a Soviet brigade in Cuba may be there to demonstrate large unit tactics and field maneuvers to Cuban soldiers."[168] If so, it was believed, a compromise was possible, for "such a mission would seem to give some credence both to U.S. official statements that the Soviet force is a cohesive unit with combat armaments, and to Soviet counter-statements that it is 'a training center' with no combat role."[169]

Before Moscow could respond, several members of Congress, fueled by intelligence leaks, reacted adversely. First came the "privately voiced concern" of unidentified United States intelligence analysts, who said that "the slow but steady growth of Soviet military systems and facilities in Cuba over the past few years represented a more serious challenge to the United States than the combat brigade."[170] The brigade was "only one part of a general increase," they said. "Everything that the Soviets have done is small in itself, but they are building a 'fortress Cuba' that down the road has strategic significance for us."

Senator Henry Jackson of Washington, a leading opponent of detente with the Soviet Union, immediately picked up the "fortress Cuba" idea, railing against the administration for permitting the Soviet Union to carry out a "major upgrading of the combat capabilities of the Cuban armed forces."[171] This meant, Jackson said from the Senate floor, that "just getting rid of Soviet combat troops was not enough." The administration must seek "to reverse the buildup of Cuban military strength with Soviet armaments that has been going on since the Cuban army began operating in Africa almost four years ago in support of Kremlin policies."

Two days later, when Jackson discovered that Secretary Vance was backing away from demanding withdrawal of the brigade, the senator charged publicly that "the Carter administration was trying to work out with the Soviet Union 'some rationalization' for resolving the problem of a Soviet brigade in Cuba without forcing its removal."[172] That, he said, "would go over like a lead balloon." The rationalization was reported to center around a Soviet affirmation that "its troops had only a training mission, that no combat exercises would be held, and that the tanks and other heavy equipment would be [placed] under Cuban control."[173]

At the same time, Senators Sam Nunn of Georgia and Fritz Hollings of South Carolina led a Senate delegation to see the president. Alarmed by the Soviet weapons buildup, they demanded "as a precondition" for supporting SALT that the president authorize a 5 percent increase in the defense budget, rather than the current plan for a 3 percent increase, which would bring the defense budget for the year to $130.6 billion.[174] Furthermore, the senators insisted that the "political challenge" of the brigade had to be removed before the Senate would ratify SALT. An AP-NBC news poll released the next day reinforced this view, saying that "by a 3-to-1 margin, Americans want the U.S. Senate to delay voting on the SALT II treaty until Soviet combat troops are pulled out of Cuba."[175]

After their third meeting, on September 14, Vance, speaking on background, noted that "instead of talking about any specific proposal . . . [we] have been discussing 'both the nature of the problem and the nature of possible solutions . . . . We have some generalized notions of the direction to which both of us should be pointed, but we also need to know more.'"[176] Stressing that "a Soviet combat capability in Cuba offended this country," he said that "the Soviet Union must respect U.S. concerns and sensitivities" even as the United States was "trying to respect Soviet concerns and sensitivities in changing the troops' status."

Three days later Vance and Dobrynin held a fourth meeting, again with no result. Immediately afterward Dobrynin left for New York to meet Soviet Foreign Minister Gromyko, who was arriving to attend the opening fall session of the United Nations General Assembly. The Carter leadership then met "to refine" the general notions discussed thus far in the talks, and to consider countermeasures "if the troops issue cannot be settled through negotiations."[177] The president was reportedly "irritated" at news accounts suggesting that the issue might be resolved by "redefining the Soviet force as a training rather than an operational unit." White House officials said Carter was "determined to reject any 'cosmetic solution' to the problem."

Within the administration a rare general agreement seemed to have coalesced on what to do about the brigade itself. Both Brzezinski and Vance were willing to treat it as a training unit, even if the president was not yet ready to do so, and they agreed that an acceptable solution was disaggregation of the brigade's headquarters and combat function rather than its formal withdrawal.[178] They disagreed sharply, however, on the brigade's role in the larger context of United States–Soviet relations.

Brzezinski pressed for "a policy decision which would put primary emphasis on the worldwide thrust of Soviet assertiveness and thus deemphasize the Cuban issue itself."[179] This would justify increases in defense spending, stepped-up condemnation of Soviet–Cuban third world activities, and a closer relationship to China. He argued that this would actually enhance chances for SALT ratification because it would demonstrate American action from strength rather than from weakness. Vance, on the other hand, supported by Vice-President Mondale, "increasingly pressed for confining the issue to Cuba itself, arguing that the wider approach would spell the doom of SALT."[180]

President Carter decided on the narrower approach, which, however, did not mean demanding that the Soviet Union remove its combat troops from Cuba. On the contrary. Vance deemed his first four talks (September 10–17) with Dobrynin "exploratory," during which he claimed merely to have asked "specific questions" about the troops, their location, mission, and length of stay.[181] He now declared that the talks had "taken a new turn." High administration officials echoed his view, saying, "We are now in a position to begin discussing with the Soviet Union steps which could be taken to relieve—or to alter—the situation in a way that would be acceptable to the United States."

In fact, what Vance sought was a face-saving way out because, during the first four so-called "exploratory" talks, Moscow had made it clear that withdrawal of the troops was out of the question.[182] Thus, on September 20, during his fifth meeting with Dobrynin, Vance proposed only that "the Soviets remove the brigade headquarters, heavy equipment, and weapons, and discontinue its field exercises."[183] (This had been Brzezinski's recommendation from the start.[184]) But once again the Soviets "refused, insisting that it had been in Cuba unchanged in its function as a training unit for over seventeen years. They said it had nothing to do with the 1962 understanding, and that the United States had no right to request any gesture from Moscow."[185]

President Carter persisted. In a briefing to congressional leaders the same day, he not only gave the impression that troop withdrawal was still a possibility, and his own preference, but suggested that unless the Soviets were accommodating the United States would apply force to resolve the issue. Carter declared, "The United States is prepared to act on its own if negotiations fail to resolve the controversy."[186]

Attempting to increase the pressure on Moscow, the administration encouraged high-ranking Democratic congressional leaders to speak out—an approach that only revealed a serious split in their ranks. Senate Majority Leader Byrd and several other senators declared that unless the brigade issue were quickly and satisfactorily resolved it was "increasingly doubtful that the nuclear arms treaty can be brought to a vote this year or next."[187]

Offering a carrot along with the stick, Byrd said that, assuming prompt resolution of the brigade incident, the Senate calendar could be stretched to accommodate debate on the treaty this year, although "we may have to be here to [*sic*] Christmas." A delay until 1980 would mean entanglement in the presidential election campaign and consignment of the treaty to political limbo. Senator Byrd said that, although it was his personal view that the treaty should not be "held hostage" to the brigade, it was unlikely Senate Foreign Relations Committee Chairman Frank Church "would permit the committee to begin voting on the treaty until the White House had made public the details of any 'resolution' of the troop issue reached with the Soviet Union."[188]

In an unusual step, probably prompted by Secretary Vance, the White House, or both, Senator Byrd went to see Ambassador Dobrynin. He warned him that "SALT would be jeopardized unless the Soviets are in some fashion accommodating."[189] But Dobrynin rejected Byrd's warning on the grounds that "the issue is a phony one." The senator immediately went to the White House for a hastily arranged meeting with President Carter, Secretary Vance, and National Security Adviser Brzezinski late on the evening of September 23 to convey Dobrynin's answer and decide what to do.

Byrd expressed his disagreement with the administration's stance on the brigade as "unacceptable," declaring, "We have to find some way to get off it in order to save SALT."[190] The president, concerned that he was "about to lose SALT," was "very impressed by what Byrd had told him," and now became more inclined to accept what he had publicly vowed not to—a "cosmetic solution." Vance had already received a negative reply the day before when he met with Foreign Minister Gromyko in New York, so Byrd's news was no surprise. Indeed, by this time, Vance, too, was prepared to back away from the quid pro quo he had offered to Moscow and proceed with ratification of the treaty.

The evening of the twenty-third, as Brzezinski noted, was "the turning point" on the brigade issue.[191] The question now was how "to get off it in order to save SALT." In a move faintly reminiscent of President Kennedy's during the Cuban missile crisis of 1962, President Carter decided to accept the suggestion of Vance's political ally

Lloyd Cutler, the president's counsel, to assemble a bipartisan panel of senior statesmen from both political parties to advise "whether we should link further efforts on SALT ratification to a satisfactory resolution of the brigade issue."[192]

Despite the fact that Brzezinski vigorously opposed the idea on the grounds that "Kennedy, Nixon, and Truman had never consulted with outside panels before they made their decisions and that Johnson had convened panels largely in order to browbeat them into support of his own policies," Carter was unmoved.[193] The administration hastily assembled half a dozen senior statesmen under Clark Clifford's chairmanship over the next several hours, and they met the next day, September 24, for "eight or nine hours."[194]

The following day, September 24, hoping to effect an eleventh hour agreement, President Carter sent a hot line message to Brezhnev noting that the issue "could adversely affect Soviet–American relations . . . and that he trusted Mr. Brezhnev would take actions to alleviate American concerns."[195] Gromyko publicly replied to Carter's message that same evening during his speech at the United Nations. He declared that Washington's claim of a Soviet combat presence in Cuba was "totally without foundation in reality and is, indeed, based on falsehoods."[196] Then, leaving no room for compromise, he said, "Our advice on this score is simple. The artificiality of this entire question must be honestly admitted and the matter closed."

Senator Church immediately protested Gromyko's speech and declared that the Senate Foreign Relations Committee "should not send the SALT treaty to the Senate for ratification 'until the current negotiations [over the brigade] have been completed and the results are known.'" Furthermore, he said, "the matter can be closed only when President Carter is able to certify to the Senate his conclusion, based on our independent intelligence assessment, that these Soviet combat forces are no longer present in Cuba."[197]

Senator Jackson called Gromyko's statement "a bald-faced lie," and judged that SALT "has been put on ice for an indefinite period." Senator Howard Baker was "astonished" at Gromyko's remarks; he said that "there is simply no basis for doubting that the Russians have a fully equipped, fully manned brigade in Cuba."[198] And President Carter, speaking to a town meeting in Queens, New York, later that same night, declared that he would be reporting to the nation the next week on the issue. "We want the Soviets to understand that the American people are exceptionally sensitive about Soviet combat troops in this hemisphere, particularly in a country like Cuba, which acts like an arm of the Soviets."[199]

As the president prepared his speech to the nation, Secretary Vance met a second and final time with Gromyko in New York on September 27, again with no result.[200] That day, Brezhnev formally replied to Carter's hot line message of the twenty-fifth, reiterating the Soviet position but declaring that "in the future the function and training status of the unit would not be changed."[201] As Vance put it, "The Soviets deemed this assurance a significant undertaking, not required of them by the Cuba understandings, which we could use to close off the issue."[202]

Checking with Dobrynin, the Soviet ambassador was authorized to confirm that the Soviet Union "would not enlarge the force or give it additional capabilities." Although some of the president's "aides described this as a new 'understanding' with Moscow on the Soviet [ground] forces in Cuba, the President himself [was] more reluctant to go that far."[203] At any rate, the stage was now set for Secretary Vance to attempt to extricate the administration from the embarrassing corner into which he had painted it.

On September 29 and 30, the panel of "wise men," enlarged from seven to sixteen in all and including representatives of the Kennedy, Johnson, and Nixon administrations, again convened.[204] After receiving briefings from Secretary Vance and other administration officials, the panel concluded, but not unanimously, that "the discovery of the brigade was in fact the rediscovery of the brigade that had been there since 1962."[205] Intelligence had made a mistake. The brigade posed no threat to the United States; therefore, "our response should be measured." Finally, the panel concluded that "we should not link SALT and the brigade issue."

Vance described the panel's conclusions as "most helpful," recommending to the president that his speech to the nation be focused on Cuba, treating the brigade issue "as a serious but isolated incident" and "not aimed at the overall U.S.–Soviet relationship."[206] He further recommended that the president announce Brezhnev's "assurances," as well as "a number of measured unilateral actions" the United States would be taking to monitor and counter Cuban activities in the hemisphere.

President Carter's Unsatisfactory Compromise

Vance's recommendations, of course, represented nothing less than a 180-degree reversal from his original plan, which was to ignore Cuba and focus entirely on the United States–Soviet relationship. Indeed, the main political purpose for convening the "wise men" was less to seek their advice on what to do than it was to obtain establishment agreement—both Democrat and Republican—for what the president had already decided to do, which was to make a major shift in the strategy the United States had been pursuing since 1973.

That strategy was the gradual withdrawal of American military power from its "containing" position around the Soviet periphery and the construction of stable, collective security structures to replace it. The central requirement of the strategy was a broad-based accommodation with Moscow, without which no restructuring around the Soviet periphery could hope to succeed. The accommodation itself—detente—would involve a quid pro quo: a major increase in trade and technology transfer in exchange for Soviet geopolitical and strategic weapons restraint.

What was most obvious from the Soviet reaction to the brigade episode was that Moscow had once again, as it had in the early seventies when Henry Kissinger first proffered it, rejected the quid pro quo.[207] Vance's deputy, Newsom, comes close to the mark in his description of the brigade crisis as Vance's "gamble" that "the Soviets were still sufficiently interested in preserving the SALT treaty that they would . . . help an American administration out of a domestic dilemma."[208] The dilemma, of course, was over strategy.

Without Soviet cooperation American strategy could not go forward and would have to be deferred. Indeed, the fundamental decision made by the president, which would become apparent over the next few weeks but well before the Soviet invasion of Afghanistan, was a temporary shift toward "containing" Soviet expansion without returning to "Containment." In making this choice the president satisfied neither of his chief advisers, both of whom continued to press for incompatible strategies, although he incorporated ideas from both.[209]

In response to Brzezinski's urging of containment, to "lay it on the line more explicitly in regard to Soviet adventurism around the world," Carter flatly declared that "he had no intention of going to war over the Soviet brigade in Cuba." Thus rebuked and believing his and his supporters' "political fortunes" were at a low point, Brzezinski revealed that the president's decision "was the only time that I ever thought seriously of the possibility of resigning."[210]

Vance, too, who after all had been responsible for promoting the strategy of accommodation with Moscow, was publicly "put down by the White House" for continuing—against explicit instructions—to express a willingness to "negotiate" with the Soviets.[211] It was reportedly "the closest thing to public humiliation that Vance [had] faced . . . over U.S.–Soviet relations." Vance revealed his dissatisfaction with the decision by indicating that he would not serve a second term if Carter were reelected, speaking of himself as a "lame duck" secretary of state.[212]

President Carter's decision included five essential policy choices. First, even though the president continued to press Congress for ratification of SALT II, which he deemed to be in the national interest (and certainly in his own political interests), bilateral relations with the Soviet Union would cool.[213] Washington would cut off high-technology transfer to the Soviet Union (a pending computer sale was disallowed), but non-strategic trade would continue (the grain sales limit was increased).[214]

Congressional sentiment against the treaty quickly grew to the point that ratification became highly unlikely. The Senate Foreign Relations Committee would conclude its hearings on the treaty on October 10, and almost a month later, November 9, would approve the resolution of ratification by a vote of nine to six. The resolution, incidentally, contained the "understanding" that before the treaty entered into effect, the president would "affirm" that Soviet troops in Cuba "are not engaged in a combat role and will not become a threat to any country . . . in the Western Hemisphere."[215]

The votes for ratification of the treaty were not there. In early December the unofficial head count stood at "53 to 55 votes for the treaty, 27 to 30 against and 15 to 20 undecided."[216] Lacking the necessary two-thirds majority needed in the Senate for ratification, on December 6, Majority Leader Byrd announced that there would be no debate of the treaty "this year," which meant in effect that debate would be put off until after the election.[217]

Second, the United States would move ahead with a stronger long-term defense program. Partly to influence the Senate vote on SALT, but partly also out of necessity, the president gave an unprecedented preview of the administration's five-year defense plan in mid-October; it revealed a commitment to an annual 3 percent real increase in defense expenditures "even if additional funds had to be requested from Congress to reach that level."[218]

This program, which included the commitment to build 200 MX missiles, announced just before the Vienna summit, and to construct the very expensive and complicated mobile "racetrack" basing scheme, announced in mid-September, offered the prospect of sharply improved defense. This would be particularly true if, as also discussed, the ballistic missile defense program was revived.[219] The defense increase would help retard the growing imbalance in the American–Soviet strategic weapons equation and demonstrate United States resolve to confront Soviet expansionism.

Third, the United States would take countermeasures to contain Soviet adventurism. The decision to move forward on NATO's long-term modernization program was already entering its final stages. A more important decision was made to strengthen security ties with China. The day after the president's speech, it was announced that Secretary of Defense Harold Brown would visit China to discuss "security issues of mutual interest" with its military leaders.[220] And in mid-October, the administration announced that it would seek most-favored-nation status for China but not for the Soviet Union.[221] The president approved MFN for China within a week.[222]

Fourth, President Carter decided to adopt a policy of containment toward Cuba, which was the central thrust of his speech to the nation on October 1 regarding the brigade. In his address, the president rejected the advice of the "wise men" and Secretary Vance to back down in the face of Soviet refusal to accommodate and say that the brigade was an intelligence mistake. Instead he stuck to his guns. Although acknowledging that the Soviet Union had had an advisory unit in Cuba since the Cuban missile crisis, he said that United States intelligence had recently obtained "persuasive evidence" that some of these forces had been organized into a "combat unit."[223] This "combat brigade," he said, had been in Cuba "for several years, probably since the mid-1970's, and possibly even longer."

The president hastened to add that while the brigade was not a threat to the United States, it was nevertheless "a serious matter" because it "contributes to tension in the Caribbean and Central American region." The brigade was, he said, "a manifestation of Moscow's dominance of Cuba." Moreover, the "strengthened" Soviet–Cuban military relationship and the presence of Soviet naval forces in Cuban waters "added to the fears of some countries that they may come under Soviet or Cuban pressure."

The Soviet Union, the president went on, "does not admit that the unit in question is a combat unit." However, he said, referring to Brezhnev's hot line message, the "highest levels of the Soviet government" have given us "assurances" that the unit in question is a training center, "that it does nothing more than training, and can do nothing more." The Soviets say that "they will not change its function or status as a training center," and that Soviet personnel in Cuba "are not and will not be a threat to the U.S. or to any other nation." Finally, the Soviets "reaffirm the 1962 understanding and the mutually agreed confirmation of this understanding in 1970."[224]

However, the president continued, the United States would not be satisfied with Soviet assurances alone. We would monitor the status of Soviet forces on the island through increased surveillance, referring to a decision to resume SR-71 overflights.[225] "We will assure that no Soviet unit in Cuba can be used as a combat force to threaten the security of the United States or any other nation in this hemisphere." Moreover, the United States would respond to any requests for assistance "in meeting any such threat from Soviet or Cuban forces."[226]

Carter then quoted President John F. Kennedy's 1963 declaration "that we would not permit any troops from Cuba to move off the island of Cuba in any offensive action against any neighboring countries."[227] Emphasizing United States treaty commitments to the Organization of American States and the Rio Treaty, he announced that he was authorizing the establishment of a Caribbean Joint Task Force Headquarters at Key West, Florida, expanded military maneuvers in the Caribbean, and increased economic assistance to the nations of the region. Finally, he said, the United States would keep its forces at Guantanamo, Cuba.

Finally, in saying that the brigade crisis was "no reason to return to the cold war" and urging the Senate to ratify SALT II, President Carter also indicated that his decisions went well beyond Cuba itself to the fundamental issue of containing the Soviet Union worldwide.

The president revealed that he had authorized the reinforcement of the United States naval presence in the Indian Ocean, the enhancement of the Rapid Deployment Force, and the strengthening of the United States' global intelligence collection capability.

Nevertheless, the president's speech could not paper over the reality that the Soviet Union had rejected Washington's demands to withdraw or alter its ground-force presence on the island of Cuba. Nor could it conceal the fact that the United States would not or could not change the status quo unilaterally. The brigade would remain despite all of the "hullaballoo" raised by Secretary Vance, thus demonstrating American weakness. Moscow's rejection, of course, related to much more than the issue of the brigade. It was a rejection of the quid pro quo which Secretary Vance had offered as the basis of a broad-based accommodation between the two countries. There would be no "restraint" of Soviet behavior, either strategic or geopolitical. And there would be no detente, either.

Still, the failure of Vance's strategy of accommodation was not followed by a return to containment. Instead, President Carter opted for a compromise solution that included elements of both strategies but that was true to neither. In this, the president's choice was strategically illogical, however understandable in terms of domestic politics. Soviet rejection of accommodation made it illogical to continue to advocate ratification of SALT II. Even if, as some insisted, an arms control treaty should be sought on its own merits, SALT II was not that treaty.

If there were to be an arms control treaty negotiated for its own sake, such a treaty would have to be much more equitable and verifiable. In short, it would in fact have to control or reduce the numbers of nuclear weapons, and it certainly would have to address the growing threat to Minuteman, which SALT II did not do. Even the administration acknowledged that the current treaty would permit the Soviet Union to deploy more warheads than the United States and construct three times their destructive potential in megatons.[228]

If Carter's continued espousal of SALT II was illogical, his effort to "contain" Soviet adventurism was ineffective. In fact, it was a charade. Washington's allies showed no inclination to adopt a less friendly posture toward the Soviet Union in the fall of 1979. The reverse was true, as the European allies led by West German Chancellor Helmut Schmidt openly urged negotiations with Moscow to remove the necessity of deploying additional nuclear weapons to Western Europe (see chapter 2). In Central America and Southeast Asia, the two areas where the containment approach was necessary, moreover, the Carter administration failed to do more than posture toward Nicaragua and Iran—two places which would shortly demonstrate the bankruptcy of the president's compromise.

Notes

1. Brzezinski, *Power and Principle*, p. 134. See also Vance, *Hard Choices*, pp. 451–52.
2. See chapter 1 for additional discussion of the concept of human rights.
3. Rex A. Hudson, *Castro's America Department* (Washington, DC: Cuban American National Foundation, 1988).
4. Vance, *Hard Choices*, p. 141.
5. Carter, *Keeping Faith*, p. 156.
6. For excellent accounts of the treaty negotiations, see Carter, *Keeping Faith*, pp. 152–85, and Vance, *Hard Choices*, pp. 140–57.
7. Cuban cooperation with Panama was an open secret by the fall of 1977. See the testimony of Lt. Gen. Gordon Sumner, *Panama Gunrunning*, Hearings of the House Subcommittee on the Panama Canal, Committee on Merchant Marine and Fisheries, June 6,7 and July 10, 1979 (Washington, DC: GPO, 1980), pp. 122–26. General Sumner was chairman of the Inter-American Defense Board during 1975–1978. He testified that Omar Torrijos had told him personally in November 1977 of Panama's cooperation with Havana to overthrow Somoza.
8. Department of State, *Cuba's Renewed Support for Violence in Latin America*, Special Report No. 90, December 14, 1981, p. 8. (Hereafter referred to as "Cuba's Renewed Support for Violence in Latin America.")
9. Robert A. Pastor, *Condemned to Repetition, the United States and Nicaragua* (Princeton: Princeton University Press, 1987), p. 49.
10. John A. Booth, *The End and the Beginning, the Nicaraguan Revolution* (Boulder, CO: Westview Press, 1985), pp. 143–44.
11. Ibid., p. 52.
12. Anthony Lake, *Somoza Falling, the Nicaraguan Dilemma: a Portrait of Washington at Work* (Boston: Houghton Mifflin, 1989), pp. 22–23.
13. See Anastasio Somoza, *Nicaragua Betrayed* (Boston: Western Islands, 1980).
14. Pastor, *Condemned to Repetition*, p. 57.
15. Ibid., p. 59, and Somoza, *Nicaragua Betrayed*, pp. 109–22.
16. See Pastor, *Condemned to Repetition*, p. 96, for a chart of the FAO membership.
17. Somoza, *Nicaragua Betrayed*, pp. 151f.
18. For the manifesto, see ibid., pp. 157–62.
19. Pastor, *Condemned to Repetition*, p. 77.
20. Carter, *Keeping Faith*, p. 178.
21. "Cuba's Renewed Support for Violence in Latin America," pp. 5–6, and "Cuban Support for Central American Guerrilla Groups," Cen-

tral Intelligence Agency Memorandum, May 2, 1979, in Robert S. Leiken and Barry Rubin, eds., *The Central American Crisis Reader* (New York: Summit Books, 1987), p. 669. (Hereafter referred to as Cuban Support for Central American Guerrilla Groups, Central Intelligence Agency Memorandum, May 2, 1979.)

22. It would not be until the end of June 1979 that the administration would publicly identify Cuban involvement in the Nicaraguan revolution. See Richard Burt, "U.S. Asserts Cubans Are Supplying and Training Rebels in Nicaragua," *New York Times*, June 23, 1979, p. 1, and Henry L. Trewhitt, "U.S. Warns Cuba on Role in Nicaragua," *Baltimore Sun*, June 27, 1979, p. 4.
23. Cf. Pastor, *Condemned to Repetition*, p. 77, who says it was "Somoza's decision to strike at the moderate opposition [that] was one of the major factors motivating the United States to review its previous policy of strict noninterference in Nicaragua's internal affairs."
24. See "Cuba's Renewed Support for Violence in Latin America," p. 6. Pastor, *Condemned to Repetition*, p. 85, skirts the issue of Costa Rican support for the September offensive by saying that before September 12, 1978, the FSLN "had used Costa Rica, but without the permission of the government."
25. Karen DeYoung, "U.S. Vetoed Panama Role in Nicaragua," *Washington Post*, December 31, 1978, p. 1.
26. Booth, *The End and the Beginning*, pp. 130–31. See also "Nicaraguan Reserves Called Up," *Baltimore Sun*, September 15, 1978, p. 1.
27. Pastor, *Condemned to Repetition*, pp. 82–83.
28. Booth, *The End and the Beginning*, p. 165.
29. As quoted in Pastor, *Condemned to Repetition*, p. 85.
30. Ibid., p. 86.
31. Ibid., p. 93.
32. Ibid., p. 106.
33. Ibid., pp. 109–110.
34. "Cuba's Renewed Support for Violence in Latin America," p. 6.
35. Asemblea Legislativa, San Jose, Costa Rica, Comision de Asuntos Especialas, *Informe sobre el trafico de armas, primera parte, epe 8768*, May 14, 1981, pp. 16–18. (Hereafter referred to as Costa Rica Commission Report.) I am indebted to Mssrs. Arthur Houston and Theodore Lapin, who, respectively, obtained and translated this report for me. For translated excerpts, see *Latin America Report*, No. 78316, Joint Publication Research Service, June 17, 1981, pp. 19–23. (Hereafter referred to as Latin America Report.) See also Pastor, *Condemned to Repetition*, p. 342 n. 13, and pp. 125–26.
36. "Cuban Support for Central American Guerrilla Groups," Central Intelligence Agency Memorandum, May 2, 1979, pp. 668–71.

37. Pastor, *Condemned to Repetition*, pp. 112–13.
38. Ibid., p. 114.
39. Gilbert A. Lewthwaite, "U.S. Drops Bid to Mediate in Nicaraguan Strife," *Baltimore Sun*, February 9, 1979, p. 1.
40. Alan Riding, "Nicaragua Crumbles as Rebels Prepare," *New York Times*, March 21, 1979, p. 2.
41. Pastor, *Condemned to Repetition*, p. 122.
42. "Cuban Support for Central American Guerrilla Groups," Central Intelligence Agency Memorandum, May 2, 1979.
43. Ibid.
44. Pastor, *Condemned to Repetition*, p. 127.
45. Costa Rica Commission Report, pp. 7–8, describes the establishment of a Cuban air company, Exaco, which had been set up specifically to transport weapons and supplies to the FSLN. The commission only identified the planes used in terms of their cargo capacity, of 30,000 to 35,000 pounds. The commission declared, however, that it had "grounds to believe that the United States Government as well as other governments of America had full knowledge of this traffic from Cuba, its destination and purpose." Aircraft cargo capacity indicated the probable use of Boeing 707 aircraft, and the claim that Washington had "full knowledge" suggested that Exaco had leased the planes from an American or Latin American leasing company. The Cuban military had no cargo planes with this capacity. The largest military transports which Cuba had in 1979 were ten IL-14s and twenty An-26s, each with a maximum cargo capacity of roughly 10,000 pounds. Cuba's civil airline, Cubana, included four of one type plane with this large a cargo capacity—the IL-62. The IL-62 could carry 168 passengers and had a maximum cargo capacity of 50,000 pounds. Thus, the possibilities are that Castro was employing a front company (Exaco) with leased aircraft or using Il-62s from Cubana Airlines. A third possibility is that the Soviet Union was directly but discreetly involved in the air transport. Several Soviet aircraft fit this description, such as the An-124, with a 44,000-pound payload. The commission report, p. 12, also identified delivery, in December 1978, of single planeloads of 707s carrying weapons from West Germany and Portugal. Washington officially ignored all of it. Pastor, incidentally, severely distorts this report by saying that the total amount of weapons carried in all of the Cuban shipments was 31,000 pounds. In fact that was the amount of a single planeload. See Pastor, *Condemned to Repetition*, pp. 127–28.
46. Richard Burt, "U.S. Is Studying Overall Buildup of Cuban Forces," *New York Times*, September 11, 1979, p. 1, and U.S. Congress, House Committee on Foreign Affairs, Subcommittee on Inter-American

Affairs, *Impact of Cuban–Soviet Ties in the Western Hemisphere, Spring 1979* (Washington, DC: GPO, April 25–26, 1979), p. 6. This highly censored testimony of Defense Intelligence Agency officers nevertheless indicates close monitoring of Cuban involvement in Nicaragua.

47. "Cuba's Renewed Support for Violence in Latin America," p. 6.
48. See Timothy Ashby, *The Bear in the Back Yard* (Lexington, MA: Lexington Books, 1987), pp. 81–84, and William F. Buckley, Jr., "Red Tide in the Caribbean," *Washington Star*, October 28, 1979, p. D3. There was also concern about growing Cuban influence in Jamaica, Guyana, Dominica, and St. Lucia.
49. Thus, on Grenada, for example, see Henry L. Trewhitt, "U.S. Cautions Grenada on Cuban Military Ties," *Washington Post*, April 17, 1979, p. 4, and Karen DeYoung, "U.S. vs. China on Caribbean Isle of Grenada," *Washington Post*, April 27, 1979, p. 27. The word "China" in the title is a misprint. It should have read "Cuba," because the article is about Cuban involvement. China is not mentioned.
50. Vance, *Hard Choices*, pp. 132–33 and 358–64. On the MiG-23s see Charles W. Corddry, "U.S. Silence on MiG's in Cuba Suggests Dilemma," *Baltimore Sun*, November 22, 1979, p. 5.
51. Karen De Young, "U.S. Vetoed Panama Role in Nicaragua," *Washington Post*, December 31, 1978, p. 1.
52. Pastor, *Condemned to Repetition*, p. 128. See also House Committee on Foreign Affairs, Subcommittee on Inter-American Affairs, *Impact of Cuban–Soviet Ties in the Western Hemisphere, Spring 1979.*
53. Ibid., p. 121.
54. Graham Hovey, "Vance Proposes Replacement of Somoza Rule in Nicaragua; Asks for an O.A.S. Peace Force," *New York Times*, June 22, 1979, p. 1. As the Somoza regime was crumbling Secretary Vance did note for the first time Cuban involvement but did not even mention the Sandinistas by name, referring only to "guerrillas."
55. Ibid., p. 135. A key component of the Policy Review Committee meeting of June 11 was to attempt to stop the flow of arms to both sides.
56. Pastor, *Condemned to Repetition*, p. 131.
57. Ibid.
58. Alan Riding, "Mexico Presses U.S. to End Somoza Aid," *New York Times*, May 22, 1979, p. 13.
59. Pastor, *Condemned to Repetition*, p. 131.
60. Alan Riding, "Nicaraguan Rebels Begin Major Drive," *New York Times*, June 2, 1979, p. 1.
61. Tom Fenton, "Nicaragua Army Said to Plan a Major Push to Recapture City," *Philadelphia Inquirer*, April 12, 1979, p. 20, and Booth, *The End and the Beginning*, p. 173.

62. Karen DeYoung, "Nicaragua Says 300 Irregulars Attack from Costa Rica," *Washington Post*, May 30, 1979, p. 28.
63. Riding, "Nicaraguan Rebels Begin Major Drive," p. 1.
64. Karen DeYoung, "Guerrilla Forces Hold Key Cities in Nicaraguan War," *Washington Post*, June 8, 1979, p. 1; Jeremiah O'Leary, "U.S. Sees Somoza Finished, Hopes for Exit to End Crisis," *Washington Star*, June 9, 1979, p. 1; and Alan Riding, "Somoza Says He Will Crush the Revolt in Two Weeks," *New York Times*, June 12, 1979, p. 4.
65. Pastor, *Condemned to Repetition*, p. 135.
66. Karen DeYoung, "61 from U.S. Pulled Out of Managua," *Washington Post*, June 13, 1979, p. 1.
67. Pastor, *Condemned to Repetition*, p. 135.
68. Ibid., p. 137.
69. Ibid.
70. Garthoff, *Detente and Confrontation*, pp. 730–31.
71. John Goshko, "Dobrynin, U.S. Officials Meet Amid Signs of Easing Trade," *Washington Post*, April 28, 1979, p. 10.
72. Brzezinski, *Power and Principle*, p. 341.
73. Vance, *Hard Choices*, p. 134.
74. Ibid. See also Talbott, *Endgame*, pp. 270ff, who notes several additional issues.
75. Brzezinski, *Power and Principle*, pp. 333–35.
76. David Binder, "Soviet Brigade: How the U.S. Traced It," *New York Times*, September 13, 1979, p. 16, notes that the first reference in radio intercept data to a brigade occurred in 1975. See also, Richard Burt, "U.S. Is Studying Overall Buildup of Cuban Forces," *New York Times*, September 11, 1979, p. 1.
77. See Charles W. Corddry, "Soviet Union Building Sub Base in Cuba," *Baltimore Sun*, March 30, 1979, p. 4, and John M. Goshko, "Soviet Construction of Pier at Cuban Base Is Reported," *Washington Post*, October 31, 1979, p. 6.
78. David D. Newsom, *The Soviet Brigade in Cuba, a Study in Political Diplomacy*, (Bloomington: Indiana University Press, 1987), p. 69, and "Drama in Cuba—Chances for SALT Now," *U.S. News & World Report*, September 24, 1979, p. 27.
79. Burt, "U.S. Is Studying Overall Buildup," p. 1, and *The Military Balance, 1980–1981* (London: International Institute of Strategic Studies, 1980), p. 142.
80. Curiously, in their memoirs neither the president, Vance, nor Brzezinski discusses the Nicaraguan revolution, but Newsom, under secretary of state for political affairs in the Carter administration, does note the relationship.

81. "Cuban Support for Central American Guerrilla Groups," CIA Memorandum, May 2, 1979, pp. 668–73.
82. For their views on the summit, see Brzezinski, *Power and Principle*, pp. 340–44, and Vance, *Hard Choices*, pp. 138–39. Both men note the issue of the Soviet use of Cuban proxy forces, but Brzezinski refers to the "Indian Ocean area" and Vance to Africa. Neither mentions Central America or Nicaragua, where Cuba was then most active.
83. For example, Vance, *Hard Choices*, p. 133, saw the MiG-23 issue as simply part of a normal, long-term Soviet effort to modernize Cuba's armed forces over many years.
84. Gloria Duffy, "Crisis Mangling and the Cuban Brigade," *International Security* (Summer 1983), p. 72.
85. Vance, *Hard Choices*, p. 358.
86. Don Oberdorfer, "Chapter 1: 'Brigada': Unwelcome Sight in Cuba," *Washington Post*, September 9, 1979, p. 1.
87. Brzezinski, *Power and Principle*, p. 340.
88. Carter, *Keeping Faith*, p. 249.
89. That this was a serious objection and not just an off-the-cuff remark emerged in the meeting between Defense Minister Dmitriy Ustinov, Secretary of Defense Harold Brown, and Joint Chiefs Chairman David Jones, in which Ustinov termed the mobile basing mode "unacceptable." See "But We Did Get to Know Each Other Better," the record of a conversation at the June 17 Vienna summit, *Wall Street Journal*, September 11, 1979, p. 22.
90. Carter, *Keeping Faith*, p. 250. Vance, *Hard Choices*, p. 139, refers to "some confusion over the acting out of the scenario Dobrynin and we had prearranged." Brzezinski, *Power and Principle*, p. 341, notes that "Brezhnev simply did not act according to script and would not give us the expected assurances on Backfire."
91. Carter, *Keeping Faith*, p. 250.
92. Ibid., pp. 250–51.
93. For a list of the president's proposals, see ibid., p. 253.
94. Ibid., p. 255.
95. Ibid., p. 247.
96. Ibid., p. 258.
97. Ibid., p. 259.
98. Garthoff, *Detente and Confrontation*, p. 733.
99. Carter, *Keeping Faith*, pp. 254–56.
100. Ibid., p. 254.
101. Ibid., p. 256. Brezhnev's answer is clearly apropos a question about a Soviet buildup, not Cuban "military activities."
102. Kissinger, *White House Years*, p. 650. Cf. Newsom, *Soviet Brigade in Cuba*, p. 27, who claims quite erroneously that "the question of what

constituted a [naval] 'base' was never clarified. The question of whether nuclear-powered submarines, submarines with nuclear missiles, or both, violated the understanding was not clear."

103. Oberdorfer, "Chapter 1: 'Brigada,'" p. 1.
104. Ibid.
105. Letter from President Carter to Senator Stone, January 27, 1978, in Newsom, *Soviet Brigade in Cuba*, appendix G, pp. 94–95.
106. Ibid.
107. Ibid., p. 20.
108. Duffy, "Crisis Mangling and the Cuban Brigade," p. 73.
109. Ibid., p. 74.
110. Ibid.
111. "How Many Russians in Cuba?" *Washington Star*, July 18, 1979, p. 4.
112. Don Oberdorfer, "Cuban Crisis Mishandled, Insiders and Outsiders Agree," *Washington Post*, October 16, 1979, p. 14.
113. John Maclean, "Cuba–Soviet 'Military Collaboration' Promised by Castro's Envoy to U.S.," *Chicago Tribune*, July 21, 1979, p. 5.
114. Graham Hovey, "U.S. Fears Unrest in Central America," *New York Times*, July 22, 1979, p. 13.
115. Vance, *Hard Choices*, p. 359.
116. Brzezinski, *Power and Principle*, p. 346.
117. Vance, *Hard Choices*, p. 359.
118. Letter from Secretary Vance to Senator Stone, July 27, 1979, in Newsom, *Soviet Brigade in Cuba*, appendix H, p. 96.
119. Ibid.
120. Oberdorfer, "Chapter 1: 'Brigada,'" p. 1.
121. Oberdorfer, "Cuban Crisis Mishandled," p. 14.
122. Vance, *Hard Choices*, p. 359.
123. Walter Pincus and George C. Wilson, "Chapter 3: Dilemma: Saving SALT II," *Washington Post*, September 9, 1979, p. 19, quote a DIA intelligence officer: "Vance was lying and we knew he was lying when he wrote Stone that there was only a Soviet command structure for a brigade that had not been fleshed out with troops."
124. Binder, "The Soviet Brigade: How the U.S. Traced It," p. 16.
125. Brzezinski, *Power and Principle*, p. 347.
126. Ibid.
127. Binder, "The Soviet Brigade: How the U.S. Traced It," p. 16.
128. Oberdorfer, "Cuban Crisis Mishandled," p. 14.
129. Martin Schram, "Chapter 2: Response: Avoiding a Crisis Tone," *Washington Post*, September 9, 1979, p. 18.
130. Oberdorfer, "Cuban Crisis Mishandled," p. 14.
131. Duffy, "Crisis Mangling and the Cuban Brigade," p. 80, suggests that Vance was led to believe that the Soviets would be accommodating

"based partly on early indications from a Soviet source he trusted that the U.S.S.R. might be flexible on this point."

132. Newsom, *Soviet Brigade in Cuba*, p. 29.
133. Vance, *Hard Choices*, pp. 360–61. Newsom, *Soviet Brigade in Cuba*, p. 32, says it was worked out on the twenty-ninth.
134. Newsom, *Soviet Brigade in Cuba*, pp. 32–33.
135. Brzezinski, *Power and Principle*, p. 347, termed the meeting a "sub-SCC committee."
136. Brzezinski, *Power and Principle*, p. 347.
137. Ibid.
138. Ibid., "Vance did not call."
139. Newsom, *Soviet Brigade in Cuba*, p. 22. Oberdorfer, "Cuban Crisis Mishandled," says that the *Aviation Week* call came on August 30. In fact, however, neither *Aviation Week* nor Copley News Service printed anything at all. In retrospect, it is not clear that a leak at this time would have been received with any less indifference than it was in July.
140. Newsom, *Soviet Brigade in Cuba*, p. 33.
141. Vance, *Hard Choices*, p. 361, and Brzezinski, *Power and Principle*, p. 347.
142. Newsom, *Soviet Brigade in Cuba*, p. 34.
143. Vance, *Hard Choices*, p. 361.
144. Ibid.
145. Brzezinski, *Power and Principle*, p. 347.
146. "2,300-Man Soviet Unit Now in Cuba," *Washington Post*, August 31, 1979, p. 1.
147. Ibid.
148. Duffy, "Crisis Mangling and the Cuban Brigade," p. 78.
149. Bernard Gwertzman, "U.S. Reports Soviet Has Combat Troops Stationed in Cuba," *New York Times*, September 1, 1979, p. 1.
150. Ibid.
151. Brzezinski, *Power and Principle*, p. 348.
152. Oberdorfer, "Cuban Crisis Mishandled," p. 14.
153. As Brzezinski, *Power and Principle*, p. 348, put it, "Heretofore (and also thereafter) all crises were handled by the SCC, under my chairmanship. However, it was evident that State wished to assert itself on this subject."
154. Vance, *Hard Choices*, pp. 360–61.
155. Ibid, p. 362.
156. Newsom, *Soviet Brigade in Cuba*, p. 38.
157. For the press conference transcript, see Newsom, *Soviet Brigade in Cuba*, appendix B, pp. 67–76.
158. Ibid., p. 68. Vance said, "My reply sounded stronger than I intended, and was widely interpreted to imply that we would demand removal

of the brigade. What I meant was that changes in the armament, structure, and function of the brigade could allay our concerns." See also Don Oberdorfer, "Vance Says Soviet Combat Unit Has Been in Cuba for Years," *Washington Post*, September 6, 1979, p. 1. Duffy, "Crisis Mangling and the Cuban Brigade," p. 79, whose analysis is sympathetic to Vance, comes to the same conclusion on the linkage.

159. George C. Wilson, "Church Says SALT Doomed in Senate If Soviet Combat Unit Stays in Cuba," *Washington Post*, September 6, 1979, p. 1, and Vernon J. Guidry, "Russia Must Quit Cuba for Pact, Church Says," *Washington Star*, September 6, 1979, p. 1.
160. Ibid.
161. Ibid.
162. "'We Are Confident of Our Ability to Defend' the Nation," *Washington Post*, September 8, 1979, p. 8.
163. "Remarks by Zbigniew Brzezinski, National Security Adviser," *Washington Post*, September 8, 1979, p. 8.
164. Henry L. Trewhitt, "U.S. Urges Soviet Units to Quit Cuba," *Baltimore Sun*, September 11, 1979, p. 1.
165. Kevin Klose and Don Oberdorfer, "Kremlin Defends Troops in Cuba as Training Unit," *Washington Post*, September 11, 1979, p. 1.
166. "Who Needs This and Why," *Baltimore Sun*, September 12, 1979, p. 23.
167. Vance, *Hard Choices*, p. 362.
168. Don Oberdorfer, "U.S. Thinks Soviet Brigade Could Be in Cuba for Training," *Washington Post*, September 13, 1979, p. 1.
169. Ibid.
170. Don Oberdorfer and Walter Pincus, "Soviet Troop Talks Continue Amid a Swirl of Controversy," *Washington Post*, September 12, 1979, p. 2.
171. Henry S. Bradsher and Lance Gay, "U.S., Russians Talk Again on Troops in Cuba," *Washington Star*, September 12, 1979, p. 1.
172. Bernard Gwertzman, "Jackson Says U.S. Seeks Deal with Soviet on Cuba," *New York Times*, September 14, 1979, p. 11.
173. Ibid.
174. Henry Trewhitt, "Senators Link SALT Votes to Military Spending," *Baltimore Sun*, September 14, 1979, p. 1.
175. "Poll Shows Link between SALT Vote, Troops in Cuba," *Washington Star*, September 15, 1979, p. 4.
176. Henry S. Bradsher, "U.S. Cautious About Hope for Cuba Troop Solution," *Washington Star*, September 15, 1979, p. 1.
177. Don Oberdorfer, "Carter Convenes Aides on Cuba Issue," *Washington Post*, September 18, 1979, p. 10.
178. Brzezinski, *Power and Principle*, pp. 348–49, and Vance, *Hard Choices*, p. 363.

179. Brzezinski, *Power and Principle*, pp. 349–50.
180. Ibid.
181. Bernard Gwertzman, "Vance Offers Ideas to Resolve Soviet Brigade Issue," *New York Times*, September 21, 1979, p. 3.
182. There is some suggestion that the Soviet Union may have proposed a trade, withdrawal of American forces from either Turkey or Guantanamo, for withdrawal of Soviet forces from Cuba, but the American side determined that Turkey and Guantanamo were "not negotiable." See Robert Toth, "Soviet Brigade in Cuba: No Easy Solution," *Los Angeles Times*, September 19, 1979, p. 8.
183. Ibid., Vance, *Hard Choices*, p. 363, and Newsom, *Soviet Brigade in Cuba*, p. 45.
184. Brzezinski, *Power and Principle*, p. 348.
185. Vance, *Hard Choices*, p. 363.
186. Phil Gailey, "Carter Says He Will 'Act' If Talks Fail," *Washington Star*, September 21, 1979, p. 3.
187. Charles Mohr, "Byrd Says Arms Pact Could Still Be Acted On in '79," *New York Times*, September 23, 1979, p. 5.
188. Ibid.
189. Brzezinski, *Power and Principle*, p. 350.
190. Ibid.
191. Ibid.
192. Vance, *Hard Choices*, p. 363. claims that the sugggestion came from both Cutler and Brzezinski's man, Hedley Donovan, but Brzezinski, *Power and Principle*, p. 350, makes plain that it was Cutler alone who "persuaded the president."
193. Brzezinski, *Power and Principle*, p. 350.
194. "Carter Asks New View of Cuba Issue," *Baltimore Sun*, September 27, 1979, p. 1. This press report identified Clark Clifford as head of a seven-member panel.
195. Hedrick Smith, "Carter Feels Certain Soviet Will Alter Brigade in Cuba," *New York Times*, October 3, 1979, p. 11.
196. Henry Trewhitt, "Soviet Calls Cuban Base 'Falsehood,'" *Baltimore Sun*, September 26, 1979, p. 1.
197. Ibid.
198. Ibid.
199. Jeremiah O'Leary and Henry S, Bradsher, "Carter to Report to Nation on Soviet Troops in Cuba," *Washington Star*, September 26, 1979, p. 1.
200. Bernard Gwertzman, "Vance and Gromyko End Talk on Troops; Impasse Is Indicated," *New York Times*, September 28, 1979, p. 1.
201. Hedrick Smith, "Carter Feels Certain Soviet Will Alter Brigade in Cuba," p. 11.

202. Vance, *Hard Choices*, p. 363.
203. Smith, "Carter Feels Certain," p. 11.
204. Ibid., and Vance, *Hard Choices*, p. 363. The sixteen senior statesmen were: George Ball, McGeorge Bundy, Clark Clifford, Roswell Gilpatric, Averell Harriman, Nicholas Katzenbach, Henry Kissinger, Sol Linowitz, John McCloy, John McCone, David Packard, William Rogers, Dean Rusk, James Schlesinger, Brent Scowcroft, and William Scranton.
205. Vance, *Hard Choices*, pp. 363–64.
206. Ibid., p. 364.
207. See the author's *Nixon–Kissinger Years, Reshaping America's Foreign Policy*.
208. Newsom, *Soviet Brigade in Cuba*, pp. 57–58.
209. Richard Burt, "Carter, Given Conflicting Advice, Chose a Middle Course on Cuba," *New York Times*, October 3, 1979, p. 14.
210. Brzezinski, *Power and Principle*, p. 351.
211. James McCartney, "Vance Is Rebuffed by White House," *Philadelphia Inquirer*, October 25, 1979, p. 6.
212. Karen Elliott House, "Mr. Zbig: Brzezinski Wins Some Loses Some but Always Brings Zest to His Job," *Wall Street Journal*, October 3, 1979, p. 1.
213. Henry S. Bradsher, "U.S.–Soviet Relations Back in Holding Pattern," *Washington Star*, October 3, 1979, p. 10.
214. Seth S. King, "U.S. Increases Limit on Grain for Soviet to Record Amount, but It Bars a Computer Deal," *New York Times*, October 4, 1979, p. 1.
215. Vernon A. Guidry, "SALT, Cuban Brigade 'Link' Approved by Senate Panel," *Washington Star*, November 3, 1979, p. 7.
216. Robert G. Kaiser, "Byrd Says SALT Debate Dead in Senate for 1979," *Washington Post*, December 7, 1979, p. 1.
217. Ibid.
218. Vance, *Hard Choices*, p. 365.
219. George C. Wilson, "Army Now Sees ABM as Blockbusters' Guard," *Washington Post*, October 15, 1979, p. 6.
220. "Brown Planning Visit to China," *Washington Star*, October 2, 1979, p. 4.
221. Henry S. Bradsher, "Carter to Seek Trade Benefits for China Ahead of Soviet Union," *Washington Star*, October 16, 1979, p. 2.
222. Don Oberdorfer, "Trade Benefits for China Are Approved by Carter," *Washington Post*, October 24, 1979, p. 2.
223. "Text of President's Speech," *New York Times*, October 2, 1979, p. 18.
224. Ibid.

225. Charles W. Corddry, "Spy Jet Sent over Cuba, U.S. Reports," *Baltimore Sun*, October 2, 1979, p. 2.
226. "Text of President's Speech," *New York Times*, October 2, 1979, p. 18.
227. Ibid. It is curious that with all the attention devoted to the 1962 "understandings" as a result of the brigade crisis, the most important position statement was never mentioned. This was, of course, the statement issued by President Kennedy on November 20, 1962, in which he declared that "if the Western Hemisphere is to continue to be protected against offensive weapons, this Government has no choice but to pursue its own means of checking on military activities in Cuba. The importance of our continued vigilance is underlined by our identification in recent days of a number of Soviet ground combat units in Cuba, although we are informed that these and other Soviet units were associated with the protection of offensive weapons systems and will also be withdrawn in due course. . . . If all offensive weapons are removed from Cuba and kept out of the Hemisphere in the future . . . and if Cuba is not used for the export of aggressive Communist purposes, there will be peace in the Caribbean." See Robert F. Kennedy, *Thirteen Days, a Memoir of the Cuban Missile Crisis* (New York: W.W. Norton & Co., 1969), pp. 217–18.
228. Senator Jake Garn, "SALT II 'Loopholes,'" *National Defense*, September–October, 1979, p. 38.

CHAPTER 9

No End of Crises: A Strategy in Disarray

The second half of 1979 saw the severe disruption of the American domestic economic base and the complete collapse of the strategy of the Carter administration to construct a new global order. President Carter's attempts to contain the Soviets without returning to containment and to rein in the allies without reinforcing the alliance, met with little success on either count.

The summer of 1979 was a period of crisis for the United States and the Western alliance as oil prices skyrocketed. These developments provided the context for a major change in American international economic policy whose consequences would be felt for years to come as the United States, West Germany, and Japan continued to struggle for global market share and access. The immediate impact of these policies, however, was on Jimmy Carter himself. By the time of the 1980 election, the American economy had careened out of control as inflation soared, interest rates surged to 20 percent, and petroleum prices climbed to $32 per barrel.

Paralleling these developments, in the context of a major crisis between the United States and Iran precipitated by the seizure of American hostages and the deterioration of the communist regime in Afghanistan, the United States and the Soviet Union gradually edged toward confrontation until the Soviet Union invaded Afghanistan in late December 1979. The Soviet invasion brought United States–Soviet relations to an impasse, shelved all prospects for arms control, and constituted a final repudiation of the detente strategy which the president and his secretary of state had been pursuing since taking office.

Replaying the Energy Card: The 1974 Oil Crisis Redux

By the time that the American–German exchange-rate crisis had been resolved in the fall of 1978 (see chapter 2), Washington was already positioned to mount another challenge to its allies—this time over energy. Indeed, the oil crisis of 1979 would be a replay of the oil crisis of 1974—and for the same reasons. Germany and Japan were once again surging ahead economically in relation to the United States, and adjustments had to be made to slow their advance and improve the United States' position. The principal means employed to make the adjustment was to raise still higher the price of oil, but the evidence suggests that the scheme got out of control, only partially accomplished the desired outcome, and actually backfired on the president.

The United States was rapidly running out of time and opportunity to attempt to re-equilibrate its position vis-à-vis Germany and Japan. The resolution of the exchange-rate crisis the previous fall meant that henceforth there would be greater exchange-rate stability. Put another way, opportunities for exchange-rate manipulation would be limited. Moreover, when the European Monetary System began to function, the United States would no longer be able to manipulate other European currencies against the deutschemark as occurred in 1978.

Time was also running out on the energy front. Though they adopted an official thesis of an impending energy crisis, the administration's leaders certainly knew that an energy shortage was not imminent. Indeed, the evidence suggested that the reverse was true. Oil analyst M.A. Adelman of MIT, for example, said in 1977 in the context of bringing oil prices down that "the next three years are our biggest last opportunity. The greater the potential surplus the more vulnerable they [OPEC] are."[1]

World crude oil production was high and rising. In 1973 output was 58.3 million b/d. Total output would be 62.5 million b/d in 1977 and 63.4 million b/d in 1978, and would peak at 65.7 million b/d in the crisis year of 1979. Thereafter production declined to 63 million b/d in 1980, 59.5 million b/d in 1981, and 56.8 million b/d in 1982.[2]

The decrease in output was not a function of shortage, but of cutbacks to maintain price in the face of increased conservation and more efficient energy use.

It was no secret that the United States had abundant coal supplies. The United States contained the largest deposits, one-third of known global supplies, 437 billion tons.[3] Environmental concerns inhibited wider use of coal, as did the availability of cheaper oil and gas. But the big story was natural gas. The administration's official position was that the nation was "running out of natural gas," which should be "disregarded as an energy resource."[4] But discovery after discovery of huge, virtually unlimited natural gas deposits was contradicting the administration's gloomy assessment.

For example, an Energy Research and Development Agency (ERDA) study completed in early April 1977, a few days before President Carter delivered his first major energy speech, concluded that natural gas reserves in the United States alone could be expected to exceed the nation's total energy needs well into the twenty-first century. The report was suppressed and the official responsible for writing it fired. Later in 1977, gas discoveries in the Tuscaloosa Trend in Louisiana and Texas were estimated by the U.S. Geological Survey to contain "as much as 50,000 trillion cubic feet (TCF)."[5] Annual national consumption of natural gas was only 20 TCF.

The director of the U.S. Geological Survey, Dr. Vincent McKelvey, declared publicly following these discoveries that America's natural gas reserves were so large that they were "about ten times the energy value of all [previously discovered] oil, gas and coal reserves in the United States combined."[6] It was his view that the geopressured zones in Louisiana and Texas alone held the equivalent in gas of "about 4 trillion barrels of oil, roughly twice the conventional estimate of ultimate *world* petroleum resources."[7] Dr. McKelvey was quickly removed as director of USGS.

There was, in short, no energy crisis. Left to run its natural course, the impending energy glut would mean low-cost energy for the United States and its allies. But a low-cost energy regime would make it difficult, if not impossible, to improve the nation's competitive position vis-à-vis Germany and Japan, which had already put in place energy conservation policies after the 1974 crisis and were more efficient users of energy than was the United States. The failure to act before the glut became apparent would mean the loss of any opportunity to adopt conservation and efficiency measures in energy in the United States and the perpetuation of competitive advantages Washington's allies were already demonstrating in the world marketplace.

Official assertions of an impending energy shortage served an important purpose, however. They offered the justification the Carter administration needed to make the changes required to improve the nation's competitive position. The coming crisis would justify reorganizing the government to deal with energy issues more efficiently and allow legislation to be put into place to promote conservation and more efficient energy use. The most important problem was how to change consumer behavior in energy production, distribution, and consumption—the key to successful conservation. Only in the context of a crisis, the administration believed, could energy usage patterns be changed.

But there was the rub. Official warnings of an impending energy crisis were viewed by the public as lacking in credibility. President Carter himself set an ambivalent tone in his address to the nation shortly after taking office. On April 18, 1977, the president declared an impending energy crisis and christened the struggle his administration would make to overcome it the "moral equivalent of war." Saying that "the energy crisis has not yet overwhelmed us, but it will if we do not act quickly," he immediately contradicted himself. "It is a problem we will not be able to solve in the next few years, and it is likely to get progressively worse through the rest of this century. . . ."[8]

Nevertheless, the Carter administration's "crisis approach" was the justification for pressing forward with conservation measures. The president began with consolidating the many energy-related departments and offices scattered throughout the federal bureaucracy into the Department of Energy and appointing James Schlesinger its head. Schlesinger had previously served as director of the Central Intelligence Agency and secretary of defense during the Nixon-Ford years.

Legislatively, the administration's energy program consisted of two broad packages. One was the energy bill, sent to Congress in April 1977 and passed only after bitter wrangling and extensive compromise eighteen months later, on October 15, 1978. The bill encouraged energy conservation but generally did not require it.[9] Key provisions included the phased decontrol of natural gas prices through 1985; encouragement of an industry-wide shift from use of oil and gas to increased use of coal; the promotion of more energy-efficient automobile engines, electrical appliances, and home construction; and incentives for the use of alternative energy sources such as solar power.

The president did not unveil the second part of his program until the spring of 1979, when oil prices had already started to climb. The second package centered around the phased decontrol of domestic oil prices, on which controls in any case were due to expire in October 1981, as required by the Energy Act of 1975. The president also sought taxation of windfall profits accruing to the oil companies as a result of decontrol, and the development of synthetic fuels.[10]

There were two aspects to the issue of the United States' competitive position vis-à-vis its allies. One was the need for greater efficiency and conservation in energy use: It was imperative that the nation begin to use less energy more efficiently. America's economic competitors were already employing energy more efficiently than was the United States. Their products—from tape cassettes to automobiles—were being manufactured at lower marginal costs than those in the United States. Unless United States industry used energy more efficiently, American exports would become increasingly uncompetitive against other nations' products.

The other aspect was to raise the unit costs of production for United States competitors. Raising the price of oil would, of course, contribute to that objective, but such a policy would raise the costs of American production, too. As it was, the United States was in the midst of a "productivity slowdown" which had been going on since 1973.[11] Presumably, in an even higher-priced energy regime than currently prevailed, Germany and Japan would suffer relatively more than the United States because they relied on imports to satisfy virtually all of their petroleum requirements.

In this sense the problem was quite similar to what had faced the nation's leaders in 1973, leading to the first oil shock.[12] By the end of 1978 Western Europe and Japan had fully recovered from the earlier oil shock. Western Europe, in another similarity with 1973, was in 1978 on the verge of monetary union, having decided in December 1977 to establish the European Monetary System (EMS). Success here would severely minimize the dollar's weight in European financial markets and strengthen the deutschemark's.

One mark of the Europeans' recovery was the rapid growth in their reserve positions. By the end of 1978, the reserves of West Germany and Japan had soared both in absolute terms and in relation to the United States. Between 1972 and 1978 the reserve holdings of the United States had improved from $13.1 billion (including gold) to $18.6 billion.[13] Over the same period Japan had improved its reserve position from $18.3 billion to $33.4 billion. But it was West Germany which had made the most astonishing gain, moving from $23.6 billion to $57.8 billion! The accumulation of official, disposable national wealth, which is what the reserve holdings signified, implied even greater accumulation of wealth in private industry, finance, and commerce. These trends carried obvious and ominous implications for the United States' overall global position.

It was thus imperative for the American leadership to stop the adverse trends and level the economic playing field to the extent possible before the last opportunity to do so had vanished. The administration had failed to equilibrate positions during the exchange-rate crisis, and oil was now the only remaining card to play. Theoretically, in the best of outcomes, raising the price of oil would be expected to siphon off some of the surplus wealth Germany and Japan had accumulated and brake their rapidly growing economies, the principal objective. There was also the outside chance that higher oil prices would disrupt the European Monetary System in much the same way that the earlier oil crisis had disrupted steps toward monetary union.

A higher price of oil would also strengthen the dollar since oil was still priced largely in dollars. In the process, the United States' position would be improved vis-à-vis its competitors by raising their costs of production. A stronger dollar would theoretically help reduce domestic inflation, already running at double-digit levels. The impact of a strong dollar on trade would be beneficial as well and help to close a growing deficit. (The United States trade deficit had climbed from $17 billion in 1976 to $39.1 billion in 1977, and to $42.3 billion in 1978.[14]) A stronger dollar would have the opposite impact on Germany's and Japan's trade positions, particularly on their energy bills.

Finally, the impact of higher oil prices presumably would be less onerous on the United States than on Germany and Japan because less than half of the petroleum consumed was imported and thus only that part was subject to rising prices. Decontrol of United States domestically produced oil, which was planned to be initiated during the crisis, would occur in a phased manner over twenty-eight months. Thus, the United States would hold a temporary and diminishing advantage, but an advantage nonetheless, as it sought to balance its economic position with its principal allies.

Shortage in a Time of Plenty

The trigger of the energy crisis was the upheaval in Iran, which resulted in the fall of the shah (see chapter 6). Iran had been exporting 5 million barrels of oil per day when petroleum exports ceased in December 1978. Over the next two years the price of oil would nearly triple; the posted price for Saudi Light marker crude would reach $32 per barrel by January 1981 (and spot market prices would reach $43 per barrel by the end of 1979).[15] In the United States, retail gasoline shortages brought long lines at filling stations and ever higher prices for gasoline and home heating oil.

In fact, petroleum producers had immediately largely compensated for the Iranian shortfall by increasing output. Saudi Arabia quickly increased production as Iranian exports declined at the end of the year.[16] The Saudi production ceiling for 1978 was 8.5 million b/d. Below average production during the early part of the year permitted Aramco to pump at a rate in excess of 10 million b/d in November and December and still remain under the prescribed annual average production ceiling of 8.5 million b/d. Riyadh raised the production ceiling to 9.5 million b/d for the first quarter of 1979.

Iraq, Mexico, and Nigeria also sharply increased production in early 1979. Iraqi output rose from 2.9 million b/d to 3.6 million b/d, Mexican output increased from 1.3 million b/d to 1.6 million b/d, while Nigerian output increased from 1.9 million b/d to 2.3 million b/d, actually surging to 2.5 million b/d in the first quarter.[17] First half 1979 production in the North Sea (Great Britain and Norway) was also up to 2.2 million b/d.[18] In fact, during the first half of 1979 world oil production was up 5.8 percent to 61.9 million b/d from 58.7 million b/d over the first half of 1978, more than compensating for the Iranian stoppage.

Increases in world crude production clearly offset the Iranian shortfall, and Iran itself resumed exports at 60 percent of the previous level in March 1979. There were shortages, nevertheless, and reasons for the shortages ranged from the curious to the bizarre. Curiously—a fact never explained—just as Iranian exports stopped, United States domestic production, according to Robert Sherrill, "went into its sharpest decline in seven years," by some 200,000 b/d, continuing until spring 1979.[19] Even more curiously, during the same time frame, the first four months of the year, the United States exported some 275,000 b/d, a sharp increase over previous practice.[20]

What made the crisis difficult to accept was the fact that the United States imported only some 10 percent of Iranian exports in 1978, slightly more than 500,000 b/d of total imports of 8.2 million b/d.[21] Iranian imports, in other words, represented only 6 percent of total United States imports. The fact was that the United States could have made up virtually all of the Iranian shortfall from its own resources by not decreasing domestic production and by exporting less. As it was, counting the losses from Iran, cutbacks in domestic production, and exports, the shortfall was approximately one million barrels per day during the first few months of 1979.

This phenomenon would be short-lived. Domestic production increased and was down by only 150,000 b/d for the entire year. Exports continued but at a lower rate, averaging 235,000 b/d for the year. Moreover, total crude imports in 1979, 8.3 million b/d, exceeded those of 1978.[22] A draft Treasury Department study concluded as early as April 1979 that the United States was actually better off without Iranian oil because the oil substituted for it was of better quality, requiring less refining and producing more gallons of product per barrel.[23] That report, too, was suppressed and its author consigned to bureaucratic oblivion.

Confounding the shortage thesis, however, was the report by Schlesinger's deputy, John O'Leary, that American consumption patterns had already begun to change. In March, O'Leary was quoted as saying that Americans were already increasing conservation and switching to alternative fuels, thus reducing consumption of oil on an anticipated annual basis by some 700,000 to 830,000 b/d![24] Schlesinger immediately denied O'Leary's report and sequestered his deputy from the public. (O'Leary had, in fact, exaggerated. Oil consumption in the United States in 1979 dropped by 400,000 b/d, the first drop since 1975, but still a substantial drop.)[25]

The administration's claims of an oil crisis rang increasingly hollow as reports accumulated of industry and firm panic buying and stockpiling; employment of idle, surplus tanker capacity for storage;[26] slowdown of tanker speed on the high seas; and slowdown of refinery production.[27] Polls showed public disbelief. One, representative of the rest, a *New York Times*/CBS poll taken in early April, found that 57 percent did not believe that the United States was "running out of oil and natural gas" as the administration claimed.[28]

But if the petroleum shortage was not real, the price increases of oil were very real indeed. In the immediate context of the Iranian shutdown, in late December 1978, OPEC met and agreed on the first increase in the price of oil in eighteen months, from $12.70 to $13.34. This was a 5 percent rise, scheduled as the first of four quarterly increases, to reach $14.54 on October 1, 1979.[29] Riyadh had hoped to hold the increase for the entire year to 5 percent but gave way to OPEC militants arguing for a larger increase.

American officials immediately began playing up the Iranian shortage as a crisis, warning of even higher prices. Energy Secretary Schlesinger, for example, declared in mid-February that "the Iranian shutdown could be more serious than the 1973 Arab oil embargo because it might last longer."[30] Two weeks later, on March 1, in testimony before the Senate Energy Committee, Schlesinger acknowledged President Carter's commitment to the allies at the Bonn summit in June 1978, that "it has been the objective of this administration to get to world prices . . . [T]he means are less important than anything else."[31] What the Carter administration did next ensured both a shortage and high prices.

In early March, Schlesinger used DOE's allocation authority to cut back gasoline production in favor of home heating oil, on the grounds of needing to build home heating oil stocks for the coming winter.[32] This was a most extraordinary decision. March is the month when refiners traditionally begin to shift away from home heating oil production to gasoline production to meet the needs of the coming summer driving season. Increasing home heating oil production in March ensured a gasoline shortage in May.

Then, also in early March, the administration prevailed upon the "majors" not to buy on the spot market, where the price was $10 above the posted January price.[33] But this policy simply intensified upward pressure on spot prices. In complying, the international oil companies reduced overall deliveries to Europe, Japan, and the United States and cut off smaller customers entirely. Predictably, the cutoff forced smaller firms into the spot market, where they competed with Europeans and Japanese, driving up prices.[34] An internal White House memorandum later described what had happened.

> The bulk of foreign oil traded in international markets and imported into the United States is controlled by a handful of major international companies. Other companies buy all or most of their foreign oil from them. In recent months, as the world oil supplies became tight, these major companies reduced their third-party sales to other companies in order to meet their own needs and/or divert supplies to take advantage of high spot market prices. At the same time, they greatly expanded their mark-ups on remaining third party sales. Their customers who were cut back were driven into very thin spot markets for oil where they bid up prices to extroardinary levels. They imported this oil at vastly inflated prices into the United States where it has had the double impact of driving up prices for both domestic crude oil and refined products.[35]

Quite clearly, the Carter administration turned what was a temporary petroleum shortfall into a major crisis, and did so principally, as argued in this chapter, in an attempt to equalize the United States economic position with that of its allies by raising energy costs. But there may have been an additional reason for what was universally interpreted as inept crisis management. That was an anticipated backlash from Saudi Arabia, an increasingly pivotal petroleum source, as American Middle East policy became clearer.

The Iranian crisis made it imperative that Washington act promptly to complete the Egyptian–Israeli peace process, to facilitate the shift of the United States anchor in the Middle East from Iran to Egypt and Israel. The cutoff of Iranian oil in December only intensified pressure on the Carter administration to complete the treaty process. But the Iranian crisis had also convinced the Israelis that Washington's leverage had diminished, and Menachem Begin remained intransigent over the West Bank, refusing to reach a compromise with Washington.[36]

The dilemma for President Carter, therefore, was that if he brought pressure to bear on the Israelis and they simply refused to cooperate—as they were very convincingly threatening to do—then at the very least there would be no treaty when Iran fell and no position for the United States in the Middle East. On the other hand, capitulating to the Israelis on the West Bank formula would lead to a treaty, but it risked a backlash from the moderate Arabs, most of all the Saudis. That backlash, of course, would obviously center around oil.

The president's decision, as noted in chapter 7, was to dilute the terms of the Camp David framework on the West Bank self-governing authority in order to obtain Israeli agreement on an Egyptian–Israeli peace treaty, and to increase the pressure on Saudi Arabia in hopes of gaining Riyadh's acquiescence to the compromise, if not acceptance of it. The odds were not good. The worst case was for a Saudi-inspired oil cutoff along the lines of 1973. Then, recall, Saudi Arabia had proclaimed the use of the "oil weapon," a 5 percent per month production cutback until Israel had withdrawn from the occupied territories and an embargo on the sale of oil to the United States.[37] Neither measure had survived the price increases of early 1974. The Carter administration was prepared to use the same tactic.

Therefore, one reason the administration deliberately turned a temporary shortfall into a crisis was to protect the United States from the worst case. Thus, what looked like administration incompetence was in reality a calculated attempt to insure against a cutoff. A preemptive raising of oil prices would be the best guarantee that oil continued to flow to the market. There would be no cutoff with oil selling at double or triple its current price. Very high prices would also attract additional non-OPEC sources of oil, diluting that organization's future influence on world oil. Finally, the rise in oil prices was fully consistent with the main objective, raising the costs of energy to the allies.

The irony was that the Saudi attitude in 1979 was fundamentally different from that of 1973. While there was a production cutback, it was not meant to enforce an embargo against the sale of oil to the United States but to support a price rise. Thus, when OPEC met in Geneva at the end of March after the signing of the Egyptian–Israeli peace treaty, the decision, which Riyadh supported, was to advance the price increases scheduled for the third and fourth quarters.[38] Thus, the price increase to $14.54, originally intended to go into effect October 1, instead took effect April 1.

The Carter administration, while declaring the price hike "untimely and unjustified," nevertheless by its reaction paved the way for further increases. State Department spokesman Hodding Carter told newsmen that Washington had no plans to retaliate. "Friends, after all, can have differences and still be friends," he said.[39] The president's anti-inflation adviser, Alfred E. Kahn, virtually invited the Arabs to raise prices again, saying, "We can expect [OPEC members] to extort from us everything they think the market will bear."[40]

Then, on April 5 the president announced the second part of his administration's energy package, the oil decontrol plan. Declaring that "energy prices are high and going higher, no matter what we do" and that "the fundamental cause of our nation's energy crisis is petroleum," Carter said that "phased decontrol of oil prices [would] begin on June 1st and continue at a fairly uniform rate over the next 28 months," until October 1, 1981.[41] "I'll give it to you straight," he declared. "Each one of us will have to use less oil and pay more for it."

Minimizing the domestic effects of higher prices, the president said, "Phased decontrol will gradually increase the price of petroleum products. In the short run it will add a small amount to our rate of inflation, but that is the cost we must pay to reduce our dependence on the foreign oil cartel."[42] But if the president truly believed that decontrol would only "gradually increase" oil prices and add only a "small amount" to the inflation rate, he was badly informed—and in for a rude awakening.

For the moment, however, despite the upward price pressure generated by the administration's actions, it appeared that prices would stabilize, if not fall. Although the Saudis had decided to abolish the 9.5 million b/d production ceiling of the first quarter and revert to an 8.5 million b/d level, by this time Iran had resumed exports at a rate of 3 million b/d.[43] As new oil also began coming onto the market, the expectation was that prices would soon level off, if not decline. (The spot market price for Arabian Light, which had risen to $23 per barrel in February, had dropped to $21 per barrel by mid-April, and Libyan Zuetina had also dropped from $26 to $24.)[44]

But at this point, in early May, the administration moved again to provide a further stimulus, opening the way to a broad price advance. As noted above, at the beginning of March, the administration had decided to cut back gasoline production in favor of increasing production of home heating oil and had forbidden the majors to buy on the spot market.[45] It had been these two decisions that had produced the gasoline shortage and higher prices. On May 7, presumably to ease the growing gasoline shortage, particularly in California, President Carter reversed these decisions. He "urged the big American oil companies to plunge back in" and buy on the spot market, and he offered a premium incentive of $5 per barrel to refineries, who shifted from refining heating oil to refining gasoline.[46]

Carter's policy reversal quickly ended the gas lines in California. By May 21 gasoline supplies had reappeared—just as suddenly as they had vanished. While there continued to be periodic shortages through the summer, especially in large cities along the East Coast, gasoline supplies became increasingly available across the country as refiners increased gasoline production. But gasoline now came at staggeringly higher prices. That summer, gasoline prices at the pump rose in places to well over a dollar per gallon, more than a 50 percent increase over the average price for leaded regular gasoline in 1978.[47]

In mid-May, the majors had, at the president's urging, returned to the spot markets "in force" and the result was "explosive."[48] The reason was that by this time one-third of all oil sold by OPEC, compared to the usual 5 to 8 percent, was moving through the spot market.[49] Within weeks the price of Arabian Light spot crude had shot up to nearly $35 per barrel, an increase of $13 per barrel and almost $20 per barrel over Saudi Arabia's official price. "From then on," as Ian Seymour notes, "the market never really looked back."[50] Part of the reason was the irrresistible upward pull exerted by the largest differential yet ($14.69) between spot and posted prices.[51] But equally important was the continued nosedive of United States relations with Saudi Arabia, the only element of restraint in OPEC.

The return of the international oil firms to the markets catapulted them into a wider political crisis, then reaching a crescendo, between Washington and Riyadh over the Camp David accords (see chapter 7). In early May, the Saudi leadership had denounced the Egyptian–Israeli treaty, excoriated the "Israeli orientation" of American policy, and boasted that Saudi Arabia could "replace the Americans any time [they] want."[52] The Carter administration's permission for the "majors" to resume operations was thus part of a larger decision, made on May 11, to attempt to restore the rapidly fraying "special relationship" with Saudi Arabia.[53]

Relations with the Saudis had suffered to the point that Secretary Vance was forced to acknowledge in public testimony before the House Foreign Affairs Committee on May 8 that "American relations with Saudi Arabia had deteriorated because of 'clear and sharp differences' over the Egyptian–Israeli peace treaty."[54] Since the Baghdad conference, November 2 through 5, 1978, he said, at which the Saudis and other Arab leaders had called on Sadat to refuse to sign the treaty and threatened an economic boycott of Egypt if he did, "the declared position of the Saudis has changed. It's a fact, and nobody can or should gloss over it."[55]

Despite a personal letter from President Carter and visits by Brzezinski and other high State Department officials, the Saudis refused to relent.[56] Indeed, they seemed bent on attempting to isolate the United States, maintaining a supply cutback to Aramco and cutting out the majors by signing bilateral deals with several West European countries. Aramco, which had been obtaining 7 million b/d, was cut back to 6.1 million b/d. Riyadh had also executed direct government-to-government contracts with France, Greece, and Spain and was negotiating with West Germany.[57]

Even more ominous was the effort by the Emir of Kuwait, supported by the Saudis and other Arabs, to sound out European leaders' interest in a "Eurabian" understanding. The emir had sent a letter to French President Valery Giscard d'Estaing in April, in his capacity as current chairman of the European Economic Community. The terms of the "understanding" were reported to be a guaranteed flow of Arab oil in return for European suppport for a Palestinian state in the Middle East. The effect of such a linkage would, of course, "progressively erode the American political and economic presence in the Mideast."[58]

When OPEC met in Geneva at the end of June, after much haggling it was agreed to establish a price ceiling on all OPEC crudes of $23.50 per barrel, an increase of almost 62 percent! Saudi Arabia jumped its marker price for Arabian Light from $14.55 to $18 per barrel but also decided to raise its production ceiling to 9.5 million b/d, a decision which presumably would stabilize prices at the higher level.[59] But although supplies were more than adequate in the second half of 1979, the price ceiling failed to hold as spot prices continued to surge. After dipping slightly to $32 per barrel in July, Arabian Light rose strongly through the second half of the year to peak in November at a price of $40. The spot price for Libyan Zuctina moved parallel but higher, hitting $43 in November.[60]

By early July, oil prices were careening skyward, seemingly with no limit in sight. The $23.50 price ceiling was widely believed to be temporary until market pressures forced another increase (which in fact occurred in November). Relations with Saudi Arabia, the key to price moderation, were in a shambles. Worse, it was not clear that high oil prices had had the desired effect of braking the economic advances of Germany and Japan.[61] Still worse, in the United States inflation had reached 14 percent and was rising. Finally, the "oil crisis" had had no impact on the European Monetary System, which after a three-month delay began to operate in March, effectively stabilizing exchange rates. In short, not only had the oil crisis gambit failed to work, it had backfired domestically, and it had to be remedied.

Carter Attempts to Salvage a Failed Policy

The Carter administration's oil strategy had succeeded in raising energy costs to Germany and Japan but had had little effect in braking their economic success. Moreover, this had been accomplished at high domestic economic costs to the United States and perhaps at even higher political costs to the president himself. On the positive side, by mid-year it was already apparent that a major shift in current account balances was under way. A strengthening dollar enabled the United States to repay all foreign currency debt owed to banks from the previous fall's $30 billion monetary package (see chapter 2). By June the dollar had recovered overall about 10 percent from its 1978 low point, but by 25 percent against the yen and 10.75 percent against the deutschemark.[62]

In fact, the United States would be the only major industrial country to record a strong improvement in its current account balance in 1979. The United States balance would improve by $13.2 billion, moving from a deficit of $13.5 in 1978 to $0.3 in 1979.[63] This was accomplished by a general economic slowdown, a reduction of imports, and—despite an $18 billion deficit in trade with OPEC—because of the rise in oil prices.

West Germany suffered a current account deficit for the year, dropping from a surplus of $8.9 billion in 1978 to a deficit of $5.8 billion, a swing of $14.7 billion.[64] Appreciation of the deutschemark and a buildup of crude oil stocks accounted for the bulk of the deficit. Bonn's trade deficit in oil went from $14.7 billion to $24.5 billion, a shift of $9.8 billion, reflecting not only the rise in oil prices but also an increase in the volume of imports by 3.5 percent due to stockpiling. Nevertheless, strong German growth in exports to the OPEC nations compensated for the increase in the oil bill.

Japan's current account balance was affected most, dropping from a $16.5 billion surplus in 1978 to a $8.6 billion deficit in 1979, a $25.1 billion swing.[65] Tokyo covered much of its deficit through short-term capital inflows of $8.9 billion and by drawing down $12.7 billion on official reserves. Three factors accounted for most of the swing: depreciation of the yen, the rise in oil prices—which increased Japan's oil bill by $9 billion—and the first drop in overall export volume in several years. Although Japan's exports to the Middle East grew, they failed to cover rising oil costs.[66]

It was therefore under relatively favorable circumstances that President Carter arrived in Japan for the seven-nation Tokyo summit, June 28 and 29. Carter's main objective was to lock in a reduction in demand for imported petroleum. He sought, among other things, to obtain national commitments from his allies for reductions in near-term petroleum imports and agreements to shift over the long term away from oil to greater use of coal and nuclear energy,[67] measures which would cause substantial short-term dislocations to their economies. He also sought to end "stockpiling of oil when supplies are short," the "erratic high bidding on the oil spot market," a "firm agreement for fuel allocation by the International Energy Agency if and when necessary," and the "specific monitoring of each nation's performance."

Britain, France, Italy, and West Germany, "the Europeans," as Carter referred to them, would have none of it, especially the idea of an external monitor of their respective performances, and were "adamantly against any sort of individual national commitment."[68] In response, they offered a formula which would allow them to comply formally with Carter's demands for reduced petroleum imports, but which would in reality permit increasing imports. The four European powers had

> decided in advance that in setting up their import goals, they should be considered as a group by the United States, Canada, and Japan, and not as individual nations. Their purpose was obvious. . . . [It was] to absorb the rapidly growing oil production in the North Sea and not have to count it in their own countries as imports.[69]

In what the president described as "an acrimonious meeting," the Europeans, led by Chancellor Helmut Schmidt, reacted heatedly to his proposals. "Schmidt got personally abusive toward me when I pushed the individual target position. . . . He alleged that American interference in the Middle East trying to work for a peace treaty was what had caused the problems with oil all over the world."[70]

At a breakfast meeting the following day, June 29, of Carter, Giscard, Schmidt, and Thatcher, President Giscard gained grudging acceptance for his proposal that each nation set import targets up to 1985. Afterward, Prime Minister Masayoshi Ohira, who had not attended the breakfast, was shocked to find that Japan had been assigned an import ceiling insufficient to sustain its projected growth rate of 6 percent.[71] Part of the shock was due to his understanding that Carter would not accept import targets to 1985, an understanding apparently reached during Carter's pre-summit meeting with him.

By the end of the day, it seemed as if key compromises would unravel, as Schmidt and Ohira attempted to wriggle out of commitments to long-term import quotas. However, Giscard "joined forces" with President Carter to keep Schmidt on board, "pointing out that we had reached 'a superb agreement based on complete misunderstanding.'"[72] And at the last minute, the Japanese prime minister also agreed to a "1985 target which would allow Japan's imports to rise by 3 per cent per year."[73]

From the perspective of Carter's main objective of locking in reduced demand for imported petroleum, the agreements reached at the Tokyo summit were positive, although they soon became irrelevant. The fact was that the agreed targets were too high and proved no burden to adhere to. Moreover, over the next several years demand for petroleum fell as all of the allies conserved more and employed less imported energy. The OECD target for imports in 1980, for example, was 27 milion b/d, but actual imports totalled 24 million b/d.[74]

But if for the moment the achievements at the Tokyo summit were positive from the Carter administration's point of view, the domestic political and economic effects of high oil prices decidedly were not. Upon the president's return home from Tokyo he learned that his "popularity had dropped to a new low." Indeed, a draft-Kennedy drive was gaining momentum, raising the prospect of a divisive intra-party struggle over the Democratic nomination. The dissatisfaction in the party reflected popular disapproval. As Carter noted, the American people had become "convinced that both the government and the oil companies were either incompetent or dishonest—or both."[75]

Moreover, the economy was heating up dangerously. Contrary to economic theory, high oil prices had fueled a virulent rise in inflation, whose origin lay in the domestic expansion of the previous three years, and it had severely eroded the administration's credibility and the president's popularity. Theoretically, the rise in oil prices should have had a deflationary effect following an initial inflationary rise in the overall price level.[76] This is because the price increase in oil was essentially a tax, whose net effect should have been to reduce demand.

Instead, different from the outcome the president was led by his advisers to expect, the rise in oil prices had stoked the inflationary trend rather than banked it. (Recall that in his April 5 speech announcing the decontrol of oil prices, President Carter had assured the nation that the rise in oil prices would add only a "small amount" to the rate of inflation.) The deflationary effects of the "oil tax" were being overridden by the growing strength of inflationary expectations that prices would continue to rise regardless of administration pronouncements to the contrary.

The effect was a determined consumer effort to shift wealth out of money into the acquisition of real assets such as gold and real estate. The price of gold would exceed $300 per ounce in July, on its way to $700 in 1980; investors and speculators acquired the precious metal as a hedge against further inflation. And for the same reason, buyers of homes and real estate were not discouraged by rising interest rates. Moreover, low real interest rates (the interest rate minus inflation was zero) and easy credit spurred real estate and home acquisition.

The domestic deterioration had a visible impact on President Carter. On July 4, the president canceled a scheduled speech on energy, which was to have been his fifth, and secluded himself with trusted aides at Camp David to decide "where we should go from here."[77] The president remained at Camp David for ten days, fueling speculation that the pressures of office had produced physical and mental collapse. But Carter thought of his seclusion as a way to "dramatize the importance of the questions I was trying to answer."

The chief policy question, of course, was how to stop the inflation that was wracking the country. And the president's response was to fire those officials who had been responsible for the failed policy, hire replacements to execute a new policy, and make yet another attempt to enforce energy conservation. After returning from Camp David, on July 15 the president delivered what was immediately dubbed the "national malaise speech." Although in fact he never used the word "malaise," that term accurately expressed the state of the national mind as the president saw it.[78]

In the course of his speech the president announced the establishment of a national "goal": To stop our growing dependence on foreign oil in its tracks. "Beginning this moment," he declared, "this Nation will never use more foreign oil than we did in 1977—never."[79] Toward this end he set import quotas to ensure compliance. He proposed creation of an Energy Security Corporation to develop synthetic fuels, asked Congress to mandate that utility companies switch from oil to coal by 50 percent over the next decade, and requested standby gasoline rationing authority.

To galvanize the national spirit, Carter also urged Congress to establish an Energy Mobilization Board along the lines of the War Production Board of World War II, "to cut through the red tape, the delays, and the endless roadblocks." It was the president's hope that "the solution of our energy crisis can also help us conquer the crisis of the spirit in our country."[80] The immediate public reaction to the president's speech was very positive. He appeared to have touched a responsive chord in the American psyche, and it may have buoyed his spirits for the more daunting task of personnel shuffling which lay before him.

According to President Carter, "the advice at Camp David had been almost unanimous" that he would have to make some major changes in his cabinet.[81] He claims that he had "argued against" firing Energy Secretary Schlesinger, Treasury Secretary Blumenthal, and HEW Secretary Califano, but that a group of his "senior political advisors" led by Charles Kirbo, Clark Clifford, and Sol Linowitz, persuaded him that these three, in particular, had outlived their usefulness and had to go.

Unfortunately, as the president noted in retrospect, he "handled the Cabinet changes very poorly." Instead of announcing the resignations of those he had desired to replace and being done with it, the president "decided that the entire [cabinet] group would offer to resign, and I would then quickly decide which resignations to accept."[82] Too clever by half, the maneuver backfired. What should have been an example of the president's resolve and determination to regain control of the government, was instead interpreted as "a great governmental crisis."

On July 19 and 20, the president accepted the resignations of Michael Blumenthal, James Schlesinger, Joseph Califano, Attorney

General Griffin Bell, and Transportation Secretary Brock Adams. The White House also announced that G. William Miller would resign his post as chairman of the Federal Reserve Board to take over Blumenthal's position at Treasury, but no replacement was announced for Miller's now vacant Fed post.[83] The Fed post was filled five days later by Paul Volcker, at the time president of the New York Federal Reserve Bank.

President Carter's choice of the man to succeed G. William Miller as the new chairman of the Federal Reserve Board was supremely ironic. Whether wittingly or unwittingly, in selecting Paul Volcker the president had chosen the man who had designed the monetary system of floating rates in 1972 which had brought the Carter administration to its current pass.[84] The float was sold then, in part, on the grounds that it would enable the United States to temper the inflationary impact of higher oil prices, which, of course, it had not done. It was as if to say, "All right, Mr. Volcker, you got us into this mess, now get us out."

Within ten days of taking the oath of office, on August 16 Volcker began to tighten monetary policy in an effort to bring down inflation. He obtained the Federal Reserve Board's approval to reduce the money supply by raising the discount rate from 10 percent to 10.5 percent, the highest in the history of the Federal Reserve. It was to no avail. Although it was too much to expect a prompt response, early indications were that the discount rate rise would not be sufficient to bring the money supply down to its targeted range. A month later, on September 18, the screws were tightened further, as the Fed Funds rate was raised to 11.75 percent.[85] Still no response.

Furthermore, by the summer of 1979 the dollar was once again exhibiting signs of weakness in the international markets. Though the dollar had strengthened through the spring, growing concerns about inflation had translated into a weakening of the dollar in the summer.[86] International interest rate differentials had also moved adversely against the dollar. The Bundesbank, for example, had tightened German monetary policy earlier in the year when the dollar was strengthening and had raised interest rates over the summer to keep the lid on inflation. Despite the slippage of the German current account balance noted above, the deutschemark rose against the dollar through the summer.[87]

The growing success of the EMS brought another concern. In

early September, the major powers agreed in Paris to support the IMF's substitution account proposal, which, if implemented, would gradually reduce the dollar's central role as a reserve asset. The plan was several years old and up to then had been spurned by the United States. The substitution account would permit the IMF to accept dollars from countries wishing to dispose of them in return for SDRs, special drawing rights. Since the establishment of the European Monetary System, Washington had become more interested in the substitution account as an alternative to the EMS monetary unit, the ECU, out of concern for the ECU's potential to evolve into a regional reserve currency.

Of course, a weakening dollar improved the United States export position in the trade competition with the allies, who complained bitterly; but it also reduced the dollar value of American investments abroad and of the billions of dollars of loans which American banks had made, especially to Latin American nations. While a weaker dollar made their debt burden less and enabled the debtor nations to import more, it made the portfolio value of the loans worth less and undermined the financial position of the American banks.[88]

Thus, a weakening dollar abroad fed surging inflation at home and forced more drastic action. By the end of September, the staff work had been completed on a plan which would, it was hoped, produce the desired result.[89] The essential objective was to bring about a rapid reduction in inflation through a sharp drop in consumption and speculative activity. The means to that end was a steep rise in interest rates. But simply to raise interest rates was not enough, because the unknown factor was how far rates would have to be increased to accomplish the objective. Moreover, the rise in the unemployment level that would inevitably accompany a steep rise in interest rates would undoubtedly redound to the president's disadvantage as the 1980 election year approached.

The Federal Reserve devised a scheme which would, to the extent possible, allow the board and the president to dissociate themselves from what was going to be an extremely unpopular policy and to place the blame on "market forces," even while it allowed more direct control over policy. This was the basic idea behind the decision of October 6, 1979, to change the operating system of the Federal Reserve. The Federal Reserve had traditionally employed an indirect approach targeting interest rates, specifically the Federal Funds rate, as the means of determining the overall growth of the money supply. This technique became increasingly unworkable as the monetary environment became more and more volatile in 1979. As Fed Governor Henry Wallich noted:

> It suffered from a reluctance of the FOMC [Federal Open Market Committee] to move the funds rate fast enough and far enough to keep the money supply on track even over intervals of several months or longer. Because nobody, including the Fed, likes to see interest rates go up, there was over time a bias in policy which allowed the money supply to expand excessively.[90]

What Volcker decided to do was to adopt a system which would eliminate that expansionary bias by shifting from the targeting of interest rates to targeting, and thus directly restraining, the growth of the money supply. The minutes of the FOMC of October 6, 1979, noted that

> the principal reason . . . for shifting to an operating procedure aimed at controlling the supply of bank reserves more directly was that it would provide greater assurance that the Committee's objectives for monetary growth could be achieved. In the present environment of rapid inflation, estimates of the relationship among interest rates, monetary growth, and economic activity had become less reliable than before, and monetary growth since the first quarter of 1979 had exceeded the rates expected despite substantial increases in short-term rates.[91]

It was understood that placing emphasis on direct control of the money supply would produce greater interest rate volatility. But that was the point. "The surge in interest rates produced by this automatic reserve control approach would eventually damp business and consumer speculative borrowing demands and help reduce money growth to a less inflationary pace."[92] The danger, however, was that a sharp spike in interest rates would precipitate a recession. The trick would be to walk the fence between inflation and recession without falling off either side.

The initial reaction to the Federal Reserve's policy change was positive. Money growth slowed sharply in October and November as interest rates rose.[93] So far so good. The general reaction was that the United States government was combating inflation in the traditional manner by severely squeezing the money supply. The impact abroad was also beneficial, particularly against the deutschemark. Three-month Eurodollar rates immediately jumped five points to 16 percent per year.[94]

As money became scarce, banks looked increasingly to the large, unregulated pool of money in the Eurodollar market. The Federal Reserve attempted to discourage use of the Eurodollar market by imposing special marginal reserve requirements on managed liabilities but could not close it off entirely. Estimated to be as large as $800 billion, the Eurodollar market was the way large banks with overseas branches evaded the restrictions placed by the Federal Reserve. As Wallich noted,

> The Federal Reserve could, of course, adjust the domestic targets so as to keep the combined amount of domestic and Euromoney on the right track. But as the Eurodollar market grows, the Federal Reserve would have to bear down increasingly hard on the domestic supply of money and credit in order to offset the expansion of Eurodollars. This would work a hardship on our domestic economy and particularly on U.S. borrowers who did not have access to the Euromarket.[95]

Upwards of $50 billion drawn from the Eurodollar market was augmenting the United States money supply. Some of the borrowing would show up as bank deposits and would be counted in the money supply. Most would be carried on the books of foreign branches of American banks, or foreign subsidiaries of American corporations borrowing the money, and would not be counted.[96] But all of it would undermine the Federal Reserve's effort to reduce the money supply and curtail inflation.

Moreover, within weeks of the October 6 policy change, a series of events occurred highlighting what apppeared to be a growing American impotence in international affairs: the Iranian hostage seizure on November 4; the attack on the Grand Mosque in Mecca on November 20; attacks on the United States embassy in Islamabad and on the consul general in Lahore, Pakistan, on November 21; rock-throwing demonstrations before American diplomatic missions in Turkey, Bangladesh, and India, on November 22–23; and an attack on the embassy in Tripoli, Libya, on December 2. Finally, the Soviet invasion of Afghanistan on December 24 stimulated a shift of funds out of dollar-denominated assets, intensifying pressure on the dollar.[97]

As part of the response to the seizure of the hostages, President Carter placed a freeze on Iranian assets on November 14. While domestically popular, the freeze had the financial effect of raising foreign investors' concerns regarding the holding of dollar assets in American banks; and they began to shift capital into the Eurodollar market, deutschemarks, and Swiss francs.[98] The attacks on the Grand Mosque in Mecca and on American overseas offices and the Soviet invasion of Afghanistan reinforced these concerns.

By January 1980, it was clear that the economy was not slowing down in the manner expected. "The psychological shock that Volcker thought might reverberate from the October 6 shift had not happened."[99] Despite nearly doubled interest rates, the economy continued to expand, confounding Volcker and the Federal Reserve. Moreover, the money supply, instead of contracting, continued to grow; and inflation was again on the rise. There was but one answer, and that was to tighten further. This would, of course, drive the economy into recession and have profound effects upon the president's electoral chances. But that takes us slightly ahead of the story. The fall of 1979 saw a more ominous turn in international events, which would also impact negatively upon the president's bid for reelection.

Crises in Southwest Asia

The Iranian revolution in early 1979 governed both Washington's and Moscow's policies in Southwest Asia, and perhaps beyond, through the year. Washington sought to recoup what had been a failed attempt to make the transition from the shah's regime to a post-shah regime without skipping a beat. There was unstated but profound concern—indeed, in some quarters gnawing worry—that failure to repair the damage to United States–Iranian relations would provide the Soviet Union with a geopolitical windfall. This unspoken concern explains why Brzezinski and Vance, who were diametrically opposed on earlier policy toward Iran, now closed ranks in the face of the common danger.[100] The persistence with which the United States pressed for a return to normal relations with

Khomeini's regime—which only excoriated American attempts—lent the Carter administration's efforts a surreal and pathetic aspect.

Moscow, on the other hand, strove to forestall an American recovery of its former relationship and toward this end moved to strengthen the Soviet position in and around Iran. Hoping to exploit what was perceived to be an historic opportunity to alter the geopolitical balance of power, Moscow maneuvered carefully to ensure that the United States would not succeed in regaining its position in Iran. Soviet policy toward Afghanistan was part of Moscow's larger regional policy mix and should be understood in this broader context.

Through the summer and fall Iran declined further into chaos. As Khomeini moved to create a theocratic dictatorship in the name of the Islamic Republic, there was constant infighting among the ayatollahs for power in the regime's revolutionary council. At the same time, tension grew between the revolutionary council and the civil government of Mehdi Bazargan as the clerics and bureaucrats maneuvered for control of state power. Multiple sources of military power also emerged with the intensification of internal and external violence. In addition to the greatly weakened regular army, Khomeini established the Revolutionary Guards under his control, the Hezbollah under control of the Islamic Revolutionary party, and a volunteer force, the Baseej, to serve as "guardians of the revolution." There was also an armed and disciplined communist element, the Tudeh party, as well as Marxist guerrilla groups, the Fedayeen and Mujahedeen.[101]

Amid daily executions and assassinations of real or presumed "enemies of the regime" inside Iran, separatist sentiment exploded in demands for greater regional autonomy. Minority peoples, who constitute 37 percent of Iran's population of 36 million, balked at the rigid strictures of the Islamic regime.[102] All around the Iranian frontier there were unrest and conflict between government forces and different separatist groups.

Continuous heavy fighting occurred in the northwest between the Kurds, who number 3.5 million, and the Revolutionary Guards. In Khuzistan, Iran's main petroleum province, government forces hastily organized as "guardians of the revolution" fought to defeat separatist efforts of the largely Arab population. And there was growing unrest among Baluchis in the southeast and Azerbaijanis in the northwest. Finally, there were also skirmishes between Iraqi and

Iranian forces as Baghdad probed Iran's defenses. By fall, oil exports had dropped from the 1979 high of 3.3 million b/d to 2 million b/d. Unemployment was over 35 percent. The Iranian economy was at a standstill.

The United States government, under Secretary Vance's direction, sought to "come to terms" with the Iranian revolution from the beginning.[103] The United States moved to dissociate itself from all ties to the shah, refusing to grant him sanctuary, and shamelessly attempted to ingratiate itself with Khomeini's new regime by muting its criticism of human rights abuses and portraying them as the temporary excesses of the revolution. Journalists were urged to restrain their criticism, and American business was encouraged to return.

American restraint was not reciprocated. Khomeini issued scathing denunciations of the Great Satan. In June, the Department of State bowed to Khomeini's refusal to accept the newly designated ambassador to Iran, Walter Cutler (William Sullivan had been withdrawn in April), and appointed Bruce Laingen as chargé d'affaires instead. Although there was little demonstrable progress in developing ties with the new regime—indeed there was no direct contact with Khomeini at all—the official, and hopeful, Washington line was that "things were improving."[104]

Behind the scenes, in July Washington had in fact initiated contact with the Bazargan government, which had expressed an interest in obtaining spare parts from the United States to restore its largely American-derived military arsenal. The regime's efforts to subdue the Kurds, which had sparked the request, was not going well.[105] Perceiving an opportunity to develop relations, the Carter administration readily agreed to resume deliveries of spare parts. There were also discreet exchanges of intelligence with the Iranian government. [106] By early October, the United States government had parlayed these efforts into a series of meetings with high-ranking Iranian government officials.

The first of these took place in New York on October 3, 4, and 6. Iranian Acting Foreign Minister Ibrahim Yazdi arrived in New York for the opening session of the United Nations General Assembly. Yazdi met with Secretary of State Vance on the third, in the first high-level meeting between representatives of the two countries since the fall of the shah. Secretary Vance expressed United States interest in Iran's continued independence and territorial integrity, denied any attempt to destabilize Iran, and recommended that the two countries "put the past behind them."[107] In response to Yazdi's questions about American policy toward the shah and his assets, Vance replied that the administration had advised the shah not to come to the United States at this time but could not rule out admitting him at some point.[108] He also advised that Iran pursue its case in American courts against the shah's assets.

The next day high State and Defense officials met with Yazdi and his aides to discuss the question of Iranian arms purchases and to clear up misconceptions relating to the tangle of contractual rights and obligations inherited from the ancien régime.[109] Reaffirming Vance's words of the day before, of the United States' interest in Iran's independence, territorial integrity, and security, American officials expressed their "willingness to cooperate with and assist Iran on defense matters where that was desired . . . and feasible."[110]

Despite Iranian "suspicions" and "bluntness," Secretary Vance and his top aides, Under Secretaries David Newsom and Harold Saunders and UN Ambassador Donald McHenry, met with Yazdi again on October 6 to make a pitch for normalizing relations. But Yazdi balked, raising a number of conditions, asserting against Vance's protestations that the United States had not yet "accepted" the revolution.[111] Yazdi asked for "concrete steps" to demonstrate Washington's acceptance, such as the extradition of "criminals" who had fled to the United States, favorable disposition of military contracts signed by the shah, and an end to criticism of the Iranian revolution.

Vance was clearly taken aback by Yazdi's demands. He had expected a more forthcoming attitude on Iran's part. In the postmortem after the meeting, Newsom expressed the optimistic view that "Iranian suspicions were only natural in the post-revolutionary situation."[112] After a cooling-off period, he believed, "common interests" could provide a basis for future cooperation. Responding to Vance's growing sensitivity on the issue of "who lost Iran," Newsom went on to note that such cooperation would not be "on the scale of before but sufficient to demonstrate that Iran has not been 'lost' to us and to the West."[113]

Despite the rebuff by Yazdi, on October 7 the Iranian government announced its agreement with Washington's intention to appoint Bruce Laingen as ambassador.[114] American officials in Tehran continued to meet with Iranian defense officials to pursue the spare-parts weapons angle, as a means of maintaining contact if nothing else. But before any meaningful dialogue could develop, the issue of the shah rose to the fore. On October 18, American officials learned for the first time that the shah was terminally ill with cancer, making it impossible to continue to refuse him entry into the United States.[115]

To explain the extenuating circumstances of the decision to admit the shah, on October 20 Vance sent Henry Precht, the State Department's country director for Iran, to Tehran for a meeting with Mehdi Bazargan. Precht, the foremost advocate within the department of pursuing normalization of relations with Iran, explained the shah's predicament, while at the same time offering to resume America's "old relationship with Iran," including arms supply.[116]

To Bazargan, however, admittance of the shah to the United States was bad news. He feared that the shah's presence would be an obstacle to improvement of relations with Washington.[117] The shah's illness had been an extraordinarily well-kept secret, and the Iranian leadership greeted its revelation with profound skepticism, suspecting an American trick. They wanted Iranian doctors to examine the ailing exile and suggested that he be treated outside the United States. They urged that if admitted the shah not be taken to New York City, where there were numerous Iranian exiles hostile to the revolution, to whom the shah would have access.[118]

But if the shah's coming to the United States (he was taken to New York Hospital and also treated at adjacent Memorial Sloan-Kettering Cancer Center in New York City) was an unwelcome roadblock to improvement of relations to Bazargan, it was a godsend to Khomeini. In the continuing power struggle between the civil and religious elements in Iran, the issue of the shah offered Khomeini the perfect pretext to take action against Bazargan and bring the civil government under his control. He was preparing a move against Bazargan in any case to head off normalization of relations with the United States, which would only strengthen the Iranian civil government. Khomeini moved to kill two birds with one stone.

After the taking of the American hostages, some of the "students" who participated in the assault on the embassy were interviewed by a Western correspondent. They declared that the planning for the attack had begun in early October, which would mean the decision to seize the embassy was made shortly after the meetings between Vance and Yazdi in New York.[119] The original idea evidently was to invade the embassy compound in order to obtain documentary support for Khomeini's charges of Washington's espionage activities. The shah's entry into the United States offered the rationale for a more decisive step against both the Bazargan government and the United States.[120]

That step was taken on October 31 when Khomeini called for a march on the American embassy the following day.[121] On November 1 a crowd of some 3,500 people demonstrated in front of the embassy to protest the shah's presence in the United States. The government turned back many thousands more marching toward the embassy from downtown Tehran. During the demonstration Khomeini's office issued a statement in the ayatollah's name. Addressed to the demonstrators, the critical thrust of the statement was the following sentence:

> It is therefore up to the dear pupils, students and theological students to expand their attacks against the United States and Israel, so that they may force the U.S. to return the deposed and criminal shah.[122]

Despite the incendiary nature of the statement, calling on the "students to expand their attacks," embassy officials professed no alarm. Chargé Bruce Laingen reported to Washington that he was "aware of no plans for further protests in the immediate future."[123]

Whether coincidentally or not, on the same day, Brzezinski was in Algiers meeting with the top officials of the Iranian government, Prime Minister Bazargan, Foreign Minister Yazdi, and Defense Minister Mustafa Ali Chamran. Brzezinski's presence in a delegation celebrating the twenty-fifth anniversary of the Algerian revolution was unusual, to say the least.[124] In fact, it was part of a premeditated attempt to make high-level contact with Iranian leaders. When Brzezinski had learned that Bazargan would be going to Algiers, he arranged to go himself. Laingen had mentioned to Bazargan that Brzezinski would be there, and the Iranian leader "seemed interested."[125]

Perhaps to protect himself against precisely the charges of collusion which would follow his meeting with Brzezinski, on October 31 Bazargan announced that Iran was planning to abrogate the 1959 United States–Iran Mutual Assistance Agreement and certain offensive clauses in the 1921 Soviet–Iranian treaty. At any rate, during their meeting, Brzezinski offered "any relationship you want. . . . We have a basic community of interests but we do not know what you want us to do. . . . The American government is prepared to expand security, economic, political, and intelligence relationships at your pace."[126]

While Brzezinski's open-ended offer produced "some exchanges" on security assistance, Bazargan and Yazdi put him off, raising again the issue of the shah and his assets, as Bazargan had to Precht on October 20 and as Yazdi had to Vance on October 6. Yazdi "mocked the idea that the shah sought asylum for medical reasons." At this, Brzezinski exploded, charging that "this discussion is humiliating and demeaning. I am not certain whether it is more humiliating for me to listen or for you to raise this." Nevertheless, Brzezinski inexplicably judged that "the discussion ended very amiably, and actually throughout the Iranians were surprisingly cordial."[127]

A few days later, when the Iranian militants seized the embassy, Brzezinski came under stringent criticism for his Algiers meeting. Vance charged that "the meeting was used by the militants in Tehran to charge Bazargan and Yazdi with being too inclined toward the United States. Their meeting . . . made Bazargan and Yazdi vulnerable to attack by extremists. . . ."[128] But the national security adviser defended his actions on the grounds that, had he refused to talk, "the Iranian radicals would have been provided with additional proof of American hostility, and the U.S. government would have been charged with rebuffing an important overture."[129]

It was undoubtedly true that Brzezinski's meeting was a factor in Khomeini's drive to oust Bazargan, but it was not the critical factor Vance asserts. At best, it was a convenient pretext. On the other hand, Brzezinski does not explain why he went to Algiers in the first place. The seizure of the hostages occurred a mere three days after the Algiers meeting. The move to block any improvement of relations with the United States, as well as to consolidate power in the hands of the ayatollah in the continuing battle between the secularists and the clerics, had been planned weeks earlier and was not a spontaneous reaction to the Algiers meeting.

In any case, the taking of 100 hostages at the American embassy (66 Americans, 63 at the embassy and 3 others incarcerated in the Foreign Ministry on November 4) not only transformed the Iranian domestic situation, as Khomeini consolidated the clerics' hold on power, but also the geopolitics of Southwest Asia, which entered a new and explosive stage.[130] The immobilization of United States–

Iran relations produced politico-military reactions by both Washington and Moscow as the two superpowers moved closer toward confrontation in Southwest Asia.

Hostage Seizure and Washington's Response

To the Carter leadership, the seizing of the hostages meant that there would be no near-term normalization of relations with Iran. Instead, the focus shifted to seeking the prompt release of the hostages. There was also the sense that Iran was on the verge of disintegration, which might require more drastic action. In addition to the economic collapse, Iranian politics was in chaos, with the dismissal of the secular government, immobilization of the bureaucracy, and continued power struggles among the ayatollahs. Militarily, the conflict with minority groups, especially the Kurds, was going badly, and the increasing pressure of Iraqi incursions along the border exacerbated confusion, dissension, and instability in Tehran.

On November 6, the Carter administration made a series of decisions designed to isolate Iran diplomatically and "to convince the revolutionary leadership . . . that it was in their interests to release the hostages promptly and safely."[131] Toward this end a major effort was undertaken to open channels of communication to Iranian authorities, as Vance put it, "to determine the condition of the hostages and give them aid and comfort, to learn the Iranians' motives and aims in holding them, and to negotiate their freedom."[132]

Publicly, a major campaign was mounted immediately to condemn Iran and to generate pressure for release of the hostages, including representations to the UN Security Council and International Court of Justice. Over the next few days, further political-economic measures were put in place. On November 10, Washington announced that it would commence deportation proceedings against all Iranians found to be residing illegally in the United States. On the twelfth, President Carter announced the termination of all petroleum imports from Iran.[133] And on the fourteenth, he signed an executive order freezing all Iranian assets, valued at over $12 billion, in American financial institutions and their foreign branches.

Secretly, the administration began contingency planning for three types of military operations: a rescue mission, a retaliatory strike if the hostages were harmed, and "in the event that Iran disintegrated as a political entity," a major ground-force deployment to take control of the oil fields of Khuzistan.[134] Of course, this last contingency would come into play if Moscow moved to take control of Iranian provinces bordering on the Soviet Union. (This was a standing contingency plan, dating back to World War II, when Great Britain, the United States, and the Soviet Union divided and occupied the country. No American administration would permit a Soviet attempt to seize control of northern Iran and its gas fields without a concomitant move into the southwest and the oil fields, although Iranian territorial integrity was obviously preferred.)[135]

The idea of an immediate rescue was considered and dropped on November 6, but contingency planning was authorized. By the middle of November the U.S. Army's elite Delta Force had prepared an emergency (and suicidal) assault plan in the event it was learned that the hostages were being harmed.[136] Brzezinski's "special small committee" consisting of himself, Defense Secretary Brown, Chief of Staff Jones, and CIA chief Turner, "had identified initial targets and would be ready to act within two days if ordered."[137] Delta Force was also making extensive preparations for a rescue mission should that option later prove feasible and desirable, although the initial reaction of the Joint Chiefs was "pessimistic."[138]

These military considerations seemed premature, for it appeared at this point that the seizure might have been the independent act of some militant students and not a deliberate act by Khomeini, and that it would be resolved in short order. The release of thirteen of the hostages (women and blacks not accused of espionage) between November 17 and 19 reinforced the "accident" hypothesis. Moreover, by this time, negotiations with Iranian representatives at the UN appeared to hold promise for release of the rest.[139]

Before negotiations got anywhere, however, Khomeini himself made it clear there would be no quick and easy solution, casting doubt on the "accident" hypothesis. Upon release of the thirteen hostages, in a major speech on November 20 Khomeini reiterated a threat made several times over the previous three days that unless the shah were returned Iran would place the remaining hostages on trial for espionage. As if to taunt the president, Khomeini declared that Carter lacked "the guts for military action."[140] Khomeini's threat forced the United States government to consider the grim possibility, however bizarre, that the hostages might be tried and executed and that retaliation would be necessary.

There were also early reports about an attack by Saudi Shiites, possibly sponsored by Iran, on the Grand Mosque in Mecca.[141] The Saudis immediately blacked out foreign communications and recalled Prince Fahd, the day-to-day leader of the monarchy, from an Arab summit in Tunisia.[142] Administration (and Saudi) concern was particularly high because most Saudi Shiites, who number only some 115,000 out of a total population of 5 million, lived in the eastern province of Saudi Arabia, where the major oil production facilities were. The threat of executions of Americans and the possible spread of Khomeini's disruptive influence beyond Iran triggered a major shift in administration thinking about the hostage problem over the next several days.

The immediate reaction to Khomeini's speech was to take a tougher public stance. From the evening of November 20, the Carter administration began to speak of the possibility that the United States would take military action against Iran. Before this, the administration had carefully ruled out the use of force. Then, suddenly, on that day following a meeting of President Carter with his top advisers, the White House issued a statement reiterating a preference for a peaceful solution to the hostage crisis but noting the availability of "other remedies" authorized in chapter 7 of the UN charter.[143] The statement cited articles 42 and 51, which, respectively, authorize the UN Security Council to employ force "to maintain or restore international peace and security" and individual nations' inherent right to employ force in self-defense.

Also on the twentieth, President Carter ordered a carrier task force from its station in the Philippines to the Indian Ocean, deployed additional tanker aircraft to support possible long-range air operations, and sent some helicopters to Diego Garcia.[144] The aircraft carrier *Kittyhawk* was accompanied by five other ships, including a guided missile cruiser.[145] It would join on arrival two other naval groups already there. One of these was a force of eight ships led by the carrier *Midway*, also in the Arabian Sea. The other was the Mideast task force, with three ships in the Persian Gulf and two in the Arabian Sea, including a command ship, a destroyer, and a frigate. This combined force of nineteen warships, with an air complement of 160 planes, constituted "the most powerful fleet the United States [had] ever sent to the Arabian Sea and Persian Gulf area."[146]

It seemed that the United States wished to draw a line beyond which Khomeini could not go without severe reaction from Washington, and also to reassure the Saudis and others that the United States would not be intimidated. The announcement of the naval movements came none too soon, however, for within forty-eight hours it seemed as if the United States was coming under attack from fanatical fundamentalists throughout the Moslem world. Moscow, too, began to prepare the ground for greater involvement in Iran, although its effort was primarily to establish "legal" justification for future action.

Following confirmation of the news of the attack on the Grand Mosque, which was complicated by erroneous and absurd reports that it was an attack by Israel with United States support, there came within hours a mob attack on the American embassy in Islamabad, Pakistan.[147] Two Americans and four Pakistanis were killed and the embassy badly burned. There was also an attack on the U.S. consul general in Lahore. The next two days, November 22 and 23, saw rock-throwing demonstrations at American diplomatic missions in Ismir, Turkey; Dacca, Bangladesh; and Srinagar, India.[148]

At the same time, presumably in reaction to Washington's announcement regarding its naval deployments, Moscow sought to have it both ways, attempting to deter Washington while preserving its own right to intervene. On the one hand, the National Voice of Iran, the Soviet-controlled, clandestine radio station in Baku, reversed position on the hostages, declaring that those remaining should be released.[149] Soviet Foreign Minister Gromyko declared that the Iranian revolution was an internal affair, toward which the Soviet Union had a "positive attitude." Indeed, he went on, "nobody should intervene from outside in the national affairs of Iran."[150]

On the other hand, Soviet sources in Washington asserted that the Soviet Union still had the right under the 1921 treaty "to intervene if it sees any U.S. military move in Iran as a threat to Soviet security."[151] As promised, Tehran had unilaterally canceled both the 1959 United States–Iran agreement and key clauses in the 1921 Soviet–Iran treaty the day after the hostage seizure. But Soviet sources noted that abrogation would not become effective for six more months and, more importantly, that those sections still intact provided a "rationale for action" should there occur "any events in Iran that threaten the security of the Soviet Union."[152]

On November 23, the president convened his top aides at Camp David to "reassess U.S. strategy." The president was most concerned that "Iran not be allowed to set the pace of events," as it would if the hostages were placed on trial.[153] Khomeini's latest threat, issued on that day and no doubt reflecting news of United States naval deployments, was that if the United States attacked Iran, the students holding the embassy "would blow it up and 'destroy' their hostages."[154]

The president, growing impatient, wanted to adopt a series of escalating measures to increase pressure on Iran, and he wanted to send a stern message to Khomeini against placing the hostages on trial. Secretary Vance, who "adamantly opposed" any military action unless the hostages were harmed, objected to sending a direct threat and urged the president to show restraint and continue with the negotiations he was conducting at the UN.[155] After a "lively debate" the president agreed to pursue "the political path" on negotiations but determined that military preparations for a punitive strike against Iran would go forward and, overruling Vance (and Mondale and Brown, who agreed with him), Carter decided that a strong warning be sent to Khomeini.[156]

The message, sent privately to Tehran through a friendly intermediary, stipulated that if the hostages were placed on trial the United States would "interrupt all commerce with Iran as soon as the first trial began."[157] The form of interruption was not spelled out in the note, but the president had decided to mine the entrances to Iran's seaports. Should any of the hostages be harmed or executed, the note went on, the president was prepared to order "a direct military attack on Iran."[158] The target for a punitive strike was Iran's domestic petroleum facilities.

The president's warning to Iran had a positive impact on the issue of hostage trials but immediately produced problems of another sort. Although no Iranian official ever publicly referred to Carter's warning message, talk of hostage trials quickly ceased.[159] Almost immediately, however, Iran placed its air force and navy on alert.[160] A few days later, Khomeini began to call for the mobilization of the entire Iranian nation against a possible United States attack. In a talk to revolutionary militiamen, he said, "Prepare yourselves. Get military training. Give military training."[161] He declared, "One thing is clear: our enemy is the United States, and all our efforts should be directed toward this."[162]

Worse, the negotiations at the UN broke down. By November 25, Iranian and American negotiators had reached a tentative agreement on a settlement. It had been arranged that Acting Foreign Minister Abolhassan Bani-Sadr would travel to the UN to address the Security Council at the end of the month and effect a resolution of the crisis. But at the last minute, on November 28, Khomeini dismissed Bani-Sadr, who had been in office all of eighteen days, scuttling the settlement. Two days later, the new foreign minister, Sadegh Ghotbzadeh, cancelled his trip to the UN, publicly repudiated the agreement, and closed off further negotiations.

The collapse of the negotiations left the administration with no ready means of resolving the crisis, so the president's top advisers met again the day of Bani-Sadr's dismissal to decide how to proceed.[163] The November 28 NSC meeting was the "turning point" in American policy and as such was "the most contentious" meeting of the entire crisis.[164] The crucial issue was whether or not the United States should employ force in an effort to save the hostages. Brzezinski—and it seems the president, although he was not present at this meeting—argued for a more forceful course of action, while Secretaries Vance and Brown, General Jones, Stansfield Turner, and Charles Kirbo argued that any use of force would place the lives of the hostages in jeopardy and should not be employed.[165]

The basis for their discussion was a list which the president had circulated earlier of possible actions the United States could take, ranging from condemnation of Iran to punitive military action. Brzezinski, arguing that the United States was becoming locked into a "litigation strategy," pressed for adoption of a series of measured, escalating military steps to bring pressure on the Iranian leadership.[166] Secretary Vance led the objections to this proposed course. After heated argument the group decided that, although military preparations for contingency purposes would continue, the best course of action to pursue would be a diplomatic approach combined with efforts to gain international cooperation to condemn and isolate Iran. There would, in short, be no use of military force to extract the hostages.[167]

But military preparations for contingency purposes would continue. The chief contingency, of course, was the question of potential Soviet involvement. Since the United States had made the firm decision to abjure the use of force, continued deployment of military power toward Iran could only have been to deter the Soviet Union from an adventurous move. It is obvious that Iran was a major geopolitical opportunity for the Soviet Union and therefore a major concern for most of the Carter leadership.[168] Secretary Vance, however, objected strongly to any hint that the United States would take action against Iran, and even to a buildup of American military presence in the area. As he put it in his memoir, in the context of growing Soviet involvement in Afghanistan,

> There were background news stories coming out of Washington to the effect that there was a possibility of some form of U.S. military action against Iran. I felt this unwise. U.S. military presence in the area would make a collapse of the Kabul regime more dangerous for the Soviets and thus enhance the possibility of Soviet intervention. In addition, a U.S. military move in Iran might diminish international reaction to a Soviet invasion [of Afghanistan], as the Anglo–French attack on Egypt had done in the Suez crisis in 1956.[169]

Despite Vance's objections, however, another carrier, the *Forrestal*, was dispatched to the Mediterranean. There were already two carriers in the Mediterranean, the *Independence* and the *Nimitz*. Combined with the *Midway* and the *Kittyhawk* in the Arabian Sea, by the second week in December the United States would have five aircraft carriers in place, with 350 planes capable of conducting long-range air strikes against Iran.[170] Air tankers were already deployed for in-flight refueling, which would enable execution of air strikes from either the Mediterranean or the Arabian Sea. And Washington had deployed two AWACs to Egypt to coordinate large-scale aerial combat.[171] Navy pilots in Norfolk, the port from which the *Forrestal* sailed, said that they "could make Iran into a parking lot."[172] This same capability, of course, could be employed against any Soviet force invading Iran.

Moscow Moves Its Queen: The Invasion of Afghanistan

If the fall of the shah had opened a major geopolitical opportunity for the Soviet Union to alter the global correlation of forces to advantage, then the hostage crisis threatened to take it away. Soviet leaders had to assume that the American leadership would employ the enormous military power being assembled near Iran to overthrow the Khomeini regime and restore relations with its formerly close ally.[173] This assumption was reinforced from November 20, when the United States abruptly began to speak of using force against Iran to gain the release of the hostages and citing international law to justify military action. It is probable that Moscow had also learned of Carter's private threat to attack Iran, but in any case Iran's war mobilization was public.

From Moscow's point of view the hostages offered Washington a justifiable opportunity to take action against Iran, and the sheer size of the American buildup—five carriers, 350 planes—suggested more than a mere rescue attempt. It bears reiterating that despite the military buildup and accompanying saber-rattling rhetoric, President Carter had decided *not* to employ force. But Soviet leaders did not know that, and if they had known, they probably would not have believed it.

The problem for Moscow, then, was how to deter the United States from taking action and preserve the opportunity to draw Iran into the Soviet orbit. That the Soviet leadership would employ its military power to deter the United States was an obvious extrapolation from the Soviet strategic and conventional weapons buildup of the past decade, and from Soviet policy behavior itself. Soviet power projection to distant points, from Angola to Ethiopia to Vietnam, had been from Moscow's point of view highly successful. Washington's responses had been, at most, feeble. There was every reason to expect that military intervention in a country on the immediate Soviet border would meet with a similar response from its global adversary. What the Soviets failed to anticipate was the response from the Afghan people themselves.

Moscow had been assessing strategic requirements in Afghanistan since January, when it had become obvious that the shah would not survive. The first of several high-level Soviet military missions occurred at that time.[174] At that point, however, Soviet calculations were no doubt defensive—to be prepared to stabilize the deteriorating situation in Afghanistan in case civil war erupted in Iran and/or the United States intervened the way it had done a quarter-century earlier to restore its ally to power.

But as United States–Iran relations collapsed following Khomeini's ascendancy and Washington took no action, Soviet calculations changed. A strong show of force in Afghanistan, where the Soviets already had a growing military involvement, potentially offered Moscow the means not only to stabilize Afghanistan but also to deter an American move against Iran. Moreover, a strong Soviet position in Afghanistan would increase leverage on Iran.

Nevertheless, while an increased Soviet role in Afghanistan was becoming inevitable, its specific application and timing would depend upon perception of American policy intentions toward Iran.[175] A decision for a preemptive show of force would only be necessary if an American military move against Iran appeared imminent. Otherwise, a simple increase in Soviet military assistance programs to Afghanistan would suffice. Until then, preparations for both courses of action would continue. The hostage seizure and Washington's response forced a choice.

Although popular disaffection in Afghanistan with the communist regime had become widespread rather quickly, armed resistance had been minor through 1978, until late in the year.[176] By then the impact of communist land and social "reforms" and purges had begun to be felt by large segments of the populace. The onset of winter had also freed farmers from the fields to fight.[177] Still, through the early spring of 1979, resistance was sporadic and confined to remote areas; the cities seemed safe and under firm communist control.

The first major crisis to the Afghan communist regime occurred in mid-March. Nuristani rebels declared the establishment of Azad (Free) Nuristan in the Kunar Valley of eastern Afghanistan.[178] The rebels had gained control of most of the upper valley, driving out government forces and administration. Their example was followed by other ethnic groups as rebellious outbursts occurred in Paktia, Nangarhar, Kapisa, Uruzgan, Parvan, Sadghis, Balkh, Ghazni, Farah, and Herat. By summer, the revolt had spread to over half of Afghanistan's twenty-eight provinces, mostly in the eastern half of the country, even though it remained uncoordinated.

But it was the rebellion at Herat, a city of 150,000 located in western Afghanistan some sixty-five miles from the Iranian border, which brought an immediate response from Moscow. The Herat uprising was brutally put down, with extensive loss of life, after almost a week of fierce fighting and the dispatch of reinforcements from the garrison at Kandahar. One estimate counted 20,000 Afghanis dead, including hundreds of government officials, Khalq officers, and twenty Soviet advisers and their families.[179]

While blaming outside forces for "instigating" the rebellion, the Soviets immediately sent additional military equipment and advisers to reinforce Afghan forces.[180] Tanks, armored personnel carriers, and helicopter gunships began arriving by the end of the month. The swift helicopter gunships (MI-24s), in particular, operated by Soviet pilots and sporting rockets and heavy machine guns, proved to be devastating against traditional guerrilla tactics of quick movement, ambush, and surprise attack.[181] In early April, Moscow sent General Alexei A. Yepishev and half a dozen other generals to Kabul for a week to assess the efficacy of the new tactics and weaponry against the growing resistance.

The Herat uprising, meanwhile, brought to a head differences within the PDPA between President and party chief Nur Mohammad Taraki and his second in command, Hafizullah Amin. On March 27, a cabinet shuffle saw Amin become prime minister, assuming direct control of the government. Taraki remained president, but was on his way to being eclipsed by his "faithful student." In effective policy control, Amin spurred a relentless campaign against the rebellion. At the same time he intensified a widespread purge of Taraki's followers within the Khalq faction of the PDPA, and of the rival Parcham faction, which the Soviets favored.

Moscow no doubt fully supported Amin's efforts to eradicate resistance to the regime; the Soviets were after all providing the military equipment, pilots, and advisers for it. In most cases, purged Afghan officials were replaced by Soviet advisers. Conservative estimates identified 1,500 Soviet advisers in the Afghan government and between 3,500 and 4,000 in the military.[182] That summer, on Soviet advice, Amin's forces carried out a scorched-earth policy, burning crops to deprive resistance groups of food.[183] Even though Moscow promised to make up any shortfalls, the net effect of such policies was further alienation of the people.

By summer, Afghanistan was headed into a downward spiral of repression, rebellion, and reprisal. The army, originally a force of 90,000, was wracked by desertion, defection, and disloyalty, and dwindled to half its original size. Perhaps reflecting growing concern about army loyalty, following an army mutiny at Jalalabad in late June, Moscow deployed the first Soviet ground-force contingent of four hundred men to secure control of Bagram airfield, north of Kabul, in early July.

But Moscow balked at Amin's brutal suppression of the Khalq and Parcham factions, for the Soviets were attempting in time-honored fashion to reduce resistance to the regime by broadening participation in it. Indeed, Moscow sought unsuccessfully to gain Taraki's and Amin's agreement to broaden the Afghan government by including Parcham members as well as noncommunists in a "united national front."[184] By July, unable to check Amin's repression of real and imagined adversaries, Moscow began searching in earnest for ways to install a more compliant successor.

From July onward, Moscow pursued a two-track policy toward Afghanistan. On the one hand, preparations continued for greater Soviet involvement to stabilize the country. In mid-August, for example, Moscow sent a major mission to Kabul, headed by General Ivan G. Pavlovsky, chief of Soviet ground forces, and also the officer who had planned the 1968 invasion of Czechoslovakia.[185] Sixty-three officers and eleven generals, the Pavlovsky mission remained in Afghanistan for two months, departing in mid-October. Pavlovsky left behind a headquarters unit staffed by a lieutenant general and a cadre of general officers large enough to command a massive Soviet troop presence.[186]

On the other hand, Moscow strove to improve both Afghan military operations and political organization with dispatch of additional equipment and advisers.[187] In this context, the Soviets sponsored at least three attempts to assassinate Amin—all of which backfired.[188] The first attempt was apparently worked out during Taraki's stopover in Moscow, September 10, on his way home from attending the so-called non-aligned conference in Havana in early September. The essence of simplicity, the plot involved luring Amin into an ambush at Taraki's office, having him killed, and restoring Taraki to power.[189] In return, Taraki would broaden the government by re-including the Parcham faction, led by Babrak Karmal.

Suspicious of a plot against him, on September 14 Amin ordered the firing of four cabinet leaders close to Taraki.[190] That same day Taraki telephoned Amin inviting him to a meeting, presumably to discuss the firings. Amin hesitated until assured of his safety by Soviet Ambassador Alexander M. Puzanov, who was with Taraki. When Amin arrived at Taraki's office in the People's Palace a gunfight ensued in which several were killed; but Amin himself escaped unhurt. He returned shortly afterward with reinforcements and captured Taraki, who may have been wounded in the fighting.[191]

On September 16, the PDPA Central Committee announced that Taraki had resigned "due to health reasons and physical incapacity . . . to continue his work," and that Hafizullah Amin had been appointed secretary general of the PDPA.[192] Foiled, the Soviets continued to cooperate with Amin, while treating him coolly. For his part, Amin, thoroughly alerted to threats against his life, also kept the Soviets at a distance. He demanded and eventually obtained Puzanov's removal as ambassador and in early October refused an invitation to go to Moscow to talk things over.[193] Frustrated at their inability to control Amin, the Soviets attempted to poison him through his cook, a KGB agent, but the wily Afghan leader avoided the bait.[194]

Moscow's third attempt to eliminate Amin occurred in mid-December as part of "plan A," the show of force. The Soviet leadership had chosen, evidently between November 26 and 28, to make all necessary preparations for a major show of force in Afghanistan, to preempt the then-expected American military move into Iran.[195] At this point (see above), the Carter administration had just made a series of decisions (November 20–26), including the issuance of a direct threat to Khomeini and the assemblage of a major naval and air force in the Arabian Sea, and had begun to speak publicly of using military force against Iran.

Thus, the decisions of November 26–28 centered on mobilizing necessary forces, securing Soviet lines of communication into Afghanistan, and obtaining the necessary "invitation" for a major Soviet military deployment. The final decision to go would not be made until the last moment, after all preparations were completed. From late November, American intelligence identified what were later established to have been the initial Soviet military preparations in the area north of the Soviet–Afghan border.[196] From November 29, Soviet transport aircraft began flying troops of the 105th Guards Airborne Division at Ferghana into Bagram airfield, including a "special brigade" of heavily armed airborne troops.[197] By December 10, the Soviets had put in over 2,700 men, reinforcing the 400-man unit sent in July.

There can be little doubt that Moscow had decided to eliminate Amin; as noted, several attempts had already been made. But now that the Soviet leadership had decided upon "plan A," there was one last duty for Amin to perform before his usefulness came to an end. To help him accomplish it, on November 29, Moscow sent the first deputy of the Interior Ministry, Victor S. Paputin, to Kabul at the head of a delegation to formally discuss internal police work with opposite numbers in the Afghan Interior Ministry.

Paputin's true mission can, of course, only be surmised. It was apparently his complicated assignment to reassure Amin of continuing Soviet confidence while obtaining from him the invitation that would "legalize" a massive Soviet intervention in Afghanistan.[198] At the same time, Paputin was to arrange for Amin's assassination once the formal request for troops was in hand, or, perhaps more likely, if Amin refused to make such a request—as he had for months. The assassination would be carried out by the very security police that Paputin's office had been training and advising since the Saur revolution.[199] Paputin, no doubt, knew the top men in the security police personally, a factor which was probably the reason for his selection.

If this was indeed Paputin's mission, and something like it is generally assumed, it met with mixed results.[200] Paputin stayed in Kabul for two weeks, meeting with officials of the Afghan security police and also with Amin himself. At first, Paputin's efforts appeared to bear fruit, as Amin publicly announced several new policy decisions which the Soviets had been pressing upon him for months. But Amin was wary of Paputin and provided him with trusted "escorts." Curiously, just before Paputin departed, Amin himself announced that a coup attempt had been "foiled," suggesting that Soviet efforts to depose him had failed again.

On December 3, Amin took a step to soften his harsh regime, urging the Council of Ministers to get closer to the people, carry out policy in the spirit of criticism and self-criticism, listen to the people, and "tolerate their criticism."[201] Three days later, Amin also agreed to the formation of a united national front, for which Moscow had been pressing since mid-year. At a Politburo session on December 6, Amin decided to inaugurate the "national organization for the defense of the revolution."[202]

Meanwhile, the next day, in discussing the first anniversary of the Soviet–Afghan treaty of 1978, Tass commentator Novikov went beyond the language of article 4 of the treaty, which called for "cooperation in the military sphere," to make reference to Soviet and Afghan forces "conducting joint measures" to ensure the security, independence, and territorial integrity of both countries.[203] The Brezhnev–Kosygin message of greeting on the anniversary of the Soviet–Afghan treaty, published in *Pravda* December 7, was more reserved, expressing confidence that the treaty would promote relations in the "spirit of equality and revolutionary solidarity." But it omitted reference to the spirit of "comradeship," which had been included in earlier messages, and to Amin personally.[204]

Amin, however, came extremely close to publicly "requesting"

Soviet troop assistance, a major shift in his own position, which he had publicly maintained for months. At a news conference on December 10, when queried by an Italian correspondent whether he would "ask for Russian soldiers in case of war with Pakistan," Amin replied:

> I wouldn't say a war between Afghanistan and Pakistan, but I would say that if we are attacked, we will ask the Soviet Union for the help we require. We are certain that whatever we ask of the USSR, it will give us.[205]

If the Soviets hoped that Amin would use the opportunity to "invite" Soviet troops, they were disappointed. In any case, the next day, December 11, the Afghan leader announced in a radio speech that "a coup plot aimed at toppling his regime" had failed. "The coup attempt was foiled," he said.[206] Amin's speech was vague. He did not disclose the identities of those involved, when the attempt had been made, or whether the coup plot was discovered beforehand.[207] Nor was there any suggestion that Paputin had had anything to do with the "coup attempt." The first deputy departed December 13, after what were described simply and briefly as "a series of friendly talks."[208]

Whether or not there had been an actual coup attempt earlier in December or whether Amin had discovered a plot and sought to preempt it by exposing it, will never be known. But a few days after Paputin had departed, on December 17 there was an attempt to assassinate Amin. This was presumably the plot that Paputin had arranged (and perhaps the one Amin had smelled) involving the Afghan security services, but they botched it.

Amin reportedly suffered a flesh wound in the leg, but the head of the security forces, Amin's nephew, Asadullah Amin, was wounded seriously enough to be evacuated to the Soviet Union for treatment.[209] It was not clear on whose side Asadullah Amin had been aligned. Nevertheless, realizing that a showdown was near, Amin called together his most trusted men, assembled eight tanks and several armored personnel carriers, and moved his entourage on December 19 to the Darulaman Palace complex seven miles outside the city.

Amin's retreat to the Darulaman redoubt to await his fate came just as Soviet forces were poised to move en masse into Afghanistan.[210] The Soviets had set up a special operational headquarters at

Termez on the Soviet side of the Soviet–Afghan border, on the main road link. And on the twentieth one of the units flown in earlier in the month, a 600-man armored force, moved to secure the main road between Kabul and Termez, including the Salang Pass tunnel, which shortly would become the main invasion route.

The Carter administration, hoping to deter the Soviets from invading, decided to send another private warning to Moscow, publicize its troop buildup, and concentrate additional forces in the Arabian Sea. A *New York Times* front-page report on December 22 revealed that American intelligence had identified three divisions, over thirty thousand men, poised to cross the Amu Darya, the river forming part of the Soviet–Afghan border.[211] The same day, the administration announced that the president had decided to send the nuclear aircraft carrier *Nimitz*, the largest warship afloat, from its station in the Mediterranean to the Arabian Sea.[212] The *Nimitz*, accompanied by two guided-missile cruisers, the *Texas* and the *California*, would arrive in late January and bring the total number of American warships in the Arabian Sea to twenty-four, including four aircraft carriers.[213]

Pravda responded quickly to the administration's charges. The next day, December 23, commentator Arkadi Maslennikov described as "pure invention" reports by the United States government that the Soviet Union had moved combat troops into Afghanistan.

> The Western, and particularly American, mass media have lately been spreading patently inspired rumors about some kind of 'interference' on the part of the Soviet Union in the internal affairs of Afghanistan. They have gone so far as to allege that Soviet 'combat units' have been moved into Afghanistan's territory. All this, of course, is pure invention.[214]

The next night, December 24, 200 troop transports began offloading Soviet combat troops at four of Afghanistan's major airports—at Kabul, Bagram, Shindand, and Kandahar. By the twenty-seventh, there were 6,000 troops on the ground, with five divisions poised on the border ready to enter.[215] That evening, following a "courtesy call" to Amin by the Soviet minister of communications, Nikolai V. Talyzin, who had arrived on the twenty-fourth, Soviet combat units began their assault on Amin's palace stronghold. Talyzin himself led an assault to secure control of Kabul's central communications complex.[216]

The failure to remove and replace Amin or to obtain a formal "invitation" before deploying massive numbers of troops made a mockery of all Soviet explanations about providing assistance to the Democratic Republic of Afghanistan (DRA). Since the Soviets had failed by various means to assassinate the Afghan leader, Soviet troops would have to do the job. Paputin evidently returned to Kabul at this point to identify Amin for them.[217] Clearly, Amin would have to be killed before his chosen replacement, Babrak Karmal, could be installed. In any case, by the morning of December 28, the deed was done and Babrak Karmal brought in to assume the "presidency" of the DRA.

What is apparent in retrospect is that factors external to Afghanistan itself drove the decision on the timing of the Soviet invasion. The internal Afghan situation was not so perilous as to require an invasion without first securing the necessary "invitation."[218] Soviet concern to legitimize the invasion surely would have counseled a delay of even a few more days until Amin had been disposed of. Although the Soviets had tried several times without success, there would be other opportunities. Surely they would eventually succeed. With Amin removed and Babrak installed *before* the invasion, a subsequent invitation from Babrak would have gone great lengths toward neutralizing the worldwide condemnation of the Soviets for their barbaric violation of international law. Indeed, it would very likely have remained a problem of national rather than of international dimensions.

The question is: What was of so much concern for the Soviet leadership that they risked an invasion before obtaining the necessary invitation? The answer, as argued in this chapter, was their perception that the United States was preparing to take action against Iran, action which Soviet leaders feared would close off the historic opportunity to draw Iran into the Soviet orbit. Needless to say, the supreme irony in the Soviet decision was that the Carter administration had decided *not* to do anything of the kind.

Moscow was hoist on its own strategic petard, borne of the Brezhnev leadership's increasing predisposition to attempt to alter the geopolitical balance by military means. Thus, when an unparalleled opportunity arose to make perhaps the most significant alteration in the global balance outside of conquering Europe, Soviet leaders were prepared to run extreme risks. Within two weeks Moscow had poured some 80,000 troops into Afghanistan, and by the end of January there were 90,000, a figure that would remain substantially constant for several months.

The pattern of Soviet deployment into Afghanistan was consistent with the view that the invasion was designed to be preemptive. The main danger to the Kabul regime came from rebel concentrations in the eastern half of the country bordering on Pakistan. The purpose of huge troop concentrations could only have been to encircle and cut off support for the rebels. Yet the Soviets deployed roughly half of the invasion force to the southwest, near the Iranian border.[219]

The conclusion seems inescapable that the *timing* of Moscow's decision to invade was for the larger purpose of deterring the United States from taking action in neighboring Iran. If Soviet thinking was that an invasion, a show of force, would be preemptive, they had simply lost touch with American political reality. If they believed that an invasion would also shore up their disintegrating regime in Kabul, they had lost touch with Afghan political reality. Afghan resistance would increase in ferocity, the puppet communist regime would continue to deteriorate, losing all credibility and drawing the Soviet Union into a costly, decade-long entanglement.

As Brezhnev declared in a mid-January interview, "It was no simple decision for us to send Soviet military contingents to Afghanistan. But the party's Central Committee and the Soviet Government acted in full awareness of their responsibility and took into account the entire aggregate of circumstances."[220] In dismissing Washington's warnings and repudiating detente, Soviet leaders were clearly willing to accept the costs of a negative American and world reaction if the reward was the exclusion of the United States from Iran.

On the other hand, there can be little doubt that the Soviets calculated they could withstand the kind of response the United States could make.[221] SALT II, after all, was already on the shelf and United States–Soviet relations already in sharp decline because of the Cuban brigade episode of a few months before. The Soviets undoubtedly anticipated that at the very least the United States would attempt to fuel the Afghan resistance, but they believed that their military power was adequate to the challenge.

However, Washington's main reaction would have to be strategic, a return to full-fledged containment, and here there would be difficulty. An American military buildup, in Southwest Asia and elsewhere, was already under way, so there was not much more to be expected on that score. Actual reinvigoration of trade and technology controls beyond allied lip service would not be easy; further development of rapprochement with China, while of concern, would have clear limits; and stimulation of dissent within the Soviet bloc could also be difficult.

Despite strong language condemning the invasion and promising "serious consequences" unless the Soviet Union withdrew, President Carter took no decisive action.[222] That was because there was none to take that would not penalize the United States as much as the Soviet Union. The president did cut off grain shipments, which caused as much concern within the United States as problems for the Soviet Union and could not be maintained indefinitely. Indeed, there were alternative suppliers of grain, but not alternative buyers. Negative world reaction was never a major factor in Soviet calculations. The American boycott of the Moscow Olympics was borne without undue difficulty. Indeed, the substantial attendance at the games was potentially embarrassing to the United States.

Indeed, one could argue that the Carter administration's weak reaction to the Afghanistan invasion further undercut the president's claim to leadership as he headed into the final year of his presidency, groping for an adequate response to a strategic failure whose origins spanned two administrations. Moscow had for the second time since 1973 emphatically rejected the strategy which the American leadership had proffered—the quid pro quo of trade and high technology exchange in return for Soviet strategic weapons and geopolitical restraint. Moscow was bent on altering the global correlation of forces by military means, acting on the assumption, reinforced by the American response to their actions in Afghanistan, that there was no power standing in the way.

Notes

1. See William Greider and J.P. Smith, "A Proposition: High Oil Prices Benefit U.S.," *Washington Post*, July 10, 1977, p. 1.
2. *World Economic Outlook*, Occasional Paper No. 27 (Washington, DC: International Monetary Fund, 1984), p. 130.
3. Jack Anderson, with James Boyd, *Fiasco* (New York: Times Books, 1983), p. 51, and Robert Sherrill, *The Oil Follies of 1970–1980, How the Petroleum Industry Stole the Show (and Much More Besides)* (New York: Anchor Press, 1983), p. 348.
4. Fred J. Cook, *The Great Energy Scam: Private Billions vs Public Good* (New York: Macmillan Publishing Company, 1982), pp. 134–37.
5. Ibid., p. 139. The rate of natural gas discoveries in the United States and Alaska accelerated thereafter for the rest of the Carter administration and beyond. See pp. 149–53.
6. Cook, *The Great Energy Scam*, pp. 141–42.
7. Ibid.
8. Carter, *Keeping Faith*, p. 91.
9. For details, see *CQ Almanac 1978*, pp. 639–67.
10. For details, see *CQ Almanac 1979*, pp. 601–61.
11. See the *Economic Report of the President, 1982* (Washington, DC: GPO, 1982), pp. 112–15.
12. For the analysis of the earlier period, see the author's *Nixon–Kissinger Years*, pp. 274–88.
13. *International Financial Statistics* (Washington, DC: International Monetary Fund, 1980), p. 165 for Germany, p. 225 for Japan, and p. 403 for the United States. If one excludes gold holdings, then the disparity between the United States and Germany and Japan is even greater.
14. *Direction of Trade Yearbook—1983* (Washington, DC: International Monetary Fund, 1983), p. 397.
15. Although the spot market would normally only handle 5 to 8 percent of market operations, essentially odd-lot and single tanker auctions, the spot price indicated the direction of change for long-term contract prices.
16. Ian Seymour, *OPEC, Instrument of Change* (New York: St. Martin's Press, 1981), p. 182.
17. *World Economic Outlook*, p. 130. For the Nigerian surge figure, see "Saudis Chop 1 Million B/D Off Output," *Oil and Gas Journal*, April 16, 1979, p. 52.
18. "Global Survey," *Oil and Gas Journal*, August 27, 1979, pp. 32–33.
19. Sherrill, *Oil Follies*, pp. 435–36, and *Monthly Energy Review*, U.S. Department of Energy (June 1981), p. 28.
20. Ibid.

21. Ibid., p. 32. Imports from Iran in 1978 had averaged 555,000 b/d.
22. Ibid., p. 30.
23. Cook, *Great Energy Scam*, p. 88.
24. Sherrill, *Oil Follies*, p. 427.
25. *CQ Almanac 1979*, p. 601.
26. The prosperity in the petroleum industry had fueled a dramatic increase in oil tanker construction. There was by 1979 a tanker surplus of over 100 million deadweight tons. See *Tankers and the Flags They Fly*, Exxon Background Series (June 1979), p. 5.
27. See Dankwert A. Rustow, *Oil and Turmoil, America Faces OPEC and the Middle East* (New York: W.W. Norton & Co., 1982), pp. 183–84.
28. Sherrill, *Oil Follies*, p. 423.
29. Seymour, *OPEC, Instrument of Change*, p. 186.
30. "Iranian Crude Exports Still in Doubt," *Oil and Gas Journal*, February 19, 1979, pp. 63–64.
31. Sherrill, *Oil Follies*, p. 420.
32. Anderson, *Fiasco*, p. 334.
33. Ibid., p. 333.
34. Ibid., pp. 333–34. For example, Japanese Foreign Minister Saburo Okita noted in December that the majors "had cut back their oil shipments to Japan from 1.4 million b/d at this time last year to 400,000 b/d now. Japan, he said, was forced by the major oil companies to buy Iranian oil on the spot market." *Japan Times*, December 14, 1979, p. 1.
35. Anderson, *Fiasco*,, p. 334.
36. See chapter 7, pp. 317–18.
37. See Seymour, *OPEC, Instrument of Change*, pp. 117–18.
38. "OPEC Accelerates Price Hike Schedule," *Oil and Gas Journal*, April 2, 1979, pp. 44–45.
39. "U.S.: Price Hikes Untimely, Unjustified," *Oil and Gas Journal*, April 2, 1979, p. 44.
40. Ibid.
41. *CQ Almanac 1979*, pp. 23–24E. For an extended discussion of energy legislation, see pp. 601–61.
42. Ibid.
43. "Saudis Chop 1 Million B/D Off Output," pp. 52–53, and "Iran Sets Crude Export Ceiling at 3 Million B/D," May 7, 1979, p. 43.
44. Seymour, *OPEC, Instrument of Change*, pp. 183, 192.
45. Anderson, *Fiasco*, p. 334.
46. Ibid., p. 335.
47. *Monthly Energy Review*, June 1981, p. 80.
48. Seymour, *OPEC, Instrument of Change*, p. 184.
49. Sherrill, *Oil Follies*, p. 461.

50. Seymour, *OPEC, Instrument of Change*, p. 184.
51. Ibid., p. 192.
52. *Middle East Economic Digest*, January 18, 1980, p. 37, and Thomas W. Lippman, "Arab Opponents of Pact Say U.S. Made Policy Error," *Washington Post*, May 2, 1979, p. 27.
53. Jim Hoagland and J.P. Smith, "U.S. Moving to Repair Saudi Ties," *Washington Post*, June 12, 1979, p. 1, and Karen Elliott House, "The Anger in Saudi Arabia," *Wall Street Journal*, June 11, 1979, p. 14.
54. "Vance Sees Decline in U.S.–Saudi Links," *New York Times*, May 9, 1979, p. 1.
55. Ibid. See chapter 7, pp. 292–93, for discussion of the Baghdad conference.
56. Hoagland and Smith, "U.S. Moving to Repair Saudi Ties," p. 1.
57. Ibid.
58. "New Arab Oil Threat Helped Push Carter to Seek Palestinian Role," *Forum Notes*, Washington Forum, August 24, 1979, p. 3. Washington's tentative exploration of better relations with the Palestinians ended in the "Andy Young affair" in July when UN Ambassador Young was forced to resign because of so-called inappropriate contacts with PLO representatives.
59. *Saudi Arabia and the United States, the New Context in an Evolving "Special Relationship,"* Report of the Subcommittee on Europe and the Middle East of the Committee on Foreign Affairs, U.S. House of Representatives (Washington, DC: GPO, August 1981), p. 27.
60. Seymour, *OPEC, Instrument of Change*, p. 192.
61. See the informative article by Robert J. Samuelson, "The International Money Tightrope," *Washington Post*, October 2, 1979, p. E1.
62. *Bank for International Settlements*, April 1979–March 1980 (Basle, Switzerland, 1980), p. 134. (Hereafter referred to as *BIS 1979–80*.)
63. Ibid., pp. 89–90.
64. Ibid., p. 92.
65. Ibid., p. 91.
66. See Ronald A. Morse, "Japan's Search for an Independent Foreign Policy: An American Perspective," *Journal of Northeast Asia Studies* (Summer 1984), pp. 34–35.
67. Carter, *Keeping Faith*, pp. 111–12.
68. Ibid.
69. Ibid.
70. Ibid., p. 112.
71. Robert Putnam and Nicholas Bayne, *Hanging Together, the Seven Power Summits* (London: Heinemann Books, 1984), p. 124.
72. Carter, *Keeping Faith*, pp. 112–13.
73. Putnam and Bayne, *Hanging Together*, p. 124.

74. Ibid., p. 126.
75. Carter, *Keeping Faith*, p. 114.
76. *BIS 1979–80*, p. 3.
77. Carter, *Keeping Faith*, p. 115.
78. "Text of the President's Televised Address," *New York Times*, July 16, 1979, p. 1.
79. Ibid. It was a reasonable objective to meet because the nation had never imported as much petroleum as it had in that year.
80. Ibid.
81. Carter, *Keeping Faith*, pp. 121 and 116. A major exception was Vice-President Mondale, who opposed the firings and thereafter, perhaps in anticipation of a presidential bid, sought to distance himself from the president.
82. Ibid., p. 121.
83. See William Greider, *Secrets of the Temple, How the Federal Reserve Runs the Country* (New York: Simon and Schuster, 1987), pp. 19–20.
84. Carter, *Keeping Faith*, pp. 116–21, omits all mention of Miller and Volcker, and, of course, of monetary policy.
85. Greider, *Secrets of the Temple*, pp. 79–80.
86. Brendan Brown, *The Flight of International Capital—A Contemporary History* (New York: Routledge, 1987), p. 375, and *BIS 1979–80*, p. 134.
87. Brown, *Flight of International Capital*, p. 376.
88. Greider, *Secrets of the Temple*, pp. 118–19, suggests that unspoken concern over the banks' international portfolio accounts was an important reason for the shift to a strong dollar at this time.
89. Solomon, *International Monetary System*, p. 354.
90. "Changes in Monetary Policy and the Fight against Inflation," Remarks to the Cato Institute, January 21, 1983, p. 2, as cited in David M. Jones, *Fed Watching and Interest Rate Projections* (New York: New York Institute of Finance, 1986), p. 70.
91. Federal Reserve Board of Governors, "Record of the Federal Open Market Committee, October 6, 1979," *Federal Reserve Bulletin* (December 1979), p. 974.
92. Jones, *Fed Watching*, p. 74.
93. Greider, *Secrets of the Temple*, p. 147.
94. Brown, *Flight of International Capital*, p. 376.
95. As quoted in Greider, *Secrets of the Temple*, p. 143.
96. Ibid., pp. 142–43.
97. *BIS 1979–80*, p. 134.
98. Brown, *Flight of International Capital*, p. 377, and Sick, *All Fall Down*, p. 269.
99. Greider, *Secrets of the Temple*, p. 147.

100. Perhaps understandably, neither Vance nor Brzezinski dwells on this prospect in his memoir.
101. Brzezinski, *Power and Principle*, p. 471.
102. See the informative article by Kenneth H. Jacobson, "The Middle East in Turmoil," *Leading Edge* (Summer 1979), p. 4.
103. Vance, *Hard Choices*, p. 347.
104. Lewis and Ledeen, *Debacle*, p. 223.
105. Indeed, Kurdish forces would shortly overrun Paveh, a town in western Iran three hundred miles northwest of Tehran. See "Kurds Overrun Iranian Forces; 13 Are Killed," *Washington Star*, August 17, 1979, p. 3.
106. Vance, *Hard Choices*, p. 368.
107. Sick, *All Fall Down*, p. 221.
108. Vance, *Hard Choices*, p. 371. Vance's response to Yazdi was equivocal because on September 28 he had been informed that the shah was seriously ill and might seek admittance into the United States for medical treatment.
109. Sick, *All Fall Down*, pp. 221–22.
110. Ledeen and Lewis, *Debacle*, p. 226.
111. Ibid., p. 227. Sick omits discussion of the October 6 meeting.
112. Ibid.
113. Ibid.
114. *The Iran Hostage Crisis, a Chronology of Daily Developments*, Report of the House Committee on Foreign Affairs, March 1981 (Washington, DC: Congressional Research Service, 1981), p. 33. (Hereafter referred to as Iran Hostage Chronology.)
115. Sick, *All Fall Down*, p. 215.
116. Ibid., p. 216, and Ledeen and Lewis, *Debacle*, pp. 228–29. Vance, *Hard Choices*, p. 372, omits any mention of Precht.
117. Ibid.
118. Sick, *All Fall Down*, p. 217.
119. Lewis and Ledeen, *Debacle*, p. 229.
120. Vance, *Hard Choices*, pp. 375–76, comes to a similar conclusion, without attributing the decision to Khomeini, noting that after the seizure of the embassy, "it became apparent that some of the Islamic figures in the revolution may have designed the seizure as a means of weakening the secular government."
121. Iran Hostage Chronology, p. 35.
122. Ibid.
123. Carter, *Keeping Faith*, p. 457.
124. Brzezinski, *Power and Principle*, p. 475, says simply that he was "heading the American delegation" and that "Mehdi Bazargan requested a meeting with me." Sick, *All Fall Down*, p. 222, says even more enig-

matically that Brzezinski "found himself in an anniversary celebration in Algiers with Bazargan, Yazdi and Mustapha Ali Chamran." Vance, *Hard Choices*, p. 373, on the other hand, who evidently was not informed of Brzezinski's trip, says disapprovingly: "To my surprise, Brzezinski, who was a member of the American delegation to Algiers, met with them."

125. Sick, *All Fall Down*, p. 222.
126. Brzezinski, *Power and Principle*, pp. 475–76.
127. Ibid., p. 476.
128. Vance, *Hard Choices*, p. 373.
129. Brzezinski, *Power and Principle*, p. 476.
130. Sick, *All Fall Down*, p. 230, says that there was "considerable evidence to suggest that Khomeini was aware of [the embassy attack plan], that he openly encouraged it, and when it succeeded, he was prepared to exploit the situation quickly and deftly for his own political purposes."
131. Sick, *All Fall Down*, p. 252.
132. Vance, *Hard Choices*, p. 377.
133. Sick, *All Fall Down*, p. 266, says that the United States was importing an average of 700,000 b/d from Iran "at that time." In fact, however, since 1973 the United States never imported more than 555,000 b/d from Iran, and that high number occurred in 1978. Moreover, by late 1979 total Iranian petroleum exports had dwindled to about 2 million b/d. United States imports "at that time" were 496,000 b/d, but the average up to that point was less than 300,000 b/d because of the shutdown earlier in the year. See *Monthly Energy Review* (June 1981), p. 32.
134. Brzezinski, *Power and Principle*, p. 482. Carter himself wanted "to punish them as soon as our people have been released; really hit them. They must know they can't fool around with us." Sick, *All Fall Down*, p. 252, omits the proposal to seize the oilfields.
135. The Soviets had sensitized the administration to this issue in recent weeks. Probably to demonstrate their ability to project force to any point where the United States might consider doing so, in late October the Soviet Union conducted a "massive airlift" exercise into South Yemen and Ethiopia. Over a 36-hour period, a fleet of AN-22 transport planes flew two brigades (10,000 men) including armored vehicles and artillery, from southern Russian bases to landing fields in South Yemen and Ethiopia. But it was the route used that was unusual. According to European intelligence sources, the transports flew "south along the Turkish–Iranian border, into Syria and Iraq for refueling stops, then over the Persian Gulf and around the Arabian Peninsula to their destinations." Then, after brief stopovers, with cargo intact, the aircraft flew back along the same route! American

intelligence denied any knowledge of the event. See "Russia's Secret Airlift," *Newsweek*, November 26, 1979, p. 33.

136. Col. Charlie A. Beckwith and Donald Knox, *Delta Force* (New York: Harcourt Brace Jovanovich, 1983), pp. 188, 198–99.
137. Brzezinski, *Power and Principle*, p. 483.
138. Vance, *Hard Choices*, p. 377.
139. Sick, *All Fall Down*, p. 266. Sick notes that Iranian treatment of the hostages, as evidenced by the thirteen who had been released, was "shocking."
140. John Kifner, "Khomeini in TV Talk," *New York Times*, November 21, 1979, p. 1.
141. The administration was undoubtedly also aware of intelligence from Omani sources claiming that those who attacked the Mosque received weapons from South Yemen and "advice" from the Soviet Union. See *Oil and Gas Journal*, January 14, 1980, p. 3.
142. Karen Elliott House, "Military Action to Free Hostages Is No Longer Ruled Out by Carter," *Wall Street Journal*, November 21, 1979, p. 2.
143. "Text of U.S. Position on Iran," *New York Times*, November 21, 1979, p. 12. See also Bernard Gwertzman, "Carter Shifts Stand," *New York Times*, November 21, 1979, p. 1, who called it the "toughest" statement yet; Edward Walsh and John Goshko, "U.S. Hints at Use of Arms against Iran," *Washington Post*, November 21, 1979, p. 1, who called it a "dramatic escalation"; and Gilbert Lewthwaite, "Carter Spokesman Hints at Military Action in Iran," *Baltimore Sun*, November 21, 1979, p. 1, who called it a "thinly veiled threat."
144. Brzezinski, *Power and Principle*, p. 483.
145. Richard Halloran, "Carter Sending 6 More Navy Ships, Including Carrier, to Arabian Sea," *New York Times*, November 21, 1979, p. 1.
146. John J. Fialka, "2nd U.S. Carrier Is Ordered to Patrol Iran Area," *Washington Star*, November 21, 1979, p. 1.
147. Sick, *All Fall Down*, pp. 273–74.
148. See "Carter Calls Camp David Crisis Talks," *Washington Star*, November 23, 1979, p. 1.
149. "Free Hostages, Pro-Soviet Iran Radio Urges," *Washington Star*, November 21, 1979, p. 6.
150. Iran Hostage Chronology, p. 41.
151. Raymond Coffey, "Soviets May Intervene If U.S. Moves on Iran," *Chicago Tribune*, November 21, 1979, p. 1.
152. Ibid.
153. Sick, *All Fall Down*, p. 275.
154. Iran Hostage Chronology, p. 43.
155. Sick, *All Fall Down*, pp. 275–76.
156. Brzezinski, *Power and Principle*, p. 483.

157. Carter, *Keeping Faith*, p. 466.
158. Ibid.
159. Sick, *All Fall Down*, p. 276.
160. Iran Hostage Chronology, p. 44.
161. Bruce van Voorst, "Khomeini Calls All Youths to Arms," *Washington Star*, November 27, 1979, p. 1.
162. Ibid. See also Jonathan Randall, "Iran Told to Prepare for War," *Washington Post*, November 27, 1979, p. 7.
163. Bernard Gwertzman, "Diplomatic Impasse: Removal of Iranian Foreign Minister Ends U.S. Hope for Quiet U.N. Talks," *New York Times*, November 29, 1979, p. 18.
164. Sick, *All Fall Down*, p. 279.
165. Three days later, Secretary Brown would change his mind. In a memorandum to the president on December 1, he said, "My own judgment is that we can go for a period of 10–15 days along the diplomatic route if it appears to be moving in a promising way and if there is not evidence or grave suspicion that any hostages have been harmed. If strong economic measures against Iran are taken by our key allies acting with us, that might give us another week or so. But even then I do not think we can delay facing up to at least the mildest military action for more than about a month from now." See Brzezinski, *Power and Principle*, p. 484.
166. Sick, *All Fall Down*, pp. 277–78.
167. Brzezinski, *Power and Principle*, pp. 483–85, leaves the pivotal November 28 meeting out of his account because it totally refutes his argument, p. 485, that "until the Soviet invasion of Afghanistan, the trend was toward more and more serious consideration of military action."
168. Brzezinski, *Power and Principle*, pp. 447–48. Since the spring, Brzezinski and others in the administration had sought to "balance" the buildup of Soviet power in the region.
169. Vance, *Hard Choices*, p. 387.
170. Shortly after December 2, six RH 53D Sea Stallion helicopters were placed aboard the USS *Kittyhawk* in the Indian Ocean. See Beckwith and Knox, *Delta Force*, p. 218.
171. Carter decided to send the AWACS on November 24. See Sick, *All Fall Down*, p. 280. Brzezinski, *Power and Principle*, p. 484, says the AWACS decision was made on December 4.
172. Richard Halloran, "Carrier Forrestal Sails to the Mediterranean, Adding to U.S. Power," *New York Times*, November 30, 1979, p. 15.
173. Immediately after the hostage seizure, all Warsaw Pact forces went on alert (except for Polish and Romanian forces), while Moscow and Berlin executed a limited call-up of reserves. East German Prime Minister Willie Stoph issued a public denial that the alert was in any

way related to the hostage crisis. See Drew Middleton, "Soviet Display of Flexibility," *New York Times*, December 28, 1979, p. 13.

174. General Vasily Kuznetzov had led a mission to Kabul in January to arrange for additional military aid.
175. It is obvious that American intelligence was alert to the various possibilities. Secretary Vance, *Hard Choices*, p. 387, for example, noted that by the late summer of 1979, "the question was not whether the Soviets would become more actively engaged in the Afghan civil war, but what form their larger involvement would take. Most intelligence analysts thought it more likely that Moscow would significantly increase its military assistance and training of the Afghan Army and assume greater operational control of the war than commit its own combat troops."
176. Louis Dupree, "Afghanistan under the Khalq," *Problems of Communism* (July–August 1979), pp. 43–44.
177. Henry S. Bradsher, *Afghanistan and the Soviet Union* (Durham: Duke University Press, 1983), p. 100.
178. Dupree, "Afghanistan under the Khalq," p. 44.
179. "Murder in the Mountains," *Time*, October 1, 1979, p. 29.
180. *FBIS-SU*, April 11, 1979, p. D1.
181. Bradsher, *Afghanistan and the Soviet Union*, p. 102.
182. Ibid., p. 123.
183. Ibid., p. 107.
184. Ibid., pp. 104–5.
185. Thomas T. Hammond, *Red Flag over Afghanistan* (Boulder: Westview Press, 1984), pp. 97–98.
186. See Cord Meyer, "The Soviet War against Afghan Self-rule," *Washington Star*, December 24, 1979, p. 9.
187. Drew Middleton, "In Afghanistan, 2 Soviet Trends Now Emerging," *New York Times*, October 30, 1979, p. 6. Middleton, drawing on "European intelligence sources," described the two trends as the "establishment of army and air bases near the Iranian frontier" and "the reconstruction of Afghanistan's internal security forces."
188. See J. Bruce Amstutz, *Afghanistan, the First Five Years of Soviet Occupation* (Washington, DC: National Defense University, 1986), pp. 43–44.
189. Kevin Klose, "Death of Soviet Official Spurs Rumors," *Washington Post*, March 14, 1980, p. A27, and "U.S. Officials Describe the Scenario of Coup," *Washington Star*, January 2, 1980, p. A8.
190. The four, who fled to the Soviet embassy, were: Colonel Mohammad Watanjar, interior minister; Major Sherjan Mazdooryar, minister of frontier affairs; Colonel Sayed Gulabzoy, minister of communica-

tions; and Asadullah Sarwari, secret police chief. See Hammond, *Red Flag over Afghanistan*, p. 85.

191. "U.S. Officials Describe the Scenario of Coup," *Washington Star*, January 2, 1980, p. A8. Bradsher, *Afghanistan and the Soviet Union*, pp. 113–16, says Taraki was not wounded in the shootout; Hammond, *Red Flag over Afghanistan*, p. 85, avoids the issue. Both agree he was killed through a combination of strangulation and suffocation by Amin's henchmen on October 8.
192. *FBIS-MENA*, September 17, 1979, pp. S1–S2.
193. Bradsher, *Afghanistan and the Soviet Union*, p. 117.
194. "Coups and Killings in Kabul: A KGB Defector Tells How Afghanistan Became Brezhnev's Vietnam," an interview with Vladimir Kuzichkin, *Time*, November 22, 1982, pp. 33–36.
195. See Bradsher, *Afghanistan and the Soviet Union*, pp. 164–65, for discussion of the November 26–28 decisionmaking process.
196. U.S. Congress, House Committee on Foreign Affairs, Subcommittee on Europe and the Middle East, *East–West Relations in the Aftermath of the Soviet Invasion of Afghanistan* (Washington, DC: GPO, 1980), pp. 39f.
197. Bradsher, *Afghanistan and the Soviet Union*, p. 176, and "U.S. Officials Describe the Scenario of Coup," p. A8.
198. Kevin Klose, "Death of Soviet Official Spurs Rumors," *Washington Post*, March 14, 1980, p. A27.
199. Bradsher, *Afghanistan and the Soviet Union*, p. 177, saw Paputin as a "curious choice" for this mission.
200. Anthony Arnold, *Afghanistan: The Soviet Invasion in Perspective* (Stanford: The Hoover Institute Press, 1981), p. 91, and Bradsher, *Afghanistan and the Soviet Union*, pp. 170–73, note the historic Soviet preoccupation with "legitimizing" their interventions.
201. *FBIS-MENA*, December 5, 1979, p. S1.
202. Ibid.
203. *FBIS TRENDS*, December 19, 1979, p. 3.
204. Ibid.
205. *FBIS-MENA*, December 11, 1979, p. S3.
206. *FBIS-MENA*, December 12, 1979, p. S1.
207. Amin's December 10 interview reappeared a few days later, on the day of Paputin's departure, as an AFP release from Islamabad, but in altered form. The AFP version included reference to the attempted coup but placed it in mid-October as the rebellion of the Riskhur garrison in Kabul. Shots heard near the People's Palace at the beginning of December were also dismissed as "only blanks for a film of the April 1978 Revolution." See *FBIS-MENA*, December 14, 1979, p. S1.

208. Ibid., p. S2.
209. Bradsher, *Afghanistan and the Soviet Union*, p. 178. Bradsher also makes reference to the presence of a "shadowy" KGB general noted by unidentified Western intelligence officials. See pp. 175–77.
210. Henry S. Bradsher, "U.S. Frustrated by Soviet Afghan Buildup," *Washington Star*, December 21, 1979, p. 1. Noting the Soviet buildup along the border with Afghanistan, Bradsher reported on "speculation high in the administration that the larger forces are poised to cross the river if the United States takes military action against neighboring Iran."
211. Richard Burt, "Soviet Buildup Seen at Afghan Frontier," *New York Times*, December 22, 1979, p. 1.
212. John J. Fialka, "Carter Sends Nuclear Carrier to Join Arabian Sea Buildup," *Washington Star*, December 22, 1979, p. 3.
213. Three days before, Washington had sent a delegation to the Middle East seeking permission to upgrade port and airfield facilities in Oman, Somalia, and Kenya. See Henry S. Bradsher, "U.S. Is Seeking Port Expansion in Indian Ocean," *Washington Star*, December 19, 1979, p. 1.
214. "Soviet Denies Charge on Afghans," *New York Times*, December 24, 1979, p. 9.
215. Bernard Gwertzman, "Afghan President Is Ousted and Executed in Kabul Coup, Reportedly with Soviet Help," *New York Times*, December 28, 1979, p. 1.
216. Arnold, *Afghanistan: The Soviet Invasion in Perspective*, p. 95.
217. Paputin evidently was killed in the process. His obituary, published in *Pravda* on January 2, 1980, noted only that he had been killed "unexpectedly" on December 28, without saying where. The fact that it appeared on page 8, instead of page 1, and was signed only by the interior minister instead of by Brezhnev and the entire Politburo, as was the custom for prominent party officials, suggested that he had failed in his mission. It was also rumored that he had taken his own life to atone for his failure, rather than face ruin upon return to Moscow. See Kevin Klose, "Death of Soviet Official Spurs Rumors," *Washington Post*, March 14, 1980, p. A27.
218. United States intelligence analysts saw the conflict as a stalemate in which "the army of President Hafizullah Amin controls Kabul and a handful of other cities, while insurgent forces operate with impunity in about half the country," See David Binder, "U.S. Experts Say Afghanistan's Civil War Has Reached Stalemate," *New York Times*, October 29, 1979, p. 3.
219. *International Defense Review*, February 1980, p. 2.

220. "Brezhnev's Responses to Questions from Pravda Correspondent," *Izvestia*, January 13, 1980, p. 1.
221. Vance, *Hard Choices*, p. 388, believed it was "possible that had there been more to lose in the relationship with the United States, the Soviet Union would have been more cautious."
222. Terence Smith, "Carter Tells Soviet to Pull Its Troops from Afghanistan," *New York Times*, December 30, 1979, p. 1. On January 8, 1980, Carter also called the Soviet invasion "the greatest threat to peace since the Second World War." For discussion of United States sanctions, see Bradsher, *Afghanistan and the Soviet Union*, pp. 189–99.

CHAPTER 10

After Afghanistan: From Fiasco to Fiasco

The Soviet invasion of Afghanistan marked the failure of the strategy that President Carter and Secretary Vance had attempted to pursue. For all intents and purposes—with a major exception to be discussed below—the invasion also brought to an end Secretary Vance's substantive role in the formulation of American foreign policy.[1] The president's decision to attempt to rescue the American hostages in Iran was, of course, the precipitating cause of Vance's actual resignation.

After the Afghanistan invasion, until the end of his term of office, President Carter attempted to straddle two strategies—the new global order from which he would never completely disengage, and containment, which he refused to fully embrace. His determination to sit on the fence was exemplified in his personnel policy. The same high officials—except for Vance after April—who had been responsible for carrying out all of the old policies remained in place.[2]

For Carter, the Soviet invasion reinforced the decision he had made following the "brigade incident," to contain the Soviet Union without moving fully to containment, per se. But in the aftermath of the invasion he would be pressed hard by Brzezinski to move further than he liked along the path to full-fledged containment. The president's ambivalence produced growing contradictions in almost every facet of American foreign policy. By the time of the election, virtually every major initiative undertaken by Carter from the beginning of his presidency had either failed or was failing, and every important relationship was in disarray. Indecisive half-measures would characterize the president's policies in 1980.

The Ambivalent Response to Afghanistan

In the immediate aftermath of the Soviet invasion, the president adopted a series of measures designed to curtail relations with Moscow, which, he believed, must be made to pay a price for its direct aggression. In a hot line message, Carter told Brezhnev that the invasion was "a clear threat to the peace" and "unless you draw back from your present course" it "could mark a fundamental and long-lasting turning point in our relations."[3] In reply, Brezhnev claimed that the Soviets had entered "at the request of Afghan leaders" because of "armed incursions from without into Afghanistan territory." The Soviets would leave, he said, "as soon as the reasons which prompted the Afghan request to the Soviet Union disappear."[4] Brezhnev's response occasioned the oft-quoted remark by Carter that the Soviet invasion "has made a more dramatic change in my own opinion of what the Soviets' ultimate goals are than anything they've done in the previous time I've been in office."[5]

The direct exchange set the stage for the application of United States sanctions against, and a sharp curtailment of relations with, the Soviet Union. Washington recalled its recently appointed ambassador, Thomas Watson, for consultations, restricted official contact, and rallied UN support against the Soviet Union. On January 14, the United Nations General Assembly condemned the Soviet invasion by a vote of 104 to 18 (following Moscow's veto of a similar measure in the Security Council).

In the meantime, several sanctions were imposed to demonstrate that there would be no "business as usual." In a letter to Majority Leader Robert Byrd, the president requested that the Senate "delay consideration" of the SALT II treaty so that the president and Congress could "assess Soviet actions and intentions."[6] To keep the door open for a resolution of the current crisis, however, Carter made what appeared to be an artificial distinction between the treaty and Soviet compliance with it, declaring in the letter that he continued to believe that the treaty was in the national security interests of the United States and that it "should be taken up by the Senate as soon as these more urgent issues have been addressed."

Similarly, given the president's evaluation of the Soviet invasion as "the most serious threat to peace since World War II," the sanctions he imposed seemed less than appropriate. As the *New York Times* immediately noted, "the steps seemed designed not so much to force the Soviet Union to withdraw its forces from Afghanistan as to persuade the leadership in Moscow that such moves would meet a sharp response from the West."[7] Yet there were those who thought the sanctions were an overreaction that hurt the United States more than they did the Soviet Union.[8]

Carter instituted an embargo on grain sales but abided by the terms of the 1976 grain agreement, which permitted annual sale of 8 million tons through 1981. He canceled 17 million tons that had been ordered (but not paid for) in excess of that agreement—grain intended to build up Soviet livestock herds, not meant for human consumption.[9] He placed an indefinite suspension on new export licenses for sale of high technology and also suspended previously issued export licenses pending review, resulting in cancellation of sales of computer and oil drilling technology.[10]

Both these measures—if enforced—carried the potential to make Moscow pay a substantial price for its aggression. But enforcement lay outside the administration's control. Within days, contrary to expectations by Department of Agriculture analyses, Argentina stepped in to replace a substantial portion of the withheld grain and severely undercut the effectiveness of the grain embargo; other suppliers would follow. The attempt to bar the transfer of high technology fared only slightly better, as West Germany, Japan, and other countries continued to function as de facto conduits for technology transfer to the Soviet Union.

Even in those areas where the United States could act unilaterally and enforce compliance, the sanctions imposed were of only marginal significance. For example, Carter cut back privileges for Soviet fishing in American coastal waters, reducing by some 330,000 tons the Soviet fish catch for the year; he froze all cultural and educational exchanges;[11] he deferred opening of two new consulates; and he limited but did not stop Aeroflot flights to the United States. The president also spoke of the possibility of boycotting the Olympic Games to be held in Moscow that summer and proposed to institute draft registration for eighteen-year-olds.

Curiously, despite his evaluation of Afghanistan's "strategic importance" as a "steppingstone to possible control over much of the world's oil supplies," the president mentioned no decision to assist the Afghanistan resistance. (Indeed, under President Carter, the United States did not adopt a public policy of providing military assistance to the beleaguered Afghan freedom fighters, although some covert aid was arranged.[12]) Only to Pakistan did the president offer to "provide military equipment, food and other assistance to help . . . defend its independence and its national security against the seriously increased threat it now faces from the north."[13] (Two weeks later, when Washington offered Pakistan $400 million, President Zia promptly rejected the American aid offer as "peanuts.")

The Gamble to Restore United States–Soviet Amity

President Carter was not comfortable with the shift he was being required to make, and when an opportunity arose which seemed to offer a possible resolution of the crisis he seized it, a step urged on him by Secretary Vance, heedless of the fact that it contradicted public policy. In his State of the Union Address to Congress January 23, the president had formulated what would be called the "Carter Doctrine."

> An attempt by any outside force to gain control of the Persian Gulf region will be regarded as an assault on the vital interests of the United States of America, and such an assault will be repelled by any means necessary, including military force.[14]

Yet, even as he was renaming the doctrine that President Eisenhower had first promulgated in 1958 (though without the courage to name the "outside force" communist as Eisenhower had done), Carter was grasping at what appeared to be a Soviet offer to negotiate a resolution to all aspects of the crisis then facing the two countries. The details of this prospective United States–Soviet "behind-the-scenes deal"—which never materialized—remain sketchy, but enough information exists to permit an analysis of its main outline.

In the second week of January, Carter recounts, Fidel Castro had "sent . . . word that he wanted to discuss Iran and Afghanistan."[15] The president immediately arranged for two of his top aides, Robert Pastor, NSC Latin America chief, and Peter Tarnoff, Department of State executive secretary, "to go to Cuba for a secret meeting with him." In an eleven-hour discussion on January 16 and 17, Castro reportedly spoke of "his desire to pull out of Ethiopia now, and Angola later; his involvement in the revolutionary movements in Central America but his aversion to sending weapons or military capability to the Caribbean countries."[16] Hurt economically by the United States embargo in place since 1962, Castro wanted to normalize relations with Washington, "but [could not] abandon his friends, the Soviets, who have supported his revolution unequivocally."

In his memoir, the president said only that "the reasons for this long discourse were unclear to us, but it was at least obvious that Cuba was embarrassed to be aligned with the Soviet Union."[17] That there was more to it than this seems clear even from the president's terse account. Embarrassment with Moscow would hardly have been sufficient reason for Castro to request a meeting with the President of the United States. Moreover, as Carter acknowledged, Castro had stated specifically that—embarrassed or not—he would not abandon "his friends, the Soviets."

Castro's proposed terms for the normalization of relations with the United States were the following: In return for lifting the embargo and not opposing a Cuban seat on the UN Security Council (which, but for American opposition, Cuba stood a fair chance of obtaining), Castro would pull out of Africa in stages (Ethiopia first, Angola later) and discontinue support for revolutionary movements in the islands of the Caribbean (Jamaica and Grenada). His involvement in Central America would not be affected but, as will be noted below, his proposal apparently involved the extension of United States aid to Nicaragua.

What Castro said about Iran and Afghanistan—the declared purpose of his message to Carter—must be deduced from subsequent events. Carter says nothing about it. It appears that the Cuban leader sought the meeting with Carter not merely to explore an American–Cuban rapprochement, but also to act as Moscow's intermediary to explore if not propose the ingredients of a settlement of the crisis in American–Soviet relations and the revival of detente. Castro evidently proposed a quid pro quo whose main elements were that if the United States removed the sanctions placed against the Soviet Union, including the Olympic boycott, ratified SALT II, and extended economic assistance to Nicaragua, the Soviet Union would withdraw from Afghanistan, leaving behind a "neutral" regime, and would also "assist" in the release of the American hostages in Iran.

What lent credibility to Castro's proposals was the fact that—at that very moment—a new channel was being opened to Tehran at the initiative of Panamanian leader Omar Torrijos. It seems that two French lawyers with connections in Tehran, Hector Villalon and Christian Bourguet, had traveled to Panama in late December for the ostensible purpose of extraditing the shah. Their real intention, however, was to employ Torrijos as an intermediary to make contact with Hamilton Jordan, Carter's close friend and political adviser, who had arranged the shah's exile in Panama.[18] After Torrijos established contact for them, they proposed to mediate a resolution of the hostage crisis.

Thus, by mid-January, the Carter leadership had received two secret proposals—one from Castro and one through Torrijos—offering solutions to the whole range of problems then bedeviling United States foreign policy but converging on the hostage problem. In view of what transpired over the next few weeks, after considering these proposals or something very much like them, in late January the president must have decided to explore them. It was a measure of Carter's desperation to resolve the crisis in American foreign policy that he acted on, and perhaps even welcomed, the possibility that Moscow was behind both initiatives and was having second thoughts about its own policy. Indeed, the belief in a Soviet hand behind these matters seems to have underlain Carter's, and particularly Vance's, thinking.

First, on the "unanimous recommendation of his advisers," Carter deferred imposition of sanctions against Iran.[19] Then Secretary Vance "urged the president to communicate with Brezhnev," ostensibly to "impress upon the Soviets that their action in Afghanistan threatened the very basis of U.S.–Soviet relations" but in reality to obtain a reading on the extent of Soviet involvement in the recent, secret proposals.[20] The president had just communicated with Brezhnev in the hot line message noted above, making it unlikely that another communication with the same content was the reason for Vance's urgency. In view of that unsatisfactory exchange it was no wonder that the president declined the secretary's suggestion that he send another message to Brezhnev; but Carter authorized Vance to write a letter to Gromyko.

The president had secretly agreed to let Vance make one last try to reach a settlement with Moscow, based on the discussion with Castro and the concurrent opening of the secret channel to Tehran.

The president's decision was not shared with Brzezinski, who meanwhile continued to attempt to build allied support for containment of Moscow, improve relations with China, and prepare military options for dealing with Iran. In agreeing to negotiate secretly with Moscow on the one hand while continuing to build public support for "containment" of the Soviet Union on the other, Carter created a basic contradiction which would grow over the next two months. And when the gamble on detente failed, Carter's credibility with the allies—who indeed learned of it—would reach its nadir.

Having agreed to Vance's request but before Vance had sent his letter, President Carter began to extend feelers along the lines of the proposed quid pro quo outlined by Castro. In his State of the Union Address the president had declared that the United States would continue to abide by the terms of the SALT II treaty if the Soviets would. A few days later, on January 29, articles appeared in the *New York Times* and *Washington Post* making the legal case for continued adherence to the treaty and the strategic case for passage of it.[21]

The same day these articles appeared, the president held a question-and-answer session with visiting editors and broadcasters, during which he expressed a new, more tolerant attitude toward the Soviet presence in the Western Hemisphere, and also toward Cuba. Asked whether the Caribbean fell into the same vital interest category as the Persian Gulf, he reversed his view of the previous fall when, during the Cuban brigade crisis, he had seen the Soviet presence in Cuba—and Cuba itself—as a distinct threat to the hemisphere (see chapter 8). He now perceived "no outside threat to the Caribbean area and, therefore . . . no reason to use military force to defend it."[22]

A few days later, Brezhnev appeared to respond to the positive signals coming from Washington. On February 4, in his first speech since the Soviet invasion of Afghanistan, Brezhnev declared that "detente is the result of many-faceted efforts" and "reckless imperialist forces must not be allowed to destroy its fruits."[23] The Soviet leader went on to say that he "did not want to give up any of the good things achieved in the 70s in the international arena." He said that "it was indispensable . . . to eliminate conflicts in the Middle and Near East and Southeast Asia." Finally, Brezhnev declared that "any road is acceptable and desirable if it leads to lasting peace."

This apparent signal from Brezhnev—tepid as it was—combined with Castro's proposals and progress in the Tehran channel, was reinforced by a communication from newly elected Iranian President Abolhassan Bani-Sadr on February 4 saying that he wished to resolve the hostage crisis. The president believed that Bani-Sadr's statement "was the most encouraging development since our embassy was seized."[24] These developments, in turn, bolstered Vance's hope that the makings of a settlement were materializing, and on February 8 he dispatched his letter to Gromyko without further ado.

In the letter, Vance says, he emphasized that Soviet withdrawal from Afghanistan "was necessary to restore a sense of stability to the region, and . . . that if there was restraint on both sides and respect for the independence and territorial integrity of the states in the region, our respective interests need not lead to confrontation." Then Vance came to the heart of it, which was to indicate that the United States was open to a negotiated settlement and to ascertain whether the Soviets had anything to do with Castro's and Torrijos' initiatives. He thus "requested that [Gromyko] indicate to us Soviet intentions in both Afghanistan and the region."[25] The reference to "the region," of course, meant Iran.

The dispatch of Vance's letter occasioned a spate of further policy shifts by the president and other administration officials over the next few weeks. For example, in mid-January, just before Castro's initiative, the administration had announced its policy regarding American participation in the Moscow Olympics. Secretary Vance had announced on January 14 that the administration had "set a deadline of not later than mid-February for the Soviet Union to withdraw its troops from Afghanistan or face the likelihood of an American boycott of the Moscow Olympics this summer."[26]

On February 11, the White House issued the first of several additional changes of policy, beginning with its position on the Olympic Games. It was now decided "not to press for an immediate decision on its request that the Summer Olympic Games be moved from Moscow, postponed or canceled unless Soviet troops are fully withdrawn from Afghanistan by February 20."[27] White House counsel Lloyd Cutler said that the International Olympic Committee should be given "a reasonable amount of time" to consider the United States Olympic Committee's request to transfer, delay, or call off the Moscow games. Asked what the president's view would be if there were a significant withdrawal of Soviet troops after the February 20 deadline originally set by President Carter but before the May 24 deadline for accepting invitations to the Moscow Games,

Cutler said, "If there were a bona fide withdrawal, or a plan for a bona fide withdrawal, it would have to be considered. After all, the objective of this is *not* to inflict a punishment, but to achieve a result."[28]

Two days later, in his first press conference in eleven weeks, the president unveiled new positions on Afghanistan and Iran. On Afghanistan, he was asked "what kind of a regime would be acceptable" if the Soviets withdrew. The president responded that "we would like to have a neutral country."[29] He suggested that after Soviet withdrawal the UN could dispatch a peace-keeping force possibly comprised of troops from Muslim countries as a transition measure "during which a neutral and responsible government might be established acceptable to the Afghanistan people." The president's careful definition of a neutral government acceptable to the Afghan people left open the door for reestablishment of the formally non-aligned but pro-Soviet regime which had existed before the invasion.

With regard to Iran, the president noted that the new Iranian president, Bani-Sadr, had announced that "an action plan for release of the hostages had been approved by Ayatollah Ruhollah Khomeini."[30] Cautioning against any excessive optimism, Carter signaled his approval of a "carefully defined" UN commission of inquiry to be set up prior to the release of the hostages, as part of the procedure for resolving the crisis. The commission's task would be to collect information on Iran's grievances against the previous regime and past American actions.

This was a major shift of position. Earlier, the president had refused to discuss the establishment of such a commission until after the hostages had been released and returned home.[31] Commenting on the president's remarks, administration officials noted that there was "no agreement yet on a formula for releasing the hostages," but implied that they were working on one.[32] They suggested privately that "the political breakthrough that would precede release of the hostages could come at any moment."[33]

The president's shift was part of the secret negotiations by the French lawyers Villalon and Bourguet deriving from the "Torrijos initiative." Washington and Tehran would move along a parallel, predetermined path whose end result would be the release of the hostages.[34] A UN commission would proceed to Tehran and interview the hostages. Pursuant to the commission's report, Bani-Sadr would arrange for the transfer of the hostages from the revolutionary students to the government. The final step in this scenario was for the commission to present its report to the UN secretary-general, and for Iran to pardon and expel the hostages from the country.

A week later, White House officials made the Soviet–American quid pro quo explicit. The president reportedly would seek Senate approval of the SALT II treaty by spring if two conditions were met. These were that the "American hostages in Iran are released" and that "there is by then a general public perception that President Carter has reacted firmly to the Soviet invasion of Afghanistan, and in so doing has contained it."[35]

> This would not necessarily require even a partial withdrawal of Soviet troops from Afghanistan, but it would be greatly aided by *some sign* that the Soviets were loosening their grip over that country, the officials say.[36]

In other words, if the hostages were released, President Carter was willing to overlook the Soviet presence in Afghanistan and proceed with ratification of SALT II. The clear assumption in this quid pro quo was that the Soviet Union could and would play a key role in arranging for the release of the hostages.

A few days later Congress enacted a bill extending economic assistance to Nicaragua—the presumed final piece of the "package." In January the Senate had passed an $80 million supplemental bill for economic support funds for Central America and the Caribbean, $70 million of which was ticketed for Nicaragua. Now, amid growing and acrimonious debate in Congress and across the nation over support for the Sandinistas, the House took up the Senate bill.

On February 25, the House held an unprecedented secret session to examine classified materials on Soviet-bloc involvement in Nicaragua.[37] The bill was passed after Congressman Jim Wright concluded that the classified information did not convince him that Nicaragua was "Communist-controlled."[38] But several amendments were appended requiring presidential verification that the Sandinistas had implemented stated commitments to human rights, free press, and so forth. In other words, there were sufficient levers to derail the package later if things went wrong.

On February 28 Carter met with Mondale, Vance, Brzezinski, and Marshall Shulman, Vance's deputy, to assess where they stood. The United States had taken several steps along the path toward a settlement, with little reciprocation from Moscow. Three weeks had passed since the secretary had sent his letter to Gromyko, and there had been no reply. There was only "an indirect communication from Moscow, through Brezhnev's son, to the effect that the Soviets might be willing to consider withdrawal from Afghanistan if the United States reconsidered its position on the Olympics."[39]

Secretary Vance seized on this remark, plus the informal comments by two Soviet officials who said that the invasion had been a mistake, to propose that Washington attempt to "reopen a dialogue" with Moscow. He urged Carter to let him meet with Gromyko "to reinforce" the message of his February 8 letter.[40] Brzezinski was "appalled at the thought that two months after the Soviet invasion of Afghanistan we might be taking the initiative to open up a dialogue with the Soviets even while pressing our allies to maintain a united front."[41] Vice-President Mondale, too, was highly skeptical, declaring that "we [could] lose everything by appearing to want a meeting. They might conclude it's a sign of weakness on our part. I don't see any hopeful signals."

Vance responded by saying that he also had a message from Ambassador Dobrynin "favoring a formal Gromyko–Vance meeting."[42] Shulman chimed in with the observation that "the time to relax our pressure" on the Soviets was now, when they were "stuck." He opined that the Soviets would leave "when an Afghan army and government were in place." President Carter noted sarcastically that this meant the Soviets would withdraw "when they can leave a puppet government in place."[43] Brzezinski said that, while he did not object to talking to the Soviets, "we should proceed very carefully lest we project the image of uncertainty and be accused of new zigzags."[44] A Vance–Gromyko meeting now, he concluded, "would confuse our allies and would be politically devastating at home." Vance, undeterred, countered by proposing that his deputy, Shulman, go to Moscow with a message from Carter to Brezhnev.

Although the February 28 meeting ended inconclusively, with Carter's approval Vance persisted in his plan, devising an ingenious way to consult with Gromyko without arousing allied or domestic concerns. The following day, he saw Dobrynin and arranged a tentative meeting with Gromyko in Belgrade for himself or Vice-President Mondale when Tito, who was gravely ill, died.[45] Two days later he put through a request to the Soviet embassy for a visa for Shulman and sent the president the draft of a proposed letter to Brezhnev.

Then, in a conciliatory speech to the Chicago Council on Foreign Relations on March 3, Vance stated that "when Soviet troops are fully withdrawn from Afghanistan, our intention is to remove the sanctions we have imposed."[46] Furthermore, Vance said, although United States relations with the Soviet Union

> have been and will be essentially competitive . . . our competition must be bounded by restraint and by sensitivity to each other's vital interests. For such a relationship between the two superpowers is central to peace. We seek no return of the cold war, of the indiscriminate confrontation of earlier times.[47]

Carter had secretly approved Vance's initiative without informing his national security adviser of the decision. Brzezinski only learned about it, to his "amazement," from Dobrynin himself during an embarrassing conversation at a Japanese embassy reception.[48] In the course of that conversation, a "sardonically smiling" Dobrynin also informed Brzezinski that "the Soviet side had rejected the initiative." Vance's last desperate gamble had failed. Once again he had trusted the Soviets, gone to embarrassing lengths to accommodate them, and been rejected. A few days later Carter "turned the entire project off."[49]

The failure of Vance's behind-the-scenes Soviet–American deal in early March was rapidly followed by the collapse of its subordinate parts. The centerpiece from Carter's standpoint—the plan to release the hostages, which had been shaky from the start—fell apart on March 10. Contrary to all previous understandings, at the last moment Khomeini refused to go along with the plan to transfer control of the hostages to the Iranian government, declaring instead that the Majlis, or parliament, would decide the hostage question. This meant that the issue would drag on for several more months because the Majlis had not yet been elected. Although elections were scheduled for mid-March, weeks if not months would pass before the process was completed and a premier and cabinet were selected.

Worse, Khomeini attempted to turn the UN commission into a vehicle for condemnation of the United States by demanding that the commission promptly issue its report, before even meeting with the hostages.[50] When the revolutionary students that same day withdrew their offer to turn their hostages over to the government, the White House immediately announced that the commission was suspending its activities and returning to the United States. As the president put it later that day, "It seemed that we had now lost our last chance to set the Americans free."[51]

Despite the obvious Iranian intent to delay resolution of the crisis, and probably to embarrass the United States, Vance would not give up. He met with the members of the commission immediately upon their return to the United States, March 12, and in conjunction with Bourguet and Villalon, worked out a "revised scenario."[52] On the assumptions that Bani-Sadr sincerely intended to resolve the issue and that an elected Majlis would strengthen his hand, Vance argued that the United States should continue on the negotiating track. He suggested that the president send a message to Bani-Sadr proposing a return of the UN commission and a transfer of the hostages to government control. This would restore the situation to the critical point where the original plan had broken down.

The breakdown of the original plan, however, had also increased pressure for some form of direct action and moved the president toward more serious consideration of a military option. The day after the failure, March 11, at an SCC meeting, Brzezinski proposed considering "at some point" the mining of Iran's ports or the seizure of Kharg Island, the main petroleum loading facility.[53] A rescue mission was not yet under consideration. Within a few days, the president, too, came to the view that "we needed to increase our pressure on Iran." At an NSC meeting on March 18 he said,

> in his judgment, the United States had been too quiet and had not taken sufficiently direct action to create the most favorable circumstances for a settlement. As a result, we seemed to be accepting the status quo. We simply could not sit until May without placing greater pressure on Iran to release the hostages.[54]

Although permitting Secretary Vance to continue along the negotiating track, Carter moved "to create the most favorable circumstances for a settlement" by accelerating preparations for more forceful sanctions, including military action, if negotiations failed. The key decisions were made on March 22, when Carter met with his top advisers at Camp David for more than five hours. Present were Vance, Mondale, Brown, Turner, Jones, Aaron, Powell, and Brzezinski.[55]

First, the president had decided to issue an ultimatum to Iran.[56]

If agreement was not reached on release of the hostages by March 31, the United States would break relations, impose trade and economic sanctions, begin to adjudicate American companies' financial claims against Iran from assets frozen earlier, and expel Iranian diplomats. Second, a strong diplomatic effort would be made to persuade United States allies to break relations with Iran when the United States did.[57] Third, Vance would be permitted to continue his negotiating effort, but the cutoff date would be March 31. Finally, the president received a full briefing on a proposed rescue mission that had been under development since the previous November, authorizing several preparatory steps, including a secret reconnaissance flight to test the acceptability of one of the sites selected for the rescue mission.[58]

When the March 31 deadline arrived with no reply from Tehran, Carter met with his top aides again to decide on the nature and extent of sanctions to be imposed. But Vance arrived at the meeting with a message from Bani-Sadr and Ghotbzadeh which stated that Iran would announce details of the hostage transfer the next day.[59] Vance urged that they wait twenty-four hours until they heard what would come from Tehran. Carter was reluctant to defer sanctions, for he had publicly let it be known he would impose them if Tehran failed to meet the deadline. It would be considered yet one more sign of presidential weakness if he failed to act. But Vance was persuasive, and the president agreed.

Bani-Sadr spoke the next day, April 1, reaffirming Khomeini's earlier position that the Majlis would determine the fate of the hostages, but said that if the United States refrained from any hostile act the government would take charge of them.[60] Hoping to encourage the Iranian government, Carter immediately announced that in light of this "positive step" the United States would defer sanctions. But despite a favorable vote in the Revolutionary Council a few days later to accept custody of the hostages, Khomeini vetoed the decision. The negotiation had fallen through.

Khomeini's veto reversed the situation which had prevailed since the seizure of the hostages. Up until this point it had been the student militants who had refused to surrender the hostages to the government. Now, the students had agreed to transfer the hostages, but the government refused to accept them. It was at last clear to everyone, including Vance, that Khomeini had never intended to negotiate the release of the hostages. They were, in effect, a shield to keep the United States at arm's length while he installed the institutions of his Islamic republic.[61]

The Consequences of Self-Deception

There would be no further talk of a Soviet withdrawal from Afghanistan in return for SALT II, which now lay dead in the water. The United States boycott of the Olympics would be pressed forward, although it would not be completely successful. United States relations with the Soviet Union and its allies would be frozen into antagonism, including relations with Cuba and Nicaragua. But the main American reaction was the president's decision to attempt a rescue of the hostages in Iran. The rescue attempt, its failure, and subsequent consequences for the United States' relations with its allies would haunt the president till his final day in office and be one of the main factors—along with mounting domestic economic woes—responsible for his electoral defeat.

On April 7 at a formal NSC meeting, in a clear repudiation of the policy of restraint that Secretary Vance had been urging, the president declared that "it had been a mistake for him not to have acted more assertively sooner."[62] The time had come, Carter indicated, "to bring things to a head." We were no longer dealing with kidnappers defying a weak Iranian government but with "a hostile government." Despite Vance's objections to the adoption of a more assertive policy course, "Mondale, Brown and others felt strongly that we should leave no ambiguity on the subject."[63] The secretary was isolated.

The president determined to impose several sanctions against Iran, including the formal break in diplomatic relations decided upon earlier.[64] All exports from the United States to Iran would be prohibited. The Department of the Treasury would begin an inventory of individual and corporate claims against Iran to be paid from assets previously frozen. And the United States would "invalidate all visas issued to Iranian citizens for future entry into the United States."

The president's decisions were immediately interpreted as "more important as a turning point than as a pressure point."[65] White House officials briefing reporters declared that "nobody" expected the break in diplomatic relations to bring an end to the crisis. Instead, they said, the hostage crisis had entered its third phase. In phase one, the period from November 4 through the early part of the year, United States policy had been essentially an attempt to exert pressure on Tehran by nonmilitary means. But in the absence of any duly constituted Iranian government, there had been no interaction and no progress.

Phase two began with the election of Bani-Sadr as president in late January. The prospect of a negotiated settlement with the Iranian government preoccupied American leaders for the next nine weeks, until early April. The United States and Iran had agreed to a "process involving reciprocal actions . . . a step by step approach on our part and on their part culminating in the release of the hostages."[66] This phase, however, was now over because "it did not work." Khomeini's decision to turn the hostage issue over to the Iranian parliament, which would not be in a position to act before the end of May, meant that there was no "functioning mechanism" capable of resolving the issue at the present time.

This, in turn, meant that the United States was now entering phase three—"a return to pressure and threats"—but in a more complicated milieu. The president's own political fortunes were increasingly at risk. There was a "clear danger" that the hostages would still be held during the Democratic National Convention in mid-August, perhaps even on election day. "The grave domestic consequences of such a continuing stalemate," the analysis concluded, "argue powerfully for strong action in the new phase of the hostage crisis."[67]

Phase three, as the president's advisers termed it, also coincided with a sharp rise in criticism of Carter's competence. A Harris survey taken on April 8 and a Gallup poll taken the following day showed a dramatic drop in public confidence regarding his handling of the hostage crisis. The Harris survey charted the shift of public opinion from mid-December 1979, when the president was given a 66 to 32 percent approval rating, to April 8, 1980, when he had a 65 to 24 percent disapproval rating.[68] The turning point was the failure of the UN commission in early March, after which public perception of the president's handling of the crisis turned increasingly negative. The Gallup poll taken April 9 showed a similar shift from a mid-December approval rating of 77 to 19 percent to the April reading of 49 to 40 percent disapproval.[69]

The Gallup poll also noted that 51 to 42 percent of those polled thought that the sanctions against Iran were "not tough enough." By a very wide margin, 71 to 25 percent, the Harris survey noted that Khomeini had made the United States look "weak and helpless." Indeed, for the first time since the outbreak of the crisis, Americans by a margin of 51 to 39 percent believed that the United States "should take military action" against Iran.[70] Whether the growing public criticism reflected in the polling data encouraged the president to take more decisive action is unknown. Clearly, however, the public's views and those of Jimmy Carter had converged.

It would also appear that this same convergence of views was the last straw for Secretary Vance. He understood, as did all of the president's advisers, that he no longer had the president's confidence. Vance also knew full well that following the rupture in diplomatic relations the president would decide upon the use of some form of military force, to which he remained fundamentally opposed. Therefore, on April 10, fully cognizant that a decision was imminent, Secretary Vance absented himself for what was described as a "much needed long-weekend vacation in Florida."[71] However, before leaving, Vance told the president that "he opposed any military action but if a choice had to be made between a rescue and a wider blockade, he preferred the rescue."[72]

The next day, April 11, in Vance's absence the president convened his top advisers and made the decision for the rescue mission to proceed "without delay."[73] The date was set for April 24, less than two weeks away. In his memoir President Carter suggested that in addition to the collapse of the negotiations, another reason for deciding to act promptly to rescue the hostages lay in Iraq's preparations to invade Iran. Carter's diary entry of April 10 was explicit. "The Iranian terrorists are making all kinds of crazy threats to kill the American hostages if they are invaded by Iraq—whom they identify as an American puppet."[74] In the face of these threats, the president concluded, "we could no longer afford to depend on diplomacy. I decided to act."[75]

But the argument that the president decided to act because the hostages' lives were in jeopardy is not supported by American intelligence. A secret report in early April had concluded that the "continuing turmoil in Iran posed no particular threat to the captives."[76] Indeed, the rescue mission itself posed a greater threat. One Pentagon analysis of the rescue mission's possible outcomes painted a "worst-case scenario" envisioning twenty casualties among the hostages and fifty or more among their rescuers, not to mention numerous casualties among the Iranian captors.[77] Another estimated fifteen hostages and thirty rescuers would have been killed "even if the commandos had made it to the embassy compound undetected."[78]

In view of the case against a rescue attempt, there must have been a compelling reason to take action, and that was domestic politics. As noted above, President Carter had slipped badly in recent public opinion polls regarding his handling of the hostage crisis. Continued inaction with the election fast approaching did not augur well for his chances against the most likely challenger, Ronald Reagan, who was scoring heavily in public opinion over the president's passive response to the crisis. It was vital for Carter to be seen taking action on the hostages' behalf.

At any rate, as discussion turned to consideration of the best means of ensuring the success of the mission, issues of secrecy and an accompanying diversion arose. To preserve secrecy Brzezinski proposed convening a formal NSC meeting to announce that the president had decided *against* a rescue attempt, then proceeding with the mission and informing only those with a "need to know."[79] On whether a diversion should be incorporated into the plan, the national security adviser also suggested that there be "an almost simultaneous retaliatory strike to provide a broader context in the event that the rescue mission should fail." Neither suggestion was accepted, although military support was to be provided once the mission got under way.

The president did attempt to employ a rhetorical diversion—implying in pubic statements that the United States was preparing to mine Iran's ports—as the rescue mission date drew close. On April 17 the president held a news conference to announce the imposition of additional sanctions against Iran.[80] Henceforth, all financial transactions between the United States and Iran were prohibited; all Iranian imports to the United States were barred; travel to Iran by American citizens was prohibited; all military equipment previously purchased by Iran but since impounded would be made available for use by United States military forces; and last, the president said he would ask Congress for discretionary authority to pay reparations to the hostages and their families out of the more than $8 billion in frozen Iranian assets.

During the ensuing question-and-answer session, the president was asked whether he had set a deadline for a new belligerent stand. In reply, the president said that there had always been three options available—economic, political, and military. "So far," he said, "we have only exercised the economic and the political measures." He then went on to say that

> if this additional set of sanctions . . . is not successful then the only next step available that I can see would be some sort of military action which is the prerogative and the right of the United States under these circumstances.[81]

The president's reply sparked a further question: Would not "military action . . . be too high a price to pay in terms of the damage to the allied oil supplies and the further risk of war?" The president answered that he would carefully assess his options and their impact on the allies, but that the United States had reserved the right to take action and the "interruption of commerce with Iran is a kind of step that would be available." Referring to his announcement of the previous November 20, the president noted, "I think we used the phrase 'interruption of commerce with Iran.'"[82]

The truth was that the president was attempting to mislead Iran as to the thrust of the imminent American action, but Carter's repeated references to the use of military force over the next week generated growing internal, domestic, and international concern. Increasing dissension within the leadership culminated on April 21 when Secretary Vance, his policy of restraint repudiated by the president and refusing to support a policy he opposed, tendered his resignation. Vance complied with Carter's request not to make his resignation public until after the rescue attempt.[83]

Vance's opposition to the use of force was paralleled by congressional demands for "consultation," which were aimed at the same objective. There was also increasing concern among the allies about a resort to use of force, which could threaten the security of the petroleum supply, and even an appeal from a group of leaders of the United Methodist church "not to give in to those who counsel military intervention, nor to take steps which will lead eventually to war."[84] Despite the extraordinary secrecy surrounding the rescue mission itself, it was apparent to a wide spectrum of concerned observers that President Carter had decided to act.

The Soviet Union, too, drew the obvious conclusion that the

United States was about to undertake some form of military action against Iran in the wake of the collapse of negotiations, and took precautionary measures. Attempting to prepare for every contingency, the Soviets strengthened military units in the Transcaucasian military district adjacent to Iran, sent naval and amphibious forces into the Persian Gulf, and offered "emergency" economic support to Tehran in the event the United States did in fact blockade Iranian ports.[85]

The Soviets also sought to derive benefits from the growing schism between Washington and its European allies. The day of Carter's press conference announcing new sanctions, Moscow announced that Soviet Foreign Minister Andrei Gromyko would travel to France within the week.[86] Soviet officials said that he would follow up the Paris trip with visits to Bonn, Brussels, Madrid, and Amsterdam. The Soviet line—which received a sympathetic hearing from the European powers—was that the crisis in detente did not originate with the Soviet invasion of Afghanistan but with American insistence upon deploying new weapons to Western Europe to counter the Soviet SS-20.[87]

The Failure of the Hostage Rescue Mission

The mission to rescue the fifty-three American hostages got under way at twilight on April 24.[88] The plan called for the surreptitious insertion into Iran of a specially trained 208-man force (118 in the rescue team and 90 in a combat-logistics support role), which would assault the United States embassy compound and the Iranian Foreign Ministry, rescue the hostages, and fly them to safety.[89] The mission was undertaken despite the fact that it would place in jeopardy the lives of some 300 other Americans in Iran, including many journalists.[90] There seemed little doubt that some of these would suffer reprisals or be seized themselves if the hostages were rescued.

The assault force was to be transported by six C-130s from Egypt via the island of Masirah to an isolated site, code-named Desert 1, near the town of Tabas, some 250 miles southeast of Tehran.[91] There they would rendezvous with eight RH-53D Sea Stallion helicopters flown in from the carrier *Nimitz* on station in the Gulf of Oman. Auxiliary fuel tanks gave the helicopters the needed range to fly the more than 600 miles from the *Nimitz* to Desert 1.

After refueling at Desert 1, the helicopters were to take the assault force 270 miles more to a mountain hideout, code-named Figbar, about 50 miles southeast of Tehran. Arriving before daylight, the assault force would rest all that day.

After nightfall, the rescue team was to travel to Tehran in trucks provided by agents in Iran, for an after-midnight assault on the compound and foreign ministry. The rescue force would then transport the freed hostages to a pickup point—either the adjacent soccer stadium, or if possible, the courtyard inside the embassy compound itself.[92] The helicopters from Figbar would swoop in to pick them up and fly them to an abandoned airfield at Manzariyeh, thirty-five miles southwest of Tehran. The airfield would have been secured by a Ranger company prior to their arrival. There they would board C-141 transports for the flight out of Iran, accompanied by a fighter escort.

As is well known, this complex rescue plan never got beyond the first step before it turned into a disaster. Two of the eight helicopters failed to make it to Desert 1 due to instrument failure resulting from an unexpected and extensive dust cloud. One helicopter returned to the *Nimitz;* the other landed en route and was abandoned, its crew picked up by one of the other helicopters. The dust cloud had also caused a delay in the remaining six helicopters' flight. Instead of arriving at 10:30 p.m. as planned, they arrived after midnight.

At Desert 1 it was discovered that a third helicopter had developed a leak in its flight controls system, causing the burnout of a backup hydraulic pump.[93] "A fitting between a pump and a hydraulic line had cracked," producing the leak.[94] It could not be repaired, and no spare pumps or fittings were available. Ironically, a spare hydraulic pump had been aboard the helicopter that had returned to the *Nimitz.* This left five helicopters capable of proceeding. It had been determined in advance that unless six helicopters were available the mission would be abandoned. After consultation with mission commanders, the president quickly ordered the rescue team to withdraw. The mission was aborted.

But in the process of departing, a helicopter collided with one of the C-130s, and the resulting explosion killed eight crewmen and severely injured three others. As the aircraft burned, the rescue team hurriedly boarded the remaining transports and departed, leaving behind all of the helicopters and their contents. The collision turned a failed rescue mission into a domestic and international crisis and was a political calamity for President Carter.[95] Coming just as the Mariel boatlift was getting under way (see next section, below), depositing thousands of Cuban refugees on American shores, the rescue debacle made the president appear to be extremely weak, indecisive, and even incompetent.

There are numerous grounds for criticizing the hasty decision to abort the rescue mission—a decision the president made in twelve minutes.[96] The abruptness with which the decision was made raised questions afterward about the president's intention to see the mission through to completion—"a failure of nerve," as one writer put it.[97] The mission commander at Desert 1, however, Colonel Charlie Beckwith, refused to proceed with five helicopters on the grounds that it had been determined beforehand that a minimum of six was necessary.

Beckwith's reasoning was that with only five helicopters he would be forced to leave behind eighteen to twenty men, which would compromise the mission. Further, he argued, if any other helicopters were lost during the mission there would not be enough to pick up the rescuers and hostages, a total of 178 people in all.[98] But Beckwith's explanation is unsatisfactory. Not only did he decline to take even minimum risks to proceed—a decision in which his superiors concurred—key parts of the explanation for abandoning the mission do not stand up to close scrutiny.

For the long-distance flight from the *Nimitz* to Desert 1 the RH-53Ds had been equipped with four auxiliary fuel tanks—two inboard 300-gallon fiberglass palletized fuel containers and two outboard 600-gallon drop tanks strapped onto both sides of the fuselage. The inboard auxiliary tanks restricted the helicopters' carrying capacity. It was the restricted capacity, in turn, that had determined the minimum requirement of six helicopters to transport 118 men and their equipment from Desert 1 to Figbar, eighteen to twenty men aboard each helicopter. Beckwith claimed that with only five helicopters available he would have had to leave behind eighteen to twenty men. This conclusion is not convincing.

Space could easily have been made for four more men and their equipment aboard each of the remaining five helicopters either by leaving behind a few of the gun crew members assigned to the helicopters (each helicopter had a crew of five men; pilot, co-pilot, crew chief, and two gunners), along with their machine guns, ammunition, and tear gas cannisters, or simply by removing one or both of the inboard auxiliary fuel tanks.[99] The palletized fuel containers were specifically designed for easy installation and removal. Thus it would seem that a simple space-weight calculation could have determined what combination of inboard tanks, gun crew members, and equipment would have to be removed from one, two, or three helicopters to obtain the needed space.

Jettisoning the inboard auxiliary fuel tanks was feasible because the remaining distance the helicopters would have to travel—under 400 miles in all—was well within the RH-53D's range with the two 600-gallon outboard auxiliary tanks. The published range of the RH53D is 685 miles (596 nautical miles).[100] Yet, at the critical moment, when on-scene mission commander Air Force Colonel James Kyle asked Marine pilot Ed Seiffert whether he could "dump gas and hack it," Seiffert said no because he would "need every gallon . . . to make it through Night Two."[101]

If six helicopters were deemed absolutely necessary, there were three possibilities. First, the decision could have been made to risk flying the helicopter with a burned-out back-up hydraulic pump—a not uncommon decision in crisis situations. The load could have been lightened to reduce the risk. The advantage in proceeding was that no additional time would have been lost. The disadvantage was that the condition of the craft would have remained precarious throughout the mission, making this the least satisfactory of the three alternatives.

Second, the damaged helicopter could have been repaired. The five flyable helicopters could have proceeded to Figbar with full Delta Force complement, rearranged as noted, leaving behind the disabled helicopter, its crew, and those crew members, machine guns, ammunition, and loaded auxiliary tanks stripped from the flyable helicopters to make extra space. A call could have been placed to the *Nimitz* to fly in a hydraulic pump kit to repair the downed helicopter. The pump itself weighed thirteen pounds, the replacement fitting a few ounces.[102] A carrier jet could have air-dropped a replacement pump with fittings to Desert 1 in a few hours, certainly by daylight.

Even though the pump replacement would take less than one hour, however, to preserve secrecy the sixth helicopter would have been required to spend the day at Desert 1, waiting until nightfall to proceed to Figbar. There was less risk here than it might seem. Although a fairly well traveled road passed close to Desert 1, the helicopters had been painted in the Iranian Air Force color scheme with appropriate decals. Iran had several RH53 helicopters, so if the helicopter was spotted during the day, there would have been no immediate cause for alarm. Finally, one of the Farsi speakers on the strike team could have been left behind, just in case a passer-by became curious.

The trip from Desert 1 to Figbar was 270 miles and would take just over two hours, flying at the RH-53D's cruising speed of 120 knots. Leaving at nightfall, the sixth helicopter would still have arrived at Figbar several hours before the embassy assault was scheduled to get under way, after midnight. Moreover, that helicopter could have hauled fuel left behind at Desert 1. There was, in short, ample time to assemble even the declared minimum number of six helicopters at Figbar prior to the rescue attempt.

The third possibility was that the helicopter which had returned to the *Nimitz* could have been sent out again, with the spare pump kit it had on board. It would have had to have gotten under way almost immediately in order to make Desert 1 before daylight, and there is some question whether it could have been made ready in time because of crew fatigue and instrument damage suffered in the dust storm.[103] If so, given the above scenario, that would have made seven helicopters available for the mission. On balance, delivery of the hydraulic pump kit by carrier jet aircraft would have been the preferred solution if the president and his advisers had given the problem sufficient thought.

Beckwith's second reason for not proceeding—that he might not have enough helicopter capacity available for retrieval of hostages and rescuers and their transport to Manzariyeh—has, as suggested above, even less merit. Maximum seating capacity of the RH-53D was fifty-six.[104] But seating capacity was reduced to twenty during the first phase, the flight from the *Nimitz* to Desert 1, because of the inboard auxiliary fuel tanks.

The inboard auxiliaries were unnecessary for the last phase of the mission because the helicopters had sufficient range without them. Moreover, without the tanks, there would be more space available for picking up the hostages and rescue team and transporting them the thirty-five miles from Tehran to Manzariyeh. In fact, the plan in any case was to jettison the inboard auxiliary tanks when they reached the mountain hideout.[105] Thus, removal of the internal auxiliary tanks would give the helicopters something like their maximum capacity of fifty-six.[106] According to Beckwith, the total number to be transported was 178 men, which four helicopters—not five or six—could accommodate, with room to spare.

This calculation also assumes that there would not be any casualties in the rescue attempt, which was not only highly unlikely but in fact not even expected. Carter later said publicly he had expected there would be casualties.[107] As noted above, Pentagon analyses predicted that there would be between forty-five and seventy casualties among hostages and rescuers. Very likely, in the darkness and chaos, some would be killed and not make it to the pickup point. In terms of lift requirements, this meant that possibly even three helicopters, with a maximum capacity of 168 people, would have been sufficient to extricate the rescue team and hostages from the embassy compound in a single trip.[108] Of course, if necessary one or more of the helicopters could have made two trips. Extra fuel would be available at Manzariyeh.

It is truly difficult to believe that there was no attempt to find precisely what was wrong with the disabled helicopter beyond the vague diagnosis of an unfixable "hydraulic problem" and that no attempt was made to find a repair solution.[109] Once the problem was identified—that continuation of the mission hinged on repair of a backup hydraulic pump—it is incredible that the idea of flying in a pump and repair kit did not occur to any of those involved.[110] If no one thought of repairing the helicopter, it simply testifies to the inadequacy of the Carter leadership under pressure. But if the repair idea was considered and rejected, there needs to be further consideration of why the mission was aborted.

The official critiques of the mission—both military and civilian—were clearly inadequate, focusing on mission mechanics but not politics. The top secret Pentagon critique charged that the helicopters were inadequately maintained, the helicopter pilots had never practiced the mission in bad weather, and the weather forecasters had missed a 200-mile-wide, 6,000-foot-high dust fog. Criticism also focused on the selection and performance of General James Vaught as overall commander, on grounds that he lacked experience in inter-service operations.[111] The Senate Armed Services Committee focused on the same areas.[112]

Two other possibilities occur, both suggested at the time. The first is that the mission was called off after the Soviet Union discovered it and "sent us a message," threatening to attack the transports as they exited Iran through Turkey.[113] The day after the failure, however, the administration went to great pains to note that mission secrecy was not compromised. In a news account of Defense Secretary Brown's press conference, "informed sources" were quoted as saying that "the military high command carefully monitored the status of Soviet forces. There was no sign that the Russians either detected the mission or put forces on higher alert."[114] AWACS planes were also continually aloft to detect any Soviet or Iranian reaction and to direct a response from carrier-based jets, if needed, but no response was detected. In fact, the actual exit plan called for a flight across Saudi Arabia, not Turkey, which largely discounts the Soviet threat argument.[115]

A second, and more likely, possibility is that the rescue mission was cut short because the president had never intended to do more than carry out a show of force in the first place. He needed to shore up a badly sagging image of ineptitude, and in an attempt to intimidate the Iranian leadership and to demonstrate to the American people his ability to take action, he authorized the "rescue." *New York Times* columnist William Safire trenchantly criticized the mission plan as Carter's "tentative, hypercautious, escape-hatch-laden foray into military force." The political question he raised at the time is well worth asking again: "Did the president see any advantage in making a feint and then withdrawing?"[116]

Whatever President Carter's original intent, the rescue mission had been a fiasco of the first order—and a fiasco tinged with blood. But it was not the only or last fiasco of 1980. Another was already in progress as the rescue mission was failing. The Mariel boatlift, which began just before the April rescue attempt and continued to the end of September, would raise further questions about the president's leadership and competency.

The Response to the Mariel Boatlift

In the January discussions American–Cuban normalization was planned to accompany the United States–Soviet accommodation. In the wake of the collapse of the behind-the-scenes rapprochement with Moscow in early March, the Cuban accommodation also foundered. Indeed, Castro responded to the collapse of the deal in a not unexpected way. Aside from publicly reaffirming his interest in and support for revolution in Africa, Central America, and the Caribbean, the Cuban leader precipitated a major international and domestic crisis for President Carter.[117] This was the Mariel boatlift, which lasted more than five months and brought more than 125,000 Cuban refugees and 8,000 Haitians to American shores.

On March 8, in a speech to the Cuban Women's Federation, Fidel Castro listed recent American offenses against Cuba, including the encouragement of "illegal departures" by boat.[118] "We trust they will take measures to discourage illegal departures from the country," Castro said. "Otherwise we would also have to take measures." Castro referred to his 1965 proposal to permit all would-be emigrants to leave the country, an offer which resulted in the emigration of several thousand Cubans by boat from the port of Camarioca to the United States, and subsequently many thousands more by an airlift which lasted until 1971. "We have warned the United States," Castro said, concluding that he hoped Cuba "won't be forced to take such measures again."[119] Although forewarned, the Carter administration was unprepared for what followed.

On Tuesday, April 1, six Cubans in a commandeered city bus crashed through the gate of the Peruvian embassy in Havana, seeking refuge.[120] A Cuban embassy guard was killed by a ricocheting bullet fired by guards in an unsuccessful attempt to stop the bus. Eighteen other supposed "dissidents" quickly joined the refugees. Two days later the Cuban government withdrew police protection from the embassy, on the grounds that the Peruvian government had "encouraged" the dissidents, and used bulldozers to demolish the guard posts and barriers in front of the embassy gate.[121]

The Cuban government's reaction to the events at the Peruvian embassy, persistent rumors in Miami among the Cuban–American community about an impending boatlift, and intelligence reinforcing the rumors, gave American officials advance warning about the possibility of mass Cuban emigration, but no prompt action was taken. American intelligence, in fact, eavesdropping on the Cuban government, had picked up as early as February 21 discussions regarding the reopening of Camarioca specifically "to allow more Cubans to migrate to the United States."[122]

The Department of State convened an interagency meeting for the specific purpose of considering the possibility of "another Camarioca" on April 3. The attending officials agreed that the situation warranted close observation but concluded—in what was a most serious misjudgment—that another Camarioca "did not appear imminent."[123] To be on the safe side, however, they decided to prepare a contingency plan. As it turned out, the contingency plan did not get beyond an initial draft before it was overtaken by events.

Within twenty-four hours of the removal of police protection from the Peruvian embassy some 3,000 Cuban citizens had poured into the embassy compound, encouraged by a Cuban government loudspeaker van announcing that any Cuban citizen going to the embassy could leave the country. The next day, Saturday, April 5, the Cuban government reaffirmed its offer and sweetened it by promising that no reprisals would be carried out if other countries agreed to accept the emigrants. (The government said, however, that the original band of twenty-four would not be permitted to leave because they had used force to enter the embassy.) By Sunday morning there were over 7,000 people jammed into the football field-size Peruvian embassy compound—sitting in trees and on the roof.[124] And the number continued to grow, exceeding 10,000 in a few days.

The Carter administration's initial reaction, on April 7, was to decline any involvement, saying that it was the Peruvian government's problem. Two days later, Secretary Vance declared that the United States was sympathetic but that it was a problem for Latin American countries to work out among themselves.[125] Then on April 14 the president agreed to assist, pledging $4.2 million for refugee relief and resettlement and agreeing to accept 3,500 Cubans under the 1980 Refugee Act, which had just come into force on April 1.[126] The administration arranged for refugee flights from Cuba to Costa Rica, where refugees would be screened prior to resettlement in countries wishing to accept them. But this arrangement lasted only three days, April 16 to 18, before Havana suspended the flights, insisting that all emigrants proceed directly to the United States.

Up to this point, the United States had reacted to the specific problem of the overcrowding of the Peruvian embassy compound. But on April 20 Radio Havana dropped the other shoe, announcing that the port of Mariel was open to anyone who wanted to come to Cuba to pick up relatives. Two days later, on the twenty-second, the government newspaper *Granma* made it official. Cuba had "withdrawn protection from the Florida peninsula" and "anyone who could get a boat from the United States to pick him up could leave."[127]

The news was electrifying. Thousands of Cuban citizens lined up outside the downtown Havana telephone company to call friends and relatives in the United States. Within three days there were over three hundred private boats in Mariel harbor, a small fishing village fifteen miles west of Havana to which Cuban authorities were directing incoming boats. Thus began an exodus from Mariel which would continue for over five months, defying the administration's attempts to stop it. The boatlift brought thousands of Cubans and Haitians to the United States and created a social, bureaucratic, and political nightmare.

For the first two weeks, President Carter proceeded on the wholly erroneous assumption that Castro had initiated the boatlift simply in order to exert pressure on the United States to negotiate a more orderly migration agreement, for which there was a precedent.[128] The president's advisers evidently believed that the Mariel exodus would be a repetition of the Camarioca boatlift in 1965, which had produced a negotiated settlement for immigration of Cuban refugees. The Department of State had set up an interests section in Havana to approve Cubans for entry, who then flew to the United States. These "freedom flights"—two flights a day, five days a week from Havana to Miami—continued for almost six years until the summer of 1971. The Camarioca boatlift had initially transported some 3,000 Cubans, and led to the orderly migration of over 260,000 subsequent refugees to the United States.

That Castro had something else in mind in 1980 became evident in short order. By May 2, in less than two weeks, over 5,000 Cubans had already arrived in Key West—almost twice the number of the entire 1965 boatlift—with as many as 2,000 more boats either on the way to Mariel, loading passengers there, or returning to the United States.[129] Hoping to move quickly to a negotiated settlement, the president arranged a secret meeting with Castro and sent the same two officials, Robert Pastor and Peter Tarnoff, he had sent in January in response to Castro's request. Although Castro had agreed to the meeting, when the two American emissaries arrived, he refused to see them. They met instead with officials from the Foreign Ministry, cabinet, and Central Committee, whose position was that no negotiations could occur until the United States and Cuba normalized relations.[130] In other words, unless Castro's January proposal to normalize relations were accepted, the Cuban leader would not cooperate.

By the middle of May over 40,000 refugees had arrived in Key

West, Florida, swamping the ability of the Coast Guard and Customs to manage the flow. And the flow was fast becoming a flood. On May 14, President Carter announced that he was determined to stop the "uncontrolled" boatlift, but he accompanied his announcement with the offer to start an "orderly" boat- or airlift.[131] The Cuban government simply derided the president's offer. A *Granma* editorial of May 15 challenged Carter to stop the boatlift. "Carter governs in Florida," said the editorial, "but in Mariel . . . Cuba governs."[132]

With the announcement of the president's intent to stop the uncontrolled boatlift, the U.S. Coast Guard began to stop, board, and inspect boats bound for Cuba and to seize and levy fines on those returning with refugees. But the administration was hesitant in applying a consistent policy of firm measures, and little effect was made on the refugee influx. By the end of May, 94,850 Cuban refugees had arrived in Key West.[133] In the meantime, holding and resettlement depots had been set up to process the refugees. Five centers were established. The main one was the Key West–Opa Locka–Miami center, which processed slightly fewer than half of the 125,000 refugees. Four others—at Eglin Air Force Base, Florida; Fort Chaffee, Arkansas; Indiantown Gap, Pennsylvania; and Fort McCoy, Wisconsin—handled the rest.[134]

The refugee flow began to taper off from the second week in June, from the 3,000 or so refugees arriving each *day* in May to a few hundred a week from June through the end of September. The boatlift ended as abruptly as it had begun, on September 25, when without warning the Cuban government closed Mariel harbor. All told, of the 125,000 arrivals 22,000 were detained by the federal government. Of these, 20,200 were political prisoners, 1,200 were suspected criminals, and 600 were serious mental cases.[135]

The administration's response to the boatlift contributed to the already strong popular impression of its general ineptitude and added one more negative to the president's reelection prospects.[136] An ABC News–Harris survey in mid-July found that by a 84 to 13 percent majority the American people gave Carter negative marks on his handling of the boatlift, his lowest rating on any issue tested. By a 73 to 23 percent majority the public felt that the president had been "wrong to allow this influx," and by a 75 to 23 percent majority they disagreed with the view that "the United States has always been a place where refugees can come, and we should let the Cubans in." By a two-to-one margin Americans believed that Castro had made the United States look "foolish."

The Mariel boatlift had a significant impact on the United States at a time of economic recession. The monetary cost of the boatlift alone through the end of 1981 was over $700 million. And the sociopolitical problem for the country of absorbing the large number of immigrants presented continuing difficulties for most of the decade. But for the Carter administration the immediate significance of the boatlift lay primarily in its timing, for the Mariel episode spanned and created the atmosphere for the final few crisis-filled months of the Carter administration. The boatlift began just prior to the ill-fated hostage rescue attempt, formed a rancorous backdrop to a deterioration of United States relations with its allies and a sharp domestic economic downturn over the summer, and ended just as relations with Nicaragua collapsed and the Iran–Iraq war commenced in late September.

Nicaragua and El Salvador: Carter's Election Dilemma

In early September 1980, Jimmy Carter was faced with a momentous decision regarding his policy toward Central America, which would have an obvious impact on his chances for reelection, less than two months away. This was American policy toward Nicaragua, which had failed in its central purposes. Nicaragua had become deeply involved in support of revolution in El Salvador. The essential question was: Should the president acknowledge the failure of his policy, or cover it up until after the election?

From the time that the Sandinistas had come to power in July 1979, the United States had pursued a strategy of cooptation toward Managua, hoping to assist the revolution to fulfill its democratic promises, to deny it an enemy and thus a reason to ally with Cuba and the Soviet Union, and most of all, to ensure the regime's noninterference in the internal affairs of its neighbors, particularly El Salvador.[137]

During the remainder of 1979, Washington had cause for modest satisfaction with its policy toward Nicaragua, even though there was but symbolic movement toward the institution of a pluralistic system. Elections were promised, but in five years—and Managua had quickly aligned itself with Havana and Moscow. The Sandinistas appeared to be intent upon consolidating control internally and showed little disposition to become entangled in the internal affairs of their neighbors, particularly El Salvador, which was undergoing considerable turmoil.

There were disturbing signs, however. At a conference September 21–23, 1979, reviewing the course of the revolution, the Sandinista Directorate had formulated its enemies list, which included what were termed the traitorous bourgeoisie, the vestiges of Somocismo, the ultra-left, and American imperialism.[138] The enemies list was hardly compatible with the policies of political pluralism, a mixed economy, and nonalignment, which the United States was urging upon the Sandinistas. Nevertheless, Washington persisted on course.

Meanwhile, El Salvador, a small country of two and a half million with a tradition of violence, had been experiencing an increase of terrorist attacks and guerrilla activity since the late seventies and was fast becoming a tinderbox. The radical left, comprising several groups which had earlier split from the Communist party of El Salvador, including the Farabundo Marti Popular Liberation Forces (FPL), the People's Revolutionary Army (ERP), and the Armed Forces of National Resistance (FARN), had intensified terrorist and guerrilla attacks since the Sandinista victory. As Archbishop Romero warned in August of 1979, "Our popular groups have been taken over by the far left. They want the church to support everything, not only justice but all their strategies."[139]

The Sandinista victory had not only encouraged the left, it had also galvanized the right. Conservative organizations, fiercely resistant to any change, such as the ORDEN, with strong ties to local security forces and the peasantry, and the White Warriors Union (UGB), a clandestine group of far-rightists, were claiming credit for the assassination of many teachers and priests whom they considered to be subversives. The violence and counterviolence that escalated after the Sandinista victory increased the pressure on El Salvador's traditional political and social structures, threatening to fragment the country into armed camps.

The government of General Humberto Romero had become paralyzed, having neither the will to impose draconian measures nor the determination to counter terrorism with a long-term reform program. In any case, whether concerned about the example of Nicaragua or the evident disintegration of their own country, or both, on October 15, 1979, a group of reform-minded army officers overthrew General Romero. In the October 15 manifesto, the new governing junta of three civilians and two military men denounced government abuse of power, proclaimed a commitment to social and economic reform, and called for a transition to a democratic political system based on free elections.

Though supported by the public, the junta never had time to put its plans for a democratic political-economic system into practice. It did manage to form a widely representative government, release political prisoners, permit the return of exiled political leaders, and outlaw extremist organizations. But the junta could not overcome internal tensions and was unable to restore order. Under the pressure of renewed attacks from both the left and the right, it gradually disintegrated and finally collapsed on January 3, 1980.[140]

The failure of the 1979 revolution in El Salvador was, in retrospect, a turning point for American policy toward Nicaragua. Although the Salvadoran Christian Democratic party agreed to form a new government later, in January 1980, and actually began to implement a far-reaching land reform program in March, the evident disintegration of the junta in late 1979 made El Salvador too tempting a target for Fidel Castro to resist.[141] Increased Cuban support for the communists in El Salvador in turn led to Sandinista involvement from mid-1980, at the latest, thus creating the crisis in American policy toward Nicaragua.

Castro met with the leaders of the three principal Salvadoran revolutionary groups—the Communist party, the National Resistance (FARN), and the Popular Liberation Forces (FPL)—in Havana in mid-December 1979. In a step reminiscent of his support for the Sandinistas during a similar stage of the Nicaraguan revolution, the Cuban leader sought to unify the three factions. As the Salvadoran revolutionaries described it in a December 16 letter of thanks, Castro had agreed to help build the "coordination and unity of our organizations."[142]

During a meeting of the Salvadoran Communist party in late April, party leader Shafik Handal stressed the need to "speed up reorganization and put the Party on a war footing" and noted Fidel's agreement to "involving everyone in the area" in the armed movement.[143] Within a month, at the end of May, after several more meetings with Castro in Havana, the unification of the Salvadoran revolutionary factions was accomplished with the addition of the

Popular Revolutionary Army (ERP) into the coalition. The coalition thereafter assumed the name of Unified Revolutionary Directorate (DRU)—a further resemblance to the Nicaraguan organization.

The newly unified Salvadoran revolutionary leadership then embarked upon a concerted effort to organize the acquisition of weaponry and supplies from friendly communist countries and to arrange for shipment to El Salvador. Shafik Handal departed Havana on May 30 for Moscow and during the next two months visited Vietnam, East Germany, Czechoslovakia, Bulgaria, Hungary, and Ethiopia in his quest to procure arms. Soviet and East German leaders agreed to provide transportation.

In the meantime, other members of the DRU went directly to Managua to discuss Nicaragua's crucial role in the Salvadoran revolution. Nicaragua would play the same role vis-à-vis El Salvador that Costa Rica played vis-à-vis Nicaragua as the principal staging area for the revolutionary struggle. Weapons would be sent first to Cuba, then to Nicaragua for delivery in El Salvador. During the early June meetings, the Sandinistas agreed to establish a secure headquarters, a specific area of operational responsibility, and also to supply weapons.[144] They also agreed to set up, at the appropriate moment, a radio station.

Representatives of the DRU spent two weeks in Managua, July 13–27, to help celebrate the first anniversary of the Nicaraguan revolution as well as to review logistical arrangements, before going once again to Havana to put the final touches on plans for the coming military campaign. Arms deliveries began in mid-August. On August 15, a shipment of Ethiopian arms departed for Cuba, and at about the same time sixty tons of captured American weaponry left Vietnam for arrival in Cuba in early September.[145] Other shipments were under way to both Cuba and Nicaragua. By early September, in other words, an upheaval in El Salvador was imminent.

At this juncture the impending explosion in El Salvador presented a crisis in American policy toward Nicaragua. As part of the cooptation approach, Carter had promised to extend economic assistance to Nicaragua. But in passing the necessary legislation in the spring, Congress had required that the president certify through consultation with the intelligence community that the Sandinista regime was not involved in support of the growing violence in El Salvador and Guatemala.

To de-certify, that is, to acknowledge Nicaragua's involvement, would lay bare the failure of his year-long policy of cooptation toward Managua and reveal the Sandinistas' cooperation with the Soviet Union, Cuba, and the El Salvadoran Communist party in the major campaign then under way to overthrow the government of El Salvador. On the other hand, to delay signing the economic assistance bill until after the election would guarantee that the president's policy toward Nicaragua would be highlighted as a campaign issue, for the revolution in El Salvador and Nicaragua's role were already prominent in the news.

President Carter decided to sidestep the issue. Despite mounting evidence in the press of the Nicaraguan government's involvement in El Salvador, he determined that though there was cause for concern—weapons were being transshipped—the evidence was not conclusive that the government of Nicaragua was responsible.[146] And on September 12 Carter "certified" that the government of Nicaragua "has not cooperated with or harbors any international terrorist organization or is abiding, abetting or supporting acts of violence or terrorism in other countries."[147]

Carter's decision flew in the face of the evidence, confounding those who were following events in Central America. The evidence—by any reasonable calculation—was conclusive. For example, from July of 1980, the CIA had watched the transformation of an 800-meter dirt airstrip used for crop dusting at Papalonal, twenty-five miles northwest of Managua, into a 1200-meter graded airfield complete with dispersal areas and storage facilities to enable its use by large aircraft. As Robert Pastor notes, "the pattern and speed of construction convinced the experts of its military function."[148]

But it was precisely because events were moving quickly that Carter made his decision. To de-certify would deprive Washington of any leverage on Nicaragua's policy and only accelerate the communists' timetable for toppling the government of El Salvador, precipitating an attack which would probably come just before the election. From the president's point of view, a pre-election explosion would have a predictably negative impact on his chances.

The charitable interpretation would be that it was sheer coincidence that the president decided to certify aid to Nicaragua immediately prior to all-out Sandinista involvement in support of Salvadoran revolution. It is far more likely that he interpreted the evidence accurately and that his decision to certify was based upon the hope he could influence the Sandinistas to delay action until after the election.

In short, Carter's decision to certify Managua's non-involvement represented a calculated, if desperate, effort to stave off a major crisis in El Salvador until after the election. Yet, even in purely political terms, this decision was flawed. Candidate Ronald Reagan had made it abundantly clear that, if elected, he would take a hard line toward the Sandinistas. Thus, there can be little doubt that the leaders in Managua understood that they could expect little sympathy from Ronald Reagan if he were elected. It followed that it was in their interests to delay an offensive against El Salvador until after the election, so as not to jeopardize Carter's chances. But Carter was unwilling to leave the issue to chance.

Immediately after certifying that Nicaragua was not "supporting acts of violence or terrorism in other countries," the president sent Deputy Assistant Secretary of State James Cheek to Managua to inform the Sandinistas that the United States government, in fact, knew otherwise. Cheek told the Sandinista leadership that "the argument that the Sandinistas could not control all activities in Nicaragua was not acceptable" and that "if the United States found that Nicaragua was cooperating with or aiding rebels in other countries, it would terminate the aid program."[149]

The demarche to Managua achieved its purpose. Despite growing stockpiles of enormous quantities of weapons in Nicaragua (120 tons) and Cuba (300 to 400 tons), in late September the Sandinistas suspended deliveries to the Salvadoran guerrillas for one month.[150] But one month was all Carter had bargained for. It delayed a growing problem—Cuban and Nicaraguan support for revolution in Central America—beyond the election but of course did not resolve it.

In any event, Carter's electoral defeat removed all reasons for restraint by the Sandinistas—indeed, now the opposite course seemed appropriate. Understanding that once in office Ronald Reagan would attempt to thwart their plans, the Sandinistas—no doubt with full Cuban approval—moved to make the revolution in El Salvador "irreversible."[151] From early November—shipments actually recommenced on election day—the Sandinistas resumed large-scale weapons shipments by air, overland through Honduras, and by water across the Gulf of Fonseca in preparation for a "final offensive," to occur in early 1981, before Ronald Reagan assumed office.[152]

The "final offensive" began on January 10, 1981, but immediately fizzled. The Salvadoran communists, now grouped under the rubric of the Farabundo Marti National Liberation Front (FMLN), had hoped that widespread guerrilla attacks, including an attempted assassination of the newly installed president of El Salvador, Jose Napoleon Duarte, would spark a popular uprising of the Salvadoran people. But nothing happened. The FMLN was weak and the populace indifferent to their cause. Within a few days the final offensive had been spent.

President Carter had certainly known in advance that the Sandinistas were preparing for a major offensive. That had, after all, been the basis for his calculations before the election. Additional hard evidence had become available by mid-December.[153] In all likelihood, this advance information provided the reason for resumption of economic aid to El Salvador on December 17.[154] No military aid was included in this package. Military aid was not resumed until after the final offensive had begun and failed. On January 14, 1981, a week before leaving office, President Carter approved $5.9 million in arms for El Salvador while reluctantly cutting off aid to Nicaragua.[155]

A few weeks after leaving office, Carter went to Nicaragua to explain. At a press conference on February 9, he expressed his attitude regarding the aid cutoff.

> I had no alternative but to cut off aid to the Sandinistas before I left office, because there was evidence that was clear to me that the Sandinistas were giving assistance to the revolution in El Salvador, and the law required me to stop the aid. I was very eager to give the people of Nicaragua economic aid after the revolution, but it was not possible under those circumstances.[156]

While the Carter administration acted to hold off military action in El Salvador prior to the election, it adopted the opposite course in its policy toward Southwest Asia as Iraq prepared to invade Iran.

The Iran–Iraq War, and Begin's Revenge

On September 22, 1980, Iraq invaded Iran in an attempt to displace the former regional hegemon, now wracked with internal upheaval. The war also held significant implications for the United

States position in the region as well as for President Carter's political future. The war, in fact, was the culmination of changes on several levels. At the superpower level, the Soviet Union had assumed the geopolitical initiative, an impression reinforced by the invasion of Afghanistan, while the United States was on the defensive, an impression reinforced by repeated setbacks throughout the Middle East–Southwest Asian region.

In the region itself, the Iranian revolution had been a strategic disaster for the United States, but it had also precipitated a regional realignment. By late 1978 the main trends had already become apparent. These were: Iraq's shift away from Moscow, Iran's intractable hostility toward Washington, and growing conflict between Iraq and Iran as Saddam Hussein's forces probed for Iranian weaknesses.

Not only had the United States failed to normalize relations with Khomeini's Iran, the hostage crisis made dubious any relationship at all for the foreseeable future, particularly after the failed rescue attempt. Furthermore, President Carter had earlier compromised his objectives regarding the Palestinians to obtain the Egyptian–Israeli peace treaty, a decision that had severely damaged relations with Saudi Arabia and Jordan. Initial efforts to repair ties to Saudi Arabia had boomeranged—with high oil prices the result—and by the end of 1979, United States relations with its two former main allies in Southwest Asia, the "twin pillars," were a shambles.

The Soviet invasion of Afghanistan had offered the United States an unexpected opportunity to recover. Through the spring of 1980 Washington had proceeded along three tracks: negotiating for the release of the hostages in Iran, restoring relations with Saudi Arabia and Jordan, and offering to cooperate with Iraq—all within the context of construction of a broader-based regional security network. The collapse of the hostage negotiations followed by the abortive rescue attempt left policy toward Iran at a dead end, but movement proceeded along the remaining two tracks as a growing coincidence of interests among the United States, Saudi Arabia, and Iraq offered the promise of compensating for the failure to reestablish relations with Tehran.

By the middle of 1979, the Iraqi leadership had determined that Iran, weakened by revolution, offered an opportunity for Iraq to become the principal Arab power.[157] Such an advance, however, would require the military defeat of Iran and reversal of the onerous terms of the 1975 treaty which Iran had imposed upon Iraq, including recovery of Shatt Al Arab, the waterway dividing the two countries. Saddam Hussein, who assumed the mantle of supreme leader at that time, commenced a shift toward Saudi Arabia, Egypt, and Jordan to strengthen his rear in any war with Iran and also provide him with necessary Arab support.

The Soviet Union had observed and attempted to counter Baghdad's shift in the spring of 1979 by promoting a rapprochement between Iraq and Syria, which had an interest in forestalling the emergence of Iraq as the principal Arab power, but it had failed. That failure clarified the strategic situation for both powers and led to policy responses which would shape the region's politics for several years. Syria, now faced with a two-front conflict situation involving Iraq and Israel, sought to counter it with a move to Iran, while Iraq, faced with a two-front conflict situation between Syria and Iran, sought to counter it with moves toward Egypt, Jordan, and Saudi Arabia.

Implicit in both shifts were improved relations between Syria and the Soviet Union, on the one hand, and improved relations between Iraq and the United States, on the other hand. Since Syria already had a long-standing relationship with the Soviet Union, its improvement was open and obvious, but since Iraq had had no relationship with the United States for many years, improvement of relations was gradual and indirect though no less real.

From early in 1980, Iraqi and American leaders indicated a growing coincidence of interests in their public statements. For example, on January 6, in a speech outlining Iraq's non-aligned foreign policy, Saddam Hussein denounced the Soviet invasion of Afghanistan and declared his intent to mobilize opposition to it. "We call upon all the peoples of the region to adopt a frank and firm stand against all forms of foreign intervention."[158]

The Carter administration, alert to the possibilities of countering Iran with Iraq, opened the door to improved relations. Following Saddam's speech, both President Carter and National Security Adviser Brzezinski laid out a broader position regarding the Gulf in which relations with Iraq could improve. Brzezinski, in an interview one week before the president announced the Carter Doctrine, declared that the United States was prepared to use force to protect "vital interests" in what he viewed as three interdependent "strategic zones": Western Europe, the Far East, and the Persian Gulf.[159]

Brzezinski announced that the United States was prepared to build a "cooperative security framework" with countries of the Middle East which would take into account local political and ideological factors and not necessarily involve formal agreements. Brzezinski declared that the United States wished to have friendly relations with all Moslem countries, specifically identifying Iraq and Libya as countries "with whom we don't have irreconcilable differences."[160]

A week later, the president used the "no irreconcilable differences" line with Muslim nations in announcing United States determination to protect its vital interests in the Gulf against "any attempt by any outside force to gain control."[161] The doctrine not only offered a rationale for the military buildup the United States was making in the region, but also indicated Washington's needs for access points on which to base its force-projection capability.

Saddam Hussein outlined his views of relations with the United States on January 31. Denouncing both the Soviet Union and the United States for their attempts to gain control of the region, Hussein nevertheless indicated Iraq's continued movement away from Moscow and willingness to deal with Washington. Iraq would continue its relationship with the Soviet Union, he said, but only to the extent that it "strengthens Iraq's independence and serves the Arab nation's cause."[162] As for the United States, while there was little reason at present to reestablish diplomatic relations, "Iraq is not absolutely and fanatically against dealing with the United States, but it supports dealings that are based on respect for the Arab nation's interests."

Hussein's willingness to support dealings with the United States on the basis of national interests—even though establishment of diplomatic relations was still far off—and his announcement on February 8 of the pan-Arab "National Charter," designed to position Iraq as the preeminent power in the Gulf, were sufficient incentive for the Carter administration to take additional steps toward Baghdad. By early February, each country had publicly and specifically indicated its willingness to cooperate with the other on an informal basis.

Moving beyond public statements, Washington attempted to secure cooperation with the countries of the region and indicate approval for Iraq's inclusion in the regional security framework it was building. In early February Brzezinski and Deputy Secretary of State Warren Christopher visited Pakistan and Saudi Arabia to discuss prospects for security cooperation. Although Pakistan dismissed an offer for $400 million over two years as "peanuts," the visit to Riyadh was more productive.

The Saudi leadership was quite receptive to Brzezinski and Christopher's proposals for strengthened security cooperation, both in terms of improving their own defense capabilities and approving a greater American presence in the region—a marked change from a year earlier, when they had publicly denounced American policy over the Israeli–Egyptian treaty and threatened to shift away from Washington (see chapter 7).[163] The Saudis now sought to enhance the capabilities of their newly acquired F-15s and to purchase AWACS, while agreeing to greater cooperation with Pakistan, including the provision of funds for Islamabad's weapons purchases.[164]

Regarding a larger American regional presence, the Saudis endorsed Washington's plans to gain base rights in Oman, Somalia, and Kenya but continued to demur on the question of providing bases in Saudi Arabia for American forces. The growing threat, however (genuine this time, not manufactured as a year earlier during the South Yemeni attack of North Yemen), prompted them to make two substantial concessions in the matter of bases. First, they agreed that the United States could use Saudi bases in a military emergency.[165] Most important for the long run, however, was Saudi agreement to construct, according to American specificiations, a greatly enlarged military base structure—over two dozen bases costing some fifty billion dollars. The United States, in return, agreed to pre-position fuel and ammunition at these bases for the use of American forces in a crisis.[166]

Aside from activating the Rapid Deployment Force,[167] a long-range project, Washington's general approach was to accelerate military sales to its allies in the region while supporting their improving relations with Iraq, even as the United States gradually permitted the transfer of military technology to Iraq. For example, on January 23, the Department of Commerce granted an export license for eight General Electric marine gas turbine engines destined for Italy, where they would be installed on four frigates being built for Iraq.[168] The ships, which were outfitted with other American technology as well, would significantly improve Iraq's naval capability in the Gulf.

From early April 1980, as Iraqi skirmishing along the Iranian border intensified, Under Secretary of State David Newsom and National Security Adviser Brzezinski each expressed United States interest in improving relations with Iraq. On April 10, Newsom declared that "the United States is prepared . . . to resume diplomatic relations with Iraq at any time."[169] Four days later, on the MacNeil–Lehrer television news show, Brzezinski proclaimed:

> We see no fundamental incompatibility of interests between the United States and Iraq. We feel that Iraq desires to be independent, that Iraq wishes a secure Persian Gulf, and we do not feel that American–Iraqi relations need to be frozen in antagonism.[170]

Publicly indicating Iraq's acceptability to the United States encouraged Washington's allies in the region to improve relations with Baghdad. On April 9, King Hussein of Jordan urged all Arabs to support Iraq and proceeded to mediate a rapprochement between Iraq and Saudi Arabia.[171] By the middle of the month, a Jordanian–Saudi–Iraqi entente, based on "Arab solidarity," was in place.[172]

Through the summer both the Soviet and American sides sought to strengthen their respective coalitions for the coming war. Iran signed technical and economic agreements with the Soviet Union, Romania, and Poland, while Iraq proceeded to normalize relations with Saudi Arabia and the moderate Arabs.[173] On the eve of Saddam Hussein's visit to Saudi Arabia, the United States announced its final decision to sell the eight marine turbine engines licensed in February and that the Commerce Department was considering the sale of five Boeing jets to Iraq as well.

By the end of August, the regional realignment precipitated by the Iranian revolution had crystallized. There is little doubt that the United States was in support of the Jordan–Saudi–Iraq entente, while the Soviet Union was backing the Iran–Syria–Libya grouping.[174] Although United States involvement in Iraq's war planning was minimal and indirect, there can be little doubt of the Carter administration's knowledge that war was imminent.

War between Iraq and Iran would advance United States interests in several ways. It would contain Iran's expansionist ambitions and perhaps even result in the removal of Khomeini from power. War would threaten both the security of regional powers and of petroleum flows through the Persian Gulf. Thus, perhaps most importantly, the war would offer the United States greater opportunities to enhance its military presence in the area and to strengthen the collective security structure which Washington was in the process of constructing.

Finally, the war could serve President Carter's personal political interests by helping to gain the release of the hostages. That this was more than a fleeting thought was revealed on the very day the war broke out. On the campaign trail in Torrance, California, the president was asked about the war's impact on the hostages. He said:

> It could convince Iran that they need peace with their neighbors, they need to be part of the international community, they need to be able to have a strong and viable economy, they need to get spare parts for their military weapons . . . and therefore induce them to release the hostages.[175]

Brzezinski acknowledges in his memoirs that the outbreak of the war raised the prospect for gaining the release of the hostages because of Iran's need for weapons spare parts.

> We began to hold out that option as a way of enticing the Iranians into a prompt settlement. By the middle of October, we were even discussing among ourselves the possibility of pre-positioning some of these spare parts in Germany, Algeria, or Pakistan, so that the Iranians could then promptly pick them up with their own aircraft.[176]

The key to American hopes was that the Iraqi invasion would generate sufficient pressure on the Iranian leadership to persuade them to reach a settlement over the hostages in return for resumption of military supply. Reference to "spare parts" was in fact simply a euphemism; it meant, at minimum, delivery of the very substantial amount of military equipment that Iran had already purchased and was in the pipeline for delivery before the assets were frozen in November 1979. This amounted to $240 million in weapons, including spare tires for Iran's American-made aircraft (F-4s, F-5s, and F-14s), several C-130 transports, over 8,600 anti-tank missiles, thousands of tank and artillery rounds, cluster bombs, land mines, and Hawk surface-to-air missiles.[177]

Success, however, hinged on two factors: the strength of the Iraqi invasion and the weakness of Iranian defenses. The president would almost immediately be disappointed on both counts. By the end of the first week of fighting, the Iraqi offensive stalled as Saddam Hussein's armor reached the cities of Khorramshahr, Abadan, Ahwaz, and Dezful. Fierce resistance in these cities quickly forced an change in Iraqi policy from attack to attrition, and Iraq turned to seige warfare. Indeed, on the twenty-eighth, Saddam Hussein offered a cease-fire and declared his willingness to accept mediation or enter into direct negotiations—as long as Iran recognized Iraq's "legitimate rights."[178] Khomeini refused.

Part of the reason for Iran's better-than-expected defense was the Soviet Union. By the end of the first week in October, Moscow had set in motion a major resupply plan (which closely resembled the supply arrangements for El Salvador) and weapons began to be delivered to Iran from Syria, Libya, North Korea, and Vietnam.[179] Soviet Ambassador to Tehran Vladimir Vinogradov had met with Iranian Prime Minister Rajai on October 4, reportedly offering to "cooperate in various fields and . . . help you with military equipment."[180] Although Rajai publicly rejected the offer of direct Soviet assistance, the flow of arms within a few days of the meeting pointed to an agreement to accept indirect aid.

Of great concern was Iran's immediate aerial counteroffensive against Iraq's petroleum installations.[181] Iranian attacks on Al-Fao at the mouth of the Shatt, Kirkuk, and Mosul forced Iraq to suspend oil exports because of damage to pipelines, pumping stations, and shipping platforms.[182] The effectiveness of the Iranian air force alarmed the Saudis, who feared that Iran might attack Saudi Arabia because Riyadh had permitted Iraq to disperse aircraft to Saudi bases after the outbreak of the war.[183]

Discovery of the reason for Iran's effective utilization of its American aircraft, however, created a dilemma for President Carter, who made a fateful choice. As Brzezinski described it,

> It was at this juncture that we learned, much to our dismay, that the Israelis had been secretly supplying American spare parts to the Iranians, without much concern for the negative impact this was having on our leverage with the Iranians on the hostage issue.[184]

After discussing the issue "at some length" with Secretary of State Edward Muskie, who had replaced Cyrus Vance, it was decided that Muskie "would make a strong demarche to the Israelis, since this was obviously undercutting our sensitive efforts." Brzezinski affirms that Muskie "did so" but that the results were less than hoped for. "As far as I know," the national security adviser recounted, "at least for a while, the Israelis held back."[185]

Brzezinski's laconic comment that the Israelis held back supply of Iran "at least for a while" masked the dilemma which Menachem

Begin had created for Jimmy Carter. Iraq's attack was weaker than expected and, in part because of Israel's resupply, Iran's defense was more effective than expected. The result, as Brzezinski concluded, was that "the Iraq–Iran war created less of an opportunity for negotiations than we may have thought."[186] The immediate question, however, was: in the face of the uncertainty of Israeli compliance, should the strategy be continued or changed?

Brzezinski and other high officials, if not the president, had believed for some time—certainly since February 1979 (see chapter 7)—that Begin sought Carter's electoral defeat.[187] Undercutting Carter's efforts to gain the release of the hostages was certainly a means to that end. Given the animosity between the two leaders, Carter evidently concluded that Begin would not stop resupplying the Iranians and that therefore the strategy of pressuring the Iranians into an arms-for-hostages deal would fail.[188]

Thus, in mid-October, with the election less than three weeks away, President Carter reversed policy from a tilt to Iraq to support of Iran. He announced the policy change on October 15, during remarks at a town meeting in Yatesville, Pennsylvania. Calling for an end to the hostilities and for immediate negotiations to settle the border dispute, the president said:

> This reflects the long-standing policy of our country that all territorial disputes should be settled peacefully and not by aggression. The United States remains committed to the proposition that the national security and integrity of Iran is in the interest of national stability [*sic*]. We oppose any effort to dismember Iran, to cut away part of it and separate it from the rest of Iran.[189]

The president's statement came in the context of the resumption of Iraq's offensive against Khorramshahr and Abadan five days before and clearly signaled to Saddam Hussein that the United States would not countenance any Iraqi plan to seize Iranian territory.[190] Carter had reversed policy 180 degrees in a desperate gamble to gain through support of Iran that which could no longer be gained through support of Iraq—the release of the hostages.

For a brief time it appeared that Carter's last-minute switch of policy would work. A week after Carter's announcement, on October 22, Tehran indicated that it was close to reaching a decision on release of the hostages.[191] But a few days later, on October 27, the day before Carter's nationally televised debate with Ronald Reagan, the Iranians postponed a decision.[192] Despite continued desperate promises over the next few days, the plan to gain the release of the hostages before the election failed.

The frenzied efforts to effect an arms-for-hostages deal before the election captured headlines, but the issue which decisively tipped the balance in the days leading up to the election was the one which struck the American voter in his pocketbook—the national economy. Here, Jimmy Carter failed as badly as in his efforts to gain the release of the hostages, and in the same way, by subordinating national priorities to personal, political needs.

The Response to Continuing Inflation

By January 1980, the shock of the October 6 policy change had been absorbed by the financial markets and was having little effect in slowing down the economy as hoped (see chapter 9). Despite nearly doubled interest rates from the previous September, the economy continued to expand. The money supply continued to grow, and inflation rose with it. The only answer was to restrict the growth of the money supply further, a step which risked throwing the economy into a recession. During an election year, this created a serious dilemma for President Carter. To bring down inflation would undermine his reelection chances, but to promote economic growth would further stimulate inflation.

In discussion with Federal Reserve chief Paul Volcker, President Carter strongly urged, indeed demanded, that the Federal Reserve put in place emergency measures to gain control of the inflation wracking the nation. Although the Federal Reserve was technically independent, as a practical matter its members were clearly influenced by the president. Some solution was sought to satisfy both the president's demands and the economy's needs. The compromise that emerged was that the president would redraft his budget to reflect greater cuts in federal spending and the Federal Reserve would install curbs on lending.[193]

The result was the imposition of emergency credit controls, announced by the president on March 14.[194] Carter coupled restrictions on the growth of bank credit to 9 percent per year with controls on retail and credit card borrowing. Volcker objected to consumer credit controls as pointless because consumer borrowing was already subsiding, but the president insisted on including the average consumer "as a unifying political message, not an economic strategy."[195] Later it would be judged that the recession of 1980 had in fact already begun in January, which meant that the president's desperate effort to place controls on the economy had been a needless excursion into economic policy.[196]

The president's calculation, or hope, was that direct controls on lending would push down interest rates and cool off the economy without precipitating a recession—the last thing desired in an election year. The president miscalculated badly. Not only did direct controls inhibit borrowing but consumers stopped buying as well, plunging the nation into recession. By mid-year the gross national product had shrunk by 10 percent, the sharpest contraction in thirty-five years.[197] Over a million and a half people were thrown out of work as the umemployment rate rose from 6.8 percent in March to 7.8 percent in July.

The sharp contraction prompted the Federal Reserve to move quickly to rescind the main components of the credit control program—to Carter's relief—and Volcker began to pump in more reserves to stimulate money growth and bring down interest rates. In early April the Fed Funds Rate—to which all lending rates were tied—had hit a peak of nearly 20 percent. By mid-June, following Volcker's corrective action, it had plummeted to 8.5 percent, and all other rates had followed. By early July the drop in interest rates produced, inevitably, the restimulation of the economy. Personal consumption was rising again. Housing starts, a key indicator, increased by 30 percent after falling for five straight months. By early August it was clear that the recession of 1980 had ended.[198]

The danger was that rapidly increasing the money supply risked restimulating the economy before inflation had been eliminated, which is exactly what happened. Carter's initial relief that the Fed was bringing the economy out of its nosedive of the second quarter quickly turned to alarm as the old bugaboo of inflation reared its head. The recession had lasted approximately one quarter, but inflation had not been conquered. By early fall the Consumer Price Index was bumping against an annual inflation rate of 11 percent.

Oddly enough, there was a positive aspect in the international financial market to the continued strong inflation wracking the domestic economic scene. During the late summer of 1980 the dollar began to appreciate against major currencies, starting a trend that would last until 1985. International financial flows began to shift to the dollar, flowing to the higher interest rates prevailing in the United States. This was particularly true with regard to the deutschemark. In what was euphemistically described as a "business cycle mismatch" the dollar once again began to dominate the dollar-mark axis.[199]

In the early fall of 1980, with the election campaign in full swing, the dollar's international rebound was hardly comforting to the president because the inflation in the domestic economy was showing no signs of abating. By September the Fed faced a Hobson's choice—that is, no choice at all. The only way to slow inflation was to restrict the money supply, election campaign or no. Thus, on September 16, the Federal Open Market Committee (FOMC) decided to push interest rates upward and reduce the money supply.[200]

Over the next seven weeks the Fed Funds Rate rose steadily from 10.5 percent, to 14 percent on election day. Other lending rates, of course, followed. The prime rate hit 20.5 percent, GNP growth was negative (–0.2 percent), the unemployment rate had rose to 7.1 percent, and the Consumer Price Index stood at 12.4 percent. In short, contrary to some campaign arguments and indeed past practice by Republican and Democratic administrations alike, there was no attempt to pump money into the economy to drive interest rates down just prior to the election of 1980.

Indeed, the president began to attack the Federal Reserve policy for not increasing the money supply as the election neared, to no avail. In fitting irony, the "misery index"—Carter's own creation in the campaign of 1976—now came back to haunt him. The rise in interest rates during the last month turned a close election, in which Carter actually held a few percentage-points lead, into a landslide victory for Ronald Reagan, by a 51 to 41 percent majority.

Notes

1. Brzezinski, *Power and Principle*, p. 437, noted that after Afghanistan "Vance . . . was clearly unhappy, feeling unfairly blamed on the Middle East issue, resentful of White House political criticism, and also deeply disappointed by the turn of the U.S.–Soviet relationship. Most of our key strategic decisions, be it on relations with China, on our defense policy, or on the response to the Soviet action in Afghanistan, were not pointed in directions that he would have naturally favored." Sick, *All Fall Down*, p. 343, goes further, noting that "the Soviet invasion was a body blow to Vance, and he seemed to age visibly under the impact. It marked the end, at least for some time, of the polices to which he had devoted his professional life. American policy was taking a dangerous new turn that he was powerless to prevent. He had run out of ideas, and he seemed to distance himself from the day-to-day policy process."
2. Rowland Evans and Robert Novak, "Changing Streams without Changing Horses," *Washington Post*, January 16, 1980, p. 21, noted that "many politicians of both parties, while applauding Carter's belated moves against Soviet expansion, believe the president's long lack of awareness is a portent of deep problems ahead. They worry that Carter himself, despite strong talk, has missed the full import of the Soviet invasion. If he has not, they ask, what makes him stick to his old mentors? These were the very officials in control for the three years during which, by his own testimony, he was so completely misled by the Soviet Union."
3. Carter, *Keeping Faith*, p. 472.
4. Ibid.
5. "Transcript of President's Interview with Frank Reynolds on Soviet Reply," *New York Times*, January 1, 1980, p. 1.
6. "Carter Letter, Byrd's Response on SALT II Debate," *Washington Post*, January 4, 1980, p. 10. The president does not have the power to withdraw a treaty once it is delivered to the Senate. A treaty can only be returned to the president by order of the Senate.
7. Smith, "Carter Embargoes Technology for Soviet," p. 1.
8. Garthoff, *Detente and Confrontation*, p. 956.
9. "Transcript of President's Speech on Soviet Military Intervention in Afghanistan," *New York Times*, January 5, 1980, p. 6.
10. Smith, "Carter Embargoes Technology for Soviet."
11. Henry L. Trewhitt, "U.S. Freezes Many Links with Soviet," *Baltimore Sun*, January 10, 1980, p. 1.
12. See Garthoff, *Detente and Confrontation*, p. 962, who details the covert

support arrangements, essentially Egyptian and Pakistani shipment of Soviet weapons.

13. "Transcript of President's Speech on Soviet Military Intervention in Afghanistan."
14. President Carter, "The State of the Union Address before Joint Session of Congress," January 23, 1980, *Public Papers of the Presidents of the United States, Jimmy Carter 1980–1981* (Washington, DC: GPO, 1981), p. 195.
15. Carter, *Keeping Faith*, p. 479. See also Garthoff, *Detente and Confrontation*, p. 976.
16. Ibid., p. 480.
17. Ibid.
18. Hamilton Jordan, *Crisis: The Last Year of the Carter Presidency* (New York: G.P.Putnam's, 1982), pp. 104–5. Jordan had become acquainted with Torrijos through his efforts to arrange exile accommodations for the shah in Panama. On January 11 Torrijos contacted Jordan to arrange a meeting the next day with his top "leftist" aide, Marcel Saliman. Saliman had just returned from Tehran and a meeting with acting Foreign Minister Ghotbzadeh, presumably to confirm their ideas and identities. It was Saliman who brought Villalon and Bourguet into contact with Jordan. The two lawyers sought a direct contact with Carter through his personal friend and political adviser Jordan because, they said, the Department of State was "controlled by Kissinger and Rockefeller."
19. Vance, *Hard Choices*, p. 402.
20. Ibid., p. 394.
21. See Carl Marcy, "SALT II Still Lives," *New York Times*, January 29, 1980, p. 19, and Paul Warnke, "SALT without Detente," *Washington Post*, January 29, 1980, p. 19.
22. Frank Cormier, "Carter Sees No Threat to Caribbean Nations," *Philadelphia Inquirer*, January 31, 1980, p. 5.
23. "Brezhnev Reaffirms Soviet Union Committed to Following Detente," *Washington Post*, February 5, 1980, p. 13.
24. Carter, *Keeping Faith*, p. 485.
25. Vance, *Hard Choices*, p. 395.
26. "Vance Sets Deadline on Olympics," *Baltimore Sun*, January 16, 1980, p. 1. Of the three options being considered, boycott, transfer, or cancellation of the games, Vance pressed for the option least offensive to Moscow.
27. Barry Lorge, "White House Deadline on Games Eased," *Washington Post*, February 12, 1980, p. 1.
28. Ibid. (Emphasis supplied.)

29. "Transcript of President's News Conference," *New York Times*, February 14, 1980, p. 16. Cf. Garthoff, *Detente and Confrontation*, p. 963.
30. Henry L. Trewhitt, "Carter Endorses Role for U.N. in Freeing Hostages," *Baltimore Sun*, February 14, 1980, p. 1.
31. See George F. Will, "What Next on the Agenda of Appeasement?" *Washington Post*, February 21, 1980, p. 17.
32. Hedrick Smith, "Carter Backs an Iran Commission As Step toward Freeing Captives; Cautions on 'Excessive Optimism,'" *New York Times*, February 14, 1980, p. 1.
33. Trewhitt, "Carter Endorses Role for U.N.," p. 1.
34. Vance, *Hard Choices*, pp. 400–1, and Sick, *All Fall Down*, pp. 301–2.
35. Edward Walsh, "White House Eyeing SALT Resurrection," *Washington Post*, February 21, 1980, p. 25.
36. Ibid. (Emphasis supplied.) Brzezinski, *Power and Principle*, pp. 434–35, says that in February he had opened "a quiet negotiating channel with the Soviets to determine if at some point they were prepared to reconsider their involvement in Afghanistan." He noted that in discussions with Dobrynin "at one point it appeared that the Soviets might be prepared to dump their newly installed puppet President, Babrak Karmal," then abruptly dropped the matter.
37. Pastor, *Condemned to Repetition*, p. 210.
38. Ibid.
39. Brzezinski, *Power and Principle*, p. 435.
40. Vance, *Hard Choices*, p. 395, and Brzezinski, *Power and Principle*, p. 435.
41. Brzezinski, *Power and Principle*, p. 435.
42. Ibid.
43. Ibid.
44. Ibid., p. 436.
45. Bernard Gwertzman, "Vance and Moscow Envoy Confer," *New York Times*, March 1, 1980, p. 5. State Department officials said that Vance or Mondale "would probably meet with Foreign Minister Andrei A. Gromyko in Belgrade when President Tito of Yugoslavia died. The Yugoslav leader is gravely ill."
46. Bernard Gwertzman, "Vance Urging a Balanced Response on Afghanistan," *New York Times*, March 4, 1980, p. 3.
47. Ibid.
48. Brzezinski, *Power and Principle*, pp. 436–37, attempts to excuse the president, explaining the "highly charged atmosphere," the president's "low" political stock, the irritation of the Kennedy challenge, and the frustration with Iran.
49. Ibid., pp. 436–37.
50. Jonathan C. Randal, "U.N. Mission to Iran Ends in Failure," *Wash-*

ington Post, March 11, 1980, p. 1, John Goshko and Don Oberdorfer, "U.S. Says Tehran Reneged on Panel," *Washington Post*, March 11, 1980, p. 1, and Sick, *All Fall Down*, p. 317.

51. Carter, *Keeping Faith*, p. 499.
52. Vance, *Hard Choices*, pp. 405–7.
53. Brzezinski, *Power and Principle*, p. 486.
54. Ibid.
55. Ibid., p. 487.
56. Sick, *All Fall Down*, pp. 321–23. The ultimatum was actually sent on March 25.
57. Vance, *Hard Choices*, pp. 406–7.
58. Brzezinski, *Power and Principle*, p. 487.
59. Sick, *All Fall Down*, pp. 322–23.
60. Ibid., p. 326.
61. Even Vance, *Hard Choices*, p. 408, had come to the conclusion that "the hostages would be freed only when Khomeini was certain all the institutions of an Islamic republic were in place."
62. Brzezinski, *Power and Principle*, p. 491.
63. Ibid.
64. "Transcript of Carter Statement on Iran," *New York Times*, April 8, 1980, p. 6.
65. Don Oberdorfer, "A Turning Point," *Washington Post*, April 8, 1980, p. 1.
66. Ibid.
67. Ibid.
68. Louis Harris, "Criticism of Carter on Iran Rises Sharply," *Chicago Tribune*, April 17, 1980, p. 5.
69. "Carter Suffers Drop in Views on Iran Action," *Washington Star*, April 14, 1980, p. 4.
70. Harris, "Criticism of Carter on Iran Rises Sharply."
71. Sick, *All Fall Down*, p. 341, and Vance, *Hard Choices*, p. 409.
72. Brzezinski, *Power and Principle*, p. 493.
73. Sick, *All Fall Down*, p. 345.
74. Carter, *Keeping Faith*, p. 506. In fact, that day Tehran radio reported "cross border assaults by small bands of Iraqi troops" had taken place a few days earlier, and announced the dispatch of Iranian naval units to the head of the Persian Gulf in a move which threatened to "choke off Iraq's narrow outlet to the sea." See "Iran Sends Naval Forces Steaming into Persian Gulf," *Washington Star*, April 11, 1980, p. 7.
75. Carter, *Keeping Faith*, p. 506.
76. Jack Anderson, "Hostage Rescue Try Wasn't Necessary," *Washington Post*, May 8, 1980, p. D9.
77. Ibid.

78. "New Light on the Rescue Mission," *Newsweek*, June 30, 1980, p. 18.
79. Brzezinski, *Power and Principle*, p. 492.
80. "Transcript of President's News Conference," *New York Times*, April 18, 1980, p. 14. See also Don Oberdorfer, "Carter Adds to Reprisals against Iran," *Washington Post*, April 18, 1980, p. 1, and Bernard Gwertzman, "Carter Says Military Action Is the Only Choice Left to U.S. If Iran Fails to Free Captives," *New York Times*, April 18, 1980, p. 1.
81. Ibid.
82. Ibid.
83. Vance, *Hard Choices*, p. 411.
84. Don Oberdorfer, "Carter Hints about Force Upset Staff," *Washington Post*, April 24, 1980, p. 1, Roberta Hornig, "Senators Ask Consultation by President," *Washington Star*, April 25, 1980, p. 1, Leonard Downie, "Allies Had Hoped to Prevent Use of Force by U.S.," *Washington Post*, April 25, 1980, p. 1.
85. Henry S. Bradsher, "Soviet Units on Iran Border Raised to Combat Strength," *Washington Star*, April 16, 1980, p. 1, and Anthony Barbieri, "Soviet Dusting Off World War II Land Route As Supply Line for Iran's Use in 'Emergency,'" *Baltimore Sun*, April 25, 1980, p. 4.
86. Ronald Koven, "Europe's Rift with U.S. Is Target of Soviet Drive," *Washington Post*, April 18, 1980, p. 25.
87. Ibid.
88. See Carter, *Keeping Faith*, pp. 506–19, Brzezinski, *Power and Principle*, pp. 487–500, Sick, *All Fall Down*, pp. 334–52.
89. Beckwith, *Delta Force*, p. 253, says there were 118 in the assault team. James H. Kyle, *The Guts to Try* (New York: Orion Books, 1990), p. 134, who was on-scene mission commander, says there were "120 in the Delta contingent, about 100 Rangers, and as many as 56 helicopter crew members." Defense Secretary Brown said afterward that there were 90 in the assault team, plus 90 in a support role. See Charles W. Corddry, "Hostage Rescue: Why It Failed," *Baltimore Sun*, April 26, 1980, p. 1.
90. Seymour M. Hersh, "The Iran Operation: 'Hard Questions That Need Answers Now,'" *New York Times*, May 1, 1980, p. 31.
91. Beckwith, *Delta Force*, pp. 253–56.
92. The hostage captors had placed twenty-foot-long poles upright around the courtyard in anticipation of a helicopter assault. Departure via the courtyard would occur only if the rescue team were able to remove them.
93. "New Light on the Rescue Mission," p. 18. See also John J. Fialka, "Helicopters' Sand Filters Removed Before Mission," *Washington Star*, April 30, 1980, p. 1. Kyle, *Guts to Try*, p. 287, notes that the leak

resulted from "a cracked nut on a servo which leads to the backup pump for the flight controls. . . . The pump was burned out because of a lack of fluid."

94. Richard Halloran, "Multiple Causes Seen in Failure of 3 Rescue Copters," *New York Times*, May 1, 1980, p. 18.
95. Brzezinski, *Power and Principle*, p. 499.
96. Carter, *Keeping Faith*, pp. 515–16.
97. William Safire, "Rescue Mission Questions," *New York Times*, June 5, 1980, p. 23.
98. Beckwith, *Delta Force*, p. 277.
99. Army Colonel (ret.) Jerry King, operations planner for the mission, said in a letter to the author of April 19, 1991, that it had been his calculation that "the entire force could have lifted on the remaining helicopters and still have a twenty-five percent backup, simply by removing one door gunner and the tear gas (intended to disperse large crowds) on each of the remaining helicopters." Kyle, *Guts to Try*, p. 291, claims that only "years later" did he hear of the suggestion to leave behind the machine gun, gunner, and ammunition, and says that Beckwith knew nothing of it either. King, who was in Egypt during the mission, believed that such a suggestion "had to have been broadcast by me or someone else during the period that the matter was under discussion by Vaught and Kyle."
100. See Douglas B. Feaver, "Sand and Distance Strained Copters," *Washington Post*, April 27, 1980, p. 15. See also John K. Cooley, "How the Failure of Three Helicopters Changed History," *Christian Science Monitor*, April 28, 1980, p. 14.
101. Kyle, *Guts to Try*, p. 289.
102. "New Light on the Rescue Mission," *Newsweek*, June 30, 1980, p. 18.
103. Ibid.
104. Feaver, "Sand and Distance Strained Copters," p. 13.
105. Kyle, *Guts to Try*, p. 226.
106. There is reason to believe that the capacity of these particular RH53Ds was somewhat greater than the published maximum because of structural reinforcements made for anti-submarine warfare duty.
107. Phil Gailey, "Carter Says Rescue Bid Worth Risk," *Washington Star*, April 30, 1980, p. 1.
108. Kyle, *Guts to Try*, p. 226, also notes about the helicopters that "at worst, we could make do with three."
109. Beckwith, *Delta Force*, p. 276.
110. According to Colonel King, letter to author, "Flying in a replacement [pump] was never considered."
111. For a synopsis, see Stewart Lytle, "Pentagon Finds Major Errors in Iran Rescue Bid," *Pittsburgh Press*, May 30, 1980, p. 1.

112. Richard Burt, "'Major' Mistakes on Iran Mission Noted in Report," *New York Times*, June 6, 1980, p. 1.
113. Safire, "Rescue Mission Questions," p. 23.
114. Corddry, "Hostage Rescue: Why It Failed."
115. Kyle, *Guts to Try*, p. 182.
116. Safire, "Rescue Mission Questions," p. 23.
117. For Castro's reversal on policy toward the Caribbean, see two articles by Gilbert A. Lewthwaite, "Cubans Bolster Unique Revolution in Grenada," *Baltimore Sun*, March 31, 1980, p. 1, and "3 Leftist Chiefs Pledge Unity in Caribbean Area," *Baltimore Sun*, March 14, 1980, p. 6.
118. Marlise Simmons, "Cuba Suddenly Permits Mass Emigration to U.S.," *Washington Post*, April 24, 1980, p. 1.
119. Ibid.
120. "7,000 Cubans at Peru Embassy," *Chicago Tribune*, April 7, 1980, p. 2.
121. Alex Larzelere, *The 1980 Cuban Boatlift, Castro's Ploy—America's Dilemma* (Washington, D.C.: National Defense University, 1988), p. 6.
122. Ibid., p. 119.
123. Ibid., p. 120.
124. "7,000 Cubans at Peru Embassy."
125. Graham Hovey, "U.S. Asks Latins to Take Lead," *New York Times*, April 11, 1980, p. 2.
126. Phil Gailey, "U.S. Will Take 3,500 Cubans, Carter Declares," *Washington Star*, April 15, 1980, p. 1.
127. Simmons, "Cuba Suddenly Permits Mass Emigration to U.S.," p. 1.
128. Larzelere, *The 1980 Cuban Boatlift*, pp. 240–41.
129. Ibid., p. 249.
130. Ibid., pp. 253–54.
131. Robert Pear, "President Toughens Curbs on Ferrying of Cuban Refugees," *New York Times*, May 15, 1980, p. 12.
132. Karen DeYoung, "Cuba Will Ignore U.S. Effort to Halt Refugee Boatlift," *Washington Post*, May 16, 1980, p. 1.
133. Larzelere, *The 1980 Cuban Boatlift*, pp. 291, 356.
134. Ibid., p. 379.
135. "What Happened to the Marielitos?" *New York Times*, November 25, 1987, p. B6.
136. See Louis Harris, "Most Disagree with Cubalift," *New York News*, July 17, 1980, p. 50.
137. The day after the Nicaraguan revolution, July 20, the SCC convened to formulate American policy. See Pastor, *Condemned to Repetition*, p. 194.
138. The conference resolution was formally titled "Analysis of the Situation and the Tasks of the Sandinista People's Revolution," but was

also known as the "72-Hour Document." It outlined the Nicaraguan as well as global situation and set forth Sandinista plans for consolidation of the revolution. See Pastor, *Condemned to Repetition*, pp. 199–200.

139. Department of State, *El Salvador: The Search for Peace*, (Washington, DC, September 1981), p. 3.
140. See Michael Radu, "The Structure of the Salvadoran Left," *Orbis*, Winter 1985, no.4, p. 675.
141. The chronology of the Mariel boatlift suggests that it was intended to provide a diversionary cover for Castro's stepped-up role in support of revolution in El Salvador.
142. Department of State, *Communist Interference in El Salvador*, Special Report No. 80, (Washington, DC, February 23, 1981), p. 4.
143. Ibid.
144. Ibid., pp. 4–5.
145. Ibid., pp. 5–7.
146. Pastor, *Condemned to Repetition*, pp. 217–18.
147. Presidential Determination No. 82–26 of September 12, 1980, *Federal Register*, vol.45, no. 185, September 22, 1980, p. 62779.
148. Pastor, *Condemned to Repetition*, p. 225.
149. Department of State, *Revolution Beyond Our Borders: Sandinista Intervention in Central America*, no. 132, (Washington, DC, September 1985), p. 21. See also Pastor, *Condemned to Repetition*, p. 218.
150. *Communist Interference in El Salvador*, p. 7.
151. David Wood, "Carter Orders Military Supplies to Embattled Junta in Salvador," *Washington Star*, January 15, 1981, p. 1.
152. *Communist Interference in El Salvador*, p. 7.
153. Cord Meyer, "Soviet Aid to Guerrillas in Salvador Documented," *Washington Star*, January 23, 1981, p. 8. Meyer's reference to "hard information" was to a document cache obtained from the Communist party of El Salvador in November 1980 which included battle plans, letters, and reports. See *Communist Interference in El Salvador*, p. 2.
154. "State Department Resumes Economic Assistance to El Salvador," *Washington Post*, December 18, 1980, p. 23.
155. Karen DeYoung, "Carter Decides to Resume Military Aid to El Salvador," *Washington Post*, January 14, 1981, p. 18.
156. Pastor, *Condemned to Repetition*, p. 228.
157. See the author's "U.S.–Soviet Strategic Balance in the Middle East, 1977–1981," *Korea and World Affairs*, Winter 1981, p. 619.
158. Baghdad Domestic Service, January 6, 1980, in *FBIS-MEA*, January 8, 1980, p. E1.
159. "An Interview with Zbigniew Brzezinski," *Wall Street Journal*, January 15, 1980, p. 20.

160. Ibid.
161. "State of the Union Address," January 23, 1980, *Public Papers of the Presidents of the United States, Jimmy Carter 1980–1981*, p. 195.
162. Baghdad INA, January 31, 1980, in *FBIS-MEA*, February 1, 1980, p. E1.
163. Brzezinski, *Power and Principle*, pp. 449–50.
164. Congressional Research Service, *Saudi Arabia and the United States: The New Context in an Evolving 'Special Relationship,'"* (Washington, DC: GPO, August 1981), p. 59.
165. Bernard Gwertzman, "Saudis Considering Military Tie to U.S.," *New York Times*, February 6, 1980, p. 1.
166. Richard Burt, "Indian Ocean Lands Reported to Agree to U.S. Use of Bases," *New York Times*, February 12, 1980, p. 1.
167. Richard Halloran, "Pentagon Activates Strike Force: Effectiveness Believed Years Off," *New York Times*, February 19, 1980, p. 1.
168. Clyde Farnsworth, "Canceling of Engines for Iraq Reported," *New York Times*, February 7, 1980, p. IV2. Direct United States trade with Iraq sharply increased between 1979 and 1980 by 64 percent, from $442 million to $722 million. See *United States Foreign Agricultural Trade, Statistical Report, Fiscal Year 1980* (Washington, DC: GPO, March 1981), p. 132.
169. David Newsom, "U.S.–Persian Gulf Relationship," Department of State *Bulletin*, August 1980, p. 62.
170. "The MacNeil–Lehrer Report: Zbigniew Brzezinski Interview," April 14, 1980 (Show no. 5206), p. 3.
171. Amman Domestic Service, April 9, 1980, *FBIS-MEA*, April 11, 1980, p. E3.
172. "Interview with the Saudi Foreign Minister," *Der Spiegel*, April 14, 1980, pp. 178–89, in *FBIS-MEA*, April 17, 1980, p. C3.
173. See Tehran Domestic Service, May 14, 1980, in *FBIS-SA*, May 15, 1980, p. I21; Tehran Bamdad, May 8, 1980, *FBIS-SA*, May 22, 1980, p. I4; and Tehran Domestic Service, June 8, 1980, in *FBIS-SA*, June 9, 1980, pp. I13–14.
174. For a detailed, day-by-day analysis of the United States role in the origins of the conflict, see the brilliant master's thesis by David Jackson Smith, *The Search for Strategic Stability in the Persian Gulf: The United States and the Start of the Iran–Iraq War* (Washington, DC: George Washington University, May 10, 1987).
175. President Carter, "Remarks and Question and Answer Session at a Town Meeting, Torrance, CA," September 22, 1980, *Public Papers of the Presidents of the United States, Jimmy Carter 1980–1981*, Book II, p. 1881.

176. Brzezinski, *Power and Principle*, p. 504.
177. Bernard Gwertzman, "U.S. Ready to Release Arms to Iran When Hostages Have Been Freed," *New York Times*, October 10, 1980, p. 1.
178. Baghdad Voice of the Masses, September 28, 1980, in *FBIS-MEA*, September 29, 1980, p. E1.
179. John Kifner, "Libya and Syria Said to Aid Iran," *New York Times*, October 10, 1980, p. 14; Bernard Gwertzman, "Iran Is Said to Be Receiving Arms and Medicines from North Korea," *New York Times*, October 9, 1980, p. 1; and Loren Jenkins, "Iraq Presses War in South, Seeking Decisive Victory," *Washington Post*, October 14, 1980, p. A1.
180. Tehran Domestic Service, October 5, 1980, in *FBIS-SA*, October 6, 1980, pp. I8–9.
181. "The Slow March into Khuzestan," *Economist*, October 4, 1980, p. 35.
182. Robert D. Hersey, "Iraq Halts Exports of Its Oil as Result of Damage by Iran," *New York Times*, September 27, 1980, p. 1.
183. Michael Getler, "U.S. Officials Say Diplomatic Action Headed Off Iraqi Escalation of War," *Washington Post*, October 4, 1980, p. A16.
184. Brzezinski, *Power and Principle*, p. 504.
185. Ibid.
186. Ibid.
187. Ibid., p. 279. In an Oval Office meeting on February 28, 1979, Brzezinski says that he "had now reached the conclusion that the Israelis would prefer Carter not to be reelected and that this objective was influencing their current tactics." By July 1980, Vice-President Mondale had also come to that conclusion, ibid., p. 433.
188. In fact, he did not. Israel shipped some 250 F-4 tires and spare tank parts to Iran via Cyprus. Through the end of June 1981, the Israelis sent nearly 400 tons of equipment, valued at $27 million. See Anthony Cordesman, *The Gulf and the Search for Strategic Stability; Saudi Arabia, the Military Balance in the Gulf, and Trends in the Arab–Israeli MIlitary Balance* (Boulder: Westview Press, 1984), p. 717.
189. President Carter, "Remarks, Question and Answer, Town Meeting Yatesville, Pennsylvania," October 15, 1980, *Public Papers of the Presidents of the United States, Jimmy Carter 1980–1981*, Book II, p. 2256.
190. Loren Jenkins, "Iraqis Bridge River Near Key Iranian Port," *Washington Post*, October 11, 1980, p. A22.
191. Bernard Gwertzman, "Tehran Indicates It Is Moving Closer to Hostage Decision," *New York Times*, October 23, 1980, p. 1.
192. Brzezinski, *Power and Principle*, p. 505.
193. Greider, *Secrets of the Temple*, pp. 182–83. The president's fiscal 1981 budget promising a deficit of only $13 billion was openly derided,

particularly after the deficit for the current fiscal year had been revised upward to $60 billion.

194. "Text of President Carter's Statement on the Nation's Economy," *New York Times*, March 15, 1980, p. 1.
195. Greider, *Secrets of the Temple*, p. 183.
196. *Economic Report of the President, January 1981* (Washington, DC: GPO, 1981), p. 136.
197. Greider, *Secrets of the Temple*, p. 185.
198. Ibid., pp. 206–7.
199. Brown, *Flight of International Capital*, p. 379.
200. Greider, *Secrets of the Temple*, p. 215.

Conclusion

The major objective of the president and his secretary of state had been to secure a new cooperative relationship—detente—with the Soviet Union, as the prerequisite to movement toward construction of a new international order. The focus of American strategy was completion of a SALT II treaty as a steppingstone to a broader relationship. The strategic bargain would involve a quid pro quo—Soviet strategic weapons and geopolitical restraint in exchange for American technological and economic largess.

Detente with Moscow would permit the United States to move toward completion of the geopolitical changes that had been set in motion in 1973—changes which would include the withdrawal of American forces from their forward containing positions around the Soviet periphery to less vulnerable, and less costly, positions off the Eurasian landmass and the establishment of stable collective security structures in place of American power. Ultimately, American strategy envisaged the establishment of a new global order based upon United States–Soviet cooperation rather than confrontation. That strategy also envisaged harnessing the growing economic power of West Germany and Japan to a broader cooperative world order, forestalling the disintegration of the global political-economic system into competitive regional blocs.

Yet it was plain from the first months of the Carter administration that the probability of success for this strategy was low. The Soviet Union was bent upon a different course, designed to exploit its growing military power. The continued buildup of Soviet strategic and conventional weapons power, combined with geopolitical activism, was clearly designed to support a broad strategy of attempting to alter the geopolitical balance by military means, and at the expense of the United States. The role of detente in such a strategy could only be to immobilize the United States, not to serve as the basis for a new cooperative world order—as some in the administration came to realize, including the president himself.

Secretary Vance, the driving force behind United States foreign policy, dismissed objections to the general strategy and doggedly pressed forward with negotiation of the SALT II treaty. Vance responded to Soviet actions inconsistent with detente by additional offers of compromise. Hoping to obtain Soviet agreement, Vance subordinated all other foreign policy initiatives to his pursuit of detente. Vance and those who supported the new strategy believed that only after detente was in place could the United States arrange for the disposition of its positions around the Soviet periphery—the new order.

Vance's determined pursuit of detente at all costs was a major error. Soviet leaders read the secretary's intentions clearly and turned his avid search for detente to their own advantage. The Soviets understood that since he put detente before all other policy ends, opportunity existed to turn American strategy to the service of the Soviet Union. Therefore, the Soviets dragged out the SALT II negotiations, enticing Vance, toying with him, leading him on—while formulating their own strategy accordingly. The fruits of this tactic, as detailed in this volume, were seen in Southwest and Southeast Asia, in Africa, and in Central America, as well as in United States–Soviet relations.

Even though Secretary Vance himself belatedly came to the realization that the Soviets were drawing out the negotiations, he was not deterred from pressing the strategy forward. Vance's single-minded focus on SALT II—it would not be too strong to call it an obsession—blinded him to the mounting evidence that Moscow was set on another, incompatible course. Compromise in the face of challenge had not changed the minds of Soviet leaders; it had only encouraged them to continue a strategy that produced results from their point of view. The fundamental lesson here was that only taking a firm stand held any promise for eventually reaching agreement. Only after establishing bedrock reality could a basis for agreement be found. Indeed, Moscow's strategy had to be defeated before Washington's could succeed. It was a lesson in strategy that President Carter never learned, but it was a course understood and pursued by his successor in the White House.

Carter's legacy to the incoming Reagan administration was burdened with failure to resolve both immediate and long-term problems. The problem of inflation continued to sap domestic economic vigor well into the incoming administration. The Iran hostage problem lingered, defeating Carter's attempts to resolve it while he was still in office. Relations with Iran remained adversarial, however, particularly in light of the late September outbreak of the Iran–Iraq war, in which the United States first tilted toward Iraq and then toward Iran. The plan to normalize relations with Nicaragua also faltered late in 1980, as Managua supported a major attempt to subvert El Salvador. Carter's economic and foreign policies left the incoming Reagan administration with immediate difficulties which persisted as long-term problems.

There were also long-term structural problems that must be counted as Carter's legacy to the Reagan administration. First was Carter's short-changing of defense. His effort to reign in inflation and restore a semblance of budget balance led to what was widely perceived to be a "defense budget shell game."[1] Torn between the desire to counterbalance growing Soviet power and the need to restore fiscal balance, the president tried to straddle the two positions. The result was that he fell in between.

Long-term geopolitical issues were also left in disarray. These centered on United States relations with the Soviet Union, China, the NATO allies, Japan, Saudi Arabia, and Israel, to name the most serious. By the end of 1980 the Soviet Union was deeply engaged in a vigorous, multi-continental effort to alter the geopolitical balance to advantage. Practically wherever one looked—in Europe, Asia, the Middle East, Africa, and the Caribbean—the Soviets were strengthening positions at American expense. The Carter administration had succeeded in neither blocking Moscow's drive nor tempering it.

As part of the effort to counterbalance Soviet power, the United States sought to improve relations with China, but they also deteriorated as the Beijing regime declined to be drawn into an antagonistic position toward Moscow. Indeed, the Chinese were intent upon pursuit of a balanced policy toward the two superpowers, and American efforts to pressure the Chinese only aggravated the newly normalized relationship.

In the Middle East, the much heralded Camp David peace

process had stagnated in stalemate as Israel flatly refused to address the issue of West Bank sovereignty. The American attempt to construct a strategic consensus based upon an Israeli–Egyptian peace treaty foundered on the failure to move even slightly toward a resolution of the Palestinian issue. Relations with Saudi Arabia teetered precariously as a result, and only the Soviet invasion of Afghanistan permitted the beginning of an improvement. The Israeli leadership clearly awaited Carter's successor and, in the Iran–Iraq conflict, undercut American policy.

Finally, problems with allies grew more intractable. West Germany, in particular, sought for the first time in the postwar era to play a "leading role" in world affairs, striking a more independent position between the United States and the Soviet Union.[2] Bonn emphasized detente and arms control at a time when the United States was shifting toward a more militant posture. The resultant rift between the United States and its European allies found expression over virtually the entire range of outstanding issues then current.

Regarding Japan, Carter entered office seeking to constrain Japanese economic growth by prompting increased defense spending and to limit continued accumulation of surplus Japanese wealth by urging domestic economic expansion. But Japanese leaders outmaneuvered the United States. During the Carter years Japan increased exports to America—despite Washington's efforts to place restraints on Japanese exports—while limiting defense spending to one percent of GNP. The beginning of a serious trade imbalance between the two countries, reflecting totally different philosophies of international behavior, became apparent during the Carter years.

President Carter left office with American strategy in disarray and with the American people confused and angry about what was perceived to be his inability to lead the nation. The problems he inherited were of great magnitude but hardly unmanageable. A failure of leadership—indecision, a lack of imagination, and, most importantly, tentative adoption of half-measures—characterized the Carter presidency. Carter attempted to accomplish through deception and diplomacy what could only be accomplished through the firm application of American power. Indeed, even in 1980, when a firm stance was the only option available, he preferred temporizing compromises to clear choices. When all is said and done, the nation was worse off in 1980 than when he entered office four years before.

The attempt to move toward a new global order based upon detente with the Soviet Union initiated in 1973 and carried forward by the Carter administration to 1980—had failed.

Notes

1. James R. Schlesinger, "The Defense Budget Shell Game," *Wall Street Journal*, October 23, 1980, p. 34. See also Samuel F. Wells, Jr., "A Question of Priorities: A Comparison of the Carter and Reagan Defense Programs," *Orbis*, Fall 1983, pp. 641–66.
2. Bradley Graham, "Schmidt Lays Claim to 'Leading Role' in World Affairs," *Washington Post*, August 12, 1980, p. 19.

Index